Rainer Albertz
Geschichte und Theologie II

Beihefte zur Zeitschrift für die alttestamentliche Wissenschaft

Herausgegeben von
John Barton, Reinhard G. Kratz, Nathan MacDonald,
Sara Milstein und Markus Witte

Band 551

Rainer Albertz

Geschichte und Theologie II

Studien zur Literatur-, Religions-
und Theologiegeschichte des Alten Testaments

Herausgegeben von
Ruth Ebach und Jakob Wöhrle

DE GRUYTER

ISBN 978-3-11-117981-0
e-ISBN (PDF) 978-3-11-120222-8
e-ISBN (EPUB) 978-3-11-120293-8
ISSN 0934-2575

Library of Congress Control Number: 2023931785

Bibliografische Information der Deutschen Nationalbibliothek
Die Deutsche Nationalbibliothek verzeichnet diese Publikation in der Deutschen
Nationalbibliografie; detaillierte bibliografische Daten sind im Internet über
http://dnb.dnb.de.

© 2023 Walter de Gruyter GmbH, Berlin/Boston
Satz: Meta Systems Publishing & Printservices GmbH, Wustermark
Druck und Bindung: CPI books GmbH, Leck

www.degruyter.com

MIX
Papier | Fördert
gute Waldnutzung
FSC® C083411
FSC
www.fsc.org

Vorwort

Rainer Albertz gehört zweifellos zu den großen Alttestamentlern unserer Zeit. Mit seinen Arbeiten hat er die gegenwärtige Forschung in vielfacher Hinsicht geprägt. Er hat zahlreiche neue Einsichten, neue Theorien und neue methodische Zugänge in das Fach eingebracht und dafür national und international, auch über die Fachgrenzen hinaus, Anerkennung erfahren.

Das Besondere am Werk von Rainer Albertz ist, dass er – als einer der letzten Allround-Gelehrten des Faches – seinen Blick nie auf einen Bereich der alttestamentlichen Wissenschaft verengt hat. Inhaltlich wie methodisch sieht er das Alte Testament und seine Umwelt stets in der gesamten Breite als Gegenstand seiner Arbeit. Er hat wichtige Überlegungen zum Pentateuch vorgestellt, ja, in den vergangenen Jahren ein eigenes Pentateuchmodell entwickelt; er hat zu den Geschichtsbüchern, der Prophetie, den Psalmen und der Weisheit gearbeitet. Seine Arbeiten umfassen historische Fragestellungen, literaturgeschichtliche und religionsgeschichtliche Themen, anthropologische und theologische Überlegungen. Methodisch basiert sein Ansatz auf einer kreativen und fruchtbaren Verbindung von literatur-, religions- und sozialgeschichtlichen Zugängen.

Bei all dem war und ist es das Anliegen von Rainer Albertz, die bleibende Relevanz und Aktualität des Alten Testaments und seiner Überlieferungen herauszustellen. Er legt die historischen Hintergründe der biblischen Literatur, die gesellschaftlichen Diskurse hinter dieser Literatur, die in ihnen verhandelten politischen und religiösen Themen frei, um so deren Bedeutung für die damalige und von hier aus auch für die heutige Zeit aufzuzeigen. Die Arbeiten von Rainer Albertz verbleiben nie im exegetischen Klein-Klein. Sie hauchen den alten Überlieferungen vielmehr ganz neues Leben ein; sie zeigen ihre zeitüberdauernde Kraft und Bedeutsamkeit.

Der hier vorgelegte Sammelband gibt Einblick in das so beschriebene breite Schaffen von Rainer Albertz. 20 Jahre nach dem ersten Band „Geschichte und Theologie" vereinigt das Werk eine Vielzahl weiterer Studien zur Geschichte Israels, zur Literatur- und Religionsgeschichte, zur Anthropologie und Theologie des Alten Testaments. Die Aufsätze befassen sich nahezu mit dem gesamten Spektrum der Geschichte des Alten Israel und der Literatur des Alten Testaments. Und in sämtlichen Arbeiten zeigt sich das Anliegen von Rainer Albertz, die Geschichte des Alten Israel und die alttestamentliche Literatur als lebendigen Diskurs über wichtige politische, gesellschaftliche und religiöse Fragen zu deuten und verständlich zu machen.

Herausgegeben wird der Band aus Anlass des 80. Geburtstags unseres verehrten Lehrers am 2. Mai 2023 – als Zeichen des Dankes, des Respekts und der Wertschätzung für alles, was wir von ihm lernen durften, sowie für alle Unterstützung

https://doi.org/10.1515/9783111202228-202

in den vergangenen Jahren und Jahrzehnten. Denn nicht nur als Autor, sondern auch als akademischer Lehrer an der Universität Münster war es Rainer Albertz stets ein Anliegen, seine Leidenschaft für das Alte Testament und seine Überzeugung von der bleibenden Relevanz der alttestamentlichen Überlieferungen an seine Studierenden und seine Schüler/innen weiterzugeben.

Zu danken haben wir all denen, die die Veröffentlichung dieses Bandes ermöglicht und bei seinem Entstehen mitgewirkt haben. Den Herausgebern und der Herausgeberin der BZAW, Prof. Dr. John Barton, Prof. Dr. Reinhard G. Kratz, Prof. Dr. Nathan MacDonald, Prof. Dr. Sara Milstein und Prof. Dr. Markus Witte, sei sehr herzlich für die Aufnahme des Buches in ihre Reihe gedankt. Dem Verlag Walter de Gruyter mit Dr. Albrecht Döhnert, Alice Meroz und Dr. Sophie Wagenhofer als den Verantwortlichen im Lektorat und Sabina Dabrowski in der Herstellung danken wir sehr für die kompetente, engagierte und freundliche verlegerische Betreuung. Ein großer Dank gilt schließlich unseren Assistent/innen Dorothea von Böhlen (Tübingen) und Gaël Carriou (Lausanne) sowie den Hilfskräften Markus Hauff und Rebekka Ursula Schwend (Tübingen) für ihre vielfältige Unterstützung bei der Erstellung des Manuskripts sowie der Verzeichnisse und Register.

Lausanne/Tübingen, im März 2023

Ruth Ebach
Jakob Wöhrle

Inhalt

1 Geschichte

Einführung

In den letzten Jahren standen für mich vor allem literaturgeschichtliche Themen im Vordergrund, insbesondere solche, die den Pentateuch betreffen. Dennoch war und ist für mich die historische Rekonstruktion der Geschichte und Sozialgeschichte des Alten Israel eine wichtige und unverzichtbare Grundlegung, auf der alle weiteren Schritte der historisch-kritischen Arbeit an der Hebräischen Bibel aufruhen. Denn wäre es so, dass – wie es in den letzten Jahrzehnten zuweilen schien – gar keine Sicherheit mehr über den Verlauf der vor- und nachexilischen Geschichte Israels zu gewinnen ist, dann bräche auch die Erforschung der Literatur-, der Religions- und Theologiegeschichte des Alten Israel in sich zusammen. Aus der Hebräischen Bibel würde dann eine Sammlung erbaulicher, aber weitgehend zeitloser Schriften, deren sachgemäßes Verständnis nicht mehr an ihrem wahrscheinlichen historischen Kontext und in ihrem entwicklungsgeschichtlichen Zusammenhang überprüft werden könnte.

Aus diesem Grunde habe ich mich viele Jahre in der Arbeitsgruppe „European Seminar in Historical Methodology" engagiert, die sich von 1996 bis 2012 regelmäßig auf den jährlichen Tagungen der „European Association of Biblical Studies (EABS)" zusammenfand. Lester L. Grabbe hatte die Gruppe gegründet, um den damals heftigen und häufig emotional geführten Streit zwischen den sogenannten „Minimalisten", welche historische Aussagen der Bibel nur anerkannten, sofern sie durch außerbiblische Quellen gestützt würden, und den sogenannten „Maximalisten", welche solche biblischen Aussagen solange anerkannten, soweit sie nicht per se unglaubwürdig erschienen und nicht durch andere Quellen widerlegt werden konnten, auf die sachliche Ebene eines akademischen Streitgespräches zu heben. Dieses Ziel wurde unter der sachkundigen, fairen und humorvollen Leitung von Lester Grabbe weitgehend erreicht; viele methodische Fragen zu den verschiedenen Epochen der Geschichte Israels wurden kontrovers diskutiert und besser geklärt, auch weil die meisten Teilnehmer – von denen mir vor allem Thomas L. Thompson, Niels Peter Lemche, Philip R. Davies, Hans M. Barstad, Bob Becking und Nadav Na'aman noch in lebendiger Erinnerung sind – trotz widerstreitender Ansichten persönlich befreundet waren. Mir kam in der Gruppe die Rolle eines „gemäßigten Maximalisten" zu. Zur Verbesserung der Auseinandersetzung wurden dabei teilweise die Manuskripte schon vor der Seminar-Diskussion ausgetauscht.

Die ersten beiden der hier aufgenommenen Beiträge stammen aus diesem intensiven Diskussionszusammenhang. Der erste Beitrag „Secondary Sources also Deserve to Be Historically Evaluated: The Case of the United Monarchy" setzt sich mit der stark methodisch ausgerichteten Darstellung der Geschichte Israels in

https://doi.org/10.1515/9783111202228-001

Lester Grabbes Buch „Ancient Israel" aus dem Jahr 2007 auseinander.[1] Gegenüber seiner Distinktion zwischen primären und sekundären Quellen, die ich grundsätzlich teile, mache ich darauf aufmerksam, dass dem eher mageren archäologischen Befund zum früheisenzeitlichen Jerusalem, der für Grabbe als Primärquelle die Existenz eines unter David vereinten Reiches unwahrscheinlich macht, der textliche Befund aus der als sekundär eingestuften Hebräischen Bibel entgegensteht, in der nicht weniger als siebenmal und davon dreimal völlig unabhängig voneinander von einem Zerfall dieses Reiches gesprochen wird. Diese offensichtliche Divergenz in der Quellenlage deutet an, dass die Frage, ob es irgendeine Art von vereintem Königreich unter David und Salomo gegeben hat oder nicht, noch keineswegs erledigt ist.

Beim zweiten Beitrag „Why a Reform like Josiah's Must Have Happened" handelt es sich um eine detaillierte Auseinandersetzung mit einem Aufsatz von Philip R. Davies, die im Methodenseminar 2002 in Berlin geführt wurde. Während die Historizität des Berichts von der Kultreform Josias (2 Kön 22–23) schon mehrfach angezweifelt und das damit in Zusammenhang stehende Deuteronomische Gesetz (Dtn 12–26) schon öfter in die nachexilische Zeit gerückt wurde, bemüht sich Davies in seinem Aufsatz „Josiah and the Law Book"[2] um einen detaillierten positiven Nachweis, dass beide nicht wie üblich in das späte 7., sondern in das 5. Jh. v. Chr. zu datieren sind. Meine Entgegnung nimmt Schritt für Schritt seine Argumente auf und versucht den Nachweis zu führen, dass die religionspolitischen Verhältnisse des 5. Jhs., soweit wir sie rekonstruieren können, keineswegs geeignet sind, den Sprachgebrauch, die Vorstellungswelt und die teilweise utopisch klingenden Reformanliegen der deuteronomischen Gesetzgebung besser zu erklären als die des ausgehenden 7. Jhs. v. Chr. Der erneute Abdruck meiner ausführlichen Auseinandersetzung mit Philip Davies ist für mich zugleich eine Form des Gedenkens an einen viel zu früh verstorbenen Freund.

Die übrigen beiden Aufsätze stammen aus anderen Zusammenhängen. Sie stellen eigene Beiträge zur Rekonstruktion der Geschichte Judas in der persischen Epoche dar, die zwar heute häufig als Hintergrund biblischer Texte in Anspruch genommen wird, aber selber noch längst nicht hinreichend genau historisch aufgeklärt und verstanden worden ist. Im ersten Aufsatz „Ethnische und kultische Konzepte in der Politik Nehemias" wird versucht, die Politik Nehemias zur Stärkung der Unabhängigkeit der Provinz Jehud mithilfe binärer ethnischer und kulti-

---

[1] S. L. L. Grabbe, Ancient Israel. What Do We Know and How Do We Know It?, London/New York 2007.

[2] Veröffentlicht in: L. L. Grabbe (Hg.), Good Kings and Bad Kings (LHBOTS 393), London/New York 2005, 65–77.

scher Oppositionen, die sonst in der Sozialanthropologie Verwendung finden,[3] genauer zu analysieren und in ihrer Strategie, aber auch ihrer Problematik besser verständlich zu machen.

Im letzten Aufsatz dieses historischen Kapitels „The Controversy about Judean versus Israelite Identity and the Persian Government: A New Interpretation of the Bagoses Story (*Jewish Antiquities* XI.297–301)" greife ich eine zwar hinlänglich bekannte, aber bis jetzt noch immer nicht historisch richtig eingeordnete Nachricht des Josephus auf, um eine ziemlich turbulente Phase der Geschichte Judas im letzten Jahrzehnt des 5. Jhs. v. Chr. aufzudecken. Sie lässt eine grundlegende Veränderung der persischen Politik gegenüber ihren Provinzen Jehud und Samarina erkennen, welche mit dem Verlust Ägyptens plötzlich die Südwestgrenze des Perserreichs bildeten. Dieser politische Umschwung ist auch für die Promulgation des Pentateuchs am Anfang des 4. Jhs. v. Chr. von Bedeutung.

---

3 Vgl. dazu grundlegend S. M. Olyan, Rites and Rank. Hierarchy in Biblical Representations of Cult, Princeton 2000.

Secondary Sources Also Deserve to be Historically Evaluated: The Case of the United Monarchy

In his recent book, *Ancient Israel: What Do We Know and How Do We Know It?* (2007), Lester Grabbe, to whom I wish to convey my warmest greetings with this essay, has drawn a fascinating outline of how a reconstruction of Israel's history from the twelfth to sixth centuries B.C.E., one that fully meets the requirements of strict historical standards, could work. Remembering the heated debate between so-called minimalists and maximalists of recent decades, I very much appreciate this attempt; it is an important step forward. I would also like to take the opportunity to thank Lester Grabbe for his constant efforts in bringing both "parties" into a critical dialogue on the panel of the European Seminar in Historical Methodology (ESHM), and his friendly invitation to me to participate. I consider the ESHM to be an important venture, forcing all of us to reconsider the material basis and methodical approach of our historical reconstructions. I hope he will enjoy the present contribution to those discussions.

Remaining Methodological Questions

Grabbe (2007, 3–36) has greatly clarified, probably more than any other historian of ancient Israel, the methodological questions of historiography. I will mention here only the question of the status of sources. Like many others, Grabbe distinguishes fundamentally between primary and secondary sources:

> Primary sources are those contemporary (or nearly so) with the events they describe and usually have some other direct connection (eyewitness report, compilation from eyewitness reports or other good sources, proximity to the events or those involved in the events). Secondary sources are those further removed in time and space from the original events. (Grabbe 2007, 220) |

He rightly concludes: "Preference should be given to primary sources ... this means archaeology and inscriptions" (2007, 35). As long as suitable sources of this first category are available, I think no one would argue against that general rule. According to Grabbe, the texts of the Hebrew Bible generally belong to the second category:

> The biblical text is almost always a secondary source, written and edited long after the events ostensibly described. In some cases, the text may depend on earlier sources, but

https://doi.org/10.1515/9783111202228-002

these sources were edited and adapted; in any case the source has to be dug out from the present context. (2007, 35)

Grabbe does not wish to attack or vilify the Hebrew Bible by categorizing the biblical texts in such a way (2007, 219). Rather, he opposes a "dogmatic scepticism that continually looks for a way to reject or denigrate the biblical text" (2007, 23), an attitude that Barstad (1998) has called "bibliophobia." In contrast to a strict minimalist view, Grabbe demands:

> The biblical text should always be considered: it is one of the sources for the history of ancient Israel and needs to be treated like any other source, being neither privileged nor rejected a priori, but handled straightforwardly and critically. (2007, 224)

According to Grabbe, "we cannot say that the biblical text is reliable or unreliable, because it all depends on which episode or text one has in mind" (2007, 219). From this insight he derives the methodical demand: "secondary sources normally need some sort of confirmation" (2007, 220). Thus, compared with some radical minimalist positions, Grabbe's methodical approach seems well-balanced and fair.

Yet some serious material and methodological questions remain. First, we must recognize that our primary sources for the pre-exilic history of ancient Israel, despite their theoretical importance, are very limited. This is especially true of the epigraphic material: unfortunately, we have not a single monumental inscription or written document from monarchic archives of Israel and Judah that would allow us to reconstruct the political history of these states. The reasons for this strange situation are not totally clear. On the one hand, they may have to do with the frequency of warfare in that area, which could have damaged many of the potential written or inscribed sources. On the other hand, official documents were mostly written on papyrus in Palestine, a medium that is rarely preserved, given the wet climate. The only two – fragmentary – monumental inscriptions from Palestine that we have come from neighbouring states, the Mesha stele from a king of Moab, and the Tel Dan stele, probably from a king of Aram (Damascus). Together with several Assyrian, and a few | Babylonian, royal inscriptions and chronicles concerning events in Palestine, these are the only epigraphic sources enabling us to control the historical data supplied by the biblical texts; unfortunately, however, these potential sources are restricted to the period from the middle of the ninth to the sixth century.

The other kind of primary source, the results of archaeological excavations including stratigraphy, architecture, pottery and other small finds, together with demographic calculations derived from surveys, comprises a huge amount of data, more than from any other place in the ancient Near East. Yet historical conclusions – especially conclusions based on an absence of evidence – are often ambiguous. While Grabbe earlier stressed the significance of "textual material, which provides much of the interpretative framework," stating that "without textual data, the archaeology is much less helpful" (2000, 217), he now grants the archaeological data the highest status of objectivity, because they "actually existed in real life," while "a text always contains human invention, and it is always possible that a text is entirely fantasy" (2007, 10).[1] But if we note the very different interpretations of archaeological results relating to the twelfth to tenth centuries, reported by Grabbe in detail, his earlier opinion seems equally to be justified. Important as such results may be for developments of the *longue* and *moyenne durée*, without the interpretative framework of epigraphic material they do not provide the exact historical data necessary for reconstructing the *histoire événementelle*, the political history of Israel and Judah. Thus, for the whole period of about 350 years from the stele of Merneptah (1209/8 B.C.E.), which mentions Israel for the first time, to the Kurkh Monolith of Shalmaneser III (853 B.C.E.), which mentions King Ahab in the battle of Qarqar, we do not have the primary sources that we need in order to control the reliability of the secondary sources in the Bible. Since the biblical texts concerning this earlier period cannot be evaluated by external primary sources, Grabbe, in accordance with his methodological demands, concludes that they cannot be used for historical reconstruction. The outcome of this procedure is demonstrated in his book: despite the many possible suggestions about the early history of ancient Israel that Grabbe discusses in detail, no reliable historical reconstruction from the twelfth to tenth centuries B.C.E. is possible. |

Can we really be satisfied with such a negative result, which depends merely on a fortuitous lack of all epigraphic inscriptions? As long as this situation is not altered by new findings, should we not make use of the possibilities provided by the Hebrew Bible?

Grabbe sometimes relativizes his strict division between primary and secondary sources, as, for example, when he concedes:

> Primary sources are not always trustworthy, and secondary sources may sometimes contain reliable information, and no two sources agree entirely. Thus, the historian has to make a critical investigation of all data, whatever the source. (2007, 220)

I appreciate this statement: it implies that the texts of the Hebrew Bible, despite being classified as "secondary sources," should be historically evaluated. Some

---

1 Thus, Grabbe is now ready to concede archaeology has paramount importance for his historiography: "The importance of archaeology cannot ... be overestimated" (2007, 6); "The proper attention to archaeology is vital for any history of ancient Israel, and it is my intention to try to give it the prominence it deserves" (2007, 10). |

may contain reliable historical information, some less, and some none. But, unfortunately, Grabbe is not really interested in developing internal criteria for distinguishing those biblical texts that may contain reliable historical information from those in which no clear external evidence is available. He reckons with the possibility that a biblical text may depend on earlier sources that might be retrieved (2007, 35), but does not offer much by way of examples. The results of literary historical exegesis seem too uncertain to him:

> The complicated history of the biblical text has been partially worked out in the past two centuries, but there is still much unknown and much on which there is disagreement. (2007, 220)

Thus in most cases he prefers to deal with the biblical text (often taken in the singular!) as if all passages stand on the same level. But can that be the solution? The disagreement about the dating and interpretation of biblical texts is no worse than about the interpretation of archaeological data. In the realm of history we can never be absolutely sure. Nevertheless, there are some literary-historical criteria that provide us with a rough guideline for the historical evaluation of biblical texts. First of all, the uniformity or non-uniformity of a given text has to be proven by literary criticism and its units have to be dated: texts that lie closer to the events are normally more reliable. Form-critical classifications are also important: reports often contain more reliable information than narratives, narratives more than sagas and legends, and prophetic accusations more than prophetic announcements. In any case, all texts have to be interpreted against their *Tendenz* or ideology, which also has to be evaluated first. Of course, identical or similar information given by more than one independent biblical source has a higher degree of historical probability. This means that the same literary tools used for the historical | interpretation of the epigraphic material are valid for evaluating the degree of historicity of a biblical text. Because of the longer editorial history of the latter, however – which Grabbe rightly notes – the historical evaluation of biblical texts is more complex and must be handled very carefully.

Grabbe has demonstrated in great detail that there is no reason for mistrusting the historicity of biblical texts in general: he has shown that in many of those cases where we have external evidence from epigraphic sources, the information in biblical texts can be confirmed or brought into a meaningful correlation with such data (2007, 144–49, 163–64, 200, 209–10, 224–25). In other cases where they deviate, the discrepancy often can be explained by the specific ideological interest of the biblical author. The importance of form-critical categories can be demonstrated in the case of Sennacherib's invasion of Judah in 701: the report of this event in 2 Kgs 18:13–16 perfectly accords with Sennacherib's inscription (see Grabbe 2007, 200), while the Isaiah-Hezekiah legend (18:17–19:10, 32*, 36*) disagrees with both, despite including some historical details (but in an inaccurate way). For Sennacherib never besieged Jerusalem, but withdrew from Lachish after Hezekiah paid him a huge tribute.[2] In any event, the Deuteronomistic author concealed Sennacherib's devastation of the Shephelah and the deportation of many of its inhabitants, presumably because he wanted to give a positive judgement on Hezekiah for ideological reasons. So, while it can be legitimately argued that without the Assyrian inscriptions and the archaeological evidence we would not see the overall extent of the catastrophe, nevertheless a sound literary-historical evaluation of the biblical accounts, giving the report priority over the legend, would not deliver entirely misleading results. I ask, therefore: Should we not similarly scrutinize the biblical texts for that period between the twelfth and the tenth centuries when no other written sources are available (especially for the tenth century B.C.E.)?

The Case of the "United Monarchy"

The archaeological results concerning Jerusalem in the tenth and early ninth centuries (Iron IIA) are unfortunately very ambiguous, and Grabbe (2007, 71–73) describes in detail the dispute between archaeologists. On one side (Ussishkin 2003; Finkelstein 2003; Steiner 2003; Lehmann | 2003; Herzog and Singer-Avitz 2004), Jerusalem was only a minor settlement, a village or possibly a citadel. On the other side (Cahill 2003; Mazar 2007), it was a substantial city, the capital of an emerging state. The uncertainty has to do not only with the heavy destruction Jerusalem suffered during its long history and the severe restrictions to which all excavations in the Old City are subjected under the complicated political and religious regime, but also with the fact that archaeology has not so far found clear answers to substantial material questions. Were the impressive fortifications of the Middle Bronze (IIB) reused in later LB and Iron IIA–B periods, or was Jerusalem an unfortified settlement until the eighth century? What was the date and the purpose of the so-called stepped structure on the south-eastern slope? Was it already built in the tenth century or later? Did it serve as a foundation of a monumental building such as a palace, or not? Depending on the answers to these and similar questions, very different reconstructions of the history of the tenth century can be supported.

---

2 The expression $URU.ḪAL-ṢU.MEŠ$ in Sennacherib's inscription does not denote "ramps," as is often suggested (*ANET* 288: "earthwork"), but "forts" which the Assyrian king had built in order to control the access to Jerusalem. So argues, rightly, Mayer (1995, 355–63). |

Weighing up these two alternative reconstructions, Grabbe tends to follow the minimal position. He does not wish to deny that Saul, David and Solomon really existed, but would severely reduce the portrait of a great and renowned Davidic empire drawn by the Hebrew Bible:

> Perhaps a city-state, much like the city-states of Shechem under Lab'aya or of Jerusalem under 'Abdi-Ḫeba, would be feasible ... It seems unlikely that David controlled anything beyond a limited territory centred on the southern hill country and Jerusalem. (2007, 121)

Moreover, following Finkelstein and Silberman (2001, 121–45; cf. Finkelstein 2003, 79) and others, Grabbe feels obliged to deny the existence of a "united monarchy" for more general reasons.[3] In his view, the ecological conditions and the economic and demographic development of northern Israel and the southern hill country were so different (2007, 70–71) that a unification of Judah and Israel in one territorial state under David "would have been an unusual development" (2007, 121) – perhaps not impossible, but rather unlikely. According to him, it is much more likely that the first Israelite state would have been established in the ecologically privileged northern area, where the Omride kingdom emerged. Thus he states: |

> The first kingdom for which we have solid evidence is the northern kingdom, the state founded by Omri. This fits what we would expect from the *longue durée*; if there was an earlier state, we have no direct information on it except perhaps some memory in the biblical text. This does not mean that nothing existed before Omri in either the north or the south, but what was there was probably not a state as such. (2007, 222–23)

As plausible as this historical reconstruction may be, our limited external sources mean that the problem remains "what to do with the biblical traditions about the rise of the Israelite kingship," as Grabbe puts it (2007, 121). He tries to explain why their authors came to the idea of a "united monarchy": the territory controlled by David "might have overlapped with territory earlier controlled by Saul, which would lead to some of the biblical traditions that made David the usurper and successor of Saul" (2007, 121). But is this a sufficient explanation? There are not just "some traditions," but dozens of texts between 1 Sam 10 and 2 Sam 21 which without exception describe the complicated start of Israel's monarchic history in this way.

There is no space here to discuss all the biblical texts concerning the "united monarchy." I would mention just two pieces of evidence which seem not to be

---

3 The main archaeological argument for a "united monarchy," the similar six-chambered gates in Gezer, Megiddo and Hazor (cf. Mazar 2007, 130–31), is no longer mentioned by Grabbe. This feature has probably lost plausibility for him, since their traditional dating in the tenth century was questioned (cf. Finkelstein 2007, 111–13) in the controversy about the low chronology. |

taken sufficiently into consideration by Grabbe. The first is the external evidence of the Tel Dan inscription, which – astonishing enough – Grabbe does not use for his reconstruction of early monarchic history.[4] In line 9 of the inscription occurs the expression *bytdwd*, which in the political context of the inscription can only be rendered "house of David." The element *beit* in this expression can have two meanings, "family/dynasty [of David]" and "state [of David]," just as we find with the expression *bît ḥumri*, "house of Omri," in the Assyrian inscriptions (Weippert 1978), one of the terms denoting the northern kingdom.[5] Thus the Aramaean ruler of the ninth century (probably Hazael) regarded David as the founder of a dynasty and a founder of a state. This evidence not only calls into question all suggestions that Judah did not become a state before the eighth century,[6] but also shows that the political organization | founded by David belonged to the same category as the Omride kingdom, even if it probably represented a less developed form of it.[7] The Tel Dan inscription does not, of course, refer to the "united monarchy," only the kingdom of Judah, but it does not exclude the possibility, since the extent of the "house of David" may have varied.

The second issue I will mention is the biblical traditions about the division of the monarchy, which seem to me overlooked in the present discussion. Relating the end of the Solomonic empire and the foundation of a separate northern kingdom makes sense only if a "united kingdom" had existed. The bulk of the traditions is collected and commented on by the Deuteronomistic historian in 1 Kgs 11–12, and a literary-critical analysis can distinguish four different sources, each with different degrees of historicity:

1. *A report of the rebellion of Jeroboam ben Nebat, an Ephraimite from Zeredah, against King Solomon.* First the rebellion failed; Solomon sought to kill Jeroboam. He had to flee to Egypt, but after Solomon's death he came back to Israel and

---

4 See his very restricted reconstruction and cautious interpretation (2007, 129–30). For a more extensive reconstruction and historical interpretation, see Kottsieper 1998.
5 Also in the Hebrew Bible the term בית can denote a nation or a state: 2 Sam 2:4; 12:8; 16:3; 1 Kgs 12:21; 20:31; Isa 8:14; Jer 2:26; 5:11; Hos 1:4; 5:12, 14 etc.
6 This view is also questioned by the discovery of 170 clay bullae from the ninth century by near the Gihon spring, on which see Reich, Shukron and Lernau 2007, 156–57. Together with a large quantity of fish bones in the same area, these bullae verify that Jerusalem was a commercial and administrative centre in the late ninth century at least. The suggestion that this centre emerged only under the | influence of the northern state, whose ally Judah was during the Omride period (Grabbe 2007, 127), is possible, but in no way necessary, and depends on the view that Judah was still much less developed than Israel.
7 Using the categories of Claessen and Skalník (1978) – namely, of an "inchoate early state" in contrast to a "typical early state" I have argued (Albertz 2007, 358–59) that the Omride state should be categorized as a "transitional early state" on the way to a "mature state," a stage reached in the eighth and seventh centuries.

was crowned as the first king of the northern kingdom (1 Kgs 11:26, 40; 12:2,[8] 20a[9]). This short report could have come from the "Chronicle of the kings of Judah and Israel." From its *Gattung* and its possible origin, it claims a high degree of historicity.[10] |

2. *The fragment of a narrative about Jeroboam's failed rebellion (1 Kgs 11:27–28)*. Its summary, probably given by the Deuteronomistic historian (v. 27), confirms that Jeroboam raised his hand against King Solomon when the latter was building the Millo. The narrative relates that Solomon had promoted Jeroboam because of his achievements and put him in charge for the labour-gangs of the tribal district of Joseph (v. 28). Unfortunately, the rest of the story is broken off, giving way to the Ahijah story. Although a narrative, the text accords with the report mentioned above. Its contention that the king himself fostered his later enemy runs against a tendency to glorify Solomon and so seems to be trustworthy.

3. *A long historical narrative about the separation of the northern tribes from the Davidic dynasty at the beginning of the reign of Rehoboam (1 Kgs 12:1*, 3b–14, 16, 18–19).*[11] The negotiations between the northern tribes and Rehoboam concerning the burdens of corvée, in which Jeroboam was originally not included (cf. v. 20) are stylized in a didactic manner and probably did not happen in this way. But the fact that the main reason for the division of the monarchy was a social conflict about compulsory labour accords with the fragmented narrative (11:27–28) and seems to be trustworthy. This is confirmed by the detail of the murder of Adoram, the commander in charge of the labour (v. 18). Since v. 19 characterizes the separation of the northern tribes as a sinful rebellion (פשע) against the Davidic dynasty, the narrative is of Judean origin. As the aetiological motive ("until the present day") at the end shows, it presupposes an interval from the events reported; yet its self-critical intention implies that the problem of the

---

8 That the verse does not really fit the narrative of 1 Kgs 12:1–19 is shown by the fact that it is missing here in the LXX; it comes at the end of ch. 11. In the MT its final clause is aligned to the context. As the deviating text of 2 Chr 10:2 and the LXX and Vulgate show, the verse should run: As Jeroboam ben Nebat heard (that), while he was still in Egypt, where he had fled from Solomon, he *came back from Egypt*. Originally the message heard by Jeroboam was not the assembly in Shechem but the death of Solomon (11:40, now explicitly reported by the Dtr's final clause, v. 43; see the LXX). Furthermore, his return did not originally lead him to the assembly, where he was only secondarily included by DtrH (12:3a, 12, 20*), but somewhere else (according to the LXX in 11:43: "straight to his town in the land of Samaria on the mountain of Ephraim"), from where he had to be called (12:20).

9 Only the words "in the assembly" are a Dtr addition. Whether v. 20b originally belonged to the report is not certain. In any case, it is a doublet to the end of the narrative in v. 19.

10 For more details, see Albertz 1994, 138–43. |

11 Verse 2 originally belonged to the report: vv. 3a, 15 are Dtr additions. Verse 17 is a different interpolation reminiscent of 1 Chr 11:16–17. |

division of monarchy was still present. Thus, it should be assigned to not later than the time of Hezekiah and can claim a kernel of historicity for itself.

4. *The prophetic narrative on how Ahijah from Shiloh anointed Jeroboam king (1 Kgs 11:29–39*).* The narrative has been heavily reworked by the Deuteronomists (vv. 32–36, 38a, 39); but the underlying plot containing Ahijah's symbolic act of tearing his new cloak in twelve pieces and offering Jeroboam ten of them already presupposes the existence of a "united monarchy." As a prophetic legend, however, its degree of historicity is rather low. | It probably originated as a legitimating story about the beginning of the northern monarchy. Nevertheless, as such it confirms that the "united monarchy" was a concept not only promoted in Judah, but also acknowledged in a foundation story within the northern kingdom.

In contrast to his sources the Deuteronomistic historian presented his own view of the "division of the monarchy." According to him, the main reason for this division was the later apostasy of Solomon, who has been seduced by his foreign wives (1 Kgs 11:1–13; generalized in 12:33). In his view the Judean state survived only because of the divine election of David, which remained valid (11:13). Such a difficult theological construction would have been superfluous had a considerable loss of power for the Davidides not taken place. Thus, even the Deuteronomistic historian, probably in the exilic period, in some way attests the division of the united monarchy.

The critical modern historian may nevertheless raise the objection that the sources intertwined in 1 Kgs 11–12 are not really independent of each other. Apart from the Ahijah legend they could perhaps have come from a similar Judean milieu. There is, however, an independent source which has nothing to do with Deuteronomistic History and its possible sources. It consists in a prophetic oracle in the book of Isaiah:

> Yhwh will bring on you [and your people] and the house of your father a time, the like of which has not been come since the time that Ephraim deviated from Judah [the king of Assur]. (Isa 7:17)[12]

This verse constitutes the final oracle of judgment uttered by Isaiah against Ahab in his activity during the Syro-Ephraimite war (Isa 7:1–17). It is generally acknowledged that the verse belongs to the earliest layer of the book, often called the *Denkschrift* (Isa 6:1–8:19*), which was probably written shortly after the events

---

12 The passages set in brackets are probably, as their syntactical isolation shows, generalizing and explaining glosses.

of 734–32 B.C.E.[13] I have pointed out above that prophetic announcements are obviously not reliable historical sources, because they can turn out to be wrong. Yet, in our case the | reference to the division of the monarchy is a memory used as a comparison for the future. Indeed, the rather surprising comparison with its unusual terminology[14] probably provides the verse with a high degree of historicity. Thus, this prophetic source confirms that even more than two centuries after the event the separation of the northern tribes from the Davidic kings was remembered as a traumatic experience. It was seen as the worst catastrophe that had ever happened in the history of Judah so far. According to this source, the "division of the monarchy" was strongly anchored in the historical memory of Judah in the eighth century; thus it seems very improbable that this event should have been an invention.

There is a second prophetic reference to the united monarchy in a salvation oracle of the book of Ezekiel, probably coming from the late exilic period. According to Ezek 37:15–22, Judah and Israel will be reunited under one king in the future. If v. 22 proposes that Judah and Israel should no longer be two separate nations and should never again split into two kingdoms, the memory of the former division is still present. The use of the verb חצה ("divide"), uncommon in this context, shows that this prophetic announcement depends neither on Isaiah nor the Deuteronomistic historian. This late text reveals that it is impossible to regard the "united monarchy" as merely a projection of an exilic hope into the past. On the contrary, the exilic hope tries to overcome the unhappy experience of a political division that occurred in the past.

Conclusion

A more detailed investigation of the biblical texts reveals that there are no fewer than seven different sources that confirm the "division of the monarchy." At least three of these are independent of each other (the Deuteronomistic historian;

---

13 Cf. Blum 1996/97, 552–57. According to Blum, this *Denkschrift* acquired its final form (including ch. 6) in the second stage of Isaiah's "testament," written at the end of the prophet's life shortly after 701 B.C.E. Liss (2003, 72–92) wants to date Isa 7:1–17 in the time of Josiah, while Becker (1997, 21–60) has even pleaded for post-Dtr dating. Nevertheless, Blum is right to argue that Isa 6–8* contains a vivid dispute with Isaiah's pupils, which cannot have taken place long after the death of the prophet. For the complex structure of the unit, cf. Steck 1982a, 1982b. |

14 In contrast to the pejorative terminology in 1 Kgs 12:19 (פשׁע ב, "sinned or rebelled against"), the expression used by Isaiah (סור מעל, "deviate from, separate from") lacks any negative assessment. |

Isa 7:17 and Ezek 37:22), and at least two of them, according to their features and content, are furnished with a high degree of reliability (1 Kgs 11:26, 40; 12:2*, 20a; Isa 7:17), while at least three come from the monarchic period (1 Kgs 11:26, 40; 12:2*, 20a; 12:1–19*; Isa 7:17). Naturally, the withdrawal of the northern tribes was remembered more in Judah, because it included here a considerable loss of power (six sources). Yet it was also preserved in the tradition of the northern kingdom (1 Kgs 11:29–39*). Although different in shape and content, each of the sources corroborates the others; there is no | single source that draws a totally different picture.[15] Assessed with the usual historical criteria, this result should be sufficient to establish the historicity of the division of the monarchy. Therefore, there is also good reason to postulate the existence of the united monarchy, whatever its shape and extent.[16]

I think Grabbe is right in pointing out that we should expect the emergence of statehood first in the more developed areas in the north. However, in accordance with the biblical tradition I think that this happened already with the arrival of Saul (1 Sam 9–11). Generally speaking, there is no fundamental doubt that a strong character like David could have been able to turn the normal development in a different direction: after having become the king of Judah he actually usurped the throne of Saul in a bloody civil war and united the three dominions of Judah, Israel and Jerusalem under his rule (2 Sam 2–5). The united monarchy was precarious from its beginnings, as reflected in the stories of the Absalom and Sheba rebellions (2 Sam 16:5–14; 19:9b–41; 19:42–20:22). Nevertheless, it strengthened, or even created, an overall Israelite identity that embraced the north and the south (2 Sam 13:12, 15–19). In spite of the division of the monarchy after Solomon's death, some kind of overall Israelite identity must have survived. This is because it is presupposed by the prophets of the eighth century (cf. Isa 5:7; 8:14; 9:7–20) and it is the prerequisite of the assumptions that thousands of refugees from the north fled to Judah when the Assyrians conquered Samaria (722–720 B.C.E.). It therefore makes sense to assume that the first history of the early monarchy from Saul to Solomon (1 Sam 10–2 Kgs 2*) was composed in the time of Hezekiah (Dietrich 2002, 259–73; Albertz 2009 [[= p. 197–214 in the present volume]]), when a compromise between the competing historical traditions of the inhabitants of Judah and the refugees from the north had to be found.

---

15 This is also true for the shape of the tradition given by Chronicles (1 Chr 10:1–12:4; 13:4–12). This source is here intentionally excluded, because it clearly depends on DtrH and is much later. Its slightly different view of the event is not derived from older traditions, but depends on its dispute with the Samarians of the fourth century B.C.E. See Bae 2005, 67–77.

16 For me, it is important to see that Na'aman (2006, 14–15), although reducing the biblical picture of David's and Solomon's rule considerably, does not deny the existence of a united monarchy. |

From these insights I would like to outline the following methodical demands: anyone who denies the historicity of the united monarchy for any reason should be obliged to answer two questions. First, how can the existence of so many biblical sources for the division of the monarchy be | explained if a united monarchy had never existed? Second, if not during the united monarchy, when should the consciousness of an overall Israelite identity have emerged – a consciousness already testified in the eighth century B.C.E.?[17]

References

Albertz, R. 1994. *A History of Israelite Religion in the Old Testament Period*. 2 vols. OTL. Louisville, Ky.: Westminster John Knox.

Albertz, R. 2005. Why a Reform like Josiah's Must Have Happened. Pages 27–46 in *Good Kings and Bad Kings*. Edited by L. L. Grabbe. JSOTSup 393; ESHM 5. London: T&T Clark International. [[= p. 21–43 in the present volume]]

Albertz, R. 2007. Social History of Ancient Israel. Pages 347–67 in *Understanding the History of Ancient Israel*. Edited by H. G. M. Williamson. Proceedings of the British Academy 143. Oxford: Oxford University Press.

Albertz, R. 2009. Israel in der offiziellen Religion der Königszeit. Pages 39–57 in *Die Identität Israels. Entwicklungen und Kontroversen in alttestamentlicher Zeit*. Edited by H. Irsigler. Herders Biblische Studien 56. Freiburg: Herder. [[= p. 197–214 in the present volume]]

Bae, H.-S. 2005. *Vereinte Suche nach JHWH: Die Hiskianische und Josianische Reform in der Chronik*. BZAW 355. Berlin: de Gruyter.

Barstad, H. 1998. The Strange Fear of the Bible: Some Reflections on the "Bibliophobia" in Recent Ancient Israelite Historiography. Pages 120–27 in *Leading Captivity Captive: "The Exile" as History and Ideology*. Edited by L. L. Grabbe. JSOTSup 279; ESHM 2. Sheffield: Sheffield Academic.

Becker, U. 1997. *Jesaja – Von der Botschaft zum Buch*. FRLANT 179. Göttingen: Vandenhoeck & Ruprecht.

Blum, E. 1996/97. Jesajas prophetisches Testament: Beobachtungen zu Jes 1–11. *ZAW* 108:547–68 and 109:12–29.

Cahill, J. M. 2003. Jerusalem at the Time of the United Monarchy: The Archaeological Evidence. Pages 13–80 in Vaughn and Killebrew, eds., 2003.

Claessen, H. J. M., and P. Skalník. 1978. *The Early State*. New Babylon 32. The Haag: Mouton.

Dever, W. G., and S. Gitin, eds. 2003. *Symbiosis, Symbolism, and the Power of the Past: Canaan, Ancient Israel, and Their Neighbors from the Late Bronze Age through Roman Palestina. Proceedings of the Centennial Symposium W. F. Albright Institute of Archaeological Research and American School of Oriental Research Jerusalem, May 29–31, 2000*. Winona Lake: Eisenbrauns.

Dietrich, W. 2002. *Die frühe Königszeit in Israel: 10. Jahrhundert v. Chr.* Biblische Enzyklopädie 3. Stuttgart: Kohlhammer.

---

17 Finkelstein and Silberman (2001, 275–88) regard Josiah's reform as the period that gave birth to such an identity, but that would be rather too late. Moreover, Josiah's interference in northern affairs was according to them rather limited (2001, 347–53); cf. my criticisms in Albertz 2005, 27–32 [[= p. 21–27 in the present volume]]. |

Finkelstein, I. 2003. City States to States: Polity Dynamics in the 10th–9th Centuries B.C.E.
Pages 75–83 in Dever and Gitin, eds., 2003. |

Finkelstein, I. 2007. King Solomon's Golden Age: History or Myth? Pages 107–16 in Finkelstein and Mazar, eds., 2007.

Finkelstein, I., and A. Mazar, eds. 2007. *The Quest for the Historical Israel: Debating Archaeology and the History of Early Israel.* ABS 17. Atlanta: SBL.

Finkelstein, I., and N. A. Silberman. 2001. *The Bible Unearthed: Archaeology's New Vision of Ancient Israel and the Origin of Its Sacred Texts.* New York: Free Press.

Grabbe, L. L. 2000. Writing Israel's History at the End of the Twentieth Century. Pages 203–18 in *Congress Volume, Oslo 1998.* Edited by A. Lemaire and M. Saebø. VTSup 80. Leiden: Brill.

Grabbe, L. L. 2007. *Ancient Israel: What Do We Know and How Do We Know It?* London: T&T Clark International.

Hardmeier, C. 1990. *Prophetie im Streit vor dem Untergang Judas. Erzählkommunikative Studien zur Entstehungssituation der Jesaja- und Jeremiaerzählungen in II Reg 18–20 und Jer 37–40.* BZAW 187. Berlin: de Gruyter.

Herzog, Z., and L. Singer-Avitz. 2004. Redefining the Centre: The Emergence of State in Judah. *Tel Aviv* 31:209–44.

Kottsieper, I. 1998. Die Inschrift vom Tell Dan und die politischen Beziehungen zwischen Aram-Damaskus und Israel in der 1. Hälfte des 1. Jahrtausends vor Christus. Pages 475–500 in *"Und Mose schrieb dieses Lied auf": Studien zum Alten Testament und zum Alten Orient.* Edited by M. Dietrich and I. Kottsieper. FS O. Loretz. AOAT 250. Münster: Ugarit-Verlag.

Lehmann, G. 2003. The United Monarchy in the Countryside: Jerusalem, Judah, and the Shephela during the Tenth Century B.C.E. Pages 117–62 in Vaughn and Killebrew, eds., 2003.

Liss, H. 2003. *Die unerhörte Prophetie: Kommunikative Strukturen prophetischer Rede im Buch Yesha'yahu.* Arbeiten zur Bibel und ihrer Geschichte 14. Leipzig: Evangelische Verlagsanstalt.

Mayer, W. 1995. *Politik und Kriegskunst der Assyrer.* ALASPM 9. Münster: Ugarit-Verlag.

Mazar, A. 2007. The Search for David and Solomon: An Archaeological Perspective. Pages 117–39 in *The Quest for the Historical Israel: Debating Archaeology and the History of Early Israel.* Edited by I. Finkelstein and A. Mazar. ABS 17. Atlanta: SBL.

Na'aman, N. 2006. The Contribution of the Amarna Letters to the Debate on Jerusalem's Political Position in the Tenth Century. Pages 1–17 in *Ancient Israel's History and Historiography: Collected Essays.* Vol. 3, *The First Temple Period.* Winona Lake, Ind.: Eisenbrauns.

Reich, R., E. Shukron and O. Lernau. 2007. Recent Discoveries in the City of David, Jerusalem. *IEJ* 57:153–69.

Steck, O. H. 1982a. Beiträge zum Verständnis von Jesaja 7,10–17 und 8,1–4. Pages 187–203 in Steck 1982c.

Steck, O. H. 1982b. Rettung und Verstockung: Exegetische Bemerkungen zu Jesaja 7,3–9. Pages 171–86 in Steck 1982c.

Steck, O. H. 1982c. *Wahrnehmungen Gottes: Gesammelte Studien.* ThB 70. Munich: Chr. Kaiser.

Steiner, M. 2003. Expanding the Borders: The Development of Jerusalem in the Iron Age. Pages 68–79 in *Jerusalem in Ancient History and Tradition.* Edited by T. L. Thompson (with the collaboration of S. K. Jayyusi). JSOTSup 381; CIS 13. London: T&T Clark International. |

Ussishkin, D. 2003. Jerusalem as a Royal and Cultic Centre in the 10th–8th Centuries B.C.E. Pages 529–38 in Dever and Gitin, eds., 2003.

Vaughn, A. G., and A. E. Killebrew, eds. 2003. *Jerusalem in Bible and Archaeology: The First Temple Period.* SBL.SS 18. Atlanta: SBL.

Weippert, M. 1978. Israel und Juda. *RLA* 5:200–208.

Why a Reform like Josiah's Must Have Happened

1 The Role of the Josianic Period for Israel's Religious and Political History

In his contribution to the present volume (pp. 65–77) [[= Davies, P. R., Josiah and the Law Book, in: Grabbe, L. L. (ed.), Good Kings and Bad Kings. The Kingdom of Judah in the Seventh Century BCE, European Seminar in Historical Methodology 5, LHBOTS 393, London/New York: T&T Clark, 2005, 65–77]], Philip R. Davies cited a statement that I made about ten years ago: 'The most important decision in the history of Israelite religion is made with a dating of an essential part of Deuteronomy in the time of Josiah' (Albertz 1994: I, 199). I had become aware that any reconstruction of Israel's religion decisively depends on whether you – in accordance with W. M. L. de Wette – equate the core of Deuteronomy with Josiah's law book (2 Kgs 22.8, 11), dating it in the last third of the seventh century, or whether you dissolve this connection and – in company with Hölscher (1922) and Kaiser (1984: 132–34) – shift the date of Deuteronomy to the post-exilic period. Since the date or even the existence of the Pentateuchal sources J and E have been heavily questioned, the dating of the Deuteronomy constitutes the last fixed point in Old Testament literary history. So, giving up the seventh-century dating of the Deuteronomy would have far-reaching consequences: not only important features of Israel's religion like monotheism, exclusivism, and brotherhood would have to be dated much later, but also most of the Deuteronomic reform ideas like the centralisation of cult or the subordination of all the state to the law would lose any connection to societal reality. In the Persian province of Yehud there was only one temple and there existed no king, thus there were no need for centralisation and subordination any longer. As a result of this, an important turning point in the development of Israel's religious history would disappear.

Recently it was shown that Josiah's reform became the decisive fixed point for the reconstruction of Israel's political history as well. In their recent book, Finkelstein and Silberman (2001)[1] developed their new view of the history of Israel and Judah, which they claimed to be based mainly on archaeological findings and not on the biblical text, whose historicity in their opinion is largely to be doubted. According to their view there was no United Monarchy under David and Solomon, and the Davidic empire never existed. The two states Israel and Judah came into existence independently, the state of Israel during the ninth, the

---

[1] The title of the German edition (2002) is more aggressive: *No Trumpets before Jericho: The Archaeological Truth about the Bible.* |

https://doi.org/10.1515/9783111202228-003

state of Judah not before the eighth century. Nevertheless, in spite of this | rather minimalistic view Finkelstein and Silberman do believe in the historicity of Josiah's reform. Moreover, they title their chapter on it 'A Great Reformation' and even call it a 'revolution' (Finkelstein and Silberman 2001: 275, 285, 288). The authors praise Josiah's reign as 'the climax of Israel's monarchic history' (Finkelstein and Silberman 2001: 275). And they add: 'During his thirty-one-year reign over the kingdom of Judah, Josiah was recognized by many as the greatest hope for national redemption, a genuine messiah who was destined to reform the fallen glories of the house of Israel' (Finkelstein and Silberman 2001: 275–76). According to the authors Josiah was not only the key figure of a 'new religious movement', but also created a new Israelite identity by attempting to unify the Judaeans with the people of the former northern state. In their view, vast parts of the biblical literature, not only Deuteronomy and the first edition of the Deuteronomistic History (DtrH) but also the stories of the Patriarchs, the Exodus, the Conquest, and the Judges were written during this great religious and national upheaval.[2] Even the stories about David and Solomon and their empire must be understood as reflections of the national hopes raised under Josiah and projected back into the past (cf. Finkelstein and Silberman 2001: 144). In 'Appendix F' of the book, which curiously enough was not included in the German edition, Finkelstein and Silberman admit on the grounds of archaeological considerations, however, that Josiah was possibly not able to realize his plans of a united monarchy to any large extent (cf. Finkelstein and Silberman 2001: 347–53).

One may ask what caused two scholars, who are inclined towards a minimal position, to reconstruct a vast religious and national movement under king Josiah that goes even beyond a scenario which 'conservative maximalists' like me would venture to draw? All methodical restrictions they made seemed to be forgotten: there are no, or no unambiguous, archaeological data which could verify Josiah's reform. The biblical text, which includes the report given by the DtrH in 2 Kings 22–23, is suddenly taken to be reliable. If we ask in amazement how that could happen, in my opinion the answer will be easy: Finkelstein and Silberman feel obliged to create a substitute for the United Monarchy that they denied. If it is right that pre-state Israel emerged from different populations and was organized in separate tribes, if it is right that the states of Israel and Judah 'represent two sides of ancient Israel's experience, two quite different societies with different attitudes and national identities' (Finkelstein and Silberman 2001: 24), then it must be

---

2 Cf. Finkelstein and Silberman 2001: 45–46, 68–71, 95, 120–22; in their early dating of the DtrH Finkelstein and Silberman are still following F. M. Cross. That they date awkwardly many of the sources of DtrH in the same years as the DtrH itself, which levels all distinctions of literary analysis, does not seem to trouble them.

explained how the unifying concept of 'Israel' was born, which included all tribes
and all the people from both states. Since the unifying concept is spread throughout all the exilic Prophets[3] and is present throughout the book of Deuteronomy,[4]
the reform of Josiah – accepting the traditional dating – is the latest | opportunity
that would explain such a development to some extent. Therefore it was taken
up by Finkelstein and Silberman and stressed so heavily. In their view the 'great
reformation' of Josiah in the late seventh century not only gave birth to Israel's
unique religion, but also to Israel's new identity as a united nation under Judaean
leadership. From this example we learn that we cannot just deal with the historicity of one period, but we are forced to observe the interdependency between the
assessments of different periods and must somehow bring them into balance.

Compared with Finkelstein and Silberman Philip Davies is more radical. In
his article he is questioning the historicity of Josiah's reform,[5] even though he
has denied the existence of the Davidic and Solomonic empire as well (cf. Davies
1992: 67–70). For the former, his main arguments are the following: first, at the
time of Josiah there existed no political vacuum after the decline of the Assyrian
empire. Davies shares the suggestion of Na'aman (1991: 39–41),[6] that the Assyrians
ceded control over Palestine 'in a more or less orderly way' to Egypt in return
for its military assistance against the Medes and Babylonians. Therefore 'the Judaean king had little or no opportunity for the exercise of political independence'
(see p. 65, below) [[= Davies, Josiah and the Law Book, 65]]. Second, since the
report of 2 Kings 18–23 does not mention any Assyrian dominance over Judah
after Hezekiah's revolt in 701 BCE, which contrasts sharply with the historical
evidence drawn from the extrabiblical sources, there is no reason to believe that
it is more reliable on what it tells about the internal political conditions of Judah,
including also Josiah's cultic measures. Third, since the book of Deuteronomy,
even in its core, does not belong to the late seventh century but is better dated
to the fifth century, there is no legislation that could serve as a base for Josiah's
reform. Davies is not quite sure about the fifth-century date; however his negative
result is clear: 'Weinfeld ..., among others, has argued, in defence of a Josianic
date for Deuteronomy, that the Assyrian vassal-treaty form (exemplified by those

---

3 Isa. 11.11–16; Jer. 30.3; 31.2–6, 15–22; Ezek. 37.15–22, etc.
4 As also stated by Philip R. Davies in his contribution to the present volume (pp. 65–77)
[[= Davies, Josiah and the Law Book, 65–77]], but with different consequences. |
5 Cf. already Davies 1992: 40–41.
6 See also Na'aman's contribution to the present volume (pp. 189–247, below) [[= Na'aman, N.,
Josiah and the Kingdom of Judah, in: Grabbe, L. L. (ed.), Good Kings and Bad Kings. The Kingdom
of Judah in the Seventh Century B.C.E., European Seminar in Historical Methodology 5,
LHBOTS 393, London/New York: T&T Clark, 2005, 189–247]].

of Esarhaddon) supplies a model for Deuteronomy. But to be valid, this argument
has to show that knowledge of such literary forms vanished at a certain point.
However, the influence of Assyria on the diplomatic rhetoric and literature (as
well as the imagination) of the ancient Near East persisted for several centuries'
(see p. 73, below) [[= Davies, Josiah and the Law Book, 73]]. In contrast to Finkelstein and Silberman the question of how the unifying concept of the 'biblical
Israel' could emerge does not bother Philip Davies. In his opinion, it was just an
idealized myth of the past, invented by the post-exilic Golah-society of Yehud
(1992: 87–93).[7]

Thus, Davies' argument has to do with the historical assessment of the international political situation during the reign of Josiah, the reliability of the DtrH,
especially in the book of Kings, and the chronological setting of the Deuteronomic
legislation in Deuteronomy 12–26. I would like to respond to that in the opposite
sequence. |

2 Dating Deuteronomy 12–26

I think Philip Davies is absolutely right when he states that any dating of Deuteronomy 12–26 must be done without the use of de Wette's hypothesis that the law
book found by Josiah (2 Kgs 22–23) can be identified with it (see pp. 69–70, below)
[[= Davies, Josiah and the Law Book, 69–70]]. Even if it is probable, that the
Deuteronomistic Historian wanted his readers to believe that the law book was
nothing else than the Deuteronomic law, which he had then included in his
work,[8] this identification could be a misleading invention. Methodologically, in-
ner-Deuteronomic observations have to decide whether a Josianic dating of the
Deuteronomic law can be accepted or not.

2.1. Davies rightly notes that the name given to the society for which the
Deuteronomy legislates is 'Israel' (see p. 71, below) [[= Davies, Josiah and the Law
Book, 71]]. One can add: the Deuteronomic legislation even stresses the concept
that Israel constitutes a unity, where all members are brothers. It does not know
any divisions concerning north or south; even a division into tribes is not mentioned in the core of Deuteronomy, where Israel is conceptualized as 'the people
of God'.[9] The alternative concept of Israel as a nation composed of twelve tribes,

---

7 The fact that the concept occurs already in the books of the exilic prophets (Ezekiel, Deutero-
Isaiah, see above) conflicts with this solution and forces us to date these later likewise. |
8 Cf. the identical expression ספר התורה in 2 Kgs 22.8, 11 and Deut. 28.61; 29.20; 31.26 (cf. 31.24)
and the scene, where Moses writes down the Deuteronomic law in Deut. 31.9–13.
9 The assumptions Philip R. Davies made in this context are not fully correct, see pp. 71–72,
below [[= Davies, Josiah and the Law Book, 71–72]]. |

which is so prominent in the Patriarchal Narratives and the Priestly Source, occurs only on the fringe of the book of Deuteronomy, in Deuteronomy 33, and has there only peripheral importance.

However, Davies' argument that this Deuteronomic concept of Israel would be historically problematic in the late seventh century and excludes such a dating is not convincing. It would be convincing only if one shares the historical and terminological reconstruction of Philip Davies: that there was no United Monarchy, that there existed only two different kingdoms, Judah and Israel, and that the meaning of the term 'Israel' in its historical sense must be restricted to the Northern Kingdom. If one takes those presuppositions for granted, the outcome that at the end of the seventh century Deuteronomy 12–26 should use only the name of the Northern Kingdom, which had perished a century before, for Judaean society would indeed be astonishing. But the presuppositions are questionable.

My first point is that already on the level of semantics the strict division that Davies made between the historical 'Israel', restricted to the Northern Kingdom, and the so-called 'biblical Israel', envisaging the ideal concept of a unified nation, is not true. I investigated the term 'Israel' in detail many years ago (Albertz 1987) and found that the name has an exclusive and an inclusive meaning. In its exclusive meaning it denotes the territory of Eshbaal (2 Sam. 2.9–10; 3.12, 21), the ten tribes of the middle and northern Palestinian hill country (2 Sam. 19.42–44), and later the Northern Kingdom (1 Kgs 12–2 Kgs 17). In its inclusive meaning it denotes all the tribes including Judah, so the 'men of Israel' (2 Sam. 15.13; 16.15, 18; 17.14, 24, etc.) and the 'elders of Israel' (2 Sam. 17.4, 15, etc.) during the Absalom revolt, when the northern and the southern tribes formed an alliance, or | the united kingdom of David and Solomon (2 Sam. 5.12; 6.20–21; 8.15; 19.23; 1 Kgs 1.34; 4.1; 11.42), that could also be called 'Israel and Judah' (2 Sam. 5.5; 11.11; 1 Kgs 1.35; 4.20). Since the exclusive and inclusive meaning are often alternating confusingly in one and the same literary unit (e.g. 2 Sam. 5.5, 12; 1 Kgs 1.34, 35), it seems to me extremely difficult to divide them diachronically and to assign them to an old historical or a late ideological level. If Davies' thesis was right, all narratives and reports on David and Solomon would have to be dated into the post-exilic period, when according to him the inclusive concept of 'biblical Israel' was invented (cf. 1992: 87–93). But even though the dating of the David narratives varies in the recent discussion,[10] there still remains one passage that clearly contradicts Davies' hypothesis: in Isa. 8.14 the prophet Isaiah could call the Southern and North-

---

10 The date of the Succession Narrative (2 Sam. 9–1 Kgs 2*) varies from the time of Solomon (L. Rost) to the post-exilic period (J. van Seters), but even very critical scholars such as D. M. Gunn ('several centuries after the events') and O. Kaiser ('between Hezekiah and Jehoiakim') defended a pre-exilic dating; see the discussion in Dietrich and Naumann 1995: 213–16.

ern Kingdom 'both houses of Israel'. Here the term 'Israel' explicitly embraces the two states (בתים). This means that unless one wants to question Isaiah's preaching during the Syro-Ephraimite crisis 734–732 BCE, the inclusive meaning of the name 'Israel' is already common during the eighth century. Therefore, it is still likely that the expansion of the term took place much earlier. In my view, 'Israel' denoted in the pre-state period a coalition of tribes in the middle and northern Palestinian hill country and was expanded in order to include the southern tribes during the late pre-state and the early monarchic period.[11] Accordingly, the fact that the Deuteronomy uses the name 'Israel' in a definitely inclusive sense is in no way astonishing and does not rule out a seventh-century date. On the contrary, the course of history in which the Northern Kingdom was destroyed and many refugees from the north joined the Judaean society in the late eighth century makes it comprehensible that the Deuteronomic legislators could easily appropriate the name 'Israel' for the Judaean society and stress – admittedly in archaic diction – the unity of the people without any tribal subdivisions.

Philip Davies suggested that the Persian period would be the most likely setting for the usage of the name 'Israel' in Deuteronomy. I have my serious doubts about this suggestion. The Nehemiah Memoir,[12] which we can date with a high degree of probability in the second part of the fifth century, does not lay any emphasis on the term 'Israel'. It uses 'Israel' only four times, two times for the people of the past (Neh. 1.6; 13.26) and just two times for those of the present (2.10; 13.18). Much more prominent is the usage of the term 'Jews', mostly with | the article 'the Jews' (ה/יהודים), which appears ten times (1.2; 2.16; 3.33, 34; 4.6; 5.1, 8, 17; 6.6; 13.23) and denotes all descendants of the inhabitants of the former kingdom of Judah wherever they live, whether in the province Yehud, in other territories of Palestine or in Babylonia or Persia. This new linguistic usage accords with Nehemiah's policy to strengthen the independence of Yehud by excluding all the non-Jewish from the community, especially the descendants of the former northern tribes in the province Samaria. For such a policy the term 'Israel', which originally had denoted and always had included the northern tribes, would be counter-productive. In the rest of the books Ezra and Nehemiah the term 'Israel'

---

11 Since not only 1 Kgs 12 but also Isa. 7.17 testify to the separation of the northern tribes from Judah, there must have existed some kind of United Monarchy under David and Solomon. Two independent and trustworthy sources cannot so easily be denied, not even by possible negative archaeological evidence. It must be taken into account that for the prophet Isaiah in the eighth century the separation of the north is still the most traumatic event in the history of Judah.

12 Neh. 1.1–7.5a; 12.21–32, 37–40; 13.4–31; probably without 7.1b; 13.24a, 30a. Cf. Mowinckel 1923: 278–322; Kellermann 1967: 4–56; Rudolph 1949: XXIV; Williamson 1985: XXIV–XXVIII; Gunneweg 1987: 176–80; Blenkinsopp 1988: 46–47; Karrer 2001: 128–213; Reinmuth 2002. |

is more prominent, but it does not include the whole people, but is mostly restricted to the emigrants of the Babylonian Golah.[13] Thus it seems to me extremely
difficult to explain the inclusive usage of the term 'Israel' in Deuteronomy from
a fifth-century background.

Progressing from the terminology to the cultural background, it must be stated that the inclusive use of the name 'Israel' was not a pure fiction but mirrors
a social reality. In spite of all political differences, the members of the northern
and southern tribes had the feeling that they shared common moral and religious
values. 'No such thing ought to be done in Israel', said the Judaean princess Tamar
to Amnon who wanted to rape her in Jerusalem. The God YHWH is always named
the 'God of Israel',[14] never the God of Judah,[15] even when he was venerated in
Jerusalem.[16] Therefore the authors of Deuteronomy could combine religious and
legal traditions from the north and the south when they stressed the ethnic, moral
and religious unity of 'Israel'.

2.2. Philip Davies thinks that the sharp distinction between Israel and the
foreign nations presented by the Deuteronomy would make no sense in a reform
under a king whose subjects include a plurality of cultures or population elements (see p. 72, below) [[= Davies, Josiah and the Law Book, 72]]. Interpreted
as a contrast between the immigrants and the indigenous population it would fit
much better in the conflict between the returnees and the 'people of the land' in
the Persian period. It can be admitted that there are material parallels between
the concepts of Deuteronomy and Ezra/Nehemiah. Nevertheless, there is the problem that the terminology in Deuteronomy and in Ezra/Nehemiah is completely
different: the foreign nations, who would seduce Israel and whom Israel should
expel, are called in Deuteronomy 12–26 generally (eighteen times) גוים, 'nations'
or 'many nations', 'big nations', 'strong nations', and so on,[17] but only four times
is עמים used.[18] But in Ezra/Nehemiah the term | גוים is used hardly at all; it
occurs only once in the expression גוי הארץ ('people of the land', Ezra 6.21) and
several times in the older Nehemiah Memoir for non-Jewish people elsewhere in

---

13 Cf. Ezra 2.2, 5, 59, 70; 3.1; 6.21; Neh. 9.2; the expression עם/ה ישראל in Ezra 2.2; 9.1; Neh. 7.7
does not appear in the Deuteronomy.

14 Altogether 202 times in the Hebrew Bible from Judg. 5.3, 5 to Mal. 2.16.

15 This result is statistically significant; the expression אלהי ירושלם occurs in the Hebrew Bible
only in 2 Chron. 32.19 and probably in the inscription A of Khirbet Bet Lei. Here it is stated, that
the hills of Judah belong to YHWH, who is also called אלהי כל ארץ; see Renz and Röllig 1995:
245.

16 Cf. the expression 'The Holy One of Israel' coined by Isaiah, Isa. 5.19, 24; 30.11, 12, 15; 31.1.

17 Deut. 7.1, 17, 22; 8.20; 9.1, 4, 5; 11.23; 12.2, 29, 30; 15.6; 17.14; 18.9, 14; 19.1; 20.15; 26.19.

18 Deut. 6.14; 17.14, 19; 20.16. |

the world.[19] In Ezra/Nehemiah the groups, from which the Golah-community should separate itself, are called עמי הארץ/הארצות ('people of the land' or 'people of the lands').[20] The same expression עמי הארץ is used in Deut. 28.10 and in the DtrH (Josh. 4.24; 1 Kgs 8.43, 53, 60) with the total different meaning 'the nations of the world', like simple עמים in Deuteronomy 12–26 and its admonitory frame.[21] Thus it is not possible to bring Deuteronomy and Ezra–Nehemiah into a literary coherence. In contrast, to date Deuteronomy to a similar time as Ezra/Nehemiah, one must suppose that both literary works emerge in two totally separated groups whose terminologies had no mutual influence. Such a suggestion would not be totally impossible, though a little bit difficult, if we take the small size of the province Yehud into account. But if we become aware that the editors of Ezra/Nehemiah cited explicitly the law of Deut. 23.4 from 'the book of Moses' as authoritative (Neh. 13.1–2), it will be more likely that the Deuteronomic legislation preceded the writing of Ezra/Nehemiah by a long time. That would not completely exclude a Persian date but would limit it to the early Persian period.

Davies' doubts that the sharp distinction between Israel and the former inhabitants of the land would not be useful for a reform in the seventh century can perhaps be dispelled. Whatever different people had formed the people of Israel and Judah during a long historical process, their differences had fused for the most part in the late seventh century. Under those conditions, the Deuteronomic demand to expel the indigenous population from the land and keep apart from their horrible customs can be understood as an attempt to denounce specific Judaean and Israelite beliefs and practices as dangerous foreign influences that must be radically removed. The Deuteronomic reformers wanted to implant a new feeling of being a particular, a 'holy people'[22] in Judaean society. Such a target would fit well the conditions of the seventh century, after Judah had suffered a century of Assyrian domination.

2.3. In his analysis, Philip Davies followed S. A. Geller (2000: 273–319) who stated that Deuteronomic legislators support an individual concept of covenant that would constitute a close parallel to the book of Nehemiah. Geller thinks that a new examination of Deuteronomy would conclude 'that the collectivity of the covenant community barely masks the fact that it is a radically new type of association of individuals' (2000: 300). Geller and Davies have rightly pointed out that many laws of Deuteronomy stress the responsibility of the individual, like Deut. 13.7–12. But their assessment that it 'negates the doctrine of collective re-

---

19 Neh. 5.8, 9, 17; 6.6, 16; 13.26.
20 Ezra 3.3; 9.1, 2; 10.2, 11; Neh. 9.24, 30; 10.29, 31; cf. גוי הארץ, Ezra 6.21.
21 Deut. 4.6, 9; 6.14; 7.6, 7, 14, 16; 10.15; 13.8; 14.2; 28.10, 37, 64; 30.3; 32.8.
22 Deut. 7.6; 14.2, 21; 26.19. |

sponsibility for sin' can be questioned in this generality, because the rule of Deut. 24.16 that a son should not be punished for the sins of his father and vice | versa is only valid for human jurisdiction. If God's jurisdiction is involved, then Deuteronomic legislators know a collective responsibility for appeasing God's anger (e.g. Deut. 21.1–9). And the same is valid for the Deuteronomic concept of covenant: in all passages where it is unfolded in some detail (Deut. 26.16–19; 28.69–29.28) it is always a collective 'you' who enters into the covenant with YHWH.[23] This collective shape of the Deuteronomic concept is a heritage of the Assyrian vassal-treaties, which gave the model. A closer comparison between the shapes of covenant in Deuteronomy and Ezra/Nehemiah reveals a decisive difference: what had been a collective covenant in accordance with the vassal-treaties in Deuteronomy became in Ezra 10 and Nehemiah 10 an individual commitment according to private contracts; no longer God but only the community made the agreement, and all leaders of the families of the different groups of society signed personally that they were going to commit themselves to specific moral and religious duties.[24] Not by chance does a different terminology for such a self-commitment (אמנה instead of ברית) occur in Neh. 10.1. These differences in the covenant concepts are so fundamental that it is unlikely that both could come from the same post-exilic period. In my view, the parallels between the Deuteronomic concept of covenant and the Assyrian vassal-treaties make a dating in the seventh or at latest in the sixth century more probable.[25]

2.4. Philip Davies reflects the somewhat utopian character of the law of kings (Deut. 17.14–20) in order to undermine the traditional seventh-century dating. Here he is in good company with G. Hölscher, who argued likewise that 'the ideological character of the Deuteronomic legislation' demonstrates 'that it could not have emerged in the pre-exilic Judah, but belongs to the period after the destruction' (1922: 228). Davies mainly pointed out that the radical limitations of monarchical power made in 17.16–20 were completely unrealistic: 'There are no plausible explanations why a king should accept a reform that deprives him of the essential powers of monarchy, justice and warfare' (see p. 74, below) [[= Davies, Josiah and the Law Book, 74]]. Admittedly, the law of kings sounds unrealistic to us; the question remains whether a later date would make its utopian concept more realistic. Moreover, there is no hint in the text that its author was

---

23 The same is true for the covenant of Josiah in 2 Kgs 23.1–3. It was the king as the representative of the people who made the covenant, the people only entered into it collectively, of course.
24 I owe this insight to Dr Ralf Rothenbusch, with whom I co-operated in the 'Sonderforschungsbereich 493' in Münster.
25 Cf. also the close material parallels between Deut. 28.20–44 and the vassal-treaties of Esarhaddon pointed out by Steymans 1995.

looking forward to the restoration of an idealized kingship (cf. Nelson 2002: 223), in contrast to many exilic and post-exilic prophetic texts.[26] Every attempt to date Deut. 17.14–20 in the Persian period is confronted with the problem that this law still held on to the divine election of the king according to the Davidic theology (Ps. 89.4, 20), whereas the Davidides disappeared from the political stage after the failure of Zerubbabel 519/518 BCE. After him, Nehemiah would be in accordance with that law in some | way: a pious, selfless ruler, one who was obedient to God's law, as he presented himself (Neh. 5). And there were some people who wanted to make this Persian governor a king (6.6–7). Anyhow, he was no Davidide; therefore he and persons like him possibly did not influence the concept of Deut. 17.14–20.[27] So there are good reasons for dating the Deuteronomic law of kings during a period when Davidic kings were still on the throne.

Philip Davies overstates a little the radicalism of that law. As Nelson rightly points out, 'it does not forbid characteristic royal activities, but rather thoroughly limits them' (Nelson 2002: 222). That the king, who traditionally had been the supreme judge and legislator in the ancient Near East, is subjected to that law must be seen as the intended consequence of all Deuteronomic legislation: Moses as mediator of the divine law is promoted in order to replace the king as legislator (cf. Albertz 1997: 124–30). In reality that does not mean that 'authority is conferred exclusively on the priests', as Davies suggested (see p. 74, below) [[= Davies, Josiah and the Law Book, 74]]. According to Deut. 17.8–13 the supreme legal authority is conferred on a kind of upper court in Jerusalem, which consists of priests and laymen (v. 9). In the matters of warfare again priests and lay officials are provided with authority (20.1–9), but the functions of the king as military leader are not excluded (17.16).[28] What the Deuteronomic legislators intended with their radical law was nothing else than the creation of what was called later a 'constitutional monarchy'. The measures may have been impractical to some degree and somewhat utopian like other archaic reform models of the ancient world,[29] but the goal was very concrete and – as we can see in the later history

---

26 Cf. Isa. 11.1–5; Jer. 23.1–7; Ezek. 34.23–24; 37.24–25; Mic. 5.1–5; Zech. 9.9–10, etc. |

27 The same would be true for Gedaliah, who otherwise would be also a good candidate for the ideal of a ruler with limited power.

28 Thus Davies' criticism of my thesis that the עַם הָאָרֶץ was the promoter of the Josianic reform falls short twice. First, his statement 'that these people would hardly have transferred authority over warfare or justice to the *priesthood*' (see p. 75, below) [[= Davies, Josiah and the Law Book, 75]] does describe the intention of the Deuteronomic legislation correctly. Second, in my opinion a broad coalition promoted the Josianic reform, consisting not only of the עַם הָאָרֶץ but also of scribal circles like the Shaphanides, priestly circles like the Hilkiades, and prophets like Huldah and Jeremiah, cf. Albertz 1994: 201–203.

29 Cf. Rüterswörden 1987: 102–105, who pointed out that the deprivation of the king's power as seen in Deut. 17 has some similarities in the Greek history of polity.

of humankind – with other measures definitely realizable. But why should such a far reaching constitutional reform be conceptualized at a time when the legal limitation of monarchic power was completely irrelevant for Judah? In my view, the most probable period for dating the Deuteronomic law of kings are the reigns of Jehoiakim and Zedekiah, when the alliances with Egypt became a new threat for Judah (17.16) and when the Shaphanide scribes, who are the best candidates for having written the Deuteronomic law, resisted the ruling kings (Jer. 26.24; 36.9–26).[30] |

2.5. Finally Philip Davies suggested that the centralization of the cult was a problem of the early Persian period, when after the reconstruction of the Jerusalem temple its claim to be the only authorized temple of YHWH had to be carried through against the claim of other cult places like that in the former capital Mizpeh. These suggestions are highly speculative. Whether there existed any YHWH-temple in Mizpeh during the period of exile is totally uncertain. The בית יהוה of Jer. 41.5, sometimes taken as a piece of evidence (cf. Veijola 1982: 190–210), probably refers to the temple in Jerusalem.[31] No archaeological evidence has been found. It seems that the sanctuary in Bethel played a role during the exilic and early post-exilic period (cf. 2 Kgs 17.24–34a; cf. Albertz 1994: II, 525), but its legitimacy was heavily questioned. Again no temple has been found, so it is difficult to assess what really happened. We can only state, that in none of the post-exilic books of the Hebrew Bible – neither in Haggai and Zechariah nor in Ezra and Trito-Isaiah – is there any hint of a dispute on the question of whether any other sanctuary than Jerusalem should be reconstructed or put into operation. On the contrary, the prophet Haggai presupposed that no other sanctuary existed apart from the Jerusalem temple that could bring about the blessing over the land (Hag. 1.7–11). Thus, we cannot rule out that there were again rivalries between different YHWH sanctuaries in the post-exilic time,[32] but we can say that cult centralization was no serious problem of that period.

---

30 The strange prohibition of bringing back the people to Egypt in order to multiply horses motivated by an oracle of YHWH (Deut. 17.16aβb), which seems to be inserted into its context, can easily have reference to the military alliance between Zedekiah and Psammetichus II in the years between 594 and 591 BCE. That alliance probably included the supply of Judaean mercenaries for Egypt, cf. Albertz 2002: 27. If this reference is accepted, we would have a *terminus ad quem* for the Deuteronomic law of kings. |

31 Not only in the tale of Jeremiah's woe (Jer. 38.14), but always in the book of Jeremiah the expression denotes the Jerusalem temple.

32 The temple of YHW in Elephantine seems to be simply disregarded by the officials of Jerusalem, cf. Cowley 1923: 31.18–19. According to Lemaire 2002: 149–56, there existed a temple or shrine of YHW (בית יהו) in Idumaea during the fourth century. But the idea that somewhere in remote southern Palestine should have existed a proper cult centre where not only YHWH, but also the Babylonian God Nabû, and the Arabic Goddess ʿUzza were venerated, sounds to me very

Thus we can conclude: None of Davies' arguments that Deuteronomy 12–26 should be better dated into the fifth century is convincing. There might be some doubts on a seventh century dating, but the Deuteronomic legislation fits rather less well the socio-political conditions and the literature of the Persian period.

3 Dating the Deuteronomistic History

Since 2 Kings does not know any Assyrian hegemony during the seventh century, Philip Davies questioned the historicity of the DtrH altogether. That seems to be appropriate in so far as Davies assigns a very late date to the DtrH. He has not dealt with it explicitly in the present article, but if he thinks of a fifth-century date for the earliest pieces of Deuteronomy, then the DtrH, which also included most of its later parts, cannot have emerged before the beginning of the fourth century. A History that is separated from Josiah's reform by more than 200 years can be of doubtful reliability. But the question must be raised: Is such a late dating of the DtrH possible at all? |

The suggestion that the report of Josiah's reform was contemporary with the events, which is advocated by most scholars of the Cross school, has led I. Finkelstein and N. A. Silberman, among others, to believe that the DtrH is completely reliable on this point. But recently Th. Römer, who sympathizes with the Cross school, has shown convincingly that 2 Kings 22–23 'should be dated from the exilic period' (Römer 1997: 10).[33] What is true for this report is also true for the whole DtrH, whose climax it constitutes. Other evidence comes from 1 Kgs 8.46–53, where Solomon's prayer refers explicitly to the exile. Since it can be shown that this passage is no later addition but belongs to the Deuteronomistic edition of the chapter (8.1, 9, 14–30, 44–53, 55–61), which includes an older prayer in 8.31–43,[34] the exilic dating of DtrH becomes unavoidable. The last piece of evidence

---

unlikely. Since the *Gattung* of text 283 is a cadaster, perhaps the names should be better interpreted as personal names of the land owners. |

33 Römer points to the Huldah oracle, which presupposes the exile (cf. 2 Kgs 22.16–17), and other features (1997: 6). As Hardmeier (2000: 81–145) has shown, the report must be seen as a mostly coherent literary unit, which included in 2 Kgs 23.4–15 an older arrangement of cultic reform measures (*waw-perfect* sentences). Only a few verses are probably later additions: 23.15*, 16–18, 19–20, 24a.

34 1 Kgs 8.46–53 belongs to the same literary layer as 8.44–45 (cf. השמעת השמים in vv. 45, 49 in distinction from the expressions used in the *Vorlage*, cf. vv. 32, 34, 36, 39, 43; and the use of דרך in the sense 'towards' in vv. 44, 48, etc.); both passages are bound to the Deuteronomistic introduction (cf. v. 44 and 18.19; vv. 48 and 16). The Deuteronomistic reworking can be seen by the fact that vv. 44–45 is a doublet of vv. 33–34. Moreover, the passage 8.46–53 contains many parallels to other Deuteronomistic texts, especially to Deut. 4 and 30.1–11.

comes from the end of the DtrH (2 Kgs 25.27–30), which reports the release of Jehoiachin by Amel-Marduk in the year 562 BCE. Leaving apart the question to what extent the Deuteronomistic Historians used older material, it becomes likely that the years after 562 are the first possible date for the DtrH, as M. Noth (1957: 91) has already proposed. If one is not tied to the model of the Cross-school, the *terminus a quo* 562 BCE will be relatively certain.

The uncertainty concerns the *terminus ad quem*. Since several scholars are inclined to date the DtrH partly or completely into the Persian period (cf., among others, Würthwein 1994: 1–11; Römer 1997: 10–11), the question arises whether it is possible to define a latest possible date. Taking into consideration some older text- and literary-critical studies of A. Rofé (1985, 1987) and E. Tov (1985, 1986), R. F. Person (2002: 31–63) recently pleaded for a longer genesis of the DtrH, starting during the period of exile and coming to an end not before the time of Ezra. Person draws a vivid picture of what he called the 'Deuteronomic School' that he imagined as a scribal guild: after it had come home from Babylonia it supported Zerubbabel, but disillusioned with his failure and a later Persian supported administration, it developed an increasingly eschatological critique. Finally, Ezra's mission and the introduction of a new law led to its demise (Person 2002: 121–22, 135, 152). Whether that all happened, we do not know, but if we ask more concretely what passages would derive from the year 520 onwards, Person can name only a small number and mostly no others than those which have often been seen to be the latest.[35] Sometimes the historical setting | given by Person remains obscure; for example, Person dates Deut. 30.1–14 during both the time of Zerubbabel and the period after him. Moreover, it remains strange that in none of the passages can we find an allusion to any event that we know from the period between Zerubbabel and Ezra: neither the reconstruction of the temple, nor the reconstruction of the Jerusalem wall is mentioned. So Person's results are not really convincing. There might have been smaller additions and limited alterations as the differences between the text traditions (MT, LXX, Samaritanus) show, but they are less substantial and may be even later than Person thinks. Rather, his investigation demonstrates that the Persian period, apart from its very beginning (539–520 BCE), did not leave any clear footprint in the DtrH.[36] The substantial redactions of DtrH seem to have happened earlier.

---

35 So Deut. 4.29–31; 30.1–14; 1 Kgs 8; 2 Kgs 17; 25.27–30 and some others: Josh. 1.1–11; Judg. 3.1–6; 17.6; 21.25; 1 Sam. 16–18; 2 Sam. 7.1–17; 23.1–7; 1 Kgs 21.1–20. |

36 Römer (1997: 11) admitted this fact, when he wrote: 'We may still ask why are there no direct allusions to the Persian period in DH?' But his answer, that the Deuteronomistic Historians – like modern ones – avoided including their own present, is not convincing. The present can be excluded or not, but in every historical work, whether ancient or modern, the reader can find out from what temporal perspective it was written.

In this connection, it is of crucial importance that, apart from a few exceptions that will be discussed below, DtrH reveals no knowledge that the exile would ever come to an end. That can be demonstrated by 1 Kgs 8.46–50, one of the passages that clearly reflect the experience of the exilic period. According to vv. 49–50 God is asked to hear the prayers of the exiles in order to forgive them 'and grant them mercy before those who have taken them captive so that they may show them mercy'. In this passage, there is no hint of knowledge that the mighty Babylonian empire could ever collapse, there are no expectations that God would liberate the exiles and bring them home. The only hope is the wish to find mercy in the eyes of the Babylonian officials, to whose despotism they are hopelessly subjected.[37] What is meant more concretely can be demonstrated by the parallel passage in Jer. 42.12: the wish that the Babylonian king would not also punish all Judaeans for the murder of Gedaliah but would spare those who were loyal to him. The Deuteronomistic Historians describe a similar event at the very end of their work (2 Kgs 25.27–30): the Babylonian king Amel-Marduk released Jehoiachin from prison and restored his position of an honoured vassal. Probably Nebuchadnezzar had sentenced him to be his hostage because of the murder of Gedaliah by a member of the royal family.[38] When after his accession Amel-Marduk reprieved Jehoiachin, he actually 'showed him mercy' in accordance with the prayer of 2 Kgs 8.49–50.

Thus, 1 Kgs 8.46–50 and 2 Kgs 25.27–30 share the same horizon of hope and probably belong to the same literary layer. Both do not expect the downfall of the Babylonian empire, but a better treatment under the Babylonian government. Thus, these texts cannot have been written after 539 BCE, when the Babylonian empire was destroyed. Since there is no hint of a major political change, it is very probable that these passages emerged before Cyrus' impressive victory over | Lydia in 547/46 BCE. As 2 Kgs 25.27–30 constitutes the compositional ending of the DtrH, therefore most of that history can be dated between 562 and 547 BCE. There are only two passages in the present DtrH that move beyond this glimmer of hope. The first is Deut. 4.25–32, the second Deut. 30.1–10. All of the long sermon of Deut. 4.1–40 is an addition to its context, which presupposes the introduction to DtrH (Deut. 1–3),[39] but is still not known by it. Nevertheless, its shape is Deuteronomistic in style and theology. Within 4.25–32, which bends the listener's eyes to the future, vv. 29–31 seem to be again a later addition (cf. Nelson 2002: 62, 68).

---

37 Cf. the same expression נתן רחמים לפני in Gen. 43.14; Jer. 42.12; Neh. 1.11; Ps. 106.46; Dan. 1.9.
38 For the historical reconstruction of this event and its far-reaching consequences, see Albertz 2001: 63–64, 89–91. |
39 Cf. Deut. 4.3–4 and 3.29; 4.21–22 and 3.23–28. The chs. 1–3 of Deuteronomy do not prepare for the sermon. With regard to the content, Deut. 4 interprets Deut. 5.

After giving a grim portrayal of the exile in vv. 25–28, the text turns abruptly to a positive viewpoint:

> You will seek YHWH your God from there and you will find him, if only you search for him with all your heart and all your being. In your distress when all these things have happened to you, in the days to come[40] you will return to YHWH your God and obey him. For a merciful God is YHWH your God. He will not desert or destroy you. He will not forget the covenant with your ancestors that he swore them.[41] (Deut. 4.29–31)

In this passage there is still no hope for a return to the homeland, though its author expects a drastic change between God and his people. YHWH will become attainable again for his people, and the people will return to its God. Israel will no longer be confronted with YHWH's jealous anger, but will experience his mercy again. The same kind of hope expressed by a very similar wording can be found in Jer. 29.10–14a.[42] As I could show elsewhere, this passage belongs to the second edition of the Deuteronomistic book of Jeremiah (JerD²).[43] This edition can probably be dated during the years 545–540, just before the downfall of the Babylonian empire.[44] During the same years the anonymous prophetical group whom we call Deutero-Isaiah proclaimed that the period of God's wrath was over and a new period of God's mercy would begin (Isa. 40.1–2). So it is highly probable that a Deuteronomistic Historian – by adding Deut. 4.29–31 – actualized the DtrH during those years when a drastic change in the Near Eastern history could be foreseen.

The second passage, Deut. 30.1–10, has so many significant features in common that it may have been written by the same author.[45] However, R. D. Nelson | 2002: 348) is right to state that '30.1–11 goes a step further than 4.29–31 to envision

---

40 The term באחרית הימים has nothing to do with eschatology as Person (2002: 125–26) suggests, but means a just and fairer future like in Gen. 49.1; Num. 24.14; Deut. 31.29; Jer. 30.24.

41 The translation is taken from Nelson 2002: 58–59.

42 Jer. 29.14bβ does not occur in LXX and is a later addition.

43 Albertz 2001: 326–55; in my opinion the second edition consists of Jer. 1–45* without the book of consolation (Jer. 30–31) and its narrative transition (Jer. 32–35).

44 Jer. 29.10 reckons a 70-year duration of the Babylonian dominion. The most probable solution to identify the beginning of that period can be seen in Nebuchadnezzar's accession to the throne in 605 or his first regnal year 604 BCE (cf. Schmid 1996: 224–25). Then the 70-years period would end in the years 535 or 534. Since the collapse of the Babylonian empire happened some years earlier, the passage must have been written before the year 539.

45 So Nelson 2002: 348. The phrase שוב עד־יהוה – with the preposition עד instead of normal אל – occurs within the DtrH only in Deut. 4.30 and 30.2, and is extremely infrequent in the Hebrew | Bible (Hos. 14.2; Isa. 19.22; Lam. 3.40); the parallelism of returning to YHWH and hearing his voice occurs in 4.30 and 30.2; cf. 30.8, 10, the phrase 'with all your heart and all your being' in 4.29 and 30.2, 6, 10, etc.

the return home from the exile'. Along with that, God promised to multiply his people and make them prosperous again (v. 5). The wide horizon of hope reminds one of the promises of salvation made in the 'Book of Consolation' (Jer. 30–31), although it is still less detailed. In my view, those belong to the third edition of the Deuteronomistic book of Jeremiah (JerD³).[46] Likewise the hope that God would circumcise the heart of his people (Deut. 30.6) and by this would restore the broken relationship from his side has its closest parallels in JerD³ (Jer. 31.31–33; 32.37–41; cf. Jer. 4.4 and Deut. 10.16). JerD³ can be dated with some probability in the years between 525 and 521/0 BCE, after Cambyses' campaign against Egypt focused the Persian interest on the southwest of the empire, including Palestine, and before Darius conquered Babylon, which rebelled against him.[47] Thus, it is very probable that Deut. 30.1–10 also has to be dated in these dramatic years when, after the Gaumata rebellion and the usurpation of Darius, the Judaean minority got the first chance of repatriation. Both passages, Deut. 4.29–31 and 30.1–10, constitute a hopeful frame around the book of Deuteronomy. Thus, their insertion is part of a deliberate redaction of the DtrH. The time when that took place cannot be determined exactly, but it is improbable that it happened much later than the year 520 BCE, when after the return of Zerubbabel and Joshua the restoration in Judah was started. Since the discernible latest passages of the DtrH belong still in the late sixth and not in the fifth century as R. F. Person suggested, its *terminus ad quem* can probably be fixed around the year 520 BCE. However, the concept and most of the text of that history was largely drafted before the rise of Cyrus in 547 BCE.

In the event that the DtrH emerged largely between 562 and 547 and its later parts followed until the year 520, then several conclusions can be drawn which are of some importance for the assessment of the Josianic reform. First, we get another important confirmation that the book of Deuteronomy could not have emerged in the later Persian period but must have been written earlier. Since Deuteronomy 4 presupposes not only the Deuteronomic core in chs. 12–26, but also includes its admonitory frame in Deut. 4.44–30.20, the book of Deuteronomy must have been largely finished by 540. Second, since most of the DtrH was composed during the 15 years following the release of Jehoiachin (562), their authors were not too far away from the period when Josiah's reform was carried through (622–609 BCE). The time covers just the range of 47 to 75 years.[48] This |

---

46 Cf. Jer. 30.18–22; 31.10–14, 21–22, 23–26; 32.37–44; 50.17–20, 33–34; 51.34–37. In my view, JerD³ consists of Jer. 1–51*, including the book of consolation and the oracles against foreign nations, cf. Albertz 2001: 255–60.

47 Cf. the last oracle of the book of Jeremiah (51.58), which expects the occupation of Babylon.

48 Handy (1995: 252–75) rightly points out that the report of Josiah's reform is not contemporary, but 'cannot have been written prior to the sixth century' (p. 259). But when he concludes that

would mean that the Deuteronomistic Historians had to be aware that there were still some eye-witnesses alive and that there were a lot of people among their audience whose fathers or grandfathers had participated in Josiah's government. So they could not invent fabulous fairy tales, whatever religious ideology they wanted to promote. They could overstate some measures and they could ignore others – and they did both: they generalized the cult reform, but they ignored the social and national reform attempts – nevertheless, they could not lie. This means that the reliability of the DtrH for the events of the late seventh and early sixth century can be assessed as good, if we take its ideology into account. For example, as it is obvious that the Deuteronomistic Historians shared a nationalistic view and therefore praised revolts against the Assyrian dominance (2 Kgs 17.2–4; 18.5–6), there is no wonder that they ignored the re-establishment of the Assyrian domination under Manasseh.[49] As far as reliability is concerned, we cannot extrapolate conclusions from their treatment of foreign policy to that of domestic policy, as Philip Davies did.[50]

Apart from the temporal proximity, there is another strong argument that excludes the suggestion of a pure invention. The Josianic reform does not really fit the DtrH. According to the theological concept of the Deuteronomistic Historians, Josiah's exceptional cult reform that met YHWH's demands as never before should have opened Judah to a wonderful future. At least, it should have averted the catastrophe, the destruction of Judah and the deportations of major parts of its inhabitants. The historians had a great deal of trouble, to bring the course of history in line with the Josianic reform: they actually invented(!) a period of horrible apostasy under Manasseh, claimed that this provoked YHWH to decide on destruction (2 Kgs 21.10–15), and explained that this decision could not be removed by Josiah's reform, but only delayed (23.25–27). The concept of such an unchangeable destiny contradicts their effort to show God's morality in history. Their will to keep the Josianic reform and to defend its correctness forced the Deuteronomistic Historians to distort their own theology in some way. So it must have been such an important event for them that they could not deny it.

---

the report cannot be reliable, because it would have been written 'a century or more' after the events | of Josiah's reign (p. 275), then it becomes apparent, that he has no clear idea about the *terminus ad quem* of the DtrH.

49 They were also forced to do so by incorporating the nationalistic Isaiah narrative (2 Kgs 18.9–10; 18.13–19.37*) into their history, which asserted the departure of the Assyrians; cf. Hardmeier 1989. The Deuteronomistic Historians also ignored that Jehu became a vassal of Assyria as can be seen and read on the 'Black Obelisk' of Shalmanesar III.

50 See pp. 65–77, below [[= Davies, Josiah and the Law Book, 65–77]]. |

4 The Historical Evidence

Finally, Philip Davies argued that the basic historical conditions during the late seventh century did not admit any significant reform movement. In his view, after the decline of the Assyrian power in Palestine, Egypt took over the hegemony directly. After having been a vassal of Assyria, Josiah became immediately an Egyptian vassal and did not have the scope of action for any bigger changes. In | this assessment, Davies agrees with H. Niehr, who stated: 'All of these statements result in a picture of Josiah as an Egyptian vassal, unable to establish an enlarged kingdom or to pursue independent politics'.[51]

However, it must be remembered that such a historical reconstruction, which has now become more popular,[52] is not attested by any source but is a conclusion of more general considerations. Neither the archaeological results of Meṣad Ḥashavyahu nor the mysterious death of Josiah at Megiddo convey a clear picture.[53] How Assyrian rule collapsed in Judah, Samaria, and the other Palestinian provinces, and when and to what degree it was replaced by Egyptian rule, we do not know exactly. Biblical sources rather suggest a break and a certain vacuum of power until the Egyptians established their hegemony over Palestine in the year 609 BCE. In Isa. 8.23b–9.6 the withdrawal of the Assyrian armies could be compared with a great victory and is experienced as liberation.[54] And according to Jer. 2.36–37 influential groups of the population of the former Northern Kingdom obviously believed that the Egyptians could help them to restore their political independence, possibly against Josiah's national ambitions (cf. Albertz 2003: 228–30). Perhaps Josiah's strange interference in Megiddo has to do with such compet-

---

51 'Aus allen diesen Angaben ergibt sich das Bild eines ägyptischen Vasallen Joschija, der keineswegs ein Großreich etablieren und eine eigenständige Politik verfolgen konnte' (Niehr 1995: 44).
52 Cf. Miller and Hayes 1986: 383–91; Na'aman 1991: 40–41, 52–53; Ahlström 1993: 763–67, 778–79.
53 See the interpretation of Na'aman, referred to by Davies (pp. 65–67, below) [[= Davies, Josiah and the Law Book, 65–67]]. Miller and Hayes 1986: 388, draw from Jer. 2.16–18, 36–37 the conclusion that in Palestine 'there was a hegemony shared between the Nile and Mesopotamian superpowers'. But this interpretation is very doubtful. Jer. 2.4–4.2 is addressed to Israel, the people of the former Northern Kingdom (2.4). The first passage, Jer. 2.14–18, does not deal with the present but with the past (cf. *waw* consecutive imperfect in v. 15), when the Northern Kingdom pursued its ruinous seesaw politics between Assyria and Egypt (cf. Hos. 5.12–14). On the contrary, Jer. 2.36–37 (and also the actualizing verse, 2.16) deals with present dangers and warns the northern brethren to place their hope in Egypt because they will fail, as their hope of Assyria had failed in the past. It can be suggested that – after becoming free from Assyrian rule – the population in the North hoped to win the restoration of their state with the help of Egypt. Thus, during the late-seventh century Egypt clearly succeeded Assyria in Palestine; cf. Albertz 2003.
54 That Isa. 8.23b–9.6 is to be dated in the late seventh century and refers to the young king Josiah was convincingly shown by Barth 1977: 141–77. |

ing political interest. There seemed to be unsettled political conditions in Judah and Israel for some years, which could raise very different expectations and options.

Whatever concrete scenario one might imagine, however, it is interesting to notice that even most of those scholars who think that the domination over Palestine passed uninterrupted from the Assyrians to the Egyptians do not want to deny the possibility of the Josianic reform. According to N. Na'aman the emphasis of the Egyptian rule 'was placed on control of the valley districts and the coast, whereas the mountain areas were considered of secondary importance' (1991: 40). So, in his view the Egyptian vassalage of Josiah was of a more nominal kind. The same is true for Finkelstein and Silberman who restricted the | Egyptian interest 'mainly to the coast' and saw the path 'open for a final fulfilment of Judahite ambitions' (2001: 283). Thus, in any case the change of hegemony in Palestine during the last third of the seventh century opened a space where a cultic, social, and national reform could take place in Judah. Even a limited expansion of Judah to the north on the hill country is conceivable under such international conditions.[55]

Admittedly, apart from the report in 2 Kings 22–23, other sources for the Josianic reform are rather scarce. The archaeologists could not provide anything essential for it.[56] Only a little bit more did the biblical scholars! The often repeated argument that contemporary texts like the book of Jeremiah[57] do not know anything of the reform is not correct. The passages of Jer. 5.4–6 and 8.7–8 refer explicitly to a law of YHWH that should give advice to the people, especially to the learned and wealthy upper class, but was neglected after Josiah's death. In Jer. 3.22–4.2; 31.2–6 the Israelites of the former Northern Kingdom are invited to come to Jerusalem and worship YHWH there, in accordance with Josiah's national

---

55 Heltzer (2000) thinks that the seventh-century bulla of the Shlomo Moussaieff Collection would testify that Josiah annexed even such a northern place like 'Arubboth in the vicinity of Taanach as early as 630/629 BCE from the Assyrians. But the evidence remains doubtful.

56 Cf. Finkelstein and Silberman 2001: 287–88. The little that was found was partly made unusable by improper excavation; cf. the unclear closure or abandonment of the temple in Arad. The only possible evidence is provided by the seal impressions of the late seventh century, which include only names, sometimes decorated with some floral ornaments, but are lacking the religious, often astral icons, in contrast to the seals before, cf. Uehlinger 1995: 67–70, as well as his contribution to the present volume (pp. 279–316) [[= Uehlinger, C., Was there a Cult Reform under King Josiah? The Case for a Well-Grounded Minimum, in: Grabbe, L. L. (ed.), Good Kings and Bad Kings. The Kingdom of Judah in the Seventh Century BCE, European Seminar in Historical Methodology 5, LHBOTS 393, London/New York: T&T Clark, 2005, 279–316]]. But they also can mean just a higher level of literate persons or simply a new fashion.

57 So again Kaiser 1984: 134.

policy. And a closer reading of Jeremiah 2–6 reveals that the accusation against syncretism, which played a prominent role in Jeremiah's preaching to the brethren in the north (2.4–4.2), does not appear in his preaching to the Judaeans at all (4.3–6.30), which could testify to the results of Josiah's reform indirectly. Sometimes it is said that the different kinds of syncretism and foreign cult practices in the accusation in Ezek. 8.7–18 contradicted any Josianic reform; but this event belongs to a much later period (593/2 BCE), 29 years after the cult reform (622 BCE). Moreover, it must be taken into account that Ezekiel could easily misunderstand or overstate a rumour from Jerusalem that he heard in Babylonia.[58]

Thus, the body of evidence that the Josianic reform happened during the late seventh century could have been much better. Often we possess only clues, not hard facts. Philip Davies is to be commended for not only denying the Josianic reform and pushing the book of Deuteronomy into any later period but also trying to give reasons for a fifth-century dating. But in my view, the evidence given by him is rather less convincing than that of the traditional hypothesis. |

Bibliography

Ahlström, G. W.
1993   *The History of Ancient Palestine from the Palaeolithic Period to Alexander's Conquest* (JSOTSup, 146; Sheffield: Sheffield Academic Press).
Albertz, R.
1987   'Israel I: Altes Testament', in *Theologische Realenzyklopädie* XVI: 368–79.
1994   *A History of Israelite Religion in the Old Testament Period* (Old Testament Library; 2 vols.; Louisville, KY: Westminster/John Knox Press).
1997   'Die Theologisierung des Rechts im Alten Israel', in *idem* (ed.), *Religion und Gesellschaft. Studien zu ihrer Wechselbeziehung in den Kulturen des Antiken Vorderen Orients* (Alter Orient und Altes Testament, 248; Münster: Ugarit-Verlag): 115–32.
2001   *Die Exilszeit, Das 6. Jahrhundert v. Chr.* (Biblische Enzyklopädie, 7; Stuttgart: Kohlhammer).
2002   'Die Zerstörung des Jerusalemer Tempels 587 v. Chr.: Historische Einordnung und religionspolitische Bedeutung', in J. Hahn (ed.), *Zerstörungen des Jerusalemer Tempels: Geschehen – Wahrnehmung – Bewältigung* (Wissenschaftliche Untersuchungen zum Neuen Testament, 147; Tübingen: Mohr Siebeck): 23–39.
2003   'Jer 2–6 und die Frühzeitverkündigung Jeremias', in *idem, Geschichte und Theologie: Studien zur Exegese des Alten Testaments und zur Religionsgeschichte Israels* (ed. I. Kottsieper and J. Wöhrle; BZAW, 326; Berlin: W. de Gruyter): 209–38 (orig. *ZAW* 94 [1982]: 20–27).
Barth, H.
1977   *Die Jesaja-Worte in der Josiazeit: Israel und Assur als Thema einer produktiven Neuinterpretation der Jesajaüberlieferung* (WMANT, 48; Neukirchen-Vluyn: Neukirchener Verlag).

---

58 Why Ezekiel personally charged with apostasy a member of the Shaphan family (Ezek. 8.12) who had been one of the promoters of the reform remains obscure. |

Blenkinsopp, J.
  1988   *Ezra-Nehemiah: A Commentary* (OTL; Philadelphia: Westminster Press).
Cowley, A.
  1923   *Aramaic Papyri of the Fifth Century B.C.* (Oxford: Clarendon Press).
Davies, P. R.
  1992   *In Search of 'Ancient Israel'* (JSOTSup, 148; Sheffield: Sheffield Academic Press).
Dietrich, W., and Th. Naumann
  1995   *Die Samuelbücher* (Erträge der Forschung, 287; Darmstadt: Wissenschaftliche Buchgesellschaft).
Finkelstein, I., and N. A. Silberman
  2001   *The Bible Unearthed: Archaeology's New View of Ancient Israel and the Origin of Its Sacred Texts* (New York: Free Press).
  2002   *Keine Posaunen vor Jericho. Die archäologische Wahrheit über die Bibel* (Munich: Beck).
Geller, S. A.
  2000   'The God of the Covenant', in B. N. Porter (ed.), *One God or the Many: Concepts of Divinity in the Ancient World* (Transactions of the Casco Bay Assyriological Institute, 1; New York: The New Yorker Collection): 273–319.
Gross, W. (ed.)
  1995   *Jeremia und die 'deuteronomistische Bewegung'* (BBB, 98; Weinheim: Beltz Athenäum).
Gunneweg, A. H. J.
  1987   *Nehemia* (KAT, XIX, 2; Gütersloh: Gütersloher Verlagshaus). |
Handy, L. K.
  1995   'Historical Probability and the Narrative of Josiah's Reform in 2 Kings', in S. W. Holloway and L. K. Handy (eds.), *The Pitcher is Broken: Memorial Essays for Gösta W. Ahlström* (JSOTSup, 190; Sheffield: Sheffield Academic Press): 252–75.
Hardmeier, Chr.
  1989   *Prophetie im Streit vor dem Untergang Judas. Erzählkommunikative Studien zur Entstehungssituation der Jesaja- und Jeremiaerzählungen in II Reg 18–20 und Jer 37–40* (BZAW, 187; Berlin: W. de Gruyter).
  2000   'König Joschia in der Klimax des DtrG (2Reg 22 f.) und das vordtr Dokument einer Kultreform am Residenzort (23,4–15*)', in R. Lux (ed.), *Erzählte Geschichte: Beiträge zur narrativen Kultur im Alten Israel* (Biblisch-Theologische Studien, 40; Neukirchen-Vluyn: Neukirchener Verlag): 81–145.
Heltzer, M.
  2000   'Some Questions Concerning the Economic Policy of Josiah, King of Judah', *Israel Exploration Journal* 50: 105–108.
Hölscher, G.
  1922   'Komposition und Ursprung des Deuteronomiums', *ZAW* 40: 161–255.
Kaiser, O.
  1984   *Einleitung in das Alte Testament: Eine Einführung in Ergebnisse und Probleme* (Gütersloh: Gütersloher Verlagshaus, 5th edn): 132–34.
Karrer, Chr.
  2001   *Das Ringen um die Verfassung Judas. Eine Studie zu den theologisch-politischen Vorstellungen im Esra–Nehemia–Buch* (BZAW, 308; Berlin: W. de Gruyter).
Kellermann, U.
  1967   *Nehemia. Quellen, Überlieferung, Geschichte* (BZAW, 102; Berlin: W. de Gruyter).
Lemaire, A.
  2002   *Nouvelle inscriptions araméennes d'Idumée*, II (Transeuphratène, Supplement, 9; Paris: J. Gabalda).

Miller, J. M., and J. H. Hayes
  1986   *A History of Ancient Israel and Judah* (Philadelphia: Westminster Press).
Mowinckel, S.
  1923   'Die vorderasiatischen Königs- und Fürsteninschriften. Eine stilistische Studie',
          in H. Schmidt (ed.), *Eucharisterion* (Festschrift H. Gunkel; FRLANT, 36; Göttingen:
          Vandenhoeck & Ruprecht): 278–322.
Na'aman, N.
  1991   'The Kingdom of Judah under Josiah', *TA* 18: 3–71.
Nelson, R. D.
  2002   *Deuteronomy: A Commentary* (OTL; Louisville, KY: Westminster/John Knox Press).
Niehr, H.
  1995   'Die Reform des Joschija: Methodische, historische und religionsgeschichtliche Aspekte', in
          Gross (ed.) 1995: 33–52.
Noth, M.
  1957 [1943]   *Überlieferungsgeschichtliche Studien* (Tübingen: Max Niemeyer, 2nd edn).
Person, Jr, R. F.
  2002   *The Deuteronomic School: History, Social Setting, and Literature* (Studies in Biblical Literature,
          2; Atlanta: Society of Biblical Literature). |
Reinmuth, T.
  2002   *Der Bericht Nehemias. Zur literarischen Eigenart, traditionsgeschichtlichen Prägung und
          innerbiblischen Rezeption des Ich-Berichts Nehemias* (OBO, 183; Fribourg: Universitätsverlag).
Renz, J., and W. Röllig
  1995   *Handbuch der althebräischen Epigraphik*, I,1 (Darmstadt: Wissenschaftliche
          Buchgesellschaft).
Rofé, A.
  1985   'The Monotheistic Argumentation in Deuteronomy 4.32–40: Content, Composition, and
          Text', *VT* 35: 434–45.
  1987   'The Battle of David and Goliath: Folklore, Theology, Eschatology', in J. Neusner, A. Levine
          and E. S. Frerichs (eds.), *Judaic Perspectives on Ancient Israel* (Philadelphia: Fortress Press):
          117–51.
Römer, Th. C.
  1997   'Transformations in Deuteronomistic and Biblical Historiography: On the "Book-Finding"
          and Other Literary Strategies', *ZAW* 109: 1–11.
Rudolph, W.
  1949   *Esra und Nehemia* (HAT, I, 20; Tübingen: J. C. B. Mohr).
Rüterswörden, U.
  1987   *Von der politischen Gemeinschaft zur Gemeinde. Studien zu Dt 16,18–18,22* (BBB, 65;
          Frankfurt/Bonn: Peter Hanstein Verlag).
Schmid, K.
  1996   *Buchgestalten des Jeremiabuches: Untersuchungen zur Redaktions- und Rezeptionsgeschichte
          von Jer 30–33 im Kontext des Buches* (WMANT, 72; Neukirchen-Vluyn: Neukirchener Verlag).
Steymans, H. U.
  1995   *Deuteronomium 28 und die Adê zur Thronbesteigung Asarhaddons: Segen und Fluch im Alten
          Orient und Israel* (OBO, 145; Fribourg: Universitätsverlag).
Tov, E.
  1985   'The Composition of I Samuel 16–18 in the Light of the Septuagint Version', in J. Tigay
          (ed.), *Empirical Models for Biblical Criticism* (Philadelphia: University of Pennsylvania Press):
          97–130.

1986 'The Nature of Differences between MT and LXX', in D. Barthélemy *et al.* (eds.), *The Story of David and Goliath: Textual and Literary Criticism* (OBO, 73; Fribourg: Universitätsverlag): 19–46.

Uehlinger, Chr.

1995 'Gab es eine joschijanische Kultreform? Plädoyer für ein begründetes Minimum', in Gross (ed.) 1995: 57–89.

Veijola, T.

1982 *Verheißung in der Krise. Studien zur Literatur und Theologie der Exilszeit anhand des 89. Psalms* (Annales Academiae Scientiarum Fennicae, Series B, 220; Helsinki: Suomalainen Tiedeakatemia).

Williamson, H. G. M.

1985 *Ezra, Nehemiah* (WBC, 16; Waco, TX: Word Books).

Würthwein, E.

1994 'Erwägungen zum sog. deuteronomistischen Geschichtswerk: Eine Skizze', in *idem*, *Studien zum Deuteronomistischen Geschichtswerk* (BZAW, 277; Berlin: W. de Gruyter): 1–11.

Ethnische und kultische Konzepte in der Politik Nehemias

Die folgenden Überlegungen gehören zu einem Forschungsprojekt, das unter dem Titel „Religiöse Gruppenbildung im Frühjudentum" innerhalb des Sonderforschungsbereichs 493 „Funktionen von Religion in antiken Gesellschaften des Vorderen Orients" in den Jahren 2000–2003 zusammen mit dem katholischen Alttestamentler Dr. Ralf Rothenbusch erarbeitet wurde.[1] Auch Erich Zenger war an diesem großen religionswissenschaftlichen Sonderforschungsbereich in Münster, der leider von der Deutschen Forschungsgemeinschaft aus der Förderung herausgenommen wurde, bevor er reife Früchte hätte tragen können, mit einem gewichtigen Teilprojekt beteiligt. Mit diesem Artikel, mit dem ich den Jubilar und geschätzten Kollegen grüßen möchte, will ich zugleich an diese schöne Zusammenarbeit in Münster erinnern.

In seinem neuen Buch „Rites and Rank. Hierarchy in Biblical Representations of Cult",[2] hat Saul M. Olyan, den wir zu diesem Thema im Jahr 2001 auch in den Sonderforschungsbereich nach Münster eingeladen hatten, überzeugend gezeigt, welche große Bedeutung binäre kultische Oppositionen wie „heilig/profan", „rein/unrein", „unversehrt/mit Makeln behaftet" und „wir/die anderen" nicht nur für das biblische Denken, sondern auch für die Determinierung und Strukturierung der gesellschaftli|chen Realität des alten Israel hatten. Solche Klassifikationen entschieden nicht nur über den Zutritt zu den Heiligtümern und die Teilnahme an Festen und Riten, sondern schufen auch eine Hierarchie in der Gesellschaft und begründeten die Zugehörigkeit zur Gemeinschaft. Dabei konnte Saul M. Olyan zeigen, dass die Grenzlinien zwischen solchen Oppositionen nicht ein für alle Mal feststanden, sondern sich im Verlauf der Geschichte verschieben konnten. Und normalerweise standen immer Riten und Strategien zur Verfügung, um verletzte Grenzlinien wiederherzustellen und zwischen den scharfen Gegensätzen zu vermitteln.

Allerdings hat Saul M. Olyan beobachtet, dass der Gegensatz „wir/die anderen" in den Büchern Esra und Nehemia seit dem 5. Jh. v. Chr. stark betont wurde: „,Alien', understood in texts antedating the fifth century to apply to persons of

---

1 Eine englische Fassung dieses Beitrags wurde unter dem Titel „Purity Strategies and Political Interest in the Policy of Nehemiah" in der Session „Uncovering Strategies of Religious and Social Control in the Post-Exilic Period" am 22. 7. 2002 auf dem International Meeting of the Society of Biblical Literature in Berlin vorgetragen. An dieser Session waren auch Ralf Rothenbusch, Saul M. Olyan, Bob Becking und Joachim Schaper beteiligt.
2 S. M. Olyan, Rites and Rank (2000). |

https://doi.org/10.1515/9783111202228-004

foreign birth or persons lacking an Israelite father, becomes in Ezra-Nehemiah a term applied to persons with any foreign blood."[3] Dabei hat Saul M. Olyan bereits gesehen, dass diese rigide Ausgrenzung damit zu tun hat, dass zwei andere binäre Oppositionen, nämlich „heilig/profan" und „rein/unrein", von ihrem ursprünglichen kultischen oder quasi-kultischen Kontext in den Bereich der sozialen Beziehungen übertragen wurden, insbesondere da, wo es um die Problematik der Mischehen ging.[4] Einen ersten Schritt in diese Richtung habe seiner Meinung nach schon das Heiligkeitsgesetz vollzogen, wenn es die Trennung Israels von allen anderen Völkern betonte und forderte, jegliche verunreinigenden Handlungen zu vermeiden (Lev 18,24–30; 20,22–26).[5] Die Bücher Esra und Nehemia seien dann auf diesem Weg noch einige Schritte weiter gegangen, indem sie Israel als „heiligen Samen" (Esr 9,2) definierten, der in der ständigen Gefahr stehe, von seinen Nachbarn mit deren Unreinheit verschmutzt zu werden: „If aliens are defiling, their ability to pollute justifies their absolute exclusion from the cult and community, both of which are constructed as holy."[6] Im Unterschied zum Heiligkeitsgesetz war damit „Heiligkeit" in Esra und Nehemia zu einer Frage der Verwandtschaft geworden.[7]

Es ist Saul M. Olyan zuzustimmen, wenn er in Bezug auf die Bücher Esra und Nehemia von einem „innovative program of exclusion" spricht. Doch hat er sich nicht weiter mit der Frage beschäftigt, wie denn ein | solch rigides „Programm", das weit über die älteren gesetzlichen Bestimmungen hinausgeht (Dtn 7,3 f; 23,4–9), überhaupt hat entstehen können. Wann wurde es entwickelt? Von wem wurde es durchgesetzt? Lassen sich verschiedene Phasen der Entwicklung unterscheiden? Das sind die Fragen, mit denen ich die Analyse von Saul M. Olyan, der ich grundsätzlich zustimme, weiter vorantreiben und stärker historisch verankern möchte. Damit möchte ich zugleich einen ersten Schritt beschreiben, den das judäische Gemeinwesen in der zweiten Hälfte des 5. Jh.s in Richtung auf die Ausbildung einer religiösen Gruppe gegangen ist.

1 Die Nehemia-Denkschrift als ältere Quelle

Ein älteres Traditionsstadium in den Büchern Esra und Nehemia stellt die sogenannte Nehemia-Denkschrift dar. Da das Buch Nehemia die Überschrift: „Worte

---

3 S. M. Olyan, Rites and Rank (2000) 89.
4 S. M. Olyan, Rites and Rank (2000) 60.
5 S. M. Olyan, Rites and Rank (2000) 90.
6 S. M. Olyan, Rites and Rank (2000) 89.
7 Vgl. S. M. Olyan, Rites and Rank (2000) 90. |

Nehemias, Sohn des Hachalja" (Neh 1,1) trägt, ist es sehr wahrscheinlich, dass der Herausgeber von Esra-Nehemia hier eine ältere Quelle verwendete, die entweder von Nehemia selbst oder einem Vertrauten aus seiner Umgebung geschrieben worden ist. Die Existenz einer solchen älteren Quelle ist breit akzeptiert.[8] J. Beckers erneuter Versuch, die Nehemia-Denkschrift als eine chronistische Erfindung zu erweisen,[9] ist nicht überzeugend, da sich ihr Stil und ihre Vorstellungswelt deutlich von ihrem redaktionellen Kontext abheben. Man kann sogar sagen, dass ein beträchtlicher Konsens hinsichtlich ihrer textlichen Rekonstruktion erreicht ist: Die meisten Exegeten schreiben der Nehemia-Denkschrift die in der 1. Pers. Sing. formulierten Passagen in Neh 1,1–7,5a; 12,31 f.37–40; 13,4–31 zu. Unsicherheit besteht nur hinsichtlich einiger Verse wie 7,1b; 13,6.7a.22.30a und einiger kleinerer Versteile, die möglicherweise auf eine Überarbeitung des Herausgebers zurückgehen. Gewichtiger ist das Problem, dass der rekonstruierte Text keine vollständige und wohlstrukturierte Einheit darstellt. In Neh 1,1–7,3 liegt ein ziemlich geschlossener Bericht Nehemias vor, wie er gegen den militanten Widerstand seiner Feinde erfolgreich die Mauer von Jerusalem wiederaufbauen konnte. Doch wird dieser zweimal unterbrochen, einmal in Neh 3,1–32 durch die | lange Liste der am Bau Beteiligten, die ein offizielles Dokument gewesen sein könnte, ein anderes Mal in Neh 5,1–19 durch einen Bericht von Nehemias sozialen Reformen und seiner Freigebigkeit als Statthalter, der fast nichts (vgl. V 16) mit dem Mauerbau zu tun hat.

Größer sind allerdings die Probleme, die dann folgen: Der Bericht von der Wiederbesiedlung Jerusalems und der Registration der Bevölkerung, der in Neh 7,4–5a beginnt, wird nicht durchgeführt. Er wurde ersetzt durch eine Liste der Heimkehrer (Neh 7,6–72), die ebenfalls in Esr 2 erscheint, und eine kurze Notiz in Neh 11,1 f, die wahrscheinlich vom Herausgeber von Esra-Nehemia geschrieben wurde. Der Bericht von der Einweihung der Mauer (12,27–43), der einmal das ursprüngliche Ende des Bauberichts gebildet haben könnte, wurde vom Herausgeber weit versetzt und stark überarbeitet. Höchstens die Verse 12,31 f.37–40 gehörten einmal zur Nehemia-Denkschrift.

Der Bericht von Nehemias kultischen und rituellen Reformen in Neh 13,4–31, der in die Periode seines zweiten Aufenthaltes in Juda datiert wird (V 6), findet sich völlig separiert. In diesem Fall schrieb der Herausgeber von Esra-Nehemia eine neue Einleitung, die von ähnlichen kultischen und rituellen Maßnahmen

---

8 Vgl. S. Mowinckel, Königs- und Fürsteninschriften (1923) 278–322; U. Kellermann, Nehemia (1967) 4–56; W. Rudolph, Esra und Nehemia (1949) XXIV; H. G. M. Williamson, Ezra, Nehemiah (1985) XXIV–XXVIII; A. H. J. Gunneweg, Nehemia (1987) 176–180; J. Blenkinsopp, Ezra-Nehemiah (1988) 46 f; Chr. Karrer, Verfassung Judas (2001) 128–213.
9 J. Becker, Ich-Bericht (1998). |

berichtet, die allerdings vom ganzen Volk freiwillig unternommen worden seien (12,44–13,3). Der Herausgeber benutzt somit den älteren Nehemia-Bericht an dieser Stelle, um auf die früheren Missstände zurückzublicken, mit denen Nehemia noch konfrontiert war, die aber später durch die feierliche Selbstverpflichtung des Volkes (Neh 10)[10] ein für alle Mal beseitigt wurden. Deswegen kann der ursprüngliche Platz, den Neh 13,4–31 einmal in der Denkschrift eingenommen hat, nicht mehr bestimmt werden. Möglicherweise handelt es sich um eine Ergänzung wie Neh 5.

Schließlich müssen wir mit der Möglichkeit rechnen, dass der Herausgeber von Esra-Nehemia am Text der Nehemia-Denkschrift, die er für seine Zwecke verwendete, einige kleinere Ergänzungen und Anpassungen vorgenommen hat. Meiner Ansicht nach stellt die Erwähnung von ammonitischen und moabitischen Frauen im Zusammenhang des Vorgehens Nehemias gegen die Mischehen (Neh 13,23) eine solche Ergänzung dar, da dieses sonst allein gegen aschdoditische Frauen zielt. Sie erklärt sich als Anpassung an die gesetzliche Bestimmung von Dtn 23,4–7, welche die Aufnahme von Ammonitern und Moabitern in die Kultgemeinde verbietet und die vom Herausgeber in Neh 13,1–3 zitiert wird. So ist wohl auch die Generalisierung „oder in einer Sprache anderer Völker", | die in 13,24b syntaktisch seltsam nachklappt, eine Ergänzung desselben Herausgebers oder sogar eine noch spätere Glosse.[11] Die abschließende Bemerkung in Neh 13,30a „So reinigte ich sie von allem Fremden", die durch ihre etwas ungeschickte Stellung nach dem kurzen Gebetswunsch (V 29) und vor Bemerkungen über weitere kultische Maßnahmen auffällt (V 30b.31a), erklärt sich am ehesten als redaktionelle Klammer zu Neh 13,3 („So trennten sie alles Mischvolk von Israel"), mit der der Herausgeber die ältere Nehemia-Quelle in seine Komposition einbinden wollte.[12] Dagegen gehörte der Versteil 22a, in dem die Leviten am Sabbat als Wächter für die Stadttore eingesetzt werden, trotz einiger Bedenken wahrscheinlich doch zur Denkschrift hinzu.[13]

---

10 Vgl. die vielen Entsprechungen zwischen Neh 13 und Neh 10. |

11 So auch S. Mowinckel, Studien (1964) 41; U. Kellermann, Nehemia (1967) 53; H. G. M. Williamson, Ezra, Nehemiah (1985) 393; A. H. J. Gunneweg, Nehemia (1987) 172; J. Blenkinsopp, Ezra-Nehemiah (1988) 362.

12 Vgl. W. Rudolph, Esra und Nehemiah (1949) 210; A. H. J. Gunneweg, Nehemia (1987) 175; J. Blenkinsopp, Ezra-Nehemiah (1988) 366.

13 Der Versteil stellt keine Dublette zu Neh 13,19 dar, da die Bewachung der Tore durch Nehemias Knechte gut als eine temporäre Maßnahme während der Krise verstanden werden kann, die durch Stationierung der Leviten später abgelöst wurde; so auch H. G. M. Williamson, Ezra, Nehemiah (1985) 396; J. Blenkinsopp, Ezra-Nehemiah (1988) 361, gegen U. Kellermann, Nehemia (1967) 169; A. H. J. Gunneweg, Nehemia (1987) 169; Chr. Karrer, Verfassung Judas (2001) 141. Der Stil des Versteils entspricht genau dem der Nehemia-Denkschrift, vgl. Neh 13,19.

H. G. M. Williamson mag mit seiner Vermutung Recht haben, dass die Nehemia-Denkschrift aus mehreren Einheiten bestand, einem älteren Baubericht aus der Anfangszeit Nehemias in Juda und einem oder mehreren Berichten über Maßnahmen aus seiner späteren Amtszeit (Neh 5; 13,4–31*). Nur letztere tragen mit ihren eingestreuten kleinen Gebetswünschen deutliche Merkmale von Votivinschriften.[14] Auch wenn die Nehemia-Denkschrift nicht vollständig rekonstruiert werden kann und auch wenn ihre Entstehung komplizierter war, als wir heute noch erkennen können, so besitzen wir mit ihr dennoch eine fast zeitgenössische Quelle, die kaum später als etwa 25 Jahre nach den historischen Ereignissen verfasst bzw. kompiliert worden ist. Dies bedeutet nicht, dass sie die historischen Ereignisse objektiv wiedergibt. Eher ist das Gegenteil der Fall. Ihre Beschreibungen sind extrem parteilich, da Nehemia seinen Bericht mit der klar erkennbaren Absicht verfasste, seine kontroverse Politik zu verteidigen, sei es in den Augen seiner jüdischen Mitbürger oder sei es | in den Augen Gottes. Stellt man ihre extrem subjektive Sicht in Rechnung, dann ist die Nehemia-Denkschrift vielleicht eine problematische Quelle, wenn es um eine faire historische Rekonstruktion der Auseinandersetzungen geht, in denen sich Nehemia befand, aber sie ist eine hervorragende Quelle, um Nehemias politische Interessen und religiös-kultischen Vorstellungen herauszuarbeiten, die seine Politik bestimmten.

2 Die politischen Interessen Nehemias

Wir wissen nicht genau, wie der politische Status Judas aussah, bevor Nehemia sein Amt antrat. Bekanntlich hat A. Alt die These vertreten, dass Juda während der babylonischen und frühen persischen Zeit Teil der Provinz Samaria gewesen sei und erst mit der Statthalterschaft Nehemias den Status einer eigenständigen Provinz erhalten habe.[15] Doch wurde diese These von M. Smith und H. G. M. Williamson[16] mit guten Gründen in Frage gestellt. Nicht nur Serubbabel trägt schon den Statthaltertitel (פֶּחָה Esr 6,7; Hag 1,1.14; 2,2.21), sondern auch Nehemia verweist auf die Statthalter vor ihm (Neh 5,15). Darüber hinaus deuten möglicher-

---

14 H. G. M. Williamson, Ezra, Nehemiah (1985) XXIV–XXVIII. Auf diesen Spuren hat jüngst T. Reinmuth, Bericht Nehemias (2002), zwischen einer „Mauerbau-Erzählung" (Neh 1,1–4,17*; 6,1–7,5*; 12,27–43*) und einer „Nehemia-Denkschrift" im engeren Sinne (5,1–19; 13,4–31*) unterschieden. |

15 Vgl. A. Alt, Rolle Samarias (1953) 316–337; unterstützt von S. E. McEvenue, Political Structure (1981) 353–364, und E. Stern, Persian Empire (1984) 82 f; zur Diskussion vgl. L. L. Grabbe, Judaism (1992) 79–83.

16 Vgl. M. Smith, Palestinian Parties (1987); H. G. M. Williamson, Governors of Judah (1988) 59–82.

weise Siegel und Münzen auf eine frühere Existenz einer Provinz Juda hin, auch wenn deren Datierung kontrovers ist.[17]

Aus der Sicht der Nehemia-Denkschrift ist die Situation völlig klar: Was immer der legale Status Judas im Perserreich gewesen sein mag, seine politische Lage war verheerend: Die Mauern und Tore seiner Hauptstadt lagen seit 140 Jahren in Trümmern, ständig regierten die Eliten der Nachbarprovinzen hinein (vgl. Neh 1,3; 2,3.17). Juda war kein respektierter Partner in der Region, sondern wurde dauernd von seinen Nachbarn beschimpft und verspottet, so dass sich seine Bevölkerung gedemütigt fühlen musste (Neh 1,3; 2,17; 3,33.36). Nehemias erstes Interesse war es darum, die Provinz Juda mit einem unabhängigeren, sichereren und geachteteren politischen Status auszustatten. Der Wiederaufbau der Jerusalemer Mauer war darum von ihm nicht nur als strategische Maßnahme gemeint, sondern zugleich auch als Symbol eines neuen Selbstvertrauens (Neh 2,17). Durch die Mauer sollten die Einflussnahmen | der Nachbarn gestoppt, durch die Tore der Zugang zur Hauptstadt kontrolliert und durch die Durchführung der Baumaßnahmen in der kürzest möglichen Zeit erwiesen werden, dass die Juden, die Sanballat als „hinfällig" verspottet hatte (Neh 3,34), in der Lage waren, durch eine gemeinsame Anstrengung ein gewaltiges Werk zu leisten. Nicht zufällig betont darum die Nehemia-Denkschrift, wie die Nachbarvölker beeindruckt und in ihrer Selbstüberschätzung gedemütigt wurden, als sie von der Vollendung des Mauerbaus erfuhren (Neh 6,15 f). Nehemia setzte darum all seine militärische und politische Macht als Statthalter ein, um sein wichtigstes Ziel, die Stärkung der Unabhängigkeit und des Ansehens Judas, zu erreichen (Neh 2,8 f; 4,9–17; 7,1–3*).

Das zweite politische Interesse Nehemias, das aus seiner Denkschrift erkennbar wird, zielte auf die Stärkung der Solidarität des Volkes. Im sozialen Konflikt zwischen den Armen und den Reichen setzte er all seine Autorität als Statthalter ein, um einen allgemeinen Schuldenerlass zu erzwingen (Neh 5,1–13). Um die Lasten der Bevölkerung zu erleichtern und zugleich ein gutes Beispiel zu liefern, verzichtete er auf die ihm zustehende Statthaltersteuer und bezahlte die Hofhaltung aus eigener Tasche (Neh 5,14–18). Es ist darum kein Zufall, dass Nehemia in seiner Denkschrift oft in der 1. Pers. Plur. formuliert; er spricht „vom Unglück, in dem wir sind" (Neh 2,17), von „unseren Brüdern" (Neh 5,8), „unserem Gott" (Neh 6,16; 13,18) und „unseren Feinden" (Neh 4,5; 6,1.16) in der Absicht, damit das *in-group-feeling* gegenüber einer feindlichen Umwelt zu stärken.

Das dritte politische Interesse Nehemias, das durch seine Denkschrift bezeugt wird, hat mit seiner religiösen Sorge zu tun, dass der Zorn Gottes, der während der Exilszeit so bitter erfahren wurde, erneut entfesselt werden könnte (Neh 13,18). Da

---

17 Vgl. dazu L. L. Grabbe, Judaism (1992) 68–72. |

dieser in der Vergangenheit durch Israels Ungehorsam gegenüber dem Gesetz des Mose hervorgerufen wurde, fühlte sich Nehemia verpflichtet, politische Rahmenbedingungen dafür zu schaffen, dass die Gebote der Tora strikt befolgt werden konnten. Das war der Grund, warum er für die Versorgung der Leviten (Neh 13,10–13; vgl. Num 18,24–31), für die Einhaltung des Sabbat (Neh 13,15–22; vgl. Ex 20,8.11; Dtn 5,12) und für die Auflösung der Mischehen kämpfte (Neh 13,23–28; vgl. Dtn 7,3).

3 Die Opposition gegen Nehemia

Die rechtfertigende Tendenz der Nehemia-Denkschrift insgesamt und viele ihrer Einzelheiten belegen, dass Nehemia seine politischen Interes|sen nur gegen erhebliche Widerstände durchsetzen konnte. Auf der einen Seite musste er mit der ihm unterstellten Provinzverwaltung kämpfen, deren 150 Bedienstete (סְגָנִים Neh 5,17) keineswegs alle Juden waren, sondern ebenso Experten aus den umliegenden Völkern.[18] Weil er offenbar Widerstand von Seiten der Provinzverwaltung erwartete, hielt Nehemia das Mauerbauprojekt vor ihr anfangs geheim (2,12.16a), solange er noch nicht die beiden jüdischen Selbstverwaltungsgremien (יְהוּדִים), das Priesterkollegium (כֹּהֲנִים) und den Ältestenrat (חֹרִים), einschließlich der jüdischen Bediensteten (סְגָנִים), benachrichtigt hatte, um zuerst ihre Unterstützung zu gewinnen (2,16b.17 f).[19]

---

18 Die Wortfolge im Satz Neh 5,17 ist syntaktisch schwierig: Mit der Formulierung: „Obgleich die Juden, die 150 Bediensteten und diejenigen, die von den Völkern kamen, die uns umgeben" sollen die Gruppen aufgezählt werden, die an Nehemias Tafel saßen. Doch gehören sie unterschiedlichen Kategorien an und können darum eigentlich nicht auf einer logischen Ebene aneinandergereiht werden. So hat W. Rudolph, Esra und Nehemia (1949) 132, vorgeschlagen, anstelle von „die Juden" וְהֹרִים „die Vornehmen" zu lesen. Doch ist diese Emendation nicht überzeugend und wurde zu Recht von den neueren Kommentaren nicht übernommen. Aber auch die Erklärung, dass der Begriff durch den zweiten und dritten expliziert werden soll (*waw-explicativum*), fällt aus, da der Begriff „Jude" zwar möglicherweise die Bediensteten umfassen kann, aber sicher nicht die Angehörigen anderer Völker. So sah H. G. M. Williamson, Ezra, Nehemiah (1985) 232–234, „die Juden" als eine Art *casus pendens* an, und J. Blenkinsopp, Ezra-Nehemiah (1988) 261, stellte die Wortfolge um, aber nannte doch immer noch die Juden und die Beamten nebeneinander. Nun hören wir aus Neh 2,16, dass zwar einige Juden zu den Bediensteten der persischen Provinzverwaltung gehörten, aber keineswegs alle Bediensteten Juden waren. Meiner Ansicht nach sollte darum Neh 5,17 auf folgende Weise verstanden werden: „Obgleich die 150 Bediensteten, d. h. die Juden und diejenigen, die von den Völkern kamen, die uns umgeben ...". Der Begriff „die Juden" wurde möglicherweise deswegen vorangestellt, weil Nehemia seine Generosität seinen Landsleuten gegenüber ganz besonders betonen wollte.

19 Unterhalb des Statthalters, der in seiner Arbeit von der persischen Provinzverwaltung unterstützt wurde, befanden sich zwei jüdische Leitungsgremien, der Ältestenrat und das Priesterkol-

Es gab in Juda viele Juden, insbesondere aus der Oberschicht, die Nehemias
negative Einschätzung der gegenwärtigen Lage ihrer Provinz nicht teilten und
darum sein politisches Programm mehr oder weniger heftig bekämpften. So lehn-
ten es etwa die Edlen (אַדִּירִים) von Thekoa ab, sich am Wiederaufbau der Mauer
von Jerusalem zu beteiligen (Neh 3,5) – trotz der breiten Solidarität, die Nehemia
in diesem Fall ansonsten erzeugen konnte. Das kann als Ausdruck einer fundamentalen Opposition gegen Nehemias Politik angesehen werden. Andere waren
nicht so radikal. Zum Beispiel nahm der Aristokrat Meschullam ben Berechja
zwar | am Mauerbau teil (Neh 3,4), verheiratete aber seine Tochter mit einem
Sohn Tobias (Neh 6,18), eines hohen Beamten aus dem nächsten Umkreis des
Statthalters der Provinz Samaria, Sanballat (Neh 3,35), der in Nehemias Augen
einer der schlimmsten Feinde Judas war. Meschullam teilte offenbar Nehemias
Ziel, Juda mehr politische Unabhängigkeit zu verschaffen, doch er war ebenso
daran interessiert, gute Beziehungen mit den wichtigen Amtsträgern der Region
zu pflegen, insbesondere dann, wenn sie ebenfalls JHWH-Anhänger waren.

Eine ähnliche Einstellung teilten offenbar viele judäische Aristokraten (חֹרֵי
יְהוּדָה), wie sich Nehemia selbst eingestehen musste. Viele von ihnen standen mit
Tobia in regem Briefverkehr, waren ihm teilweise sogar durch Eid verpflichtet,
versuchten ihn vor dem Statthalter zu verteidigen und arbeiteten sogar als seine
Spione hinter dem Rücken des Statthalters (Neh 6,17–19). Tobia stand in verwandt-
schaftlicher Beziehung zum Priester Eljaschib, der offenbar nichts dabei fand,
seinem Verwandten einen Vorratsraum im Jerusalemer Tempel zu dessen Gebrauch zu überlassen (14,4–5), als Nehemia abwesend war. Sogar die Familie des
Hohenpriesters sah keinerlei Hinderungsgrund, einer Heirat des Sohnes bzw. Enkels des Amtsinhabers mit der Tochter des samarischen Statthalters Sanballat
zuzustimmen (Neh 13,28), obgleich dieser Nehemias Erzfeind war. Wie wir aus
anderen Quellen wissen, war er immerhin ein Anhänger des JHWH-Glaubens.[20]
So war ein beträchtlicher Teil der Priester- und Laienaristokratie sehr daran interessiert, gute Beziehungen zu den Amtsträgern der benachbarten Provinzen zu
unterhalten. Dabei mögen die Priester ein besonderes Interesse daran gehabt
haben, den Jerusalemer Tempel für alle JHWH-Verehrer offen zu halten. So opponierten sie teilweise demonstrativ gegen die exklusive Tendenz der Politik Nehe-

---

legium, denen eine Volksversammlung zur Seite stand. Zu dieser Rekonstruktion der Verfassung
von Jehud vgl. R. Albertz, Religionsgeschichte Israels (1992) 472–474; Ders., Thwarted Restoration
(2002) 11–13. |

20 Die Juden von Elephantine hatten auch an die Söhne Sanballats einen Brief gesandt und sie
um Unterstützung beim Wiederaufbau ihres zerstörten Jahu-Tempels gebeten, vgl. EP 30, Z. 29
(= A 4.7 bei: B. Porten – A. Yardeni, Textbook, Vol. I [1986] 68 f.). Darüber hinaus tragen die Söhne
Sanballats, Delaja und Schelemja, JHWH-haltige Namen. |

mias. Die Mehrheit der Aristokraten wollte definitiv kein isoliertes Juda. Was die innerjudäischen Beziehungen betraf, verfolgten sie selbstverständlich ihre eigenen ökonomischen Interessen. |

4 Die ideologischen Konzepte Nehemias

Die ideologischen Konzepte, die Nehemia verwendete, um seine jüdischen Gegner zu überzeugen, lassen sich zwei verschiedenen Vorstellungskreisen zuordnen. Der erste Kreis dreht sich um seine Vorstellung vom jüdischen Volk. Hier ist er stark von der deuteronomischen und deuteronomistischen Tradition beeinflusst. Der zweite Vorstellungskreis hat es mit kultischen und rituellen Oppositionen wie „heilig/profan" oder „rein/unrein" zu tun. Hier bewegt sich Nehemia in den Bahnen der priesterlichen Tradition, speziell des Heiligkeitsgesetzes.

4.1 Die Vorstellung von einem jüdischen Volk

Auf den ersten Blick wirken Nehemias Vorstellungen von seinem Volk nicht außergewöhnlich: Israel ist Volk Gottes (Neh 1,10), und seine Angehörigen sind dessen Diener (Neh 1,10; 2,20). Doch ihre Besonderheit wird schon daran erkennbar, dass in der Nehemia-Denkschrift häufig (10-mal) der Begriff יְהוּדִים gebraucht wird (Neh 13,23) – meist versehen mit Artikel הַיְּהוּדִים (Neh 1,2; 2,16; 3,33.34; 4,6; 5,1.8.17; 6,6) –, der mit „(die) Judäer" oder „(die) Juden" wiedergegeben werden kann. Dagegen taucht der traditionelle Name „Israel" nur viermal auf und bezeichnet davon zweimal das Volk der Vergangenheit (Neh 1,6; 13,26) und nur zweimal das der Gegenwart (Neh 2,10; 13,18).

Der Begriff יְהוּדִים ist erst seit dem 8. Jh. v. Chr. bezeugt; er bezeichnet die Bewohner Judas im Unterschied zu anderen Nationen (2 Kön 16,6; 25,25; Jer 41,3) oder Personen, die aus Juda kamen, aber nun in anderen Ländern leben (Jer 40,11.12; 43,9; 44,1). Dabei scheint der Terminus zuerst von Fremden benutzt worden zu sein.[21] Jedenfalls werden die Gruppen, die aus Juda deportiert wurden (Jer 52,28.30), von den Babyloniern *Ja-ḫu-da-aja* genannt,[22] was eine Transkription des aramäischen *Jəhudaje* „die Judäer" (*st. emph. plur.*) darstellt und genau dem hebräischen *hajjəhudim* mit Artikel entspricht. Darum ist es sehr wahrscheinlich, dass Nehemia diese übliche Fremdbezeichnung der babylonischen und persi-

---

21 Vgl. R. Albertz, Exilszeit (2001) 76 f.
22 So auf der sog. Weidner-Tafel, Babylon Nr. 28178 II, 40, TGI 78 f; ANET 308b. |

schen Diaspora aufnahm und bewusst als Selbstbezeichnung verwendete und so zu einer ganz bestimmten Sicht seiner selbst und seiner Volksgruppe gelangte. |

Die folgenden Merkmale sind dafür charakteristisch: Erstens waren „die Juden" alle Nachkommen der Bewohner Judas, die die judäische Katastrophe, die Kriege und Deportationen der Jahre 598/7, 587 und 582 v. Chr., überlebt hatten. In Neh 1,2 werden sie mit den „Entronnenen" (הַפְּלֵיטָה) gleichgesetzt, „die von der Gefangenschaft übrig geblieben sind" (אֲשֶׁר־נִשְׁאֲרוּ מִן־הַשֶּׁבִי).[23] Der Begriff bezeichnet dabei nicht nur die gegenwärtigen Einwohner von Juda, die in Neh 1,3 „Rest, der von der Gefangenschaft übrig geblieben ist, dort in der Provinz" genannt werden, und die auch in den meisten Fällen gemeint sind (2,16; 3,33.34; 5,1.17; 6,6; 13,23), sondern auch die Juden in der babylonischen und persischen Diaspora (5,8) und darüber hinaus alle kleineren jüdischen Gruppen, die wohl in Palästina, aber außerhalb der Provinz Juda lebten, so etwa in der Provinz Samaria (Neh 4,6). Der Begriff יְהוּדִים umfasst somit alle Menschen judäischer Abstammung. Im Unterschied zum übrigen Buch Esra-Nehemia unterscheidet die Nehemia-Denkschrift nicht zwischen der babylonischen Gola (הַגּוֹלָה) und den Daheimgebliebenen. Aus Nehemias Sicht waren alle judäischen Nachkommen Juden, egal wo sie gerade lebten.[24]

Zusammen mit diesem Begriff übertrug Nehemia zweitens auf alle Juden die typischen Erfahrungen, die jüdische Diasporagruppen in Babylonien und Persien unter den Bedingungen einer ethnischen Minorität gemacht hatten.[25] Wie alle ethnischen Minoritäten mussten die kleinen jüdischen Gemeinschaften in Babylonien und Persien ständig in einer doppelten Frontstellung um ihr Überleben kämpfen, einerseits gegen den kulturellen Druck von außen, andererseits gegen die Gefahr der Assimilation von innen. Daher sind für solche Minoritäten eine

---

23 Der Streit, ob in Neh 1,2 die Heimkehrer aus der Gola oder die Bewohner Judas, die nicht deportiert worden waren, gemeint seien (vgl. W. Rudolph, Esra und Nehemia [1949] 104 f; H. G. M. Williamson, Ezra, Nehemiah [1985] 169 f o. a.), geht von der falschen Voraussetzung aus, dass Nehemia zwischen diesen beiden Gruppen habe unterscheiden wollen. Doch bezeichnet der Ausdruck „Rest des Exils", wie Neh 1,3 eindeutig zeigt, sowohl die Einwohner von Juda als auch alle anderen Überlebenden; so richtig Chr. Karrer, Verfassung Judas (2001) 151–153.

24 Das bedeutet, dass sich alle Juden, in der Diaspora und in der Heimat, grundsätzlich auf demselben Niveau befinden. Natürlich schließt das für bestimmte Situationen Nehemias Anspruch auf Führerschaft nicht aus, insbesondere dann, wenn, wie in Neh 5, die Juden in Juda nicht seinen Diaspora-Standards von Judentum entsprechen. Die These von P. R. Bedford, Diaspora (2002) 163, dass im Buch Esra-Nehemia die zurückgekehrten Judäer „as a colony of and dependent on the Babylonian-Elamite diaspora" angesehen werden, gilt ganz sicher nicht für die Nehemia-Denkschrift und ist wahrscheinlich auch für den Rest dieser Bücher weit übertrieben.

25 Chr. Karrer, Verfassung Judas (2001) 149–163, betont richtig das ethnische Konzept hinter dem Begriff יהודים, aber sie übersieht die Minoritätskomponente. |

hochgradige | Gruppensolidarität im Innern und eine scharfe Abgrenzung von der gesellschaftlichen Umwelt typisch.[26]

Welch hoher Standard von *in-group* Solidarität von den Diasporajuden praktiziert wurde, wird aus Neh 5,8 ersichtlich. Hier konfrontiert Nehemia die Aristokraten Judas, die nichts dabei fanden, ihre ärmeren jüdischen Mitbürger in die Schuldsklaverei zu pressen, mit dem leuchtenden Beispiel, dass wohlhabende Diasporajuden wie er ihre „jüdischen Brüder, die an die Heiden verkauft worden waren", zurückgekauft hätten, so viele sie nur konnten. Nach Meinung Nehemias waren alle Juden „Brüder", waren alle miteinander verwandt (5,1.5.8). Deswegen musste die Solidarität der Juden untereinander die höchste Priorität haben. Indem Nehemia die deuteronomische Bruderschafts-Ethik unterstrich, weitete er die Solidaritätsverpflichtung auf alle Juden in der ganzen Welt aus. So fühlte er sich selbst verpflichtet, seine hohe Position, die er am persischen Hof erlangt hatte, zur Hilfe für seine jüdischen Landsleute in der entlegenen Provinz Juda einzusetzen (1,4–2,10). Darum, so meinte er, müssten auch die Juden der Provinz Juda darauf erpicht sein, das hohe Maß an Solidarität zu erlangen, das die Diasporajuden erreicht hatten.

Die Abgrenzungsstrategien, die von den Diasporajuden praktiziert wurden, werden nicht direkt in der Nehemia-Denkschrift belegt. Aber es ist sehr wahrscheinlich, dass die stark abgrenzende Tendenz in der Politik Nehemias von seiner Erfahrung beeinflusst war, dass die Juden in der Persis eine ethnische Minorität darstellten. Es ist doch wohl kein Zufall, dass die wichtigsten Strategien, welche das Überleben der kleinen und verstreuten jüdischen Gruppen in ihren Gastgesellschaften sichern sollten, die Einhaltung des Sabbats und das Verbot von Mischehen, auch im Zentrum der politischen Maßnahmen Nehemias standen (Neh 13,15–22.23–29). Auch der Umstand, dass Nehemia nicht mehr wie im ursprünglichen Mischehenverbot Dtn 7,3 in der religiösen Verführung die zentrale Gefahr sah, sondern im drohenden Verlust der hebräischen Sprache (Neh 13,24), kann am besten aus der Problemlage einer ethnischen Minorität erklärt werden, welche zwar ihre religiöse Identität gefestigt hatte, sich aber dennoch gezwungen sah, von der Mehrheitsgesellschaft, in der sie lebte, andere kulturelle Werte, wie die Sprache, bis zu einem gewissen Grad zu übernehmen. Dieselbe Minderheitenmentalität kommt wahrscheinlich auch in dem Umstand zum Ausdruck, dass Nehemia alle seine politischen Feinde ständig als Angehörige fremder Völker denun|zierte, so Sanballat als Horoniter (Neh 2,10.19) – was immer das heißen mag –, Tobia als Ammoniter (Neh 3,35) oder noch geringschätziger als ammoniti-

---

26 Vgl. die soziologischen Überlegungen, die D. L. Smith, Religion of the Landless (1989) 93–126, zu ethnischen Minderheiten angestellt hat. Er hat sie weiter ausgeführt in: Ders., Politics of Ezra (1991) 80–86. |

schen Knecht (Neh 2,10.19) und Geschem als Araber (Neh 2,19; 6,1). Der Logik der ethnischen Minorität entsprechend erklärte er damit seinen politischen Konflikt als einen vornehmlich ethnisch bedingten. Die Konstruktion von Ethnizität ist hier mit Händen zu greifen.

Nehemia beschrieb die Lage der Juden in Juda so, als seien sie von lauter Feinden umgeben. Damit übertrug er auf sie eine extreme Weltsicht, die wahrscheinlich unter den gefährdeten jüdischen Minoritäten in der Diaspora entstanden war. Allerdings bestand folgendes Problem: Die Juden in der Provinz waren keine Minorität. Sie lebten zwar mit vielen Fremden zusammen, aber bildeten immer noch die Mehrheit der Provinzbevölkerung. Vor allem die Angehörigen der Oberschicht waren in ihrer Existenz völlig gesichert und sahen keinerlei Probleme darin, Kontakte mit Nichtjuden innerhalb und außerhalb der Provinz zu pflegen. Es ist wohl diese strukturelle Differenz, die meiner Meinung nach den wichtigsten Grund dafür liefert, warum so viele judäische Aristokraten der Politik Nehemias ablehnend gegenüberstanden. Dennoch versuchte Nehemia seine Landsleute in Juda davon zu überzeugen, dass sie keinerlei Chance auf politisches, kulturelles und religiöses Überleben hätten, wenn sie nicht bereit wären, das in der Diaspora geprägte Konzept von Judentum zu übernehmen.

Nehemias Konzept von Judentum hatte nun weitreichende Konsequenzen bei der Bestimmung der Gruppengrenzen. Da es auf die Bewohner des früheren Staates Juda beschränkt war, der nur noch das Gebiet Benjamins umfasste, schloss es automatisch alle anderen Nachkommen des früheren Israel aus, insbesondere diejenigen, die aus dem ehemaligen Nordreich stammten. Wir wissen, dass es viele Menschen auf dem Gebiet der Provinz Samaria gab, die JHWH auf die eine oder andere Weise verehrten. Auch der Statthalter von Samaria und sein hoher Bediensteter Tobia gehörten zu ihnen. Aus Neh 13,4f können wir schließen, dass Tobia regelmäßig an den Gottesdiensten am Jerusalemer Tempel teilnahm. So ist es verständlich, dass er und andere wie er Einfluss auf die Angelegenheiten des Tempels und Mitsprache in der judäischen Selbstverwaltung erlangen wollten. Da nur Angehörige registrierter Sippenverbände (בֵּית־אָבוֹת) Mitspracherechte im politischen Gemeinwesen und in kultischen Angelegenheiten hatten,[27] versuchten Sanballat und Tobia, in | angesehene Laien- oder Priesterfamilien einzuheiraten (6,18; 13,28). Doch beide Versuche scheiterten. Besorgt darüber, dass die Provinz Juda fremden Interessen ausgeliefert sein und die jüdische Identität beschädigt werden könnte, benutzte Nehemia sein ethnisches Konzept von Judentum, um

---

27 Vgl. den *terminus technicus* התיחש „sich registrieren lassen, registriert werden" in Neh 7,5 und die Listen in Esr 2 und Neh 7. Letztere stellen eher eine Liste der regist|rierten Sippen des judäischen Gemeinwesens während der Zeit Nehemias dar als eine Liste der Rückwanderer unter Serubbabel.

alle nicht-jüdischen Ansprüche abzuwehren. Brüsk wies er Sanballat und Tobia mit dem Argument zurück, sie hätten „keinen Anteil, keine Berechtigung und keinen traditionellen Anspruch in Jerusalem",[28] da allein die Juden Gottes Diener seien (2,20). So lieferte ihm sein spezifisches Konzept von Judentum starke Argumente, um seine Politik einer Stärkung der politischen und kultischen Selbständigkeit Judas durchzusetzen.

4.2 Die binären kultischen Oppositionen

Es hat nun allerdings den Anschein, dass während der Regierung Nehemias als Statthalter weder seine politischen Maßnahmen wie der Mauerbau noch sein Diaspora-Konzept von Judentum ausgereicht hätten, ein exklusives und solidarisches jüdisches Gemeinwesen in Juda und Jerusalem zu schaffen. Es wurde schon erwähnt, dass ein beträchtlicher Teil der judäischen Aristokraten und führenden Priester seiner Politik Widerstand leistete und seine eigenen Interessen verfolgte. Als Nehemia aus irgendeinem Grunde Jerusalem für eine Weile verlassen hatte, verschaffte der Priester Eljaschib, der über die Magazine des Tempels gesetzt war, seinem Verwandten Tobia einen großen Vorratsraum, in dem zuvor Opfermaterialien und der Zehnte für die Leviten gelagert worden waren (Neh 13,4 f). Man kann nicht genau sagen, wofür Tobia diesen Raum verwenden wollte. Entweder hatte er irgendwelche politischen und wirtschaftlichen Interessen an der Tempelwirtschaft, worüber wir aber nichts wissen, oder aber er hatte nur das persönliche Interesse, all die Opfermaterialien, die er für seine große Familie während der Tempelfeste brauchte, vor Ort zu lagern. Ein Indiz für die zweite Erklärung könnte der Hinweis auf das „Haus Tobias" (בֵּית־טוֹבִיָּה) in 13,8 sein. In jedem Fall war dies eine klare Verletzung der Abgrenzungspolitik Nehemias und möglicherweise | auch als Affront gegen ihn gemeint. Schon aus dem Grunde, dass die Priester daran interessiert sein mussten, die Menge der dargebrachten Opfer zu steigern, weil sich dadurch auch ihre Opferanteile erhöhten, aber möglicherweise auch aus theologischen Gründen plädierte Eljaschib offenbar für ein umfassenderes Konzept von kultischer Gemeinschaft, das alle JHWH-Verehrer, ob sie nun in Juda, Samaria oder irgendwo in der Diaspora lebten, vereinen sollte. Darum unterstützte er den hohen Amtsträger Tobia, der außerhalb Judas lebte, und ge-

---

28 Der Ausdruck אֵין־חֵלֶק meint die politische Trennung, vgl. 2 Sam 20,1; 1 Kön 12,16 und J. Blenkinsopp, Ezra-Nehemiah (1988) 220, ähnlich Chr. Karrer, Verfassung Judas (2001) 184; צְדָקָה meint den Rechtsanspruch (vgl. 2 Sam 19,29), der verneint wird; זִכָּרוֹן drückt wahrscheinlich das Mitspracherecht in kultischen Angelegenheiten aus, vgl. H. G. M. Williamson, Ezra, Nehemiah (1985) 193. |

währte ihm gewisse Privilegien im Tempel, als wäre er ein Mitglied des judäischen Gemeinwesens.

Als Nehemia jedoch zurück nach Jerusalem kam, war er außer sich über das Übel, das während seiner Abwesenheit geschehen war. Er warf allen „Hausrat" Tobias aus dem Vorratsraum hinaus und befahl, ihn rituell zu reinigen (טהר, pi.); sodann ließ er die Vorratskrüge des Tempels mitsamt der Opfermaterie zurückbringen (Neh 13,7–9). Da Tobia seinen Vorratsraum unter priesterlicher Aufsicht genutzt hatte, ist es höchst unwahrscheinlich, dass er ihn durch irgendwelche unreinen Nahrungsmittel oder eine falsche Einlagerung kultisch verunreinigt haben könnte. Dann war es aber nicht die eingelagerte Materie, die eine rituelle Reinigung des Vorratsraumes nötig machte, sondern allein die Tatsache, dass diese von einer Person stammte, die Nehemia als Nichtjuden betrachtete, und die darum über „keinen Anteil, keine Berechtigung und keinen traditionellen Anspruch in Jerusalem" verfügte (Neh 2,20). Durch seine radikale Reaktion tat Nehemia so, als hätte Tobia nicht nur einen illegalen Anspruch erhoben oder eine unerwünschte politische Einmischung begangen, sondern als hätte er auch eine schwere kultische Verunreinigung des Tempelareals verursacht. Da Tobia als Fremder die Heiligkeit des Tempels bedrohte, war seine Vertreibung unumgänglich und in jedem Fall gerechtfertigt. Dies bedeutet, dass es Nehemia erst durch die Verwendung des kultischen Konzepts von „Rein und Unrein" gelang, sein Ziel, den ewigen politischen Gegner aus dem judäischen Gemeinwesen auszuschließen, endgültig durchzusetzen.

Eine ähnliche Verwendung des kultischen Konzepts lässt sich in einem weiteren Fall erkennen, in dem es um das Problem der Mischehen geht. Hier kämpfte Nehemia an der inneren Front. Seiner Meinung nach musste die Heirat mit einer fremden Frau selbst schon als ein Sakrileg (מעל) gegen Gott (Neh 13,27) angesehen werden, d. h. in der Formulierung von H. G. M. Williamson als „breaking the faith ... either by trespas|sing onto holy things or by violating an oath sworn in God's name".[29] Nehemia nennt die Juden zwar noch nicht „heiliger Same" wie der spätere Redaktor von Esra-Nehemia (Esr 9,2), aber er berührt zweifellos schon die Sphäre der Heiligkeit.[30]

Im Fall einer Mischehe innerhalb der hohepriesterlichen Familie wird der kultische Hintergrund der Anklagen Nehemias noch sehr viel klarer. Einer der Söhne Jojadas hatte eine Tochter Sanballats geheiratet (Neh 13,28). Das öffnete dem samarischen Statthalter Tor und Tür zur judäischen Selbstverwaltung auf ihrer obersten Ebene. Wahrscheinlich war auch der Hohepriester daran interes-

---

29 H. G. M. Williamson, Ezra, Nehemia (1985) 132, der sich dabei J. Milgrom anschließt.
30 Nehemia verwendet das Verb מעל noch einmal in Neh 1,8, hier aber in einem allgemeinen Sinn. Die Wurzel macht dann im späteren Buch Esra-Nehemia Karriere, vgl. Esr 9,2.4; 10,2.6.10.

siert, bessere und verlässlichere Beziehungen zu allen JHWH-Verehrern in der nördlichen Provinz aufzubauen. Doch in den Augen Nehemias war diese diplomatische Heirat eindeutig ein Sakrileg. Darum zögerte er nicht, den Sohn Jojadas aus der Provinz Juda zu vertreiben. Welche Beweggründe ihn dazu veranlassten, lässt sich noch aus dem folgenden kleinen Gebet erkennen: „Gedenke ihnen, mein Gott, dass sie das Priestertum und den Bund des Priestertums [und der Leviten][31] befleckt haben!" (Neh 13,29). D. h. seiner Meinung nach wurde durch die Mischehe nicht nur der Sohn bzw. Enkel des amtierenden Hohenpriesters, sondern die gesamte hohepriesterliche Familie befleckt (II גאל). Alle ihre Amtsträger waren verunreinigt, und dies bedeutet – wenn man die Formulierung ernst nimmt – nicht länger fähig, ihren priesterlichen Dienst am Jerusalemer Tempel zu versehen (vgl. Esr 2,62; Neh 7,64). Schlimmer noch, der besondere Bund, den JHWH mit den Priestern geschlossen hatte, war schwer beschädigt (vgl. Mal 2,1–9).

Damit waren Nehemias Anklagen deutlich radikaler als die gesetzlichen Einschränkungen, die für die Priester galten: Das Heiligkeitsgesetz verbietet den Priestern, eine Prostituierte, eine Frau, die ihre Jungfräulichkeit verloren hat, oder eine geschiedene Frau zu heiraten (Lev 21,7). Hier werden nur solche Frauen ausgeschlossen, deren Sexualität mit einem Makel behaftet ist. Allein der Hohepriester unterliegt stärkeren Einschränkungen. Er darf nur eine Jungfrau aus seiner eigenen Verwandtschaft heiraten (21,14), weil er andernfalls seinen Samen in seinem Volk entweihen könnte (V 15). Diese Regeln zielen primär auf Heiraten inner|halb der oberen priesterlichen Familien, schließen allerdings das Verbot von Mischehen ein. Nehemia nahm somit diese Heiratsbeschränkungen für den Hohenpriester auf, wandte sie aber speziell gegen fremde Frauen und erweiterte ihre Gültigkeit auf die gesamte hohepriesterliche Familie. Darüber hinaus übertrug er die Vorstellung, dass die Heiligkeit eines Priesters dauerhaft durch eine Ehe mit einer mit Makeln behafteten Frau beschädigt werden könne, wie sie schon im Heiligkeitsgesetz angelegt war, auf die soziale Sphäre, nämlich auf die Beziehung zwischen Juden und Fremden. Durch ein solcherart verändertes rituelles Konzept kam er unausweichlich zu der Schlussfolgerung, dass die gesamte hohepriesterliche Familie infolge des Kontaktes eines einzigen Mitglieds zu einer fremden Frau befleckt worden sei. Die Vertreibung des verunreinigten Paares kann dann am ehesten als erster Akt der Reinigung für den Rest der hohepriesterlichen Familie verstanden werden. In der Logik der kultischen Oppositionen war der Ausschluss absolut notwendig. Auf diese Weise war Nehemia in der Lage, die

---

31 Der Ausdruck „und der Leviten" passt nicht zu dem Abstraktum „Priesterschaft" und ist wahrscheinlich eine spätere Ergänzung, die an den Bund mit Levi in Dtn 33,8–11 und Mal 2,4.8 erinnern will, so J. Blenkinsopp, Ezra-Nehemiah (1988) 362. |

politische Einmischung Sanballats zu beenden und seine Ausgrenzungspolitik an dieser wichtigen Stelle durchzusetzen.

Ein dritter Fall, in dem Nehemia kultische Reinheitskonzepte zur Durchsetzung seiner Politik verwendete, lässt sich hinsichtlich der Sabbatobservanz beobachten (Neh 13,15–22). Hier bediente er sich erst einmal politischer Mittel, um den Sabbatmarkt vor den Toren Jerusalems zu beenden: Er befahl, die Stadttore während des Sabbats geschlossen zu halten, und stellte seine Truppen auf, um die Tore zu bewachen und die fremden Händler zu vertreiben (13,19–21). Doch damit nicht genug. Um seine jüdischen Mitbürger zu überzeugen, dass der Sabbat nicht entheiligt werden dürfe (13,17 f), erinnerte er sie an die traurigen Lehren, die sie aus ihrer Geschichte ziehen mussten (13,18). Wenn er schließlich auch noch den Leviten befahl, sich zu reinigen (טהר, hitp.) und die Tore zu bewachen, um die Heiligkeit des Sabbattages zu bewahren (קדשׁ, pi.; 13,22), dann wollte er offenbar ein öffentliches Symbol für die Heiligkeit dieses Tages etablieren, das allen Juden dessen Würde vor Augen führen sollte. In diesem Fall hatte somit die Einbeziehung ritueller Konzepte eine eher unterstützende und erzieherische Funktion, um eine strengere Lebenspraxis durchzusetzen.

Zusammenfassend können wir also feststellen, dass Nehemia in der späteren Zeit seiner Regierung das kultische und rituelle Konzept binärer Oppositionen in seine politischen Strategien einbezog, um die Durchsetzung seiner exklusiven Abgrenzungspolitik, die sonst fehlgeschlagen wäre, zu erzwingen. |

Es konnte gezeigt werden, dass das politische Interesse Nehemias dahin ging, ein exklusives jüdisches Gemeinwesen in einer unabhängigen Provinz Juda zu schaffen, das seinen Nachbarn keine Gelegenheit mehr bot, sich einzumischen. Und seiner religiösen Vorstellung entsprechend sollte dieses Gemeinwesen das Zentrum aller jüdischen Gruppen bilden, die über das persische Reich verstreut waren. Zur Durchsetzung dieses Zieles war ihm das kultische Weltverständnis sehr hilfreich. Sein Charakteristikum binärer Oppositionen bot, wie Saul M. Olyan gezeigt hat, ein einfaches Schema, um die Welt, die Tiere und die Menschen in zwei gegensätzliche Sphären oder Gruppen einzuteilen: heilig oder profan, rein oder unrein, unversehrt oder mit Makeln behaftet. Damit half das kultische Schema dabei, die Komplexität der Welt drastisch zu reduzieren und klare Entscheidungen zu ermöglichen. Indem Nehemia diese rituellen Oppositionen auf die gesellschaftliche Unterscheidung von „wir und die anderen" übertrug und dabei dieses „wir" als jüdisch im engen ethnischen Sinne definierte, war er in der Lage, klar zwischen dem jüdischen Gemeinwesen und seinen Nachbarn zu unterscheiden. Indem er ferner unterstellte, dass diese Nachbarn allein deswegen kultisch unrein seien, weil sie Fremde waren und damit die kultische Reinheit der jüdischen Gemeinschaft bedrohten, provozierte er starke Emotionen gegen sie. Und indem er schließlich die Fremden als Menschen stigmatisierte, die mit einem gefährlichen Makel versehen und deswegen abzusondern seien, gelang es Nehemia, den Ausschluss einflussreicher Ausländer wie Tobia und Sanballat samt deren Gefolgsleuten durchzusetzen und zu rechtfertigen, wozu er allein mit politischen Argumenten nicht in der Lage gewesen wäre. So halfen ihm die kultischen Oppositionen substantiell dabei, die harten und umstrittenen Entscheidungen zu treffen, die er für notwendig hielt.

Dennoch ist die Verwendung kultischer Oppositionen auf dem Feld der Politik höchst problematisch. Die politische Welt ist nicht in „schwarz und weiß" eingeteilt. Im Gegenteil, hundert verschiedene Graustufen und fließende Übergänge sind gerade in diesem Bereich typisch. Darum können hier binäre Kategorien, mit denen man scharfe Gegensätze markiert, leicht zu einer Übersimplifikation führen. Man mag einwenden, dass die Politik Nehemias notwendig war, um eine wirklich unabhängige Provinz Juda zu schaffen und die Juden in ihr mit einer neuen Identität und einem neuen Selbstvertrauen auszustatten. Und man kann sicher sagen, dass Nehemia durch die Verwendung solcher kultischen Kategorien die Entwicklung des Judentums in Richtung auf eine religiös konstituierte Gruppe ein gutes Stück voran gebracht hat. Dennoch war die Vertreibung des Sohnes bzw. Enkels des Hohenpriesters, der die Tochter Sanballats | geheiratet hatte, sicher eine der beleidigenden Provokationen, die später zur kultischen Trennung der Samarier von den Juden geführt hat.[32] Außerdem bleibt zu bedenken, dass die Vorstellung, die Nehemia aus politischen Gründen „erfand", dass nämlich ein Fremder allein aufgrund seiner Fremdheit als unrein angesehen werden müsse, gefährliche und inhumane Konsequenzen in sich birgt. Ein Fremder, der durch ein solches Urteil stigmatisiert wurde, hat keinerlei Chance mehr, je wieder rein zu werden, egal welche rituellen Mittel er auch benutzen würde. Trotzdem wurde die Vorstellung im Buch Esra-Nehemia weiterentwickelt,[33] mit weitreichenden Folgen für das spätere Judentum.[34]

Literaturverzeichnis

Albertz, Rainer, Die Exilszeit. Das 6. Jahrhundert v. Chr. (BE 7), Stuttgart 2001.
Albertz, Rainer, Religionsgeschichte Israels in alttestamentlicher Zeit, 2 Bde. (GAT 8,1–2), Göttingen 1992 (I: ²1996, II: ²1997).

---

32 Josephus berichtet in seinen Antiquitates (XI, 302 f) von einem weiteren, ähnlich gescheiterten Versuch von Einheirat unter Darius III. (338–331 v. Chr.), der dann den Bau des Garizim-Tempels unmittelbar provozierte.
33 Vgl. Esr 9,10–12; Neh 13,30a; vgl. Esr 9,1 f; Neh 9,2.
34 Vgl. den schweren Konflikt zwischen den konservativen Kreisen und den sogenannten Hellenisten im makkabäischen Bürgerkrieg. |

Albertz, Rainer, The Thwarted Restoration, in: Ders. – B. Becking (eds.), Yahwism after Exile (STAR 5), Leiden 2002, 1–17.

Alt, Albrecht, Die Rolle Samarias bei der Entstehung des Judentums (1934), in: Ders., Kleine Schriften zur Geschichte des Volkes Israel, Bd. II, München 1953, 316–337.

Becker, Joachim, Der Ich-Bericht des Nehemiabuches als chronistische Gestaltung (fzb 87), Würzburg 1998.

Bedford, Peter R., Diaspora: Homeland Relations in Ezra-Nehemiah: VT 52 (2002) 147–165.

Blenkinsopp, Joseph, Ezra-Nehemiah. A Commentary (OTL), Philadelphia 1988.

Grabbe, Lester L., Judaism from Cyrus to Hadrian, Vol. I, Minneapolis 1992.

Gunneweg, Antonius H. J., Nehemia (KAT XIX,2), Gütersloh 1987.

Karrer, Christiane, Das Ringen um die Verfassung Judas. Eine Studie zu den theologisch-politischen Vorstellungen im Esra-Nehemia-Buch (BZAW 308), Berlin 2001.

Kellermann, Ulrich, Nehemia. Quellen, Überlieferung, Geschichte (BZAW 102), Berlin 1967. |

McEvenue, Sean E., The Political Structure in Judah from Cyrus to Nehemiah: CBQ 43 (1981) 353–364.

Mowinckel, Sigmund, Die vorderasiatischen Königs- und Fürsteninschriften. Eine stilistische Studie, in: H. Schmidt (Hg.), Eucharisterion. FS H. Gunkel (FRLANT 36), Göttingen 1923, 278–322.

Mowinckel, Sigmund, Studien zum Buche Esra-Nehemia, Bd. II, Oslo 1964.

Olyan, Saul M., Rites and Rank. Hierarchy in Biblical Representations of Cult, Princeton, NJ 2000.

Porten, Bezalel/Yardeni, Ada (eds.), Textbook of Aramaic Documents from Ancient Egypt, 4 Vol., Jerusalem 1986–1999.

Reinmuth, Titus, Der Bericht Nehemias. Zur literarischen Eigenart, traditionsgeschichtlichen Prägung und innerbiblischen Rezeption des Ich-Berichts Nehemias (OBO 183), Fribourg-Göttingen 2002.

Rudolph, Wilhelm, Esra und Nehemia (HAT I,20), Tübingen 1949.

Smith, Daniel L., The Politics of Ezra: Sociological Indicator of Postexilic Judaean Society, in: P. R. Davies (ed.), Second Temple Studies I: Persian Period (JSOT.S 117), Sheffield 1991, 73–97.

Smith, Daniel L., The Religion of the Landless: The Social Context of the Babylonian Exile, Bloomington 1989.

Smith, Morton, Palestinian Parties and Politics that Shaped the Old Testament, London ²1987.

Stern, Ephraim, The Persian Empire and the Political and Social History of Palestine in the Persian Period, in: W. D. Davies – L. Finkelstein (eds.), The Cambridge History of Judaism, Vol. I, Cambridge 1984, 70–87.

Williamson, Hugh G. M., Ezra, Nehemiah (WBC 16), Waco, TX 1985.

Williamson, Hugh G. M., The Governors of Judah under the Persians: TynB 39 (1988) 59–82.

The Controversy about Judean versus Israelite Identity and the Persian Government: A New Interpretation of the Bagoses Story (*Jewish Antiquities* XI.297–301)

In recent years, we have become more and more aware of the significance of the controversy about an exclusive Judean or Jewish versus an inclusive Israelite concept of identity permeating more or less most of the postexilic literature, be it Ezra–Nehemiah, the Chronicles, or the Hexateuch and Pentateuch redactions. This controversy included the Judean claim to leadership in all matters of YHWH religion. A possible but so far mostly neglected piece of evidence for this controversy is given by the so-called Bagoses story transmitted by Josephus in his *Jewish Antiquities* 11.297–301. It sheds light not only on a bloody internal conflict of the high priestly family but also on a severe Persian intervention in the affairs of the Judean community.

The Bagoses Story of Josephus

Because the story is widely unknown, I would like to cite it here in the translation of Ralph Marcus (1937):

> (§ 297a) On the death of the high priest Eliasib his son Jōdas succeeded him in the high priesthood. (b) And, when he also died, Jōannēs, who was his son, assumed this office; (c) it was through him that Bagōsēs, the general of the second Artaxerxes (ὁ στρατηγὸς τοῦ ἄλλου Ἀρταξέρξου), defiled the sanctuary and imposed tribute on the Jews, so that before offering the daily sacrifices they had to pay from the public treasury fifty drachmae for every lamb. (§ 298a) The reason for this was the following happening:
> (b) Jōannēs had a brother named Jēsūs, and Bagōsēs, whose friend he was, promised to obtain the high priesthood for him. (§ 299a) With this assurance, therefore, Jēsūs quarrelled with Jōannēs in the temple and provoked his brother so far that in his anger he killed him. (b) That Jōannēs should have committed so impious a deed against his brother while serving as priest was terrible enough, but the more terrible in that neither among Greeks nor barbarians had so savage and impious a deed | ever been committed. (§ 300a) The Deity, however, was not indifferent to it, and it was for this reason that the people were made slaves and the temple was defiled by the Persians. (b) Now, when Bagōsēs, the general of Artaxerxes, learned that Jōannēs, the high priest of the Jews, had murdered his own brother Jēsūs in the temple, he at once set upon the Jews and in anger began to say, "You have dared to commit murder in your own temple." (§ 301a) But, when he attempted to enter the temple, they sought to prevent him, whereupon he said to them, "Am I, then, not purer

https://doi.org/10.1515/9783111202228-005

than he who was slain in the temple?" and, having spoken these words, he went in to the temple.

(b) This, then, being the pretext which he used, Bagōsēs made the Jews suffer seven years for the death of Jēsūs.

At the first glance, the story looks like a personal quarrel between a high priest and his brother, because the political and religious background of this murder is not reported. But, because this murder was induced by a Persian official, who was interested to replace the high priest with his preferred brother, and because it had severe consequences for the temple cult in Jerusalem and the whole Judean community, one is entitled to presume a more extensive conflict. In any case, the massive intervention of Bagoses in internal Judean affairs differs so remarkably from the picture drawn of the Persians in the book of Ezra–Nehemiah that it was not really integrated into the Judean history of the Persian period. In the first part of the 20th century, after the discovery of the Elephantine papyri, smaller attempts were made to connect the Bagoses story with Judean-Samarian struggle (C. Steuernagel 1909; A. Cowley 1923; R. Marcus 1937; J. Morgenstern 1935, 1938; K. Galling 1964; cf. M. Smith 1971), but they were almost not taken up by the text books of Israelite history. Apart from A. H. J. Gunneweg (1972: 139), who assumed a connection with the Elephantine affairs, and J. M. Miller and J. H. Hayes (1986: 475), who presumed an intervention of unknown reason in the late Persian period, in the histories of ancient Israel, the Bagoses story is just shortly mentioned (H. Tadmor 1978) or totally forgotten (M. Noth 1963; S. Herrmann 1973; M. Metzger 1977; A. Soggin 1991).

Historical Reliability and Setting

Although Josephus's knowledge of the Persian period is rather limited, the historical reliability of the Bagoses story is widely accepted, even by critical scholars such as Lester Grabbe (1992a: 62; 2004: 320). Hugh Williamson (2004b: 75–79) has pointed out that Josephus probably was drawing on an independent source (§§ 298b–301a), which he has framed by his own introduction (§§ 297–98a) and conclusion (§ 301b). We cannot prove the accuracy of this source, because other sources are | lacking, "but the story of the murder in the temple is not likely to be simply a Jewish invention" (Grabbe 1992a: 62). The event is important enough that the source could have been handed down in the temple archive.[1]

---

1 This is probably not a Samarian but a Judean source, because the suffering of the people and the defilement of the sanctuary is regarded as a divine judgment for Joḥanan's sin (§ 300a). |

There has been a long scholarly debate over with which historical person the Bagoses of the story can be identified. Before the discovery of the Elephantine papyri, according to Cowley (1923: 109), "the Bagoses of Josephus has generally been identified with the minister under Artaxerxes III (358–337), mentioned by Diodorus Siculus (XVI, 47)." But after the papyrus TAD A4.7–9 (EP 30–32) verified a Persian governor in Judah, named Bagohi, who was a contemporary of the high priest Joḥanan at the end of the 5th century (410–407), this identification was generally preferred (C. Steuernagel 1909: 5; Cowley 1923: 109; Marcus 1937: 501; Morgenstern 1935: 127; 1938: 364). However, following Torrey (1939: 300–301), Hugh Williamson (2004a: 21–23; 2004b: 81–89) questioned this identification and returned to the older solution. His main argument points to the fact that Bagoses is given the title στρατηγός not only in the frame formulated by Josephus (§ 297c) but also in the source itself (§ 300b). According to Williamson, this term points to a military office, which perfectly accords with Bagoas under Artaxerxes III as one of the military leaders who reconquered Egypt 343 B.C.E. (Diodorus, XVI.47–50) but does not go well with the office of a "governor" (פחה), which is attested for Bagohi in TAD A4.7:1. But meanwhile, Grabbe (1992b; 2004: 320–21) has completely invalidated Williamson's argument; on the one hand, he could show that the title στρατηγός in Hellenistic Greek could denote both military and civil offices, including the office of a provincial governor or a satrap. On the other hand, the high official under Artaxerxes III was never called a στρατηγός in the ancient sources; he was more frequently a "general," namely a "commander over the thousands," in charge of the king's bodyguard and the chief friend of King Artaxerxes. On the contrary, there is no evidence at all that this one of the most powerful men of the late Persian Empire had anything to do with Judean affairs (Schwartz 1990: 194). Moreover, J. C. VanderKam (1991: 86) has rightly pointed out that "this Bagoas differs markedly from the modest official of Josephus's story." And I would like to add that a man such as this, who did not hesitate to poison two Persian kings (Artaxerxes III and Arses) in order to replace them with his favorites (first Arses, then Darius III; see Diodorus, XVII.5), would not | have only promised to his favorite the high priesthood but would have also killed the high priest, whom he did not like, immediately.

Williamson's second argument against the traditional identification is less significant. He argues that Bagoses of Josephus's story is apparently a Persian (cf. § 300a), while the governors of Judah generally were Jews (2004a: 21; 2004b: 83–84).[2] This is, however, a weak argument, because we do not know all Judean

---

2 Williamson (2004b: 83–84) points to Zerubbabel, Nehemiah, and Hezekiah, verified by coins. In addition to that, he assumes that also Shezbazzar and Hananiah, the brother of Nehemiah, were Persian governors.

governors of the Persian period (Grabbe 1992b: 53). We know that Bagohi, the Aramaic spelling of Bagavahya (A. Lemaire 2007: 54), is clearly a Persian name without any doubt, even if Jews may have adopted it in some way (cf. Bigwai in Ezra 2:2, 14; Neh 7:7; 10:17). There is no evidence that the Bagohi of the Elephantine letters is a Jew; on the contrary, he obviously neglected Judean claims and cooperated with the Samarians (TAD A4.9). Moreover, it makes sense that the Persian king would have appointed a more neutral Persian as a governor, after the Jewish governor Nehemiah had provoked several conflicts with his harsh dissociating policy (cf. Morgenstern 1935: 128; Galling 1964: 162). Thus, Bagohi as well as Bagoses should be regarded as a Persian.

Apart from this, Williamson's historical identification leads to another problem: because the Bagoses story knows of a high priest Joannes, Williamson is forced to postulate an office holder of this name in the middle of the 4th century (2004b: 85–88), which is not attested in the biblical lists (Neh 12:10–11, 22, 23). However, for a candidate of this sort, a piece of evidence seemed to be found when D. Barag (1986–87: 10–15) interpreted the inscription of a small silver coin as "Joḥanan, the priest" and tried to connect Josephus's story with the Tennes rebellion (350–345 B.C.E.).[3] But the coin does not really mention a high priest (Rooke 2000: 233, 236–37), and it probably should be dated later (J. Dušek 2007: 508).[4] Whether the Tennes rebellion, which was mostly restricted to Sidon and its environment, has any impact on Judah is highly questionable (Grabbe 2007: 129–32). Moreover, there is a growing | consensus that the biblical list of the high priests, which knows only the high priest Jaddua' in the later fourth century, is complete (VanderKam 1991; R. G. Kratz 2004a: 106–11; J. Dušek: 2007: 549–98).[5]

Compared with the increasing number of arguments against identifying Bagoses with the high official under Artaxerxes III, the problems with identifying him with the governor of Judah attested in the Elephantine papyri are many fewer. Apart from the problem concerning the title στρατηγός already solved by

---

3 D. W. Rooke (2000: 234) rightly argued against Barag's identification, pointing out the "huge discrepancy between the Yoḥanan who was in a position to issue coins and was supposedly of similar status to a provincial governor ... and the Temple-based Joannes who according to Josephus was overridden decisively by another Persian official and was unable to retaliate." Barag's argument concerning the Tennes rebellion (1966: 8–11) was only cautiously taken up by Williamson (2004a: 21–23).

4 The opposite attempt of L. S. Fried (2003: 79) to date the coin earlier (378–368 B.C.E.) and connect it with high priest Joḥanan of the Elephantine papyri (TAD A4.7:18), according to Lemaire (2007: 54), is not impossible but "far from certain." |

5 For reconstructing the list of the high priests, F. M. Cross (1975: 5) dated the Bagoses story in the fourth century in order to gain two additional candidates; but his attempt was refuted by J. C. VanderKam (1991: 70–89).

Grabbe, there is only one smaller difficulty, that the Josephus story attributes Bagoses to Artaxerxes II (§§ 297c, 300b), whereas the papyri deal with the last years of his forerunner Darius II. But this can be explained by the fact that he was kept in office also by his successor. In any case, the juxtaposition of Bagoses and the high priest Joannes fits perfectly with Bagohi and Joḥanan in TAD A4.7–8.[6] Thus, an increasing number of scholars is pleading again for this well-founded identification (Galling 1964: 162–64; D. R. Schwartz 1990: 193–94; VanderKam 1991: 81–87; Grabbe 1992a: 62–63, 141; 1992b: 54–55; 2004: 320–21; Rooke 2000: 236; Dušek 2007: 593–97).[7] Therefore, the Bagoses story can possibly be dated in the late fifth century.[8]

A Historical Reconstruction of the Conflict

Lester Grabbe has rightly pointed out: "If Josephus's story is credible" – what he is inclined to suppose – "it helps to fill in the long gap in our knowledge of events in Yehud after the governorship of Nehemiah" (2004: 321). But so far only a few scholars actually tried to use the story for filling the gap (Morgenstern 1935: 126–32; 1938: 360–67; Galling 1964: 161–65; Gunneweg 1972: 139). Thus, I would like to make a new attempt. |

The International Background of Late Fifth-Century Judah

The ruthless intervention of the Persian governor reported by the Bagoses story, which seems to be somehow strange in our picture of the Persian provincial government, may have to do with important international changes, of which former scholars, who tried to integrate the story, were not aware: the loss of Egypt for the Persian Empire and the establishment of a YHWH temple in the province of Samaria.

---

6 That Joḥanan was in office in the late fifth and the early fourth centuries can be also drawn from Ezra 10:6, if one is ready to date Ezra's mission to the reign of Artaxerxes II.

7 Cf., with some reservations, also Lemaire (2007: 54).

8 Dated in third quarter of the forth century, the possible historical background of the Bagoses story became much more vague. Miller and Hayes (1986: 474–75), who saw no possibility of connecting it with any Egyptian invasion into Syro-Palestine or the Tennes revolt, stated: "Unfortunately this little vignette provided by Josephus casts no major light on the course and shape of Jewish history." Williamson (2004a: 23–24), however, more on general considerations, postulated the long lasting Samarian-Judean conflict in behind, although he could not make use of the data given by Elephantine papyri. |

Oded Lipschits has pointed out that in the early Persian period the settlement development of the Levant shows a clear distribution: "urbanization along the coast and ruralism in the hill country" (2006: 26–30). From this result, he convincingly concluded that the Persians had only limited interest in their provinces Samaria and Judah for most of the fifth century; their main interest was directed to the coastal plain, where they built many fortresses, fostered urban life and supported the Phoenicians in order to safeguard their roads and harbors on the way to their province Egypt. But, as Lipschits demonstrated, this situation underwent a considerable change at the end of the fifth and beginning of the fourth centuries, "when the Egyptians freed themselves from the Persian yoke" (2006: 38). The province Yehud, then becoming part of the southwestern borderline of the empire, came into the Persians' field of view and under stricter control. For the latter, we have archaeological evidence: according to Alexander Fantalkin and Oren Tal, the Persian fortress of Lachish (level I) is to be dated not in the middle but at the end of the fifth century. Together with the forts in the Negev and other fortified administrative centers in Tell Jemmeh, Tel Haror, Tel Sera', Tel Ḥalif, Bet-Zur, and Ramat Raḥel, it must be seen "as a response to a new political reality: Egypt was no longer part of the Persian Empire" (2006: 186).

From the historical point of view, we can add the insight that the Egyptian fight for independence was a longer process. It already started with smaller riots from 410 B.C.E. onwards, which we can notice in some of the Elephantine papyri (TAD A4.5:1; 6.7:6; 6.10:4; 6.11:2, 4); also, the encroachment on the Jewish temple in Elephantine, initiated by the Khnum priests, can be seen not only as a religious but also as a political demonstration against foreign elements in the Persian garrison.[9] Especially for the troubles in Lower Egypt (TAD A6.10:4; 6.11:2, | 4), Amyrtae-

---

[9] Contrast the accentuation of the loyalty of the Jewish troop with detachments of the Egyptians that had already rebelled before 410 B.C.E. in the letter of complaint to Persian satrap of Egypt Arsames or his deputy (TAD A4.5:1). The reason for the conflict with the Khnum priests cannot have been purely religious, for instance, because of their anger on the sacrifice of rams, the symbol animal of Khnum (refer to the ram cemetery found in the precinct of the Khnum temple of Elephantine; | S. G. Rosenberg 2004: 8–9), because they had already tolerated those sacrifices for more than a century. One of the main reasons seems to be that the self-confident Khnum priesthood wanted to extend their big temple area, and the much smaller Yahu Temple with its courtyard stood in the way of it (cf. TAD A4.5 I:5, II:6–8 and the archaeological evidence shown by Rosenberg 2004: 8–10). According to C. von Pilgrim (2003: 316–17), it is likely that the Khnum priests used the restoration of the main street between the two temples by a protecting wall, which forced the removal of the southeastern courtyard wall of the Yahu Temple (see the map, von Pilgrim 2003: 308), as a pretext to destroy the entire temple building. This political explanation accords with the additional information given by TAD A4.3:7 that the hostility with the Khnum priests had arisen since Hananiah had been in Egypt, because it is very probable that the mission of Hananiah on behalf of the central Persian government enhanced the public reli-

us from Saïs, the grandson of one of the protagonists of the Inarus rebellion and the first pharaoh of independent Egypt, probably was already responsible. With the death of Darius II in the year 405 and the following long-lasting battles of Artaxerxes II against his brother Cyrus for carrying through his claim on the Persian throne (404–401), Amyrtaeus seized the opportunity to throw off the Persian yoke with the help of Sparta. In the year 404, his rule was acknowledged in the Delta (TAD B4.6), between 402 and 400 also in Upper Egypt (B3.12; 4.6).[10] The Persians never put up with the loss of Egypt. But an attack on it possibly planned in 401 was not materialized (P. Briant 2002: 619), and a serious attempt in 383 to reconquer it failed. With the end of the fifth century, the coastal plain of the southern Levant including the Phoenician cities became a bone of contention between the two rivals, both of them using different Greek powers for their advantage. All the more, it was important for the Persians to keep a tight hold on their provinces in the Palestinian hill country.

In the closer environment of the province of Jehud, things changed dramatically with the fact that the Samarians built their own temple on Mount Gerizim and gained their cultic independence from Jerusalem. As the excavations on Mount Gerizim have turned out, the cultic splitting between the two communities did not happen in the late fourth century under Darius III and Alexander (336–332 B.C.E.; *Ant.* XI.306–25), | but already in the fifth century.[11] When it exactly happened is not totally clear; according to the excavator Yitzak Magen, the first temple on the Gerizim was constructed in the mid-fifth century (2007: 176). However, Magen connected Nehemiah's expulsion of a member of the high priestly family, who married a daughter of Sanballat (Neh 13:28), the governor of the province Samaria (TAD A4.7:29), to the foundation of the temple; that would lead us to a date of around 430 B.C.E.[12] Perhaps we can link the same event with

---

gious status of the Jewish minority in the multiethnic society of Elephantine, for example, the official acknowledgment of its holidays during the feast of Unleavened Bread (TAD A4.1; Kottsieper 2002: 150–57; Kratz 2004b: 65–67).

10 According to Lemaire (1995: 52–54, 59–60) the Persians lost their control in Memphis not before 403 and in Elephantine not before 398, the possible year of Ezra's mission. But this depends on ascribing two inscriptions to Artaxerxes II that have often been attributed to Artaxerxes I. |

11 In this, I must correct my older statements on the subject in Albertz (1994: 2:523–33).

12 Nehemiah's tenure of office is unclear. According to Neh 1:1 and 13:6, he was from the 20th to the 32nd year of Artaxerxes in Judah, which means between 445 and 433 B.C.E. But Neh 13:6 mentions a second term, the length of which is unknown. It might be that Nehemiah was removed from his office of governorship after a short period because of his severe conflict with the high priestly family (Neh 13:28) around 430, because he does not report anything about the efforts to establish a Samarian sanctuary. However, Galling (1964: 157) still assumed that he served until the death of Artaxerxes I in 425 B.C.E.

Josephus's information that a brother of the high priest, Jaddua' called Manasse, married Sanballat's daughter Nikaso and was expelled from Jerusalem (*Ant.* 11.302, 306–11). Then, Manasse would actually have been the son of the high priest Joiada' and a brother or a nephew of the later high priest Joḥanan.[13] In any case, this expulsion, which deprived Sanballat of any right to have a say in the Judean self-government (Albertz 1994: 2:530–31), constituted the reason for the decision of the Samarians to build their own temple; and if we take in our account that such an important building needed some preparations and the approval of the Persian government, the temple on Mount Gerizim was built sometime in the 20s of the fifth century. Perhaps one should date it shortly after the accession of Darius II in 424 B.C.E., because the new Persian king was certainly much | less obliged to foster the Judean interest than his father Artaxerxes I, who had supported Nehemiah's mission.

Relating the Bagoses Story with Elephantine: The Papyri TAD A4.7–9

It was often assumed that the conflict told in the Bagoses story has something to do with letters from Elephantine (TAD A4.7–8), in which the leader of the Jewish garrison asked for support, that their Yahu Temple, which had been destroyed by local authorities, would be allowed to be rebuilt (Cowley 1923: 109; Morgenstern 1935: 128–32; Galling 1964: 162–64; Gunneweg 1972: 139). In both texts the same persons, the governor Bagohi and the high priest Joḥanan, are acting, and both letters read together with their answer (A4.9) reveal a conflict between the two.

From the first draft of the letter (TAD A4.7), which is written on November 26, 407 B.C.E., we hear that a previous letter was sent three years before (410) to the governor Bagohi and to both councils of the Judean self-government, namely, the high priest Joḥanan, leader of the priestly congregation, and Ostanes, the

---

13 The genealogy of Jerusalem's high priests remains unclear. Neh 12:10–11 reports a genealogy that contains Joshua', Joiakim, Eliashib, Joiada', Jonatan, and Jaddua'. But Neh 12:22 lists the sequence as Eliashib, Joiada', Joḥanan, Jaddua'. Here, Jonatan seems to be replaced by Joḥanan. Because Jonatan is not mentioned any more, the genealogy of Neh 12:10–11 often is corrected according to 12:22 (VanderKam, Kratz, and others). In a reconstruction of this sort, the son of Joiada', who was expelled by Nehemiah (cf. *Ant.* 11.297b), would be the brother of Joḥanan. However, in other passages, Joḥanan is regarded not as son of Joiada' but as son of Eliashib (Neh 12:23, Ezra 10:6); therefore, one should perhaps prefer the reconstruction of Dušek (2007: 585–91), who distinguished between the genealogy, which mentions the first-born in all cases, even if he never held the rank of a high priest (Neh 12:10–11), and the list of the (later) high priests in Neh 12:22, which should not genealogically be misunderstood. Then Joḥanan is regarded as a younger brother of Joiada', and Joiada''s son expelled by Nehemiah is his nephew. |

leader of the assembly of the elders.[14] But this letter was not answered (lines 18–19). After three years, Jedoniah, the priest of the Elephantine garrison, sent a second letter to Jerusalem, but directed it only to the governor Bagohi. Having repeated his petition regarding the destroyed Yahu Temple in Elephantine, Jedoniah mentioned that the garrison had sent a similar letter also to the sons of the Samarian governor Sanballat, Delaiah, and Shelemiah (line 29). This time, Bagohi acted without hesitation, together with Delaiah, who possibly acted for his old father. They formulated a message sent back to Arsames, in which both governors would support the reconstruction of the destroyed Yahu Temple (A4.9).

From this difference of addresses, the conflict behind becomes apparent: as a Persian governor, Bagohi was very interested that the Jewish garrison became satisfied as we can see from his quick positive response after the second letter: the morality of Jewish mercenaries in the Persian garrison must be supported; the nationalistic Egyptian riots must be stopped. But the high priest Johanan and the Judean self-government were obviously against the reconstruction of the Yahu Temple; for them, it was a denial of the exclusivity of the Jerusalem temple founded on the law of centralization (Deuteronomy 12). They were probably happy that this cult was destroyed, which was not controlled by a Zadokide priesthood and did not correspond to the rules of | exclusive YHWH veneration. Therefore, Johanan opposed the governor by claiming a Judean leadership in all matters of YHWH religion. He obviously prevented the Judean assemblies from making any decision. As the Samarians were included in the decision, they became part of the conflict. In the past, scholars were incredulous as to why the Elephantine Jews could address their petition also to the Samarians (Herrmann 1973: 396–97) and supposed that they were not informed about the Judean-Samarian conflicts of the time of Nehemiah (Noth 1963: 319; Donner 1995: 2:468). Or scholars considered this address to be an indication that Judah and Samaria had not yet split (Galling 1964: 163) or even that conflicts told in the book of Nehemiah must be doubted (Kratz 2004a: 94–95).[15] Today, we definitely know that the cultic separation of the Samarians had already taken place at least 10 years before the Elephantine letters were written. And rightly understood, they presuppose it.[16] In

---

14 For this polity of Yehud, already derived from the address of TAD A4.7:18–19 by Galling (1964: 162–63), see Albertz (1994: 2:446–47). |

15 Kratz refers to Galling's statement but tacitly generalizes it. Galling stated that the letter shows that the schism between the Judean and Samarian communities, which became manifest about 330, did not yet exist; Kratz stated that nothing points to a schism between Samaria and Judah: "Auf ein Schisma zwischen Samaria und Juda deutet nichts." Based on the results of the excavations on Mount Gerizim, both statements turned out to be untrue.

16 That the letter of the Elephantine Jews directed to the Samarian governor family presupposes their knowledge of the conflict between Judah and Samaria was already rightly discerned by Steuernagel (1909: 5) and Marcus (1937: 507). |

their first letter, the Elephantine Jews still acknowledged the Judean claim to leadership. But after they received no response, they included the Samarians in their petition, acknowledging them as a second center of YHWH religion. They hoped that they would have a wider understanding of Israelite identity, because they had opposed the claim of Jerusalem's exclusivism themselves. The Elephantine Jews were very well informed about the inner Israelite rivalry, and their attempt to annul the Judean exclusivism with the help of the Samarians was successful.

Thus, it is highly probable that this conflict between Judean exclusivism and Persian interest in stabilizing the Persian government against the new Egyptian unrest and in minimizing possible conflicts between their southern Levantine provinces also constitutes the background of the severe confrontation told in the Bagoses story.

Reconstructing the Course of Events

There are not too many possibilities of integrating the events of Josephus's story, the murder of Joḥanan and the seven-year-long punishment of the Judean community ordered by Bagohi, into the course of events in the Elephantine letters mentioned above. The first possibility | could be that they happened more than seven years before the first letter, 410 B.C.E. In this case, they perhaps could have something to do with the Persian decision to approve the Samarian temple, possibly during the years after 424. But because the high priest under Nehemiah was Eliashib, his son Joiada' was probably still in office at that time and not Joḥanan as mentioned in the Bagoses story. Morgenstern presumed that the conflict broke out shortly before the first letter (412 or 411), when according to him the election of one of the brothers for the high priestly office took place (1935: 129–31 and n. 212; 1938: 60–65).[17] But the address of this letter naming Bagohi and Joḥanan close together – in the first draft, TAD A4.7:18–19, simply connected with וְעַל, "and to" – shows no indication of any conflict between the Persian governor and the high priest. Therefore, Morgenstern is forced to suppose that the Elephantine Jews "were not yet intimately acquainted with the new conditions which had come to obtain Jerusalem" (1935: 131 n. 212). But this assumption is rather improbable, if we take the sensation of the murder and the effectiveness of the Persian

---

17 Morgenstern still regards the year 411 as the date of the first letter. His assumption that Bagohi already intervened in the election of the high priest could more easily explain why the governor promised one of the candidates his support. But this solution is questioned by the fact that according to the Bagoses story Joḥanan already held the high priestly office when he killed his brother (§ 300b). |

postal system into account. More probable is the conclusion that in 410 the conflict had not yet broken out. Thus, the murder could not have happened fewer than seven years before 410.

The second possibility is that the murder happened after Bagohi's and Delaiah's decision to support a reconstruction of the Elephantine temple, in the year 407 itself or shortly after. In this case, Johanan felt ignored and protested against the high-handed decision of the governor in religious affairs of Jewish interests; therefore, Bagohi tried to get rid of him by promoting his brother to high priest. Because Joshua' was said to be a friend of Bagohi, he probably had more sympathy for the Persian interests and supported a less exclusive concept of Judaism and a wider understanding of Israelite identity. By eliminating him cruelly, Johanan carried through a rigid policy similar to Nehemiah's (for the latter, see Albertz 2006: 203–5).

This kind of solution has already been proposed by Cowley (1923: 109) and Galling (1964: 164–65). It has the advantage that, according to it, one could date all or most of the seven years of punishment during the reign of Artaxerxes II (405–359), who is regarded as the governor's lord in the Bagoses story (so explicitly Cowley). Thus, there is good reason to fix the period of punishment in the years 406–399 or | 405–398 B.C.E. An even later date would be problematic[18] because, in this case, the period of punishment would overlap Ezra's mission (398), so this is the latest date that should be preferred. This nice solution has only one disadvantage: it cannot explain why Bagohi did not initiate the positive decision, which we know he would like to have done, immediately after the first letter of the Elephantine Jews.[19] If there were still good relations between Bagohi and Johanan before 407, it should have been no problem to find a compromise.[20] The question remains: What is the reason for the long delay, lasting three years?

---

18 See below, pp. 497–99 [[= p. 76–78 in the present volume]].

19 Galling (1964: 163) seems to have been aware of this problem. He explains Bagohi's policy of waiting by arguing that Bagohi knew that the satrap Arsames was still outside Egypt. But this cannot be the main reason. The Persians had a very effective postal system. If Bagohi had wanted, he could have reached Arsames anywhere in the Persian Empire; and Arsames could have given his approval for reconstructing the Jewish temple in Elephantine from any place in the empire in written form.

20 Often the fact that Bagohi's and Delaiah's approval (TAD A4.9:9) only mentions meal-offerings and incense but no bloody sacrifices is seen as a compromise with the Judeans. But because bloody sacrifices were already offered at the Samarian temple of Mount Gerizim, this restriction would not help to defend the exceptional status of the Jerusalem cult. Moreover, it cannot be explained why a compromise of this sort could not already be found in response to the first petition (in 410). Thus, the restriction should rather be seen as consideration for the Persian concepts of the holiness of fire (cf. Albertz 1994: 2:648–49; I. Kottsieper 2002: 169–75). As we know from TAD A4.10:10–11, it was finally accepted by the Jewish community in Elephantine.

Therefore, the most probable solution seems to be that the incident happened between the two letters of the Elephantine Jews (410–407). Presupposing the usual good relationship between the Persian governor and the Judean self-government, Jedoniah, the priest and leader of the Jewish garrison in Elephantine, sent a letter to Bagohi, Joḥanan, and Ostanes. Concerned by the newly started Egyptian unrest, Bagohi was interested in preventing any success of Egyptian nationalism and in strengthening the morality of the Jewish mercenaries in the Persian garrison. But the high priest Joḥanan, who probably had entered his office just before,[21] refused to agree. He used the matter of the Elephantine temple as an opportunity to demonstrate the cultic exclusivity of the Jerusalem temple and the Judean leadership in all matters of YHWH | religion. As his brother Joshuaʻ verifies, among the leading priests and aristocrats there was also a party that pleaded for a wider concept of Israelite identity and for more understanding of the Persian governmental interest. However, it does not seem to have been the majority in the two councils of the Judean self-government. Thus, Joḥanan notoriously used his authority to prevent them from making any decision.

Reconstructed in this way, the first letter from Elephantine can actually provide a suitable reason for the emergence of the deep conflict, reported by Josephus. Frustrated by Joḥanan's delaying resistance, the Persian governor was no longer ready to accept that Judean religious ambitions should disturb Persian strategic interest in safeguarding the empire at its southwestern wing. Thus, he intervened in the Judean self-government. By promising Joshuaʻ his support in overtaking the high priestly office (§ 298b), he tried to replace Joḥanan, to change the majority in the Judean councils and to pave the way for a reasonable decision. However, this attempt failed; the priestly brothers got into an argument about their opposite political options, and provoked by Joshuaʻʻs assurance the high priest Joḥanan killed his brother while he was serving in the sanctuary (§ 299a).

One can imagine that Bagohi was disappointed and angry about the failure of his more indirect intervention. However, the shocking sacrilege provided him with the opportunity to teach the entire Judean community a harsh lesson: by imposing a high tax of 50 drachmae on all the daily sacrifices, which must be paid from the public treasury (§ 297c), the governor not only imposed a severe restriction on the steady temple cult (תמיד) and shrank the income of the priests but also caused heavy financial losses for all the Judean community (§ 301b). And

---

21 This assumption depends on the problem that – presupposing that the lists of high priests in Neh 12:10–11, 22, 23 are complete – the last two candidates, Joḥanan and Jadduaʻ, must cover the long period between Darius II and Alexander (424–331 B.C.E.). Because Joḥanan must still have reigned in the first decades of the fourth century (down to 370; cf. at least Ezra 10:6), his reign cannot have begun long before 410, the first date on which he is attested. |

by defiling the sanctuary deliberately, forcing his way into the temple (§§ 300a, 301a), and speaking in a mocking tone about the high priest who had defiled the sanctuary with a corpse (§ 301a), Bagoas wanted to humiliate the Judeans and their ambitious priesthood. With all these measures, Bagoas wanted to demonstrate that, in spite of all their ambitious claims, the Judeans were subjected to the Persian government, including their temple and their priests. During the long period of seven years of punishment, they were to learn that their claim to religious leadership was very restricted and should never contradict Persian strategic interest.

The murder and the beginning of the punishment could well have happened in the year 408, some time after the first letter from Elephantine and some time before the second. In this case, the period of punishment would run until 401, approximately until the end of the succession wars between Artaxerxes II and his brother Cyrus. Thus, the | severe punishment could last that long, because the king was busy with more important affairs and had no ears for Judean complaints.

During the years 408 and 407, the Jews of Elephantine heard about the serious disagreement between Bagohi and the Judean community. They regarded it as their best opportunity to push their request. Thus, they decided to write new letters, one directed to Bagoses only and the other to the sons of Sanballat, deliberately excluding the High Priest Johanan and the Judean councils of self-government. There is even a little indication that the Elephantine Jews actually knew about the disagreement in Jerusalem. In the second draft of the letter, TAD A4.8:17, they changed a little bit the syntax of the address of their previous letters: "We sent to our lord, ev[en] ([ף]א) to Jehohanan ... and Ostanes." Using the emphatic particle אף in place of a simple copula, the writers expressed that in their present view their former address to the leaders of the Jewish councils would no longer be natural but may even be superfluous, because the leaders' negative position had already come out. The Elephantine Jews should have written to the governor alone from the beginning; in their present view, he alone was responsible.[22]

---

22 Also Kottsieper (2002: 171–72 n. 78) considered dating the conflict between Bagohi and Johanan before the second letter (407), pointing to the fact that the Elephantine Jews demonstratively call themselves Bagohi's friends who desires the best from him (TAD A4.7:23–24; verbatim: "those who are entitled of your goodness and your mercy"). But because he believes that the address "our lord" (line 18) of the first letter refers not to Bagohi but to Arsames, he looses the criterion for a terminus a quo. His assumption, however, that the same phrase in line 18, without introducing a new name, should mean a different person than in lines 1–2 remains doubtful, even if the letter does not show – Kottsieper's main argument (2002: 163) – that Bagohi has already been informed before. In order to appeal to Bagohi's only responsibility, it is reasonable that Elephantine Jews made a new case and told him the whole incident once more.

It seems that Bagohi very well understood the hint given in the letter. Because of his disagreement with the Judeans he felt no longer obliged to consult the High Priest and the Judean self-government. On the contrary, he consulted his Samarian colleague Delaiah,[23] whose wider concept of Israelite identity he knew. We have no sources about how Delaiah came to his positive decision; but because – as his name shows – he belonged to the believers of YHWH, he probably would have consulted the Samarian religious community. Obviously, the latter did | not see any problem in allowing the Jews in Elephantine the reconstruction of their temple. Thus, Bagohi and Delaiah made their positive cultic-political decision on the Persian governmental level without any participation of the Judeans (TAD A4.9).[24]

Therefore, we can conclude that the Bagoses story told by Josephus perfectly accords with all details given in the Elephantine texts, if it is dated between the two letters to Jerusalem (410–407 B.C.E.). Moreover, with the story about Persian-Judean disagreement in between, a good reason can be given for why two similar letters of petition were sent to Jerusalem with different addresses in a short period. There is only one problem with this solution: Dated from 408 to 401, the period of punishment would not be restricted to the reign of Artaxerxes II, starting in 405, but would already have begun during the last years of Darius II. But, I think, this problem is minor, because the period of punishment would considerably overlap the first years of his successor.

An Outlook on Ezra's Mission

In recent years, more and more scholars have pleaded on several grounds that the mission of Ezra should be dated in the 7th year not of Artaxerxes I but rather

---

23 Apart from the Elephantine papyri, Delaiah is probably verified by a Samarian coin (no. 22) as governor of the province of Samaria (Eshel 2007: 228–29); according to TAD A4.9:1, it was he who made the decision together with Bagohi. His brother Shelemiah, who is probably attested by ten types of Samarian coins (nos. 61–70), seems to have followed him in office (Eshel 2007: 229, 234). |

24 The support of both governors was successful. Accepting the restriction on burning holocaust sacrifices (TAD A4.10:10–11), the Elephantine Jews were allowed to rebuild their temple. The reconstruction must have happened before 402, because the Temple of Yahu is mentioned in a contract of this year (B3.12:18–19). The second phase of the tiled floor found in the new German excavation can be probably connected with this reconstruction (Rosenberg 2004: 10). After the Persians were driven out of Upper Egypt, the temple was not destroyed but abandoned. The independence of Egypt constituted the end of the Jewish garrison in Elephantine; the last letter comes from 399 B.C.E., the year of enthronement of Pharaoh Nepherites. According to the archeological evidence, the Temple of Yahu was later used as a stable, and its floor was covered with

of Artaxerxes II, which means in the year 398 B.C.E. Presupposing this late date, the mission would have taken place immediately after the period of punishment for the Judean community (408–401) had ended. Already, Kurt Galling (1964: 165–78) has closely connected Bagohi and Ezra.[25] According to him, during the years of punishment, the Judeans tried to lodge a complaint with Bagohi at the Persian royal court with the help of the Diaspora Jews. And as an answer, Artaxerxes and his counselors gave Ezra the task of investigating in Yehud and Jerusalem (Ezra 7:14). The cult of Jerusalem, heavily reduced by Bagohi, was supported by royal donations (7:15–17); Ezra's investigation, however, was deliberately restricted on the cultic and | religious realm in order to prevent any political disturbances in Judah, which – after the loss of Egypt – had become a border province of the Persian Empire. Therefore, Ezra had nothing directly to do with Bagohi.

We can doubt whether the connection between the Bagohi conflict and Ezra's mission is that close. The historical value of the Ezra tradition is difficult to determine (cf. Grabbe 2004: 324–32), and any evaluation of the Artaxerxes rescript should be more critical than Galling's. However, his idea that Ezra's mission constitutes some kind of reaction of the conflict between Bagohi and the Judean community is helpful, because it provides the former with some reason.

In short, I would try to reconstruct the connection in the following way, taking the implementation of the divine law as the most probable element of Ezra's mission: One can be sure that the Judeans tried to submit their complaints about Bagohi's interference in their cultic affairs at the Persian court; but they probably did not gain hearing as long as Artarxerxes II was involved in the fights against his brother (404–401). After the wars had ended, Artaxerxes should have been very interested in restraining all possible religious and cultic conflicts in his southwestern provinces, because they recently had become the borderline against possible Egyptian attacks. Thus, there is good reason to believe that he actually induced the final redaction, publication, and implementation of a document, which, on the one hand, could help to prevent Persian interventions in Jewish cultic and religious affairs such as Bagohi's and, on the other hand, might be able to limit the internal religious conflicts between the different Jewish groups, be it priests and laymen, Diaspora and provincial Jews, or – most important of all – Judeans and Samarians. Thus, Ezra was ordered to prepare, publish, and implement a document that can be inferred from the Artaxerxes rescript (Ezra 7:14, 25–26). This document, called "the law of the God of heaven" (v. 21), probably consists of the entire Pentateuch.

---

animal dung, which is probably to be regarded as "an act of deliberate desecration" (Rosenberg 2004: 9).

25 This is so even in the title of his famous article, "Bagoas und Esra." |

If we look at the Pentateuch with regard to the Judean-Samarian rivalry, it looks like a compromise: neither Jerusalem nor Gerizim is standing in the center; both are mentioned only incidentally (Gen 14:18–20, 22:2; and Deut 11:29, 27:12). The question of which location YHWH would like to choose as a dwelling place for his name (12:5, 11; 14:23; 16:6, 11; 26:2) is deliberately left open to future interpretation. According to the Pentateuch, more important than the place of YHWH's cult were its rites properly performed by an authorized Aaronide priesthood, which was the case in both places. Thus, the Pentateuch considerably lowered the Judean claim to religious leadership; other places for legitimate YHWH cult were possible. Likewise, a way for a coexistence of a more exclusive and a more inclusive concept of Jewish identity was | paved. Considered in this way, the publication and implementation of the Pentateuch in the provinces Judah and Samaria, induced by the Persian king, can be seen as a religious-political device for helping to stabilize and pacify the southwestern border of the empire at the beginning of the fourth century B.C.E.

Conclusion: Jewish Identities and Persian Control

Let me draw some conclusions from this historical reconstruction for the topic of this conference and integrate them into a little wider context: As far as we can see, the controversy about an exclusive or inclusive concept of Jewish identity started with Nehemiah in the middle of the fifth century B.C.E. In order to strengthen the independence of the little province of Yehud against constant interference of its much stronger Samarian neighbor, Nehemiah imposed on the Judean community a rigid concept of an exclusive Jewish identity, which had emerged among the ethnic minority of the Babylonian Diaspora (cf. Albertz 2006: 200–205). According to this concept, only believers in YHWH who were descendants of former Judah and Benjamin belong to the Jews, be they somewhere in the Diaspora or in the province. By stigmatizing all others, including the believers in YHWH in Samaria, as being alien or even unclean (Neh 13:7–9, 28–29), Nehemiah was able to carry through his exclusive policy against outer and inner resistance. Even a member of the high priestly family such as the son of Joiada', who married the daughter of the Samarian governor Sanballat and so stood up for a wider inclusive concept of Israelite identity, was expelled (13:28).

However, this rigid, exclusive concept of Jewish identity probably provoked the cultic separation of the Samarians. Sanballat and his Zadokide son-in-law founded their independent Samarian sanctuary on Mount Gerizim at least after the accession of Darius II (424 B.C.E.). And obviously, the High Priest Joiada', who seems to have advocated a more inclusive concept of a Jewish identity, was ready to accept this fact. From this time onward, there were two different cultic centers with different concepts of Judaism. Naturally, the Samarians refused the exclusive Jewish identity and advocated a wider, inclusive concept. And in return, the new rivalry provoked an even stronger Judean claim to religious leadership.

During this phase, from 445 to about 415 B.C.E., the Persians let the Judeans and Samarians do what they wanted as far as their inner affairs were involved; they were not really interested in their remote provinces of the Palestinian hill country (cf. Lipschits 2006: 29–30). Anyhow, this lack of interest underwent a considerable change in the last decade | of the fifth and the beginning of the fourth centuries. Being confronted with new revolts in Egypt and the gradual loss of this important province during the years 410–401, the Persians tried hard to tighten their control over their border provinces in the southern Levant, including Samaria and Judah.

An example of a stricter Persian rule over Judah occurred when the Jewish garrison of Elephantine wrote a letter of petition in the year 410. Their request to reconstruct their temple destroyed by the Egyptians concerned both the Persian political and the Judean religious competence; therefore, the letter is directed to the Persian governor Bagohi and the leaders of the Judean self-government, still acknowledging the religious leadership of the latter. But when the high priest Johanan used this matter as an opportunity to demonstrate the cultic exclusivity of Jerusalem and refused any permission, Bagohi was no longer ready to accept his claim to religious leadership. Facing new Egyptian riots, he wanted to demoralize Egyptian nationalism and strengthen the morality of the Jewish mercenaries in Persian service. Thus, he intervened in the Judean self-government and tried to replace Johanan with his brother Joshua', who promised to advocate a more liberal and inclusive concept of identity. In this, Bagohi, although a Persian, still acknowledged Judean authority in religious affairs. When, however, this attempt failed with the murder of Joshua', Bagohi left the Judeans with no doubt that they would be subjected to severe Persian rule. He imposed a heavy tax on all their official sacrifices for seven years, demonstratively defiled the temple, and humiliated the Judean leaders in order to cure them of their religious arrogance. After the second letter of the Elephantine Jews (in 407), he even interfered in the religious autonomy of the Judean self-government and made his own decision for approving the reconstruction of the Elephantine temple. Without consulting the Judean officials but with the consent of the Samarian governor, the Persian governor of Judah operated with an inclusive and liberal concept of Judaism in a case of strategic Persian interest.

Of course, the Judeans could not accept interference of this sort in their traditional religious rights. They probably lodged a complaint with Bagohi at the Persian court but did not gain hearing as long as Artaxerxes II was involved in the succession wars (404–401). Confronted with the loss of Egypt and the task of safeguarding the new borderline of the southwest wing of his empire, Artaxerxes became personally interested in limiting religious conflicts in the provinces of Judah and Samaria as much as possible. Thus, he ordered Ezra to prepare and publish a religious document that would allow several central sanctuaries to exist and pave the way for a coexistence of a more inclusive and | a more exclusive concept of Jewish identity. In contrast to Bagohi, Artaxerxes did not deny any Judean claim to religious leadership, but he restricted this claim to an extent that would no longer disturb Persian security policy.

Bibliography

Albertz, R.
  1994   *A History of Israelite Religion in the Old Testament Period.* 2 vols. Old Testament Library.
          Louisville, KY: Westminster John Knox.
  2006   Purity Strategies and Political Interests in the Policy of Nehemiah. Pp. 199–206 in
          *Confronting the Past: Archaeological and Historical Essays on Ancient Israel in Honor of
          William G. Dever,* ed. S. Gitin, J. E. Wright, and J. P. Dessel. Winona Lake, IN: Eisenbrauns.
Barag, D.
  1966   The Effects of the Tennes Rebellion on Palestine. *BASOR* 183: 6–12.
  1986-87 A Silver Coin of Yoḥanan the High Priest and the Coinage of Judea in the Fourth
          Century B.C. *INJ* 9: 4–21 and pl. 1.
Briant, P.
  2002   *From Cyrus to Alexander: A History of the Persian Empire.* Winona Lake, IN: Eisenbrauns.
Cowley, A. E.
  1923   *Aramaic Papyri of the Fifth Century B.C.* Oxford: Clarendon.
Cross, F. M.
  1975   A Reconstruction of the Judean Restoration. *JBL* 94: 4–18.
Donner, H.
  1995   *Geschichte des Volkes Israel und seiner Nachbarn in Grundzügen.* 2 vols. GAT 4/1-2. 2nd ed.
          Göttingen: Vandenhoeck & Ruprecht.
Dušek, J.
  2007   *Les Manuscrits araméens du Wadi Daliyeh et la Samarie vers 450–332 av. J.-C.* Culture and
          History of the Ancient Near East 30. Leiden: Brill.
Eshel, H.
  2007   The Governors of Samaria in the Fifth and Fourth Centuries B.C.E. Pp. 223–34 in *Judah
          and the Judeans in the Fourth Century B.C.E.,* ed. O. Lipschits, G. N. Knoppers, and R.
          Albertz. Winona Lake, IN: Eisenbrauns.
Fantalkin, A., and Tal, O.
  2006   Redating Lachish Level I: Identifying Achaemenid Imperial Policy at the Southern Frontier
          of the Fifth Satrapy. Pp. 167–97 in *Judah and the Judeans in the Persian Period,* ed.
          O. Lipschits and M. Oeming. Winona Lake, IN: Eisenbrauns.
Fried, L. S.
  2003   A Silver Coin of Yoḥanan. *Transeuphratène* 26: 65–85 and pls. II–V.

Galling, K.
 1964   Bagoas and Esra. Pp. 149–84 in *Studien zur Geschichte Israels im persischen Zeitalter.*
        Tübingen: Mohr Siebeck. |
Grabbe, L. L.
 1992a *Judaism from Cyrus to Hadrian.* 2 vols. Minneapolis: Fortress.
 1992b Who Was the Bagoses of Josephus (Ant. 11.7.1, §§ 297–301)? *Transeuphratène* 5: 49–55.
 2004   *A History of Jews and Judaism in the Second Temple Period,* vol. 1: *Yehud: A History of the
        Persian Province of Judah.* Library of Second Temple Sources 47. London: T. & T. Clark.
 2007   Archaeology and *Archaiologias*: Relating Excavations to History in Fourth-Century B.C.E.
        Palestine. Pp. 125–35 in *Judah and the Judeans in the Fourth Century B.C.E.,* ed. O. Lipschits,
        G. N. Knoppers, and R. Albertz. Winona Lake, IN: Eisenbrauns.
Gunneweg, A. H. J.
 1972   *Geschichte Israels bis Bar Kochba.* TW 2. 2nd ed. Stuttgart: Kohlhammer.
Herrmann, S.
 1973   *Geschichte Israels in alttestamentlicher Zeit.* Munich: Chr. Kaiser.
Kottsieper, I.
 2002   Die Religionspolitik der Achämeniden und die Juden von Elephantine. Pp. 150–78 in
        Religion und Religionskontakte im Zeitalter der Achämeniden, ed. R. Kratz. Veröffentlichungen
        der Wissenschaftlichen Gesellschaft für Theologie 22. Gütersloh: Chr. Kaiser and
        Gütersloher Verlagshaus.
Kratz, R.
 2004a Statthalter, Hohepriester und Schreiber im perserzeitlichen Juda. Pp. 93–119 in *Das
        Judentum im Zeitalter des Zweiten Tempels.* FAT 42. Tübingen: Mohr Siebeck.
 2004b Der zweite Tempel zu Jeb und zu Jerusalem. Pp. 60–78 in *Das Judentum im Zeitalter des
        Zweiten Tempels.* FAT 42. Tübingen: Mohr Siebeck.
Lemaire, A.
 1995   La fin de la première période perse en Égypte et la chronologie judéenne vers
        400 av. J.-C. *Transeuphratène* 9: 51–61.
 2007   Administration in Fourth-Century B.C.E. Judah in the Light of Epigraphy and Numismatics.
        Pp. 53–74 in *Judah and the Judeans in the Fourth Century B.C.E.,* ed. O. Lipschits,
        G. N. Knoppers, and R. Albertz. Winona Lake, IN: Eisenbrauns.
Lipschits, O.
 2006   Achaemenid Imperial Policy, Settlement Processes in Palestine, and the Status of
        Jerusalem in the Middle of the Fifth Century B.C.E. Pp. 19–52 in *Judah and the Judeans in
        the Persian Period,* ed. O. Lipschits and M. Oeming. Winona Lake, IN: Eisenbrauns.
Magen, Y.
 2007   The Dating of the First Phase of the Samaritan Temple on Mount Gerizim in Light of
        Archaeological Evidence. Pp. 157–211 in *Judah and the Judeans in the Fourth Century B.C.E.,*
        ed. O. Lipschits, G. N. Knoppers, and R. Albertz. Winona Lake, IN: Eisenbrauns. |
Marcus, R.
 1937   *Josephus,* vol. 6: *Jewish Antiquities, Books IX–XI.* London: Heinemann/Cambridge: Harvard
        University Press. Repr., 1958.
Metzger, M.
 1977   *Grundriß der Geschichte Israels.* 4th ed. Neukirchen-Vluyn: Neukirchener Verlag.
Miller, M., and Hayes, J. H.
 1986   *A History of Ancient Israel and Judah.* Philadelphia: Westminster.
Morgenstern, J.
 1935   Supplementary Studies in the Calendars of Ancient Israel. *HUCA* 10: 1–148.
 1938   A Chapter in the History of the High-Priesthood. *AJSL* 55: 1–24, 183–97, 360–77.

Noth, M.

1963   *Geschichte Israels*. 5th ed. Göttingen: Vandenhoeck & Ruprecht.

Pilgrim, C. von

2003   Tempel des Jahu und "Straße des Königs": Ein Konflikt in der späten Perserzeit auf Elephantine. Pp. 303–17 in *Egypt – Temple of the World. Ägypten – Tempel der ganzen Welt*, ed. S. Meyer. Studies in the History of Religion 47. Leiden: Brill.

Rooke, D. W.

2000   *Zadok's Heirs: The Role and Development of the High Priesthood in Ancient Israel*. Oxford Theological Monographs. Oxford: Oxford University Press.

Rosenberg, S. G.

2004   The Jewish Temple at Elephantine. *NEA* 67: 4–13.

Schwartz, D. R.

1990   On Some Papyri and Josephus' Sources and Chronology for the Persian Period. *JSJ* 21: 175–99.

Smith, M.

1971   *Palestinian Parties and Politics That Shaped the Old Testament*. New York: Columbia University Press.

Soggin, A. J.

1991   *Einführung in die Geschichte Israels und Judas: Von den Ursprüngen bis zum Aufstand Bar Kochbas*. Darmstadt: Wissenschaftliche Buchgesellschaft.

Steuernagel, C.

1909   Bemerkungen über die neuentdeckten jüdischen Papyrusurkunden aus Elephantine und ihre Bedeutung für das Alte Testament. *Theologische Studien und Kritiken* 82: 1–12.

Tadmor, H.

1978   Die Zeit des Ersten Tempels, die babylonische Gefangenschaft und die Restauration. Pp. 115–228 in *Geschichte des jüdischen Volkes*, vol. 1: *Von den Anfängen bis zum 7. Jahrhundert*, ed. H. H. Ben-Sasson. Munich: Beck. |

Torrey, C. C.

1939   The Two Persian Officers Named Bagoas. *AJSL* 56: 300–301.

VanderKam, J. C.

1991   Jewish High Priests of the Persian Temple Period: Is the List Complete? Pp. 67–91 in *Priesthood and Cult in Ancient Israel*, ed. G. A. Anderson and S. M. Olyan. JSOTSup 125. Sheffield: Sheffield Academic Press.

Williamson, H. G. M.

2004a   Early Post-Exilic Judaean History. Pp. 3–45 in *Studies in the Persian Period: History and Historiography*. FAT 38. Tübingen: Mohr Siebeck.

2004b   The Historical Value of Josephus' Jewish Antiquities XI. 297–301. Pp. 74–89 in *Studies in the Persian Period: History and Historiography*. FAT 38. Tübingen: Mohr Siebeck.

2 Literaturgeschichte

Einführung

Solange die Palästina-Archäologie kaum literarische Texte zutage fördert, bildet immer noch die historisch-kritische Auslegung und literaturgeschichtliche Einordnung der biblischen Texte eine wesentliche Quelle für das tiefere Verständnis der Geschichte und der Religions- bzw. Theologiegeschichte des Alten Israel. Meine Aufsätze zur Literaturgeschichte des Pentateuchs, die mit der Herausarbeitung meines Exoduskommentars verbunden waren, sind schon gesondert veröffentlicht worden.[1] Die ersten beiden Beiträge dieses Kapitels bilden dazu noch zwei Nachträge, die zwar von einiger Bedeutung, aber erst in jüngster Zeit entstanden sind. Sie handeln von zwei wichtigen formativen Stufen in der Entstehung des Pentateuchs.

Der erste Beitrag „Die erstmalige Konstituierung des Pentateuch durch die spät-deuteronomistische Redaktionsschicht (K^D bzw. D)" wendet sich noch einmal speziell der spät-deuteronomistischen Bearbeitung des Pentateuchs zu, die Erhard Blum vor über 30 Jahren entdeckt hat und K^D nannte.[2] Mit ihr gelang es Blum nicht nur, viele der seit Anfang des 19. Jhs. immer wieder diskutierten deuteronomisch bzw. deuteronomistisch klingenden Passagen im Pentateuch einer bestimmten Redaktionsschicht zuzuordnen, sondern es gelang ihm auch, erstmals genauer zu erklären, wie das Deuteronomium, das ursprünglich zum Deuteronomistischen Geschichtswerk gehörte, in den entstehenden Pentateuch einbezogen wurde. Im ersten Teil des Aufsatzes reflektiere ich ausführlich über die Gründe, warum diese ertragreiche und anfangs vielfach positiv gewürdigte Hypothese im Verlauf der neuesten Pentateuchforschung seltsamerweise immer weiter in den Hintergrund gedrängt und vielfach abgetan wurde. Im zweiten Teil versuche ich zu zeigen, dass diese Hypothese – nur leicht modifiziert – nach wie vor in der Lage ist, ein entscheidendes literarisches Stadium der Entstehung der Gründungsgeschichte Israels, nämlich ihren Ausbau zu einem „fünf-rolligen Buch", einem Pentateuch, angemessen zu beschreiben – besser jedenfalls als manche der gegenwärtig diskutierten Alternativen. Zu beachten ist allerdings, dass mit der D-Redaktion der Pentateuch noch lange nicht fertig gestellt war.

Der zweite Beitrag „Der kompositionelle Abschluss des Pentateuchs (Dtn 31–34): Zur Rekonstruktion der nicht-priesterlichen Pentateuchredaktion" unternimmt den Versuch, in der noch weitgehend ungeklärten Frage der Endredaktion(en) des Pentateuchs ein Stück weiter voranzukommen. Die Quellentheorie war

---

1 S. R. Albertz, Pentateuchstudien, hrsg. von Jakob Wöhrle unter Mitarbeit von Friederike Neumann (FAT 117), Tübingen 2018.
2 Vgl. E. Blum, Studien zur Komposition des Pentateuch (BZAW 189), Berlin/New York 1990, 102–218.

https://doi.org/10.1515/9783111202228-006

davon ausgegangen, dass die Endredaktion im Zuge der Vereinigung der Priester-
schrift mit den älteren nicht-priesterlichen Quellen erfolgt sei, hatte allerdings
einen solchen Endredaktor textlich kaum nachweisen können. Weiter führte die
Einsicht, die heute von einer ganzen Anzahl von Exegeten geteilt wird, dass der
Kanonisierung des Pentateuch eine Hexateuchredaktion vorausging, die darauf
zielte, eine verbindliche Gründungsgeschichte Israels zu schaffen, die das Josuabuch mit einbezog.[3] Denn vor diesem Hintergrund lassen sich dann einige Textpassagen innerhalb des Pentateuch, die geeignet sind, eine Art Ersatz für das
letztlich doch wieder abgespaltene Josuabuch zu schaffen, als Teil einer späteren
Pentateuchredaktion klassifizieren. So hatte ich die Kapitel Num 25–36, welche
die Einnahme und Verteilung des verheißenen Landes detailliert vorbereiten,
schon vor einiger Zeit einer priesterlichen Pentateuchredaktion zugeschrieben.[4]
Die wenigen kurzen priesterlichen Passagen am Ende des Buches Deuteronomium (Dtn 32,48–52; 34.1*.7–9) tragen allerdings kaum etwas zur Abrundung des
Pentateuchs als ein eigenes Werk bei. Es muss somit daneben mindestens eine,
wenn nicht mehrere nicht-priesterliche Pentateuchredaktionen gegeben haben.
Unter dieser Fragestellung werden die abschließenden Kapitel des Buches Deuteronomium, insbesondere der Einbau des Moseliedes (Dtn 31–32) und des Mosesegens (Dtn 33), einer ausführlichen Untersuchung unterzogen. So erweiterte ein
erster nicht-priesterlicher Redaktor den Abschluss des Pentateuch im Moselied
um eine warnende Zukunftsperspektive als Ersatz für das abgetrennte Deuteronomistische Geschichtswerk, ein zweiter begründete dann ausdrücklich die Erweiterung des deuteronomischen Torabuchs zum Gesamtpentateuch und stattete
ihn im hymnisch gerahmten Mosesegen mit einer heilvollen Zukunftsperspektive
aus, die das gesicherte Leben der Stämme im Lande nach der erfolgreichen Landnahme schildert. Damit wird die Erfüllung der Landverheißung in den Pentateuch hineingezogen (Dtn 33,26–28) und das Josuabuch erneut antizipiert.

Nachdem ich schon früher die „priesterlichen" Passagen im Buch Josua als
nachträgliche Angleichungen an die Vorstellungen und Normen des bereits kano-
nisierten Pentateuchs erwiesen hatte,[5] zeigt der dritte Beitrag „How Jerusalem's
Temple Was Aligned to Moses' Tabernacle: About the Historical Power of an Invented Myth" auf, dass auch die „priesterlichen" Ergänzungen zum dtr. Bericht
vom Tempelbau Salomos in 1 Kön 6–8 bemüht sind, den Jerusalemer Tempel
literarisch an das inzwischen normativ gewordene „Zelt der Begegnung", dessen
Bau in Ex 25–40 berichtet worden war, anzugleichen. Die beiden an sich recht
unterschiedlichen „priesterlichen" Ergänzungen setzen somit gleichermaßen die

---

3 Vgl. zusammenfassend zu dieser Hypothese Albertz, Pentateuchstudien, 449–470.
4 S. Albertz, Pentateuchstudien, 357–373.
5 Vgl. Albertz, Pentateuchstudien, 375–390.

Verselbständigung des Pentateuch als autoritative Gründungsgeschichte voraus und können daher nicht für die Konstituierung eines Enneateuchs in Anspruch genommen werden. Daneben möchte dieser Beitrag aufzeigen, dass dieses von den Minimalisten gern der „mythic past" zugerechnete Wüstenzelt nichtsdestoweniger die historische Kraft entwickelt hat, nicht nur die literarische Gestalt der Berichte vom Jerusalemer Tempel, sondern auch dessen reale bauliche Gestalt und Ausstattung zu verändern.

Der letzte Aufsatz dieses Kapitels „On the Structure and Formation of the Book of Deutero-Isaiah" widmet sich der Literaturgeschichte des Deuterojesajabuches. In meinem Buch „Die Exilszeit" hatte ich im intensiven Gespräch mit der Forschung die ersten drei Stadien der Entstehungsgeschichte nachgewiesen, die dieses Prophetenbuch im 6. Jh. v. Chr. durchlaufen hat.[6] Meine Überlegungen zu weiteren Redaktionen, die erst nach der Exilszeit erfolgten, konnte ich dort nicht entfalten. Der hier aufgenommene Aufsatz möchte diese Lücke schließen, indem er auch die Bearbeitungen, die das Buch noch in späterer Zeit, wahrscheinlich vom 5. bis 3. Jh. v. Chr., erfahren hat, in die redaktionsgeschichtliche Untersuchung einbezieht. Da einige dieser Bearbeitungen Verklammerungen zum Proto- und Tritojesajabuch herstellen, müssen die sie betreffenden Überlegungen allerdings solange einigermaßen hypothetisch bleiben, bis sie durch entsprechende Untersuchungen zu den anderen beiden Teilen des Jesajabuches bestätigt sind.

---

6 S. R. Albertz, Die Exilszeit. 6. Jahrhundert v. Chr. (BE 7), Stuttgart 2001, 283–323.

Die erstmalige Konstituierung des Pentateuch durch die spät-deuteronomistische Redaktionsschicht (K^D bzw. D)

Erhard Blum, dem ich mit diesem Beitrag zu seinem 70. Geburtstag herzlich gratulieren und ihn ehren möchte, hat in der neueren Pentateuchforschung ganz Außergewöhnliches geleistet. Sein erstes Buch zur Komposition der Genesis, mit dem er sein kompositions- und redaktionsgeschichtliches Modell begründete,[1] hat eine Vielzahl neuerer Entwürfe zur Pentateuchentstehung beeinflusst.[2] Sein zweites Buch, das den Pentateuch aus der spannungsreichen Vereinigung zweier Großkompositionen erklärt, einer spät-deuteronomistischen K^D und einer priesterlichen K^{P},[3] hat international eine außergewöhnlich breite Beachtung gefunden. Ich stieß dazu auf nicht weniger als 14 Buchbesprechungen und ausführlichere Auseinandersetzungen.[4] Jean-Louis Ska etwa fand die These des Buches | so bestechend,[5] dass er seinen Beitrag mit der respektvollen Frage „Un nouveau Wellhausen?" überschrieb.

---

1 E. Blum, Die Komposition der Vätergeschichte (WMANT 57), Neukirchen-Vluyn 1984.

2 Vgl. nur die Entwürfe von E. Zenger u. a. (Hg.), Einleitung in das Alte Testament (Kohlhammer Studienbücher 1,1), Stuttgart ⁵1995, 105; D. M. Carr, Reading the Fractures of Genesis. Historical and Literary Approaches, Louisville 1996, 150–151; R. G. Kratz, Die Komposition der erzählenden Bücher des Alten Testaments (UTB 2157), Göttingen 2000, 331; E. Otto, Das Deuteronomium im Pentateuch und Hexateuch. Studien zur Literaturgeschichte von Pentateuch und Hexateuch im Lichte des Deuteronomiumrahmens (FAT 30), Tübingen 2000, 264; R. Albertz, Pentateuchstudien (FAT 117), Tübingen 2018, 485, u. a.

3 E. Blum, Studien zur Komposition des Pentateuch (BZAW 189), Berlin/New York 1990.

4 Vgl. W. Gross, Review, ThQ 171 (1991) 132–133; H.-C. Schmitt, Review, ZAW 103 (1991) 148–149; J. Blenkinsopp, Review, CBQ 54 (1992) 312–313; H. Seebass, Review, ThRv 88 (1992) 17–21; J. Van Seters, Review, JBL 111 (1992) 122–144; G. I. Davies, Review, VT 43 (1993) 135–137; dazu: T. Römer, L'école de Heidelberg a 15 ans … À propos de deux ouvrages sur une nouvelle approche de la formation du Pentateuque, ÉTR 67 (1991) 77–81; J.-L. Ska, Un nouveau Wellhausen?, Bib. 72 (1991) 253–263; E. Otto, Kritik der Pentateuchkomposition, ThR 60 (1995) 163–191; G. I. Davies, The Composition of the Book of Exodus. Reflections on the Theses of Erhard Blum, in: M. V. Fox u. a. (Hg.), Texts, Temples, and Traditions. A Tribute to Menachem Haran, Winona Lake 1996, 71–85; H. Ausloos, The Need for Linguistic Criteria in Characterising Biblical Pericopes as Deuteronomistic. A Critical Note to Erhard Blum's Methodology, JNSL 23 (1997) 47–56; D. M. Carr, Controversy and Convergence in Recent Studies of the Formation of the Pentateuch, Religious Studies Review 23 (1997) 22–29; G. I. Davies, K^D in Exodus. An Assessment of E. Blum's Proposal, in: M. Vervenne/ J. Lust (Hg.), Deuteronomy and Deuteronomic Literature. FS C. H. W. Brekelmans (BEThL 133), Leuven 1997, 407–420; | J. Van Seters, The Deuteronomistic Redaction of the Pentateuch. The Case against It, in: Vervenne/Lust, Deuteronomy and Deuteronomic Literature, 301–319.

5 Siehe Ska, Un nouveau, 257: „L'idée centrale de cette thèse, celle de deux compositions principales dans le Pentateuque, est séduisante à plus d'un égard."

https://doi.org/10.1515/9783111202228-007

I Blums epochale K^D-Hypothese und ihr merkwürdiges Verschwinden aus den meisten neueren Pentateuchmodellen

So anregend Blums Überlegungen zum literarischen Charakter der priesterlichen Komposition (K^P) gewesen sind,[6] so darf doch, wie schon Graham I. Davies 1997 feststellte, Blums „thesis of a wide-ranging ‚D-Komposition' in Exodus and Numbers (as well as in Genesis) [...] be regarded as his main new contribution."[7] Bei einem engen Blick auf die Forschungsgeschichte könnte man zwar meinen, Blum habe hier nur eine These ausformuliert und besser begründet, die sein Lehrer Rolf Rendtorff zuvor noch recht vage und vorsichtig angedacht hatte – war dieser doch bei seiner Untersuchung der Verheißungen in der Genesis auf eine Gruppe von Landgabeschwüren an die Erzväter gestoßen (Gen 22,16; 24,7; 26,3; 50,24), die sprachlich den typisch dtn. Landverheißungen entsprachen (Dtn 1,8.35; 6,10.18.23 u. ö.) und sich ebenfalls über die Bücher Exodus (Ex 13,5.11; 32,13; 33,1) und Numeri (Num 11,12; 14,23; 32,11) hinweg zogen.[8] Doch blickt man auf die gesamte Forschungsgeschichte zur Thematik, wie sie Hans Ausloos detailreich, wenn auch leider aus einer etwas engen Perspektive, nachgezeichnet hat,[9] dann erkennt man, dass Blums K^D-Hypothese die sehr respektable Lösung eines uralten Problems darstellt, um das seit dem Anfang des 19. Jahrhunderts gerungen wird: Wie nämlich die von Rendtorff beobachteten und viele weitere Textpassagen in Gen–Num, die Anklänge an die dtn./dtr. Sprache und Gedankenwelt erkennen lassen, aus der Entstehungsgeschichte des Pentateuch heraus erklärt werden können.

Hier ist nicht der Ort, diese Forschungsgeschichte im Einzelnen nachzuzeichnen, der deutliche Fortschritt, den die Blum'sche Hypothese darstellt, zeigt sich jedoch genügend, wenn man sie mit einigen vorausgehenden Positionen ver|gleicht. Julius Wellhausen konnte im Rahmen seiner Drei-Quellentheorie mit den besagten Passagen nicht recht etwas anfangen. Er erklärte sie entweder aus der Geistesverwandtschaft, die der die Quellen J und E zusammenfügende Jehowist mit dem Deuteronomium geteilt hat, oder aber aus der Redaktionsarbeit des

---

6 Vgl. seine Einschätzung „Weder ‚Quelle' noch ‚Redaktion'", Blum, Studien, 229–285. Zur anhaltenden Diskussion vgl. Albertz, Pentateuchstudien, 255–276.

7 So Davies, K^D in Exodus, 407.

8 R. Rendtorff, Das überlieferungsgeschichtliche Problem des Pentateuch (BZAW 147), Berlin/New York 1976, 75–79.163–173.

9 H. Ausloos, The Deuteronomist's History. The Role of the Deuteronomist in Historical-Critical Research into Genesis–Numbers (OTS 67), Leiden/Boston 2015. Da Ausloos selber auf eine protodtn. Erklärung festgelegt ist, kann er Blums Lösung des Problems kaum angemessen würdigen, vgl. ebd., 209–219. |

Deuteronomisten, der das Deuteronomium in den Hexateuch eingesetzt habe.[10] Doch kann er nicht aufzeigen, wie letzteres stattgefunden hat, schwankt nicht selten zwischen beiden Erklärungsmöglichkeiten und zeigt kein Interesse, stilistische oder konzeptionelle Zusammenhänge zwischen den betreffenden Passagen aufzuzeigen. Geradezu in Widersprüche verwickelte sich Martin Noth, der zwar konsequenter als andere nicht weniger als acht gewichtige „deuteronomistisch stilisierte Zusätze" im Buch Exodus aufspürte,[11] dennoch aber auf der Meinung beharrte: „In den Büchern Gen.–Num. fehlt jede Spur einer ‚deuteronomistischen Redaktion',"[12] wohl um deren Differenz zu dem von ihm entdeckten Deuteronomistischen Geschichtswerk (DtrG) in Dtn–2 Kön herauszustreichen. Bei dieser Unsicherheit in der Forschung verwundert es nicht, dass die beiden Entwürfe, die vor und neben Blum den Pentateuch ebenfalls aus der Verbindung eines deuteronomistischen und eines priesterlichen Werks erklären wollten, nämlich die von Ivan Engnell und Joseph Blenkinsopp,[13] sowohl bei der textlichen Zuweisung als auch bei der zeitlichen Ansetzung recht vage bleiben. Auch die Skizze einer Endredaktion aus prophetischem oder spät-dtr. Geiste, die Hans-Christoph Schmitt über Rendtorff hinausgehend anhand einiger Motivlinien in dtr. klingenden Passagen entwarf, konnte, was die Bestimmung des Charakters und den Umfang einer solchen Redaktion betraf, noch keine Sicherheit gewinnen.[14] |

In dieser eher verworrenen Diskussionslage ist es Erhard Blum mit seiner K[D]-Hypothese erstmals gelungen, einen großen Teil der im Pentateuch schon seit langer Zeit beobachteten Passagen mit dtn. oder dtr. Sprachmerkmalen als Teil

---

10 Vgl. J. Wellhausen, Die Composition des Hexateuch und der historischen Bücher des Alten Testaments, Leipzig [6]1899 = Berlin [4]1963, 74.79.86.94 mit Anm. 2.115.205–206 mit Anm. 1.

11 Vgl. M. Noth, Überlieferungsgeschichte des Pentateuch, Stuttgart [2]1948, 32–33. Das Zitat findet sich in Anm. 106. Es handelt sich um Ex 12,24–27; 13; 15,25b–26; 16,4bβ.28; 19,3b–9a.(9b); in Ders., Das zweite Buch Mose. Exodus (ATD 5), Göttingen [4]1968, 156.200.215, kommen dann noch Ex 23,20–33; 32,9–14; 34,11b–13 hinzu.

12 M. Noth, Überlieferungsgeschichtliche Studien. Die sammelnden und bearbeitenden Geschichtswerke im Alten Testament, Tübingen [3]1967, 13.

13 Siehe I. Engnell, The Pentateuch, in: Ders., A Rigid Scrunity. Critical Essays on the Old Testament, Nashville 1969, 50–67; J. Blenkinsopp, The Pentateuch. An Introduction to the first Five Books of the Bible (The Anchor Bible Reference Library), New York u. a. 1992, 229–241; Ders., Deuteronomic Contribution to the Narrative in Genesis–Numbers. A Test Case, in: L. S. Shearing/ S. L. McKenzie (Hg.), Those Elusive Deuteronomists. The Phenomenon of Pan-Deuteronomism (JSOT.S 268), Sheffield 1999, 84–115. Letzterer war weniger von Blum als von Rendtorff angeregt.

14 Vgl. H.-C. Schmitt, Redaktion des Pentateuch im Geiste der Prophetie. Beobachtungen zur Bedeutung der „Glaubens"-Thematik innerhalb der Theologie des Pentateuch, in: Ders., Theologie in Prophetie und Pentateuch. Gesammelte Schriften (BZAW 310), Berlin/New York 2001, 220–237, von 1982 mit Ders., Das spätdeuteronomistische Geschichtswerk Gen I–2 Regum XXV und seine theologische Intention, ebd., 277–294, von 1997. |

einer einheitlichen Redaktion wahrscheinlich zu machen, welche die vorgegebenen Erzähl- und Gesetzesüberlieferungen von Gen–Dtn untereinander verbindet,
durch eigene Texte ergänzt und teilweise neu gestaltet. Blum kann den Umfang
der D-Komposition klar benennen, sie reicht von Gen 15 bis Dtn 34,10, d. h. von
der Vätergeschichte der Genesis bis zum Ende des Deuteronomiums. Und im Unterschied zu Rendtorff, der sich hinsichtlich der zeitlichen Ansetzung noch vorsichtig zurückhielt, kann Blum einen eindeutigen *terminus a quo* für die von ihm
rekonstruierte Komposition bestimmen: Da die von ihr geschaffene Motivlinie
vom Begegnungszelt außerhalb des Lagers (Ex 33,7–11; Num 11,14–17.24b–30; 12,4–
8) mit Dtn 31,14–15.23 in das Dtn hineinreicht und hier klar eine Ergänzung zum
schon dtr. gerahmten Gesetzeswerk darstellt, ist K^D zeitlich nach dem DtrG, d. h.
schon in die frühnachexilische Zeit anzusetzen, was sich auch durch traditionsge-
schichtliche Untersuchungen wichtiger K^D-Passagen (z. B. Ex 19,3–9) bestätigen
lasse.[15] Dadurch war nicht nur die proto-dtn. Datierung der betreffenden Passagen abgewiesen, wie sie unter der Ägide der Quellentheorie üblich war,[16] sondern
auch ihre Herleitung von den Verfassern des DtrG. Blum will die D-Komposition
ausdrücklich unter den Erben der klassischen dtr. Schule beheimaten, die sich in
Sprache und theologischer Orientierung ein Stück weit von dieser unterscheiden.[17] Die Bestimmung des *terminus ad quem*, d. h. die vor-priesterliche Ansetzung von K^D, die Blum im Anschluss an Rendtorff vornahm, war demgegenüber
schon 1990 weniger eindeutig.[18]

Besser als allen vor ihm gelang es Blum, durchlaufende Anliegen der D-Komposition zu benennen: die Wichtigkeit der Verheißungen, insbesondere der Land-

---

15 Vgl. Blum, Studien, 85–87.164–172.
16 Vgl. Ausloos, History, 113–166. Ders., Need, missversteht Blum, wenn er meint, dieser wolle
die Stilkritik generell ablehnen. Dieser weist nur auf, dass eine solche ohne redaktionskritische
Kriterien uneindeutig bleibt, vgl. Blum, Komposition, 373–375; Ders. Studien, 167–168. Interessant
ist, dass Ausloos' Doktorvater, M. Vervenne, The Question of ‚Deuteronomic' Elements in Genesis
to Numbers, in: F. García Martínez u. a. (Hg.), Studies in Deuteronomy. FS C. J. Labuschagne
(VT.S 53), Leiden/New York/Köln 1994, 243–268, hier 266, durchaus seine Sympathie für Blums
Lösung des Problems ausdrücken konnte, obwohl er einer proto-dtn. Einordnung der Stellen
zuneigte und im Einzelfall Zweifel an seiner Zuweisung von Ex 14,13–14 zur nach-dtr. D-Komposition hegt.
17 E. Blum, Israël à la montagne de Dieu. Remarques sur Ex 19–24; 32–34 et sur le contexte
littéraire et historique de sa composition, in: A. de Pury (Hg.), Le Pentateuque en question. Les
origines et la composition des cinq premiers livres de la Bible à la lumière des recherches
récentes, Genève 1989, 271–295, hier 288–290.
18 Vgl. das frühe Plädoyer einer nach-priesterlichen Ansetzung von Gen 15 eines weiteren Rend-
torff-Schülers, T. Römer, Genesis 15 und Genesis 17. Beobachtungen und Anfragen zu einem Dog-
ma der „neueren" und „neusten" Pentateuchkritik, DBAT 26 (1989/90) 32–47.

verheißungen an die Erzväter,[19] die große Bedeutung des Glaubens Israels | an Gottes Verheißungen und an Mose als Rettungs- und Offenbarungsmittler[20] und schließlich die alle Priester und Propheten überragende Rolle des Mose als der Übermittler der göttlichen Gesetze, erst am Sinai und dann am Begegnungszelt.[21] Vor allem Blums präzise und einfühlsame Nachzeichnung der kompositionellen Erzähllinie der Exodus- und Sinai-Texte (Ex 1–14; 19–24; 32–34), welche durch die Quellenscheidung oft verstellt worden war, hat viele Exegeten beeindruckt. Graham I. Davies, eigentlich ein Anhänger der Quellentheorie, konnte einräumen, „at the very least Blum's approach sheds a fresh light on the dominant themes of this material as a whole and promises a way out of the impasse of previous source-critical debates."[22] Und Thomas Römer wagte sogar trotz einiger kritischer Einwände an der These seines früheren Heidelberger Kollegen die Prognose, „le modèle de l',école de Heidelberg' s'imposera peut-être à une grande partie des exégètes vétérotestamentaires, probablement dans une version revue et corrigée."[23]

Doch diese Prognose hat sich in der weiteren Forschungsgeschichte nicht erfüllt. Trotz ihres beträchtlichen und anfangs auch gewürdigten innovativen Potentials wurde Blums K[D]-Hypothese in den neueren Entwürfen zur Entstehung des Pentateuch kaum rezipiert.[24] John Van Seters sah keinen Bedarf an einer „so-called Dtr redaction in the Pentateuch"[25] und Christoph Levin bestritt sogar vehement deren Existenz.[26] In der Darstellung der aktuellen Forschung von Reinhard G. Kratz auf dem Pentateuchkongress in Zürich von 2011 spielt Blums K[D]-Hypothese fast gar keine Rolle mehr. Er nennt sie nicht unter den wichtigen Thesen, die einen möglichen Forschungskonsens tragen könnten, sondern erwähnt sie nur noch beiläufig und zudem kritisch.[27] Nach seinem eigenen Modell

---

19 Gen 15; 22,15–18; 24,7; 26,3bβ–5.24*; Ex 13,5.11; 32,13; 33,1; Num 11,12; 14,16.23; Dtn 34,4*. |
20 Gen 15,6; Ex 4,1.8.9.31; 14,31; 19,9; Num 14,11.22.
21 Ex 19,9; 33,7–11; Num 11,14–17.24b–30; 12,4–8; Dtn 31,14–15.23; 34,10.
22 Davies, Composition, 84.
23 Römer, L'école, 81.
24 Daran konnte auch mein Versuch wenig ändern, die Hypothese in R. Albertz, Religionsgeschichte Israels in alttestamentlicher Zeit, 2 Bde. (GAT 8,1–2), Göttingen ²1996/1997, 504–516, zu popularisieren und der D-Komposition im nachexilischen Selbstverwaltungsgremium „Ältestenrat" einen institutionellen Hintergrund (vgl. Num 11,16–17.24–25) zu verschaffen.
25 Siehe J. Van Seters, The So-Called Deuteronomistic Redaction of the Pentateuch, in: J. A. Emerton (Hg.), Congress Volume. Leuven 1989 (VT.S 43), Leiden u. a. 1991, 58–77, hier 77; vgl. Ders., Case, 319.
26 Siehe C. Levin, Der Jahwist (FRLANT 157), Göttingen 1993, 436.
27 Siehe R. G. Kratz, The Pentateuch in Current Research. Consensus and Debate, in: T. Dozeman/ K. Schmid/B. J. Schwartz (Hg.), The Pentateuch. International Perspectives on Current Research (FAT 78), Tübingen 2011, 31–61, hier 41–42 und 54, Anm. 73.

handelt es sich bei den dtr. klingenden Passagen um vereinzelte spät- oder nach-dtr. Ergänzungen, die in zwei Schüben in der exilischen und nachexilischen Zeit in den Hexateuch eingefügt worden seien, was wieder an die Mutmaßungen Wellhausens erinnert.[28] Im Pentateuchmodell von Eckart Otto fehlt K^D | vollständig. Die Einbindung des Deuteronomiums (plus Josua) wird hier von der nach-priesterlichen Hexateuchredaktion übernommen, die Gestaltung der Sinaiperikope erfolgt gar erst durch die Pentateuchredaktion, die sich „in nicht geringem Maß dtr Sprachklischees" bediene.[29] Selbst in den neueren Arbeiten von Thomas Römer spielt Blums K^D nur noch eine begrenzte und untergeordnete Rolle. Zwar rechnet er noch, besonders in Ex 1–14, mit einer „composition deutéronomiste",[30] doch weist er inzwischen immer mehr Passagen, die Blum für die D-Komposition in Anspruch genommen hatte, der abschließenden Pentateuchredaktion zu.[31] So ist die innovative Hypothese aus den neueren Modellen zur Entstehung des Pentateuch fast verschwunden.

II Gründe für die spärliche Rezeption der K^D-Hypothese

Fragt man, was wohl die Gründe für die erstaunlich spärliche Rezeption von Blums K^D-Hypothese gewesen sein könnten, so lassen sich aus meiner Sicht zumindest drei benennen: erstens ihre inneren Schwachstellen, zweitens ihre Konkurrenz zu Alternativmodellen, drittens ihr nachträglicher Umbau, mit dem Blum selber ihren Geltungsbereich einschränkte.

1 Innere Schwachstellen

Bei aller Würdigung der beachtlichen Syntheseleistung, die Erhard Blum mit seiner K^D-Hypothese vollbracht hatte, wurden schon von den Rezensenten einige Schwachstellen benannt, die sie in der 1990 präsentierten Form aufweise: Erstens wurde vielfach Blums Verzicht bedauert, die der D-Komposition vorgegebenen

---

28 So Kratz, Komposition, 312–313. |

29 Das Zitat findet sich in Otto, Kritik, 180. Vgl. sonst die zusammenfassende Darstellung des Modells in Ders., Deuteronomiumstudien III. Die literarische Entstehung und Geschichte des Buches Deuteronomium als Teil der Tora, ZAR 17 (2011) 79–132, hier 99–108.

30 So T. Römer, Moïse en version originale. Enquête sur le récit de la sortie d'Égypte (Exode 1–15), Montrouge Cedex/Genève 2015, 20–22.

31 Vgl. im neusten Studienbuch T. Römer, Der Pentateuch, in: W. Dietrich/H.-P. Mathys/T. Römer/R. Smend (Hg.), Die Entstehung des Pentateuch. Neuausgabe (ThW 1), Stuttgart 2014, 53–166, hier bes. 86–87.98.115–116, darunter Gen 15; 50,24; Ex 4,1–17; 14,31; 19,9; 32,13; 33,1; Dtn 34,4*.10–12.

Erzähl- und Gesetzesüberlieferungen genauer zu bestimmen, wodurch auch die Textzuweisungen an K^D nicht immer zwingend erscheinen würden.[32] D. h. es würde nicht kritisch genug überprüft, ob die aufgewiesenen kompositionellen Linien wirklich alle auf derselben Redaktionsebene angesiedelt sind. Zweitens | wurde auf das Problem hingewiesen, dass bei der Moseberufung in Ex 3,8 nicht auf die Landverheißungen an die Erzväter zurückverwiesen würde, mit denen K^D die Vätergeschichte strukturiert hatte.[33] Wenn die Moseberufung durchweg von K^D formuliert worden ist, wie Blum annimmt, wäre das sehr merkwürdig. Stand damit die Kohärenz der D-Komposition über Genesis und Exodus hinweg auf dem Spiel, auch wenn solche Rückverweise dann in Ex 32,13 und 33,1 sehr wohl auftauchen? Oder stammte Ex 3 nicht insgesamt von K^D? Immerhin war ja für Rendtorff das auffällige Phänomen ein Grund, die ursprüngliche Eigenständigkeit der Exoduserzählung gegenüber der Vätererzählung anzunehmen.[34] Drittens wurde von Römer bemängelt, dass die Hypothese im Numeribuch noch nicht voll ausgearbeitet sei und hier Korrekturen nötig sein könnten.[35]Und viertens wurde schließlich von ihm, Hans-Christoph Schmitt und besonders von Eckart Otto die vor-priesterliche Datierung von K^D in Frage gestellt.[36] So gab es einige Punkte, die Anlass zu einer weiteren Ausarbeitung und besseren Absicherung der These geboten hätten.

2 Konkurrenz zu Alternativmodellen

Während alle Pentateuchmodelle einen Platz für die priesterlichen Texte bereithalten, so herrscht auf Seiten der nicht-priesterlichen Texte an konkurrierenden Erklärungshypothesen kein Mangel. Als Blum seine K^D-Hypothese veröffentlichte, hatte John Van Seters die Herausforderungen, welche die erneute Wahrnehmung zahlreicher dtn./dtr. klingender Wendungen in den Büchern Gen–Num an die klassische Quellentheorie stellten, dadurch aufzunehmen versucht, dass er den

---

32 Vgl. Blenkinsopp, Review, 312; Gross, Review, 132; Otto, Kritik, 165; Römer, L'école, 78–79; Van Seters, Review, 124; vgl. J.-L. Ska, Introduction to Reading the Pentateuch, Winona Lake 2006, 136. Blum, Studien, 214–218, begründet seine Zurückhaltung an dieser Stelle ausführlich methodisch, aber der einzige Rezensent, der sie positiv würdigt, ist Carr, Controversy, 25. |

33 Vgl. dazu ausführlich Ska, Un nouveau, 258–259; sodann Römer, L'école, 81, der erstmals einen Beginn von K^D in Ex 1 erwog. Blum, Studien, 189–190, hatte gemeint, K^D wolle mit dieser Eigenheit „eine zweite eigengewichtige Fundierung der Gottesbindung an Israel" (190) profilieren. Doch ist das Argument offensichtlich nicht so ganz überzeugend.

34 Vgl. Rendtorff, Problem, 66–67.

35 So Römer, L'école, 81.

36 Vgl. Römer, L'école, 81; Schmitt, Review, 149; und ausführlich Otto, Kritik, 172–180.

Jahwisten in die Exilszeit nach der Entstehung des DtrG datierte.[37] Dieser späte jahwistische Historiker, der dtr. Sprachklischees verwenden kann, aber unter Aufnahme älteren Materials seine eigenen Anliegen vertritt, hat manche Ähnlichkeit mit dem Verfasser von Blums D-Komposition und macht für Van Seters eine gesonderte spät-dtr. Redaktion überflüssig. Doch es bleibt die Frage, ob Blums sorgfältige Beobachtung der Kompositionsbögen, welche die Urgeschichte Gen 1–11 nicht einbeziehen,[38] und seine Charakterisierung der Gesamtkomposition als Autorität heischendes „Torabuch" des Mose[39] dem wer|denden Pentateuch nicht besser gerecht werden als Van Seters Sicht von einem selbstverständlich mit der Schöpfung beginnenden „prologue to the national history of DtrH", der niemals als ein gesondertes Werk existiert habe.[40]

Ein Beispiel dafür, dass Blums K[D]-Hypothese sehr wohl rezipiert wurde, aber unter dem Mantel einer abweichenden Hypothese völlig verschwand, liefert das Pentateuchmodell von David M. Carr. Er rekonstruierte eine „Post-D Hexateuchal Compositional layer", die sich aus dem schriftgelehrten Bemühen um Harmonisierung des Tetrateuch mit dem ursprünglich zum DtrG gehörenden Deuteronomium erklären lasse.[41] Hinsichtlich Textauswahl und vor-priesterlicher Ansetzung stimmt dieses Werk weitgehend mit K[D] überein. Carr beharrt nur auf einer Einbeziehung des Josuabuches, weil er die Differenzierung zwischen K[D] und einer nach-priesterlichen „Jos-24-Bearbeitung", die Blum gegenüber seinem ersten Buch vorgenommen hatte, nicht mitging.[42] Doch stellt sich die Frage, ob Carr dem Abschluss, den der Preis des Mose als „Superpropheten" für alle Zeiten in Dtn 34,10 darstellt, wirklich gerecht wird.[43]

---

37 Vgl. J. Van Seters, Prologue to History. The Yahwist as Historian in Genesis, Louisville 1992; Ders., The Life of Moses. The Yahwist as Historian in Exodus–Numbers, Louisville 1994.
38 So Blum, Studien, 107–108.
39 So ebd., 88. |
40 So Van Seters, Case, 302–303.
41 Vgl. D. M. Carr, The Formation of the Hebrew Bible. A New Reconstruction, Oxford 2011, 256–285; Ders., Scribal Processes of Coordination/Harmonization and the Formation of the First Hexateuch(s), in: T. Dozeman/K. Schmid/B. J. Schwartz (Hg.), The Pentateuch. International Perspectives on Current Research (FAT 78), Tübingen 2011, 63–83, hier 75–82.
42 Vgl. Blum, Studien, 363–365, gegenüber Ders., Komposition, 255–257.392. Für Carr könnte sprechen, dass in Gen 50,24–26 der Landschwur an die Erzväter und das Motiv von den Josephgebeinen, das auf Jos 24,32 zielt, kombiniert vorkommen. Blum hat zuerst allein Gen 50,25–26 für die Jos-24-Bearbeitung in Anspruch genommen, später aber konsequenter die ganze zusammenhängende Passage der Hexateuch-Bearbeitung zugeschrieben, vgl. Ders., Die literarische Verbindung von Erzvätern und Exodus. Ein Gespräch mit neueren Endredaktionshypothesen, in: Ders., Textgestalt und Komposition. Exegetische Beiträge zu Tora und Vordere Propheten (FAT 69), Tübingen, 2010, 85–121, hier 114–117.
43 Carr, Formation, 270, schreibt: „The superlative emphasis on Moses may point to a particular emphasis on Moses in the post-D Hexateuch rather than an effort to conclude a particular composition."

Ein Beispiel dafür, dass Blums Hypothese allein schon wegen der vor-priester-lichen Ansetzung der D-Komposition zurückgewiesen wird, liefert Eckart Otto. Seiner Ansicht nach hat erst der Pentateuchredaktor die Komposition der nicht-priesterlichen Texte in Ex 19–24 und 32–34 unter Verwendung von Dekalog und Bundesbuch geschaffen. Auffällig ist nun, dass Otto der von Blum herausgearbei-teten „redaktionellen Höhenlinie" weitgehend folgt, jedoch meint, ihre Zugehörig-keit zu K^D bestreiten zu müssen, indem er für einzelne Passagen aufzeigt, dass sie schon die Kenntnis der priesterlichen Texte voraussetzen. Damit erweise sich das Ganze aber als Produkt der nach-priesterlichen Pentateuchredaktion.[44] Auf-grund nach-priesterlicher Ansetzungen schreibt auch Thomas Römer eine | im-mer größer werdende Zahl von K^D-Passagen der Pentateuchredaktion zu.[45] Mö-gen Otto und Römer bei der relativen Chronologie der Texte zuweilen richtig liegen, so stellt sich doch die Frage, ob man mit einer nach-priesterlichen Einord-nung gleich schon an das Ende der Entstehungsgeschichte des Pentateuch gerät. Immerhin liegen zwischen der Priesterschrift am Ende des 6. Jahrhunderts und dem Abschluss des Pentateuch am Anfang des 4. Jahrhunderts v. Chr. nach traditi-oneller Sicht über hundert Jahre!

3 Schwächender Umbau der Hypothese

Nachdem Konrad Schmid und Jan Christian Gertz unabhängig voneinander nach-gewiesen hatten, dass der literarische Übergang zwischen der Väter- und der Exodusgeschichte nicht schon von K^D, sondern erst durch die priesterlichen Texte geschaffen worden ist,[46] sah sich Blum im Jahr 2002 veranlasst, seine K^D-Hypothe-se tiefgreifend umzubauen.[47] Er begrenzte den Umfang der D-Komposition auf Ex 1–Dtn 34 und ordnete nun die Landgabeschwüre an die Erzväter in der Gene-sis und darüber hinaus (Gen 15,7–21*; 22,15–18; 24,7?; 26,3bβ–5; Ex 13,5.11; 32,13;

---

44 Vgl. Otto, Kritik, 176–177.179–180. Diese Zuweisung ist allerdings schon aus dem Grund nicht zwingend, weil sich diese Redaktion nach Otto nicht über bestimmte Sprachstile identifizieren lässt; sie verwende sowohl dtr. als auch priesterliche Sprachklischees. |
45 Vgl. T. Römer, Provisorische Überlegungen zur Entstehung von Ex 18–24, in: R. Achenbach/ M. Arneth (Hg.), „Gerechtigkeit und Recht zu üben" (Gen 18,19). Studien zur altorientalischen und biblischen Rechtsgeschichte, zur Religionsgeschichte Israels und zur Religionssoziologie. FS E. Otto (BZAR 13), Wiesbaden 2009, 128–154, hier 132–152.
46 Vgl. K. Schmid, Erzväter und Exodus. Untersuchungen zur doppelten Begründung der Ur-sprünge Israels innerhalb der Geschichtsbücher des Alten Testaments (WMANT 81), Neukirchen-Vluyn 1999, 69–73.152–153; J. C. Gertz, Tradition und Redaktion in der Exoduserzählung. Untersu-chungen zur Endredaktion des Pentateuch (FRLANT 186), Göttingen 2000, 357–366.
47 Vgl. Blum, Verbindung, 99–121.

33,1b u. ö.) sowie das Glaubensmotiv (Gen 15,1–6; Ex 4,1–17.27–31; 14,31; 19,9 u. ö.) einer „nachpriesterlichen Fortschreibung" von K^D zu. Dagegen beschränkte er die „Hauptschicht" von K^D auf die kompositionelle Gestaltung der Exodus-Sinai-Geschichte (Ex 3–14; 19–24; 32–34) samt dem verkettenden Motiv vom Begegnungszelt und Moses überragender Offenbarungsmittlerschaft (Ex 33,7–11; 34*; Num 11*; 12*; Dtn 31,14–15.23; 34,10).[48] Es gereicht Erhard Blum zur Ehre, dass er sich von anderen Exegeten überzeugen ließ, dass Teile der von ihm rekonstruierten D-Komposition nach-priesterlich einzuordnen sind. Doch hat er damit selber zur Schwächung seiner Hypothese beigetragen, zumal er die K^D-„Fortschreibung" bisher kaum genauer profiliert hat. Doch ob allein schon durch den Verlust an Überzeugungskraft der K^D-Hypothese die alternativen Modelle zur Erklärung der dtn./dtr. klingenden Passagen in Gen–Num überzeugender werden, ist doch sehr die Frage. |

III Wer hat den Pentateuch zum ersten Mal konstituiert?

Angesichts der diffusen Diskussionslage soll im Folgenden versucht werden, nach einer klareren literaturgeschichtlichen Einordnung der D-Komposition zu fahnden. Von Wellhausen bis Carr wurde immer wieder vermutet, dass die dtn./dtr. klingenden Passagen in den Büchern Gen–Num mit der Einbindung des Buches Deuteronomium in den werdenden Pentateuch zusammenhängen. Dadurch erklärt sich die Anpassung der Väterverheißungen an den im Dtn üblichen Landgabeschwur. Auch die Aufwertung Moses zum alle weit überragenden Offenbarungs- und Gesetzesmittler mitsamt dem zugehörigen Motiv vom Zelt der Begegnung findet nicht zuletzt vom Dtn her ihren Sinn. Ist dieses Buch doch – anders als die vorangehenden Bücher, die viele Gottesreden enthalten – ausschließlich als Rede des Mose stilisiert, in der dieser die von Gott empfangenen Gesetzesoffenbarungen vollmächtig auslegt. Aufgrund der vorgenommenen Aufwertung kann niemand mehr bezweifeln, dass Mose im Dtn den Gotteswillen authentisch verkündet. Auch der Ausbau des Glaubensmotivs zum Leitfaden für die Gründungsgeschichte Israels könnte vom Dtn her veranlasst sein (vgl. Dtn 1,32; 9,23?). Hinzu kommen viele kleinere terminologische und sachliche Verklammerungen wie die Einführung der dtn. Bezeichnung für den Sinai, „Horeb", schon in Ex 3,1; 17,6; 33,6 und die Einfügung der drei Patriarchennamen ins Dtn.[49]

---

48 So ebd., 101.119–121. |

49 Vgl. Dtn 1,8; 6,10; 9,5.27; 29,12; 30,20; 34,4; dass diese erst nachträglich zu einigen der dtn. Landgabeschwüre, die nur allgemein die Väter nennen, hinzugefügt worden sind, hat T. Römer, Israels Väter. Untersuchungen zur Väterthematik im Deuteronomium und in der deuteronomistischen Tradition (OBO 99), Freiburg i. Ue./Göttingen, 1990, 196–206.251–256.269–271.390–394, nachgewiesen.

Geht man davon aus, dass ein wesentliches Anliegen der Redaktion darin bestand, das Buch Deuteronomium, das eigentlich zu einem anderen literarischen Zusammenhang, dem DtrG, gehörte,[50] in den entstehenden Pentateuch einzubeziehen, dann bekommen die schon erwähnten literarischen Klammern zwischen dem Dtn und den vorangehenden Büchern, die Blum in Dtn 31,14–15.23 und 34,10 aufzeigen konnte,[51] eine entscheidende Bedeutung. Sind sie auf der nicht-priesterlichen Textebene doch die sichersten Belege, an denen sich der redaktionelle Vorgang der Verklammerung konkret ablesen lässt. An ihnen muss sich darum zeigen, wer hinter der vereinenden Redaktion stand und wie sie zeitlich einzuordnen ist.

Die kleine Szene von der Amtseinführung Josuas im Zelt der Begegnung (Dtn 31,14–15.23) stellt eindeutig ein fremdes Element im Dtn dar. Der אהל מועד | kommt in diesem Buch sonst nicht vor; selbst die Rede-Einleitung „Da sprach JHWH zu Mose" (ויאמר יהוה אל־משה), die in den Büchern Ex–Num nicht weniger als 64-mal begegnet, erscheint im ganzen Dtn nur hier in 31,14 und davon abgeleitet in V. 16. Dass die Szene sekundär an Dtn 31,1–13 angehängt wurde, wird daran erkennbar, dass die Beauftragung Josuas durch Gott in V. 23 eine Doublette zu seiner Beauftragung durch Mose in V. 7–8 darstellt. Allerdings wurde die sekundäre Szene durch den Einschub der Einleitung zum Moselied in V. 16–22 nachträglich aufgesprengt, wodurch das ungenannte Subjekt von V. 23 undeutlich geworden ist. Nach V. 22 würde man an Mose denken, es ist aber, wie die Zusage „Ich werde mit dir sein" zeigt, eindeutig der in V. 15 genannte JHWH gemeint.

Die Identität des Verfassers dieser kleinen Szene hat Blum meiner Meinung nach immer noch am überzeugendsten bestimmt: Es ist der Autor, von dem die ganze nicht-priesterliche Motivkette von einem Offenbarungszelt außerhalb des Lagers (Ex 33,7–11; Num 11,14–17.24b–30; 12,4–8) stammt, auch wenn die Theophanieschilderung in Dtn 31,15 etwas vom Üblichen abweicht.[52] Schon dadurch, dass

---

50 So bekanntlich Noth, Studien, 12–18. Die Einschätzung von Kratz, Pentateuch, 40–41, dass auch Blums K[D]-Hypothese keinen Ausgleich zwischen Noths DtrG-Hypothese und der kanonischen Abtrennung des Pentateuchs habe schaffen können, ist nicht zutreffend. Erklärt sie doch gerade, wie das Dtn aus dem DtrG in ein neu entstehendes Werk hinübergezogen wurde.
51 Siehe Blum, Studien, 85–88.109. |
52 Während in Ex 33,9 und Num 12,5 davon die Rede ist, dass JHWH in der Wolkensäule herabfährt und an den Eingang des Zeltes der Begegnung tritt, heißt es in Dtn 31,15, dass JHWH am (?) Zelt in einer Wolkensäule erscheint und die Wolkensäule über dem Eingang des Zeltes steht. Auffällig ist בָאֹהֶל neben בְעַמוּד עֲנָן; ersteres kann kaum „im Zelt" bedeuten, da die Wolkensäule im zweiten Versteil außen über den Eingang steht. Vielleicht liegt ein Textfehler vor, da die LXX den ersten Versteil nach Num 12,5 angleicht, vgl. R. N. Nelson, Deuteronomy. A Commentary (OTL), Louisville/London 2002, 354. Da sich aber Mose und Josua eindeutig im Zelt befinden (vgl. Ex 33,8.11), bleibt die Zugehörigkeit zur nicht-priesterlichen Offenbarungszeltvorstellung gewahrt. Auch in Num 11,25 weicht die Terminologie leicht ab. |

er in Ex 33,11 Josua eine enge Affinität zu diesem Zelt zuschrieb, bereitete er dessen Amtseinführung dort vor. Hier zeigt sich eindeutig ein kompositionelles Konzept: Das Zelt, das Moses einzigartig direkte Kommunikation mit Gott auch fern vom Sinai sichern sollte, ermöglicht auch, dass Josua von Gott selber ausdrücklich zum Nachfolger des Mose bestimmt werden kann, um das Befreiungswerk zum Abschluss zu bringen. Auch mit seinen letzten Worten (Dtn 31,7–8) drückt Mose nichts anderes als den Willen Gottes aus (V. 23).

Was die Datierung der expliziten Verklammerung betrifft, so ist Blums Schlussfolgerung zwingend, dass die Szene das DtrG voraussetzt, da sie nicht nur nachträglich in es eingeschoben ist, sondern auch dessen Fortgang der Handlung als göttliche Zusage für die Zukunft neu gestaltet und sich auch sprachlich in Dtn 31,23 eng an die vorgegebene Amtsübertragung in V. 7–8 anlehnt. Nun könnte man meinen, dass V. 15 mit der Formulierung, dass „JHWH im" oder besser „am Zelt erschienen sei" (ראה ni.), schon an die spät-priesterliche Vorstellung anspielen wolle, dass die Herrlichkeit Gottes in Konfliktsituationen regelmäßig im Zelt der Begegnung erschienen sei (ebenfalls mit ראה ni.; Num 14,10; vgl. 16,19; 17,7; 20,6). Doch fehlt das entscheidende Stichwort כבוד יהוה, die Anlässe sind zu unterschiedlich, und der Text von Dtn 31,15 ist nicht ganz sicher über | liefert.[53] So ist ein *terminus ad quem* aus dieser verklammernden Szene nicht zu gewinnen. Doch setzt allein schon die Tatsache, dass sie durch die Einführung des Moseliedes in V. 16–22 nachträglich in zwei Teile aufgespalten wurde, hinter eine Zuweisung an die Pentateuchredaktion ein dickes Fragezeichen. Ist doch das Buch Dtn auch noch nach Einfügung der Szene nachweislich angewachsen (Dtn 32; 33).

Eine eindeutigere Auskunft lässt sich aus den das Buch abschließenden Versen Dtn 34,10–12 entnehmen. Blum hat mit guten Gründen insbesondere den V. 10 der D-Komposition zugewiesen, führt er doch mit der feierlichen Feststellung, dass Mose alle vergangenen und zukünftigen Propheten überragt, die Motivlinie von der einzigartigen Offenbarungsmittlerschaft des Mose (vgl. Num 12,6–8) zu ihrem Abschluss und verweist in ihrer Begründung explizit auf die face-to-face Kommunikation mit Gott im Zelt der Begegnung zurück (Ex 33,11). „Das ‚Torabuch' des Mose klingt mit einem neuen kräftigen Akkord aus."[54] Dadurch wird nach dem Tod des Mose ein feierlicher Abschluss in den fortlaufenden Erzählfluss des DtrG gesetzt. Allerdings blieb Blum hinsichtlich der Zuweisung der noch folgenden Verse Dtn 34,11–12 unentschieden, mal nahm er sie in Klammern dazu,[55] mal

---

53 Otto, Deuteronomium, 187–188, will die Szene dem Pentateuchredaktor zuschreiben, weil Dtn 31,15 angeblich wörtlich an Num 14,14 anknüpfe. Doch ist in diesem Vers vom Zelt der Begegnung gar nicht die Rede.
54 So Blum, Studien, 88.
55 Ebd., 76.110.

meinte er, ihre von einigen Exegeten vertretene literarkritische Abtrennung könne „für unsere Diskussion [...] auf sich beruhen."[56]

Doch möglicherweise hat Blum damals die Bedeutung der Frage unterschätzt.
Dtn 34,11–12 wenden wortreich den Blick auf die großen Zeichen und Wunder
zurück, die Mose im göttlichen Auftrag in Ägypten getan hat. Sie wollen damit
dem Dtn eine kompositionelle Abrundung in Richtung auf die Exodusereignisse
verschaffen, von denen in den vorangehenden Büchern die Rede ist und damit
dieses Buch noch klarer, als es V. 10 gekonnt hatte, vom Josuabuch abgrenzen.
Die Verse 11–12 kann man mit Fug und Recht einem Pentateuchredaktor zuweisen, der die Bücher Gen–Dtn gegenüber dem DtrG als eigene literarische Einheit
konstituieren wollte. Wenn auch V. 10 zu ihnen gehören würde, dann löste sich
die D-Komposition in der Pentateuchredaktion auf.

So ist es kein Wunder, dass die Exegeten, die die Blum'sche K[D] mehr oder
weniger durchgreifend durch die Pentateuchredaktion ersetzen, Dtn 34,10–12 als
eine literarische Einheit auffassen.[57] Otto möchte die Einheit der Verse damit
begründen, dass die Worte „in Israel" in V. 10a und „vor den Augen Israels" in
V. 12b einen Rahmen um sie bilden würden. Doch ist das ein relativ schwa|ches
Argument, da die Wendungen nicht identisch und wenig spezifisch sind. Eher
könnte man schon die parallelen Relativsätze in allen drei Versen als verbinden-
des Strukturelement werten, wobei allerdings auffällt, dass die ersten beiden
JHWH und der letzte Mose zum Subjekt haben. Es ist nun allerdings der ausgesprochen lockere, wenn nicht brüchige syntaktische Anschluss von V. 11 und 12
durch zwei mit spezifizierendem ל vorangestellte Objekte („in Bezug auf all' die
Zeichen und Wunder" und „in Bezug auf all' die starke Hand"),[58] welche eine
ganze Reihe von Exegeten an der ursprünglichen Zusammengehörigkeit der Verse
zweifeln lassen.[59] Die beiden Verse wollen offenbar die preisende Aussage über
Moses überlegene Wortoffenbarung in V. 10a auf weitere Tätigkeitsfelder des
Mose umlenken. Der syntaktisch komplizierte Rückgriff ist aber nur deswegen
nötig, weil in V. 10b ein Subjektwechsel erfolgt, wodurch plötzlich JHWHs außer-
gewöhnliches Handeln an Mose im Fokus steht. Darum fühlt sich der Autor von

---

56 Ebd., 88, Anm. 189.
57 Vgl. Römer, Moïse, 130–131; Ders., Pentateuch, 86; Otto, Deuteronomium, 228–233; Ders., Deuteronomium 12–34. Zweiter Teilband: 23,16–34,12 (HThKAT), Freiburg i. Br./Basel/Wien 2017,
2279.2284–2285. |
58 Vgl. B. C. Waltke/M. O'Connor, An Introduction to Biblical Syntax, Winona Lake 1990, 206–207:
§ 11.2.10d. Als Beispiel nennen die Autoren Gen 17,20.
59 Vgl. C. Steuernagel, Das Deuteronomium (HK I,3,1), Göttingen ²1923, 183; L. Perlitt, Mose als
Prophet, EvTh 31 (1971) 588–608, hier 591, Anm. 14; J. Blenkinsopp, Prophecy and Canon. A Contribution to the Study of Jewish Origins (Center for the Study of Judaism and Christianity in Antiquity 3), Notre Dame/London 1977, 86–89.

V. 11 zu der gezwungen klingenden Formulierung veranlasst, dass JHWH Mose die Wunder in Ägypten zu tun gesandt habe, bis er schließlich in V. 12 bei dem von ihm eigentlich intendierten Lobpreis angekommen ist, dass Mose all' die Macht- und Wundertaten vor Zeugen getan hat. D. h. die syntaktisch komplizierten und wortreichen Ausführungen von V. 11–12 lassen sich am besten daraus erklären, dass ihrem Verfasser das wuchtige Statement über Mose in V. 10 schon vorgegeben war. Die Motive, die er verwendet, sind weitgehend aus dem Deuteronomium gewonnen,[60] wobei sie dort durchgängig das göttliche Handeln beschreiben. So wird Mose in dieser Schlussapotheose auch im Bereich des magischen Handelns in einer Weise Gott angenähert, die den Texten der D-Komposition fremd ist.[61] Da Dtn 34,11–12 eine stilistisch und thematisch abweichende Ergänzung zum Schlussvers der D-Komposition in Dtn 34,10 darstellt, ist diese klar von einer Pentateuchredaktion zu trennen; sie geht einer solchen eindeutig voran. Damit ist auch ein relativer *terminus ad quem* für sie gewonnen.

Ist damit die Identität der D-Komposition deutlicher abgegrenzt, so lässt sich ihre relative zeitliche Einordnung noch genauer bestimmen. Denn die Einbeziehung des Dtn in den entstehenden Pentateuch durch die kompositorischen Klammern Dtn 31,14–15.23 und 34,10 ist auf die Motivkette vom Offenbarungs|zelt angewiesen, die ausgehend von Ex 33,7–11 über Num 11 und Num 12 verläuft. Nun setzt aber die Wachtelerzählung Num 11,4–35, die vom D-Autor zu einer Geschichte von der Verleihung eines Anteils des mosaischen Geistes an die 70 Ältesten umgestaltet wurde, wie ich an anderer Stelle gezeigt habe,[62] die priesterliche Manna-Erzählung von Ex 16 eindeutig voraus, wird doch in Num 11,6–9 ausdrücklich auf die regelmäßige Gabe des Mannas am Morgen jeden Tages zurückverwiesen und dabei speziell priesterliche Motive wie das Kochen des Mannas (Ex 16,23) und das dort verwendete seltene Leitwort für das Sammeln (לקט; V. 16–18.21.26–27) aufgegriffen (Num 11,8). Für Num 12,1–16 hat Römer wahrscheinlich gemacht, dass der Bearbeiter hier eine Erzählung verwendet hat, welche die priesterlichen Bestimmungen über den Aussatz in Lev 13–14 voraussetzt.[63] Nun hatte Blum die

---

60 Vgl. Dtn 4,34; 26,8; 29,1–2; die Ausdrücke „Zeichen und Wunder" (Ex 7,3) und „starke Hand" (Ex 3,19; 6,1; 13,9) kommen auch im Exodusbuch vor.
61 Zwar arbeitet die D-Komposition in Ex 4,1–17 auch die magischen Fähigkeiten des Mose heraus, doch „zum Gott" wird er gegenüber Aaron nur bezüglich seiner Wortoffenbarungen (V. 16). |
62 Siehe Albertz, Pentateuchstudien, 221–223.
63 T. Römer, Nombres 11–12 et la question d'une rédaction deutéronomique dans le Pentateuque, in: M. Vervenne/J. Lust (Hg.), Deuteronomy and Deuteronomic Literature. FS C. H. W. Brekelmans (BEThL 133), Leuven 1997, 481–498, hier 492–493. Nach Römers Urteil können Num 11 und 12 keiner zusammenhängenden Kompositionsschicht angehört haben, weil sie seiner Meinung nach gegensätzliche Tendenzen vertreten würden: Num 11 leite in V. 27–29 die Prophetie vom Geist des Mose her, Num 12,6 stelle ihn dagegen über alle Propheten. Doch geht es in Num 11 vornehmlich um die Vermittlung einer theologischen Kompetenz an die Ältesten, an der auch einige

gesamte Motivkette einschließlich der beiden Numeri-Erzählungen beim Umbau seiner Hypothese noch der vor-priesterlichen Hauptschicht von K^D zugerechnet,[64] wohl hauptsächlich darum, weil er ihren Ausgangspunkt Ex 33,7–11 als originären Bestandteil der sicher in ihrem Kern vor-priesterlichen Kapitel Ex 33–34 ansah. Doch wurde dies inzwischen von vielen Forschern angezweifelt, ist doch der Einwand des Mose in Ex 33,12 unmittelbar auf den göttlichen Aufbruchsbefehl in V. 1a.3 zurückbezogen. Ich selber habe nachzuweisen versucht, dass das ganze Konzept eines speziellen Offenbarungszeltes außerhalb des Lagers das priesterliche Kultzelt von Ex 25–31; 35–40 und Lev 9 voraussetzt.[65] Da nun Blum inzwischen schon selber eine beträchtliche Anzahl seiner K^D-Belege nach-priesterlich ansetzt, darunter Ex 32,13 und 33,1b, die einzigen, die wie 33,7–11 über das Exodusbuch hinausweisen, spricht einiges dafür, auch die Motivkette vom Offenbarungszelt diesem späteren Strang zuzuweisen. Da dann aber erst die nach-priesterliche Schicht die kompositorische Einbindung des Dtn leistet, legt es sich nahe, Blums K^D-Fortschreibung zur nach-priesterlich anzusetzenden Hauptschicht der D-Komposition zu erklären.[66] Der vor-priesterliche Rest, der sich damit ganz auf das Exodusbuch beschränkt, lässt sich dagegen nach meinen Untersuchungen besser einer vorgegebenen Ex|oduskomposition (K^{EX}) zuschreiben,[67] die allerdings auch schon das DtrG voraussetzt.[68] Viele der guten Beobachtungen, die Blum für deren Aufbau gemacht hat, behalten weiter ihre Gültigkeit. Von den Vorteilen dieser Lösung seien hier nur zwei wichtige genannt: Erstens, die D-Komposition umfasst wieder den ganzen Pentateuch von der Genesis bis zum Buch Deuteronomium, wie es sich für eine Kompositionsschicht, die das Dtn in ein neu entstehendes Werk einbinden will, gehört. Zweitens, die irritierende Tatsache, dass die erste Landverheißung des Exodusbuches in Ex 3,8 nicht auf die Landgabeschwüre der Vätergeschichte zurückverweist, erklärt sich einfach dadurch, dass diese Stelle der vorgegebenen Exoduskomposition angehört, die einmal eigenständig gewesen ist.

Propheten Anteil haben, in Num 12 dagegen um eine den Propheten und Priestern überlegene Offenbarungsqualität. Das verbindende Motiv vom Zelt der Begegnung wird von Römer eigenartigerweise gar nicht gewürdigt.

64 Vgl. Blum, Verbindung, 119–120.

65 Vgl. Albertz, Pentateuchstudien, 225–248.

66 Vgl. meine Rekonstruktion der spät-deuteronomistischen Redaktion D in Albertz, Pentateuchstudien, 478–479; ich datiere sie etwa in die Mitte des 5. Jahrhunderts v. Chr. |

67 Vgl. ebd., 187–205; dazu R. Albertz, Exodus 1–18 (ZBK.AT 2.1), Zürich ²2017; Ders., Exodus 19–40 (ZBK.AT 2.2), Zürich 2015.

68 Siehe Albertz, Exodus 19–40, 323–324.

IV Lohnt es sich, an der K^D-Hypothese festzuhalten?

Sofern man sich entschließt, die D-Komposition, wie oben skizziert, zeitlich etwas später anzusetzen und sie von der kleinteiligen Komposition der Exodus-Sinai-Erzählung (Ex 1–34*) zu entlasten, möchte ich diese Frage gegen den Trend der jüngsten Forschungsgeschichte eindeutig bejahen. Durch diese Modifikation wird die Kompositionsarbeit dieser Schicht deutlich homogener, sie beschränkt sich in Genesis, Exodus und im Deuteronomium großteils auf kleinere redaktionelle Einschübe und steuert hier nur selten ganze Kapitel (Gen 15*; Ex 4*; 13*) und grundlegende Passagen (Ex 12,21–27; 33,7–11) bei. Erst im Buch Numeri scheint sie aus mehreren Einzelüberlieferungen eine lockere Kette von Erzählungen geschaffen zu haben (zumindest Num 11; 12; 13–14*). Sie ist darum mehr als eine reine Redaktionsschicht.[69]

Die leistungsstarke These von Erhard Blum macht konkret beschreibbar, wann und auf welche Weise das Buch Deuteronomium in den entstehenden Pentateuch einbezogen und damit ein Stück weit aus dem DtrG herausgelöst wurde, worüber ohne sie nur Mutmaßungen angestellt werden könnten. Bei einer schematisch „nach-priesterlichen" Datierung scheint nun allerdings das Problem aufzutauchen, dass diese Integrationsleistung möglicherweise einer vorgängigen priesterlichen Redaktion zugeschrieben werden müsste, deren redaktionelle Klammern in Dtn 1,3; 32,48–52 nachweisbar sind. Doch muss auf Seiten der priesterlichen Texte sehr wahrscheinlich eine stärkere zeitliche Differenzierung vorgenommen werden, als sie Blum mit seiner K^P-Hypothese vorschwebte.[70] | Denn die priesterlichen Texte, welche die D-Komposition schon voraussetzt, beschränken sich allesamt auf den Bereich Gen–Lev. Dagegen scheinen die priesterlichen Texte des Numeribuches ihrerseits wieder die D-Komposition vorauszusetzen, wie beispielhaft die priesterliche Meriba-Erzählung von Num 20,1–13 verdeutlicht, die in V. 12 das typische Glaubensmotiv aus der D-Komposition aufgreift. Auf Num 20 bezieht sich wiederum Dtn 32,48–52 zurück. So war der Autor der D-Komposition sehr wahrscheinlich wirklich der Erste, der die redaktionelle Integration des Dtn in den Pentateuch vorgenommen hat. Die These Blums bewährt sich also auch bei ihrer veränderten zeitlichen Ansetzung.

---

69 Vgl. meine Rekonstruktion in Albertz, Pentateuchstudien, 346–348.

70 Vgl. Blum, Studien, 223–228, wo dieser mit einer einheitlichen priesterlichen Kompositionsschicht rechnet, die bis Num 27 laufe und damit auch das Heiligkeitsgesetz (Lev 17–26) umgreife. Kritische Anfragen hierzu finden sich schon früh, vgl. etwa Ska, Un nouveau, 260–|261. Allerdings sieht auch Blum in Lev 26 eine wichtige thematische Linie von K^P, die schon in Gen 1 beginnt, zum Abschluss kommen (Studien, 326).

Der vollen Leistungskraft der Blum'schen Hypothese wird die Forschung wohl erst ansichtig werden, wenn sie den grundlegenden Einsichten von Eckart Otto und Thomas Römer folgt, dass der Pentateuch aus zwei Kristallisationskernen entstanden ist, den stark priesterlich redigierten Büchern Genesis–Leviticus einerseits und dem Buch Deuteronomium andererseits, zwischen denen das Buch Numeri eine spätere Brücke darstellt.[71] Denn wenn die erste priesterliche Komposition nur bis Lev 16 und die zweite nur bis Lev 26 reichte, wie ich herauszuarbeiten versucht habe,[72] dann war es der Autor der D-Komposition, der überhaupt zum ersten Mal eine literarische Brücke zum DtrG schlug, um diesem mit dem Dtn sein normatives Kopfstück zu entwinden. Dann entpuppt sich dieser spät-dtr. Autor als Schöpfer des gesamten Pentateuchkonzeptes, der, indem er die Idee von einem „Torabuch des Mose" vom Deuteronomium auf die gesamte nicht-priesterliche und priesterliche Sinaigesetzgebung ausweitete, die beiden bis dahin konkurrierenden Gründungsgeschichten Israels, die priesterlich redigierte (Gen–Lev) und die dtn./dtr. (Dtn), in einem Werk miteinander verknüpfte. Aus dieser Perspektive markiert die D-Komposition eine entscheidende Entwicklungsstufe; sie hat den Pentateuch überhaupt zum ersten Mal konstituiert.

Zwar werden bis zur Fertigstellung des Pentateuch noch eine ganze Reihe weiterer Bearbeitungen folgen, von denen zwei ebenfalls mehr oder minder starke spät- oder nach-dtr. Einflüsse erkennen lassen: nämlich die sog. Mal'akredaktion, die bis in die Richterzeit ausgriff (Ri 2,1–5), und die Hexateuchredaktion, die aus dem DtrG noch das Josuabuch in die Gründungsgeschichte einbeziehen wollte (Jos 24). Auch hierzu hat Blum, was zuweilen übersehen wird, Pionierarbeit geleistet.[73] Aber schließlich wird sich am Ende das schon von der D-Kom | position entwickelte Konzept durchsetzen, die normative Gründungsgeschichte Israels mit dem Tode des Mose enden zu lassen. In der langen Entstehungsgeschichte des Pentateuch war kaum eine Bearbeitungsschicht einflussreicher!

---

71 Vgl. Otto, Deuteronomiumstudien III, 99–104; T. Römer, Das Buch Numeri und das Ende des Jahwisten. Anfragen zur ‚Quellenscheidung' im vierten Buch des Pentateuch, in: J. C. Gertz/ K. Schmid/M. Witte (Hg.) Abschied vom Jahwisten. Die Komposition des Hexateuch in der jüngsten Diskussion (BZAW 315), Berlin/New York 2002, 215–231, hier 220–224.

72 Albertz, Pentateuchstudien, 297–326.

73 Vgl. Blum, Studien, 363–378; dazu Ders., Der kompositionelle Knoten am Übergang von Josua und Richter. Ein Entflechtungsvorschlag, in: Ders., Textgestalt und Komposition. Exegetische Beiträge zu Tora und Vordere Propheten (FAT 69), Tübingen, 2010, 249–280, hier | 256–274; Ders., Verbindung, 110–119. Es trifft somit keineswegs zu, wie zuweilen unterstellt wird (vgl. Kratz, Pentateuch, 54, Anm. 73), dass Blum die dtr. klingenden Passagen in Gen–Num alle derselben literarischen Schicht zuweisen wolle.

Der kompositionelle Abschluss des Pentateuchs (Dtn 31–34): Zur Rekonstruktion der nicht-priesterlichen Pentateuchredaktion

Reinhard Achenbach gehört zu den Mitbegründern einer modernen redaktionsge-schichtlich arbeitenden Pentateuchforschung, die sich aus den Systemzwängen der älteren Quellentheorie befreit hat. Besonders beeindruckt hat er mich mit seiner detaillierten Bearbeitung der jüngsten Partien des Pentateuchs im Numeri-buch, die zuvor häufig als späte Ergänzungen der Quellenwerke ausgeschieden wurden und nicht die Beachtung erhalten haben, die sie verdienen.[1] So möchte ich meinen geschätzten Münsteraner Kollegen mit einer Untersuchung ehren, die sich den spätesten Partien des Buches Deuteronomium in Kapitel 31–34 zuwendet, dem Buch, an dem Reinhard Achenbach seine Forschungen am Pentateuch be-gann.[2]

Es ist immer wieder vermutet worden, dass die poetischen Schlusskapitel des Buches Deuteronomium, das Moselied (Dtn 32) und der Mosesegen (Dtn 33) mit der Entscheidung zusammenhängen, die Gründungsurkunde Israels mit dem Tode des Mose (Dtn 34) enden zu lassen. Mit ihnen sollte der nunmehr von den Geschichtsbüchern abgetrennte Pentateuch einen volltönenden kompositionellen Abschluss erhalten. So schreibt etwa Thomas Römer: „When Deuteronomy was cut off from the following books, new chapters were added: the blessings of Moses in Deut. 33, which parallel him with Jacob (Gen. 49) and reinforce the structural and narrative coherence of the Pentateuch. ... The editors of the Pentateuch inser-ted perhaps also Deut. 32, the ‚song of Moses'. Since the Pentateuch ended with Moses' death, Deut. 32 offers a summary of the coming negative events in the land, even if these are not part of the Torah."[3]

Allerdings besteht über die literarkritische Abgrenzung und literaturge-schichtliche Zuordnung der verschiedenen Textpartien der Schlusskapitel noch erhebliche Unsicherheit. Nachweislich spielen in ihnen Passagen priesterlicher Herkunft nur eine relativ bescheidene Rolle (Dtn 32,48–52; 34,1*.7–9).[4] Einflussrei-

---

1 Vgl. Reinhard Achenbach, *Die Vollendung der Tora: Studien zur Redaktionsgeschichte des Nume-ribuches im Kontext von Hexateuch und Pentateuch*, BZAR 3 (Wiesbaden: Harrassowitz, 2003).
2 Reinhard Achenbach, *Israel zwischen Verheißung und Gebot: Literarkritische Untersuchungen zu Deuteronomium 5–11*, EHS XXIII/422 (Frankfurt am Main et al.: Peter Lang, 1991).
3 S. Thomas Römer, *The So-called Deuteronomistic History: A Sociological, Historical and Literary Introduction* (London and New York: T&T Clark, 2009), 181–182; vgl. Rainer Albertz, *Pentateuchstu-dien*, ed. Jakob Wöhrle, FAT 117 (Tübingen: Mohr Siebeck, 2018), 483.
4 S. unten S. 277–278 [[= S. 111–113 im vorliegenden Band]]. |

https://doi.org/10.1515/9783111202228-008

cher waren hier ganz offensichtlich nicht-priesterliche Redaktoren. Darum soll im Folgenden gefragt werden, ob und wieweit sich in der Gestaltung von Dtn 31–34 eine – möglicherweise mehrstufige – nicht-priesterliche | Pentateuchredaktion (PentR^L) greifen lässt. Dabei muss ich mich auf eine Skizze meiner Überlegungen beschränken, da der Raum in dieser Festschrift begrenzt ist.

1 Der deuteronomistische Abschluss des Deuteronomiums

Als das Deuteronomium noch als Einleitung des Deuteronomistischen Geschichtswerks (DtrG) fungierte, sah der Abschluss des Buches, der vor allem die Funktion hatte, von der Gesetzgebung zur Mission Josuas überzuleiten, noch recht schlicht und bescheiden aus. Nachdem Mose seine Lehr- und Mahnreden, mit denen er die Offenbarung am Horeb auslegte, abgeschlossen hatte,[5] hielt er noch eine Abschiedsrede an das Volk (Dtn 31,1–13). In ihr ermutigte er es kurz vor seinem Tode, die Eroberung des Westjordanlandes unter Leitung Josuas in Angriff zu nehmen, nachdem ihm Gott die Überschreitung des Jordans versagt hatte (V. 1–6), und beauftragte Josua öffentlich mit dieser Aufgabe unter JHWHs Führung (V. 7–8). Darauf schrieb er die Tora, die er bislang mündlich verkündet hatte, schriftlich nieder (V. 9). Bei ihr kann es sich auf dieser Stufe der Überlieferung nur um das dtn. Gesetz handeln. Mose übergab dieses den levitischen Priestern und Ältesten mit dem Auftrag, es alle sieben Jahre beim Laubhüttenfest vor allem Volk zu verlesen, um unter ihm Gottesfurcht und Gebotsgehorsam zu mehren und so das Leben im verheißenen Land zu sichern (V. 10–13).

Nach meiner Meinung gibt es keinen Grund, von der Einschätzung Martin Noths abzuweichen, dass diese Abschiedsrede, jedenfalls in ihrem Grundbestand, vom Deuteronomisten, dem Autor des DtrG stammt.[6] Nur kann man fragen, ob

---

5 Lies in Dtn 31,1 mit 1QDeut^b und LXX ויכל משה לדבר לדבר „Als Mose geendet hatte zu reden".
6 Vgl. Martin Noth, *Überlieferungsgeschichtliche Studien: Die sammelnden und bearbeitenden Geschichtswerke im Alten Testament* (Tübingen: Niemeyer, ³1967), 39–40; so auch etwa Richard D. Nelson, *Deuteronomy: A Commentary*, OTL (Louisville und London: Westminster John Knox, 2002), 354–356, und viele andere. Die Ansicht von Eckart Otto, *Das Deuteronomium im Pentateuch und Hexateuch: Studien zur Literaturgeschichte von Pentateuch und Hexateuch im Lichte des Deuteronomiumrahmens*, FAT 30 (Tübingen: Mohr Siebeck, 2000), 175–187, dass Dtn 31,1–8 von der Hexateuch- und V. 9–13 von der Pentateuchredaktion stammen, beruht auf bestimmten Einschätzungen von Parallelen zu und Abhängigkeiten von anderen Passagen des Dtn, die aber keineswegs zwingend sind. So braucht man die „private" Ermutigung Josuas durch Mose in Dtn 3,21–22 keineswegs als eine Dublette zu seiner öffentlichen Beauftragung von 31,7–8 zu bewerten, sondern kann darin auch eine Vorbereitung auf letztere sehen, so Otto selber in Eckart Otto, *Deuteronomium 1,1–4,43*, HThKAT (Freiburg et al.: Herder, 2012), 493. Auch die sprachliche Nähe von Dtn 31,12 zu 4,10 kann eine Zuweisung von 31,9–13 zur Pentateuchredaktion kaum tragen, denn

die Rede in Dtn 31,13 schon an ihr Ende gelangt ist. Denn da sie als eine Rede an das ganze Volk begonnen hatte (V. 1), kann sie eigentlich nicht gut mit speziellen Anweisungen an eine Gruppe ausklingen. So möchte ich die These vertreten, dass sich der ehemalige Abschluss der Abschiedsrede noch in Dtn 32,45–47 greifen lässt,[7] d. h. hinter den Versen, die zwar jetzt als hinterer Rahmen für das Moselied verwandt werden, aber – wie häufig beobachtet – wieder zu einer Mahnung | zum Gehorsam gegenüber all den Worten der Tora zurücklenken (vgl. כל־דברי התורה הזאת V. 46), von denen schon in 31,12 die Rede war. Auch die Benennung der Adressaten in der Redeeinleitung 32,45 ist mit der von 31,1 identisch (אל־כל־ישראל). Mit ihrer schönen Schlussmahnung:

> Dtn 32,47   Denn es ist kein leeres Wort für euch, vielmehr ist es euer Leben, und durch dieses Wort werden eure Lebenstage lange währen in dem Lande, in das ihr über den Jordan zieht, um es in Besitz zu nehmen,

klingen diese Verse nach der ernsten Warnung des Moseliedes, wie schon Paul Sanders bemerkte,[8] erstaunlich optimistisch; sie wären aber ein passender Schlussakkord für die hoffnungsvolle dtr. Abschiedsrede des Mose nach seiner Gesetzesverkündigung, zumal 32,47 noch einmal die Perspektive des gesicherten Lebens im verheißenen Land aus 31,13 aufnimmt. Nach solchen erbaulichen Worten kann sich Mose nun endlich auf den Berg Pisga zum Sterben zurückziehen (Dtn 34,1*.4aα₁.b.5–6).[9] Er hatte alles, was er tun konnte, zur Sicherung einer heilvollen Zukunft seines Volkes getan.

---

erstens bleibt die Zuordnung von Dtn 4 zu dieser unsicher und zweitens ahmt 31,12 eine besondere Stileigentümlichkeit von 4,10 (finales אשר) gerade nicht nach. Jedenfalls lässt sich aus dieser unsicheren Beziehung nicht folgern, mit התורה הזאת sei in Dtn 31,9 schon der gesamte Pentateuch gemeint (gegen Otto, *Deuteronomiumrahmen*, 175–182). |

7 Dass Dtn 32,44 von V. 45–47 zu trennen ist, hat schon Willy Staerk, *Das Deuteronomium: Sein Inhalt und seine literarische Form* (Leipzig: Hinrich'sche Buchhandlung, 1894), 75, erkannt. Dazu s. unten S. 279–280 [[= S. 115–116 im vorliegenden Band]]. |

8 So Paul Sanders, *The Provenance of Deuteronomy 32*, OTS 37 (Leiden et al.: Brill, 1996), 337–338.

9 Zu dieser Rekonstruktion des dtr. Anteils vgl. Thomas Römer, "Deuteronomium 34 zwischen Pentateuch, Hexateuch und deuteronomistischem Geschichtswerk," *ZAR* 5 (1999): 167–178, 173–174.

2 Die Verklammerung des Deuteronomiums mit dem entstehenden Pentateuch durch die spät-deuteronomistische Redaktion (D)

In die Abschiedsrede des Mose wurde mit Dtn 31,14–15.23 eine kleine Theophanie-Erzählung eingeschoben, in der JHWH Mose und Josua zum Zelt der Begegnung beordert und höchst persönlich Mose seinen nahen Tod ankündigt, selber die Beauftragung Josuas zu seinem Nachfolger vornimmt und ihm bei der Realisierung der Landverheißung direkt seinen Beistand zusagt. Dass diese Szene einen Fremdkörper im Dtn darstellt, wird selbst von solchen Forschern gesehen, die sich um eine synchrone Auslegung bemühen.[10] Nirgends sonst kam im Dtn bisher der מועד אהל, das „Zelt der Begegnung", vor. Selbst die an sich unspektakuläre Einleitungsformel ויאמר יהוה אל־משה „Da sprach JHWH zu Mose", die nicht weniger als 64-mal im sonstigen Pentateuch belegt ist, begegnet im Dtn, das sonst konsequent als Moserede gestaltet ist, nur in 31,14 und davon abgeleitet dann in V. 16. Frühere Ausleger meinten, hier ein versprengtes Fragment der Quelle E oder JE zu finden.[11] Doch spricht dagegen, dass der jetzt durch eine noch spätere Einfügung abgesprengte V. 23 eindeutig Wendungen aus der dtr. Abschiedsrede des Mose aufnimmt (vgl. V. 7–8).[12] Eine bessere | redaktionsgeschichtliche Lösung des Problems hat Erhard Blum damit gefunden, dass er den Einschub auf den spät-deuteronomistischen Redaktor (K^D) zurückführte, der über das von ihm geschaffene Motiv eines unkultischen Offenbarungszeltes (Ex 33,7–11; Num 11,14–17.24b–30; 12,4–8) das Buch Dtn, das eigentlich zum DtrG gehörte, mit dem entstehenden Pentateuch verklammern wollte.[13] Hatte dieser Redaktor das Motiv vom Zelt der Begegnung geschaffen, um sicherzustellen, dass Mose auch fernab vom Sinai unmittelbare *face-to-face*-Offenbarungen von Gott erhalten konnte, so sollte dessen Einfügung in das Dtn demonstrieren, dass Mose auch hier, selbst wenn er außerhalb der Vermittlung seiner Gesetzesoffenbarungen eigenmächtig zu handeln schien, allein den göttlichen Willen eins-zu-eins umsetzte.

Weil dieser spät-dtr. Redaktor mit Dtn 31,14–15.23 das Buch Dtn nachweislich in den Pentateuch einbindet, haben Eckart Otto und Reinhard Achenbach ihn

---

10 Vgl. z. B. Jean-Pierre Sonnet, *The Book within the Book: Writing in Deuteronomy*, BibInt 14 (Leiden et al.: Brill, 1997), 147–148.160–162.

11 Vgl. für viele Gerhard von Rad, *Das fünfte Buch Mose: Deuteronomium*, ATD 8 (Göttingen: Vandenhoeck & Ruprecht, ²1968), 135.

12 So sind in Dtn 31,23 die Wendungen ואמץ חזק und אל־ארץ ישראל את־בני תביא אתה כי נשבעתי אשר־ fast identisch mit den in V. 7 gebrauchten; die Mitseins-Zusage Gottes אהיה ואנכי עמך entspricht der Gewissheit des Mose in V. 8. |

13 Vgl. Erhard Blum, *Studien zur Komposition des Pentateuch*, BZAW 189 (Berlin und New York: de Gruyter, 1990), 85–88.109.

schon mit dem Pentateuchredaktor gleichsetzen wollen.[14] Dies wäre allerdings nur berechtigt, wenn man die das Buch abschließenden Verse 34,10–12 insgesamt auf ihn zurückführen könnte. Für den V. 10, in dem Mose als unvergleichlicher Prophet gepriesen wird, der so eng mit Gott kommunizierte wie kein Prophet nach ihm, ist das unstrittig, weist dieser Vers doch explizit auf Ex 33,11, die *face-to-face*-Offenbarung im Zelt der Begegnung, zurück. Doch habe ich andernorts aufgezeigt, dass die Verse Dtn 34,11–12, welche wortreich den Blick auf die magischen Wundertaten des Mose in Ägypten zurücklenken und damit dem Pentateuch eine thematische Abrundung verschaffen, syntaktisch so brüchig an V. 10 angeschlossen sind, dass sie eher auf einen noch späteren Redaktor zurückgehen.[15] Der spät-dtr. Redaktor D hat zwar den Tod des Mose zu einer Epochenwende stilisiert und damit erstmals die im Pentateuch erzählten Ereignisse von den dann ab dem Josuabuch geschilderten ein Stück weit qualitativ abgesetzt, aber er hat noch nicht die Abtrennung des Pentateuchs von den Geschichtsbüchern vollzogen. Da er jedoch – wahrscheinlich erstmals – das Buch Dtn in den entstehenden Pentateuch einbezog, sind alle redaktionellen Tätigkeiten, die nach ihm in Dtn 31–34 folgten, schon aus der pentateuchischen Perspektive heraus zu interpretieren.[16] |

3 Die Verklammerung des Deuteronomiums mit dem entstehenden Pentateuch durch die spät-priesterliche Redaktion (PB³)

Nach dem mutmaßlichen Ende der dtr. Abschiedsrede des Mose wurde in Dtn 32,48–52 noch eine weitere Gottesrede eingefügt, in der Mose von Gott aufge-

---

14 So Otto, *Pentateuchrahmen*, 187–188; Achenbach, *Vollendung*, 321–322.

15 Vgl. Rainer Albertz, „Die erstmalige Konstituierung des Pentateuch durch die spät-deuteronomistische Redaktionsschicht (K^D bzw. D)," in *Eigensinn und Entstehung der Hebräischen Bibel: Erhard Blum zum siebzigsten Geburtstag*, ed. Joachim Krause et al., FAT 136 (Tübingen: Mohr Siebeck, 2020), 129–154, hier 138–141 [[= S. 98–102 im vorliegenden Band]]. Anders als Blum setze ich die D-Schicht zeitlich erst nach den ersten beiden priesterlichen Bearbeitungen (PB¹ und PB²) in den Büchern Gen–Lev an, vgl. a. a. O., 141–143. In Dtn 34 gehört noch V. 4aα₂β der D-Schicht an; vgl. die entsprechenden Landverheißungen in Gen 12,7 und Ex 33,1b.

16 So mit Recht Raik Heckl, „Die Präsentation tradierter Texte in Dtn 31 zur Revision der dtr Geschichtstheologie," in *Deuteronomium – Tora für eine neue Generation*, ed. Georg Fischer et al., BZAR 17 (Wiesbaden: Harrassowitz, 2011), 227–246, hier 227–228, gegen Eep Talstra, „Deuteronomy 31: Confusion or Conclusion? The Story of Moses' Threefold Succession," in *Deuteronomy and Deuteronomic Literature. FS C. H. W. Breckelmans*, ed. Marc Vervenne und Johan Lust, BETL 133 (Leuven: Leuven University Press und Peeters, 1997), 87–110, hier 87–88. |

fordert wird, sich unmittelbar auf seinen Tod auf dem Berg Nebo vorzubereiten (V. 49–50). Wenn Mose dabei an den Tod seines Bruders Aaron und ihrer beider Treulosigkeit in Meribat-Kadesch erinnert wird, die zu Gottes Strafankündigung führte, dass er das verheißene Land nicht betreten dürfe (V. 50–52), dann wird damit eine direkte Verbindungslinie über die Grenzen des Buches Dtn hinweg zu den priesterlichen Erzählungen in Num 20,1–13.22–29 aufgebaut. Was Gott dort angekündigt hat, wird sich jetzt erfüllen. Auch wenn Dtn 32,48–52 den dtr. Kontext voraussetzt und einige wenige dtr. Sprachmerkmale aufweist,[17] ist es immer noch die naheliegendste Lösung, den Text dem spät-priesterlichen Bearbeiter zuzuweisen, dem wir auch die genannten Passagen von Num 20 und weite Teile des Numeribuches verdanken und ich PB³ nenne.[18] Dagegen ist die ausgeführtere Variante in Num 27,12–23 späteren Ursprungs und wieder von unserem Text abhängig.[19] An Num 20,12 lässt sich übrigens nachweisen, dass der PB³ die spät-dtr. D-Redaktion bereits voraussetzt.[20] Die bewusst theologische Stilisierung von Dtn 32,48–52 als Gottesrede ist somit wahrscheinlich von Dtn 31,14–15.23 angeregt.[21] In ihrer Thematik war jene allerdings stärker festgelegt als diese, denn der göttliche Befehl an Mose, den Berg Nebo zu besteigen, musste eigentlich umgehend vollzogen werden, was dann in den priesterlichen Anteilen der Erzählung vom Tod des Mose in Dtn 34,1*.7–9 auch ausgeführt wird. Wenn in diese enge

---

17 So die in Dtn 32,49.52 gebrauchte partizipiale Konstruktion der Landverheißung (vgl. Dtn 1,20.25; 11,31; 15,7 u. ö.), die in priesterlichen Texten gerne perfektisch formuliert ist (Num 20,12.24; 27,12; vgl. allerdings 13,2) und die Wendung „dorthin wirst du nicht hineinkommen" in Dtn 32,52, die an Dtn 1,37.38.39 erinnert, während in Num 20,12 von „nicht hineinführen" die Rede war (vgl. allerdings V. 24). Sofern man die priesterlichen Passagen nicht als Teil eines unabhängigen Quellenwerks, sondern als Bearbeitung versteht, sind solche Angleichungen an den jeweiligen Kontext nicht weiter auffällig.
18 Vgl. Albertz, *Pentateuchstudien*, 348–350.397–399. Achenbach, *Vollendung*, 322–324, möchte die Passage ebenfalls der Pentateuchredaktion zuweisen; Otto, *Deuteronomiumrahmen*, 222–225, denkt eher an die Hexateuchredaktion, bzw. an eine nicht genauer zu bestimmende nachexilische Fortschreibung im Dtn, vgl. Eckart Otto, *Deuteronomium 23,16–34,14*, HThKAT (Freiburg et al.: Herder, 2017), 2171–2173.
19 So auch Achenbach, *Vollendung*, 323–324, der den Text Num 27,12–23 seiner ersten Theokratischen Bearbeitung zuweist, u. a. weil er Josua der Aufsicht des Hohenpriesters unterstellt. Ich rechne ihn, wie auch sonst den gesamten Abschnitt Num 25–36 der priesterlichen Pentateuchredaktion (PentR^P) zu, weil diese hier mit einer aufwändigen Vorbereitung der Landverteilung im Rahmen des Pentateuch eine Art Ersatz für das abgespaltene Josuabuch schafft, vgl. Albertz, *Pentateuchstudien*, 357–373.
20 Vgl. den Rekurs in Num 20,12 auf das für die D-Redaktion typische Glaubensmotiv (Gen 15,6; Ex 4,1.8.9.31; 14,31; 19,9; Num 14,11).
21 Auch die von priesterlichen Autoren bevorzugte Einleitungsformel für die Gottesrede (וידבר יהוה אל־משה), die 90-mal im übrigen Pentateuch begegnet, taucht im Deuteronomium in Dtn 32,48 nur dieses einzige Mal auf. |

Geschehensfolge mit dem Mosesegen in Dtn 33 dennoch noch etwas eingeschoben wurde, dann konnte das nur außerhalb der von der Gottesrede vorgezeichneten Erzähllinie geschehen. Mit seinem auf Josua ausgerichteten Erzählabschluss in 34,9 ebnete der PB³ den vom D gesetzten Schlusspunkt in V. 10 wieder ein Stück weit ein. | So hat der PB³ zwar die Verklammerung des Dtn mit den vorangehenden Büchern des Pentateuchs gestärkt, aber ein Pentateuchredaktor war er noch weniger als jener.

4 Der Einbau des Moseliedes; das Werk eines ersten nicht-priesterlichen Pentateuchredaktors (PentR^L1)?

In die kleine Szene einer göttlichen Offenbarung am Zelt der Begegnung, die der D-Redaktor in Moses Abschiedsrede gesetzt hatte (Dtn 31,14–15.23), findet sich eine längere JHWH-Rede an Mose eingeschoben (V. 16–22),[22] welche auf den Vortrag und die Verschriftung des Moseliedes hinausläuft, das in 32,1–43 in aller Länge zitiert wird. Man hat den Eindruck, dass hier ein Redaktor tätig wurde, der sich in Kenntnis der schon vollzogenen Niederschrift der Tora durch Mose in 31,9 und eingedenk der Kanonformel, dass man eigentlich nichts zu der am Horeb offenbarten Tora hinzufügen oder von ihr wegnehmen dürfe (13,1; vgl. 4,2), aufgrund der überraschenden erneuten Gottesoffenbarung am Begegnungszelt legitimiert sah, das Buch Deuteronomium noch um einen gewichtigen Text, nämlich um das Moselied samt einer längeren Einleitung, zu erweitern. Jean-Pierre Sonnet drückt diesen Eindruck treffend mit den Worten aus: „What Deuteronomy 31 tells is thus the story of a process of completion – a process turned dramatic by the unexpected theophany and by the ensuing interpolation of the Song in the already written Torah."[23] Ein solcher ausdrücklich von Gott her legitimierter redaktioneller Erweiterungsprozess ist einzigartig; er dient dem Redaktor dazu, das von ihm neu geschaffene Buchende mit einer speziellen göttlichen Autorisierung auszustatten.

In der eingefügten Gottesrede lässt der Redaktor JHWH Mose mitteilen, dass das Volk der Israeliten nach seinem Tod schon bald zu fremden Göttern abfallen und damit den mit ihm geschlossenen Bund brechen würde (Dtn 31,16), nämlich – satt und fett geworden – gleich nach der Einwanderung in das verheißene Land (V. 20). Darum würde sich JHWH zornig von seinem Volk abwenden und schlimme Übel und Nöte über es kommen lassen, selbst dann noch, wenn das Volk erste

---

22 Der Einschub wird literarkritisch darin erkennbar, dass durch ihn das ungenannte Subjekt von Dtn 31,23 verunklart wird. Von V. 22 her würde man Mose erwarten; aus der Mitseins-Zusage V. 23b wird aber erkennbar, dass JHWH selber das Wort ergriffen hat.
23 S. Sonnet, *Book*, 159–160.

Schritte der Buße tun würde (V. 17–18). Für diese zukünftige Katastrophe soll Mose – mit Unterstützung von Josua – ein bestimmtes, von Gott mitgeteiltes Lied aufschreiben und so intensiv unterrichten, dass es dann als Zeuge gegen das abtrünnige Israel auftreten könne (V. 19.21). Israel hätte es besser wissen können, nicht etwa JHWH, sondern es selbst war an seinem Unglück schuld! Eilig führt Mose den göttlichen Auftrag aus. Wenn es V. 22 heißt, dass er das Lied nicht nur aufschrieb, sondern auch schon lehrte, dann ist letzteres prospektiv gemeint und drückt hier nur seine Absicht aus.[24] Indem der Redaktor nach dieser harten Gerichtsrede die ältere Zusage JHWHs an Josua in V. 23 stehen lässt, will er wohl damit aussagen, dass trotz aller erwarteten Undankbarkeit Israels | der göttliche Zorn letztlich begrenzt bleibt; zumindest die Landverheißung wird JHWH getreulich erfüllen.

Eigentlich würde man nach Beendigung der Theophanie sogleich die Verkündigung des Liedes erwarten. Es folgt allerdings erst noch eine Moserede an die Leviten (Dtn 31,24–30), die zunächst dem vervollständigten Torabuch ebenfalls eine Zeugenfunktion zuschreibt (V. 24–27) und erst dann auf einen Vortrag des Liedes bei einer Volksversammlung in Gegenwart der Ältesten und Amtsträger hinsteuert (V. 28–30). Wie sich die beiden Liedeinleitungen zueinander verhalten, wird in der Forschung seit langem kontrovers diskutiert. Hier nur so viel: Eine Lösung, einfach beide Reden zusammenzunehmen, kann schlecht erklären, warum in V. 24–27 plötzlich die Tora und nicht das Lied im Mittelpunkt steht. Die älteren Exegeten meinten das Problem einfach dadurch beseitigen zu können, dass sie in V. 24.26 ziemlich willkürlich das störende Wort התורה „die Tora" in השירה „das Lied" änderten.[25] Aber auch die jüngste Lösung von Petra Schmidtkunz, nur die Verse, die das Lied betreffen, nämlich V. 16–22 und V. 28–30 zu einer Schicht zusammenzuziehen,[26] bleibt fragwürdig, weil zwischen V. 27 und 28 kein

---

24 Das impf. cons. kann zuweilen auch eine Absicht ausdrücken, vgl. Otto Eißfeldt, „Die Umrahmung des Mose-Liedes Dtn 32,1–43 und des Mose-Gesetzes Dtn 1–30 in Dtn 31,9–32,47," in idem, *Kleine Schriften, Bd. III* (Tübingen: Mohr Siebeck, 1966), 322–334, hier 327 Anm. 2, und GK § 120–121. |

25 Vgl. Staerk, *Deuteronomium*, 75; Carl Steuernagel, *Das Deuteronomium*, HKAT I, 3/1, (Göttingen: Vandenhoeck & Ruprecht, ²1923), 163, u. a.; Eißfeldt, „Umrahmung," 326, ersetzt umgekehrt השירה durch התורה in V. 30. Wenn Otto, *Deuteronomiumrahmen*, 191 Anm. 165, ausführt, schon Steuernagel habe gezeigt, „daß es keinen ausreichenden Grund gibt, Dtn 31,16–22.24–30 auf zwei voneinander getrennte Schichten zu verteilen, sondern beide Abschnitte eine Einheit bilden," dann versäumt er, darauf hinzuweisen, dass dessen Einschätzung nicht zuletzt auf einer Textänderung beruht. Vgl. auch Eckart Otto, „Moses Abschiedslied in Deuteronomium 32: Ein Zeugnis der Kanonsbildung in der Hebräischen Bibel," in idem, *Die Tora: Studien zum Pentateuch: Gesammelte Aufsätze*, BZAR 9 (Wiesbaden: Harrassowitz, 2009), 641–678, hier 652–654.

26 Vgl. Petra Schmidtkunz, *Das Moselied des Deuteronomiums: Untersuchungen zu Text und Theologie von Dtn 32,1–43*, FAT II/124 (Tübingen: Mohr Siebeck, 2020), 317.329–333. Weder ihre Behaup-

literarischer Bruch nachzuweisen ist. Im Gegenteil, die rahmende Wendung עד
תמם „bis zu ihrer Vollständigkeit" in V. 24 und V. 30 weist eher darauf hin, dass
die Verse 24–30 als eine literarische Einheit konzipiert worden sind. Zudem
spricht die Tatsache, dass die beiden Reden, und zwar wo es um das Lied geht,
für die sachlich gleiche Aussage, dass Israel vom Übel betroffen sein wird, unterschiedliche hebräische Wendungen gebrauchen,[27] stark dafür, dass sie von verschiedenen Autoren stammen. Den Ausschlag für die literaturgeschichtliche Zuordnung der beiden Reden gibt meiner Meinung nach die Einsicht, dass der Vers
Dtn 32,44, der jetzt als Ausleitung des Moseliedes verwendet wird, eigentlich eine
offenbar ältere Einleitung zum Lied darstellt,[28] die durch die jetzige | Liedeinlei-
tung nach der Moserede (31,30) verdrängt worden ist, aber einmal direkt hinter
31,23 gestanden haben könnte:[29]

> Dtn 32,44   Da kam Mose und redete alle Worte dieses Liedes in die Ohren des Volks, er
> und Hosea ben Nun.

Die sonst kaum erklärliche Ortsveränderung des Mose[30] wird von der Szene am
Zelt der Begegnung her sofort verständlich: Mose kam vom Zelt, das nach Ex 33,7
außerhalb des Lagers aufgebaut werden soll, wieder zurück in die Versammlung
des Volkes hinein; auch die Begleitung durch Josua bekommt von daher ihren
Sinn: Er war im Zelt der Begegnung anwesend gewesen und war mit dem in
Dtn 31,19 verwendeten pluralischen Imperativ vom Redaktor schon stillschwei-
gend an der Verschriftung des Liedes mitbeteiligt worden. Wenn der Redaktor
dabei den in Num 13,8.16 von PB³ erfundenen älteren Namen für Josua, nämlich
Hosea, mit der Bedeutung „Er hat gerettet" verwendet, will er wohl das Hoff-

---

27 So in Dtn 31,17a.b.21 die Aussage, es werde Israel מצאו רעות „Unheil finden", dagegen קראת
הרעה „Unheil treffen" in V. 29.

28 So schon am deutlichsten von Eißfeldt, „Umrahmung," 327, erkannt. Aber auch wenn Norbert
Lohfink, „Zur Fabel in Dtn 31–32," in idem, *Studien zum Deuteronomium und zur deuteronomischen Literatur, Bd. IV*, SBAB 31 (Stuttgart: Katholisches Bibelwerk, 2000), 219–245, hier 221, erwägt, ob Dtn 32,44 dasselbe wie 31,30 aussage oder „einen zweiten Vortrag des Moseliedes vor
einem anderen Publikum" meine, hat er den Einleitungscharakter des Verses gespürt. |

29 Dass die LXX vor Dtn 32,44 noch einmal 31,22 wiederholt, zeigt vielleicht an, dass sie noch
Manuskripte kennt, in denen die Verse näher beieinanderstanden. Allerdings formulierte sie
dann V. 44 – wohl mit Rücksicht auf V. 46 – schon zu einer Verkündigung der Worte des Gesetzes
um.

30 Dass die Aussage ויבא משה „Da kam Mose ..." unverständlich oder rätselhaft bleibt, wird
von einer Reihe von Auslegern notiert, vgl. Steuernagel, *Deuteronomium*, 172; Eduard Nielsen,
Deuteronomium, HAT I/6 (Tübingen: Mohr Siebeck, 1995), 293; Nelson, *Deuteronomy*, 378, u. a.

nungspotential unterstreichen, das in dem folgenden anklagenden Lied auch zum Ausdruck kommt (vgl. 32,36). Damit kann Dtn 31,16–22.(23) + 32,44 als die ursprüngliche Einleitung des Moseliedes 32,1–43* gelten, während die Verse 31,24–30 einer späteren Redaktionsstufe angehören.[31]

Doch was ist wohl der Grund, warum dieser Redaktor, der sowohl die spät-dtr. als auch eine spät-priesterliche Bearbeitung des werdenden Pentateuch schon voraussetzt, mit derartigem redaktionellen Aufwand und unter Rückgriff auf eine göttliche Autorisierung das Moselied in die Schlusskapitel des Dtn einfügte? Auch wenn er in seiner Einleitung schon auf Begriffe und Wendungen aus dem Lied anspielte,[32] griff er wahrscheinlich mit dieser umfangreichen hymnischen Lehrdichtung (Dtn 32,1–43) einen ihm bereits vorliegenden Text auf,[33] der aus nachexilischer Perspektive[34] über die Grundlagen des Gottesverhältnis Israels angesichts der erlebten Exilskatastrophe reflektierte. Nach Aussage des Liedes hatte das | seinem Gott untreu gewordene Israel diese Katastrophe nur deswegen überlebt, weil JHWH seinen Beschluss zu dessen totaler Vernichtung, der angesichts der Hybris der Feinde seine alleinige Weltregierung hätte infrage stellen können (V. 26–27), nicht ausführte, sondern stattdessen beschloss (V. 39–42), seine einzigartige Göttlichkeit im Kampf bloß gegen seine Feinde und Hasser, seien sie innerhalb oder außerhalb Israels, durchzusetzen.[35] Auch schon dem DtrG war es ja

---

31 Ähnlich auch Nelson, *Deuteronomy*, 356.
32 Vgl. zu 31,16 נכר אלהי 32,12 נכר אל, zu 31,17.18 פני והסתרתי 32,20 פני אסתירה, zu 31,17 והיה לאכל 32,22 הארץ ותאכל, zu 31,20 דשן 32,15 שמן, zu 31,20 ונאצוני 32,19 וינאץ mit JHWH als Subjekt.
33 So die Einschätzung der Mehrheit der Ausleger, vgl. etwa Steuernagel, *Deuteronomium*, 164; Sanders, *Provenance*, 343–348; Nelson, *Deuteronomy*, 360. Auch Reinhard Achenbach, „Die Prophezeiungen des Mose in Deuteronomium 28–32," ZAR 20 (2014): 147–179, 170 Anm. 30, scheint dieser Ansicht zu sein. Während Otto, „Moses Abschiedslied," 654–656; idem, *Deuteronomium IV*, 2104.2163–2164, meinte, aus den Anspielungen in den Einleitungsreden schließen zu können, dass der Redaktor das Lied selber für den jetzigen Zusammenhang gedichtet habe, kommt Schmidtkunz, *Moselied*, 234–258, aufgrund einer neuen ausführlichen Untersuchung der Bezüge zu dem Urteil: „Trotz der äußerlichen Ähnlichkeiten deutet der Sprachgebrauch also darauf hin, dass Lied und Rahmen unterschiedliche Verstehenshorizonte repräsentieren" (a. a. O., 335). Ihrer Meinung nach erscheint „ein gemeinsamer Ursprung als sehr unplausibel" (a. a. O., 355).
34 Dass die späte Exilszeit den *terminus a quo* für die Datierung des Liedes darstellt, zeigt die zentrale Rolle, die das monotheistische Bekenntnis darin spielt, mit deutlichen Anklängen an Deuterojesaja (vgl. Dtn 32,39 mit Jes 41,4; 43,11.13; 48,12). |
35 Mit dieser äußerst knappen Zusammenfassung des Gedankenganges des Liedes folge ich der neusten, meiner Meinung nach zutreffenden Auslegung von Schmidtkunz, *Moselied*, 48–94. Gegenüber der seit Steuernagel, *Deuteronomium*, 170–172, vorherrschenden Deutung, dass das Lied auf einen Völkerkampf Gottes hinauslaufe – Otto, *Deuteronomium IV*, 2195–2196, spricht gar von einem „apokalyptischen Völkerkampf" – kann sie sich auf die Beobachtung stützen, dass in Dtn 32,40–42 nicht von den Feinden Israels, sondern von Gottes Feinden die Rede ist. Dass, wie

darum gegangen, das Exil aus der anhaltenden Untreue Israels gegenüber JHWH zu begründen und JHWHs Göttlichkeit angesichts der Katastrophe Israels zu verteidigen. So war es wohl eine ganz wesentliche Absicht des Redaktors, die spätere Geschichte von Israels Untreue und Scheitern, welche die Geschichtsbücher erzählt hatten, schon als Zukunftsperspektive in die Gründungsgeschichte Israels hineinzuziehen. Dies setzt aber voraus, dass zu seiner Zeit die völlige Abtrennung der Geschichtsbücher vom Pentateuch vollzogen oder zumindest ernsthaft erwogen wurde. Das Moselied ist somit als eine Art von „Ersatz" für das DtrG im Rahmen des Pentateuchs gemeint. Es soll dessen Absicht, die richtigen Lehren aus der fehl gelaufenen weiteren Geschichte und der Exilskatastrophe zu ziehen, schon in der Gründungsurkunde zur Geltung kommen lassen. Darin besteht die Zeugenfunktion des Liedes, zumal es anders als das DtrG ein Stück weit über die Katastrophe hinausweist, indem es alle Überlebenden, die sich zum Gottesvolk zählen, eindringlich mahnt, sorgfältig darauf zu achten, dass sie zu JHWHs Knechten und nicht zu seinen Feinden gehören (V. 43).

Die These, dass das Moselied vornehmlich die Funktion hat, das DtrG zu ersetzen, lässt sich noch durch einige motivliche Beobachtungen weiter erhärten: Während das Lied im Rückblick ein sehr eigenes, vom Pentateuch abweichendes Bild von der Gründungsgeschichte Israels entwirft, Exodus und Sinai nicht erwähnt, sondern Israels Erwählung in den Himmel verlegt (V. 8–9) und das Bild eines ungestörten Gottesverhältnisses während der Wüstenzeit zeichnet (V. 10–14), stimmt es im Vorausblick an einem entscheidenden Punkt mit dem DtrG darin überein, dass es den Abfall Israels zu fremden Göttern erst nach der Landnahme beginnen lässt (V. 15–18; vgl. Ri 2–2 Kön 25). Wenn aber das Lied weniger eine genaue Zusammenfassung des im Pentateuch geschilderten Geschehens darstellt, sondern ein betont theologischer Ausblick auf das Geschehen in der Zukunft sein soll, das im DtrG in aller Breite aus menschlicher Perspektive erzählt worden ist, dann ist es relativ wahrscheinlich, dass seine Einfügung mit der Konstituierung des Pentateuchs als einem gegenüber dem DtrG unabhängigen Werk zu tun hat. Somit können wir den Redaktor als einen ersten wirklichen Pentateuchredaktor bezeichnen, der angesichts seiner dtr. beeinflussten Sprache eher in einem laizistischen Milieu anzusiedeln ist (PentR[L1]). Mit dem sprachlich und theologisch eindrucksvollen hymnischen Lehrgedicht verschaffte er dem Pentateuch zugleich einen würdigen Ausklang und einen zur kritischen Selbstprüfung anregenden Ausblick. |

---

schon Eduard König, *Das Deuteronomium*, KAT 3 (Leipzig: Deichtersche Verlagsbuchhandlung Werner Scholl, 1917), 214, annahm, letztlich ein göttliches Reinigungsgericht gemeint ist, das in erster Linie Israel betrifft, wird durch die letzte Aussage des Liedes bestätigt, dass Gott damit den Ackerboden seines Volkes entsühnen werde (V. 43). |

5 Die Vervollständigung des Torabuchs und der Einbau des Mosesegens; das Werk eines zweiten nicht-priesterlichen Redaktors (PentR^L2)?

Doch mit der Einfügung des Moseliedes waren die Redaktoren, die sich für den kompositionellen Abschluss des Pentateuchs verantwortlich fühlten, offenbar noch nicht zufrieden. Wie die dessen Einleitung verdoppelnde Moserede in Dtn 31,24–30 aufweist, hat es mindestens noch eine weitere Abschlussredaktion aus nicht-priesterlichem Milieu gegeben.

Wenn der Autor dieser Rede im Anschluss an die erweiterte Szene von der göttlichen Theophanie am Begegnungszelt noch einmal den Fokus ganz auf die Tora, auf ihre Verschriftung und Funktion ausrichtet (Dtn 31,24–27), um erst danach wieder auf das ihm vorgegebene Lied zurückzulenken (V. 28–30), dann muss er damit ein ihm zentral wichtiges Ziel verfolgt haben. Einerseits griff er damit die dtr. Aussage von der Verschriftung der Tora in V. 9 wieder auf; andererseits betonte er davon abweichend, dass Mose aus der Erfahrung der Gottesoffenbarung heraus „die Worte dieser Tora ... bis zu ihrer Vollständigkeit (עד תמם)" in ein Buch geschrieben und damit abgeschlossen habe (V. 24). Erst als vervollständigtes materiales Schriftstück konnte die Tora den Leviten zur Positionierung neben der Bundeslade übergeben, um damit neben seiner primären Funktion der Belehrung auch – wie schon das Lied – eine Zeugenfunktion für die Zukunft übernehmen (V. 25–26). Mir scheint, dass die Dimension der Herstellung eines vollständigen Torabuchs, die hier beschrieben wird, von der bisherigen Forschung noch nicht voll erfasst wurde. Die meisten Exegeten deuten sie vom Kontext her dahingehend, dass Mose das von Gott neu offenbarte Lied (V. 19–21) noch in die schon V. 9 verschriftete Tora aufgenommen habe.[36] Dies kann sehr wohl auch gemeint sein, aber die Formulierungen von V. 24 klingen viel allgemeiner, viel grundsätzlicher. Raik Heckl hat darum zurecht die übliche Deutung ein Stück weit ausgeweitet: Insgesamt diene „der nochmalige Verweis auf die Abfassung der Tora in Dtn 31,24 dazu, Form und Umfang des Deuteronomiums ab Dtn 32 zu erklären."[37] Das vervollständigte Torabuch des Mose würde demnach auch schon

---

36 Vgl. König, *Deuteronomium*, 205; Martin Rose, *5. Mose. Teilband II: 5. Mose 1–11 und 26–34: Rahmenstücke zum Gesetzeskorpus*, ZBK.AT 5/2 (Zürich: TVZ, 1994), II:562; Sanders, *Provenance*, 342; Talstra, „Deuteronomy 31," 100; Sonnet, *Book*, 159–160; Nelson, *Deuteronomy*, 361–362; Otto, *Deuteronomium IV*, 2105.2125.

37 S. Heckl, „Präsentation," 235. Leider verfolgt Heckl diese richtige Spur nicht weiter, weil er, a. a. O., 236–239, aus terminologischen Gründen meint annehmen zu müssen, dass es in Dtn 31,9 um den Pentateuch und in V. 24 nur um das Buch Deuteronomium gehe. Doch ist das alles andere als zwingend. Denn mit der Bezeichnung ספר התורה, die in Dtn 31,26 gebraucht ist, wird in Texten, die jünger als das DtrG sind, sehr wohl der gesamte Pentateuch bezeichnet (vgl. Neh 8,3; vgl. 8,1).

den Mosesegen in Kap. 33 und vielleicht auch die Erzählung vom Tod des Mose
in Kap. 34 umfassen. Mir scheint allerdings auch damit die volle Dimension des
in Dtn 31,24 Ausgesagten noch nicht erschlossen. Immerhin erinnert die Wendung
עד תמם ... כלה an Bemerkungen, mit denen Schreiber in Kolophonen den vollständigen Abschluss ihrer Arbeit notieren.[38] Meiner Meinung nach soll in den
knappen, aber grundsätzlichen Worten nicht weniger gesagt werden, als dass
Mose durch die erneute Theophanie JHWHs im Begegnungszelt befähigt wurde,
über das Lied (V. 22) und das Deuteronomium (V. 9) hinaus das vollständige Torabuch, d. h. den gesamten Pentateuch, der ja im Buch Genesis von Ereignissen
handelte, die noch vor der Geburt des Mose stattgefunden | hatten, niederzu-
schreiben. D. h. aber, der zweite nicht-priesterliche Redaktor will in V. 24 kurz
davon berichten, wie dank göttlicher Intervention die dtn. Tora von Mose zur
pentateuchischen Tora ausgeweitet und damit komplettiert werden konnte. Das
neben der Bundeslade deponierte vervollständigte Torabuch (V. 25–26), das Israel
auf seinem weiteren Weg begleiten und es vor Widerspenstigkeit gegenüber seinem Gott eindringlich warnen sollte (V. 27), war schon der gesamte Pentateuch.
Der Verfasser dieser Verse entpuppt sich damit als Pentateuchredaktor *par exel-
lence*. Er sei hier darum PentR^L2 genannt.

Es ist darum kein Zufall, dass dieser Redaktor gegenüber dem Moselied auch
inhaltlich die pentateuchische Perspektive dadurch zur Geltung brachte, dass er
Mose aus der eigenen Erfahrung heraus feststellen ließ, dass die Untreue Israels
gegenüber JHWH keineswegs erst, wie es das Lied (32,15–18) und entsprechend
die erste Einleitungsrede (31,16.20) darstellten, nach der Einwanderung in das
verheißene Land erfolgte, sondern schon beim Abfall zum Goldenen Kalb in der
Wüstenzeit geschehen war. Mit seinem Rückblick (V. 27.29) griff er dazu vornehmlich auf Begriffe der Darstellung in Dtn 9 zurück,[39] rief damit aber zugleich auch
die Erzählungen von Ex 32–34 in Erinnerung, in denen die Anklage, Israel sei ein
halsstarriges Volk (עַם קְשֵׁה־עֹרֶף), ein regelrechtes Leitmotiv bildete (Ex 32,9;
33,3.5; 34,9; vgl. Dtn 9,6.13). Die Notwendigkeit der Zeugenfunktion von Tora und
Lied wurde damit durch eine genuin pentateuchische Thematik untermauert.

Wenn derselbe Redaktor seinen Einschub damit rahmt, dass er auch Mose
die Worte des Liedes „bis zu ihrer Vollständigkeit" (עַד תֻּמָּם) vortragen lässt
(Dtn 31,30), dann spielt er vielleicht darauf an, dass dieses Moselied in verschiedenen Varianten bekannt war und er sich für die vollständige Fassung verbürgen
wollte. Schon Petra Schmidtkunz hatte erwogen, ob nicht die in der zweiten Person sing. formulierten Anklagen in 32,14b.15aβ, welche die Erzählung des Liedes

---

38 Vgl. Sonnet, *Book*, 159. |
39 Vgl. zu Dtn 31,27 ממרים הייתם עם־יהוה gleichlautend 9,24, zu 31,29 וסרתם מן־הדרך ähnlich
in 9,12.16; vgl. Ex 32,8 u. a. m.

sprengen, von dem Redaktor eingefügt wurden, der in seiner Einleitung angekündigt hatte, das Lied würde dem abtrünnigen Volk in sein Angesicht als Zeuge aussagen (31,21).[40] Das wäre nach der hiesigen Nomenklatur der PentR[L1]. Nun sind aber, wie auch Schmidtkunz erneut bestätigte, im Lied auch noch weitere Passagen als Zufügungen verdächtig (bes. V. 30.31.32–33).[41] Dem zweiten Pentateuchredaktor wäre davon durchaus die umfangreiche Sodom-Anklage (V. 32–33) als Explikation der Frevel Israels (!) zuzutrauen. Auch sie greift ja ein Thema aus dem Pentateuch auf (Gen 19). Indem er schließlich die ältere, noch vom PentR[L1] formulierte Liedeinleitung (Dtn 32,44) hinter das Lied verschob, deutete er an, dass Mose und Josua das Lied nicht nur einmal vor den Leitern der Volksversammlung, sondern mehrfach im Volk vortrugen.

Der Mosesegen in Dtn 33,1–29, der eindeutig sekundär in den vom PB³ gestalteten Weg des Mose zum Ort seines Sterbens (32,48–52+34,1*) eingeschoben wurde, scheint auf den ersten Blick völlig isoliert dazustehen. Doch sieht man genauer hin, so ergeben sich mehrfache Verknüpfungen hin zum Moselied[42] und vielfache Rückverweise in den Pentateuch hinein.[43] Schon allein aus der Tatsache, dass der Mosesegen ein Pendant zum Jakobsegen (Gen | 49,1–28) darstellt, auf den er sich insbesondere in der Josephstrophe explizit zurückbezieht,[44] ist schon häufiger vermutet worden, dass Dtn 33 der Pentateuchredaktion zugewiesen werden kann.[45] Diese habe mit den beiden Segenstexten am Ende des ersten und des letzten Buches des Pentateuchs einen kompositionellen Rahmen um das ganze Werk herumlegen wollen.[46]

---

40 Vgl. Schmidtkunz, *Moselied*, 361–363.

41 Vgl. Schmidtkunz, *Moselied*, 77–79.361–364.

42 Die eigenartige Aussage von Dtn 33,3 ist nur in Rückbezug auf 32,8–9 verständlich; vgl. die Ehrenbezeichnung Jeschurun, die im Pentateuch nur in Dtn 32,15; 33,5.26 vorkommt, u. a. m.

43 S. unten S. 285 [[= S. 121–122 im vorliegenden Band]]. |

44 Vgl. Dtn 33,15 גבעות עולם mit Gen 49,26a und Dtn 33,16 ולקדקד נזיר אחיו mit Gen 46,26b.

45 So schon Filemon A. Puukko, *Das Deuteronomium: Eine literarkritische Untersuchung*, BWANT 5 (Leipzig: Hinrichs, 1910), 116, sodann Henrik Pfeiffer, *Jahwes Kommen von Süden: Jdc 5; Hab 3; Dtn 33 und Ps 68 in ihrem literatur- und theologiegeschichtlichen Umfeld*, FRLANT 211 (Göttingen: Vandenhoeck & Ruprecht, 2005), 185; Martin Leuenberger, *Segen und Segenstheologien im Alten Israel: Untersuchungen zu ihren religions- und theologiegeschichtlichen Konstellationen und Transformationen*, AThANT 90 (Zürich: TVZ, 2008), 347–350; Römer, *Deuteronomistic History*, 181–182; s. oben S. 273 [[= S. 107 im vorliegenden Band]].

46 Ich konnte jüngst sogar wahrscheinlich machen, dass erst der nicht-priesterliche Pentateuchredaktor, der die Einleitung zum Mosesegen formulierte (Dtn 33,1), die Stammessprüche, die einmal in Gen 35 gestanden hatten, durch Versetzung nach Kapitel 49 zu einem Sterbesegen Jakobs umgeformt und neu gerahmt hat (49,1b.28bβ), um so eine genaue Entsprechung zum Segen des Mose kurz vor seinem Tode zu schaffen, vgl. Rainer Albertz, *Die Josephsgeschichte im Pentateuch. Ein Beitrag zur Überwindung einer anhaltenden Forschungskontroverse*, FAT 153 (Tübingen: Mohr Siebeck, 2021), 143–149.

Für die genauere literaturgeschichtliche Einordnung des hier tätigen Pentateuchredaktors ist zu berücksichtigen, dass in Dtn 33 die eigentlichen Stammessprüche V. 6–25 durch einen kleinen Hymnus gerahmt sind (V. 2–5+26–29), der seit Carl Steuernagel gerne als spätere Ergänzung von ihnen abgehoben wird.[47] Folgt man dieser Einschätzung, dann müsste man vielleicht noch mit einem weiteren nicht-priesterlichen Pentateuchredaktor rechnen. Doch hat schon Gerhard von Rad die Notwendigkeit einer solchen Aufteilung in Frage gestellt,[48] und inzwischen hat Hans-Peter Mathys im Gefolge von Raymond Tournay so viele sprachliche Beziehungen zwischen dem Rahmen und den Sprüchen aufgezeigt, dass das Kapitel als literarische Einheit aufgefasst werden kann.[49] Dann hätte hier ein Autor unter Verwendung von ihm vorliegenden Hymnen- und Stammesspruchmaterial eine komplexe, volltönende Einheit für den Abschluss des Pentateuchs komponiert. Denn erst der Hymnus und die Sprüche zusammen erreichen den vollen kompositionellen Abschluss.

Dass wir es bei diesem Autor von Dtn 33 erneut mit dem PentR[L2] zu tun haben, wird aus den folgenden Beobachtungen wahrscheinlich: Hatte dieser schon in Dtn 31,24–27 die überragende Bedeutung, die der PentR[L1] dem Moselied für die Zukunft Israels eingeräumt hatte, insofern eingeschränkt, als er erneut die Wichtigkeit der Tora ins Spiel brachte, so ergänzte er hier die Gerichtsperspektive des Liedes, die nur die Möglichkeit des Überlebens nach der Exilskatastrophe aufgezeigt hatte, durch eine facettenreiche Schilderung der großen Heilschancen, die sich Israel nach und trotz der Katastrophe auftun würden. Dank der Fürbitten und guten Wünsche des Mose würde den Stämmen Israels mit JHWHs Hilfe in Zukunft die Möglichkeit zu einem reich gesegneten, gesicherten und ungestörten Leben erwachsen (33,28). Und hatte der PentR[L2] schon in Dtn 31,27.29 auf ein zentrales Ereignis im Pentateuch | Bezug genommen, so ließ er Mose in den hymnisch gerahmten Segenssprüchen fortlaufend Erinnerungen an die in ihm erzählte Gründungsgeschichte wachrufen: Der von ihm gestaltete Hymnus räumte der Sinaitheophanie, die im Moselied übergangen worden war, einen gebührenden Platz ein (33,2),[50] an die hier Mose zuteil gewordene Berufung erinnerte die Rede vom „Dornbuschbewohner" (V. 16). Der Levi-Spruch weckte in V. 8

---

47 Vgl. Steuernagel, *Deuteronomium*, 173–175.
48 Vgl. von Rad, *Deuteronomium*, 149.
49 Vgl. Hans Peter Mathys, *Dichter und Beter: Theologen aus spätalttestamentlicher Zeit*, OBO 132 (Fribourg: Universitätsverlag; Göttingen: Vandenhoeck & Ruprecht, 1994), 170–174, und Raymond Tournay, „Le Psaume et les Bénédictions de Moïse (Deutéronome XXXIII)," *RB* 65 (1958): 181–213, bes. 202–208. |
50 Der Begriff „Sinai" fällt nur hier im ganzen Buch Dtn anstelle der hier sonst üblichen Bezeichnung „Horeb"!

die Erinnerung an Moses Bewährung in Massa und Meriba (Ex 17,1–7) und der Josephspruch in Dtn 33,16 an Josephs Sonderstellung als „Geweihter seiner Brüder" (Gen 49,26). Und falls man den Lobsatz in Dtn 33,4, dass Mose „uns" die Tora befahl und diese somit zum stolzen Besitz der Versammlung Israels wurde, nicht als spätere Ergänzung aussondert,[51] würde der PentR[L2] sogar noch einmal auf seine Szene von der Übergabe des vervollständigten Torabuchs an die Leviten Bezug nehmen (31,24–27).

An zwei markanten Punkten zeigt sich, dass auch der Mosesegen mit der Entscheidung zu tun hat, die Gründungsgeschichte Israels auf den Pentateuch zu begrenzen: Indem der PentR[L2] im Eingangshymnus schilderte, wie JHWH vom Sinai aus mit seinen himmlischen Heerscharen aufbrach, um in der Versammlung der Stämme Israels zu deren König zu werden (Dtn 33,2–5), spielte er, wie bereits mehrere Exegeten erkannten,[52] auf den sog. „Landtag von Sichem" in Jos 24 an, bei dem die Stämme JHWH zu ihrem Gott erkoren (vgl. V. 1.15.21–22). Jos 24 war aber der Abschlusstext des Hexateuchs gewesen, des vorangehenden Versuchs, eine Gründungsurkunde Israels unter Einschluss des Josuabuches zu schaffen.[53] Der PentR[L2] revidierte diesen Versuch: „Dtn 33,5 verlegt den historischen Anfang der Theokratie vom Abschluss der Landnahme an das Ende der Abschiedsrede des Mose," formulierte Henrik Pfeiffer;[54] oder um es mit den Worten von Eckart Otto auszudrücken: „Dtn 33,5 weist ... auf Jos 24 und holt so den Landtag von Sichem in den Pentateuch."[55] Des weiteren konstatierte der PentR[L2], was besonders Henrik Pfeiffer herausstellte,[56] im Schlussteil seines Hymnus ausdrücklich, dass JHWH – zur Hilfe Israels am Himmel daher fahrend – dessen Feinde vertrieb und Israel eine sichere und fruchtbare Wohnstätte verschaffte (Dtn 33,26.27b–28). Damit waren, aber ohne dass die Erzählungen von der Eroberung und Verteilung des Landes im Josuabuch noch im Einzelnen nötig wären, die den Vätern gegebe-

---

51 Für letzteres plädiert erneut Pfeiffer, *Jahwes Kommen*, 185–186. Doch wenn man berücksichtigt, dass Dtn 33 ja keine Erzählung von der Segnung der Stämme durch Mose darstellt, sondern sein Vermächtnis, das referiert wird, dann ist es nicht ausgeschlossen, dass der Hymnus, der Mose in den Mund gelegt wird, auch einen Lobpreis des Volkes über Mose enthält. Otto, *Deuteronomium IV*, 2242, belässt etwa den Vers im Hymnus.

52 Vgl. Pfeiffer, *Jahwes Kommen*, 197–199; Leuenberger, *Segen*, 349–350; Otto, *Deuteronomium IV*, 2236.

53 Zur These, dass der Pentateuchredaktion eine Hexateuchredaktion voranging, vgl. zusammenfassend Albertz, *Pentateuchstudien*, 449–470. Meiner Ansicht nach ist der Hexateuchredaktor an Dtn 31–34 möglicherweise nur in 34,1bβ–3 beteiligt, vgl. a. a. O., 463.

54 S. Pfeiffer, *Jahwes Kommen*, 199.

55 S. Otto, *Deuteronomium IV*, 2242.

56 Vgl. Pfeiffer, *Jahwes Kommen*, 199.

nen Landverheißungen schon innerhalb des Pentateuchs erfüllt.[57] So konnte, ohne den Verlust eines Teils der | Heilsgeschichte in Kauf zu nehmen, die Gründungsgeschichte Israels in der Tat mit dem Tod des Mose in Dtn 34 abgeschlossen werden.

So spricht einiges dafür, dass auch die kompositionelle Abrundung des Pentateuchs in Dtn 34,11–12 vom PentR^{L2} gestaltet worden ist. Hatte er in Dtn 33,2.4(?) die Bedeutung des Sinai resümierend hervorgehoben, so richtete er in 34,11–12 abschließend noch einmal den Blick zurück auf den Exodus, das zweite Grunddatum der im Pentateuch erzählten Heilsgeschichte, das im Moselied übergangen worden war. In der Einleitung des Mosesegens (33,1) hatte er Mose als „Gottesmann" (אִישׁ הָאֱלֹהִים) bezeichnet, d. h. mit einem Titel, mit dem gern solche Propheten benannt wurden, die wie etwa der Prophet Elisa nicht nur über mantische, sondern auch magische Fähigkeiten verfügten (2 Kön 4,7.21.40; 5,8; 6,6; 7,1–2; 8,4 u. ö.). Die einzigartigen mantischen Qualifikationen des Mose hatte schon der spät-dtr. D-Redaktor in 34,10 abschließend preisend hervorgehoben. Diese Einschätzung bildete ja auch schon die Basis für Moses weitreichende Zukunftsschau, welche der PentR^{L1} mit Dtn 32 und der PentR^{L2} in Dtn 33 entwickelten; sie wurde schon von Reinhard Achenbach gebührend gewürdigt.[58] Der PentR^{L2} ging in Dtn 34,11–12 nun aber noch einen Schritt weiter und pries die großen magischen Wundertaten, die Mose sowohl in den Plagen an Pharao, seinen Knechten und am ganzen Land Ägypten getan (V. 11) als auch vor den Augen Israels, etwa am Schilfmeer, gewirkt hatte (V. 12). Dabei benutzte er Formulierungen, die sonst nur für die Beschreibung göttlichen Handelns verwendet werden.[59] Gott hatte somit nicht nur mit Mose auf eine besonders intime Weise kommuniziert wie sonst mit keinem anderen Menschen, sondern sich auch mit seiner Macht so eng an Mose gebunden, dass dieser in Ägypten überragende Wundertaten vollbringen konnte,

---

57 Der Hexateuch hatte mit der Beschreibung der Landverteilung an alle zwölf Stämme und dem abschließenden Landtag von Sichem auch den Samariern eine gebührende Rolle in der Gründungsgeschichte Israels zuerkannt, vgl. Albertz, *Pentateuchstudien*, 469–470. Der PentR^{L2} zollt den Samariern trotz | Ausschlusses des Josuabuches aus der Gründungsurkunde insofern Respekt, als er im Unterschied zum Jakobsegen, der Juda eine Führungsstellung einräumte (vgl. Gen 49,8–12), in dem von ihm formulierten Mosesegen eindeutig die nördlichen Stämme bevorzugt. Vielleicht stammte er aus dem Norden. In jedem Fall wollte er einen für Judäer und Samarier tragbaren Kompromiss!

58 Vgl. Achenbach, „Prophezeiungen," 169–179. Auch wenn ich anders als er den Schluss des Moseliedes nicht auf einen Völkerkampf deute, stimme ich seiner Einschätzung zu, dass die Prophezeiungen des Mose – noch mehr in seinen Segenswünschen als in seinem Lied – bereits eine eschatologische Dimension öffnen.

59 Vgl. zu Dtn 34,11 אֹתוֹת וּמוֹפְתִים „Zeichen und Wunder" Dtn 4,34; 26,8; 29,2; Ex 7,3; zu Dtn 34,12 יָד חֲזָקָה „starke Hand" Dtn 4,34; 26,8; Ex 3,19; 6,1; 13,9 und zu Dtn 34,12 מוֹרָא גָּדוֹל „großer Schrecken" Dtn 26,8 und pluralisch 4,34. |

die zur Befreiung Israels führten. Mit dem Tod dieses einzigartigen Gottesmannes hatte der Pentateuch, die Gründungsurkunde Israels, wirklich seinen endgültigen Abschluss gefunden.

6 Zusammenfassung

Abschließend seien hier die Ergebnisse der redaktionsgeschichtlichen Untersuchung nur noch einmal tabellarisch zusammengefasst:

Redaktionsschicht	zugewiesene Texte	Entstehung
DtrG	Dtn 31,1–13; 32,45–47; 34,1*.4aα_1.b.5–6; Jos 1 …	um 560 v. Chr. |
D	Dtn 31,14–15.23; 34,4a$\alpha_2\beta$.10	Mitte 5. Jh. v. Chr.
PB^3	Dtn 32,48–52; 34,1*.7–9	Mitte 5. Jh. v. Chr.
HexR	Dtn 34,1bβ–3(?) ……………… Jos 24,1–32	um 420 v. Chr.
PentR^{L1}	Dtn 31,16–22; 32,44 + Moselied (32,1–43)	Ende 5. Jh. v. Chr.
PentR^{L2}	Dtn 31,24–30; Umstellung von 32,44 hinter das Moselied; 33,1–5.(6–25).26–29; 34,11–12	Anfang 4. Jh. v. Chr.

How Jerusalem's Temple Was Aligned to Moses' Tabernacle: About the Historical Power of an Invented Myth

Thomas Thompson, whom I warmly congratulate on the occasion of his 80th birthday, is a pioneer in questioning more or less weak historical reconstructions done by Old Testament scholars, reconstructions that were mainly based on biblical texts and only sometimes supported by a few arbitrarily selected extra-biblical data. I still remember how his Tübinger Dissertation on the historicity of the patriarchal narratives (Thompson 1974) struck like a bomb in Heidelberg during the preparation stage of the second volume of Westermann's commentary on Genesis. Claus Westermann – after Wellhausen's influential scepticism – had always been inclined to follow the reconstructions of a 'Patriarchal Period' put forward by William Foxwell Albright and several other American scholars on the basis of comparison with terms and customs in the Mari and Nuzi texts from the second millennium BCE. He now, however, felt compelled by the strong arguments of Thomas Thompson and others,[1] who referred to similar customs in much later texts of the first millennium, thus declaring the dating of the 'Patriarchal Period' an open question (see Westermann 1981: 52–5, 73–90; the more detailed discussion in Westermann 1975: 69–93, in which I was involved as his assistant), although he did not give up the concept completely. In my book, *A History of Israelite Religion*, I myself felt obliged to define the religion shown by the patriarchal narratives 'not as a preliminary stage but as a substratum of Yahweh religion' (Albertz 1994: 1:29). Thus, Thomas Thompson belongs to the few scholars in our field whose dissertation already had a considerable influence on Old Testament research. |

Later on Thompson extended and radicalized his historical scepticism with regard to the Hebrew Bible. According to him, all the texts from Genesis to 2 Kings constitute a 'mythic past' composed by redactors of the Persian and Hellenistic periods from many traditions (Thompson 1999). They show no historiographical interest, but are intended to construct a Judean or Samarian identity and to enfold a theological and philosophical worldview (Thompson 1992: 353–423). I think Thompson is right as far as those biblical texts are not historiographical in the modern sense (similar Blum 2015: 31–54), but I think that their relation to a possible historical background can be very different and that – read against the grain – some historical and sociological information can be detected from many

---

1 Besides Thompson, Westermann was also impressed by Van Seters (1975). |

https://doi.org/10.1515/9783111202228-009

of them. We had detailed discussions about these questions over the years when participating in the 'European Seminar on Methodology in Israel's History' led by Lester L. Grabbe. In order to continue those discussions I would like to present to Thomas Thompson a little case study, which shows that a clearly unhistorical passage of the 'mythic past' became nevertheless historically powerful, shaping not only the literary history of other texts but also changing the historical reality of some details: I refer to the priestly tabernacle texts of Exodus 25–31; 35–40. I hope this study will be to his enjoyment.

1 The Priestly Tabernacle Texts – An Invented Myth

Up to the eighteenth century, the priestly tabernacle texts were regarded as historical, serving as a model for Solomon's temple in Jerusalem. In the nineteenth century, however, serious doubt was cast on their historicity.[2] According to Wilhelm Martin Leberecht de Wette, it is highly improbable that the liberated Israelite slaves would have possessed such large quantities of precious metals, luxurious textiles and exotic perfumes, which these texts deemed to be necessary for construction of the tabernacle (Exod. 25:1–7; 30:22–38; 35:5–35), let alone the significant technical skills needed for it (de Wette 1806/7 [1971]: 1:259; 2:265–70).[3] The expensive purple wool must have been imported from Phoenicia, pure gold from south Arabia or east Africa and cinnamon from Ceylon or the Moluccas, none of which would have been attainable for the Israelites in the desert without any state-run trade. Moreover, the wooden planks, beams and pillars alone needed for the substructure of the tent would have | been too heavy to be carried through the mountainous wilderness (26:15–37). Depending on their thickness, the 56 Acacia wood planks alone would have weighed between 12.3 and 72.8 tons, far too much for those four wagons with eight oxen from Num. 7:8 to be able to move.[4] You would need two or three lorries! Thus, Julius Wellhausen, after having ascribed the tabernacle text to the early post-exilic P source, rightly understood Moses' tabernacle not as an early prototype, but as a late copy or a back projection of Solomon's temple (see Wellhausen 1927 [2001]: 36–7). Considering the conceptual and material differences between the two, however, it would perhaps be better to speak of an ideal counter model to the pre-exilic Jerusalem temple now

---

2 For a history of research see Houtman (1993–2002: 3:325–35).
3 He called the reports about Moses' tabernacle a 'holy fairy tale' (de Wette 1806/7 [1971]: 1:259) belonging to the 'realm of myth' (2:269). |
4 See for this calculation Albertz (2012/15: 2:176–7). The thickness of the planks is not indicated, but one cubit seems to be assumed. Josephus reckons with four fingers (*Ant.* 3.116, 119).

fallen into ruins, which was implanted into the foundation history of Israel.[5] Thus, Moses' tabernacle is clearly an element of the mythic past in Thompson's terms, but it was nevertheless conceptualized to exert some influence on the future.

2 The Reports on Solomon's Temple – Secondarily Connected to the Tabernacle

The reports on the building and inauguration of Solomon's temple in 1 Kings 6–8 are literarily disputed and in some respects difficult to understand. They cannot be discussed here in detail. However, whatever the date of their original composition,[6] this must have been earlier than the tabernacle texts in the book of Exodus, because in spite of some similarities concerning the structure (holy and holy of the holies) and several furnishings (ark, incense altar, table), the described Jerusalem temple shows important differences to Moses' tabernacle: it possesses a huge cherub throne for the deity in the holy of the holies (1 Kgs 6:23–28) instead of two small cherubs installed on the top of the ark, called *kapporet* (Exod. 25:17–22). Its inner rooms are enclosed by walls with wooden doors (1 Kgs 6:31–35), while the tabernacle uses an inner (*pāroket*) and an outer curtain (*māsāk*) for the same purpose (Exod. 26:31–37).[7] Its holy main room is illuminated by ten lamp stands (1 Kgs 7:49), while the tabernacle has one big lamp stand with seven arms (*měnôrah*) | instead (Exod. 25:31–39). Apart from the outer altar,[8] Solomon's temple has many more bronze objects in the courtyard, not just one water basin like the tabernacle (Exod. 30:17–21), but a decorated sea of cast metal (1 Kgs 7:23–26) and ten ornamented trolleys of bronze (vv. 27–39), which are later partly deconstructed (2 Kgs 16:17).

Although Solomon's temple and Moses' tabernacle differ in so many respects, some later priestly scribes seemed to be obliged to bring them closer together literarily. They introduced into 1 Kings 8 that somewhat strange idea that not only the ark, on which the Dtr inauguration report was focussed (vv. 1, 3–4, 5–9), but also the tabernacle, the tent of meeting and all its holy devices, were brought

---

5 For such an appraisal see Albertz (2012/15: 2:24, 142–85).
6 The proposed dates vary between the time of Solomon, such as Noth (1968: 106), and the period of exile, such as van Seters (1997: 56–7).
7 There is no reason for the supposition that the word *pāroket* in 1 Kgs 6:21 should be added, *pace* Rudolph (1955: 204–5) and others. |
8 The outer bronze altar is missing in the building report for reasons unknown; nevertheless, it is presupposed in 1 Kgs 8:64; cf. 2 Kgs 16:14, 15.

up into Solomon's temple. Verse 4aα₂βb, however, is clearly secondarily intruded.[9] The practical difficulties – where to appropriately store all these planks, beams, stands and rolls of textiles from the tabernacle in the rooms of Solomon's temple without disrupting its own service – remain unsolved.[10] It is not just by chance that the tabernacle is never mentioned again in the book of Kings. Those priestly scribes, however, inserted some other additions in order to bring the inauguration of Solomon's temple in contact with the mythic past told in the Pentateuch: interpreting the term 'elders of Israel' in v. 1 they record the fact that 'all the heads of tribes and the chiefs of the families of the Israelites' were present at the inauguration of the temple, a description similar to that used for the tabernacle's inauguration (Num. 7:2).[11] For similar reasons they changed the term 'all Israel' (כל־ישראל) in 1 Kgs 8:5, often used in the DtrH (cf. 4:1, 7; 5:27; 8:62, 65), to 'the whole congregation of Israel' (כל־עדת ישראל) in order to be reminiscent of the people of the foundation period in its priestly perspective (cf. Exod. 12:3, 47; Lev. 4:13). Therefore, it is highly probable that the additional | dating of Solomon's temple building from 1 Kgs 6:1* in the 480th year after the exodus of the Israelites from Egypt does not come from the Deuteronomistic historian as often thought (see, e.g., Noth 1968: 110; Fritz 1996: 68–9), but from the same late priestly scribes, who intend to connect the Jerusalem temple with the mythic past of the Pentateuch.[12] To this past belongs a short theophany event, where YHWH entered the erected tabernacle in the form of a cloud and filled it with his glory (Exod. 40:34–35). Thus the late priestly scribes included a similar event in their revision of the inauguration report (1 Kgs 8:10–11), doubling the divine promises for Solomon's temple of 9:1–3 already given in the DtrH:[13] after the priests had

---

9 In 1 Kgs 8:3 only the priests are regarded as carriers of the ark, while in v. 4b the Levites are mentioned next to the priests as carriers of all the holy equipment, because the former were commissioned to do so in Num. 4. Without the intrusion in v. 4* (from 'and the tent of meeting' onwards) the plot becomes clear: gathered by the king, the elders of Israel came, and the priests picked up the ark (v. 3) and brought up the ark together (beginning of v. 4), while Solomon and the assembled people offered sacrifices in front of it (v. 5).

10 Although Friedman (1980: 241–8) tried hard to find a technical solution, Hurowitz (1995) made a compelling case for rejecting it.

11 The terminology used in 1 Kgs 8:1 does not exactly agree with the typical priestly terms of the Pentateuch; the closest parallels can be found in its late priestly layers (Num. 30:2; 36:1). |

12 The dating follows stylistically exactly those priestly dating formulas of the books of Exodus and Numbers, cf. Exod. 19:1; Num. 33:38, cf. Exod. 16:1; Num. 1:1; 9:1. Thus, Achenbach (2007: 252) has appropriately assigned it to his theocratic editions.

13 To create a frame together with 1 Kgs 9:1–3 a divine promise was inserted in 6:11–13 by an editor, who uses Dtr language, but who refers to the priestly topic that YHWH will dwell among the Israelites (cf. Exod. 25:8; 29:45–46). The passage is still missing in Chronicles and LXX, but presupposed by Josephus (*Ant.* 8.125–26). Thus, it must be very late.

left the temple, it was filled by a cloud and divine glory so that they could not carry out their service. Thus Solomon's temple received the same visible confirmation of God's presence as had been given to Moses' tabernacle.[14]

What is the reason for this rather strange combination and parallelization of two sanctuary passages of the Hebrew Bible? What is the force behind it? It has nothing to do with a mutual adaptation. Only the tabernacle texts from the Pentateuch show an impact on the report on Solomon's temple building, not vice versa. Although invented they seem to have become powerful, probably a result of the authorization and implementation of the Pentateuch in the early fourth century BCE. Moses' tabernacle, as one of the most important institutions of Israel's foundation period, became so authoritative that some late Jerusalem priests felt compelled to connect their temple to it in some way. The relation to Moses, which the Dtr historian had already established via the Decalogue tablets of the ark (1 Kgs 8:9; Deut. 10:1–5), was no longer sufficient for them to defend the legitimacy and reputation of the Jerusalem temple.[15] |

3 The Jerusalem Temple in Chronicles – as a Right Follower of the Tabernacle

The authors of the books of Chronicles already presuppose the late priestly revisions in the books of Kings (cf. 2 Chron. 5:2, 5, 11–14),[16] but they were dissatisfied with them: How could the tabernacle be brought convincingly into the Jerusalem temple, if it had never been mentioned and honoured before?[17] Thus, in their

---

14 Since the shorter report of the LXX in 3 Kgdms 8:1–11 presupposes the main late priestly additions in vv. 4, 10–11, it cannot represent an older text tradition as sometimes thought; for details see Van der Keulen (2005: 151–63).

15 A similar late priestly alignment to the canonized Pentateuch can be found in the book of Joshua; see Albertz (2007). It also mentions the tent of meeting in Josh. | 18:1; 19:51, erected in Shilo. Since this Joshua revision is more interested in the High Priest Eleazar as guarantor of a just land distribution than in the tabernacle and differs from the terminology of the people's leaders used in 1 Kgs 8:1 (see Josh. 14:1; 19:51; 21:1; cf. Num. 32:28), it does not seem to come from the same authors as the late priestly revision of 1 Kings 6–8. In any case, the different late priestly groups did not intend the edition of an Enneateuch; likewise Achenbach (2007: 253), although he did not distinguish between them.

16 Only the reference to the exodus in 1 Kgs 6:1 is missing in 2 Chron. 3:2, because the Chroniclers generally neglected this date of Israel's foundation myth in order to emphasize the crucial importance of the David and Solomon period; see Kegler (1989). Instead, they refer in 2 Chron. 3:1 to another element of Israel's mythic past: Abrahams offering at Moriah in Gen. 22:2.

17 In the priestly revised DtrH the tabernacle is forgotten after Josh. 19:51. The mention of it in 1 Sam. 2:22bβ is still missing in the LXX and 4QSam[a] and seems to be a very late addition. |

new work the Chroniclers first constructed an unbroken historical continuity between Moses' tabernacle and Solomon's temple. From its beginning onwards they made clear that there was a regular cult at the tabernacle on the high place of Gibeon – besides a smaller cult at David's tent for the ark in Jerusalem (1 Chron. 16:1–38; 2 Chron. 1:4) – before Solomon built the temple (1 Chron. 6:17; 16:39–41; 21:29; 2 Chron. 1:3–6). Thus, it became logical that Moses' tabernacle was integrated into this temple together with the ark (5:5). Secondly, the Chroniclers adjusted the preparations for the temple building to those of the tabernacle: the inspired David presented a model (*tabnît*) of the temple to his son (1 Chron. 28:11) as God had shown it to Moses for the tabernacle (Exod. 25:9, 40). The temple was no longer financed only by the state as in 1 Kings 5–7 (cf. 1 Chron. 29:2), but also by private donations from David (29:3–5a) and the representatives of the people (vv. 6–9). Typical for the tabernacle texts is the call for donations (Exod. 25:2–8; 35:4–19) enthusiastically followed by all the people (35:20–36:7). Such a call is imitated in 1 Chron. 29:5b. Thus, the Chroniclers' account of 1 Chronicles 29 looks like an adjustment to the wilderness scenario under the conditions of statehood. |

The authors of the books of Chronicles surpassed their priestly forerunners in adjusting thirdly Solomon's temple to the tabernacle even in terminological and architectural concerns. Thus, in 1 Chron. 28:11 they called the holiest inner part of the temple the 'shrine of expiation' (*bêt hak-kapporet*), using the technical term from Exod. 25:17–22, as if the cult symbol for divine presence and expiating power conceptualized here and in Lev. 16:2 had really been present there.[18] Moreover, they introduced an inner curtain into Solomon's temple (2 Chron. 3:14) to separate the holy of the holies from the holy main room. Not only did they use the same term *pāroket* for this, as in the tabernacle text (Exod. 26:31, 33, 35), but they also described it as having been made from identical luxurious materials. In preparation for this innovation they broadened the skills of the craftsman Hiram from Tyre – called Huram-Abi here – a famous expert of bronze work in 1 Kgs 7:13–47, to all kinds of handicraft, including working with precious textile materials (2 Chron. 2:6, 13), thus putting him on a par with Bezalel, the leading craftsman and artist of the tabernacle (Exod. 31:1–5; 35:30–33; cf. 2 Chron. 1:5). We are not sure whether in the time of Chroniclers during the last half of the fourth or the early third century BCE the Jerusalem temple was actually provided with an inner curtain[19] as evidenced in later times.[20] But taking into consideration

---

18 In their description of the holy of the holies (2 Chron. 3:8–13), however, the Chroniclers did not follow the concept of Exod. 25:17–22 but that of the *Vorlage* 1 Kgs 6:23–28.

19 This was supposed by Rudolph (1955: 204–5) and Japhet (2003: 53).

20 Cf. 1 Macc. 4:51; Josephus, *B.J.* 5.219; Heb. 6:19; 9:3; 10:20. |

that the authors explicitly mention doors between the two inner rooms (4:22b), where 1 Kgs 7:50 only speaks of door-hinges, the idea of an additional curtain inspired by the example of the tabernacle would seem to be rather a new architectural concept to be realized later. Finally the Chroniclers further extended the inauguration of the temple in accordance with the tabernacle scenario, when they described not only how the completed temple was accepted by God (2 Chron. 5:11–14; cf. 1 Kgs 8:10–11), but also how the first prayers and offerings were answered by him through a further theophany (2 Chron. 7:1–3): the offerings were consumed by a heavenly fire as in Lev. 9:24a and the temple was so impressively filled with God's glory (cf. v. 23) that all people fell down and praised YHWH (cf. v. 24b).

Thus, the authors of the books of Chronicles invested a lot of energy not only in relating but to almost identifying the Jerusalem temple with the sanctuary of Israel's famous mythic past. In order to bring the two together as closely as possible, they added to the former specific items | from the latter, such as the inner curtain, or largely removed from the former what was missing from the latter, such as the bronze trolleys (2 Chron. 4:6, 14). Even in those cases where the number of devices differs, such as the ten lamp stands in Solomon's temple (4:7), the Chroniclers assured that they would accord to the law (vv. 7, 20). There can be no doubt that, for the Chroniclers, the tabernacle texts of the Pentateuch constituted the decisive norm to which they felt obliged to align their report of the foundation and inauguration of Jerusalem's temple. But why were they so eager? An answer may be given by 2 Chron. 29:6, where the Chroniclers once more took up one of the two old terms for the tabernacle, *miškān*, to denote the temple of Jerusalem just at the time, when King Hezekiah reopened it and invited all Israel, including the population of the former Northern Kingdom, to participate in the cult of Jerusalem. Thus, in aligning Jerusalem's temple as closely as possible with Moses' tabernacle, the Chroniclers intended to bestow upon their sanctuary the highest degree of legitimacy and authority in the eyes of the Samarians. We know that the Samarians had also accepted the Pentateuch as their Holy Scripture; and if we trust a much later note from Josephus (*Ant.* 18.85), the Samarians likewise legitimated their own sanctuary on Mount Gerizim by referring to vessels from Moses' tabernacle that were buried next to it. Thus, there were competing claims to the mythic past making this even more powerful. Therefore, the Chroniclers worked hard to prove that their temple in Jerusalem was the rightful successor to the normative tabernacle of Moses, that is, the only legitimate sanctuary of YHWH.

4 The Appearance of Jerusalem Temples – Changed by the Tabernacle

As time passed the tabernacle texts of the Pentateuch not only influenced increasingly other literary concepts of the Jerusalem temple, but also changed the real appearance of later temple buildings in Jerusalem. The most impressive change was the installation of a coloured outer curtain at the entrance to the sanctuary. The tabernacle texts envision such a curtain (*māsāk*) at the entrance to the main holy room, made 'from finely woven linen, embroidered with violet, purple, and scarlet' and hung on five columns (Exod. 26:36–37). It is less artistic than the inner curtain (*pāroket*) dividing the main room from the holy of the holies (vv. 31–35), but still provides the tabernacle with an impressive appearance in spite of its mobile construction. An even more impressive outer curtain of tremendous size (55 times 16 cubits) is certainly testified | for the Herodian temple of Jerusalem, installed within the vestibule before the golden doors of the main hall. Josephus describes it as 'a Babylonian curtain, embroidered with blue, and fine linen, and scarlet, and purple, and of a texture that was truly wonderful' (*B.J.* 5.211–112), which is clearly reminiscent of the tabernacle texts. Josephus describes such an installation of wooden doors covered by a curtain already existing at Solomon's temple (*Ant.* 8.75), but this seems to be clearly an anachronism; according to its oldest description Solomon's building only had decorated wooden doors and no curtains at all (1 Kgs 6:31–35). Even in the Chronistic description an outer curtain is still missing. The references that the entrance of the Second Temple was covered with a curtain come from the second century BCE (Sir. 50:5;[21] 1 Macc. 1:22; 4:51; *Ant.* 12.318) and later (*Let. Arist.* § 85; *Ant.* 14.107) (cf. Légasse 1980). A possible hint that an outer curtain for the temple obtained more importance already during the second half of the third century BCE may be given by the Septuagint. While their translators generally use the term καταπέτασμα for both curtains[22] of the tabernacle (Exod. 26:31, 33–35, 37 etc.),[23] they speak once of an ἐπίσπαστρον, where the outer curtain is introduced (v. 36). This term, used in one

---

21 Since the High Priest Simon becomes visible to the congregation, the curtain of the temple, by which he leaves, can only be the outer one, although the Hebrew text uses the expression *bêt hap-pāroket* 'house of the curtain', the term for the inner one. The Hebrew expression shows that curtains are regarded as distinct features of the Jerusalem temple at the beginning of the second century BCE.

22 The term means verbatim 'a piece of hanging material serving to conceal what is behind it'.

23 The Vaticanus even mentions a καταπέτασμα of the inner temple court in 3 Kgdms 6:36a, while Exod. 27:16 uses the term κάλυμμα for this type of curtain. The text, however, seems to be defective; see Van der Keulen 2005: 134–5.

of the Greek inscriptions from Delos, denotes "'un article comprenant un système à cordon de tirage", du type qui ornait l'entrée des sanctuaires grecs' (see Légasse 1980: 571). Thus, the Greek translators – by interpreting the normative tabernacle texts – seem to intend the authorization of a bigger curtain installation for their contemporary temple.[24] |

References to the inner curtain are fewer, probably because this one could not be seen from outside. Josephus already presupposed it inside the Solomonic temple, where it separated – along with a wooden door – the most holy chamber from the rest (*Ant.* 8.71–72). This is, however, a back projection. After being conceptually introduced by the Chroniclers as an innovation (2 Chron. 3:14), the inner curtain also seems to have been installed in the Second Temple during the second century BCE (1 Macc. 4:51; *Ant.* 12.318; cf. 14.107). The best piece of evidence comes from the Herodian temple, where Josephus no longer mentions any wooden wall or doors next to it (*B.J.* 5.219).[25] This indicated that an important relic of Solomonic architecture was completely removed in favour of the textile structure of the tabernacle. Thus, it took 300–500 years for an invented text, which had become part of the mythic past, to obtain so much power that it even changed parts of the existing reality.

5 Concluding Remarks

This short case study has shown that literary passages of the Hebrew Bible, which are evidently unhistorical, can develop an astonishing power that shapes not only the further literary history of other biblical passages but also elements of the historical reality. The priestly tabernacle texts from the book of Exodus are a good example of this. The dynamic power has to do with the decision made in the Judean and Samarian communities of the fourth century BCE to accept a bigger part of their literary tradition, the *tôrat Mošeh*, as authoritative. By doing so, they did not only concede that the concepts and rules of the Pentateuch should

---

24 This is one of the few examples where a Pentateuchal sanctuary text is changed to suit contemporary interests. Another example is the description of the tabernacle by Josephus, where he adds a fine linen veil to be drawn over the entrance in order to protect the outer curtain from bad weather. From this Josephus even deduces a later custom for the period after the temple was built (*Ant.* 3.128–129), but as far as I see he never came back to this topic. |
25 The juxtaposition of the wooden doors and the inner curtain, which might have been a compromise between the older Jerusalem temple architecture and the structure of the tabernacle found in the Second Temple during the Hellenistic period, stands possibly behind later Rabbinic disputes, whether the sanctuary had one or two veils for separating the holy of the holies from the rest (see *Yom.* 5:1 and Légasse 1980: 580–2). |

have more or less influence on their lifestyle, but they also obtained a powerful basis, on which they could found their theological claims and the legitimacy of their cultic institutions. Because of this authoritative textual corpus priests and other responsible persons felt obliged to change the appearance of the Jerusalem temple in order to align it with aspects of Moses' famous tabernacle. Thus, we should perhaps not classify all texts from Genesis to 2 Kings as 'mythic past' on the same level because of their common contrast to modern historiography. Some of them, especially those of the | Pentateuch, possess more 'mythical dynamic' than others. I agree with the statement Thomas Thompson made in his dissertation: 'In fact, we can say that the faith of Israel is not an historical faith, in the sense of a faith based on historical event; it is rather a faith within history' (see Thompson 1974: 328–9). I would like just to emphasize that this faith – expressed by biblical texts – cannot only change the mind and behaviour of people, but is also able in some way to change historical reality.

Bibliography

Achenbach, R. (2007), 'Der Pentateuch: Seine theokratischen Bearbeitungen und Josua – 2 Könige', in T. Römer and K. Schmid (eds), *Les dernières rédactions du Pentateuque, de l'Hexateuque et de l'Enneateuque*, 225–53, BEThL 203, Leuven: University Press and Peeters.

Albertz, R. (1994), *A History of Israelite Religion in the Old Testament Period*, 2 vols, Louisville, KY: Westminster John Knox Press.

Albertz, R. (2007), 'The Canonical Alignment of the Book of Joshua', in O. Lipschits, G. N. Knoppers and R. Albertz (eds), *Judah and the Judeans in the Fourth Century B.C.E.*, 287–303, Winona Lake, IN: Eisenbrauns.

Albertz, R. (2012/2015), *Exodus*, 2 vols, ZBK.AT 2/1–2, Zürich: Theologischer Verlag Zürich.

Blum, E. (2015), 'Historiographie oder Dichtung? Zur Eigenart alttestamentlicher Geschichtsüberlieferung', (repr.) in *Grundfragen der historischen Exegese*, 31–54, FAT 95, Tübingen: Mohr Siebeck.

Friedman, R. E. (1980), 'The Tabernacle in the Temple', *BA*, 43: 241–8.

Fritz, V. (1996), *Das erste Buch der Könige*, ZBK.AT 10/1, Zürich: Theologischer Verlag Zürich.

Houtman, C. (1993–2002), *Exodus*, 4 vols, Kampen: KOK; Leuven: Peeters.

Hurowitz, V. A. (1995), 'The Form and Fate of the Tabernacle: Reflections on a Recent Proposal', *JQR*, 86: 127–51.

Japhet, S. (2003), *2 Chronik*, HThKAT, Freiburg: Herder.

Kegler, J. (1989), 'Das Zurücktreten der Exodustradition in den Chronikbüchern', in R. Albertz, F. W. Golka and J. Kegler (eds), *Schöpfung und Befreiung: Für Claus Westermann zum 80. Geburtstag*, 54–66, Stuttgart: Calwer.

Légasse, S. (1980), 'Les voiles du temple de Jérusalem: essai de parcours historique', *RB*, 87: 560–89.

Noth, M. (1968), *Könige: 1. Teilband: 1. Könige 1–16*, BK IX/1, Neukirchen-Vluyn: Neukirchener.

Rudolph, W. (1955), *Chronikbücher*, HAT I/21, Tübingen: Mohr Siebeck.

Thompson, T. L. (1974), *The Historicity of the Patriarchal Narratives: The Quest for the Historical Abraham*, BZAW 133, Berlin: de Gruyter.

Thompson, T. L. (1992), *Early History of the Israelite People: From the Written and Archaeological Sources*, SHANE 4, Leiden: E. J. Brill.

Thompson, T. L. (1999), *The Mythic Past: Biblical Archaeology and the Myth of Israel*, New York: Basic Books.

Van der Keulen, P. S. F. (2005), *Two Versions of Solomon Narrative: An Inquiry into the Relationship between MT 1 Kgs. 2–11 and LXX 3 Reg. 2–11*, VTSup 104, Leiden: E. J. Brill. |

Van Seters, J. (1975), *Abraham in History and Tradition*, New Haven: Yale University Press.

Van Seters, J. (1997), 'Solomon's Temple: Fact and Ideology in Biblical History and Near Eastern Historiography', *CBQ* 59: 45–57.

Wellhausen, J. (1927), *Prolegomena zur Geschichte Israels*, 6th ed., Berlin: Reimer (repr. Berlin: de Gruyter, 2001).

Westermann, C. (1975), *Genesis 12–50*, EdF 48, Darmstadt: Wissenschaftliche Buchgesellschaft.

Westermann, C. (1981), *Genesis. 2. Teilband, Genesis 12–36*, BK I/2, Neukirchen-Vluyn: Neukirchener.

Wette, W. M. L. de (1806/7), *Beiträge zur Einleitung in das Alte Testament*, 2 vols, Halle: Schimmelpfennig (repr.: Darmstadt: Wissenschaftliche Buchgesellschaft, 1971).

On the Structure and Formation of the Book of Deutero-Isaiah

At the end of the last century, when I wrote my book on the history and literature of the Babylonian exile, which included – among other issues – a study on Deutero-Isaiah,[1] I was not aware that Joseph Blenkinsopp had prepared a commentary on Isaiah 40–55 nearly at the same time (published 2002),[2] which was part of the enormous project of interpreting the entire book of Isaiah in three volumes.[3] I am happy to be given the opportunity to appreciate this sophisticated and thoughtful commentary, which I think is one of the best written since the commentary of Bernhard Duhm.[4] For me, as one who tries to resist the pressure of specializing in our field, Joseph Blenkinsopp is an outstanding example of a learned Old Testament scholar. He has a competent overview of all research fields in scholarship, not only of all the books of the Hebrew Bible, including their ancient Near Eastern background and their | *Wirkungsgeschichte*,[5] but also of the historiography of all periods including archaeology.[6] Therefore, it is a great privilege for me to contribute some ideas about the structure and formation of the book of Deutero-Isaiah to this volume in his honor.

1 Basic Insights in the Structure of Isaiah 40–55

Blenkinsopp discussed the structure of Deutero-Isaiah in some length.[7] He was aware of many different proposals, but wisely did not follow one fixed scheme.

---

1 See Rainer Albertz, *Israel in Exile: The History and Literature of the Sixth Century B.C.E.*, Studies in Biblical Literature 3 (Atlanta: Society of Biblical Literature, 2003), pp. 376–438. The German original is titled: Rainer Albertz, *Die Exilszeit: 6. Jahrhundert v. Chr.*, Biblische Enzyklopädie 7 (Stuttgart: Kohlhammer, 2001).
2 See Joseph Blenkinsopp, *Isaiah 40–55: A New Translation with Introduction and Commentary*, The Anchor Yale Bible 19A (New Haven and London: Yale University Press, 2002).
3 See Joseph Blenkinsopp, *Isaiah 1–39: A New Translation with Introduction and Commentary*, The Anchor Yale Bible 19 (New Haven and London: Yale University Press, 2000) and Joseph Blenkinsopp, *Isaiah 56–66: A New Translation with Introduction and Commentary*, The Anchor Yale Bible 19B (New York, London, Toronto, Sidney, and Auckland: Doubleday, 2003).
4 See Bernhard Duhm, *Das Buch Jesaia*, 5th ed., Göttinger Handkommentar zum Alten Testament III/1 (Göttingen: Vandenhoeck & Ruprecht, 1968). The first edition was published in 1892. |
5 Cf., with regard to the book of Isaiah, the interesting study of Joseph Blenkinsopp, *Opening the Sealed Book: Interpretations of the Book of Isaiah in Late Antiquity* (Grand Rapids and Cambridge, U.K.: Eerdmans, 2006).
6 Cf. for example, Joseph Blenkinsopp, "The Age of the Exile" in *The Biblical World*, vol. 1, ed. John Barton (London and New York: Routledge, 2002), pp. 416–39.
7 *Isaiah 40–55*, pp. 59–61.

https://doi.org/10.1515/9783111202228-010

He rightly maintained, against Kiesow,[8] that the two parts of the book, the Jacob/Israel section (Isa 40–48) and the Zion/Jerusalem section (Isa 49–55), conceptually belong together.[9] Therefore the call to flee from Babylon (48:20–21) constitutes just the end of the first section, but not an end of an earlier book. Interestingly, he observed that the second section is structured by an alternation between Servant and Zion passages, but suggested that the last sequence, the fourth servant song (52:13–53:12) and promises for Zion (54:1–17a), "might ... appear to have been added subsequently."[10]

Perhaps one could emphasize a little bit more explicitly than Blenkinsopp that the joyous report of YHWH's arrival at Zion in 52:7–12, which runs parallel to 48:20–21 at its end, constitutes a first epilogue, where several visions of the prologue in 40:1–11, the announcement of good news and YHWH's return to Zion, become true. Because of this obvious *inclusio* already Elliger concluded that 52:7–12 may have constituted the end of the book at an earlier stage.[11] This view, which is now shared by several recent scholars,[12] is supported by the | observation that only Isa 40:1–52:7 are structured by so-called "eschatological hymns" (42:10–13; 44:23; 45:8; 48:20–21; 49:13; 52:9–10) into meaningful segments.[13]

---

8 Cf. Klaus Kiesow, *Exodustexte im Jesajabuch: Literarkritische und motivgeschichtliche Analysen*, Orbis et Biblicus Orientalis 24 (Fribourg and Göttingen: Universitätsverlag and Vandenhoeck & Ruprecht, 1979), p. 165.

9 Following Hans-Jürgen Hermisson, *Studien zur Prophetie und Weisheit*, Forschungen zum Alten Testament 23 (Tübingen: Mohr-Siebeck, 1998), pp. 117–23, 148–49.

10 *Isaiah 40–55*, p. 61.

11 See Karl Elliger, *Deuterojesaja in seinem Verhältnis zu Tritojesaja*, Beiträge zur Wissenschaft vom Alten und Neuen Testament 63 (Stuttgart: Kohlhammer, 1933), pp. 265–67.

12 Thus, Odil Hannes Steck, *Gottesknecht und Zion: Gesammelte Aufsätze zu Deuteroje | saja*, Forschungen zum Alten Testament 4 (Tübingen: Mohr-Siebeck, 1992), p. 125; Reinhard Gregor Kratz, *Kyros im Deuterojesaja-Buch: Redaktionsgeschichtliche Untersuchungen zu Entstehung und Theologie von Jesaja 40–55*, Forschungen zum Alten Testament 1 (Tübingen: Mohr-Siebeck, 1991), p. 217; Jürgen van Oorschot, *Von Babel zum Zion: Eine literarkritische und redaktionsgeschichtliche Untersuchung*, Beihefte zur Zeitschrift für die alttestamentliche Wissenschaft 206 (Berlin and New York: de Gruyter, 1993), p. 345; Ulrich Berges, *Das Buch Jesaja: Komposition und Endgestalt*, Herders Biblische Studien 16 (Freiburg, Basel, Vienna, Barcelona, Rome, and New York: Herder, 1998), p. 549; Jürgen Werlitz, *Redaktion und Komposition: Zur Rückfrage hinter die Endgestalt von Jesaja 40–55*, Bonner Biblische Beiträge 122 (Berlin and Bodenheim: Philo, 1999), pp. 319–23. This view is also indicated by Blenkinsopp, *Isaiah 40–55*, p. 372.

13 Cf. Roy F. Melugin, *The Formation of Isaiah 40–55*, Beihefte zur Zeitschrift für die alttestamentliche Wissenschaft 141 (Berlin and New York: de Gruyter, 1976), pp. 90–175. Isa 51:3 is just a fragment of such a hymn at best; it will prove to be a late insertion; see below. Isa 54:1–2 is no religious hymn at all, but a call to joy, *pace* Claus Westermann, *Das Buch Jesaja: Kapitel 40–66*, 5th ed., Das Alte Testament Deutsch 19 (Göttingen and Zürich: Vandenhoeck & Ruprecht, 1986), pp. 19–20.

It is generally acknowledged that the present book of Deutero-Isaiah comes to its end in Isa 55:13. Among others, Kiesow has convincingly shown that 55:6–13 constitutes a second epilogue, whose praise of YHWH's creative word in 55:10–11 refers back to 40:6–8* of the prologue, where the eternity of the divine word is reflected.[14] These verses constitute an outer *inclusio*. From these observations Elliger concluded that an earlier Deutero-Isaiah collection (40:1–52:7*) was expanded by the fourth servant song (52:13–53:12) first, and by chapters 54–55 later. He regarded Trito-Isaiah as responsible for these later editions of the book.[15] This last suggestion became less convincing, since it turned out that Isa 56–66 do not originate from a single person, but constitute a multi-layered composite in itself. His basic insight, however, that the doubled structure of the book points to two major editions of the book of Deutero-Isaiah, remains true; likewise that the second edition generally shows a closer relationship with Isa 56–66 than the first. |

2 Consequences for Reconstructing the Formation of Isaiah 40–55

In his commentary, Joseph Blenkinsopp deals with the formation of Isa 40–55 in some detail.[16] After having referred to the theories of some scholars, Blenkinsopp identified a "current confused situation" and maintained that "our text exhibits a relatively high level of coherence,"[17] especially in chapters 40–48, where he noted only a few possible additions.[18] With regard to chapters 49–55 he accepted the evidence of a Trito-Isaianic editor, who has added the last three servant songs (49:1–6; 50:4–9; 52:13–52:12) including the comments to the first two (49:7, 9–12; 50:10–11). He also added some smaller passages in their immediate surroundings (50:1–3; 51:1–6) and some sporadic insertions in chapters 54–55.[19] Thus, Blenkinsopp sensitively noticed different styles and concepts in such passages,[20] but he hesitated to go further in order to differentiate and classify these insertions. That may be wise for writing a commentary, which will still be read when most of the recent redactional theories will have been forgotten.

---

14 Kiesow, *Exodustexte*, pp. 65–66, 165.
15 Cf. Elliger, *Verhältnis*, pp. 265–71. |
16 See Blenkinsopp, *Isaiah 40–55*, pp. 69–81.
17 For both citations see Blenkinsopp, *Isaiah 40–55*, p. 73.
18 So Isa 46:12–13; 48:16b, 17–19, 22; see Blenkinsopp, *Isaiah 40–55*, pp. 73–74, 80.
19 For example Isa 54:17b; 55:13b; see Blenkinsopp, *Isaiah 40–55*, pp. 74, 80, 366.
20 Especially in Isa 48; cf. Blenkinsopp, *Isaiah 40–55*, pp. 288–90, going beyond the introductory remarks.

The current situation, however, is not as confused as Blenkinsopp has stated.[21] Nearly all proposals for reconstructing the formation of the book which have been recently published converge – in spite of all differences in detail – on the result that there is ample evidence to distinguish two major editions of the book of Deutero-Isaiah, an earlier one, which was restricted to Isa 40:1–52:12* and a later one, which comprised Isa 40:1–55:13*. What was identified as "Jerusalem redaction" by van Oorschot (Dtjes Z) in the earlier edition, substantially corresponds to Berges's "Golah redaction" and "first Jerusalem redaction" and Werlitz's "book edition."[22] Even the "supplementary Cyrus stratum" reconstructed by Kratz is similar.[23] The four scholars even agree on dating; they all propose the origin of the earlier edition around the year 520 B.C.E., although they concede the incorporation of older material. With regard to the later book edition, three of these scholars argue for a later | redaction during the fifth century, be it the "Servant Israel stratum" of Kratz, the "secondary Zion stratum" of van Oorschot, or the "second Jerusalem redaction" of Berges.

Among these recent attempts to reconstruct the earlier edition of the book of Deutero-Isaiah, the methodological reflections of Jürgen Werlitz are of major importance.[24] Werlitz connects the diachronic literary critical and redaction historical approach, on the one hand, with a synchronic composition critical approach, on the other hand. In his view, the composition criticism must provide a constant frame of reference and corrective for redaction criticism, and vice versa. A satisfactory literary and redactional study must yield a book with a distinct beginning and end, a clear structure, and a meaningful sequence of texts. By this methodological innovation, the redaction critical results can be controlled much better and provided with a higher degree of probability. Following these methodological lines, Werlitz was able to reconstruct a first book edition, which runs from a reduced prologue (40:1–2, 3–5*) through the Jacob/Israel and the Zion/Jerusalem portions to an epilogue (52:7–12).[25] Both portions are linked by the second servant song (49:1–6), including its commentary (49:8–12). The entire book is structured by the eschatological hymns in two introductions (40:12–31; 49:14–50:2*) and five segments (41:1–42:13; 42:14–44:23; 44:24–48:21; 49:1–13*; 50–52*). Interestingly, Werlitz has recognized that the structuring elements – the prologue, epilogue, eschatological hymns, and the commentaries on the first two servant songs – are all editorial. By these, the prophetic editor not only brought the older material

---

21 For a more detailed study of the research history see Albertz, *Israel*, pp. 378–93.
22 See the schemes or summaries mentioned above in note 12.
23 Kratz, *Kyros*, p. 217, mainly differs as far as he included also the fourth servant song into this stratum and suggested Isa 55:3–5 as a possible end. But there is no need to go beyond 52:12. |
24 See Werlitz, *Redaktion*, pp. 237–82.
25 See his summary, Werlitz, *Redaktion*, pp. 319–23.

into a meaningful sequence, but also actualized it for a new purpose. According to Werlitz, this older material also includes the first three servant songs and parts of the polemics against the idols, because they are firmly anchored in the composition. Thus, the composition critical approach detected the original compositional setting of some of those texts, which, since Bernhard Duhm, were often regarded as secondary.[26]

3 A Possible Reconstruction of the Formation of Isaiah 40–55

Along the methodological lines elaborated by Jürgen Werlitz, I presented a reconstruction of the book of Deutero-Isaiah, which comprised the first three | editorial stages, the first book edition (40:1–52:12*: DtIE[1]), the appendix of the fourth servant song (52:13–53:12), and the second edition of the book (40:1–55:13*: DtIE[2]).[27] These strata include about 87 percent of the present text. The book of this stage, however, was later expanded by a number of insertions, which I did not deal with before in detail, because my earlier publication was restricted to the exilic period. Thus, I would like to take the opportunity to complete my view of the formation of Isa 40–55 here.

3.1 The First Edition of the Book of Deutero-Isaiah (DtIE[1])

The first book edition, which was already reconstructed and described elsewhere in detail,[28] consists of the following passages:

DtIE[1]
Isa 40:1–2, 3aβ–5ba, 9–11, 12–31*; 41:1–42:16, 18–19a, 20, 22–24aα$_1$, 25; 43:1–44:8, 10–17, 20, 21–24, 26b–28; 45:1–8, 11a, 12–13ba, 14–15,[29] 18–20a, 21–25; 46:1–7, 9–13; 47:2, 5–8a, 10–15; 48:1aba, 3, 6–7a, 8a, 11aα, 11b–16a, 20–21; 49:1–6, 8–21*; 50:1–2, 4–9; 51:4–5, 9–10, 17–19; 52:1–2, 7–12

---

26 See for example Duhm, *Jesaia*, pp. 14–15; Westermann, *Jesaja*, pp. 27–28. |
27 See Albertz, *Israel*, pp. 393–438.
28 See Albertz, *Israel*, pp. 393–425.
29 In contrast to the table in Albertz, *Exilszeit*, p. 297, I include also the difficult verses Isa 45:14–15 in the first edition. They seem to reflect – like 43:3b–4 – the conquest of Egypt by Cambyses (525 B.C.E.); for additional reasons, see Rainer Albertz, "Loskauf umsonst? Die Befreiungsvorstellungen bei Deuterojesaja," in *Freiheit und Recht*, ed. Christof Hardmeier, Rainer Kessler and Andreas Ruwe (Gütersloh: Chr. Kaiser and Gütersloher Verlag, 2003), pp. 360–79, esp. pp. 366–75. In the English edition (Albertz, *Israel*, p. 398), these verses are already included (see also p. 415). But in the table on p. 398 the misprint of the first line (40:12–1) should be corrected to 40:12–15. |

According to my view, it was written during the years 521–520 B.C.E., after the group of the anonymous prophet, who had preached before among the Babylonian exiles from about 547 B.C.E. onwards, came to Judah in order to bring the good news to Zion that YHWH had decided to show pity to his people, to release his capital and bring the exiles home (40:1–2, 9–11; 52:9–10). The political events in the background are probably the usurpation of Gaumata by Darius I, the following revolts against Darius throughout the empire, especially those in Babylon during the years 522 and 521, and the suppression of these revolts by Darius. Under these conditions, Darius was probably ready to repatriate a loyal group of | Judean exiles around Zerubbabel and Joshua in order to stabilize the western wing of his empire. Against these dramatical historical events, the book describes how the message of comfort – from the first victories of Cyrus to the conquest of Babylon by Darius – extended from Babylonia to Jerusalem through all resistances and disappointments. The book proclaims divine salvation without any conditions, but its probable public recitation was intended to encourage the lethargic and reserved population of Judah to grab the opportunity of salvation and welcome the returnees from Babylonia. As shown elsewhere in detail,[30] this reconstructed edition can be understood as a well-structured, coherent, and meaningful rhetorical unit in a concrete historical situation.

3.2 The Appendix of the Fourth Servant Song

That the fourth servant song (52:13–53:12) has to be regarded as an appendix was already seen by Elliger.[31] As shown by the framing divine speeches in 52:13–15 and 53:11aβ–12 it is a rhetorical unit of its own. The fact that this song follows a call to leave Babylon as does the second one (48:20–21; 49:1–6), which was rightly observed by Blenkinsopp,[32] may be one reason for adding it at this place. There is a link to the given context: the term "arm of YHWH" in 53:1 refers back to 52:10. Thus, the song was composed with knowledge of the final passage of DtIE[1]. Since 49:7, which constitutes a second divine answer to the complaint of the Servant (49:4) and is completed by 49:8–12, directly refers to the beginning of the fourth servant song (cf. 52:15), it serves to link this song with DtIE[1]. Its position indicates that the fourth servant song should be read as a commentary to the second one, especially to the universal salvific task of the Servant mentioned in 49:6. Here, it is not the place to discuss the highly disputed meaning of the fourth

---

30 Cf. Albertz, *Israel*, pp. 404–25.
31 See Elliger, *Verhältnis*, pp. 266–67.
32 Blenkinsopp, *Isaiah 40–55*, p. 74. |

servant song. Considering the given links to 49:1–7 and 52:10, however, one should rather think of a collective understanding: By all his suffering during the exile the Servant Israel has taken on an atoning and salvific function for all the nations. These deep reflections about a possible positive meaning of the distress of exile may come from the years after 515 B.C.E., when Israel's "renewal" had begun but was not yet complete. The author was still a member of the Deutero-Isaiah group, but – as some differences in language and concept show – not the redactor of the DtIE[1]. |

3.3 The Second Edition of the Book of Deutero-Isaiah (DtIE[2])

The author of the second edition of the book (DtIE[2]) added the new chapters Isa 54–55* and tied them to the DtIE[1] through a framework of appeals to hear around the appendix of the fourth servant song (51:1–2, 7–8; 55:1–5). In addition, by inserting 40:6, 8 into the prologue and composing a new epilogue (55:6–13), the editor created a new framework for his entire book (55:10–11), which intended to emphasize the persistence and effectiveness of the divine word in the face of all earthly obstacles. Thus, he sporadically intervened also in the first edition. As explained elsewhere in more detail,[33] DtIE[2] consists of DtIE[1] including its appendix plus probably the following passages:

DtIE[2]
Isa 40:3aα, 6, 8; 44:25–26a; 45:9–10, 11b, 13bβ; 47:3–4, 8b–9; 51:1–2, 7–8, 12–15, 20–23; 52:3; 54:1–17a; 55:1–6, 8–13[34]

The message of the DtIE[2] cannot be unfolded here in detail.[35] But it should be mentioned that the second edition of the book is characterized by a defense of the prophetical message against substantial obstacles and doubts. In the beginning of the fifth century, the reality lagged far behind the enthusiastic message of the Deutero-Isaiah group. It is true that a sizable group of exiles had returned and

---

33 See Albertz, *Israel*, pp. 428–33.

34 In the table of Albertz, *Israel*, p. 429, the verses Isa 45:11a, 13bα have to be corrected to 45:11b, 13bβ. Isaiah 51:12–15 has to be added to the list, because in this divine answer to the lament of 51:9–10, which is secondary with regard to the primary answer in 51:17–19, the warning about fear of human beings, who are transient like grass, reminds one of 40:8, a verse which certainly belongs to DtIE[2]. The gloss in 40:7b, which relates the grass to people, is wrong; the enemies of Israel are meant. Also Oorschot, *Babel*, pp. 253–55, includes the passage in his "secondary Zion stratum."

35 See for more details Albertz, *Israel*, pp. 430–33. |

the temple had been rebuilt, but Jerusalem lay still in ruins until the middle of the fifth century, and several foreign leaders whom the Persians settled in Samaria interfered in Judah (Ezra 4:9–10). With several exhortations, the author of DtIE[2] intended to encourage those faithful adherents, who still waited for the complete fulfillment of the announced salvation, to maintain their hopes against all obstacles, threats and mockeries (51:1–2, 7–8, 12–15; 55:1–5). He never tired of assuring the ruined capital of YHWH's irremovable love (54:4–6, 7–9), of its wonderful reconstruction (54:11–13) and a peaceful existence (54:10, 14–17a). Since the new book edition reveals fear about | new military threats (51:12–13, 20–23; 54:15–17a), it was perhaps prompted by Xerxes' campaigns against Greece (484–479 B.C.E.), which were accompanied by new uprisings of Babylon (cf. 47:3–4, 8b–9). In DtIE[2] the prologue was converted by small intrusions (40:3aα, 6) into a kind of call narrative corresponding to Isa 6:4, 8. Now, the commission of comforting the people and Zion (40:1–2) was interpreted as an explicit annulment of the heavenly judgment of doom, which the prophet Isaiah had experienced (6:9–11). Thus, it may have happened at this stage of redactional history that the enlarged book of Deutero-Isaiah was physically connected with the existing book of Isaiah (roughly Isa 1–32*).

3.4 Alignments with the Book of Trito-Isaiah (DtIT)

After the second book edition, Deutero-Isaiah seems to have been subject only to sporadic insertions or smaller redactions. One group of insertions is characterized by the intention of aligning the book of Deutero-Isaiah with topics that can be found in the book of Trito-Isaiah. The following passages can be ascribed to it:

DtIT
Isa 48:16b; 49:22–23, 24–26; 54:13

The secondary character of 48:16b is generally acknowledged.[36] After a divine oracle, which commissioned an anonymous king – after the fall of Babylon (Isa 47) probably Darius I[37] – to carry through the salvific will of God (48:12–16a), the short self-report of a prophetical figure about his call seems to be out of

---

36 Duhm, *Jesaia*, p. 365; Elliger, *Verhältnis*, pp. 213–15; Oorschot, *Babel*, pp. 277–78; Werlitz, *Redaktion*, p. 275; Blenkinsopp, *Isaiah 40–55*, p. 294; Blenkinsopp, *Isaiah 56–66*, p. 64, among many others.

37 For the thesis that the commission of Cyrus (Isa 41:1–4; 44:24–28; 45:1–7) is tacitly substituted for that of Darius in the DtIE[1] (42:5–9; 45:11a, 12–13abα; 48:12–16a), see Albertz, *Israel*, pp. 399–404, 408–9, 418, and Albertz, "Darius in Place of Cyrus: The First Edition of Deutero-Isaiah (Isaiah 40.1–52.12) in 521 B.C.E.," *Journal for the Study of the Old Testament* 27 no. 3 (2003): pp. 371–83.

place. It may even be an anacoluthon: "And now Adonay-YHWH has sent me, and his spirit ...," as Blenkinsopp considered.[38] The phrase takes up the | presentation of the Servant Israel in 42:1 and clearly refers to the self-presentation of the prophetical Servant in 61:1. The anacoluthon may even have the rhetorical function that the reader should complete it from there in the sense: "and his spirit is laid on me." In my view, the insertion has two intentions: on the one hand, it aims at relating the royal oracle to the prophetical figure, whom we call Trito-Isaiah. It was no longer the Persian king Darius, but the Israelite prophet in the succession of Deutero-Isaiah and his group who would conduct the salvific will of YHWH in the future. On the other hand, the insertion indicates where Trito-Isaiah's promises for Zion (Isa 60–62), which run partly parallel to those of Deutero-Isaiah (49:14–54:17), should be placed in the process of Israel's salvation: just before the return of the prophetical group to Jerusalem (48:20–21).

In the contentious comfort of Zion (49:14–26), the last two passages, 49:22–23 and 49:24–26, probably constitute later additions.[39] In contrast to the announcement of 49:14–21, which belongs to DtIE[1], both small units use the messenger formula in their introduction. They both end with recognition formulas, whose stylistic features (with *waw*-perfect) remind one more of Ezekiel (Ezek 16:62; 22:16; 25:11, 17 passim) than of Deutero-Isaiah (with *lěma'an* and imperfect in 45:3); a similar construction occurs in Trito-Isaiah (60:16). Moreover, 49:22 gives an answer to Zion's question (49:21), although it was only rhetorical, and 49:24–25 imitate the rhetorical question-answer play of 49:14–15 in an artificial and slightly unclear manner. As Elliger already pointed out,[40] the language and motives of the two passages remind one of Trito-Isaiah. The first passage intends to support the hopes in the repopulation of Jerusalem with the notion that YHWH would stimulate the nations by his banner (similar to 62:10) announcing his intentions to bring home the sons and daughters of Zion (49:22). This notion is not totally absent from the DtIE[1] (43:6), but is displayed in detail by Trito-Isaiah (cf. 60:4, 9; 66:20). The idea that kings and queens will serve Zion and its people like vassals (49:23) has its closest parallels in the descriptions of salvation of Trito-

---

38 See Blenkinsopp, *Isaiah 40–55*, p. 294. Nowhere else is the divine spirit an object of God's sending. |

39 Westermann, *Jesaja*, pp. 175–80, regarded Isa 49:14–26 as a compositional unity following the three addressees of complaint, but this was already questioned by Melugin, *Formation*, pp. 148–52. Oorschot, *Babel*, pp. 151–52, 247–48, and Hans-Jürgen Hermisson, *Deuterojesaja, 3. Teilband: Jesaja 49,14–55,13*, Biblischer Kommentar Altes Testament XI/3 (Neukirchen-Vluyn: Neukirchener Verlag, 2007), pp. 17–18, 25, attribute the first passage (49:22–23) to an early book edition, but regarded the second (49:24–26) as clearly secondary. The secondary character of both passages is stressed by Werlitz, *Redaktion*, pp. 308–13.

40 See Elliger, *Verhältnis*, pp. 124–29. |

Isaiah (60:16; 61:5–6; cf. already 49:7). Against the fear that mighty earthly powers might cost YHWH his victory, the | second passage (49:24–26) encourages the audience to believe that YHWH himself will litigate with the nations and save Zion's children. The somewhat cruel notion that YHWH will feed Zion's enemies with their own flesh and make them drunk from their own blood has no parallel at all, but the final recognition formula is a citation of Isa 60:16. It is possible that especially the second passage responds to a similar military threat during the first part of the fifth century B.C.E., like DtIE².

Finally, 54:13 interrupts the report of the wonderful reconstruction of Jerusalem (from DtIE²) by interpreting the precious stones of Zion's gates as its sons, who would all become "pupils of YHWH" and enjoy peace.[41] This idea reminds one of the pupils of the prophet Isaiah (8:16) and the Deutero-Isaiah group (50:4), but is also paralleled by the notion of 61:6 that all inhabitants of restored Judah will become priests and servants of YHWH. Isaiah 54:13 intended to emphasize that not only the city but also its inhabitants would have to be transformed in the direction of a close relationship with the divine, as shown by the prophetic group itself.

It is not quite clear whether all these additions come from the same hand and from the same time, but they all intend to replenish the salvific notions of Deutero-Isaiah with ideas developed by the prophetic circle behind Trito-Isaiah. Since these ideas all are taken from the kernel of this book (Isa 60–62), these alignments must not be much later than DtIE² and probably still belong to the first part of the fifth century B.C.E.

3.5 The Scholastic Redaction (DtIS)

A more coherent reworking of the book happened by the so-called scholastic redaction, which is characterized by a closer relationship to styles and concepts of Deuteronomistic literature and other prophetic books, such as Jeremiah and Ezekiel. This redaction was first discovered by Hans-Christoph Schmitt long ago,[42] but meanwhile can probably be expanded by some other secondary verses. In my view, it comprises the following passages: |

---

41 The verse was regarded as secondary to its context by Oorschot, *Babel*, p. 268. The variant reading of 1QIsa ("your builder" instead of "your sons") can be regarded as an attempt to align the verse a little bit more with its context. Its intrusion also disturbs the *stichoi* of the passage.
42 See Hans-Christoph Schmitt, "Prophetie und Schultheologie im Deuterojesajabuch: Beobachtungen zur Redaktionsgeschichte von Jes 40–55*," *Zeitschrift für die alttestamentliche Wissenschaft* 91, no. 1 (1979): pp. 43–61. Schmitt calls this redaction "schultheologische Bearbeitung." |

DtIS

Isa 42:19b, 21, 24aα₂b; 46:8; 48:1bβ, 2, 4–5, 7b, 8b–10, 11aβ, 17–19; 50:10–11; 55:7

The best evidence for this redaction comes from Isa 48, a chapter which is thoroughly reworked in the course of this redaction.[43] Originally, 48:1–11 was an editorial unit, by which the redactor of DtIE[1] intended to prepare his Judean audience for the surprising message (48:6) that YHWH had decided to commission anew a king with the salvation of his people (48:12–16a), who – after the fall of Babylon (47:1–15*, referred to in 48:1) – could only be Darius I. He would carry through God's salvific will, what Cyrus had only started, but not completed.[44] This preparation for a salvific message was secondarily converted into a penitential sermon:[45] In 48:1bβ, 2, which constitutes a doublet to 48:1abα, the people are accused of referring to Zion and YHWH in a dishonest and immoral way. The delay of fulfilling the given prophetic announcements (48:3) is now secondarily founded on the stiff-necked character of the people (48:4; cf. Ezek 2:4; 3:7), who would rather ascribe the fulfillment to their idols (48:5). The surprising character of the good news (48:6–7a) is interpreted as a divine strategy against the arrogant attitude of the people that they already knew all that the prophets would say (48:7b). Finally, the divine statement that YHWH would save Israel for his own sake (48:11aα, b) is interpreted by a long accusation (48:8b–10, 11aβ), in which Israel is characterized as a treacherous and notorious rebel from its origins (cf. Jer 3:8, 11; 5:11; 9:1; Isa 1:2). Only because YHWH wanted to care for his name did he remain patient and not destroy Israel (cf. Ezek 20:9, 14, 22), but tested it in the smelting furnace of exile (cf. Jer 6:27–30; Ezek 22:18–22). Thus, the scholastic redaction (DtIS) used an earlier text, which reflected the delay of salvation in some way, for the purpose | of introducing accusations of the pre-exilic prophets of doom – not only of Isaiah, but also of Jeremiah and Ezekiel – into the book of Deutero-Isaiah. It intended to demonstrate that Israel, not God, is to be blamed

---

43 See already Duhm, *Jesaia*, pp. 360–66, Westermann, *Jesaja*, pp. 159–62, and Werlitz, *Redaktion*, pp. 348–53. Also Blenkinsopp, *Isaiah 40–55*, pp. 288–90, 295, noticed in Isa 48 passages of a different language and concept, which are "difficult if not impossible to reconcile with the outlook, the tone, and even the religious vocabulary of the 'prophet of consolation'" (p. 290).

44 As is known, Cyrus did not conquer Babylon in 539 B.C.E., but cooperated with its aristocracy and its Marduk priests, not with the exiled Judean groups. He only sent some temple vessels back to Jerusalem at best (Ezra 1:7); see Albertz, *Israel*, pp. 113–32.

45 Some recent scholars argue that the passage gains its specific profile only by the accusations (cf. Kratz, *Kyros*, pp. 114–17; Hans-Jürgen Hermisson, *Deuterojesaja, 2. Teilband: Jesaja 45,8–49,13*, Biblischer Kommentar Altes Testament XI/2 [Neukirchen-Vluyn: Neukirchener Verlag, 2003], pp. 210–13), but they seem to overlook its important function to introduce the commission of a new Persian king after the fall of Babylon. |

for the delay of salvation. From his post-exilic experience the redactor wanted to make Deutero-Isaiah's unconditional message of salvation conditional.

The intention of providing the salvific message of Deutero-Isaiah with a strong ethical commitment becomes obvious in 48:17–19, which the redactor put in the mouth of the prophet introduced by DtIT in 48:16b. Here YHWH is presented as a helpful guide of Israel who wishes to keep Israel on the right way (48:17). But God has to complain that the people missed the chance to obey his commandments and reflects about how Israel could have been multiplied and lived in peace, if it had done his will (48:18). According to the scholastic redactor, the misery of the people from the exilic past up to the present was a consequence of its disobedience (48:19 with a reference back to 48:9). The concept expressed in these verses is clearly Deuteronomistic; the language partly reminds one of Trito-Isaiah (60:17; 66:12), but also of patriarchal promises (Gen 22:17; Exod 32:13) and of Ps 81:14–17 (13–16).

The scholastic redactor seems to have reworked also Isa 42:18–25, the first one of the two judgment speeches on Israel (cf. 43:22–28*) in DtIE[1].[46] Here Deutero-Isaiah had criticized his companions in Babylon for being blind and deaf to his message of salvation, because they did not understand that their exilic situation was caused by YHWH and nobody else (42:18–19a, 20, 22–24aα_1, 25).[47] Thus, for the prophet and his group, the acceptance of the divine punishment was crucial for salvation, but that did not explicitly include new rules of conduct. The scholastic redactor wanted to make this explicit. He probably inserted the repeating questions of 42:19b in order to emphasize the scandal that even "Meshullam," the post-exilic substitute for the dead exilic generation, persisted in the blindness of YHWH's servant.[48] He interpreted | Israel's disorientation as divine strategy of magnifying the Torah as a new rule of conduct (42:21).[49] And he inserted an

---

46 Cf. the identical expression *hālak bᵉderek* "to go on the way" in Isa 42:24bβ and 48:17; 55:7, and the similar phrases *šāma' bᵉtôrâ* in 42:24bβ and *qāšab* hif. *lᵉmiṣwôt* "to listen to the torah/commandments" in 48:18. All these phrases have their parallels in Deuteronomic and Deuteronomistic texts (Deut 8:6; 1 Kgs 3:14; Jer 32:23; Neh 9:34).

47 Hans-Christoph Schmitt, "Erlösung und Gericht: Jes 43,1–7 und sein literarischer und theologischer Kontext," *Alttestamentlicher Glaube und Biblische Theologie: Festschrift für Horst Dietrich Preuß*, ed. Jutta Hausmann and Hans-Jürgen Zobel (Stuttgart: Kohlhammer, 1992), pp. 120–31, ascribed the ground level to the DtIS and the additions to a late Torah piety (pp. 122–25), but such a solution would distort the clear structure of DtIE[1].

48 Meshullam is a very common personal name given to a child who is regarded as a substitute for his elder brother who has died. Thus there is no reason for believing that it should have a completely different meaning as a symbolic name for Israel. |

49 The personal pronoun *wᵉhû'* "but he" in Isa 42:22 refers back to the subject of 42:20b and proves that 42:21 is an insertion.

explicit confession of sins through 42:24aα₂b in order to clarify that only an honest repentance of the people would pave the way of salvation. According to the scholastic redactor, Israel's sin was characterized by its unwillingness to listen to the Torah and to follow God's way, similar to 48:17–18. Thus, Israel's lesson to learn from the exile should be to keep God's Torah in the future.

After the third servant song (50:4–9), there is a short admonition that takes the faithful prophet as an example for the pious, but as a warning to his enemies (50:10–11). The text clearly depends on the song, but interprets it in a generalized way. Since 50:10 partly speaks in Deuteronomistic language,[50] the admonition probably also belongs to the DtIS. Anyone who is still living in darkness but "leans on his God" should be encouraged by the faithful confession of the prophet (50:10). But all those who no longer wait for the light of salvation, but kindle their own fire, are warned that they will be killed by their own hostile actions (50:11). This argument reveals that the scholastic redactor seems to belong to a prophetic group in succession of Deutero-Isaiah, which enjoyed some agreement but suffered much rejection. According to him, Israel, or at least the pious, did not only have to listen to the Torah but also to the voice of YHWH's prophet.

There are two other small admonitions, secondary to their context, which can probably be ascribed to the scholastic redaction. The first, 46:8, addresses the "rebels" (cf. 48:8) and warns them about the idols in which they may trust: they are not able to save human beings (48:7). The verse depends on its context, but draws a conclusion that moves clearly beyond.[51] The accusation of idolatry corresponds with 48:5b. The second admonition, 55:7, addresses the "wicked" (*rāšā'*) and calls him to leave "his way" (*darkô*) (cf. 42:24; 48:17) and return to YHWH. For this case, it promises him the pity and the forgiveness of "our God" (55:7; cf. 50:10; 42:24). The verse shows its secondary character by doubling the final admonition ("seek YHWH!") of DtIE² in 55:6 and focusing it on the specific group of the wicked (*rᵉšā'îm*). It takes up terms from its context but uses them in a different sense: in 55:7 *derek* denotes, for example, no longer | the plan for salvation as in 55:8, but the way of life. The call for repentance is typical for the Deuteronomistic theology (cf. 1 Kgs 8:33–34; Jer 36:3 among others). Thus the language and the concept of Isa 55:7 fit the characteristics of the scholastic redactor. From Isa 46:8; 50:10–11; and 55:7 it becomes clear that the scholastic redactor already knows a split of the Judean society into "the pious" and "the wicked"

---

50 For the phase *šāma' bᵉqôl* "to listen to one's voice" cf. Deut 4:30; 8:20; 1 Sam 8:19; 15:22 and others. These affinities in language are the main reason why I no longer assign this passage to DtIT as done before in Albertz, *Israel*, p. 397, note 778.

51 The addressees in the second person plural of Isa 46:5, 9 are not the evildoers, but all the Israelites. |

factions. This points to the social reality of the middle of the fifth century (cf. Neh 5). For the redactor, however, this split is not completely settled. He still tried hard to lead the wicked to repentance, so that they would listen to the Torah and the prophetic word and would improve their conduct. Verbal and conceptual parallels to later layers of the book of Trito-Isaiah (especially, Isa 59) suggest that the scholastic redactor – or a companion of his – was also involved in the formation of that book; but this suggestion needs further study.

3.6 Late Idol Additions

While earlier scholars regarded all idol polemics as later additions,[52] Jürgen Werlitz has shown that a major portion of them are well integrated into the composition (Isa 40:19–20; 41:6–7; 44:10–17, 20; 46:6–7).[53] They already belong to DtIE[1] and function to convince the audience of the monotheistic belief in a more amusing manner.[54] From these early passages, which reflect the Babylonian polytheistic background in a sarcastic way, those later polemics have to be distinguished. The late idol additions are secondarily placed into their contexts, and they criticize the producers and venerators of idols in a more schematic way:[55]

> **Late idol additions**
> Isa 42:17; 44:9, 18–19; 45:16–17, 20b

These passages accuse all those who create idols for their own needs, trust in them (42:17), pray to them (45:20b), and call them "our gods" (42:17). The idolators all have no understanding and will be ashamed, because these idols | would not save them (45:20b), in contrast to YHWH (45:16–17). Since the DtIS is also concerned with adherents of idols (46:[6–7], 8; 48:5), these late idol additions may come from a similar background. That some kind of idolatry became popular in post-exilic Judah can be seen from Isa 57:5–8; 66:17.

3.7 A Great Isaianic Redaction (DtIG)

Odil Hannes Steck elaborated several indications that the entire book of Isaiah including Proto-, Deutero- and Trito-Isaiah may have undergone "*großjesajanische*

---

52 For example, Elliger, *Verhältnis*, pp. 305–7, Westermann, *Jesaja*, p. 27.
53 See Werlitz, *Redaktion*, pp. 221–37.
54 These passages have an impressive rhetorical function: When a student group in my seminar in 2002 performed a recitation of DtIE[1] on stage, the audience laughed every time during the polemical idol passages.
55 See Werlitz, *Redaktion*, pp. 231–32. |

Fortschreibungen."[56] Steck observed several redactional links running through the book of Isaiah. According to him Isa 34–35 played a major role in connecting the books of Proto- and Deutero-Isaiah. He dated this redaction in the early Hellenistic period.[57] Meanwhile, several scholars postulate such a redaction,[58] but neither its scale nor its date is settled. In my view, within Isa 40–55, the following passages could most likely belong to such a redaction:

DtIG

Isa 40:5bβ; 48:22; 51:3, 11, 16; 52:4–6(?); 54:17b

The concluding formula in Isa 40:5bβ "For the YHWH's mouth has spoken" turns out to be secondary, because the order to build a "highway of YHWH" through the desert was originally spoken by the prophetic group (DtIE¹), and later – in the sight of DtIE² – by a heavenly figure (cf. 40:3aα), but not by God himself. All the more, the formula is not integrated in the poetic structure of the text. Since it also appears in Isa 1:20, its major function seems to be in aligning the beginning of Deutero- with that of Proto-Isaiah. What is said in both parts of the book comes from the very voice of YHWH. In Trito-Isaiah, the formula occurs a third time (58:14), but not in such a prominent position. At any rate, the promises of the book's third part are also provided with the same divine sanction as the first two.

At the end of Isa 48 an isolated statement is made in v. 22: "There is no peace – says YHWH – for the wicked," which has no connection to the | following second servant song (49:1–6) and only a weak linguistic link with the preceding context in 48:18 ("peace"). While the admonition speech calls all Israel to repentance (48:17–19), v. 22 presupposes a manifest split into a "pious" and a "wicked" faction. Thus, the verse is clearly an addition to its context. Nearly the same statement about the wicked is made in Isa 57:21, where it is much better integrated into its context (57:20–21; cf. the contrasting frame with 57:1–2). There, it functions to restrict the cited promise of Trito-Isaiah (57:14–19) to the pious. Thus, the Great Isaianic editor clearly borrowed the statement from 57:21. When he inserted it in 48:22, just before the prophetic group had returned from Babylon to Jerusalem (48:20–21) and passed the good news to Zion (49:14–26), he intended to exclude the wicked (*rešāʿîm*) from all the salvific promises to Jerusalem and the Judean population given in Deutero-Isaiah (49–55). They would not be includ-

---

56 Thus, in Odil Hannes Steck, *Bereitete Heimkehr: Jesaja 35 als redaktionelle Brücke zwischen dem Ersten und dem Zweiten Jesaja*, Stuttgarter Bibelstudien 121 (Stuttgart: Katholisches Bibelwerk, 1985), p. 76.
57 Cf. Steck, *Heimkehr*, pp. 65–80.
58 See the discussion in Werlitz, *Redaktion*, pp. 332–41, and the considerations of Berges, *Buch*, pp. 533–46, 551. |

ed into the eternal "covenant of peace" (54:10) that YHWH would establish with Jerusalem in the future. In contrast to the scholastic redactor, the Great Isaianic book editor presupposed a manifest split of the Judean society, which can likewise be noticed in the latest layers of Trito-Isaiah (Isa 57; 65–66). Thus, he erected a barrier in the "book of consolation," which should hinder the arrogant, antisocial, and godless people from getting an easy access to its promises.

In 54:17b there is a concluding statement which defines all the promises for Zion given in that chapter as the heritage of the "servants of YHWH." Since such "servants" are never mentioned before, the statement is clearly secondary to its context. With the same terminology ("my servants") the pious faction is named at the end of Trito-Isaiah (65:8–9, 13–15; 66:14).[59] Thus, the restriction comes from a similar milieu as 48:22 and probably also belongs to the DtIG. Both statements, 48:22 and 54:17b, constitute brackets around the promises for Zion and its people, which intended to protect the treasure of the "book of consolation" in between from any misuse by the wicked faction.

Among the promises for Zion, there are some extensions, which can probably be ascribed to DtIG. The complaint of the people in 51:9–10 that YHWH has forgotten his mighty deeds of the days of chaos and the time of the exodus is amplified by a description of the joyful wanderings of the released to Zion in 51:11. The complaint does not only burst the shape of the *Gattung*, but also has a parallel in Isa 35:10. Since the verse is firmly anchored in the salvific description of 35:1–10, where it constitutes its final climax, it is highly probable that the verse was taken from there and inserted in 51:11. According to Steck, Isa 35, which reminds one of Isa 40 in many aspects (cf. 35:2b–4 with 40:5, 9–10), was | created for the purpose of connecting the books of Proto- and Deutero-Isaiah.[60] Thus, the primary function of 51:11 would be to fasten this redactional bridge by stretching a rope back to chapter 35. In that case, we would have to do with a basic editorial work of the DtIG. There are, however, some doubts about such an appraisal. According to my observations the literary connection between Proto- and Deutero-Isaiah was rather established already by DtIE².[61] Moreover, Joseph Blenkinsopp has rightly pointed out that Isa 35 presupposes not only Deutero- but also Trito-Isaiah (cf. 35:1–2a with 60:13, 61:10; 65:18–19; 66:10).[62] According to him, chapters 34–35 – the final judgment of the nations, exemplified by the destruction of Edom, and the final salvation of Zion including a miraculous transformation of nature (35:2, 7–9) – should rather be regarded as an eschatological interpretation of Deutero-

---

59 Cf. the similar assessment of Blenkinsopp, *Isaiah 40–55*, pp. 74, 366. |
60 See Steck, *Heimkehr*, pp. 13–64.
61 See above p. 29 [[= p. 144 in the present volume]].
62 See Blenkinsopp, *Isaiah 40–55*, pp. 44–46.

and Trito-Isaiah's prophecies, which were intended to conclude the first part of the Isaiah book (cf. the references of 34:8, 17 back to 13:9, 17). Thus, the effort of the Great Isaianic redactor was of a smaller scale: he already presupposed the literary connections between the three parts of the book including the eschatological finale of the first part (34–35), but he wanted to align the prophecies of Deutero-Isaiah with the eschatological message already addressed in Isa 35. Since 51:10 speaks of the "released" (*gᵉ'ûlîm*), who have passed through the chaos waters, and 35:9 also mentions the "released" (*gᵉ'ûlîm*) on their wonderful way back to Zion, the redactor saw an appropriate place here to include a reminder of the eschatological events described by Isa 35 in the Deutero-Isaianic context of Isa 51. By this, he intended to synchronize the process of salvation between the first and second part of the book of Isaiah. Zion's preparations for the arrival of salvation dealt with in chapters 51–52 should be understood by the reader as that period when the eschatological events of chapter 35 would take place.

It is probable also that 51:3, sometimes regarded as a displaced fragment of an "eschatological hymn,"[63] belongs to the same reworking of the chapter, because it includes the identical expression "joy and gladness" (*śāśôn wᵉśimḥâ*), found in both 35:10 and 51:11.[64] Through this insertion the Great Isaianic redactor intended to focus the scope of the entire chapter on Zion; in addition, he described the wonderful transformation of the city into the garden of Eden in accord with the visions of Isa 35.

Finally, the surprising address to a prophetic figure in 51:16 may be also | ascribed to the DtIG. The verse is clearly an insertion, after the divine answer to the lament (51:12–15a) has ended with a concluding hymnic formula in 51:15b (DtIE²).[65] If one takes the verse as it is transmitted in the Masoretic text the prophet is commissioned to "plant" (*nāṭaʿ*) heaven and to ground earth through the divine word, before he should assure Zion of God's solidarity with its people. The motives are partly taken up from the context (cf. 51:13; 49:2); the commission also reminds one of Jer 1:9–10.[66] While the prophet Jeremiah was ordered to pull out and plant the nations through his divine message, the Isaianic prophet would be able to plant a new heaven through his divine word. Steck has proposed to

---

63 See for example Westermann, *Jesaja*, p. 192.
64 Apart from these passages the expression only occurs in Isa 22:13 and Ps 51:10(8). |
65 The insertion probably caused the textual problem that resulted in the addressee of the divine speech varying between the female (Zion) and male (prophet) gender.
66 In the phrase "I put my words in your mouth" only the verb differs (*śîm* instead of *nātan*). The verb *śîm* is used also in Exod 4:15; Num 23:5; and Isa 59:21. Whether the last verse, which indicates a succession of the prophetic office, also belongs to DtIG, is not clear, because it is formulated in prose.

interpret Isa 51:16 in such an eschatological horizon.[67] Then, it would refer to the creation of a new heaven and a new earth announced in 65:16b–23, which also aims at a wonderful transformation of Jerusalem and the circumstances of its inhabitants. If such an interpretation is accepted, the verse will fit perfectly the concept of the Great Isaianic redactor. In the same Deutero-Isaianic chapter, where he referred back to Proto-Isaiah, he also pointed forward to Trito-Isaiah. By doing so, he united the three parts of the book under the same eschatological perspective. According to him, at that moment (Isa 51), when the wonderful salvation of Zion described in Isa 35 is prepared, the Isaianic prophet of the book is commissioned to start the creation of the new world according to Isa 65.[68] Since DtIG lacks historical allusions, it is difficult to date. Its fully developed eschatological concept, however, points to the end of the fifth or to the fourth century B.C.E.

3.8 Apocalyptic Additions

Within Isa 40–55 there are two additions, which can be labeled as "apocalyptic," since they describe a cosmological dissolution of heaven and earth (Isa | 50:3; 51:6). They may have to do with the insertion of Isa 24–27 in the book of Isaiah. Especially 51:6 could perhaps be assigned to the DtIG described above. But since a similar apocalyptic perspective seems to be an expansion even in 34:4, the apocalyptic additions may be later.[69]

4 Conclusion

The redaction historical hypothesis elaborated above covers about 98 percent of the text of Isa 40–55 with an explanation of its formation. This is not a bad portion. Many redaction-critical proposals in our research field suffer from the fact that they are not tidied up for the entire text unit. It is not necessary to emphasize that my results are hypothetical to one degree or another. They can only be regarded as preliminary, as long as they are not controlled, revised and

---

67 See Steck, *Zion*, pp. 70–72.

68 Steck, *Heimkehr*, p. 80; Steck, *Zion*, pp. 124–25, also ascribed the prose extension, Isa 52:4–6, to the DtIG. The passage, however, has more interest in historical connections than in an eschatological unification of the book. Thus, the affiliation is rather improbable. Whether one has to distinguish different Great Isaianic redactions needs further research. |

69 A few additions to the book can be characterized as glosses: Isa 40:7a, 7b, 14bα; 43:28a; 49:21bα$_1$.

expanded by similar redactional and compositional critical studies of Proto- and Trito-Isaiah. Joseph Blenkinsopp would be one of the few scholars in the world who would be able to carry out such a tremendous task, since he has thoroughly studied all three parts of Isaiah. But I am afraid he would not like to do so, even in his younger years. I wish him more healthy years of study and hope that he may acknowledge that my attempts at reconstructing the formation of the book of Deutero-Isaiah are not totally superfluous, but can lead to a better understanding of some difficult passages.

3 Religionsgeschichte

Einführung

Nach der Veröffentlichung meiner „Religionsgeschichte Israels in alttestamentlicher Zeit"[1] am Ende des letzten Jahrhunderts, haben mich auch am Anfang dieses Jahrhunderts weiterhin religionsgeschichtliche Fragen beschäftigt, die nach meinem Verständnis nicht nur die religiösen Einflüsse von außen, sondern ebenso auch die innerisraelitischen theologischen Entwicklungen umfassen. Die ersten vier der hier aufgenommenen Aufsätze betreffen ein genaueres und detaillierteres Verständnis dessen, was in der „Religionsgeschichte" als Entwicklung der „offiziellen Theologie" in Israel und Juda beschrieben worden war. Der fünfte Aufsatz wendet sich noch einmal abschließend dem religionsinternen Segment der „Persönlichen Frömmigkeit" bzw. „Familienreligion" zu, ein Thema, das mich während meiner gesamten akademischen Tätigkeit beschäftigt hat.[2]

Die ausführliche Untersuchung der erzählerischen Darstellung des Auszugs Israels aus Ägypten in meinem Exoduskommentar[3] gab mir die Möglichkeit, mich noch einmal eingehend mit den vielgestaltigen Exodustraditionen zu beschäftigen. Der erste Aufsatz „Ausprägungen der Exodustradition in der Prophetie und in den Psalmen" kommt zu dem Ergebnis, dass der Exodus zwar schon im 7. Jh. v. Chr. in Juda zum Gründungsmythos Gesamtisraels aufstieg, es aber bis zum Ende des 5. Jhs. keine verbindliche Darstellung der Exodusereignisse gab. Vielmehr wurden die recht eigenständigen Ausprägungen der Exodustradition bei den Propheten und in den Psalmen erst ab dem 4. Jh. von der inzwischen kanonisch gewordenen Erzählüberlieferung normiert.

Die zweite Untersuchung „Israel in der offiziellen Religion der Königszeit" führte mich zu der Einsicht, dass sich die in den beiden Reichen Juda und Israel entwickelten offiziellen Theologien deutlicher voneinander unterschieden haben, als ich dies in meiner „Religionsgeschichte" gesehen hatte: Einer mythisch begründeten, um das territoriale Zentrum Jerusalem kreisenden universalen Zions-, Königs- und JHWH-Königs-Theologie im Süden stand im Norden – soweit noch erkennbar – eine heilsgeschichtlich begründete, partikulare Gottesvolk-Theologie

---

1 S. R. Albertz, Religionsgeschichte Israels in alttestamentlicher Zeit, Bd. 1: Von den Anfängen bis zum Ende der Königszeit, Bd. 2: Vom Exil bis zu den Makkabäern (GAT 8/1+2), Göttingen 1992; 2. Aufl. Bd. I, Göttingen 1996; Bd. II, Göttingen 1997. Die englischen Ausgaben erschienen 1994 in London und Louisville, KY, die koreanische 2003/04, die italienische Ausgabe 2005, die spanische und griechische 2006.

2 Vgl. R. Albertz, Persönliche Frömmigkeit und offizielle Religion. Religionsinterner Pluralismus in Israel und Babylon (CThM A9), Stuttgart 1978 = Atlanta 2005; Ders./R. Schmitt, Family and Household Religion in Ancient Israel and the Levant, Winona Lake, IN 2012.

3 S. R. Albertz, Exodus 1–18 (ZBK.AT 2.1), Zürich 2012, ²2017; Exodus 19–40 (ZBK.AT 2.2), Zürich 2015.

https://doi.org/10.1515/9783111202228-011

gegenüber, auf die auch das menschliche und göttliche Königtum bezogen sind. Zu einer Synthese beider Staatstheologien kam es erst nach dem Untergang des Nordreichs in der Hiskia- und Josia-Zeit.

Bekanntlich geriet die nunmehr stark heilsgeschichtlich begründete offizielle Religion Israels mit dem babylonischen Exil, das für alle den Verlust des davidischen Königtums und des Jerusalemer Tempels sowie für viele auch den Verlust des Landes bedeutete, in eine tiefe Krise. Als eine wichtige Gruppe, die sich um die theologische Aufarbeitung dieser Krise bemühte, gelten gemeinhin die „Deuteronomisten", die sich an Sprache und Theologie des Deuteronomiums orientierten. Dass allerdings zwischen den Deuteronomisten, die das Deuteronomistische Geschichtswerk (DtrG) verfassten, und denen, die das Jeremiabuch redaktionell bearbeiteten (JerD), unterschieden werden muss, war mir schon früher aufgefallen; zu divergent sind zwischen beiden Werken die politischen, sozialen und geschichtstheologischen Positionen.[4] Die zwischenzeitliche Herausarbeitung des Profils weiterer deuteronomistischer Literaturen – des dtr. Vierprophetenbuchs (Hos, Am, Mi, Zeph) und des dtr. Zweiprophetenbuchs (Hag, Sach 1–8) – sowie die Unterscheidung dreier Ausgaben des dtr. Jeremiabuchs (JerD$^{1-3}$)[5] erweitert das Spektrum der dtr. Geschichtsdeutungen noch einmal erheblich. Sie werden im dritten Aufsatz „Der Streit der Deuteronomisten um das richtige Verständnis der Geschichte Israels" entfaltet. Zwischen den verschiedenen deuteronomistischen Literaturwerken lässt sich ein regelrechtes Streitgespräch über die Frage rekonstruieren, welche theologischen und politischen Lehren aus der Katastrophe des babylonischen Exils gezogen werden müssen. Auch die unterschiedlichen dtr. Trägergruppen, die hinter diesen Literaturen stehen, lassen sich damit genauer einschätzen.

Das Spektrum der Konzepte, die für einen Neubeginn nach der Exilskatastrophe entwickelt wurden, erweitert sich noch einmal erheblich, wenn man das Deuterojesaja- und das Ezechielbuch in die Untersuchung einbezieht. Beide Bücher hatte ich in meinem Werk über die Exilszeit[6] in ihrer literarischen Gestalt und theologischen Aussage eingehend analysiert. Der vierte Aufsatz „How Radical Must the New Beginning Be: The Discussion between the Deutero-Isaiah and the Ezekiel School" unternimmt eine vergleichende Auswertung: Obgleich beide Pro-

---

4 S. R. Albertz, Geschichte und Theologie. Studien zur Exegese des Alten Testaments und zur Religionsgeschichte Israels, hrsg. von Ingo Kottsieper und Jakob Wöhrle (BZAW 326), Berlin/New York 2003, 279–301.

5 Vgl. R. Albertz, Die Exilszeit. 6. Jahrhundert v. Chr. (BE 7), Stuttgart 2001, 164–185.231–260; J. Wöhrle, Die frühen Sammlungen des Zwölfprophetenbuches. Entstehung und Komposition (BZAW 360), Berlin/New York 2006, 51–284.285–385.

6 Vgl. Albertz, Exilszeit, 260–326.

phetenbücher in der ausgehenden Exilszeit entstanden sind und von der offiziellen Jerusalemer Theologie herkommen, vertreten sie doch bezüglich der Frage, wie der Neustart nach dem Exil vonstatten gehen und wer daran beteiligt sein sollte, geradezu gegensätzliche Ansichten. Daran wird noch einmal deutlich, welch kreative Herausforderung die Exilskrise für die offizielle Theologie Israels darstellte.

Eine Tagung über „Religionspraxis und Individualität", die 2019 in Marburg veranstaltet wurde, gab mir Gelegenheit, noch einmal abschließend über das Verhältnis von Familie und Individuum in der von mir herausgearbeiteten Familienreligion nachzudenken, die sich auch in der von mir gebrauchten, schwankenden Nomenklatur – „personal piety" und „family and household religion" – widerspiegelt.[7] So gelange ich im fünften und letzten Aufsatz dieses Kapitels „Welche Art von Individualität förderte die altisraelitische Familienreligion?" zu der Ansicht, dass der letztgenannte Begriff wohl die sachgemäßere Bezeichnung für das gemeinte Religionssegment darstellt, aber die Gebetsrituale, welche die Familien für ihre in Not geratenen Mitglieder veranstalteten, durchaus geeignet waren, deren Individualität zu stärken.

---

7 Vgl. die oben Anm. 2 genannten Titel.

Ausprägungen der Exodustradition
in der Prophetie und in den Psalmen

Die Exodustradition gehört zu den am weitest verbreiteten Überlieferungen der Hebräischen Bibel. Sie füllt nicht nur weite Teile der Erzählungen des Buches Exodus (Ex 1–15), sondern begegnet ebenso in den Gesetzessammlungen,[1] in den Prophetenbüchern und in den Psalmen. Nur in den Weisheitsschriften der Hebräischen Bibel kommt sie nicht vor. Bei den Propheten und in den Psalmen, die hier das Thema sein sollen, lassen sich gut 100 Verse der Exodustradition zuordnen, wobei die Abgrenzung zur Wüsten- und Sinaitradition nicht immer ganz eindeutig ist.[2] Dabei sticht sogleich ein erstaunlich großer Variantenreichtum der Exodustradition ins Auge. Im Folgenden werden als erstes einige Beobachtungen zum Traditionsverständnis vorgestellt, das sich aus den hier untersuchten Texten ablesen lässt. Als zweites wird aufgezeigt, in welchen Gattungen von Prophetie und Psalmen Bezüge auf den Exodus auftauchen und welche pragmatische Funktion sie hier übernehmen. Drittens wird ein Blick auf die Motivvielfalt geworfen; dabei werden einige auffällige Gestaltungen der Tradition betrachtet. Als viertes und letztes soll versucht werden, diachron zu beschreiben, wie sich die Exodustradition in den Psalmen und bei den Propheten gegenüber der erst spät normierend wirkenden Pentateucherzählung entwickelt hat. |

1 Zum Traditionsverständnis

Am Anfang von Ps 78, der neben den Wüstenepisoden gleich mehrfach auf Exodusereignisse zu sprechen kommt (V. 12–13.42–51.52–53), findet sich eine Reflexion über den sich hier vollziehenden Vorgang des Tradierens:

---

1 Vgl. Ex 20,2; 22,20; 23,9; Lev 11,45; 18,3; 19,34.36; 22,32–33; 23,43; 25,38.42.55; Dtn 5,6; 13,6.11; 15,15; 16,12; 17,16; 23,5; 24,9.18.22; 25,17; 26,5–8.
2 Vgl. die Aufstellung im Anhang. Die hier aufgenommenen Belegstellen sind auf der einen Seite etwas umfangreicher als die in älteren einschlägigen Werken etwa bei Galling, Erwählungstraditionen, 5–65; Lauha, Geschichtsmotive, 45–72; Kühlewein, Geschichte, 134–138; Preuss, Theologie I, 43–51, aufgeführten, andererseits wurden einige oft mitbehandelten Stellen nicht einbezogen, weil es sich hier meiner Meinung nach entweder um unspezifische Theophaniemotive (Ps 18,15–16; 76,7; Nah 1,4; Hab 3,8.11) oder um Anspielungen auf den urzeitlichen Chaoskampf handelt (Ps 74,13–17; 89,10–13), die zwar Verbindungen mit den Exodusschilderungen eingehen, aber doch daneben eigene Motivzusammenhänge darstellen. Das Moselied Ex 15,1–18 und das Mirjamlied Ex 15,21 werden in der Aufstellung bewusst nicht zu den Psalmen gerechnet, sondern als Teil des Pentateuch betrachtet. |

https://doi.org/10.1515/9783111202228-012

Ps 78,1	Höre, mein Volk, auf meine Weisung,
	neigt euer Ohr zu den Worten meines Mundes!
2	Ich will öffnen meinen Mund mit einem Spruch,
	will Rätsel der Vorzeit verkünden,
3	was wir gehört und kennengelernt haben,
	und uns unsere Väter erzählten.
4	Nicht wollen wir (das) vor ihren Kindern verhehlen,
	die (wir) einer nachkommenden Generation weitererzählen
	die Ruhmestaten JHWHs und seine Stärke
	und seine Wundertaten, die er getan.

Der Vorsänger, der seinen Psalm hier wie ein Weisheitslehrer eröffnet, schließt sich einerseits mit der Gemeinde, zu der er redet, zusammen. Was er zur Sprache bringen will, ist eine ihnen allen gemeinsame Tradition, die sie von ihren Vätern empfangen haben und die sie kennen (Ps 78,3). Anderseits stellt er sich ihnen als einzelner gegenüber und fordert die Gemeinde auf, seinen Worten und seiner Weisung genau zuzuhören (V. 1). Denn die allseits bekannte Tradition aus alter Zeit weist seiner Meinung nach nichtsdestoweniger Rätsel auf, die er vor und mit der Gemeinde bedenken und klären will (V. 2), damit sie beide, der Vorsänger und die Gemeinde, als Kinder ihrer Väter dafür sorgen, dass auch diese neuen Einsichten in die empfangene Tradition in den zukünftigen Traditionsvorgang gegenüber der nachkommenden Generation einfließen, welche die Ruhmes- und Wundertaten JHWHs zum Gegenstand hat (V. 4).[3] Konkret geht es im Psalm um das Rätsel, warum JHWH, obgleich ganz Israel seine rettenden Wundertaten in seiner Frühgeschichte immer wieder vergessen hat,[4] was den göttlichen Zorn | hervorrief und schließlich zur Zerstörung des Heiligtums von Silo führte, aus der

---

3 Gegen Spieckermann, Heilsgegenwart, 134 Anm. 2, und Hossfeld/Zenger, Psalmen II, 421–422, besteht kein Anlass, die Integrität von Ps 78,1–4 anzuzweifeln. Der Wechsel zwischen der ersten und dritten Person Plural hängt damit zusammen, dass sich der Vorsänger abwechselnd mit seinen Adressaten zusammenschließt und wieder distanziert. Der pauschale Anschluss mit אֲשֶׁר „was" in V. 3 ist nicht auffälliger als der in V. 5, vgl. die syntaktische Beschreibung von Hieke, Weitergabe, 57–59, und die Auslegung von Gärtner, Geschichtspsalmen, 50–55. Zum theologischen Profil des Prologs Ps 78,1–8 vgl. auch Witte, Exodus, 25–29.

4 Trotz des berechtigten Einspruchs von Weingart, Juda, 447–449, halte ich weiterhin mit vielen Auslegern den Vers Ps 78,9 (so z. B. Kraus, Psalmen II, 698–702) bzw. die Verse 9–11 (so z. B. Witte, Exodus, 39) für einen Einschub, der den Rückblick auf die Geschichte des Unglaubens nachträglich auf das Nordreich bzw. die Samarier verengen will. Weingart, a. a. O., 455, konzediert selber, dass im Rückblick auch die Judäer mitgemeint sind, weil die Jakob-Israel-Titulatur, die in V. 21 für die sündigen Väter gebraucht wird, in V. 5.71 ganz Israel umfasst. Eine theologische Differenzierung zwischen Ephraim und Juda tritt nach der Darstellung des | Psalms erst im Rahmen der Philisternot ein (V. 67.68). Die Schwierigkeiten, in die eine Auslegung des Psalms gerät, die V. 9–11 voll berücksichtigt, zeigt beispielhaft Emanuel, Psalmists, 90. Er schreibt: „A difficult question

Philisternot heraus Juda gegenüber den Nordstämmen bevorzugt hat, indem er dessen Heiligtum auf dem Zion und dessen König David erwählte (V. 56–72). Nach der langen Sündengeschichte Israels konnte sich nach Meinung des Vorsängers niemand mehr so einfach auf das Erwählungspotential des Exodus berufen; auch die Brüder im Norden sollten vielmehr dankbar sein, dass JHWHs Erbarmen, das schon zuvor immer wieder seinen Zorn begrenzt hatte (V. 32–39), in der Erwählung Judas manifest geworden war.

Wir können also festhalten: Zur Zeit des Ps 78 – wegen seines kultpolitischen Appells an die Brüder im Norden kommt dafür am ehesten die 2. Hälfte des 5. Jahrhunderts in Frage –[5] gehörte die Exodustradition in Jerusalem zu den allseits bekannten Geschichtsüberlieferungen, die man von seinen Vorfahren ererbt hatte. Sie war auf die gesamte Volksgruppe bezogen und galt als gesamtgesellschaftlich getragen. Einzelne Intellektuelle entwickelten aber von ihren Anliegen in der Gegenwart her immer wieder neue Ausprägungen und Verständnisse der Tradition, die – sofern breiter akzeptiert – als eine weitere Variante in den gesamtgesellschaftlichen Traditionsprozess einbezogen wurden.

Die belehrende Erinnerung an JHWHs Wundertaten in der Vergangenheit, wie sie in den sogenannten Geschichtspsalmen (Ps 78; 105; 106) zur Sprache kommt, ist nur eine Weise des Umgangs mit der Exodustradition in den Psalmen. In ihnen kommt es an einigen Stellen zu andersgearteten Vergegenwärtigungen, bei denen die Zeitdifferenz zu den Exodusereignissen regelrecht übersprungen wird. So heißt es etwa in Ps 66,5–6:

Ps 66,5	Geht und schaut die Taten Gottes,
	ein furchterregendes Werk an den Menschenkindern!
6	Er verwandelte das Meer in trockenes Land,
	durch den Strom gehen sie zu Fuß,
	dort wollen wir uns über ihn freuen.

Der Ort, an dem JHWH das Meer trockenlegte und die Israeliten zu Fuß den Strom überquerten – womit wohl schon Schilfmeer- und Jordandurchzug in eins gesetzt werden sollen –[6] wird durch die Deixis שָׁם, die von einem eigenartigen | Kohorta-

---

arises: where was Judah during the rebellions enumerated throughout the psalm? Verse 69 suggests they had no role of any transgressions listed, and were consequently eligible for selection." Doch V. 69 sagt explizit weder das eine, noch das andere. Der nachträgliche Versuch, den Ephraimiten bzw. Samariern die ganze Last der Schuldgeschichte aufzubürden, ist aus den später immer heftiger werdenden Auseinandersetzungen mit ihnen verständlich.

5 Siehe unten S. 127 [[= S. 181–182 im vorliegenden Band]].

6 Mit Recht stellen Hossfeld/Zenger, Psalmen II, 223, fest, dass der (schmale) Jordan sonst niemals נהר „Strom" genannt wird, doch kann die Wahl dieses Begriffs einer Angleichung an | das Schilfmeer oder dem gerne übertreibenden Charakter des Gotteslobes geschuldet sein. Auf den

tiv gefolgt wird, unmittelbar auf den Ort, an dem die gottesdienstliche Gemeinde ihr Loblied singt, bezogen. Mit der Selbstermunterung „dort wollen wir uns über ihn freuen" denkt sich die versammelte Kultgemeinde direkt in das Exodusgeschehen hinein und reagiert so, als habe es gerade erst vor ihren Augen stattgefunden.

Neben dieser kultischen Vergegenwärtigung der Exodustradition, die in vielen Hymnen erfolgt, ohne dass wir dies sprachlich so klar wie in Ps 66 nachweisen können, scheint es mir noch eine mehr spielerische zu geben, die auch außerhalb des Gottesdienstes stattgefunden haben kann. In Ps 114, einem Psalm, der oft zwar unter die Hymnen gerechnet wird, aber aller typischen Merkmale eines Hymnus entbehrt,[7] findet sich ein ganz eigenartiges Rollenspiel:

Ps 114,3	Das Meer sah (es) und floh,
	der Jordan wandte sich rückwärts.
4	Die Berge hüpften wie Widder
	und die Hügel wie junge Lämmer.
5	Was hast du, Meer, dass du fliehst,
	du, Jordan, dass du dich rückwärts wendest?
6	Ihr Berge, dass ihr hüpft wie Widder,
	ihr Hügel, wie junge Lämmer?
7	Vor dem Angesicht des Herrn tanze,
	Erde, vor dem Angesicht des Gottes Jakobs!
8	Der den Fels zum Wasserteich verwandelt,
	den Kieselstein zur Wasserquelle.	

Schilfmeer und Jordan – übrigens wieder parallel zueinander – werden personalisiert, ebenso die Berge und Hügel; sie alle werden zu Akteuren auf einer imaginären Bühne. Es wird im Gesang geschildert, wie das Meer unter dem Eindruck

---

Jordan beziehen etwa Gunkel, Psalmen, 277, und Norin, Meer, 124–125, die zweite Aussage. Dass eine solche Parallelisierung der beiden Wasserwunder vorkam, belegt eindeutig Ps 114,3.5.

7 Es fehlen dem Psalm ein imperativischer Aufruf zum Lob, eine כִּי-Einleitung oder die Kette von Partizipien. Nur in Ps 114,8 findet sich ein vereinzelter Partizipialsatz. Entsprechend unsicher sind die Gattungszuweisungen. Gunkel, Ausgewählte Psalmen, 163, rechnete Ps 114 noch unter „die Erzählungen im Hymnenstil", in Ders., Psalmen, 493, bestimmte er seine Grundstimmung als „die des Hymnus", stellte ihn aber in die Nähe zu den Geschichtspsalmen (Ex 15; Ps 105). Norin, Meer, 126, hielt es für zweifelhaft, dass wir „dieses Stück Poesie einen Psalm nennen können", da Gott nicht angeredet werde. Und auch Leuenberger, Konzeptionen, 292, spricht immer noch von einem „gattungsmäßig wenig typische[n]" Psalm. Meine Überlegungen sind von der Beobachtung angeregt, dass auch der gattungsmäßig wenig typische Wallfahrtspsalm Ps 126, der ebenfalls mit infinitivisch konstruiertem Temporalsatz beginnt, von Ben-Chorin, Volkslied, 47, im Anschluss an Max Brod „das Volkslied der Juden" genannt wurde. Gilt diese Einschätzung auch vornehmlich für den heutigen Gebrauch des Psalms in Israel, so hat Seybold, Wallfahrtspsalmen, 52–60, literarhistorisch wahrscheinlich gemacht, dass diese Gruppe von Liedern auf Laiengedichte zurückgeht. Ähnliches halte ich auch im Fall von Ps 114 für möglich. |

eines nicht näher benannten Geschehens plötzlich die Flucht ergreift, der Jordan seine Fließrichtung umkehrt und die Berge und Hügel aufgeregt herumhüpfen (Ps 114,3–4). Nur ganz von Ferne klingen bei dieser Schilderung einer verrückten Welt einige Chaoskampf- und Theophaniemotive an (Ps 104,7; 29,6; Hab 3,6). Mit einer halb besorgten, halb übermütigen Frage katapultieren sich die Sängerinnen und Sänger selber auf die Bühne (Ps 114,5–6). Indem sie Meer, Jordan, Berge und Hügel spielerisch fragen, warum sie sich denn so verrückt verhalten, werden sie selber zu Akteuren des Exodusgeschehens. Sie allein wissen, dass Gottes Erscheinen das Erschrecken und die Aufregung unter den Naturelementen ausgelöst hat, und so fordern sie fröhlich die Erde zum Tanz vor dem Herrn, dem Gott Jakobs, auf,[8] weil derjenige, der das bedrohliche Meer in die Flucht schlug, auch der ist, der die Erde auf wunderbare Weise bewässert (V. 7–8). Wegen seiner spielerischen, ja, sogar ein wenig frechen Vergegenwärtigung der heilsgeschichtlichen Ereignisse klingt Ps 114 wie ein Volkslied. Wegen der Eingangsverse, die wieder auf den Vorrang Judas mit seinem Heiligtum abheben (V. 1–2), könnte man an ein Lied denken, das von den Pilgern auf ihrem Weg zum Passa-Massot-Fest in Jerusalem seit frühnachexilischer Zeit gesungen wurde.[9] Wenn diese Vermutung richtig ist, hätten wir hier einen Beleg dafür, dass die Exodustradition sehr wohl auch von nicht-professionellen Kreisen der Bevölkerung getragen wurde. |

2 Gattungen und pragmatische Funktion

An den Psalmen und den Propheten lässt sich studieren, wie stark die Konstruktion und Transformation der Exodustradition von der jeweiligen Kommunikati-

---

8 Oft wird der Imperativ חולי in Ps 114,7 mit der Wurzel חיל „kreißen" zusammengebracht (so schon die Septuaginta und erneut Spieckermann, Heilsgegenwart, 150–151); doch liegt es von der Form und vom beschwingten, leicht übermütigen Ton des Liedes her näher, ihn von der Wurzel חול „tanzen" abzuleiten, so etwa auch Seybold, Psalmen, 449; Hossfeld/Zenger, Psalmen III, 262; Klein, Geschichte, 50–51. Zum übermütigen Ton des Liedes gehört auch, die große Kulturnation Ägypten in V. 1 despektierlich „ein stammelndes Volk" zu nennen.
9 Ps 114 kann schon deswegen kaum vorexilisch sein, weil V. 8 wahrscheinlich auf einen Satz der Prophetie Deuterojesajas (Jes 41,18) anspielt. Die eigenartige, die ganze Geschichte Israels in einem Satz zusammendrängende Aussage von Ps 114,1–2, dass nach dem Auszug aus Ägypten Juda zu JHWHs Heiligtum und Israel zu seinem Herrschaftsgebiet wurde, lässt sich dann so ausdeuten, dass Juda nach Wiederaufbau des Tempels beansprucht, das religiöse Zentrum für alle JHWH-Anhänger zu sein, während die Provinz Samaria für sich in Anspruch nimmt, schon von ihrer Größe und Wirtschaftskraft her das wichtigere politische Zentrum zu bilden. Das würde durchaus zur geschichtlichen Lage der frühnachexilischen Zeit passen, vgl. die Erwägungen von Leuenberger, Konzeptionen, 293 Anm. 80. Dass man das kleine Liedchen in das fünfte Psalmenbuch aufgenommen hat, setzt meiner Meinung voraus, dass es zu dieser Zeit schon zum

onssituation abhängt, in der sie zur Sprache gebracht wird. Abgesehen von dem vermuteten Pilgerlied (Ps 114) begegnet diese in den folgenden Psalmengattungen: im Hymnus (Ps 66,6; 77,17–21; 135,8–9; 136,10–15), in der Klage des Volkes (Ps 80,9; Jes 51,9–10; 63,10–14),[10] in den Geschichtspsalmen (Ps 78,12–16.43–53; 105,23–38; 106,7–12.21–22) und in einer liturgischen Mahnrede (Ps 81,6–11). In den Hymnen wird die Exodustradition überall dazu genutzt, die Macht JHWHs als Herrn der Geschichte zu preisen. Entsprechend wird überall die in den Exodusereignissen erkennbare weltüberlegene Wundermacht hervorgekehrt. JHWH ist es, der das Meer trockenlegt (Ps 66,6), er ist es, der die Urfluten erzittern lässt und sich einen Weg durch das Meer bahnt (Ps 77,17.20); er erschlägt die ägyptische Erstgeburt, wie er mächtige Könige bei der Einwanderung erschlagen hat (Ps 135,8–9), er zerschneidet das Schilfmeer in zwei Teile, um sein Volk hindurchzuführen (Ps 136,13–14). Diese machtbetonte Ausrichtung der Exodustradition gilt auch für den hymnischen Geschichtspsalm 105, der am Ende einer ausführlichen Schilderung der göttlichen Zeichen und Wunder in den ägyptischen Plagen (V. 29–36) einen triumphalen Auszug Israels schildert, der an einen Heereszug der assyrischen Truppen erinnert (V. 37)[11] und bei dem sich nicht etwa die Israeliten über ihre Befreiung, sondern die Ägypter über ihre Erlösung von den Schrecken göttlicher Machterweise freuen (V. 38).

In den Klagen des Volkes dagegen, in denen – im Kontrast zur Anklage – Rückblicke auf sein früheres Heilshandeln JHWH dazu bewegen wollen, die aktuelle Not Israels zu wenden, zielen die Erinnerungen an die Exodusereignisse immer auf die in allen Machterweisen erkennbare Güte Gottes. JHWH hatte den Weinstock, den er aus Ägypten ausgehoben hatte, mit so viel Sorgfalt in Palästina eingepflanzt, ihm Raum geschaffen, ihn gepflegt und umhegt (Ps 80,9–12); wie konnte er ihn jetzt den wilden Tieren preisgeben (V. 13–14)? Er hatte mit seinem starken Arm die Chaosungeheuer niedergekämpft, um seinen Erlösten einen Weg in die Freiheit zu bahnen (Jes 51,9–10); wie konnte er jetzt im Exil untätig bleiben? Auch in der exilischen oder frühnachexilischen Volksklage Jes 63,7–64,11, nach der JHWH – angesichts der ihm zugefügten Kränkungen (V. 10) – das Schilfmeerwunder letztlich vollführt, um sich einen ewigen und herrlichen Namen zu schaffen (V. 12.14), bleibt die gesamte Szenerie dennoch von seiner tiefen Zuwendung

---

unverzichtbaren Kulturgut gehörte und darum bereits eine ganze Anzahl von Jahrzehnten im Gebrauch gewesen sein muss. Es wird daher kaum erst im 4. Jh. v. Chr. geschaffen worden sein, so Hossfeld/Zenger, Psalmen III, 264, schon gar nicht erst für seinen jetzigen Kontext. |
10 Vgl. zu diesem Vorkommen schon grundlegend Westermann, Vergegenwärtigung, 306–311.
11 Eigenartigerweise nimmt Ps 105,37 nicht nur auf das Motiv von der Beschenkung der Abschied nehmenden Israeliten mit Preziosen (Ex 11,2; 12,35) Bezug, sondern auch auf die Schilderung der in Reih und Glied marschierenden Assyrer in Jes 5,27. |

zu Israel bestimmt. Auch die Geschichtspsalmen, welche die | Erinnerung an die Heilstaten JHWHs in der Vergangenheit mit dem dauernden Ungehorsam Israels konfrontieren (Ps 78; 106), weisen in der Darstellung der Exodusereignisse vornehmlich die darin zutage tretende göttliche Gnade auf. Nach Ps 106,7–12 hat JHWH die Israeliten sogar am Schilfmeer gerettet, obgleich sie seine Wundertaten, die er zuvor für sie in den Plagen veranstaltet hatte, nicht begriffen hatten und in der Not zu trotzen anfingen (vgl. Ex 14,11–12). Er tat es um seines Namens willen (Ps 106,7–8). Hier wird schon deutlich prophetischer Einfluss sichtbar (vgl. Ez 20,9.14.22.44).

Noch weiter in Richtung gnädiger Zuwendung verschoben, finden sich eine Reihe von Exodusmotiven in der liturgischen Mahnrede Ps 81,6–17. Hier ist es Gott selber, der gegenüber dem ihm untreu gewordenen Volk daran erinnert, dass er es von den Lasten der Fronarbeit befreit (V. 7) und auf dessen Klage hin aus der Not gerettet habe (V. 8).[12] Umso unverständlicher muss Israels Übertretung des ersten Gebots des Dekalogs erscheinen (V. 9.12). So übernimmt hier die Exodustradition schon eine ganz ähnliche rhetorische Funktion wie in den Anklagen der Propheten.

Innerhalb der Prophetenbücher begegnet die Exodustradition in folgenden Gattungen: als Kontrast zur Anklage im prophetischen Gerichtswort (Hos 11,1; 13,4; Am 2,10; 5,25; Jer 2,6),[13] als kontrastiver Rückblick in prophetischen Gerichtsreden (Jer 7,22; 11,3–4.7; 34,13), als Gegenstand von oder Argument in Bestreitungen (Am 3,1; 9,7; Mi 6,4; Jes 50,2), als kritisches Element in prophetischen Geschichtsdeutungen (Hos 12,14; Ez 20,6–10.13.15), als Deutungskategorie in prophetischen Gerichtsankündigungen (Hos 8,13b; 9,3; 11,5a; 12,10; Ez 20,36–37), selten auch im Völkerwort (Jes 10,26) und häufig – als Zukunftsprojektion – in prophetischen Heilsankündigungen (Hos 2,16–17; 11,11; Mi 7,15; Jes 43,16–20; 48,20–21; 52,11–12; Jer 16,14–15 par. 23,7–8; Ez 20,38).

Im Hoseabuch (s. Anhang 1.1–2) ist es die enge personale Liebesbeziehung zwischen JHWH und Israel, die durch den Exodus begründet wird (Hos 11,1; 13,4). Vor diesem Hintergrund erscheinen Israels gegenwärtige Gottvergessenheit und Untreue noch unverständlicher als sie es so schon sind. Ganz ähnlich steht bei

---

12 Ps 81,7 ist die einzige Stelle, in der innerhalb der Psalmen einmal das soziale Befreiungspotential der Exodustradition stark gemacht wird! Die Gebetserhörung in V. 8a kann sich auf mehrere Gelegenheiten (Ex 2,24–25; 3,7–10; 14,10–11; 15,24–25) beziehen. Die eigenartige Aussage, „dass Gott Israel im Versteck des Donners geantwortet (עֲנֵךְ) habe" bezieht sich wohl auf die Sinaitheophanie (Ex 19,19), fasst aber die dortige majestätische Reaktion als ein Zeichen der besonderen Zuwendung. Ps 81 gehört wohl wie die verwandte göttliche Mahnrede von Jes 48,17–19 in die Mitte des 5. Jhs. v. Chr., vgl. Albertz, Structure, 31–34 [[= S. 146–149 im vorliegenden Band]].
13 Vgl. dazu grundlegend Westermann, Grundformen, 131–132. |

Jeremia die liebende Fürsorge im Vordergrund, die Israel durch den Gott des
Exodus auf dem Weg durch die Wüste und bei der Landnahme erfuhr (Jer 2,6–
7); doch die gegenwärtige Führungselite verhält sich so, als habe es diese nie
gegeben. Solche kontrastiven Rückbezüge auf den Exodus im Prophetenwort set-
zen, wie schon Kurt Galling feststellte, voraus, dass „die Auszugstradition | [...]
dem Volk selbst lebendig gewesen sein" muss.[14] Auch wenn wir inzwischen gelernt haben, dass die Prophetenbücher nicht direkt die originale mündliche Verkündigung der Propheten widerspiegeln, sondern nachträglich reflektierende
Kompositionen aus der Hand der Propheten oder ihrer Schüler darstellen, bleibt
doch der Öffentlichkeitsbezug der meisten prophetischen Schriften gewahrt.[15]
Spätestens seit der zweite Hälfte des 8. Jahrhunderts war somit im Nordreich
die Exodustradition allgemein geläufig, und spätestens ab der zweiten Hälfte des
7. Jahrhunderts konnte jedermann im Südreich auf sie angesprochen werden,
auch wenn die überlieferten Hymnen- und Volksklagen, die maßgeblich für ihre
Verbreitung sorgten, meist späteren Datums sind.

   Da sich die Propheten kritisch mit ihren Adressaten auseinandersetzten, gehen sie noch freier mit der Exodustradition um als die Psalmen. Hatte der Exodus
in den Hymnen und Klagen fraglos immer als ein grundlegendes Heilsdatum in
Israel gegolten, so ist dies in den Prophetenbüchern keineswegs immer der Fall.
So bestreiten etwa die dtr. Bearbeiter des Amosbuches grundsätzlich (s. Anhang 1.2),[16] dass die Herausführung aus Ägypten durch JHWH ein Ereignis sei,
auf das sich Israel etwas einbilden könne (Am 9,7). Im Gegenteil, die sich darin
ausdrückende Erwählung unterwerfe Israel einer besonders strengen göttlichen
Kontrolle (3,1–2). Für die dtr. Bearbeiter des Jeremiabuches (s. Anhang 1.3) blieb
zwar der Auszug aus Ägypten das grundlegende Datum, an dem JHWH seine
Geschichte mit Israel begann, doch dieses war nach ihrer Sicht sogleich mit einer
Verpflichtung auf das göttliche Wort verbunden (Jer 7,22; 11,3–4.7; 34,13). So entzogen sie ihren Adressaten jede Möglichkeit, die Exodus-Erwählung gegen den Sinai-
bund auszuspielen.[17] Noch einen Schritt weiter gingen die Schüler des Propheten

---

14 S. Galling, Erwählungstradition, 14.
15 Ein Beleg dafür ist die Erzählung von der Verlesung einer frühen Form des Jeremiabuches
durch Baruch (Jer 36) in einer Seitenhalle des Tempels. Ich selber habe aus der Rhetorik und der
literarischen Gestalt der ersten Ausgabe des Deuterojesajabuches (Jes 40,1–52,12*) nachzuweisen
versucht, dass diese für eine öffentliche Rezitation bestimmt war, s. Albertz, Public Recitation.
16 Die Exodusbezüge im Amosbuch (Am 2,10; 3,1b; 5,25; 9,7) gehören allesamt nicht zu dessen
frühester Schicht. Vielmehr hat Wöhrle, Sammlungen, 135–137, gute Gründe geltend gemacht,
dass sie allesamt einer dtr. Bearbeitungsschicht zugewiesen werden können, die erstmals aus
Hos, Am, Mi und Zeph ein Vierprophetenbuch komponierte (vgl. a.a.O., 229–284).
17 In ähnliche Richtung geht die Aussage der liturgischen Mahnrede in Ps 81,6, dass JHWH „ein
Gesetz in Joseph niedergelegt hat bei seinem Auszug gegen Ägypten." Dass dabei singulär von
einem Auszug „gegen Ägypten" (עַל־מִצְרָיִם) und nicht wie gewöhnlich von einem solchen „aus

Ezechiel (s. Anhang 1.4) mit ihrer großen Geschichtsdeutung in Ez 20: Sie verorteten Israels Erwählung und Verpflichtung, keinerlei Götzen zu verehren, sogar
noch vor den Auszug aus Ägypten (V. 5–7). Und indem sie darstellten, dass Israel
schon in Ägypten nicht bereit gewesen war, dieser | grundlegenden Verpflichtung
nachzukommen, formten die Prophetenschüler die Herausführung aus Ägypten
zu einem Reinigungsgericht um, das JHWH vollzog, um sein Volk auf radikale
Weise von den Götzen Ägyptens zu trennen (V. 8–10). Ihrer Meinung hatte es
überhaupt kein heilvolles Gründungsdatum in Israels Geschichte gegeben, auf
das sich jedermann bedingungslos hätte berufen können.[18]

Als Kontrastmotiv zur kritisierten Gegenwart wanderte der Exodus auch in
die prophetische Gerichtsankündigung und wurde damit zu einer Deutungskategorie für die Zukunftserwartung (s. Anhang 3.2). Schon der Prophet Hosea kündig-
te die zu erwartenden Deportationen der Bevölkerung nach Assyrien als eine
Rückkehr nach Ägypten (Hos 8,13b; 9,3; 11,5a.11) und damit als eine Annullierung
der dort begonnenen Heilsgeschichte an. Als Gott „von Ägypten her" konnte
JHWH die gewährte Kulturlandexistenz Israels auch wieder beenden und sein
Volk in die nicht-sesshafte Anfangsphase zurückwerfen (Hos 12,10). Doch da sich
JHWH gerade damals als treuer Retter Israels erwiesen hatte, deutete schon Hosea vorsichtig an, dass es aus dieser erzwungenen Fremdlingsexistenz heraus
einen neuen Exodus geben könnte (Hos 2,16–17; 11,11). Die Hoffnung auf einen
neuen Exodus ist dann während des babylonischen Exils besonders von der Deu-
terojesajagruppe (s. Anhang 3.3) in glühenden Farben ausgemalt worden. Anders
als der alte Exodus sollte der neue nicht mehr von ängstlicher Eile oder Durst
geprägt sein, weil JHWH die Rückwanderer selber begleiten und die Wüste in
fruchtbares Land verwandeln würde (Jes 43,18–20; 48,20–21; 52,11–12). Nach Sicht
der Ezechielschüler würden allerdings nur diejenigen die Heimat wirklich erreichen, die nach der Herausführung „aus dem Land ihrer Fremdlingsschaft" ein
erneutes Reinigungsgericht JHWHs erfolgreich durchlaufen hätten. Die notori-
schen Übeltäter würden ausgesondert werden; sie sollten den Neuanfang nicht
gleich wieder gefährden (Ez 20,37–38).[19]

Ägypten" (מִמִּצְרָיִם; so die LXX) gesprochen wird, ist, sofern es sich nicht um einen Textfehler
handelt, vielleicht ein Ausdruck der Distanzierung, die durch die göttliche Gesetzgebung eintritt.
Andere vermuten eine Anspielung auf die Plagen, etwa Hossfeld/Zenger, Psalmen II, 474; Klein,
Geschichte, 162–163. |

18 Vgl. zu Ez 20 grundlegend Krüger, Geschichtskonzepte, 206–214.

19 Zur kontroversen Diskussion der Deuterojesaja- und der Ezechielschule über die Bedingungen der Möglichkeit für einen Neuanfang vgl. Zimmerli, Exodus, 193–204; Albertz, Beginning, 10–
19 [[= S. 242–251 im vorliegenden Band]]. Jüngst hat Hendel, Remembering, 332–338, die beiden
exilischen Neuinterpretationen der Exodustradition in Ez 20 und Jes 43,16–21 einer eingehenden
vergleichenden Untersuchung unterzogen. Er hält sie für eigentlich unvereinbare „counter-

Auch wenn hier nicht alle Belegstellen, die im Anhang aufgelistet sind, ausdrücklich behandelt werden konnten, zeigt sich doch deutlich, dass das Anwendungsspektrum, das die Exodustradition in der Prophetie gewonnen hat, noch über das der Psalmen hinausgeht. Für den behandelten Traditionsausschnitt insgesamt kann man sagen, dass die Exodustradition sehr stark formbar war und je nach Anlass und Verwendungsabsicht in ganz verschiedene Richtungen akzentuiert und weiterentwickelt, das heißt transformiert werden konnte. |

3 Motivliche Ausgestaltungen der Exodustradition

Überblickt man die Belege für die Exodustradition bei den Propheten und in den Psalmen insgesamt,[20] so ist auch eine erstaunlich breite motivliche Ausgestaltung erkennbar. Die prophetischen und psalmistischen Träger der Tradition waren offenbar nur wenigen Festlegungen unterworfen und hatten eine große Gestaltungsmöglichkeit.

Inhaltlich lassen sich die Belege zwei großen Motivkreisen zuordnen, erstens der Herausführung bzw. Befreiung aus Ägypten, wozu auch die Plagen zu rechnen sind, und zweitens der Rettung am Schilfmeer. Da die beiden Motivkreise in einer ganzen Reihe von Texten je für sich gesondert vorkommen,[21] hatte unter anderem Johannes Kühlewein die These aufgestellt, dass beide „von Hause aus Einzeltraditionen darstellen und als solche bis in die Spätzeit hinein belegt sind."[22] Doch sind Zweifel an dieser These angebracht.[23] So begegnen beide Motivkreise in einigen Psalmen sehr wohl nebeneinander (Ps 78; 114; 136). Dazu weist Ps 106, der selber um die Schilfmeerereignisse kreist (V. 7–12), nicht nur implizit auf die Plagewunder zurück (V. 7), sondern stellt in V. 22 die „Wunder im Lande Hams" und die „Wunder am Schilfmeer" sogar ausdrücklich nebeneinander. Außerdem scheint sich die Darstellung Deuterojesajas, wie Gott durch sein Schelten das Meer trockenlegte und Ströme zur Wüste machte (Jes 50,2b), in der Schilderung der Auswirkung dieses göttlichen Eingriffs an der ersten Plage zu orientieren (vgl. Ex 7,18.21). So haben wir wohl eher zwei thematische Schwerpunkte einer gemeinsamen Exodustradition vorliegen, die beide ihren Trägern bekannt

---

memories", die erst später durch dialogischen Austausch der biblischen Bücher beide zu einem Teil des kulturellen Gedächtnisses des alten Israel werden konnten (a. a. O., 343). |

20 S. unten die Tabelle im Anhang.

21 Die Herausführung aus Ägypten etwa in Ps 80,9; 81,6.11; 105; Ez 20; die Rettung am Schilfmeer etwa in Ps 66,6; 77; 106; Jes 51,9–10.

22 S. Kühlewein, Geschichte, 134–138, das Zitat befindet sich auf S. 138.

23 So etwa auch Preuss, Theologie I, 49.

waren und derer sie sich gleichermaßen bedienen konnten, wie dies am deutlichsten bei Deuterojesaja belegt ist.[24]

Besonders groß ist der Motivreichtum bei der Darstellung des Schilfmeerwunders (s. Anhang 2.1). In Jes 51,9–10 wird die Trockenlegung des Meeres,[25] um den erlösten Israeliten einen Weg durch dessen Tiefen zu bahnen, als ein göttlicher Kampf gegen die Chaosungeheuer Rahab und Tannin geschildert.[26] Dies | ist aber der einzige Beleg dafür, dass das Schilfmeerwunder mit dem Chaoskampf gleichgesetzt wird; in den übrigen vergleichbaren Passagen (Ps 74,13–17; 89,10–13; Hiob 26,7–13) steht der Kampf in einem schöpfungstheologischen Kontext.[27] Auch das Moselied Ex 15,1–18, das gerne als Kern und Ausgangspunkt dieser mythologischen Überhöhung des Geschehens angesehen wird,[28] wandelt das Chaoskampfmotiv schon wieder derart ab, dass das Meer nicht als Gegner, sondern als eine Waffe Gottes gegen seine Feinde fungiert (V. 6–10).

Allerdings gibt es eine ganze Reihe von Stellen, an denen das Schilfmeerwunder mit Anspielungen an den Chaoskampf oder an eine Theophanie geschildert wird (s. Anhang 2.2). So bringt in Ps 77,17 der Anblick Gottes das Meer zum Erbeben (חיל) und die Urflut zum Erzittern (רגז), doch unterscheidet sich der hier zitierte Hymnus dadurch von der in Jes 51,9–10 imaginierten Szenerie, dass es Gott selber ist, der sich unter weiteren theophanen Machterweisen (Ps 77,18–19) seinen Weg durch die gewaltigen Wasser bahnt (V. 20).[29] Weiter vom Kampfgeschehen ist schon die Vorstellung entfernt, dass JHWH das Meer durch sein Schelten (גער) trocken legt (חרב, Jes 50,2b; Ps 106,7) oder das Meer vor dem bloßen Anblick Gottes die Flucht (נוס) ergreift (Ps 114,3.5).

Größer ist die Stellengruppe, in denen die Rettung am Schilfmeer ohne Anspielungen auf den Chaoskampf dargestellt wird (s. Anhang 2.3). Schon allein

---

24 Vgl. die Bezugnahmen auf die Rettung am Schilfmeer in Jes 43,16–17; 50,2b; 51,9–10, wo es um Gottes machtvolles Eingreifen zugunsten seines Volkes geht, und die Anspielungen auf die Herausführung aus Ägypten in Jes 43,18–20; 48,20–21; 52,11–12, wo die Rückführung der Exilierten im Zentrum steht.

25 Das artikellose ים kann hier vom vorausgehenden Zusammenhang her den Meergott Yam bezeichnen (vgl. Ps 74,13), der aus der ugaritischen Mythologie bekannt ist, doch wenn hier nicht mehr von seiner Besiegung, sondern von seiner Trockenlegung gesprochen wird, dann wird er schon ein gutes Stück weit entpersonalisiert und depotenziert.

26 Vgl. die Kampfesverben חלל pol. „durchbohren" und חצב hif. „niederhauen" (?), wobei | das zweite wahrscheinlich mit 1QSᵃ besser von dem Verb מחץ „zerschmettern" abzuleiten ist, das auch in Hiob 26,12 in einem ähnlichen Zusammenhang begegnet.

27 Albertz, Weltschöpfung, 110–116; dagegen ordnete Norin, Meer, 110–117, die Chaoskampfmotive in Ps 74 und 89 noch dem Schilfmeerwunder zu.

28 So etwa Norin, Meer, 77–107.

29 Zum Ineinander von Chaoskampf- und Theophaniemotiven in Ps 77 vgl. Jeremias, Theophanie, 26–28.

diese Tatsache macht die These von Stig Norin unwahrscheinlich, sie als entmy-
thisierende Abwandlung der Chaoskampfdarstellungen zu erklären.[30] Nach
Jes 63,12–13 spaltete (בקע) Gott das Meer, indem er seinen wunderbaren Arm zur
Rechten Moses führte und die Israeliten in Fluten führte wie Pferde in der Wüste
(vgl. Ps 78,13a). Von einem Zerschneiden (גזר) des Meeres ist in Ps 136,13 die Rede.
In Ps 78,13b wird das Wasser wie ein Wall aufgestellt (נצב כמו־נד). Nach Jes 43,16–
17 legte JHWH völlig undramatisch (נתן) einen Weg in das Meer, während die
schwer bewaffnete Streitmacht, die er in Fluten hinausführte (יצא hif.!), sich
hinlegt und nicht mehr aufsteht.[31] Vom Wasser bedeckt (כסה) werden die | Feinde
in Ps 78,53b und 106,11. In Ps 66,6 ist schlicht von einer Umwandlung (הפך) des
Meeres in Trockenes die Rede.[32] Interessant ist eine parallelisierende Darstellung
von Schilfmeer- und Wasserwunder in Ps 78,13–16: So wie Gott einerseits das
Meer spaltete und die Israeliten hindurchführte, so spaltete er andererseits die
Felsen in der Wüste und ließ Wasserströme hervorsprudeln (s. Anhang 2.4). Damit
erhält das Schilfmeerereignis auf ganz unmythologische Weise eine schöpfungs-
theologische Dimension, die in Ps 114,5–8 mit Anspielungen an den Chaoskampf-
mythos realisiert wurde.

Die Motive, mit denen die Herausführung Israels aus Ägypten geschildert
wird, sind nicht ganz so variantenreich. Dies gilt insbesondere für die Belege,
welche die Herausführung nur kurz ohne weitere Details erwähnen, aber auch
deren prophetische Abwandlungen als Zeitpunkt der Verpflichtung Israels oder
als Reinigungsgericht (s. Anhang 1.1–4).[33] Hier begegnet häufig ein eher formel-
hafter Sprachgebrauch,[34] dass JHWH Israel „aus (dem Lande) Ägypten heraufgeführt (עלה hif.)"[35] oder „herausgeführt (יצא hif.)"[36] habe, bzw. dass Israel „aus

---

30 Norin, Meer, 119–128, zieht viele dieser Stellen unter die Überschrift „Der entmythisierte Was-
sergott".

31 Elliger, Deuterojesaja, 346, notiert zu diesen Versen: „Es ist nicht der geringste Zweifel, daß
hinter dieser Darstellung die Tradition vom Auszug aus Ägypten steht. Aber die Sprache und die
Art der Darstellung hat gerade mit den bekanntesten Ausprägungen dieser Tradition in Ex 14
und 15, von Grundgedanken und dem einen oder anderen Motivwort abgesehen, merkwürdig
wenig gemein." Die Verwunderung, die Elliger hier ausdrückt, könnte auch für manch andere
Ausprägung der Exodustradition bei den Propheten und in den Psalmen gelten. |

32 Der fehlende Artikel vor ים in Ps 66,6 und Ps 78,13 reicht meiner Meinung nach nicht aus,
hierin noch eine Reminiszenz an das Chaosungeheuer Yam (so in Ps 74,13) zu sehen, so etwa
Norin, Meer, 124.128. Eine Umwandlung in etwas Trockenes spricht doch eher dafür, dass das
bloße Element gemeint ist.

33 Siehe oben S. 116–117 [[= S. 170–171 im vorliegenden Band]].

34 Vgl. dazu die umfassende Untersuchung von Gross, Herausführungsformel, auch wenn sein
Anliegen, den Sprachgebrauch syntaktisch sehr genau zu differenzieren, den Gesamteindruck
etwas verwischt.

35 Hos 12,14; Am 2,10; 3,1b; 9,7; Mi 6,4; Jer 2,6; 11,7; 16,14–15; 23,7–8; Ps 81,11.

36 Jer 7,22; 11,4; 32,21; 34,13; Ez 20,6.9.10.

(dem Lande) Ägypten heraufgestiegen (עלה q.)"[37] oder „herausgezogen (יצא q.)"[38] sei. Dabei mag die Formulierung mit dem Verb עלה durch den Kultruf geprägt sein, der unter dtr. Übermalung noch in 1 Kön 12,28 für das Heiligtum von Bethel belegt ist (vgl. Ex 32,4.8). Die Formulierung mit dem Verb יצא könnte von der Dekalogeinleitung her ihre Verbreitung erfahren haben (Ex 20,2). Doch kann der Vorgang der Herausführung auch mit verschiedenen Metaphern ausgedrückt werden, so wie das Verpflanzen eines Weinstocks (Ps 80,9), das Herausrufen eines Sohnes (Hos 11,1) oder das Aufbrechen-Lassen einer Herde (Ps 78,52). In Hos 12,14 wird betont, dass die Heraufführung Israels durch einen Propheten stattgefunden habe, in Ps 105,26 wird die Sendung Moses und Aarons, in Mi 6,4 die derselben und Mirjams erwähnt. Der Befreiungsvorgang, der damit verbunden war, wird nur relativ selten hervorgekehrt, so in Mi 6,4, wo JHWH betont, dass er Israel „aus dem Sklavenhaus befreit" (פדה) habe. Wenn Ps 81,11 sehr konkret formuliert, Gott habe Israels „Schulter von der Last befreit (סור מסבל hi.), und seine Hände seien vom Lastkorb losgekommen" (עבר מדוד q.), dann fühlt man sich fast an die Schilderungen der Fronarbeit erinnert, die im | Atramḫasîs-Epos den Igigu-Göttern aufgeladen war.[39] Die Auskunft von Ps 105,43, dass die Herausführung unter dem Jubel der Beteiligten stattgefunden habe, ist offenbar schon von der Vorstellung vom neuen Exodus beeinflusst (Jes 51,11).

Größerer Detailreichtum findet sich allerdings in den Schilderungen der ägyptischen Plagen, die in Ps 78,44–51 und 105,28–36 mit zahlreichen Abweichungen untereinander und zur Plage-Auszugs-Erzählung von Ex 7,14–12,39* überliefert sind.[40] Sie sollen im nächsten Abschnitt behandelt werden. Beide Motivkomplexe, die Herausführung aus Ägypten und die Rettung am Schilfmeer, werden über das häufige Reden von den Zeichen und Wundern in Ägypten zusammengebunden (s. Anhang 1.5).[41] Es handelt sich also insgesamt, auch von ihrer breiten motivlichen Ausprägung her, um eine ausgesprochene lebendige, vielstimmige Tradition.

---

37 Hos 2,17.
38 Mi 7,15; Ps 114,1. |
39 Vgl. das Nebeneinander von *abšānu* „Joch" und *t/šupšikku* „Tragkorb" auf Tafel I, Z. 196–197 u. ö. vgl. Lambert/Millard, Atra-ḫasīs, 56–57. Motivlich kommt dem Psalm aus der Hebräischen Bibel Lev 26,13 am nächsten.
40 Hinzu kommt die kurze Erwähnung der zehnten Plage in Ps 135,8; 136,10–12.
41 So Mi 7,15; Jer 32,20–21; Ps 78,12.43; 105,27; 106,21.22; 135,9. Interessant ist dabei, dass Ps 105,27 Gott für „die Worte seiner Zeichen" lobt und so auch die Wunderzeichen in Ägypten in die Kette der heilvollen Worte, die JHWH in der Heilsgeschichte spricht, einordnet (vgl. V. 8.19.42 und V. 31.34). |

4 Die Entwicklung der prophetischen und psalmistischen Exodustradition in Bezug auf deren erzählerische Ausformung im Pentateuch

Die Exodustradition bei den Propheten und in den Psalmen war bis hierher bewusst ohne jeden Vergleich zur ihrer Ausprägung in den Exoduserzählungen beschrieben worden. Dies scheint mir wichtig zu sein, um sie überhaupt erst einmal als eine eigene Größe wahrzunehmen, die ihr eigenes Gewicht hat. Wie das Verhältnis der beiden genannten Stränge der Exodustradition zutreffend beschrieben werden kann, ist eine schwierige Frage, die mit einigen methodischen Tücken belastet ist. Einerseits wissen wir nämlich nicht genau, wieweit uns der Bestand der Tradition, den sie einmal in der erzählerischen, prophetischen und psalmistischen Überlieferung gehabt hat, erhalten ist; es mag Bezüge gegeben haben, die wir in der Auswahl, die uns die Hebräische Bibel bewahrt hat, nicht mehr, oder nicht mehr zutreffend, erkennen können. Es ist darum riskant, überall direkte literarische Abhängigkeiten zwischen den uns mehr oder minder zufällig erhaltenen Textbeständen finden zu wollen. Andererseits hängt die Festlegung der Richtung der Abhängigkeit erheblich von der Datierung der Texte ab, die häufig schwierig ist. Dies gilt insbesondere für die Psalmen; doch auch die Da|tierung der Pentateuchtexte ist heute, da die klassische Drei-Quellen-Theorie ihre beherrschende Überzeugungskraft verloren hat, erneut Gegenstand heftiger Kontroversen.[42] Tendenziell schält sich heraus, dass die Exoduserzählungen des Pentateuch teilweise deutlich später anzusetzen sind als in der Quellentheorie veranschlagt. Eine gewisse zeitliche Orientierung können allerdings die Prophetentexte bieten.

Drei Positionen, die das Verhältnis der Exodusdarstellungen in den Psalmen zu denen der Erzählungen zu bestimmen, sollen hier kurz skizziert werden: Aare Lauha geht 1945 unter der damals üblichen Annahme eines frühen Jahwisten grundsätzlich davon aus, dass die Belegstellen in den Psalmen vom Pentateuch abhängig sind. Die Abweichungen erklärt er entweder aus „einer mündlich nebenher laufenden Überlieferung" oder „mit dichterischer Freiheit" der Psalmendichter.[43] Aufgrund der vielen Abweichungen, welche die Exodusmotive in den Psalmen gegenüber den Exoduserzählungen aufweisen, kommt Johannes Kühlewein 1973 zu einer gegenteiligen Einschätzung: „Gewiß mag die Geschichtsdarstellung im Pentateuch da und dort auf die der beiden Psalmen (sc. Ps 78 und 105) eingewirkt haben, aber grundsätzlich stehen sie in einem eigenen und vom ausgestalteten Pentateuch unabhängigen Traditionszusammenhang."[44] Demgegenüber

---

42 Vgl. nur die neueste Übersicht über die Forschung von Römer, Pentateuch, 53–166.
43 Vgl. Lauha, Geschichtsmotive, 60–61.
44 So Kühlewein, Geschichte, 146.

ordnet Judith Gärtner 2012 die Geschichtstraditionen der Psalmen einem Konzept „paradigmatischer Geschichte" zu, für das ein fortlaufender Rezeptions- und Interpretationsprozess typisch ist. „Somit beschreibt das Verständnis von ‚paradigmatischer Geschichte' weniger einen Zustand, sondern vielmehr einen Prozess historischer Deutungen."[45] In diesem Prozess übernehmen für Frau Gärtner die Geschichtspsalmen eindeutig die Rolle „der Interpretation eines nahezu vollständigen Pentateuchs", sie sind eine „relecture der Tora".[46] Mag auch diese Einschätzung für die von Frau Gärtner untersuchten Psalmen 78, 105, 106, 135 und 136 zum großen Teil zutreffen, so wird von ihr doch der Interpretationsvorgang, bezieht man das gesamte Material mit ein, vielleicht zu einseitig auf eine Richtung festgelegt und zu stark auf das erhaltene Textmaterial eingeengt. Hier war der Ansatz von Lauha mit der Annahme einer nebenher laufenden mündlichen Überlieferung weiter. Der Rekurs auf den Rezeptions- und Interpretationsbegriff durch Frau Gärtner ist sicher ein Fortschritt gegenüber der Rede von „dichterischer Freiheit", auch für das Verständnis der Exodustradition. Allerdings sollte er nicht den Blick dafür verstellen, dass innerhalb des Traditionsprozesses auch kreativ Neues geschaffen werden konnte, das teilweise so eigenständig ist, dass es Kühlewein zur Annahme einer | gesonderten Exodustradition in den Psalmen veranlasste. Doch ging er mit dieser Einschätzung wahrscheinlich zu weit. Wahrscheinlicher ist nach meiner Sicht die Annahme einer einzigen, aber sehr vielstimmigen Exodustradition, in der sich die erzählerischen und die psalmistischen und prophetischen Ausgestaltungen gegenseitig beeinflussten.

Nach meiner Übersicht über die Exodusbelege in den Psalmen und bei den Propheten auf der einen Seite und den Erzählungen vom Exodus auf der anderen, deren literaturgeschichtliche Entwicklung ich in meinem Exoduskommentar zu beschreiben versucht habe,[47] ergibt sich für die Rekonstruktion der Exodustradition grob das folgende Bild. In der frühen Phase, die das 10.–7. Jahrhundert v. Chr. umfasst, aber teilweise auch noch bis in das 6. Jahrhundert hineinreicht, sind die Präsentationen des Exodusgeschehens, die sich in den Texten erhalten haben, in den drei Traditionsbereichen recht verschieden und haben nur wenig miteinander zu tun. Das hängt erstens damit zusammen, dass das Exodusgeschehen, soweit wir erkennen können, anfangs noch wenig detailliert ausformuliert war. Die Belege, die sich aus dem Ende des 10. Jahrhunderts erhalten haben, wie der Kultruf von Bethel (1 Kön 12,18) und das sogenannte Mirjamlied (Ex 15,21), treffen nur die recht pauschalen Aussagen, dass JHWH Israel aus Ägypten heraufgeführt und

---

45 So Gärtner, Geschichtspsalmen, 11–24, im Anschluss an Eric Voegelin und Aleida und Jan Assmann; das Zitat befindet sich auf S. 15.
46 Die Zitate befinden sich bei Gärtner, Geschichtspsalmen, 8 und 10. |
47 S. die Übersichten Albertz, Exodus 1–18, 19–26; Ders., Exodus 19–40, 9–18.

dass er seine göttliche Macht gegen eine menschliche Militärmacht eindrucksvoll erwiesen habe. Zweitens hängen die mangelnden Bezüge auch damit zusammen, dass die Exodustradition anfangs vor allem im Nordreich gepflegt wurde[48] und nach dessen staatlichem Untergang 722 v. Chr. im Südreich zwar aufgegriffen, aber stark selektiert und verändert wurde.

In einer mittleren Phase, die etwa von der Mitte des 6. bis zum Ende des 5. Jahrhunderts v. Chr. läuft, liegen zwar die meisten der nicht-priesterlichen und priesterlichen Exodus- und Wüstenerzählungen des Exodus- und Numeribuches in großen kompositionellen Zusammenhängen vor, aber sie bilden nur einen Strang der Exodustradition neben den anderen. Die Rückbezüge der Exodusdarstellungen in der Propheten- und Psalmenüberlieferung auf diejenigen der Erzähltradition werden deutlich dichter. Doch kann noch immer sehr frei mit Letzterer umgegangen werden. Sie hat noch keine normierende Wirkung.

Es scheint mir, dass die Exodus- und Wüstenerzählungen des Pentateuch erst ab dem 4. Jahrhundert v. Chr. eine erkennbare prägende und normierende Wirkung auf die Darstellung der Exodusthematik in den Psalmen erhalten haben. Dies hängt vermutlich mit der Kanonisierung des Pentateuch am Anfang dieses Jahrhunderts zusammen. Erst dadurch, dass der Pentateuch zur offiziellen | Gründungsurkunde der Judäer und Samarier wurde, orientierten sich auch die Psalmendichter bei ihren Exodusdarstellungen bewusst an ihm, auch wenn sie es sich nicht nehmen ließen, dabei auch auf andere Ausprägungen der Exodustradition anzuspielen und ihre eigenen Akzente zu setzen. Erst jetzt kann man ihre Arbeit als eine „relecture der Tora" bezeichnen.

4.1 Zur frühen Phase der Exodustradition

Es ist hier nicht möglich, die Entwicklung der Bezüge zwischen der prophetischen, psalmistischen und erzählerischen Exodustradition im Einzelnen zu verfolgen. Einige Beobachtungen zur Erläuterung meiner These müssen genügen.

Eigentlich sollte man erwarten, dass die ältesten Texte einer Tradition deren Kern bildeten. Doch eigenartigerweise werden gerade die ältesten in Ex 1–15 verarbeiteten Exoduserzählungen, die meiner Meinung nach noch aus dem

---

48 Vgl. zu der weithin akzeptierten These z. B. Albertz, Religionsgeschichte Israels I, 212–226, und Becker, Exodus-Credo, 88–91. Die Tatsache, dass im Nordreich die Exodustradition sogar Teil der Staatstheologie wurde, wie Becker zurecht betont, schließt allerdings deren sozialrevolutionären Impuls keineswegs aus, wenn man berücksichtigt, dass sich der Nordstaat aus einer Aufstandsbewegung unter Jerobeam I. herleitete (1 Kön 11,26–28; 12,1–18). |

Nordreich des 9. Jahrhunderts stammen,[49] in Prophetie und Psalmen gar nicht oder nur spärlich aufgenommen: die politische Mose-Erzählung (Ex 1,15–2,23aα; 4,19–20a.24–26) überhaupt nicht, die Erzählung von der Verschärfung der Fron (Ex 5,3.4*.6–19) höchstens einmal in Ps 81,7 und die Schilfmeererzählung (Ex 14,5a.6–30*) erst in ihrer priesterlichen Umgestaltung (Ps 78,13.53; 106,10–11). Der Höhepunkt der nicht-priesterlichen Version (Ex 14,27), dass JHWH die Ägypter mitten ins Meer schüttelt (נער pi.), wird nur einmal in dem späten Psalm 136,15 aufgegriffen. Umgekehrt steht die eindrucksvolle Exodus-Metaphorik von der Verpflanzung eines Weinstocks, welche die relativ frühe Volksklage in Ps 80,9–12 überliefert, völlig isoliert da;[50] ihr Grundbestand stammt wohl noch aus dem Nordreich des 8. Jahrhunderts.[51] Auch die überaus positive Charakterisierung der Exodus- und Wüstenzeit durch den Propheten Hosea als Epoche einer ungetrübten Liebes- und Vertrauensbeziehung zwischen Israel und JHWH (Hos 2,17; 11,1; 13,4) hat keinerlei Berücksichtigung in den Pentateucherzählungen gefunden. Sie spiegelt sich hier höchstens noch indirekt im Konzept eines idealen engen Bundes am Sinai, der aber schon nach wenigen Tagen durch Israels Abfall zum Goldenen Kalb gebrochen wurde (Ex 24; 32). Hier drängen sich in die erzählerische Ausprägung der Tradition durch den Verfasser der Exoduskomposition (Ex 1,9–34,32) schon exilische Erfahrungen hinein, die | Hosea so noch nicht kannte.[52] Hoseas Präsentation JHWHs als Gott von Ägypten her (Hos 12,10; 13,4) stand aber wahrscheinlich bei der Formulierung der Dekalogpräambel Pate (Ex 20,2).

Nachdem die Exodustradition mit dem Untergang des Nordreiches in den Süden gewandert war, wurde sie hier teilweise im 7. Jahrhundert v. Chr. unter Aufnahme kanaanäischer und babylonischer Chaoskampfvorstellungen mythisch überhöht und schöpfungstheologisch fundiert, um sie damit besser in die Jerusalemer Gott-König-Theologie einbinden zu können.[53] Die Schilderungen der Schilf-

---

49 Vgl. Albertz, Exodus 1–18, 21.64–65.113.247–248.
50 Als motivliche Parallele könnte man höchstens Jer 2,21 anführen, doch ist unsicher, ob Jeremia hier auf den Exodus anspielen will. Beim jungen Jeremia sind auch sonst Nordreichtraditionen nachweisbar.
51 Vgl. Hossfeld/Zenger, Psalmen II, 456–458; Albertz, Israel, 46–49 [[= S. 204–207 im vorliegenden Band]]. Von einem „erstaunlich langen ‚Exodusschweigen'" wie Becker, Exodus-Credo, 83, kann man nur reden, wenn man wichtige Texte (Hosea u. a.) spät datiert. Doch scheint auch er zumindest die Belege Num 22,5; 24,8 für das 8.–7. Jh. v. Chr. gelten zu lassen. |
52 Hosea hat aber die Verunglimpfung des Stierkultes von Bethel (und Samaria?) entscheidend vorbereitet, vgl. Hos 8,5; 13,2.
53 Vgl. Ex 15,6–9.18 und dazu Spieckermann, Heilsgegenwart, 96–115; Jeremias, Königtum, 93–106; Leuenberger, Konzeptionen, 221–244. Ob allerdings überall, wo im Zusammenhang mit dem Exodusmotiv auf die Chaoskampftradition angespielt wird, auf eine JHWH-Königs-Theologie geschlossen werden kann (so etwa Hossfeld/Zenger, Psalmen III, 265–273, in Bezug auf Ps 114), ist die Frage.

meerereignisse als Chaoskampf (Jes 51,9–10) oder unter Verwendung von Chaos-kampf- und Theophaniemotiven (Ex 15,6–18*; Ps 77,14–21) sind meiner Meinung in dieser Zeit entstanden. Alle drei genannten Texte sind uns nur als Fragmente überliefert, die in anderen Zusammenhängen zitiert werden.[54] Dies gilt meiner Meinung nach auch für das Moselied, das in Ex 15,1–5 eine neue Einleitung erhal-ten hat, um es glatter in den erzählerischen Kontext einfügen zu können.[55] Durch diese Beispiele wird erwiesen, dass keineswegs der gesamte Überlieferungsbe-stand auf uns gekommen ist. Wahrscheinlich war diese Jerusalemer Ausprägung der Schilfmeertradition einmal breiter, da sie in der Propheten- und Psalmenüber-lieferung in abgemilderter Form noch länger nachwirkt (Jes 50,2b; Ps 114; 106,9). In die Erzählüberlieferung, zu der sie motivlich nicht so recht passt, ist sie mit dem Moselied (Ex 15,1–18) meiner Meinung nach erst relativ spät, nämlich in der zweiten Hälfte des 5. Jahrhunderts durch den Hexateuchredaktor, integriert worden.[56] |

4.2 Zur mittleren Phase der Exodustradition

Nach meiner Sicht ist eine zusammenhängende erzählerische Darstellung der Exodusereignisse erstmals in der zweiten Hälfte des 6. Jahrhunderts, etwa um 540 v. Chr., durch den Verfasser der nicht-priesterlichen Exoduskomposition (R[EX]) geschaffen worden (Ex 1,9–34,32*), allerdings unter Verwendung älterer Teilkom-positionen wie etwa der Plagen-Auszugs-Erzählung (Ex 5,3–21 + 7,14–12,39*), die wohl aus dem 7. Jahrhundert, und einer Schilfmeererzählung, die in ihrer Grund-fassung (Ex 14,5a.6–30*) meiner Meinung nach noch aus dem 9. Jahrhundert v. Chr. stammt.[57] Damit lag zum ersten Mal eine umfassende Gesamtdarstellung

---

54 Jes 51,9–10 wird ein kurzer Abschnitt aus einer Volksklage innerhalb des größeren Imperativ-gedichts (Jes 51,9–52,2*) zitiert (vgl. Westermann, Jesaja 40–66, 192–200); in Ps 77 dient einem Einzelnen das Zitat aus einem Hymnus (V. 14–20 vgl. die Trikola) als Trost in seiner Glaubensnot (vgl. Hossfeld/Zenger, Psalmen II, 404–405). V. 21 könnte auch eine Neubildung sein.
55 Während der aufgenommene JHWH-Hymnus (Ex 15,6–18*) bis auf V. 18 in Du-Anrede formu-liert ist und kaum Bezüge zur Ex 14 aufweist, stellt der in der dritten Person formulierte Ein-gangsteil Ex 15,1–5 vielerlei Verbindungen zur Schilfmeererzählung (vgl. 15,3 mit 14,14.25; 15,4–5 mit 14,4.7.25.28), zur weiteren Exoduserzählung (vgl. 15,2b mit 3,6; 18,4) und zur übrigen Psalmen-überlieferung her (vgl. 15,2b mit Ps 118,14). Dabei übernimmt Ex 15,5 die Funktion einer Überlei-tung zum zitierten Hymnus. Schon Jeremias, Königtum, 98–99, hatte den sekundären Charakter der Verse V 2.4.5 erkannt.
56 Zur Identifizierung und Datierung dieses Redaktors vgl. Albertz, Exodus 1–18, 234–236.314; Ders., Formative Impact. |
57 Zur Begründung vgl. Albertz, Exodus 1–18, 21.215–216.247–248.

vor, an der sich alle Tradenten orientieren konnten. Doch wie wenig prägenden Einfluss sie lange Zeit hatte, wird schlaglichtartig daran deutlich, dass ihr dramatischer Höhepunkt, nämlich die Abkehr vom Gott des Exodus durch die Verehrung des goldenen Kalbes (Ex 32), nirgends bei den Propheten und nur ein einziges Mal in den Psalmen aufgegriffen wurde (Ps 106,19–23), einem Psalm, der erst in die Spätphase nach der Kanonisierung des Pentateuchs gehört.[58]

Einige Zeit später ist dann diese Exoduskomposition in die erste priesterliche Fassung der Gründungsgeschichte Israels (PB[1]) eingearbeitet worden, welche in Analogie zum babylonischen Schöpfungsmythos Enuma-Elisch von der Schöpfung bis zur Kultgründung reichte (Gen 1–Lev 16*) und damit das Exodusgeschehen auf andere Weise schöpfungstheologisch fundierte.[59] In diesen Zusammenhang gehört auch die Umarbeitung der Schilfmeererzählung, mit welcher der geschichtliche Kampf gegen den Pharao an die Stelle des mythischen Chaoskampfes trat. Dabei ist es durchaus möglich, dass sich der priesterliche Verfasser bei seiner Darstellung, wie Mose auf Gottes Befehl hin das Meer durch seine erhobene Hand spaltet (בקע, Ex 14,16.21), von einer Ausprägung der Psalmentradition hat inspirieren lassen, die in Jes 63,10–14 bezeugt ist, wird hier doch erstaunlich detailliert geschildert, wie Gott „seinen herrlichen Arm zur Rechten des Mose führte" und damit „das Wasser vor ihnen spaltete" (בקע, V. 12). Der Priester hätte dann das dortige komplizierte Ineinander von göttlichem und mosaischem Wirken in seine typische Struktur von göttlichem Befehl und menschlicher Ausführung transponiert und so einfacher vorstellbar gemacht. In jedem Fall konnte der Priester durch die Aufnahme des Motivs von einem Durchzug Israels durch das gespaltene Meer die Wunderhaftigkeit des Rettungsvorgangs gewaltig steigern.

Typisch für den Umgang mit der Erzähltradition durch einen Psalmendichter in der mittleren Traditionsphase ist der Ps 78. Häufig wird der Psalm noch in die | vorexilische Epoche angesetzt.[60] Doch da er die priesterliche Fassung der Schilfmeerereignisse voraussetzt, nämlich eine Spaltung (בקע) des Meeres und

---

58 Siehe unten S. 130–132 [[= S. 185–187 im vorliegenden Band]].
59 Vgl. zum Umfang und theologischen Konzept der ersten priesterlichen Bearbeitung Albertz, Exodus 19–40, 379–380. |
60 Zur älteren Forschung s. Mathias, Geschichtstheologie, 69 Anm. 138; vgl. dazu Hiebert, Psalm 78, 202–211 (10. Jh. v. Chr.); Weber, Psalm 78, 211–212 (um 700); Weingart, Juda, 452–454 (kurz nach 701); Emanuel, Psalmists, 96–97 (unter Josia). Die jüngste Arbeit von Weingart zeigt, dass eine solche frühe Datierung u. a. nur um den Preis erreicht werden kann, dass solche Partien, die priesterliche oder noch spätere Passagen des Pentateuchs voraussetzen (Ps 78,13–14.40–55) ausgegliedert werden. Doch bleiben daneben auch noch dtr. und weisheitliche Sprachmerkmale, die eher für eine spätere Ansetzung sprechen. Dezidiert für eine nachexilische Datierung plädierten z. B. schon Kraus, Psalmen II, 704, und erneut Klein, Geschichte, 104. Witte, Exodus, 37–39, will sogar bis zum Ende des 3. Jhs. v. Chr. hinabgehen.

einen Durchzug (עבר) der Israeliten in V. 13a, gehört er eher in die nachexilische Zeit. Mehr noch, da der Psalm in V. 13b fast wörtlich eine Formulierung aus dem Moselied aufnimmt, dass Gott „die Wasser wie ein Wall aufstellte" (ויצב־מים כמו־נד, vgl. intransitiv Ex 15,8aβ: נצבו כמו־נד נזלים),[61] setzt er dessen Einfügung hinter Ex 14 schon voraus. Die Schilderungen der Ereignisse in der Erzählung und im Hymnus werden so einfach miteinander kombiniert. Damit gelangen wir aber nach meiner redaktionsgeschichtlichen Einschätzung des Exodusbuches in das letzte Drittel des 5. Jahrhunderts v. Chr., als die Samarier darangingen, in Konkurrenz zu Jerusalem ein neues Heiligtum auf dem Garizim zu bauen (um 425 v. Chr.).[62] In diese Zeit passt auch das Anliegen des Psalmendichters, am Ende warnend auf die Zerstörung Silos (Ps 78,60) und werbend auf die Erwählung des Zion zu verweisen (V. 68), hervorragend hinein.

Nachdem der Dichter von Psalm 78 im ersten Durchgang durch die Heilsge- schichte (V. 12–31) die Schilfmeer-Ereignisse nur kurz abgehandelt hatte (V. 13), kommt er in seinem zweiten Durchgang (V. 40–55)[63] ausführlich auf die Plagen zu sprechen (V. 43–51). Wie die zahlreichen terminologischen und sachlichen Übereinstimmungen zeigen (s. Anhang 1.6), setzte er dabei die Plage-Erzählungen von Ex 7–12 in ihrer heutigen kombiniert nicht-priesterlichen–priesterlichen Fas- sung voraus, geht aber relativ frei und eigenständig mit ihnen | um.[64] Wie der priesterliche Bearbeiter spricht er eingangs von JHWHs „Zeichen und Wundern" in Ägypten (Ps 78,43; vgl. Ex 7,3), doch sind diese für ihn nicht wie für jenen Demonstrationswunder, sondern Machttaten Gottes zur Befreiung Israels aus der

---

61 Das Nomen נד wird nur noch zweimal für das Aufstauen der Jordanwasser (Jos 3,13.16) und einmal der Himmelswasser (Ps 33,7) gebraucht, aber nie mehr zusammen mit dem Verb נצב.

62 Zur Datierung des perserzeitlichen Heiligtums auf dem Garizim vgl. Magen, Dating, 176; Al- bertz, Controversy, 489–491 [[= S. 69–70 im vorliegenden Band]].

63 Während Hossfeld/Zenger, Psalmen II, 425, die nach Ps 78,13 zweite Bezugnahme auf die Exodusereignisse in V. 40–51 einer späteren Redaktion zuweisen, hat Gärtner, Geschichtspsalmen, 46–49, eine Struktur des Psalms aufgewiesen, nach der sich zwei Rückblicke auf Israels Geschich- te, V. 12–31 und V. 40–64, um ein zentrales Mittelstück (V. 32–39), das grundsätzlich über Israels und Gottes Verhalten reflektiert, herumlegen. Die Wiederholung ist damit gewollt. Zu einer ähn- lichen Strukturbeschreibung war kurz zuvor auch schon Emanuel, Psalmists, 21–25, gekommen. Eine solche synchrone Lösung ist auch deswegen zu bevorzugen, weil sich zwischen der Schilde- rung der Schilfmeer- und Wüstenereignisse (V. 13–31) und der Darstellung der Plagen (V. 42–51) keine diachrone Differenz in den Bezugstexten feststellen lässt; beide setzen beispielsweise die priesterliche Bearbeitung von Ex 7–15 voraus. |

64 Für eine literarische Abhängigkeit spricht nicht nur die Übereinstimmung in der Bezeichnung der Plage-Instrumente, sondern auch die einiger übereinstimmender Einzelmotive, etwa dass man das Wasser des Nil nicht mehr trinken (שתה) konnte (Ps 78,44; vgl. Ex 7,18.21a), der Hagel das Vieh (מקנה) in Mitleidenschaft zog (Ps 78,48; vgl. Ex 9,19–26) oder alle Erstgeburt (כל־בכור) bei der letzten Plage geschlagen wurde (Ps 78,51; vgl. Ex 12,12.29).

Not (Ps 78,42), wie dies ebenfalls die nicht-priesterlichen Plage-Erzählungen hervorkehren. Dies mag ein Grund gewesen sein, warum sich der Psalmendichter auf nicht-priesterliche Plage-Erzählungen beschränkt und damit ein älteres Traditionsstadium als das, was ihm vorliegt, restituiert. Allerdings weicht er in der Abfolge und Gewichtung der sieben Plagen stark von seiner Vorlage ab. Am Anfang seiner Darstellung steht hier wie dort die Blutplage, die der Psalmendichter schon in der Ausweitung, die sie durch die priesterliche Bearbeitung erfahren hat, schildert (V. 33; vgl. Ex 7,19.20). Stechfliegen und Froschplage werden gegeneinander vertauscht (Ps 78,45). Auffälliger ist jedoch das Vorziehen der Heuschreckenplage, die in den nicht-priesterlichen Plage-Erzählungen den Höhepunkt vor der abschließenden Tötung der Erstgeburt bildete (V. 46; vgl. Ex 10,1–19.23–29*), der starke Ausbau der Hagelplage (Ps 78,47–49) und die Nachordnung der Pest (V. 50). Diese Umstellungen und Neugewichtungen lassen erkennen, dass der Psalmendichter mit der ihm vorgegebenen Erzähltradition unzufrieden war. Er wollte ihr gegenüber eine klarere Steigerung der göttlichen Sanktionen zugunsten Israels abbilden: Die ersten drei Plagen (Blut, Stechfliegen, Frösche) beeinträchtigen nur das menschliche Leben, die vierte, die Heuschreckenplage, vernichtete die mühsam erarbeite Ernte und damit die Lebensgrundlage. Doch die stark betonte Hagelplage zerstörte erstmals nachhaltig das außermenschliche Leben, sie „tötete" die Nutzpflanzen und das Vieh (V. 47–48).[65] Sie war nach Darstellung des Dichters mit einer besonderen Aufwallung göttlichen Zorns und dem Eingreifen überirdischer Unheilsboten verbunden (V. 49). Indem Gott seinem Zorn freien Lauf ließ, so schilderte es der Psalmendichter abschließend, ging er sogar gegen die Menschen selbst vor. Er lieferte alles menschliche Leben, wie der Dichter die Tradition von der Viehpest (Ex 9,1–7) ausweitete, der Pestseuche aus und erschlug darüber hinaus sogar noch alle Erstgeburt in Ägypten (Ps 78,50–51). So ist die Szene von der Tötung der Erstgeburt in Ps 78 sachlich und theologisch deutlich besser eingebunden als in den Plage-Erzählungen des Exodusbuches. Die Tötung des für die Angehörigen kostbarsten menschlichen Lebens erscheint als der logische Schluss- und Höhepunkt göttlicher Sanktionen und als Folge eines außergewöhnlichen Ausbruchs | des göttlichen Zorns. So bildet die Plagendarstellung von Ps 78 eine kreativ gestaltete Variante eines Stücks der Exodustradition, die zwar die Erzähltradition kennt, aber ihr keineswegs eine höhere Autorität einräumt, sondern sich selbstbewusst als eine verbesserte Fassung neben sie stellt. Etwa zur gleichen Zeit hat nach meiner Sicht der Hexateuchredaktor, dem es zum ersten Mal darum ging, eine offizielle Gründungsgeschichte Israels zu etablieren, die

---

65 Die Verwendung des Verbs הרג „töten, erschlagen" für die Einwirkung des Hagels auf Weinstock und Sykomoren in Ps 78,47 ist ganz ungewöhnlich. Sie lässt erkennen, dass der Dichter des Psalms die Nutzpflanzen ganz bewusst als Lebewesen den Haustieren zur Seite stellen wollte. |

Exodustradition in den Psalmen für so wichtig erachtet, dass er einen eindrucks-
vollen Hymnus daraus (Ex 15,6–18*) in sein großes Erzählwerk integrierte, den
er in V. 1–5 zur besseren Einbindung in den Erzählkontext neu einleitete und so
zum Moselied ausbaute.[66]

4.3 Zur späten Phase der Exodustradition

Deutlich gewandelt hat sich das Verhältnis zu den Exoduserzählungen des Pentateuch in den Geschichtspsalmen 105 und 106 sowie in den späten Hymnen Ps 135
und 136. Auch sie bedienen sich durchaus noch einzelner Motive aus der ihnen
vorangehenden prophetischen oder psalmistischen Exodustradition, aber sie räu-
men doch den erzählerischen Darstellungen des Pentateuch eindeutig den Vorrang ein und folgen an vielen Stellen deren Abfolge. Das wird etwa in Ps 105
daran sichtbar, dass er in V. 23–38 die Abfolge der Ereignisse von Ex 1,1 bis 12,39
mit nur geringen Abweichungen einfach nacherzählt (s. Anhang 1.6). So ist von
Israels Wanderung nach und Mehrung in Ägypten die Rede (Ps 105,23–24) wie in
Ex 1,1.7, von Israels Unterdrückung und der Sendung von Mose und Aaron
(Ps 105,25–26) wie in Ex 1,9–2,15 und Kapitel 3–4. Schließlich folgen die Plagen
und die Herausführung aus Ägypten (Ps 105,27–38) wie in Ex 7–12. Allerdings
werden alle diese Ereignisse – der Hymnentradition folgend – streng aus theologischer Perspektive, als Wundertaten Gottes berichtet (vgl. Ps 105,5). Selbst, dass
die Ägypter die Israeliten zu hassen begannen und arglistige Anschläge auf sie
machten, wird von Gott verursacht (V. 25).[67]

   Dem entspricht, dass die Plagenschilderung von Ps 105 in V. 27–36 der Darstellung im Exodusbuch deutlich näherstetht als die von Ps 78.[68] Es werden zwar
auch nicht alle zehn Plagen erwähnt, sondern nur acht, aber immerhin darunter
zwei spezifisch priesterliche, die Mückenplage in V. 31 und die Finsternisplage in
V. 29. Mit einer Ausnahme folgt die Schilderung der Reihenfolge der Plage in |
der Exoduserzählung, die Heuschreckenplage steht wie dort nach der Hagelplage

---

66 Wie die zitierende Aufnahme in Ex 15,1b zeigt, lag dem Redaktor, der das sog. Moselied (V. 1–
18) einfügte, das Mirjamlied (Ex 15,21) an dieser Stelle schon vor. Da die Einleitung dieses kleinen
Liedes (V. 20–21a) sich syntaktisch eng (vgl. לָהֶם) auf die priesterliche Rückblende auf Ex 14 in
Ex 15,19 zurückbezieht (vgl. בְנֵי יִשְׂרָאֵל), halte ich es für wahrscheinlich, dass dieses alte Kultlied
aus Bethel wahrscheinlich erst vom ersten priesterlichen Bearbeiter in den Erzählkontext eingebunden worden ist, s. Albertz, Exodus 1–18, 253–255.
67 Vgl. ebenso die Hungersnot, die Jakob zur Abwanderung nach Ägypten zwang, Ps 105,18.
68 So wird etwa das Erzählmotiv aufgenommen, dass die Frösche in den königlichen Gemächern
wimmelten (Ps 105,30; vgl. Ex 7,28). |

(V. 34–35), die auch weit weniger ausgestaltet ist als in Ps 78,47–49.[69] Die einzige originelle Abweichung besteht nur darin, dass der Dichter von Ps 105 die Finsternisplage von der neunten an die erste Stelle rückt, so wie eine Schilderung der düsteren chaotischen Verhältnisse den priesterlichen Schöpfungsbericht einleitet. Der Psalmendichter wollte mit dieser Anordnung vielleicht ausdrücken, dass seiner Meinung nach die Plagen eine partielle Zerstörung der von Gott geordneten Schöpfungswelt darstellen.[70] Dass er auch sonst an den priesterlichen Schöpfungsbericht anspielen will, zeigt die Rückführung der Stechfliegen/Mücken und Heuschrecken-Plage auf ein göttliches Sprechen (Ps 105,31.34); hatte doch Gott hier die ganze Welt durch sein Wort erschaffen (beide Male mit אָמַר vgl. Gen 1,3.6.9 u. ö.). Wie sehr sich der Psalmendichter an dem theologischen Konzept orientierte, das der erste priesterliche Bearbeiter der Exoduserzählung aufgeprägt hatte (vgl. Ex 2,24; 6,3–5), sieht man daran, dass auch für ihn JHWHs Treue zum Bund, den er mit Abraham geschlossen hatte, den entscheidenden Beweggrund für Israels Herausführung aus Ägypten lieferte (Ps 105,42–43), nur lässt er darin – entsprechend der prophetischen Tradition – schon die Hoffnung auf einen neuen Exodus anklingen (vgl. Jes 51,11). So kann man in Ps 105 mit Fug und Recht von einer Auslegung der Exoduserzählung des Pentateuch sprechen. Zwar werden immer noch einige Elemente der prophetischen und psalmistischen Exodustradition aktualisierend aufgegriffen, aber doch dem Pentateuch und den in ihm enthaltenen theologischen Linien eindeutig die Priorität zuerkannt.

Ähnliches lässt sich auch für Ps 106 feststellen, der Ps 105 nahesteht,[71] obwohl er die Heilsgeschichte nicht als eine Abfolge der Heilstaten Gottes, sondern des fortlaufenden Unglaubens Israels darstellt. Dieser äußert sich gerade darin, dass die göttlichen Gnadentaten schnell vergessen werden (106,7.13). In den Versen 7–12 findet sich eine recht ausführliche Schilderung der Schilfmeerereignisse (s. Anhang 2.3), die dem Ablauf der Ereignisse in der erzählerischen Darstellung von Ex 14 erkennbar folgt.[72] Wohl schildert der Psalmendichter das eigentliche |

---

69 Ps 105,32–33 hat nicht mehr die Tötung der Tiere, sondern nur noch die Zerstörung der Pflanzen im Blick, wobei die spezielle Nennung von Weinstock und Feigenbaum wohl durch Ps 78,47 angeregt wurde. Über die Plage-Erzählung hinaus geht die Erwähnung von Feuerflammen, doch könnte diese Ausgestaltung schon durch die Glosse in Ex 9,24 angeregt sein, die von einem hin- und herzuckenden Feuer inmitten des Hagels spricht (vgl. Ez 1,4).

70 So nach der anregenden und vielfach übernommenen These von Lee, Genesis, die allerdings nicht überstrapaziert werden sollte.

71 Vgl. dazu die eingehenden Untersuchungen von Gärtner, Geschichtspsalmen, 244–259, und Klein, Geschichte, 185–218. Ersterer nennt die beiden Psalmen einen großen „Parallelismus membrorum der Heilsgeschichte" (a. a. O., 135), letztere spricht im Gefolge von Zimmerli von „Zwillingspsalmen" (a. a. O., 185).

72 Die eigentümliche Behauptung in Ps 106,7, dass die Israeliten am Schilfmeer getrotzt und der Gnadentaten JHWHs nicht mehr gedacht hätten, obgleich solche zuvor im Psalm noch gar nicht

Schilfmeerwunder in Anlehnung an die Anspielungen auf den Chaoskampf in der prophetischen Tradition (vgl. zu Ps 106,9; Jes 50,2b; 51,10; 63,13), aber er fühlt sich doch an die Exoduserzählung so stark gebunden, dass er am Ende Israels Glaube und Gotteslob erwähnt (Ps 106,12 entsprechend Ex 14,31; 15,1–18), obgleich dies eigentlich zu seiner Konzeption, nach der Israel auf Gottes Heilstaten immer mit Unglauben reagiert, nicht passt. Er muss darum gleich die Aufstände Israels, von denen das Numeribuch berichtet, bemühen (Ps 106,13–33),[73] um seiner Sicht der Heilsgeschichte gegenüber dem positiven Schluss von Ex 14–15 das nötige Gewicht zu verleihen.

Sehr eng am Sprachgebrauch und der Vorstellungswelt des Pentateuch sind auch die beiden Hymnen Ps 135 und 136 in ihren Schilderungen der Exodusereignisse orientiert (s. Anhang 1.6), etwa darin, dass Gottes Schlag gegen die Erstgeburt „vom Menschen bis zum Tier" reichte (Ps 135,8; vgl. Ex 12,12) oder der Auszug mit Gottes „starker Hand und ausgerecktem Arm" erfolgte (Ps 136,10; vgl. Ex 6,1.6; 13,6 u. ö.). Der historisierende Bezug ist bei beiden Hymnen so stark, dass sie und nur sie die Stilform der poetischen Verhüllung verlassen und den Pharao offen als Israels Feind benennen (Ps 135,9; 136,15); in Ps 106,10 war dieser noch unter dem psalmistischen Feindbegriff „Hasser" versteckt worden. Der Autor von Ps 136 variiert die Vorstellungswelt von Ex 14 nur insofern ein wenig, als er von einem Zerschneiden des Meeres statt von seinem Spalten spricht (Ps 136,13; vgl. Ex 14,16.21), aber er fühlt sich doch so stark an den Pentateuchtext gebunden, dass er sogar die sonst nie beachtete alte Aussage vom Hineinschütteln der Ägypter ins Meer aufgreift (Ps 136,15; vgl. Ex 14,27). So scheinen auch hier die Pentateucherzählungen eine prägende Autorität für die Psalmendichter gewonnen zu haben.

Auf den Grund, warum es in der Spätphase der Exodustradition zu einer solchen Aufwertung der Erzählüberlieferung gekommen ist, gibt der Vers Ps 135,9 den entscheidenden Hinweis (s. Anhang 1.5). Hier wird von Gott gesagt:

> Ps 135,9   Er schickte (שׁלח) Zeichen und Wunder in die Mitte Ägyptens an Pharao und an allen seinen Knechten.

---

erwähnt worden waren, wird verständlich aus der Klage der Israeliten in Ex 14,11–12. Die | vorausgreifende Aussage, dass JHWH Israel um seines Namens willen gerettet habe (Ps 106,8), erklärt sich aus dem tröstenden Heilsorakel des Mose in Ex 14,13–14. Der Vers Ps 106,9 fasst unter theologischer Perspektive den in Ex 14,15–29 kompliziert geschilderten Rettungsvorgang zusammen. Ps 106,10 konstatiert wie Ex 14,30 das erfolgte Rettungsgeschehen, wobei Ps 106,11 zur Illustration des Feindesschicksals noch einmal auf Ex 14,28 zurückgreift. Ps 106,12 schildert wie Ex 14,31 zusammen mit Kap. 15 die abschließende Reaktion der geretteten Israeliten.
73 Verstärkt durch einen einzigartigen Rückgriff auf die Geschichte vom Goldenen Kalb (Ps 106,16–23; vgl. Ex 32). |

Die Aussage, dass Gott Zeichen und Wunder geschickt habe (שלח), ist ungewöhn-lich. Sonst wird sie gerne mit dem Verb שׂים „setzen" konstruiert (Ps 78,43; 105,27; Jer 32,20). Die erste priesterliche Bearbeitung benutzte das Verb רבה im hif. „viel machen" (Ex 7,3). In vergleichbaren Wendungen steht das | Verb עשׂה „tun" (Ps 78,12; 106,21).[74] Es gibt in der Hebräischen Bibel nur eine einzige Stelle, in der eine ähnliche Konstruktion vorkommt. Sie steht ganz am Ende des Pentateuch:

> Dtn 34,11   in Bezug auf die Zeichen und Wunder, die JHWH ihm (Mose) geschickt hat (שלח), um sie im Lande Ägypten zu tun an Pharao und an allen seinen Knech-ten und an seinem Land.

Da auch noch der Bezug auf „den Pharao und alle seine Knechte" bis auf die verwendete Präposition wörtlich übereinstimmt, ist es wahrscheinlich, dass der Dichter von Psalm 135 bei der Formulierung von V. 9 den Vers Dtn 34,11 vor Augen hatte. Das im Zusammenhang seltsame Verb שלח erklärt sich daraus, dass auch er, wie es Dtn 34,11 ausdrücklich formuliert, an eine Vermittlung der „Zeichen und Wunder" durch Mose dachte.[75] Da nun aber die Verse Dtn 34,11–12 die kom-positorische Funktion haben, durch Rückblick auf die Ereignisse des Exodus, das Deuteronomium vom Josuabuch ein Stück weit zu trennen und den Pentateuch als eigenständige Größe abzurunden, gehören sie zu einer seiner letzten Redakti-onen, die der Kanonisierung des Pentateuch am Anfang des 4. Jahrhunderts un-mittelbar vorangingen. Damit ist es aber sehr wahrscheinlich, dass dem Dichter von Ps 135 schon der abgeschlossene Pentateuch vorlag, dem als der von Esra offiziell promulgierten Gründungsgeschichte eine erhöhte Autorität zukam. Glei-ches gilt wahrscheinlich auch für den verwandten Psalm 136. Die Geschichtspsal-men 105 und 106 sind wohl etwas älter. Da sie aber Ps 78 schon voraussetzen und in 1 Chr 16 ausschnittsweise zitiert werden,[76] gehören sie ebenfalls bereits in das 4. Jahrhundert. Dadurch erklärt sich ihr Charakter als „relecture der Tora".

In der sich seit dem 10. Jahrhundert v. Chr langsam ausbildenden, vielstimmi-gen Exodustradition galten über die längste Zeit deren prophetischen und psal-

---

74 Daneben wird auch das Verb נתן „geben" verwandt, vgl. Neh 9,10; ebenso in Dtn 6,22; Jes 8,18.
75 Auch Gärtner, Geschichtspsalmen, 331 Anm. 114, hat schon gesehen, dass sich Ps 135,9 „beson-ders eng" an Dtn 34,11 anlehnt, aber daraus noch keine redaktionsgeschichtlichen Konsequenzen gezogen. Sie hat recht, dass sich die Personen, an welche die göttlichen Wunder geschickt wer-den, in den beiden Versen unterscheiden. Doch lässt man Mose auch in Ps 135,9 als implizit gemeinten Vermittler zu, fällt dieser Unterschied dahin.
76 Dass Ps 105 den Ps 78 schon kennt, lässt sich z. B. in V. 33 (vgl. 78,47), V. 36b (vgl. 78,51b) und V. 41 (vgl. 78,20) erkennen. Ähnliches zeigt sich für Ps 106 z. B. in V. 14 (vgl. 78,40), V. 15 (vgl. 78,18) und V. 22 (78,51). Ps 105,1–15 wird in 1 Chr 16,8–22 und Ps 106,1.47–48 in 1 Chr 16,34–36 zitiert. Letzterer sogar zusammen mit der Schlussdoxologie des vierten Psalmenbuches. |

mistischen Ausprägungen gegenüber den erzählerischen Ausgestaltungen als mehr oder minder gleichwertig. Nachdem sich die drei Stränge der Tradition anfangs weitgehend unabhängig voneinander entwickelt hatten, konnten sie sich allesamt gegenseitig beeinflussen; Anleihen konnten in die eine oder die andere Richtung gemacht werden. Als die Exodus-Erzähltradition in der späten | Exils- und frühen nachexilischen Zeit ihre volle Ausgestaltung erfahren hatte, gewann sie auch für die Psalmentradition während des 5. Jahrhunderts v. Chr eine größere Bedeutung. Doch wurde in dieser Zeit auch der Psalmentradition noch eine derartige Wichtigkeit beigemessen, dass man einen ganzen Psalm in die Exoduserzählung integrierte (Ex 15). Dass schließlich der erzählerischen Ausprägung der Exodusüberlieferung im Pentateuch eine so klare Vorrangstellung eingeräumt wurde, dass sich die Psalmendichter und Redaktoren von Prophetenbüchern zuvörderst an ihr orientierten, hängt mit der Kanonisierung der Tora am Anfang des 4. Jahrhunderts zusammen.

Anhang

Stelle	Begriffe	Text	Vergl. m. Pentateuch
1.1 Herausführung aus Ägypten ohne weitere Spezifikationen			
Hos 12,10	מארץ מצרים	ואנכי יהוה אלהיך מארץ מצרים עד אושיבך באהלים כימי מועד	vgl. Ex 20,2
Hos 13,4	מארץ מצרים	ואנכי יהוה אלהיך מארץ מצרים ואלהים זולתי לא תדע ומושיע אין בלתי	vgl. Ex 20,2
Am 2,10	עלה מארץ מצר"	ואנכי העליתי אתכם מארץ מצרים ואולך אתכם במדבר ארבעים שנה לרשת את־ארץ האמרי	vgl. Ex 32,4.8; (1 Kön 12,28!)
Am 3,1b	עלה מארץ מצר"	על כל־המשפחה אשר העליתי מארץ מצרים	vgl. Ex 32,4.8
Am 9,7	עלה מארץ מצר"	הלוא כבני כשיים אתם לי בני ישראל נאם־יהוה הלוא את־ישראל העליתי מארץ מצרים ופלשתיים מכפתור וארם מקיר	vgl. Ex 32,4.8
Ps 78,52	נסע כצאן	ויסע כצאן עמו וינהגם כעדר במדבר	vgl. Ex 13,20 (Ps 77,21)
Ps 80,9	נסע ממצרים	גפן ממצרים תסיע תגרש גוים ותטעה	
Ps 81,11	עלה מארץ מצר"	אנכי יהוה אלהיך המעלך מארץ מצרים	vgl. Ex 20,2; 32,4.8
Ps 114,1	יצא ממצרים	בצאת ישראל ממצרים בית יעקב מעם לעז	

(fortgesetzt)

Stelle	Begriffe	Text	Vergl. m. Pentateuch
1.2 Herausführung/Befreiung aus Ägypten mit weiteren Spezifikationen			
Hos 2,17b	עלה מארץ מצר"	וענתה שמה כימי נעוריה וכיום עלתה מארץ־מצרים	(vgl. Jer 11,7)
Hos 11,1	קרא ממצרים	כי נער ישראל ואהבהו וממצרים קראתי לבני	
Hos 12,14	עלה ממצ", נביא	ובנביא העלה יהוה את־ישראל ממצרים ובנביא נשמר	vgl. Ex 3,10; Dtn 18,15
Mi 6,4	עלה מארץ מצר" מבית עבדים שלח משה, אהרן מרים	כי העלתיך מארץ מצרים ומבית עבדים פדיתיך ואשלח לפניך את־משה אהרן ומרים	vgl. Ex 32,4.8 Dtn 7,8; 13,6 Ex 3–4; 15,20
Jer 2,6	עלה מארץ מצר"	ולא אמרו איה יהוה המעלה אתנו מארץ מצרים המוליך אתנו במדבר בארץ ערבה ושוחה בארץ ציה וצלמות בארץ לא־עבר בה איש ולא־ישב אדם שם	vgl. Ex 32,4.8 (Ps 81,11) vgl. Dtn 8,15 (Am 2,10)
(Jes 52,4)	ירד, מצרים, גור	כי כה אמר אדני יהוה מצרים ירד־עמי בראשנה לגור שם ואשור באפס עשקו	vgl. Dtn 26,5
Ps 81,7	סור, סבל, דוד	הסירותי מסבל שכמו כפיו מדוד תעברנה	סבלה vgl. Ex 1,11 u. ö.
Ps 81,8	קרא, חלץ, ענה	בצרה קראת ואחלצך אענך בסתר רעם אבחנך על־מי מריבה	?ענה vgl. Ex 19,19
Ps 105,23	בוא, מצרים, גר	ויבא ישראל מצרים ויעקב גר בארץ־חם	vgl. Ex 1,1; Dtn 26,5
Ps 105,24	פרה, עצם, מאד	ויפר את־עמו מאד ויעצמהו מצריו	Ex 1,7
Ps 105,25	הפך לב	הפך לבם לשנא עמו להתנכל בעבדיו	vgl. Ex 1,8–10
Ps 105,26	שלח משה, אהרן	שלח משה עבדו אהרן אשר בחר־בו	שלח vgl. Ex 3–4; 3,12
Ps 105,42	זכר, אברהם	כי זכר את־דבר קדשו את־אברהם עבדו	Ex 2,24b
Ps 105,43	יצא בששון, רנה	ויוצא עמו בששון ברנה את־בחיריו	(Jes 51,11)
1.3 Exodus als Zeitpunkt der Verpflichtung Israels			
Jer 7,22	יצא מארץ מצר"	כי לא־דברתי את־אבותיכם ולא צויתים ביום הוציאי אותם מארץ מצרים על־דברי עולה וזבח	vgl. Ex 20,2
(Am 5,25)		הזבחים ומנחה הגשתם־לי במדבר ארבעים שנה בית־ישראל	

(fortgesetzt)

Stelle	Begriffe	Text	Vergl. m. Pentateuch
Jer 11,3–4	יצא מארץ מצר״ כור הברזל	...את־דברי הברית הזאת אשר צויתי את־אבותיכם ביום הוציאי־אותם מארץ מצרים מכור הברזל לאמר שמעו בקולי ועשׂיתם אותם...	vgl. Ex 20,2; Dtn 4,20; (1 Kön 8,51)
Jer 11,7	עלה מארץ מצר״	כי העד העדתי באבותיכם ביום העלותי אותם מארץ מצרים ועד־היום הזה השכם והעד לאמר שמעו בקולי	
Jer 34,13	יצא מארץ מצר״	כה־אמר יהוה אלהי ישראל אנכי כרתי ברית את־אבותיכם ביום הוצאי אותם מארץ מצרים מבית עבדים...	vgl. Dtn 20,2
Ps 81,6	יצא על ארץ מצ״	עדות ביהוסף שׂמו בצאתו על־ארץ מצרים	

1.4 Exodus als Reinigungsgericht

Stelle	Begriffe	Text	Vergl. m. Pentateuch
Ez 20,6–7	נשׂא יד יצא מארץ מצר״	ביום ההוא נשׂאתי ידי להם להוציאם מארץ מצרים אל־ארץ אשר־תרתי להם... ואמר אלהם איש שׁקוצי עיניו השׁליכו ובגלולי מצרים אל־תטמאו אני יהוה אלהיכם	vgl. Ex 6,8 vgl. Ex 6,6
Ez 20,9		ואעשׂ למען שׁמי לבלתי החל לעיני הגוים	
	יצא מארץ מצר״	אשׁר־המה בתוכם אשׁר נודעתי אליהם לעיניהם להוציאם מארץ מצרים	(Ez 20,14.22) vgl. Ex 7,5
Ez 20,10	יצא מארץ מצר״	ואוציאם מארץ מצרים ואבאם אל־המדבר	
Ez 20,36–37	מדבר ארץ מצר״	כאשׁר נשׁפטתי את־אבותיכם במדבר ארץ מצרים כן אשׁפט אתכם נאם אדני יהוה והעברתי אתכם תחת השׁבט והבאתי אתכם במסרת הברית	(vgl. Ez 20,8.13.15)

1.5 Wunder in Ägypten

Stelle	Begriffe	Text	Vergl. m. Pentateuch
Mi 7,15	יצא מארץ מצר״ נפלאות	כימי צאתך מארץ מצרים אראנו (הראנו) נפלאות	vgl. Dtn 16,3 vgl. Ex 34,10
Jer 32,20	אות ומופת במצ״	אשׁר־שׂמת אתות ומפתים בארץ־מצרים עד־היום הזה ובישׂראל ובאדם ותעשׂה־לך שׁם כיום הזה	Ex 7,3 (vgl. Dtn 6,22 u. ö.)

(fortgesetzt)

Stelle	Begriffe	Text	Vergl. m. Pentateuch
Jer 32,21	יצא מארץ מצר״ אות ,מופת ,מורא	וַתֹּצֵא אֶת־עַמְּךָ אֶת־יִשְׂרָאֵל מֵאֶרֶץ מִצְרָיִם בְּאֹתוֹת וּבְמוֹפְתִים וּבְיָד חֲזָקָה וּבְאֶזְרוֹעַ נְטוּיָה וּבְמוֹרָא גָּדוֹל	vgl. Dtn 26,8
Ps 78,12	פלא בארץ מצר״	נֶגֶד אֲבוֹתָם עָשָׂה פֶלֶא בְּאֶרֶץ מִצְרַיִם שְׂדֵה־צֹעַן	vgl. Ex 15,11 עָשָׂה פֶלֶא
Ps 78,43	אות ומופת במצ״	אֲשֶׁר־שָׂם בְּמִצְרַיִם אֹתוֹתָיו וּמוֹפְתָיו בִּשְׂדֵה־צֹעַן	Ex 7,3
Ps 105,27	אות ומופת ב״	שָׂמוּ־בָם דִּבְרֵי אֹתוֹתָיו וּמֹפְתִים בְּאֶרֶץ חָם	Ex 7,3
Ps 106,7a	נפלאות	אֲבוֹתֵינוּ בְמִצְרַיִם לֹא־הִשְׂכִּילוּ נִפְלְאוֹתֶיךָ	
Ps 106,21	גדולה במצרים	שָׁכְחוּ אֵל מוֹשִׁיעָם עֹשֶׂה גְדֹלוֹת בְּמִצְרָיִם	(vgl. Hiob 5,9)
Ps 106,22	נפלאה ,נוראה	נִפְלָאוֹת בְּאֶרֶץ חָם נוֹרָאוֹת עַל־יַם־סוּף	(vgl. Mi 7,15)
Ps 135,9	אות ומופת ב״	שָׁלַח אֹתוֹת וּמֹפְתִים בְּתוֹכֵכִי מִצְרָיִם בְּפַרְעֹה וּבְכָל־עֲבָדָיו	Ex 7,3; Dtn 34,11; (Neh 9,10)

1.6 Plagen an Ägyptern

Stelle	Begriffe	Text	Vergl. m. Pentateuch
Ps 78,44	הפך לדם ,שתה	וַיַּהֲפֹךְ לְדָם יְאֹרֵיהֶם וְנֹזְלֵיהֶם בַּל־יִשְׁתָּיוּן	I, Ex 7,17.20.18.21
Ps 78,45	ערב ,צפרדע	יְשַׁלַּח בָּהֶם עָרֹב וַיֹּאכְלֵם וּצְפַרְדֵּעַ וַתַּשְׁחִיתֵם	IV+II, Ex 8,20 שָׁחַת (vertauscht)
Ps 78,46	הסיל ,ארבה	וַיִּתֵּן לֶחָסִיל יְבוּלָם וִיגִיעָם לָאַרְבֶּה	VIII
Ps 78,47	ברד	יַהֲרֹג בַּבָּרָד גַּפְנָם וְשִׁקְמוֹתָם בַּחֲנָמַל	VII
Ps 78,48	מקנה ,רשף	וַיַּסְגֵּר לַבָּרָד בְּעִירָם וּמִקְנֵיהֶם לָרְשָׁפִים	Ex 9,19–21; V.23: אֵשׁ
Ps 78,49	שלח חרון	יְשַׁלַּח־בָּם חֲרוֹן אַפּוֹ עֶבְרָה וָזַעַם וְצָרָה מִשְׁלַחַת מַלְאֲכֵי רָעִים	vgl. Ex 15,7 vgl. מַשְׁחִית in Ex 12,23?
Ps 78,50	מות (Nomen) דבר	יְפַלֵּס נָתִיב לְאַפּוֹ לֹא־חָשַׂךְ מִמָּוֶת נַפְשָׁם וְחַיָּתָם לַדֶּבֶר הִסְגִּיר	VI vgl. Ex 9,6 מות Verb; Menschenpest wie 9,15
Ps 78,51	נכה כל־בכור	וַיַּךְ כָּל־בְּכוֹר בְּמִצְרָיִם רֵאשִׁית אוֹנִים בְּאָהֳלֵי־חָם	X, Ex 12,12.29 (Ps 105,36)
Ps 105,28	חשך	שָׁלַח חֹשֶׁךְ וַיַּחְשִׁךְ וְלֹא־מָרוּ אֶת־דְּבָרוֹ	IX vgl. Ex 10,22
Ps 105,29	הפך לדם ,דגה	הָפַךְ אֶת־מֵימֵיהֶם לְדָם וַיָּמֶת אֶת־דְּגָתָם	I, Ex 7,17.20.18.21
Ps 105,30	שרץ צפרדע חדר	שָׁרַץ אַרְצָם צְפַרְדְּעִים בְּחַדְרֵי מַלְכֵיהֶם	II, Ex 7,28
Ps 105,31	בוא ערב ,כנים	אָמַר וַיָּבֹא עָרֹב כִּנִּים בְּכָל־גְּבוּלָם	IV, III, Ex 8,20
Ps 105,32	ברד ,אש	נָתַן גִּשְׁמֵיהֶם בָּרָד אֵשׁ לֶהָבוֹת בְּאַרְצָם	VII, Ex 9,23
Ps 105,33	נכה ,עץ ,גפן	וַיַּךְ גַּפְנָם וּתְאֵנָתָם וַיְשַׁבֵּר עֵץ גְּבוּלָם	Ex 9,25; (Ps 78,47)
Ps 105,34	בוא ,ארבה	אָמַר וַיָּבֹא אַרְבֶּה וְיֶלֶק וְאֵין מִסְפָּר	VIII, Ex 10,4
Ps 105,35	אכל כל־עשב פרי	וַיֹּאכַל כָּל־עֵשֶׂב בְּאַרְצָם וַיֹּאכַל פְּרִי אַדְמָתָם	Ex 10,15
Ps 105,36	נכה כל־בכור	וַיַּךְ כָּל־בְּכוֹר בְּאַרְצָם רֵאשִׁית לְכָל־אוֹנָם	X, Ex 12,12.29; (Ps 78,51)

(fortgesetzt)

Stelle	Begriffe	Text	Vergl. m. Pentateuch
Ps 105,37	יצא ,כסף ,זהב	ויוציאם בכסף וזהב ואין בשבטיו כושל	Ex 12,35.36; (vgl. Jes 5,27)
Ps 105,38	נפל פחד	שמח מצרים בצאתם כי־נפל פחדם עליהם	vgl. Ex 12,33; 15,16
Ps 135,8	נכה בכור מאדם עד־בהמה	שהכה בכורי מצרים מאדם עד־בהמה	X, Ex 12,12
Ps 136,10	נכה בכור	למכה מצרים בבכוריהם	Ex 12,12.29
Ps 136,11	יצא מן	ויוצא ישראל מתוכם	Ex 12,31
Ps 136,12	יד ,זרוע	ביד חזקה ובזרוע נטויה	Ex 6,1.6; 13,9

2.1 Rettung am Schilfmeer als Chaoskampf

Jes 51,9	מחץ ,חלל	עורי עורי לבשי־עז זרוע יהוה עורי כימי קדם דרות עולמים הלוא את־היא המחצ(ב)ת רהב מחוללת תנין	(vgl. Hiob 26,12–13)
Jes 51,10a	ים חרב	הלוא את־היא המחרבת ים מי תהום רבה	vgl. Ex 14,21; 15,5.8
Jes 51,10b	דרך עבר	השמה מעמקי־ים דרך לעבר גאולים	

2.2 Rettung am Schilfmeer mit Anspielungen an Chaoskampf oder Zügen einer Theophanie

Jes 50,2b	גערה ,חרב ים דגה ,באש ,מות	הן בגערתי אחריב ים אשים נהרות מדבר תבאש דגתם מאין מים ותמת בצמא	(Ps 106,9); vgl. Ex 14,21 Ex 7,18.21 (Plage I)?
Ps 77,17	ראה ,חיל רגז	ראוך מים אלהים ראוך מים יחילו אף ירגזו תהמות	(vgl. Hab 3,10 Berge) vgl. Ex 15,14 (Völker)
Ps 77,20	דרך ,שביל	בים דרכך ושביליך במים רבים ועקבותיך לא נדעו	
Ps 77,21	נחה כצאן	נחית כצאן עמך ביד־משה ואהרן	vgl. Ex 15,13; (Ps 78,52–53)
Ps 106,9	גור ,חרב ,הלך	ויגער בים־סוף ויחרב ויוליכם בתהמות כמדבר	(Nah 1,4; Ps 104,7; Jes 50,2; 63,13); vgl. Ex 14,21
Ps 114,3	נוס	הים ראה וינס הירדן יסב לאחור	חרבה (vgl. Ps 104,7)
Ps 114,5	נוס	מה־לך הים כי תנוס הירדן תסב לאחור	

2.3 Rettung Schilfmeer ohne Anspielungen an Chaoskampf

Jes 43,16	נתן דרך בים	כה אמר יהוה הנותן בים דרך ובמים עזים נתיבה	
Jes 43,17	יצא רכב ,סוס חיל	המוציא רכב־וסוס חיל ועזוז יחדו ישכבו בל־יקומו דעכו כפשתה כבו	vgl. Ex 14,9.23 vgl. Ex 14,30
Jes 63,12	בקע עשה ל״ שם	מוליך לימין משה זרוע תפארתו בוקע מים מפניהם לעשות לו שם עולם	בקע Ex 14,16.21 (vgl. Jer 32,20)

(fortgesetzt)

Stelle	Begriffe	Text	Vergl. m. Pentateuch
Jes 63,13	הלך	מוליכם בתהמות כסוס במדבר לא יכשלו	
Ps 78,13a	בקע ,עבר	בקע ים ויעבירם	בקע Ex 14,16.21
Ps 78,13b	נצב ,נד	ויצב־מים כמו־נד	Ex 15,8aβ
Ps 78,53b	כסה אויב	ואת־אויביהם כסה הים	המים כסו Ex 14,28
Ps 106,7b	מרה ,ים־סוף	לא זכרו את־רב חסדיך וימרו על־ים בים־סוף	vgl. Ex 14,11–12
Ps 106,8	ישע ,למען שמ"	ויושיעם למען שמו להודיע את־גבורתו	vgl. Ex 14,13.30 (Ez 20,9–44)
Ps 106,10	ישע ,גאל	ויושיעם מיד שונא ויגאלם מיד אויב	Ex 14,30
Ps 106,11	כסה ,מים ,אחד	ויכסו־מים צריהם אחד מהם לא נותר	Ex 14,28; 15,10
Ps 106,12	אמן ,תהלה	ויאמינו בדבריו ישירו תהלתו	Ex 14,31; 15,1–18
Ps 136,13	גזר ים־סוף	לגזר ים־סוף לגזרים	vgl. Ex 14,22
Ps 136,14	עבר בתוך	והעביר ישראל בתוכו	(vgl. Ps 66,6; 78,13)
Ps 136,15	נער בים־סוף	ונער פרעה וחילו בים־סוף	Ex 14,27; 15,4

2.4 Rettung am Schilfmeer und Wasserwunder als umwandelndes Handeln in Natur

Ps 66,6	הפך ,יבשה ,עבר	הפך ים ליבשה בנהר יעברו ברגל שם נשמחה־בו	vgl. Ex 14,16.22 יבשה
Ps 78,13	בקע ים	בקע ים ויעבירם...	Ex 14,16.21
Ps 78,15	בקע צור	יבקע צרים במדבר וישק כתהמות רבה	vgl. Ex 17,6 נכה בצור
Ps 78,16	יצא מים	ויוצא נוזלים מסלע ויורד כנהרות מים	vgl. Ex 17,6 יצא מים
Ps 114,5	נוס	מה־לך הים כי תנוס הירדן תסב לאחור	(Ps 104,7)
Ps 114,7	מלפני אדון	מלפני אדון חולי ארץ מלפני אלוה יעקב	(vgl. Ps 97,5)
Ps 114,8	הפך צור	ההפכי הצור אגם־מים חלמיש למעינו־מים	vgl. Ex 17,6; (Jes 41,18)

3.1 Schilfmeer als Beispiel für zukünftiges Eingreifen Gottes gegen Feinde

Jes 10,26		ועורר עליו יהוה צבאות שוט כמכת מדין בצור עורב	(vgl. Ri 7,25)
	מטה על־הים	ומטהו על־הים ונשאו בדרך מצרים	Ex 14,16

3.2 Rückkehr nach Ägypten/Assur und neuer Exodus

Hos 8,13b	שוב מצרים	עתה יזכר עונם ויפקד חטאותם המה מצרים ישובו	vgl. Dtn 28,68
Hos 9,3	שוב מצרים	לא ישבו בארץ יהוה ושב אפרים מצרים ובאשור טמא יאכלו	dto.
Hos 11,5a	שוב אל ארץ מצרים	(לא) ישוב אל־ארץ מצרים ואשור הוא מלכו	dto.

(fortgesetzt)

Stelle	Begriffe	Text	Vergl. m. Pentateuch
Hos 11,11	חרד ממצרים	יחרדו כצפור ממצרים וכיונה מארץ אשור והושבתים על־בתיהם נאם־יהוה	

3.3 Neuer Exodus als Überbietung bzw. restriktive Wiederholung des alten

Stelle	Begriffe	Text	Vergl. m. Pentateuch
Jer 16,14–15; vgl. 23,7–8	עלה מארץ מצר"	לכן הנה־ימים באים נאם־יהוה ולא־יאמר עוד חי־יהוה אשר העלה את־בני ישראל מארץ מצרים כי אם־חי־יהוה אשר העלה את־בני ישראל מארץ צפון ומכל הארצות אשר הדיחם שמה והשבתים על־אדמתם אשר נתתי לאבותם	vgl. Ex 32,4.8; vgl. Gen 15,7
Jes 43,18–19.20b	במדבר דרך, נהר	אל־תזכרו ראשנות וקדמניות אל־תתבננו הנני עשה חדשה עתה תצמח הלוא תדעוה אף אשים במדבר דרך בישמון נהרות כי־נתתי במדבר מים נהרות בישימן להשקות עמי בחירי	(vgl. Jes 41,18)
Jes 48,20–21	יצא מן בקע צור, נזל	צאו מבבל ברחו מכשדים בקול רנה... ולא צמאו בחרבות הוליכם מים מצור הזיל למו ויבקע־צור ויזבו מים	vgl. Ex 23,15 vgl. Ex 17,6 (Ps 78,15–16)
Jes 52,11–12	יצא מן בחפיון יצא	סורו סורו צאו משם... כי לא בחפזון תצאו ובמנוסה לא תלכון כי־הלך לפניכם יהוה ומאספכם אלהי ישראל	vgl. Ex 23,15 Dtn 16,3; vgl. Ex 12,11
Ez 20,38	יצא מארץ מגור	וברותי מכם המרדים והפושעים בי מארץ מגוריהם אוציא אותם ואל־אדמת ישראל לא יבוא וידעתם כי־אני יהוה	vgl. Ex 6,4 (vgl. Ez 20,6.15)

Literaturverzeichnis

Albertz, R., Weltschöpfung und Menschenschöpfung. Untersucht bei Deuterojesaja, Hiob und in den Psalmen, CThM A3, Stuttgart 1974.

Albertz, R., Religionsgeschichte Israels in alttestamentlicher Zeit 1, GAT 8/1, Göttingen ²1996.

Albertz, R., Israel in der offiziellen Religion der Königszeit. In: Irsigler, H. (Hg.), Die Identität Israels. Entwicklungen und Kontroversen in alttestamentlicher Zeit, HBS 56, Freiburg i. Br. u. a. 2009, 39–57. [[= S. 197–214 im vorliegenden Band]]

Albertz, R., Public Recitation of Prophetical Books? The Case of the First Edition of Deutero-Isaiah (Isa. 40:1–52:12). In: Edelmann, D. V./Ben Zvi, E. (Hg.), The Production of Prophecy, Sheffield 2009, 96–110.

Albertz, R., How Radical Must the New Beginning Be? The Discussion between the Deutero-Isaiah and the Ezekiel School. In: Middelmas, J. u. a. (Hg.), The Centre and the Periphery. A European Tribute to Walter Brueggemann, Sheffield 2010, 7–21. [[= S. 239–253 im vorliegenden Band]]

Albertz, R., The Controversy about Judean versus Israelite Identity and the Persian Government. A New Interpretation of the Bagoses Story (Jewish Antiquities XI.297–301). In: Lipschits, O. u. a. (Hg.), Judah and the Judeans in the Achaemenid Period. Negotiating Identity in an International Context, Winona Lake, IN 2011, 483–504. [[= S. 63–82 im vorliegenden Band]]

Albertz, R., Exodus 1–18, ZBK.AT 2/1, Zürich 2012.

Albertz, R., On the Structure and Formation of the Book of Deutero-Isaiah. In: Bautch, R. J./ Hibbard, J. T. (Hg.), The Book of Isaiah. Enduring Questions Answered Anew, FS Joseph Blenkinsopp, Grand Rapids, MI/Cambridge, U. K. 2014, 21–40. [[= S. 137–155 im vorliegenden Band]]

Albertz, R., Exodus 19–40, ZBK.AT 2/2, Zürich 2015.

Albertz, R., The Formative Impact of the Hexateuch Redaction. An Interim Result. In: Giuntoli, F./ Schmid, K. (Hg.), The Post-Priestly Pentateuch. New Perspectives on its Redactional Development and Theological Profiles, FAT 101, Tübingen 2015, 53–74.

Becker, U., Das Exodus-Credo. Historischer Haftpunkt und Geschichte einer alttestamentlichen Glaubensformel. In: Ders./van Oorschot, J. (Hg.), Das Alte Testament – ein Geschichtsbuch?! Geschichtsschreibung und Geschichtsüberlieferung im Antiken Israel, ABIG 17, Leipzig 2005, 81–100.

Ben-Chorin, S., Das Volkslied der Juden. In: Becker, H./Kaczynski, R. (Hg.), Liturgie und Dichtung. Ein internationales Kompendium I: Historische Präsentation, St. Ottilien 1983, 47–54.

Elliger, K., Deuterojesaja, Band I: Jesaja 40,1–45,7, BKAT 11/1, Neukirchen-Vluyn 1978.

Emanuel, D., The Psalmists' Use of the Exodus Motif. A Close Reading and Intertextual Analysis of Selected Exodus Psalms, Diss. (Masch.) Hebrew University, Jerusalem 2007.

Gärtner, J., Die Geschichtspsalmen. Eine Studie zu den Psalmen 78, 105, 106, 135 und 136 als hermeneutische Schlüsseltexte im Psalter, FAT 84, Tübingen 2012.

Galling, K., Die Erwählungstraditionen Israels, BZAW 48, Gießen 1928.

Gunkel, H., Ausgewählte Psalmen übersetzt und erklärt, Göttingen ⁴1917.

Gunkel, H., Die Psalmen, HKAT II/2, Göttingen ⁵1968.

Hendel, R., Remembering the Exodus in the Wake of Catastrophe. In: Dubovský, P. u. a. (Hg.), The Fall of Jerusalem and the Rise of Torah, FAT 107, Tübingen 2016, 329–345.

Hiebert, P. S., Psalm 78. Its Place in Israelite Literature and History, Diss. Theol. Havard 1992, Ann Abor, MI 1994. |

Hieke, T., „Weitergabe des Glaubens" (Ps 78,1–8). Versuch zu Syntax und Struktur von Ps 78. In: BN 78 (1995), 49–62.

Hossfeld, F.-L./Zenger, E., Psalmen 51–100, HThKAT, Freiburg i. Br. u. a. 2000.

Hossfeld, F.-L./Zenger, E., Psalmen 101–150, HThKAT, Freiburg i. Br. u. a. 2008.

Jeremias, J., Theophanie. Die Geschichte einer alttestamentlichen Gattung, WMANT 10, Neukirchen-Vluyn 1965.

Jeremias, J., Das Königtum Gottes. Israels Begegnung mit dem kanaanäischen Mythos in den Jahwe-Königs-Psalmen, FRLANT 141, Göttingen 1987.

Klein, A., Geschichte und Gebet. Die Rezeption der biblischen Geschichte in den Psalmen des Alten Testaments, FAT 94, Tübingen 2014.

Kraus, H.-J., Psalmen, BKAT 15/1–2, Neukirchen-Vluyn [5]1978.

Krüger, T., Geschichtskonzepte im Ezechielbuch, BZAW 180, Berlin/New York 1989.

Kühlewein, J., Geschichte in den Psalmen, CThM 2, Stuttgart 1973.

Lauha, A., Die Geschichtsmotive in den alttestamentlichen Psalmen, AASF B 56, Helsinki 1945.

Lambert, W. G./Millard, A. R., Atra-ḫasīs. The Babylonian Story of the Flood, Oxford 1969.

Lee, A. C. C., Genesis I and the Plagues Tradition in Psalm CV. In: VT 40 (1990), 257–263.

Leuenberger, M., Konzeptionen des Königtums Gottes im Psalter. Untersuchungen zur Komposition und Redaktion der theokratischen Bücher IV und V im Psalter, AThANT 83, Zürich 2004.

Magen, Y., The Dating of the First Phase of the Samaritan Temple on the Mount Gerizim in the Light of Archaeological Evidence. In: Lipschits, O. u. a. (Hg.), Judah and the Judeans in the Fourth Century BCE., Winona Lake, IN 2007, 157–211.

Mathias, D., Die Geschichtstheologie der Geschichtssummarien in den Psalmen, BEAT 35, Frankfurt a. Main 1993.

Norin, S. I. L., Er spaltete das Meer. Die Auszugsüberlieferung in Psalmen und Kult des alten Israel, CB.OT 9, Lund 1977.

Preuss, H. D., Theologie des Alten Testaments, Band 1: JHWHs erwählendes und verpflichtendes Handeln, Stuttgart 1991.

Römer, T., Der Pentateuch. In: Dietrich, W. u. a. (Hg.), Die Entstehung des Alten Testaments, TW 1, Stuttgart 2014, 53–166.

Seybold, K., Die Psalmen, HAT 1/15, Tübingen 1996.

Seybold, K., Die Wallfahrtspsalmen. Studien zur Entstehungsgeschichte von Ps 120–134, BThSt 3, Neukirchen-Vluyn 1978.

Spieckermann, H., Heilsgegenwart. Eine Theologie der Psalmen, FRLANT 148, Göttingen 1989.

Weber, B., Psalm 78: Geschichte mit Geschichte deuten. In: ThZ 56 (2000), 193–214.

Weingart, K., Juda als Sachwalter Israels. Geschichtstheologie nach dem Ende des Nordreiches in Hos 13 und Ps 78. In: ZAW 127 (2015), 440–458.

Westermann, C., Das Buch Jesaja. Kapitel 40–66, ATD 19, Göttingen [5]1986.

Westermann, C., Grundformen prophetischer Rede, München [2]1964.

Westermann, C., Vergegenwärtigung der Geschichte in den Psalmen. In: Ders., Forschung am Alten Testament. Gesammelte Studien, TB 24, München 1964, 306–335.

Witte, M., From Exodus to David – History and Historiography in Psalm 78. In: Calduch-Benages, N./ Liesen, J. (Hg.), History and Identity. How Israel's Late Authors Viewed its Earlier History, Deuterocanonical and Cognate Literature. Yearbook 2006, Berlin/New York 2006, 21–42. |

Zimmerli, W., Der „neue Exodus" in der Verkündigung der beiden großen Exilspropheten. In: Ders., Gottes Offenbarung. Gesammelte Aufsätze, TB 19, München 1969, 192–204.

Israel in der offiziellen Religion der Königszeit

Welchen Einfluss die offizielle Religion der Königszeit auf das Selbstverständnis Israels bzw. Judas gehabt hat, ist auf den ersten Blick gar nicht so einfach abzuschätzen. Soweit erkennbar, sind die beiden grundlegenden Konzeptionen, Israel als Volk JHWHs (Ri 5,11.13 [em.]; 2 Sam 1,12) und Israel als Stämmeverband (Ri 5,2.3–18), der idealerweise 12 Stämme umfasste (Gen 29,31–30,22 + 35,16–20), schon in der späten vorstaatlichen und der frühen staatlichen Zeit ausgebildet worden (R. Albertz 1987, 371–377).[1] Man kann vermuten, dass die Etablierung der staatlichen Königs- und Tempeltheologie im Davidisch-Salomonischen Reich und in den beiden Teilreichen Israel und Juda diese traditionellen Konzepte der Identität Israels mehr oder minder stark veränderte. Doch sind solche Veränderungen aus den in der Hebräischen Bibel stark selektiert überlieferten Texten nur schwer zu fassen; und brauchbare epigraphische Zeugnisse fehlen.[2] Es ist und bleibt immerhin ein auffälliger und bis heute nicht hinreichend erklärter Tatbestand, dass in der späten Königszeit (7. Jh. v. Chr.) plötzlich eine massiv heilsgeschichtlich fundierte Gottesvolk-Theologie in das Zentrum der offiziellen Religion des Südreiches einrücken konnte (Exodus, Erwählung, Bund), die zuvor in Juda, wie am klarsten der Prophet Jesaja noch für das 8. Jh. belegt, kaum eine Rolle gespielt hatte. Da in diesem Band die Propheten und die deuteronomisch-deuteronomistische Literatur gesondert behandelt werden,[3] beschränkt sich | der vor-

---

1 Immerhin sind in der späten vorstaatlichen Zeit erstmals die stämmeübergreifenden Institutionen der „Ältesten Israels" (1 Sam 4,3) und „Männer Israels" (1 Sam 11,15; 13,6) erwähnt. Und letztere umfassten – zumindest im Abschalomaufstand gegen David – auch den Heerbann des Stammes Juda (2 Sam 17,11; 19,10–12.41–44).

2 Es kann nur immer wieder daran erinnert werden, wie sehr für Israel die epigraphischen Befunde einfach dadurch verzerrt sind, dass literarische Texte hier meist auf Papyrus geschrieben wurden, der sich im relativ feuchten Klima Palästinas nur in Ausnahmefällen über die Jahrhunderte gehalten hat. Zum Beispiel wurde in den letzten Jahren durch Raubgrabungen ein großes offizielles Archiv ans Licht gebracht, das offenbar in der Nähe von Khirbet el-Qôm gelegen war (R. Deutsch 2003a; 2003b; A. Lemaire 2006, 236). Mehr als 500 Siegelabdrücke auf Tonklümpchen (Bullae) wurden gefunden, mit denen Schriftstücke gesiegelt waren, darunter mehrere vom König Hiskija und von einigen seiner Beamten. Hätten sich nur 100 dieser Schriftstücke erhalten, hätten wir ein viel genaueres Bild vom Juda der Hiskijazeit aus offizieller Perspektive. Auch von den Monumentalinschriften in Stein, die es durchaus gegeben hat (vgl. J. Naveh 2000, 1), haben sich leider nur unbedeutende Reste oder wenig aussagekräftige Exemplare erhalten (etwa die Schiloach-Inschrift, TGI 66 f.).

3 S. u. die Beiträge von Hubert Irsigler und Walter Dietrich [[= Irsigler, H., Der Streit um die Identität Israels in der vorexilischen Prophetie. Besonders am Beispiel von Hosea 12, in: ders. (Hg.), Die Identität Israels. Entwicklungen und Kontroversen in alttestamentlicher Zeit, HBS 56, Freiburg u. a.: Herder, 2009, 59–86; Dietrich, W., Israel in der Perspektive des deuteronomisch-deuteronomistischen Literaturkreises, in: a. a. O., 87–99]]. |

https://doi.org/10.1515/9783111202228-013

liegende Beitrag auf die Psalmen und die Geschichtsüberlieferung der vorexilischen Zeit.

1 Ein Blick von außen: Die Meša'-Stele

Aus dem zu untersuchenden Zeitraum (10.–8. Jh. v. Chr.) gibt es immerhin ein berühmtes authentisches inschriftliches Zeugnis, in dem der Begriff ‚Israel' nicht weniger als 6-mal begegnet: Die Stele des moabitischen Königs *Meša'*, die 1868 in der Nähe des ostjordanischen Diban gefunden wurde (KAI 181; H.-P. Müller 1985, 646–650). Sie stammt aus der Mitte des 9. Jh.s und kann bezeugen, wie die Größe ‚Israel' von seinen ostjordanischen Nachbarn zu dieser Zeit wahrgenommen wurde. Da Fremd- und Selbstwahrnehmung zusammenhängen, eröffnet die Stele eine erste Annäherung des Verständnisses, die zugleich den Grad der Verlässlichkeit der biblischen Aussagen besser einschätzen lässt. Erst einmal ergeben sich viele Gemeinsamkeiten: Wie sich *Meša'* als „König von Moab" einführt, so tituliert er seinen Gegner Omri als מלך ישראל (Z. 5; vgl. 10 f. 18). ‚Israel' meint also zuerst einmal – genauso wie ‚Moab' – das Herrschaftsgebiet eines Königs, konkret das Nordreich, so wie durchgängig in 1 Kön 12–2 Kön 17. Auch wenn *Meša'* sagt, sein Vater sei 30 Jahre „König über Moab" gewesen (מלך על מאב; Z. 2), und damit stärker das Staatsvolk oder das Territorium heraushebt, dann gibt es auch dazu viele entsprechende biblische Formulierungen mit Israel (2 Sam 5,3; 1 Kön 2,11 von David). Auf seiner Stele rühmt sich *Meša'* großsprecherisch, er habe die Oberhand über die Nachkommen Omris gewonnen und damit Israel vernichtet (אבד; vgl. von Moab Num 21,29); der Stellenwert des Reiches Israel hängt somit für ihn direkt von der militärischen Stärke seines Königshauses ab. Daneben berichtet *Meša'*, er habe Nebo (im Kampf) „gegen Israel eingenommen" (Z. 14); hier bezeichnet ‚Israel' das gegnerische Reich bzw. konkret seine Truppen. Auch diese Bedeutung kann ‚Israel' bzw. ‚Mannschaft Israels' in alttestamentlichen Texten häufig annehmen (1 Sam 13,1.5 f.). Auffälligerweise versteht *Meša'* unter Israel immer ein Kollektiv; einzelne Personengruppen daraus differenziert er durch Bildung einer *constructus*-Verbindung, so wahrscheinlich אסרי ישראל „die Gefangenen Israels", die er für seine Bauarbeiten einsetzt (Z. 25 f.). Auch im Alten Testament ist ‚Israel' meist ein ethnischer Kollektivbegriff. Ähnlich kollektiv zur Bezeichnung der Angehörigen seines Reiches kann *Meša'* allerdings auch den Begriff ‚Moab' verwenden (Z. 20; vgl. 1 Sam 13,2). D. h. in der Fremdwahrnehmung scheint es bis hierhin – sieht man einmal von den verschiedenen Herrschern und Göttern ab – keine gravierenden Unterschiede zwischen dem staatlichen Israel und dem staatlichen Moab zu geben; und | diese Sicht kommt durchaus mit Teilen der israelitischen Selbstwahrnehmung der Königszeit überein.

Der kritische Betrachter erkennt allerdings zwei Differenzen, die *Meša'* selber wohl kaum bewusst waren: Die erste Differenz ist eine theologische: Im Rückblick auf die Zeit der Vasallität, in die Moab unter dem israelitischen König Omri geraten war, formuliert *Meša'*:

Z. 4–6   Omri war König von Israel. Er unterdrückte Moab lange Zeit; denn *Kamoš* zürnte seinem Lande (כי יאנף כמש בארצה).

D. h. *Meša'* sieht den moabitischen Nationalgott *Kamoš* in einem primären Verhältnis zum Territorium seines Staates, nicht zu seiner Bevölkerung.[4] Diese Sicht, dass die Götter Herren oder Eigentümer von Ländern und Städten sind, ist im Vorderen Orient weit verbreitet (vgl. R. Albertz 1978, 161–163). Sie begegnet teilweise auch in Israel, etwa in der Zionstheologie, in der Jerusalem „Stadt Gottes" genannt werden kann (Ps 46,5; vgl. 48,2 f.), oder in der Vorstellung von Israels Siedlungsraum als „Erbbesitz JHWHs" (1 Sam 26,19; 2 Sam 14,16; vgl. Lev 25,23). Dennoch steht in Israel eindeutig das personale Verhältnis zu einer großen Gruppe von Menschen, einem Volk, im Vordergrund: Das häufigste Epitheton JHWHs, das seit vorstaatlicher Zeit in der Hebräischen Bibel 198-mal bezeugt wird, ist אלהי ישראל „Gott Israels" (Ri 5,3.5; 1 Sam 14,41; 1 Kön 1,30); d. h. dieser Gott wird primär über seinen Bezug auf eine Menschengruppe definiert. Und seit der gleichen Zeit kann sich diese Menschengruppe, oder doch zumindest deren kampfbereiter Teil, als „Volk JHWHs" verstehen (Ri 5,11.13cj.; 2 Sam 1,12; 6,21). Anders als in Moab war somit in Israel der Volksbegriff religiös aufgeladen und suggerierte einen engen Zusammenhalt.

Die zweite Differenz ist eine politische: *Meša'* berichtet, dass die Gaditer (אש גד) seit jeher (מעלם) im Lande Ataroth gesiedelt hätten, der König von Israel ihnen aber eine Stadt gleichen Namens gebaut habe, die er erobert und ihre Einwohner getötet habe (Z. 10 f.). *Meša'* verschweigt wohl absichtlich, dass es sich dabei um Angehörige Israels gehandelt hat, um nicht zugeben zu müssen, dass Israel in der Region uralte Siedlungsrechte besaß. Er definiert ihre Identität bewusst auf der niedrigeren Ebene einer regionalen Stammesgruppierung. Diese sei bloß in einem gewissen Schutzverhältnis zum König von Israel gestanden. Nachdem dieses beendet worden sei, könnten die überlebenden Gaditer umso leichter zusammen mit umgesiedelten Gruppen aus anderen Regionen dem moabitischen Herrschaftsbereich eingegliedert wer|den, zumal sie ihrer Kultsymbole beraubt

---

4 Wenn in Num 21,29 Moab im poetischen Kontext mit ironischem Unterton der Ehrentitel עם כמוש „Volk des *Kamoš*" verliehen wird, so wie Israel als עם יהוה „Volk JHWHs" gilt, dann handelt es sich um eine *interpretatio israelitica*, die den entscheidenden Unterschied aus israelitischer Sicht verwischt. |

worden sind (Z. 12–14). Beide Differenzen bedingen möglicherweise einander: Weil in Moab nicht ein Volk, sondern ein Land im Zentrum der Gottesbeziehung stand, konnten auf dem Territorium des moabitischen Staates Bevölkerungsgruppen unterschiedlicher nationaler und ethnischer Identität siedeln, sofern sie die Oberhoheit des Königs und des Staatsgottes anerkannten. Einen religiös aufgeladenen Volksbegriff gab es hier nicht.

2 Israel in der Königs- und Tempeltheologie des Südreiches

Ich verstehe unter offizieller Religion im weiteren Sinne alle auf Israel als Ganzes bezogenen religiösen Symbolwelten und Praktiken, die gesamtgesellschaftliche Bedeutung beanspruchten, egal ob sie Gültigkeit erlangten oder nicht, d. h. nicht nur die Theologie und die rituellen Praktiken der staatlichen Institutionen, sondern ebenfalls alle nur möglichen Theologien und Reformprogramme gesellschaftlicher Oppositions- und Reformgruppen.[5] Beschränkt man sich erst einmal auf die offizielle Religion der Königszeit im engeren Sinn als die Theologie und kultische Praxis, die von den staatlichen Institutionen konzipiert und propagiert wurde, dann ist man an die Königs- und Tempeltheologie gewiesen. Breiter sind wir darüber allerdings nur in Bezug auf das Südreich informiert; für das Nordreich haben wir nur ganz wenige Hinweise.

Den besten Zugang zur religiösen Symbolwelt der Jerusalemer Königs- und Tempeltheologie ermöglichen die Königs- (Ps 2; 18; 20; 21; 45; 72; 89; 110; 132; 144) und Zionspsalmen (Ps 46; 48; 76; 84; 87); hinzu kommen die JHWH-Königspsalmen, sofern sie mit einiger Wahrscheinlichkeit vorexilischer Herkunft (Ps 24; 29; 47; 93) sind.[6] Sieht man nun diese Psalmen durch, so stößt man auf das überraschende Ergebnis, dass der Begriff ‚Israel' in diesen 19, teilweise umfangreichen Texten nur zweimal begegnet: In Ps 76,2 bezeichnet er neben Juda den Bereich, in dem JHWH bekannt und gerühmt wird; in der schon frühexilischen Volksklage Ps 89 wird in V. 19 bekannt, | dass JHWH, „dem Heiligen Israels", trotz Verlustes

---

5 Hier bestehen zuweilen Missverständnisse in die Richtung, dass unter ‚offizieller Religion' nur das verstanden wird, was normativ galt, vgl. R. Albertz 1995, 199.
6 Dass ein Grundstock der Primärfassungen der Königs-, Zions- und JHWH-Königspsalmen aus der vorexilischen Zeit stammt, wird meist anerkannt, vgl. E. Zenger 2004, 362 f. Die Königstheologie wird in dem frühexilischen Ps 89 schon in einer entwickelten Form vorausgesetzt; das Gleiche gilt für die Grundelemente der Zionstheologie bei den Propheten des 8. und 7. Jh.s (Jes 8,17; Mi 3,11; Jer 7,4), selbst wenn Einzelmotive wie der ‚Völkersturm' erst nach 701 entfaltet sein sollten (vgl. G. Wanke 1966, 109–113). Jesaja setzt ebenfalls schon die JHWH-Königstheologie in Jerusalem voraus (Jes 6,1–5), zum ganzen s. R. Albertz 1996 I, 174–212. Da es im Folgenden um eine negative Evidenz geht, ist der Kreis der einbezogenen Texte bewusst weit gehalten. |

des Königtums der König und damit der Schild der Redenden gehört. Auch wenn man die Suche auf parallele Begriffe wie יעקב „Jakob" oder עם „Volk" ausweitet, erhöht sich die Trefferquote nur unwesentlich: Es wird bloß erkennbar, dass auch in den Königs- und Zionspsalmen vorausgesetzt wird, dass JHWH als ‚Gott Jakobs' (Ps 20,2; 46,8.12; 76,7; 84,9; vgl. 132,2.5)[7] und das Volk, das der König mit Gerechtig-keit richten soll, als JHWHs Volk gilt (Ps 72,2).[8] Aber dies wird nirgends eigens thematisiert und steht ganz im Hintergrund.[9]

Fragt man nach den Gründen für diesen eigenartigen Befund, so ist die Ant-wort eindeutig: Es mag verwundern, aber Israel war in der offiziellen Theologie des Südreiches bis in die mittlere Königszeit hinein nicht eigens konzeptionell verankert. Nach der davidischen Königstheologie ist der König Sohn Gottes (Ps 2,7), völlig unabhängig von dessen Beziehung zu Israel. JHWH regiert mit Hilfe seines Königs die aufbegehrende Völkerwelt (2,2–6); und der König unterwirft in seinen Kriegen die Völker unter JHWHs Regentschaft (2,8–11). Natürlich profitiert Israel bzw. Juda von dieser imperialen Kooperation zwischen Gott und König; aber das wird nicht eigens erwähnt; der Horizont der davidischen Königstheolo-gie ist primär universal (18,44.48; 72,8–11); Israel kommt nur da in den Blick, wo es um die innenpolitischen Funktionen des Königs als Rechtshelfer (72,2) oder Segensmittler geht (72,3 f.).

Ebenfalls von der Konzeption her universal ist die Jerusalemer Tempeltheolo-gie. Nach ihr wohnt JHWH auf dem Zion (Ps 76,3; 87,1 f.), der als mythischer Götterberg und Weltmittelpunkt vorgestellt wird (48,3; Ez 38,12). Aufgrund seiner Anwesenheit in Jerusalem (Ps 46,5 f.) macht er die Gottesstadt zum Bollwerk ge-gen den Ansturm der Chaosmächte (46,2–4) und gegen den Ansturm der Völker (46,7; 48,5–8; 76,4–6). Er verleiht von diesem Zentrum aus dem ganzen Erdkreis Stabilität und macht durch Unterwerfung der | Völker den Kriegen in der Welt überhaupt ein Ende (46,9–11). Natürlich versprach diese Theologie, die JHWH fast

---

7 In Ps 24,6 ist wahrscheinlich ein אלהי vor יעקב ausgefallen; wenn dies mit 2 MSS, LXX und Syr ergänzt wird, erhöhen sich die Belege für אלהי יעקב in den Königs- und Zionspsalmen auf immerhin sechs; hinzu kommt der Ausdruck אביר יעקב „Starker Jakobs" in Ps 132,2.5. Daneben begegnet der „Stolz Jakobs" in Ps 47,5 (Land oder König?); und die „Wohnungen Jakobs" in Ps 87,2.

8 Die beiden übrigen Belege für suffigiertes עם in Ps 29,11 sind sekundär, s. u.

9 Aus anderer Perspektive ist schon einmal H. Spieckermann auf die ‚Fremdheit' dieser Jerusale-mer Theologie gestoßen, die sich deutlich vom heilsgeschichtlichen Aufriss des Pentateuchs un-terscheide (1989, 14 f.). Auf der Grundlage von Ps 29; 93; 48; 24; 21 beschreibt er sie als „Dialektik von Präsenz und Kontingenz der Gottesgegenwart" (223) „Sie gründet den Menschen und gewährt ihm Heil, ohne auf Heilsgeschichte zu basieren" (225). Allerdings verallgemeinert Spieckermann diese Sicht zu schnell zu einer allgemeinen „Psalmentheologie" und berücksichtigt nicht die Unterschiedlichkeit der Gattungen und deren Herkunft. Gegenteilige Beispiele, wie Ps 80, werden in die exilisch-nachexilische Zeit abgeschoben (160). |

völlig mit einer Stadt identifizierte, den in und um Jerusalem Wohnenden in ganz besonderer Weise Heilssicherheit (46,8.12; Mi 3,11; Jer 7,4), aber konzeptionell beanspruchte sie, dass die Hauptstadt Judas „Wonne der ganzen Welt" sei (Ps 48,3).

Ähnlich mythologisch und universal ist von Hause aus die Konzeption von JHWHs Königtum, die in Jerusalem entwickelt wurde. Es beruht darauf, dass es JHWH gelungen sei, die Chaosfluten dauerhaft zu bändigen (Ps 29,10; 93,1–4; vgl. 24,2). Mit Israel hatte das erst einmal gar nichts zu tun; die Verse Ps 29,11 und 93,5, die den mythologischen Sieg auf Israel oder seine Institutionen applizieren, sind eindeutig sekundär und wahrscheinlich erst exilisch.[10] Einen Bezug zwischen Israel und JHWHs Königtum stellt in vorexilischer Zeit allein Ps 47[11] her: An die Stelle des Sieges über die Chaosfluten tritt hier die Bezwingung der Völker unter Israels Herrschaft (47,4). Es ist nicht ganz sicher, ob in V. 5 mit den metaphorischen Ausdrücken:

> Ps 47,5   Er erwählt uns unseren Erbteil, den Stolz Jakobs, den er liebt.

auf die Landnahme oder die Thronerhebung Davids angespielt werden soll,[12] aber in jedem Fall wird damit JHWHs Königtum erstmals auf ein Ereignis in | der Geschichte Israels bezogen. Dennoch behält das Königtum JHWHs universale Dimensionen:

---

10 Dies ist für den Ps 93,5 ziemlich sicher, wegen des verwandten Begriffs עדות, vgl. J. Jeremias 1987, 25 f.; K. Seybold 1996, 124; F.-L. Hossfeld/E. Zenger 2000, 646. Nicht ganz so sicher ist die Datierung von Ps 29,11, doch setzt die Bitte um Anteil an der Macht des Gottkönigs wohl eine anhaltende Ohnmachtssituation des Gottesvolkes voraus, vgl. H. Spieckermann 1989, 169; F.-L. Hossfeld/E. Zenger 1993, 182.

11 Zur vorexilischen Datierung von Ps 47 vgl. J. Jeremias 1987, 68 f. F.-L. Hossfeld/E. Zenger (1993, 290) nehmen zwar noch eine vorexilische Herkunft von Ps 47 an, denken aber bezüglich der Verse 3b–5b und 10 an eine nachexilische Überarbeitung. Doch gerade V. 10 hat, wie schon J. Jeremias (1987, 67 f.) feststellte, eine klare politische Konnotation: Die נדיבים „Edlen" der Völker sind versammelt; diese werden durch die Aussage, dass „Gott die Schilde der Erde gehören", als Gesandte der besiegten Vasallenvölker qualifiziert. Diese imperiale Konkretion unterscheidet aber Ps 47,10 deutlich von den späteren Vorstellungen einer Völkerwallfahrt zum Zion (Hag 2,6–9; Jes 60,5–7; 2,1–4). Ps 47,10 erklärt sich am besten als konkreter Anknüpfungspunkt für die späteren Vorstellungen.

12 Zwar bezeichnet der Begriff נחלה „Erbbesitz" häufig das Land Israels (mit dem gleichen Suffix Klgl 5,2), kann sich aber auch metaphorisch auf andere Größen, etwa auf JHWH, beziehen (Dtn 10,9). Nicht recht zum Land will das Verb בחר „erwählen" passen, das sonst seit dtn Zeit auf das Volk Israel (Dtn 7,6) oder den Zion bezogen wird (Ps 132,13), früher allerdings auf den König (2 Sam 6,21; 16,18; vgl. Ps 89,4.20 und den Namen von Davids Sohn Jibḥar in 2 Sam 5,15). In der Königstheologie ist auch das Verb אהב „lieben" zuhause (2 Sam 12,24; Jes 48,14). So könnte mit den Ausdrücken „unser Erbteil" und „Stolz/Pracht Jakobs" auch der König gemeint sein. |

Ps 47,9   König wurde Gott über die Völker,
           Gott hat Platz genommen auf seinem heiligen Thron.
     10   Die Edlen der Völker sind versammelt
           als das Volk / mit dem Volk des Gottes Abrahams.
           Denn Gott gehören die Schilde der Erde,
           hoch erhaben ist er.

Im Unterwerfen der Feinde Israels richtet JHWH sein Königtum über die Völker auf. Dieses manifestiert sich darin, dass sich die Abgesandten der unterworfenen Vasallen in Jerusalem versammeln, um diesem Völkerkönig zu huldigen. Eigenartig ist dabei die Rede vom „Volk des Gottes Abrahams", die nur hier vorkommt. Sollten die Abgesandten der Völker direkt diesem Volk angehören, wie der masoretische Text kühn behauptet? Oder sollte gemeint sein, dass die Gesandten der Völker gemeinsam mit Israel die Huldigung vollziehen, wie die Septuaginta und Peschitta vorsichtiger nahelegen?[13] In jedem Fall wird die Verehrerschaft JHWHs erweitert; um diesem universalen Gottkönig zu huldigen, reichen Israel oder Juda allein nicht aus. In der offiziellen Religion Jerusalems wird damit die Identität Israels auf imperial-religiöse Weise transzendiert. Wenn dabei JHWH nicht – wie üblich – „Gott Israels", sondern „Gott Jakobs" (Ps 20,2; [24,6]; 46,8.12; 76,7; 84,9; vgl. Ps 132,2.5)[14] oder „Gott Abrahams" (47,10) genannt wird, dann soll sehr wahrscheinlich ein Ausgleich zwischen der universalen Jerusalemer Gottesvorstellung und der vorgegebenen partikularen JHWH-Religion erreicht werden: Ist doch Abraham nicht nur Stammvater Israels, sondern auch einer Reihe von Nachbarvölkern.[15]

So ging die offizielle Theologie des Südreiches ganz eigene Wege. In den Vordergrund stellte sie die engen Beziehungen JHWHs zum davidischen Kö|nig und zur Stadt Jerusalem, die sie in einen universalen Horizont einordnete. Demgegenüber wurde die Beziehung zwischen JHWH und seinem Volk Israel deutlich in den Hintergrund gerückt und teilweise in Richtung auf den universalen Horizont hin geöffnet.

---

13 MT liest עַם אֱלֹהֵי אַבְרָהָם, die LXX setzt mit der Lesung μετὰ τοῦ θεοῦ Αβρααμ eine Präposition עַם „mit" voraus. Die Lesart der LXX könnte auf eine Haplographie des עם hindeuten.
14 Nimmt man noch die weiteren mit „Jakob" gebildeten Gottesbezeichnungen (2 Sam 23,1; Jes 2,3; 41,21; 49,26; 60,16) hinzu, die alle Jerusalemer Milieu atmen, dann scheint es sich hier um eine spezifische judäische Terminologie zu handeln; vgl. auch die Rede vom „Haus Jakob" (Jes 2,6; 8,17; Mi 2,7; 3,1.9) bzw. „Jakob" (Mi 3,8) zur Bezeichnung des Südreiches bei den Propheten Jesaja und Micha.
15 So konkret der Ismaeliter (Gen 16) und der Araber (Gen 25,1–5); nahe mit ihm verwandt sind die Aramäer (Gen 11,27–30; 22,20–24) und die Ammoniter und Moabiter (Gen 19,30–38); die Priesterschrift machte Abraham später programmatisch zum „Vater vieler Völker" (17,5). |

3 Israel in der offiziellen Theologie des Nordreiches

Von der Königs- und Tempeltheologie des Nordreiches haben sich im Alten Testament kaum direkte Zeugnisse erhalten. Eine gewisse Ausnahme bildet die Volksklage Ps 80, die immerhin einige ihrer Elemente enthält. Sonst ist man auf Rückschlüsse aus dem DtrG und dem Hoseabuch angewiesen.

Wichtig für die Geschichte der Identität Israels ist der Umstand, dass mit Gründung des Nordreiches der Begriff ‚Israel' eine klare politische, ja, wenn man so will, staatsrechtliche Konnotation erhielt. Hatte der Begriff in vorstaatlicher Zeit einen lockeren Stämmeverband mit unterschiedlicher Reichweite bezeichnet – mit deutlicher lokaler Zentrierung auf das mittel- und nordpalästinische Bergland –, und konnte das davidisch-salomonische Reich mal additiv ‚Israel und Juda' (2 Sam 3,10; 11,11; 1 Kön 1,35; 4,20), mal inklusiv ‚Israel' genannt werden (2 Sam 5,12; 6,20 f.; 1 Kön 1,34),[16] so wurde der Begriff nun auf das Staatsvolk und das Territorium des Nordreichs festgelegt. Schon die Wahl dieser Selbstbezeichnung lässt erkennen, dass sich das Nordreich als der eigentlich legitime Erbe und Wahrer israelitischer Identität betrachtete. Und darum ist zu vermuten, dass sich auch die offizielle Religion des Nordreiches mehr in den Bahnen der traditionellen JHWH-Religion der vorstaatlichen Zeit bewegte als die des Südreichs.

Aus dieser Einengung des Begriffs ‚Israel' im politischen Bereich erwuchsen nun erhebliche Probleme für die Bestimmung der religiösen Identität. Es lässt sich nämlich erkennen, dass der Begriff ‚Israel' im kulturellen und religiösen Bereich immer weiter blieb und die Bevölkerung beider Teilreiche umfasste. Wenn die Königstochter Tamar in Jerusalem zu ihrem Halbbruder Ammon, der sie zu vergewaltigen suchte, sagte: „So etwas tut man nicht in Israel" (2 Sam 13,12),[17] so fühlte sie sich offenbar in eine gesamtisraelitische Wertegemeinschaft eingebunden. Jesaja konnte sogar von den „beiden Häusern Israels" sprechen (Jes 8,14) und verstand damit unter ‚Israel' so etwas wie eine gemeinsame Nation, die in zwei Teilstaaten organisiert war. Und Ähnliches gilt nun erst recht für die religiöse Einschätzung: Trotz politischer Trennung waren und blieben JHWH und sein Volk als „Gott Israels" und „Volk Israel" gesamtisraelitisch definiert; es wurde offenbar nie versucht, | einen „Gott Judas"[18] oder ein „Gottesvolk Juda"[19] im

---

16 Vgl. dazu genauer R. Albertz 1987, 370–372.

17 Vgl. 2 Sam 13,13; Gen 34,7; Ri 20,6.10.13; Jos 7,15; Dtn 17,4; 22,21. |

18 Der Begriff יהודי אלהי kommt in der ganzen Hebräischen Bibel nicht ein einziges Mal vor, gegenüber 198 Belegen für ישראל אלהי. Nur in Jer 2,28; 11,13 wird vereinzelt in polemischer Absicht von „deinen Göttern, Juda" gesprochen, aber damit ist nicht etwa JHWH, sondern sind die Fremdgötter gemeint.

19 Es begegnet in der Hebräischen Bibel bisweilen (7-mal) ein יהודה עם „Volk Juda" (2 Sam 19,41; 2 Kön 14,21; 2 Chr 26,1; Esr 4,4; Jer 25,1.2; 26,18), aber dieses wird nie durch Suffixe oder

Südreich zu etablieren. Doch allein schon aufgrund der Namensidentität konnten Theologen des Staates Israel behaupten, dass JHWH in erster Linie der Gott ihres Reiches sei. Und es mag sein, dass der Befund, dass in den Zeugnissen der Staatstheologie des Südreiches der JHWH-Titel „Gott Israels" gemieden (erst frühexilisch Ps 89,19) und stattdessen die Bezeichnung „Gott Jakobs" (Ps 20,2; 46,8.12; 76,7; 84,9; vgl. 24,6; 132,2.5) oder „Gott Abrahams" (Ps 47,10) verwendet wird, auch damit zu tun hat, dass man hier den falschen Eindruck, dass JHWH allein oder in erster Linie der Gott des Nordreiches sei, auf alle Fälle vermeiden wollte.

Von der offiziellen Tempeltheologie der Staatsheiligtümer Bet-El und Dan ist dem polemischen Bericht des DtrG zumindest so viel zu entnehmen, dass mit deren tauromorphen Gottessymbolen der Kultruf: „Siehe, dein Gott, Israel, der dich aus dem Lande Ägypten heraufgeführt hat" verbunden war (1 Kön 12,28).[20] Dies bedeutet: Die personale Beziehung JHWHs zu Israel, d. h. genau das Element, das in der Jerusalemer Staatsreligion ganz in den Hintergrund getreten war, bildete offenbar ein zentrales Element der offiziellen Nordreichtheologie. Dabei wurde diese personale Gottesbeziehung ganz offensichtlich nicht kosmo-mythologisch, sondern durch die geschichtlichen Urdaten von Exodus und Landnahme begründet, egal ob man diese als historische Erinnerung oder als geschichtlichen Gründungsmythos versteht.[21] Deren Wichtigkeit ergibt sich daraus, dass sehr wahrscheinlich schon der Aufstand gegen die salomonische Fronarbeit, der in die Gründung des Nordrei|ches mündete, mit Berufung auf den Gott des Exodus geführt worden ist.[22] Die Prominenz der Exodus-Landnahmetradition in der offiziellen Theologie des Nordreiches wird indirekt durch den Propheten Hosea bestätigt (Hos 11,1; 12,10.14; 13,4–6 u. ö.).

Der einzige Text aus dem Umkreis der staatlichen Religion, der zu einem wesentlichen Teil aus dem Nordreich stammt, ist die Volksklage Ps 80. In ihr

Appositionen als ‚Volk JHWHs' gekennzeichnet. Nur ein einziges Mal erscheint die additive Wendung „mein Volk Israel und Juda" (Jer 30,3), aber selbst wenn Juda hier nicht erst redaktionell hinzugefügt wurde, bleibt es doch dem Gottesvolk Israel ein- und untergeordnet.

20 Der dtr Historiker konstruiert אלהים pluralisch, wahrscheinlich nicht nur, weil es sich ja um zwei ‚Kälber' handelt, von denen je eines in Bet-El und Dan aufgestellt werden soll, sondern auch, weil er polemisch einen Vielgötterglauben unterstellen will; das gleiche geschieht noch offensichtlicher in der Erzählung vom goldenen Kalb in Ex 32,4.8, in der sogar die deiktische Partikel in den Plural gesetzt ist. Doch belegt die singularische Fassung des Kultrufs in Neh 9,18 dessen ursprünglichen Sinn, den man getrost auch aus 1 Kön 12,28 rekonstruieren kann.

21 Vgl. die Diskussion zwischen K. van der Toorn (2001, 113–127) und R. Albertz (2001b, 128–143). Auch wenn man Exodus und Landnahme als Gründungsmythos betrachtet, bleibt dieser doch als Geschichtsmythos klar vom kosmologischen Mythos, der die Jerusalemer offizielle Religion kennzeichnet, geschieden. |

22 Vgl. die auffälligen Parallelen zwischen Mose und Jerobeam I.; genauer dazu R. Albertz 1996 I, 215–219.

wurde, wahrscheinlich nach herben Landverlusten, die das Nordreich nach der assyrischen Strafaktion 732 v. Chr. hinnehmen musste,[23] JHWH als Hirte Israels angerufen, der vor den Stämmen Efraim, Benjamin und Manasse, machtvoll erscheinen solle, um den damit bezeichneten samarischen Rumpfstaat vor völliger Zerstörung zu retten (80,2–3). Mit der Hirtenmetaphorik wird JHWH auch im Nordreich als König vorgestellt, allerdings nicht als universaler Völkerkönig wie im Süden, sondern als König Israels, der Josef wie Schafe leitet (V. 2). Die JHWH-Königs-Theologie blieb somit im Nordreich in die personale Gottesbeziehung Israels eingebunden. In Vers 5 präsentieren sich die Klagenden ausdrücklich als JHWHs Volk. Nicht zufällig wird im weiteren Klagepsalm versucht, JHWH durch einen heilsgeschichtlichen Rückblick auf die Exodus- und Landnahme-Ereignisse zum Einlenken zu bewegen (V. 9–12). Es ist nicht ganz sicher, ob die Fürbitte für den König in V. 18 noch aus der nordisraelitischen Fassung des Psalms stammt, oder schon zu dessen judäischer Adaption gehört:

> Ps 80,18   Deine Hand sei über den Mann deiner Rechten,
> über den Sohn {des Menschen}, den du dir großgezogen hast.[24]

Wenn das Erstere zutrifft, dann hätten auch die Nordreichkönige beansprucht, Söhne JHWHs zu sein und sein Mandat auszuführen, ähnlich wie dies im | Südreich der Fall war (Ps 2,7; 110,1). Soweit erkennbar, bewegt sich allerdings ihre besonders enge Gottesbeziehung ganz im Rahmen der grundlegenden Beziehung JHWHs zu Israel. Leider haben wir keine weiteren expliziten Belege für die Königstheologie des Nordreiches. Aber wenn man berücksichtigt, dass im Norden anders als im Süden Residenz und Staatstempel räumlich weit voneinander getrennt waren[25] und man es hier offenbar als Sakrileg ansah, wenn die Könige

---

23 Diese Datierung von Ps 80 nach der ersten Exilierung des Nordreiches 732 wurde schon von O. Eißfeldt 1953, 75, vorgeschlagen; sie wurde von F.-L. Hossfeld/E. Zenger 2000, 456 f., erneut für den Grundbestand des Psalms aufgenommen; ihrer Meinung nach gehören nur die Kehrversbitten V. 4.8.20 einer späteren judäischen Bearbeitung an; 16b ist eine glossarische Textvariante zu V. 18b. Wenn M. Emmendörffer 1998, 121–147, eine vorexilische Datierung von Ps 80 bestreitet, dann entspringt dies seiner vorgefassten Meinung, dass es vorexilisch keine heilsgeschichtlich gegründete ‚Psalmentheologie' gegeben haben kann. Doch kann er diese von seinem Lehrer H. Spieckermann übernommene Ansicht (s. o. Anm. 9) nicht aus der Traditionsgeschichte der Klage des Volkes plausibel machen; vgl. zur Kritik im Einzelnen R. Albertz 2001, 127.
24 Wie Ps 80,16b belegt, handelt es sich bei dem Wort אדם „Mensch" um eine nachträgliche Ergänzung, die den König wahrscheinlich auf die apokalyptische Menschensohn-Gestalt (Dan 7,13) beziehen will. Die Glosse V. 16b macht deutlich, dass sich die Abschreiber noch der Variante, die den älteren Text bewahrt, bewusst waren. |
25 Dass das ca. 50 km von der Hauptstadt Samaria entfernte Bet-El tatsächlich als ‚königliches Heiligtum' und als ‚Tempel des Königreiches' fungierte, belegt unabhängig von 1 Kön 12,28–31 Am 7,13. Zudem beschreibt die Erzählung von der Ausweisung des Amos (Am 7,10–17) recht

selber den Opferkult vollzogen (1 Sam 13,9–13; 1 Kön 13,1–9), was den Davididen ganz selbstverständlich zugebilligt wurde (1 Kön 8,63–66; Ps 110,4),[26] dann spricht doch einiges dafür, dass im Norden eine weniger massive Form von sakralem Königtum realisiert worden ist als im Südreich.[27] Dieser Umstand ist wohl auch der Hauptgrund dafür, dass im Nordreich die Könige weit häufiger als im Süden Opfer von Usurpationen wurden; sie waren sakral weniger massiv geschützt.

So hielt sich die offizielle Religion des Nordreichs, soweit wir erkennen können, weit mehr als die des Südens in den Bahnen der traditionellen JHWH-Religion. Hier stand das Konzept von Israel als Gottesvolk – allerdings nunmehr direkt gleichgesetzt mit dem Staatsvolk des Reiches – im Mittelpunkt. |

4 Israel in der Synthese der offiziellen Religionen von Nord- und Südreich in der Hiskijazeit

Erst wenn man sich der wahrscheinlich starken Unterschiede zwischen den Staatsreligionen von Nord- und Südreich bewusst geworden ist, kann man wohl richtig erahnen, welche tiefgreifenden Veränderungen sich im Selbstverständnis Israels nach dem Untergang des Nordreiches Israel 722 v. Chr. ereignen mussten. Plötzlich fiel nicht nur im politischen, sondern auch im theologischen Bereich der zwei Jahrhunderte während Konkurrenzdruck fort und damit der Zwang, die lokalen Besonderheiten der jeweiligen Staatstempel und Königtümer herauszustellen. Der Terminus ‚Israel' verlor seine scharfe politische Festlegung und wurde

---

plastisch, wie der Priester Amazja zwar in Abstimmung mit dem König, aber doch recht eigenverantwortlich die Geschäfte des Tempels führt.

26 Diese Differenz zwischen den Königtümern von Nord- und Südreich ist bisher noch nicht voll wahrgenommen worden. Dies führte bis heute dazu, dass der Grund für die Verwerfung der Sauliden in 1 Sam 13,7b-14 nicht richtig gewürdigt werden konnte, vgl. die vagen Formulierungen von H. J. Stoebe (1973, 251 f.) und F. Stolz (1981, 85 f.) zur Stelle. Die Differenz hinsichtlich der kultischen Kompetenz der Nordreichkönige war offenbar auch den späteren Tradenten nicht mehr plausibel, weswegen sie mit 1 Sam 15 eine weitere Begründung für die Verwerfung Sauls einschoben, die auf einer Übertretung des dtn Banngebots (Dtn 20) beruht. Die priesterliche Funktion der Davididen ist wahrscheinlich jebusitisches Erbe, vgl. Gen 14,18; Ps 110,4.

27 Dass sich die altorientalischen Königtümer trotz ihrer gemeinsamen Zugehörigkeit zum Typ des ‚Sakralen Königtums' hinsichtlich des Grades ihrer Sakralität unterschieden haben, kann ein Vergleich zwischen assyrischem und babylonischem Königtum verdeutlichen: Während die assyrischen Könige persönlich das Amt des obersten Priesters (*šangû*) ausübten und sich deswegen regelmäßig Ritualen zur Herstellung ihrer kultischen Reinheit unterziehen mussten (vgl. die an den Thronsaal angegliederten Ritualbäder), übernahmen in Babylon die Priester die kultische Vermittlung zwischen dem König und der Götterwelt (vgl. das berühmte Relief aus Sippar, auf dem ein Priester den König zum Sonnengott führt; bei O. Keel 1972, 153, Nr. 239). |

für breitere theologische Interpretationen frei verfügbar. Hinzu kam, dass Tausende von Flüchtlingen vor den assyrischen Truppen aus dem Norden nach Jerusalem strömten und sich nunmehr das Südreich mit einiger Berechtigung als Heimstätte des wiedervereinigten Gesamtisrael verstehen konnte.[28] Da die deuteronomische Theologie später im 7. Jh. starke Einflüsse des Propheten Hosea aufweist, müssen unter den Flüchtlingen auch einflussreiche Theologen aus dem Nordreich gewesen sein, die wesentliche Elemente der offiziellen Theologie des Nordreiches, allerdings in der zugespitzten Form, die sie im hoseanischen Oppositionszirkel gewonnen hatte, in das Südreich hinein vermittelten. Und offenbar waren auch die Träger der offiziellen Religionen des Südreiches aufgrund der tiefen Erschütterungen, die der Zusammenbruch des Bruderstaates ausgelöst hatte, bereit, über eine tiefgreifende Revision ihrer Theologie nachzudenken. Einige Auffälligkeiten in der überlieferten Form von Ps 80, etwa der Umstand, dass in Vers 6 von den Klagenden in der 3. Person gesprochen wird („Du speistest sie mit Tränenbrot, du tränktest sie mit Tränen über alle Maßen"), könnten darauf hinweisen, dass offizielle Kreise Judas die Klage ihrer Brüder aus dem Norden aufgenommen und solidarisch mitgesprochen haben.[29]

So kommt es wohl in der Hiskijazeit zu ersten bewussten Synthesen zwischen den offiziellen Religionen des Nord- und Südreichs, die dann in der deuteronomischen und deuteronomistischen Theologie weitergeführt werden. Hier soll vor allem auf das „Erzählwerk über die frühe Königszeit" 1 Sam 9–1 Kön 2* eingegangen werden. W. Dietrich hat 1997 – auch wenn er hinsichtlich der literarischen Abgrenzung und Rekonstruktion noch vieles | offen lässt[30] – überzeugend gezeigt, dass dieses Erzählwerk, das die Geschichte der ersten Könige Israels als göttliche Erwählungsgeschichte durchsichtig machen will, am besten aus der Hiskijazeit erklärt werden kann: Schon in politischer Perspektive war das Werk um einen Kompromiss zwischen Nord- und Südreich bemüht. Dietrich fasst ihn so zusammen: „Das Königtum Sauls war ein respektgebietendes, letztlich aber zum Scheitern verurteiltes Unternehmen. David war der richtige Mann, um Juda und

---

28 So übrigens explizit die Einschätzung der Hiskijazeit in 2 Chr 28–30, vgl. H.-S. Bae 2005, 104–116.

29 Ob die Anrede JHWHs als „Kerubenthroner" in Ps 80,2 einen Eintrag aus Jerusalemer Theologie darstellt (2 Kön 19,15; Ps 99,1) oder ob der Titel letztlich auf das Nordreichheiligtum Schilo zurückgeht (1 Sam 4,4; 2 Sam 6,2), kann hier offen bleiben. |

30 Insbesondere ist sich W. Dietrich 1997, 259, nicht ganz sicher, ob das Erzählwerk schon in 1 Kön 2, oder erst in 1 Kön 12 endete. Doch scheint mir allein die Tatsache, dass die dtr Redaktion ab 1 Kön 3 wieder sehr viel stärker als in 1 Sam 9–1 Kön 2 präsent ist, dafür zu sprechen, dass das ihr vorgegebene Erzählwerk in 1 Kön 2 endete. Auch der thematische Bogen über die Festigung des Königtums (ממלכה mit den Verben כון oder קום) in 1 Sam 13,13 f.; 24,21; 2 Sam 3,10; 5,12; 7,12; 1 Kön 2,46) endet in 1 Kön 2. Ich rechne vorläufig zum Textbestand des Erzählwerks 1 Sam 9,1–10,16; 13–14; 16–31*; 2 Sam 1–20*; und 1 Kön 1–2*.

Israel zu einen und auf ungeahnte Höhen zu führen" (1997, 267). David habe den Untergang Sauls nicht betrieben, sondern sich fair gegenüber seinen Nachkommen verhalten. So spitzt Dietrich die Intention des Werks für die Hiskijazeit zu: „Die Botschaft des Geschichtswerkes (war möglicherweise) … eine sehr konkrete: Ihr Nordisraeliten habt vom Hause Davids nichts zu befürchten, aber viel zu erhoffen" (267).

Nach der Sicht dieser staatlichen Gründungsgeschichte gibt es eigentlich nur ein einziges Königtum, „das Königtum Israels" (1 Sam 24,21). JHWH hatte es zuerst Saul übergeben und hätte „sein Königtum über Israel" auch „bis in Ewigkeit" befestigt, wenn jener nicht gegen Gottes Gebot verstoßen und eigenmächtig in den Opferkult eingegriffen hätte (1 Sam 13,13). So hat sich JHWH einen anderen „Mann seines Herzens" gesucht (1 Sam 13,14), David vor Saul und dessen Familie erwählt (2 Sam 6,21) und zum Fürsten über sein Volk bestellt (5,2; 7,8). Auf Davids frommen Wunsch hin, ihm einen Tempel in Jerusalem zu bauen, habe JHWH ihm durch Natan nicht nur den ewigen Bestand seiner Dynastie zugesagt (7,16), sondern ihm auch noch versprochen, seine Nachkommen, falls sie fehlen sollten, nur begrenzter Strafen zu unterziehen, ihnen aber nie wieder, wie Saul gegenüber geschehen, seine Gnade zu entziehen (V. 15).[31] Damit hatte das eine Königtum mit der | davidischen Dynastie gegen alle möglichen Widerstände und Krisen seine nötige Festigkeit gewonnen, wie am Schluss des Werks in Bezug auf Salomo konstatiert wird (1 Kön 2,46).

Fragt man nach den Gründen für diese stark vereinheitlichende Sicht des Werks, so ist erst einmal an die politische Zielrichtung zu erinnern: Hier soll eine Gründungsgeschichte für das teilweise schon wiedervereinigte staatliche Israel geschrieben werden. Doch damit ist die theologische Sicht noch nicht erfasst: An allen zentralen Stellen des Werks, wird das Königtum betont auf das Gottesvolk bezogen („über mein Volk Israel" 1 Sam 9,16; 2 Sam 7,8; vgl. 5,2; „um seines Volks Israel willen" 2 Sam 5,12; „über das Volk JHWHs, über Israel" 6,21). Weil aber aus streng theologischer Perspektive das Gottesvolk, besonders wenn man mit Hosea die Exklusivität seiner Beziehung zu JHWH erkannt hat, immer nur eines sein kann, kann es auch nur ein von JHWH legitimiertes Königtum über es geben.

---

31 Die wesentliche Textstufe von 2 Sam 7 (V. 1a.2–5a.8aβb-9.11b-12.14–16.17–22a.27–29), die ich früher eher in die Joschijazeit datieren wollte (R. Albertz 1996 I, 178), gehört auf die Ebene des Erzählwerks und damit in die Hiskijazeit. Dies kommt in etwa mit der klassischen Sicht von L. Rost 1965, 170–175, überein. Die Beobachtung von E. J. Waschke 1987, 167, die mich zur späteren Datierung bewog, dass nämlich die nominale Sohnes- (Ps 2,7) bzw. Vater-Deklaration (89,27) zwischen Gott und König in 2 Sam 7,14 schon im Sinne der verbalen Bundesformel (vgl. 2 Sam 7,24; Jer 11,4 u. ö.) umgebogen sei, ist vielleicht doch nicht zwingend, da die Wechselbeziehung zwischen Gott und König in der Sicht des Erzählwerks von vornherein in einen geschichtlichen Horizont gestellt ist (vgl. V. 15 mit dem Rückblick auf Saul). |

Und dies konnte nach Sicht der offiziellen Religion des Südreiches, die ja nicht zuletzt durch den Untergang des Nordreichkönigtums Bestätigung erhielt, nur das davidische Königtum sein. Insofern vertrat das Erzählwerk judäische Führungsansprüche. Doch das eine Königtum ließ sich nun nicht einfach allein für judäische Interessen okkupieren; es blieb ein Königtum über Israel und bezog damit immer auch die Nordisraeliten, insbesondere die geflüchteten, mit ein und hatte gleichfalls deren Ansprüche zu berücksichtigen.

Vertraten die Autoren des Erzählwerks von seinem Verlauf her eher eine judäische Sicht, so kamen sie den Nordisraeliten bei der inhaltlichen Bestimmung des Verhältnisses von Gott, König und Volk offenbar weit entgegen. Dies zeigt sich besonders in den Königsdesignationen, die das Werk wie ein roter Faden durchziehen:

1 Sam 9,16 Salbe ihn zum נגיד über mein Volk Israel,
dass er mein Volk aus der Hand der Philister rette!
Denn ich habe mein Volk angesehen und sein Schreien ist zu mir gelangt.

2 Sam 5,2 Du sollst mein Volk Israel weiden und sollst zum נגיד werden über Israel!

2 Sam 7,8 Ich habe dich hinter den Schafhürden weggenommen,
damit du נגיד über mein Volk Israel sein sollst.[32]

An diesen sorgfältig formulierten Aussagen ist dreierlei auffällig: Erstens, der Königstitel wird vermieden. Von Gott her gesehen, ist der König nur נגיד, | d.h. nur ‚Thronprätendent‘;[33] mit der Wahl dieses eigenartigen Titels soll festgehalten werden: der eigentliche König Israels ist JHWH, wie dies in der offiziellen Theologie des Nordreiches gesagt wurde (Ps 80,2); der irdische König ist nur beauftragter Mitregent und bleibt der göttlichen Regentschaft immer untergeordnet. Zweitens: die Einsetzung des Königs geschieht um des Gottesvolks Israel willen (so explizit 2 Sam 5,12), d.h. die Beziehung JHWHs zu seinem Volk wird seiner Beziehung zum König vorgeordnet; letztere kann erstere nicht monopolisieren und schon gar nicht ersetzen, wie dies nach der judäischen Königstheologie zumindest möglich war.[34] Und drittens: Das Königtum wird eingeordnet in das geschichtliche

---

32 Vgl. die weiteren Belege (1 Sam 10,1; 13,14; 25,30; 2 Sam 6,21), die zusammen mit den genannten eine regelrechte Kette durch das Erzählwerk bilden. |
33 So mit Recht E. Lipiński 1974 und T. N. D. Mettinger 1976, 155–162, auf der Grundlage von 1 Kön 1,35; 2 Chr 11,22.
34 Vgl. z.B. 2 Sam 8,1–15 und Anm. 38. Wie sehr die Rangfolge der Gottesbeziehungen Israels und des Königs ein kontroverses theologisches Streitthema blieb, lässt sich daran erkennen, dass sich die dtr Historiker nicht mit dem im Erzählwerk gefundenen Kompromiss abfanden, sondern die Bestandszusage der davidischen Dynastie in 2 Sam 7,12.14–16 mit einem Rahmen göttlicher Verheißungen und Bundeszusagen für Israel umgaben (2 Sam 7,10–11a.22b-26). Darin preist David die einzigartige Stellung Israels als JHWHs Volk auf Erden (V. 23) und schreibt dessen Status als

Heilshandeln JHWHs an seinem Volk; es hat keine eigene kosmo-mythologische Basis. Vor allem andern hat es die Aufgabe, das rettende Handeln Gottes an Israel zu vermitteln (1 Sam 9,16; 2 Sam 3,18; vgl. 19,10); von der Durchsetzung einer göttlichen Weltregierung ist keine Rede mehr. So wird der politische Macht- und religiöse Monopolanspruch des Königtums gegenüber der früheren judäischen Staatstheologie stark reduziert.

T. N. D. Mettinger hatte die נגיד-Designationen aus frühen Prophetenkreisen des Nordreichs hergeleitet (1976, 152–164), die in der mittleren Königszeit von den davidischen Hoftheologen übernommen worden seien; ich hatte diese These in meiner Religionsgeschichte übernommen und als Ausdruck einer relativ frühen Vermittlungsposition zwischen Staatstheologie und radikaler Königskritik gedeutet (R. Albertz 1996 I, 187–190). Doch da die Belege, die sich auf Saul beziehen (1 Sam 9,16; 10,1) fest in die kompositionelle Kette des Erzählwerks aus der Hiskijazeit eingebunden sind, und der eine Beleg, der sich auf Jerobeam I. bezieht (1 Kön 14,7), als deuteronomistisch eingestuft werden muss[35] und damit vom Erzählwerk abhängig ist, möchte ich die Aussagen jetzt eher als judäische Adaption nordisraelitischer | Königstheologie aus der Hiskijazeit werten, die einer Synthese der offiziellen Religionen von Nord- und Südreich dienen sollte.

Ein andersartiges Beispiel für einen bewussten Kompromiss zwischen der offiziellen Theologie von Süd- und Nordreich stellt der Hymnus dar, der in Ex 15,1–18 Mose in den Mund gelegt worden ist. Seine Grundstruktur, die in 6 Strophen (V. 1b–3.4–7.8–10.11–13.14–16.17–18) der Abfolge von Exodus und Landnahme folgt, nimmt wesentliche Elemente der offiziellen Theologie des Nordreiches auf (vgl. Ps 80,9–12). Doch werden diese heilsgeschichtlichen Urdaten erheblich im Sinne der Jerusalemer Theologie abgewandelt: Der Schilfmeerdurchzug wird zu einem mythischen Chaoskampf überhöht (V. 4–10); die triumphale Einwanderung Israels in das Land zielt sogleich auf Jerusalem und seinen Tempel (V. 15–17) und mündet letztlich in die Errichtung der Königsherrschaft JHWHs (V. 18). An die Stelle der kosmo-mythologischen Begründung des göttlichen Königtums ist eine mythisiert heilsgeschichtliche getreten. Bewusst werden beide Erwählungstaten JHWHs, die Erlösung und Erwerbung Israels zu seinem Volk (V. 13.16) und die Schaffung und Gründung des Zion zu seinem Wohnort (V. 17), parallel zueinander dargestellt. Nicht allein die Bindung JHWHs an eine Menschengruppe, sondern

---

Gottesvolk den gleichen ewigen Bestand zu (V. 24), der seiner Dynastie verheißen war. Hier wird die Königstheologie eindeutig der Bundestheologie untergeordnet; das besonders enge Gottesverhältnis des Königs wird zu einem *exemplum* für die Gottesbeziehung ganz Israels.
35 Vgl. das Urteil E. Würthweins 1977, 174: „Die Verse 7–11 sind nach Wortschatz und Gedankengang dtr. Auch stören sie den Gang der Erzählung". Zudem fehlen die Verse 7–9 in der Sonderüberlieferung der LXX 3 Reg 12,24g–n. |

auch seine Bindung an einen Ort bilden nach diesem Hymnus die Basis für Israels Gottesbeziehung. Das ist eine klare Synthese.[36] Leider ist die Datierung des Moseliedes nach wie vor stark umstritten;[37] ich war wegen der Prominenz des Jerusalemer Tempels bislang einer Datierung in die Zeit Joschijas zugeneigt (R. Albertz 1996 I, 353), doch ist angesichts der mythisierenden Tendenz des Hymnus auch eine etwas frühere Entstehung denkbar, als die von Hause aus kosmo-mythologische Jerusalemer Theologie noch stark präsent war.

So schufen erst diese und andere Synthesen der Hiskijazeit, welche bewusst zahlreiche Elemente der Nordreichstheologie aufgriffen, die Voraussetzung dafür, dass von nun an auch in der offiziellen Theologie des Südreiches ‚Israel' nicht mehr primär über seinen König (2 Sam 8,15)[38] oder seine | Hauptstadt (Ps 87,2), sondern über seinen Gott definiert wurde. Die zunehmend als exklusiv verstandene personale Beziehung zwischen JHWH und Israel trat von nun an in den Vordergrund der religiösen Symbolwelt und schuf die Basis, auf der die deuteronomischen und deuteronomistischen Theologen des 7. und 6. Jh.s aufbauen konnten.[39] Die kosmo-mythologischen Elemente mit ihrem universalen Horizont traten hinter die partikular heilsgeschichtlichen Konzeptionen zurück; sie wurden aber erneut in der Krise der Exilszeit bedeutsam, nachdem auch der zweite israelitische Staat untergegangen war.[40]

---

36 Wenn H. Spieckermann 1989, 114, schreibt: „So enthält das Schilfmeerlied keine Israel-ferne, wohl aber geschichtsferne Theologie. Ihr Mittelpunkt ist der Deus praesens im Tempel, der in seiner Wohnstatt ewig thront", dann verschiebt er die Synthese wohl zu stark in Richtung der Jerusalemer Theologie. Entsprechend fraglich ist seine frühe Datierung des Textes in die „nachsalomonische und vorjesajanische Zeit" (113).

37 Nach der Übersicht von C. Houtman 1996 II, 241 f., reicht sie vom 12. bis zum 3. Jh. v. Chr.

38 2 Sam 8,15 ist die einzige Stelle im Erzählwerk, an der Israel als Volk des Königs bezeichnet wird. Wahrscheinlich liegt in 2 Sam 8,1–15 ein älterer höfischer Bericht vor, der Davids große Taten preisen will. Für seinen Autor reduziert sich JHWHs Aktivität auf seinen Beistand für David (V. 6.14); seine Beziehung zu Israel gerät völlig aus dem Blick. So ist 2 Sam 8,15 ein Beleg dafür, dass in der Jerusalemer Hoftheologie Israel zu einem bloßen Anhängsel königlicher Ruhmestaten werden konnte. |

39 Indem sie die Theologumena ‚Erwählung', ‚Bund' und ‚Tora' in das Zentrum der offiziellen Religion Israels stellten, verschoben sie die Synthese nochmals in Richtung auf eine heilsgeschichtliche Volk-Gottes-Theologie. Doch hielten sie daneben durchaus auch an Elementen der offiziellen Religion des Südreiches, der göttlichen Erwählung Jerusalems (Dtn 12,11; 14,23; 16,2.6.11; 26,2; vgl. 1 Kön 11,32.36; 14,21) und der Erwählung des Königs (Dtn 17,15; vgl. 1 Kön 8,16; 11,12 f.; 15,4; 2 Kön 8,9), fest.

40 Vgl. nur die Rückblicke auf den Chaoskampf JHWHs in den exilischen Volksklagen (Ps 74,12–17; 89,10–13; Jes 51,9 f.) und die nachexilischen JHWH-Königs-Psalmen (Ps 96–99). |

Literaturverzeichnis

Albertz, R.
  1978 Persönliche Frömmigkeit und offizielle Religion. Religionsinterner Pluralismus in Israel
        und Babylon: CThM 9, Stuttgart 1978.
  1987 Israel. Altes Testament: TRE 16 (1987) 369–379.
  1995 Wieviel Pluralismus kann sich eine Religion leisten? Zum religionsinternen Pluralismus im
        alten Israel, in: Mehlhausen, J. (Hrsg.), Pluralismus und Identität: Veröffentlichungen der
        Wissenschaftlichen Gesellschaft für Theologie 8, Gütersloh 1995, 193–213.
  1996 Religionsgeschichte Israels in alttestamentlicher Zeit, 2 Bde.: GAT 8,1–2, 2. Auflage,
        Göttingen 1996–1997.
  2001a Die Exilszeit. 6. Jahrhundert v. Chr.: BE 7, Stuttgart 2001.
  2001b Exodus: Liberation History against Charter Myth, in: van Henten, J. W./Houtepen, A.
        (Hrsg.), Religious Identity and the Invention of Tradition: STAR 3, Assen 2001, 128–143.
Bae, H.-S., Vereinte Suche nach JHWH. Die Hiskianische und Josianische Reform in der Chronik:
        BZAW 355, Berlin/New York 2005.
Deutsch, R.
  2003a A Hoard of Fifty Hebrew Bullae from the Time of Hezekiah in the Shlomo Mousaieff
        Collection, in: ders. (Hrsg.), Shlomo. Studies in Epigraphy, Iconography, History and
        Archaeology in Honor of Shlomo Moussaieff, Tel Aviv-Jaffa 2003, 45–98. |
  2003b Biblical Period Hebrew Bullae. The Josef Chaim Kaufman Collection, Tel Aviv 2003.
Dietrich, W., Die frühe Königszeit in Israel. 10. Jahrhundert v. Chr.: BE 3, Stuttgart 1997.
Donner, H./Röllig, W., Kanaanäische und Aramäische Inschriften, 3 Bde., 3.–4. Auflage, Wiesbaden
        1973–1979.
Eißfeldt, O., Psalm 80, in: Albright, W. F. (Hrsg.), Geschichte und Altes Testament. FS Albrecht Alt,
        Tübingen 1953, 65–78.
Emmendörffer, M., Der ferne Gott. Eine Untersuchung der alttestamentlichen Volksklagelieder vor
        dem Hintergrund der mesopotamischen Literatur: FAT 21, Tübingen 1998.
Galling, K., Textbuch zur Geschichte Israels, 2. Auflage, Tübingen 1968.
Hossfeld, F.-L./Zenger, E.
  1993 Die Psalmen I. Psalm 1–50: NEB 29, Würzburg 1993.
  2000 Psalmen 51–100: HThKAT, Freiburg/Basel/Wien 1993.
Houtman, C., Exodus, Historical Commentary on the Old Testament, 4 Vols., Kampen/Leuven 1993–
        2002, zit. 1996.
Jeremias, J., Das Königtum Gottes in den Psalmen. Israels Begegnung mit dem kanaanäischen
        Mythos in den Jahwe-Königs-Psalmen: FRLANT 141, Göttingen 1987.
Keel, O., Die Welt der altorientalischen Bildsymbolik und das Alte Testament. Am Beispiel der
        Psalmen, Zürich/Neukirchen-Vluyn 1972.
Lemaire, A., Khirbet el-Qôm and Hebrew and Aramaic Epigraphy, in: Gitin, S./Wright, J. E./Dessel, J. P.
        (Hrsg.), Confronting the Past. Archaeological and Historical Essays on Ancient Israel in
        Honor of William G. Dever, Winona Lake, IN 2006, 231–243.
Lipiński, E., Nāgīd, der Kronprinz: VT 24 (1974) 497–499.
Mettinger, T. N. D., King and Messiah. The Civil and Sacral Legitimation of the Israelite Kings:
        CB.OT 8, Lund 1976.
Müller, H.-P., Moabitische historische Inschriften: TUAT I,6 (1985) 646–650.
Naveh, J., Hebrew and Aramaic Inscriptions, in: Ariel, D. T., Excavations at the City of David 1978–
        1985 directed by Y. Shilo, Bd. VI: Inscriptions: Qedem 41, Jerusalem 2000.

Rost, L., Die Überlieferung von der Thronnachfolge Davids (1926), in: ders., Das kleine Credo und andere Studien zum Alten Testament, Heidelberg 1965, 119–253.

Seybold, K., Die Psalmen: HAT I,15, Tübingen 1996.

Spieckermann, H., Heilsgegenwart. Eine Theologie der Psalmen: FRLANT 148, Göttingen 1989.

Stoebe, H. J., Das erste Buch Samuelis: KAT VIII,1, Gütersloh 1973.

Stolz, F., Das erste und zweite Buch Samuel: ZBK.AT 9, Zürich 1981. |

van der Toorn, K., The Exodus as Charter Myth, in: van Henten, J. W./Houtepen, A. (Hrsg.), Religious Identity and the Invention of Tradition: STAR 3, Assen 2001, 113–127.

Wanke, G., Die Zionstheologie der Korachiten in ihrem traditionsgeschichtlichen Zusammenhang: BZAW 97, Berlin/New York 1966.

Waschke, E.-J., Das Verhältnis alttestamentlicher Überlieferungen im Schnittpunkt der Dynastiezusage und die Dynastiezusage im Spiegel alttestamentlicher Überlieferungen: ZAW 99 (1987) 157–179.

Würthwein, E., Die Bücher der Könige. 1. Könige 1–16: ATD 11,1, Göttingen 1977.

Zenger, E., u. a. (Hrsg.), Einleitung in das Alte Testament: Kohlhammer Studienbücher 1,1, 5. Auflage, Stuttgart 2004.

Der Streit der Deuteronomisten um das richtige Verständnis der Geschichte Israels

Winfried Thiel, den ich zu seinem 70. Geburtstag herzlich grüßen möchte, hat sich seit seiner bahnbrechenden Dissertation (1970), in der er erstmals eine deuteronomistische (dtr.) Redaktion und Edition des Jeremiabuches detailliert nachwies,[1] bis heute immer wieder eingehend mit der dtr. Literatur beschäftigt[2] und wird es dank seiner Bereitschaft, den Noth'schen Kommentar zu den Königsbüchern[3] in der Reihe des Biblischen Kommentars fortzuführen,[4] noch über viele Jahre tun, für die ich ihm Gesundheit und Gottes Segen wünsche. Dabei hat Thiel mit Recht mehrfach hervorgehoben, dass die theologische Deutung der Geschichte des vorexilischen Israel, die in den Untergang der beiden Teilstaaten Israel (722 v. Chr.) und Juda (587 v. Chr.) führte, eines der Hauptanliegen der dtr. Literatur gewesen sei; so schreibt er schon in seinem Aufsatz von 1985: „Vom Schutthaufen der Geschichte her versuchten nun diese Kreise, die wir mit einem wissenschaftlichen Terminus die ‚Deuteronomisten' nennen, die erlebte Katastrophe und die hoffnungslose Gegenwart zu deuten. Dazu boten sie die ganze Geschichte Israels auf, sammelten die Überlieferungen, disponierten und interpretierten sie".[5] Und noch 2007 hält er fest, dass es nahezu unbestritten sei, dass das Deuteronomistische Geschichtswerk (DtrG: Dtn 1–2. Kön 25) „verfaßt wurde, um eine theologische Interpretation der Katastrophe Judas und Jerusalems von 587 v. Chr. zu liefern".[6] Deutlicher als andere hat Thiel allerdings betont, dass diese dtr. Geschichtsinterpretation keinesfalls selbstverständlich war, sondern sich gegen andere mögliche Geschichtsdeutungen richtete: „Die schockierenden Vorgänge standen an sich verschiedenen Deutungen offen: von der Niederlage des Gottes Israels gegen die übermächtigen babyloni|schen Götter bis zur Auswirkung des Zornes über die eigenmächtigen Maßnahmen der josianischen Reform. Gegen diese und ähnliche Interpretationen boten die dtr. Redaktoren die ganze Geschichte ihres Volkes auf, um sie als Kette des Abfalls Israels von seinem Gott, als einen fortgesetzten Ver-

---

1 Vorgelegt in den beiden Bänden: „Die deuteronomistische Redaktion von Jeremia 1–25" (1973) und „Die deuteronomistische Redaktion von Jeremia 26–45" (1981), die wegen der schwierigen Verhältnisse, unter denen Thiel bis 1982 in der DDR wissenschaftlich arbeiten musste, leider nur in weitem zeitlichen Abstand voneinander publiziert werden konnten.
2 Vgl. W. Thiel, Verfehlte Geschichte (1985); ders., Deuteronomistische Redaktionsarbeit (2000); ders., Grundlinien der Erforschung (2007).
3 M. Noth, Könige 1.
4 W. Thiel, Könige 2; bisher sind 2000 bis 2009 vier Lieferungen zu 1. Kön 17–20 erschienen.
5 Verfehlte Geschichte, 71.
6 Grundlinien, 79. |

https://doi.org/10.1515/9783111202228-014

stoß gegen das erste Gebot, zu kennzeichnen".[7] Im Einzelnen hatte Thiel anhand von Jer 44,15–19 gezeigt, wie sich die Redaktoren des dtr. Jeremiabuchs (JerD), mit dem Vorwurf der judäischen Frauen, es sei ihnen in der Zeit, als sie noch der Himmelskönigin ihre Opfer dargebracht hätten, d. h. vor der Josianischen Kultreform, besser als zum Zeitpunkt der Eroberung Jerusalems und ihrer Flucht nach Ägypten gegangen, mit einer solchen entgegenstehenden Geschichtsdeutung auseinandersetzen mussten.[8] Weniger Augenmerk hat Thiel dagegen bis jetzt darauf gelegt, dass „die Deuteronomisten", wiewohl sie alle – einer Definition O. Eißfeldts folgend, die Thiel gerne zitiert – „andere Bücher in Geist und Stil des Deuteronomiums überarbeiten oder ergänzen",[9] dennoch in den von ihnen redigierten Werken voneinander abweichende, ja, sogar gegensätzliche theologische Geschichtsdeutungen vorgelegt haben. Wohl vermerkt Thiel an einigen Stellen, dass JerD in einigen Punkten, etwa hinsichtlich der Zukunftsperspektive Israels, deutlich vom DtrG abweicht,[10] und er war sich des Facettenreichtums der dtr. Literatur durchaus bewusst;[11] dennoch stellt sich die Frage, ob der Streit, den verschiedene dtr. Gruppen um das richtige Verständnis der fehlgelaufenen Geschichte Israels geführt haben, heute nicht deutlicher und pointierter beschriebenen werden kann. Dies gilt um so mehr, als seit in jüngster Zeit, neben dem DtrG und dem JerD, zwei weitere dtr. gestaltete Werke einigermaßen sicher literarisch rekonstruiert werden konnten, das dtr. Vierprophetenbuch (VPB: Hos; Am; Mi; Zeph*) und die spätdtr. „Wortredaktion", die das Haggai- und Sacharjabuch überarbeitete und zu einem Zweiprophetenbuch vereinte.[12] Damit vergrößert sich das Spektrum der dtr. geprägten theologischen Geschichtsdeutungen erheblich und macht neuerliche Überlegungen sinnvoll.[13]

---

7 A. a. O., 79 f.

8 Jeremia 26–45, 75 f.

9 O. Eißfeldt, Einleitung, 19 Anm. 2, zitiert bei Thiel, Grundlinien, 65.

10 Jeremia 26–45, 112; dagegen meinte er etwa, beide dtr. Werke stimmten hinsichtlich ihrer Einstellung zum Kult in etwa überein, a. a. O., 110 f.; vgl. hierzu aber unten S. 10 [[= S. 225–226 im vorliegenden Band]].

11 Jeremiabuch, 84; vgl. Jeremia 26–45, 122.

12 Siehe dazu die nach mehreren Anläufen anderer Forscher umfassende redaktionsgeschichtliche Analyse von J. Wöhrle, Die frühen Sammlungen, 51–284; 285–385.

13 Vgl. dazu schon R. Albertz, Intentionen und Träger, 170–176; ders., Religionsgeschichte II, 390–413; ders., Wer waren die Deuteronomisten?, 286–300; ders., Exilszeit, 210–260.

1 Geschichtsdeutung des Deuteronomistischen Geschichtswerks (DtrG)

W. Thiel hat jüngst gegenüber neueren kritischen Anfragen die Existenz eines Deuteronomistischen Geschichtswerks im Sinne Noths[14] nochmals | überzeugend verteidigt.[15] Er hat mit recht auf die Schwächen des Göttinger Schichtenmodells und des Cross'schen Blockmodells hingewiesen[16] und für ein „flexibleres Modell" plädiert, „das von der Grundkonzeption Noths nicht allzuweit entfernt ist: *ein* DtrG., das zu unterschiedlichen Zeiten (vor allem in der Exilszeit, aber auch in der frühnachexilischen Zeit) mit unterschiedlichen Akzenten und Interessen an unterschiedlichen Textstellen erweitert worden ist".[17] Da das DtrG fast nirgends über die Exilszeit hinausblickt (Ausnahmen sind nur Dtn 4 und 30,1–10), spricht noch immer viel dafür, von einer Datierung des Grundstocks des Zusammenhangs von Dtn 1 bis 2. Kön 25 zwischen dem Jahr 560 und dem sich 547 v. Chr. abzeichnenden Aufstieg des Perserkönigs Kyros auszugehen.[18]

Grundsätzlich hat Thiel sicher recht, wenn er feststellt, es sei die Intention des DtrG, „die Katastrophe von 587 v. Chr. und die gegenwärtige heillose Exilsituation als Gericht Gottes über die Treulosigkeit Israels in seiner gesamten Geschichte zu interpretieren".[19] Doch vergleicht man diese Geschichtsdeutung mit der von JerD und dem Vierprophetenbuch, welche die gesamte Geschichte Israels total unter die Perspektive der Treulosigkeit des Volkes und des Gerichtes Gottes rücken, dann wird deutlich, dass die dtr. Historiker eine moderatere Sicht der Geschichte Israels vertreten und gegen eine allzu radikale prophetische Kritik verteidigen wollten. Wohl waren auch nach ihrer Sicht längere oder kürzere Epochen vom Abfall Israels bestimmt, so besonders die Geschichte des Nordreichs, in der schon die Übertretung des Zentralisationsgebots durch Jerobeam I. (1. Kön 12,25–33) auf den staatlichen Untergang hinauslief (14,15 f.), aber auch in der Geschichte des Südreichs während der Abirrungen Rehabeams, Ahas' oder Manasses, die kleinere und größere Katastrophen hervorriefen. Aber es gab für sie daneben auch heilvolle Epochen, so die beiden heilvollen Gründungsperioden unter Moses und Josua und unter David und Salomo, in denen Israel von JHWH

---

14 Vgl. Überlieferungsgeschichtliche Studien, 3–110. |
15 Vgl. Grundlinien, 63–81.
16 So a. a. O., 69–79; vgl. ähnlich R. Albertz, Exilszeit, 212–214.
17 Grundlinien, 79. Dies kommt – trotz Abweichungen im Einzelnen – grundsätzlich mit den Modellen überein, die u. a. auch R. Albertz, Exilszeit, 210–231, und T. Römer, Deuteronomistic History, 43; 67–178, vorgeschlagen haben.
18 Ausführlicher begründet in Albertz, Why a Reform, 36–41 [[= S. 32–37 im vorliegenden Band]].
19 Grundlinien, 80.

die Heilsgaben des Gesetzes, des Landes, des davidischen Königtums und des Jerusalemer Tempels geschenkt bekam.[20] Von einer fortlaufenden Abfolge von Abfall, Umkehr, göttlicher Zuwendung und neuem Abfall war nach ihrem Verständnis die Richterzeit geprägt (Ri 2); große Epochen der Umkehr und der Kultreform waren nach ihrer Sicht auch die Regentschaften Asas (1. Kön 15,9–15), Hiskias (2. Kön 18,1–7) und vor allem Josias (22–23). D. h. die dtr. Historiker wollten mit ihrer Interpretation der Geschichte Israels | deutlich machen, dass neben der Treulosigkeit Israels und seiner Könige immer auch wieder Umkehr (Ri 6,25–31; 1. Sam 7,3 f.) und die Reinigung des Kultes im Sinne des Fremdgötter- und Bilderverbots möglich waren und mit göttlicher Hilfe zu einem besseren Verlauf der Geschichte führten. Wichtig war ihnen dabei auch zu demonstrieren, dass die gegenüber dem Nordreich längere und im ganzen katastrophenärmere Geschichte Judas auf der Wirkung der göttlichen Bestandsgarantie für das davidische Königtum (2. Sam 7,14–16; 1. Kön 2,4; 8,25; 9,5) und der göttlichen Erwählung Jerusalems und seines Tempels beruhten (Dtn 12,8; 1. Kön 8,16–19). Obwohl von den dtr. Historikern unter die Bedingung des Toragehorsams gestellt (1. Kön 2,1–4; 9,3–5), waren diese beiden staatlichen Heilsgaben doch in der Lage, das Gericht JHWHs über Juda abzumildern oder herauszuzögern (11,12 f.; 15,4; 2. Kön 8,19; 19,34; 1. Kön 11,32.36; 14,21). Auf diese staatlichen Heilsgaben, über die das Nordreich nicht verfügte, konnten die judäischen Exilierten bauen, auch wenn die vorstaatliche Heilsgabe des Landes weitgehend verloren war (2. Kön 17,23; 25,21b); darum ließen die dtr. Historiker ihr Geschichtswerk mit der Nachricht von der Befreiung Jojachins aus der babylonischen Kerkerhaft enden (2. Kön 25,27–30). Ebenso gab die Heilsgabe des Gesetzes nach wie vor Orientierung für die Zukunft. Wie es in der fehlgelaufenen Geschichte Israels durchaus lichte Momente gegeben hatte, so war auch die exilische Gegenwart nicht ganz hoffnungslos.

Das schwerste theologische Problem für dtr. Historiker war es, eine Erklärung dafür zu finden, warum Juda trotz der großen Kultreform Josias, die den Jerusalemer Tempel ganz im Sinne der dtn. Tora von allen fremdreligiösen Einflüssen gereinigt und eine Stellung als einzig legitimes JHWH-Heiligtum durchgesetzt hatte (2. Kön 23,4–15), untergehen konnte. Da sie um der Orientierung für die Zukunft willen unter allen Umständen an der Richtigkeit dieser Reform festhalten wollten,

---

20 Die Parallelität der beiden heilvollen Gründungsperioden wird von den dtr. Historikern dadurch hervorgehoben, dass sie jeweils an deren Ende die vollständige Erfüllung der von Gott gegebenen Verheißungen konstatieren (Jos 21,45; 1. Kön 8,56). Erst David war es möglich, Israel den schon Dtn 12,9 f.; 25,19 verheißenen sicheren Ruheplatz unter den Völkern zu schaffen (Jos 21,44; 2. Sam 7,1.10 f.; 1. Kön 5,18; 8,56). Auch die Erwählung Jerusalems und Salomos Tempelbau wird von den dtr. Historikern in die Fluchtlinie der Befreiung Israels aus Ägypten gerückt (8,16–21). |

konstruierten sie einen beispiellosen Abfall des Königs Manasse, der alles überboten habe, was es je in der Geschichte des Südreichs an synkretistischer Verirrung gegeben hatte (21,1–9); allein diese schlimme Treulosigkeit Manasses habe den Vernichtungsbeschluss JHWHs über Juda provoziert (21,10–15), der durch Josia zwar noch hinausgeschoben werden konnte (22,18–20), aber nicht mehr zu annullieren gewesen sei (23,26 f.). D. h. nach der Geschichtsdeutung der dtr. Historiker war der Untergang Judas die Folge einer schlimmen, aber doch zeitlich begrenzten Fehlentwicklung. Ohne die Sünden Manasses hätte Juda aufgrund der Kultreform Josias überleben können. Die Lehre, die für die Verfasser des DtrG aus der fehlgelaufenen Geschichte zu ziehen war, blieb darum, unbeirrt auf dem von Josia gewiesenen Weg der Umkehr zu einer exklusiven, auf den Jerusalemer Tempel ausgerichteten JHWH-Verehrung weiter voranzuschreiten. Die Wiedererrichtung des Jerusalemer Tempels nach den Normen der Mose-Tora und unter Leitung des davidischen Königs war somit für die dtr. Historiker die Option für die Zukunft, die sich nach ihrer Sicht aus der vergangenen Geschichte Israels ergab. |

2 Die Geschichtsdeutung des deuteronomistischen Vierprophetenbuchs (VPB)

Nachdem W. H. Schmidt schon 1965 eine deuteronomistische Redaktion des Amosbuches beobachtet hatte,[21] hat J. Nogalski 1993 erstmals die These von einem „Deuteronomistic Corpus" aufgestellt,[22] das die Prophetenbücher Hosea, Amos, Micha und Zephanja umfasst habe. Inzwischen ist durch die Untersuchungen von A. Schart (1998), R. Albertz (2001) und J. Wöhrle (2006) der Textbestand der Redaktion – trotz einiger kleinerer Differenzen – soweit gesichert,[23] dass das

---

21 Deuteronomistische Redaktion, 168–193.

22 Literary Precursors, 278–280; Redactional Processes, 247 f. J. Nogalski erkannte vor allem die gleichgebauten Überschriften der vier Bücher und den redaktionell gestalteten Übergang von der Nordreichs- zur Südreichsprophetie in Mi 1,5b–7.9.

23 Vgl. A. Schart, Entstehung, 156–233; R. Albertz, Exilszeit, 164–184; J. Wöhrle, Die frühen Sammlungen, 245–284. Wöhrle kommt aufgrund eingehender redaktionsgeschichtlicher Analysen aller vier Bücher zu dem folgenden Textbestand (245): Hos 1,1; 3,1–4.5*; 4,1abα.10.15; 8,1b.4b–6.14; 13,2–3; 14,1; Am 1,1*; 2,4–5.9–12; 3,1b.7; 4,13*; 5,11.25–26; 7,10–17; 8,5.6b.11–12; 9,7–10; Mi 1,1.5b–7.9.12b; 5,9–13; 6,2–4a.9aα.10–15; Zeph 1,1.4–6.13b; 2,1–2.3*.4–6.8–9a; 3,1–4.6–8a.11–13. Meiner Meinung nach sollten der Redaktion noch die Verse Hos 1,5.7; Mi 1,13b und Zeph 1,17aβ zugeordnet werden, die alle – wie auch Mi 5,9–13 – das Vertrauen auf Waffen und Festungen geißeln; meiner Meinung nehmen hier die Redaktoren auch Impulse von Jesaja auf.

Vierprophetenbuch (VPB) zu einem Vergleich deuteronomistischer Geschichtsdeutungen herangezogen werden kann.

Nach den den vier prophetischen Büchern vorangestellten Überschriften (Hos 1,1; Am 1,1; Mi 1,1; Zeph 1,1) wollen die dtr. Redaktoren das Ergehen des prophetischen Gotteswortes von der Zeit Jerobeams II. bis zur Zeit Josias verfolgen, das zum Untergang von Nord- und Südreich führte. Dazu stellen sie die literarische Hinterlassenschaft von zwei Nord- (Hosea, Amos) und zwei Südreichpropheten (Micha, Zephanja) zusammen und rücken sie unter die vereinheitlichende Perspektive des *einen* JHWH-Worts, das von ihnen allen – wenn auch in unterschiedlichen Akzenten – verkündet worden sei. Zutreffend schreibt J. Wöhrle: „Durch die Datierungen in den Buchüberschriften gestalten die dtr. Redaktoren ihre Sammlung gewissermaßen als Geschichte der Prophetie. ... Das dtr. Vierprophetenbuch ist demnach geradezu ein theologischer Kommentar zur vorexilischen Geschichte der beiden Teilreiche von Jerobeam II. bis Josia".[24]

Auch die dtr. Redaktoren des DtrG waren der Meinung, dass JHWH sich der Propheten bedient, um den Verlauf der Geschichte Israels zu lenken und sein Volk immer wieder vor dem Unheil zu warnen (2. Kön 17,13). Auch sie ließen den Untergang der Teilreiche durch Propheten ankündigen (1. Kön 14,15 f.; 2. Kön 21,10 ff.). Allerdings übergingen sie geflissentlich die bekannten Gerichtspropheten wie Amos oder Micha, deren Botschaft ihnen offenbar zu radikal war.[25] Wenn die dtr. Redaktoren des VPB gerade die | Botschaft dieser radikalen Gerichtspropheten als wegweisend für ein richtiges Verständnis der fehlgelaufenen Geschichte Israels erachteten, dann wollten sie offenbar gegen die Geschichtssicht des DtrG opponieren.

Eine erste Differenz bezieht sich auf die Geschichte der Teilreiche; während die dtr. Historiker viel Mühe darauf verwenden, die Geschichte Judas mit ihren Höhen und Tiefen von der total fehlgelaufenen Geschichte Israels abzuheben, ordnen die dtr. Redaktoren des VPB (VPR) den Untergang von Nord- und Südreich in eine kontinuierliche Linie: Beide hatten gleichermaßen gegen JHWH gesündigt; kaum dass das Unheil Samaria getroffen hatte, pochte es auch schon gegen die Tore Jerusalems (Mi 1,5b–7.9). Ein zweiter Unterschied lässt sich hinsichtlich der näheren Bestimmung des Fehlverhaltens Israels erkennen, das in die Katastrophe führte. Wohl stimmten die VPR mit ihren Historiker-Kollegen darin überein, dass der Ungehorsam gegenüber der mosaischen Tora zum Untergang geführt hatte (Am 2,4), das hieß zum einen Fremdgötterkult und Bilderdienst (Hos 3,4; 8,4b–6;

---

24 Die frühen Sammlungen, 256.
25 K. Koch hatte in diesem Zusammenhang vom „Prophetenschweigen" des DtrG gesprochen (Profetenschweigen, 123–128); bekanntlich wird von den namentlich | bekannten „Schriftpropheten" nur Jesaja im DtrG erwähnt (2. Kön 18–20), aber dieser tritt hier als ein Heilsprophet auf.

13,2; Am 5,26; Mi 1,7; 5,11–13; Zeph 1,4–5), wie dies schon an Hosea zu lernen, aber auch aus dem Ersten und Zweiten Gebot des Dekalogs ableitbar war (Dtn 5,7–9). In sofern war man sich einig. Aber die VPR beharrten darauf, dass auch das soziale und wirtschaftliche Fehlverhalten, wie es Amos, Micha und Zephanja benannt hatten, ebenfalls zur Treulosigkeit Israels gegenüber JHWH dazugehöre (Am 5,11; 8,5; Mi 6,10–12; Zeph 3,1–4), während die dtr. Historiker jegliche sozialen Kriterien für die Beurteilung des Verhaltens der Könige und des Volkes geflissentlich ausgeblendet hatten.[26] Hier zeigt sich ein grundsätzlicher Dissens der beiden dtr. Gruppen hinsichtlich der Verbindlichkeit der sozialen Gebote und Gesetze im Deuteronomium. Zur Treulosigkeit Israels gehörte, und das markiert einen dritten Unterschied, für die VPR auch das falsche Vertrauen auf Waffen und Festungen hinzu (Hos 1,5.7; 8,14; Mi 1,13b; 5,9 f.13; Zeph 1,17aβ), wie es aus den politischen Anklagen Hoseas und Jesajas ablesbar war (Hos 5,12–14; 7,8 f.; Jes 30,1–5.15–17; 31,1–3), während die dtr. Historiker etwa den König Hiskia für seine Aufstandspolitik gegen die Assyrer ausdrücklich belobigt hatten (1. Kön 18,5–8).

Noch grundsätzlicher war der Unterschied hinsichtlich des Verlaufs der Geschichte. Die VPR sahen die gesamte Geschichte Israels seit Jerobeam II. (ca. ab 760 v. Chr.) durch eine Folge von Reinigungsgerichten JHWHs an Israel und Juda bestimmt (Hos 3,1–5*; Am 9,7–10; Mi 5,9–13; Zeph 1,4–6; 3,9–11), zu denen sie die totalen Gerichtsankündigungen der von ihnen vereinigten Propheten uminterpretierten. Damit gab es nach ihrer Sicht in dieser Periode keine positiven Phasen mehr, wie das DtrG behauptet hatte. Stattdessen suchten die VPR in der anhaltenden Gerichtsperiode von fast 200 Jahren eine untergründig wirksame pädagogische Absicht Gottes zu entdecken: Mit seinen Reinigungsgerichten, so erkannten sie, wollte JHWH selber | alle Merkmale staatlicher Existenz, die sich störend zwischen ihn und sein Volk gedrängt hatten, sukzessive beiseite räumen: das Königtum (Hos 3,5; Am 9,8), die Beamtenschaft (Hos 3,5; Zeph 3,3.11), den festlichen Opferkult (Hos 3,5; Am 5,25), die Gottessymbole (Hos 3,5; Mi 5,12), das professionelle Orakelwesen (Hos 3,5; Mi 5,11), die Waffen (Hos 1,5.7b; Mi 5,9), die Festungen (Hos 8,14; Mi 5,10; Zeph 1,17aβ) und alle fremdländischen Götzen und ihre Pfaffen (Zeph 1,4–6). Es ist schon häufiger aufgefallen, dass das letztgenannte Reinigungsgericht über die fremdländischen Kulte auffällige sprachliche Parallelen mit dem Bericht von Josias Kultreform (2. Kön 22–23) aufweist.[27] Das bedeutet: Was im DtrG als Höhepunkt der königlichen Kultreform gepriesen wurde, wird im VPB als ein Reinigungsgericht Gottes interpretiert! Ähnliches gilt wahrschein-

---

26 Wohl berichtet das DtrG u. a. auch von sozialen Konflikten (1. Kön 12; 21,1–20), aber diese spielen in den dtr. Anklagen keine Rolle und bestimmen den Geschichtsverlauf nicht. Einzige Ausnahme ist die nachgetragene Anklage gegen Manasse 2. Kön 21,16. |
27 Vgl. zusammenfassend Wöhrle, Die frühen Sammlungen, 202.

lich für Mi 5,9–13, das wohl die verheerenden Zerstörungen, die Sanherib 701 in
Juda anrichtete, als ein Reinigungsgericht JHWHs ausdeutet und an die Stelle der
Kultreform Hiskias setzt, von der das DtrG berichtete (2. Kön 18,4). Es sind nach
Sicht der VPR nicht mehr die Könige, die mit ihren Kultreformen die Umkehr zu
JHWH bahnen, sondern es ist JHWH selber, der seinem Volk die liebgewonnenen
Götzen aus der Hand schlägt, damit diejenigen, die nach ihm suchen, ihn unge-
stört finden können (Hos 3,5; Zeph 1,6; 2,3). Zurecht stellt J. Wöhrle fest, dass
das VPB auf das „Prophetenschweigen" des DtrG mit einem „Königeschweigen"
reagiere.[28]

Da nach Meinung von VPR die Josianische Reform nur eines der göttlichen
Reinigungsgerichte war, stellte sich für sie das große theologische Problem, mit
dem die dtr. Historiker gerungen hatten, so nicht. Ein erneutes, letztes Reinigungsgericht JHWHs wurde nach ihrer Sicht nötig, weil, wie Zephanja aufgedeckt hatte,
nicht nur die Beamten und Königssöhne weiter ausländischen Sitten frönten, sondern auch die wohlhabende Oberschicht erneut ihren erbeuteten Reichtum ver-
götzte und keinerlei soziale Verantwortung zeigte (Zeph 1,7–13). Da sich die stolze
Oberschicht in ihrem Treiben (3,1–4) auch nicht von JHWHs Gericht über die
Nachbarvölker warnen ließ (3,6–8a), habe JHWH auch diese beseitigt und auf
dem Zion nur noch ein armes und geringes Volk übriggelassen, das sich im Namen JHWHs berge und dem Unrecht und Betrug fremd sei (Zeph 3,11–13). Schul-
dig für den staatlichen Untergang Judas war nach Sicht der VPR somit die Oberschicht, die darum zurecht von JHWH deportiert worden sei. Darum bedeutete
der staatliche Untergang Judas auch keine unerwartete Katastrophe, sondern war
nur der letzte und konsequente Schritt JHWHs, der armen und frommen Unter-
schicht eine neue, ungestörte Lebensmöglichkeit zu schaffen. Während die dtr.
Historiker, diejenigen, die nach der Exilierung „Judas" (2. Kön 21b) im Lande zu-
rückblieben, herablassend „die Geringen (des Volkes) des Landes" tituliert hatten
(24,14; 25,12), scheuten sich die VPR nicht, diesen den Ehrentitel „Rest Israels" zu
verleihen (Zeph 3,13). Sie repräsentierten in ihren Augen das wahre Gottesvolk,
das sich JHWH durch alle Reinigungsgerichte hindurch aufbewahrt habe.

Die Lehren, die aus dieser dtr.-prophetischen Interpretation der vorexilischen
Geschichte gezogen werden mussten, waren somit völlig andere als | die, welche
das DtrG nahelegte. Den VPR ging es um die Begründung und Verteidigung der
relativ ärmlichen substaatlichen Verhältnisse in der babylonischen Provinz Juda
ohne Königtum und Tempel, ohne größeren Beamten- und Priesterapparat; sie
waren von Gott so gewollt, von ihm durch seine Reinigungsgerichte absichtsvoll
herbeigeführt. Während die dtr. Historiker auf die Wiederaufrichtung des Jerusa-

---

28 Die frühen Sammlungen, 277. |

lemer Kultes durch einen Davididen hofften und die dtr. Bearbeiter des Jeremiabuches einen Neuanfang zunehmend von einer Rückkehr der Exulanten erwarteten (Jer 29,10–14aα), sprachen sich die dtr. Redaktoren des VPB gegen jegliche
Restauration vorexilischer Verhältnisse aus; eine Wiederbelebung der davidischen Dynastie war für sie nicht mehr vorgesehen und mit der Exilierung der
Oberschicht war für sie ein *status quo* erreicht, hinter den es kein Zurück mehr
gab.[29]

J. Wöhrle hat gezeigt, dass die VPR sich bei ihrer kompositorischen Arbeit –
über die hier angesprochenen Beispiele hinaus – thematisch unmittelbar an den
geschichtlich entsprechenden Abschnitten des DtrG orientiert haben;[30] sie gehören darum sehr wohl zum Spektrum deuteronomistischer Tradition.[31] Aber es
ging ihnen, wie Wöhrle ebenfalls herausgearbeitet hat, offenbar darum, geradezu
„ein Gegenkonzept zum DtrG" zu entwickeln.[32] Obwohl gleichfalls dtr. geprägt,
lagen die VPR mit den Verfassern des DtrG um die richtige Deutung der Geschichte ihres Volkes in einem offenen Streit.

3 Die Geschichtsdeutung der deuteronomistischen Jeremiabücher (JerD$^{1-3}$)

Wie schon erwähnt, ist es W. Thiel gewesen, der den Nachweis erbrachte, dass das
Jeremiabuch nicht bloß dtr. Ergänzungen, sondern eine planvolle dtr. Redaktion
erfahren hat, welche die Gestalt und den theologischen Gehalt dieses Prophetenbuches nachhaltig prägte.[33] Über das von ihm erreichte Ergebnis hinaus lassen
sich allerdings nach kompositionskritischen Kriterien drei verschiedene Ausgaben des dtr. Jeremiabuches unterscheiden (JerD^1, JerD^2, JerD^3), die in ihren theolo-
gischen Aussagen etwas variieren.[34] |

---

29 So mit Recht J. Wöhrle, Die frühen Sammlungen, 281.
30 Vgl. a. a. O., 255–271.
31 Da die Sprache der VPR sich noch stärker als die von JerD an die Sprache der bearbeiteten
Prophetenschriften anlehnt, hatte ich früher für eine lockere Beziehung zur dtr. Tradition plädiert (Albertz, Exilszeit, 166); doch hat Wöhrle engere terminologische Bezüge zum DtrG aufgezeigt als sie mir damals bewusst waren (vgl. die Tabelle, Wöhrle, Die frühen Sammlungen, 269).
Wenn M. Beck, „Tag YHWHs", 120 f.; 316, die Existenz eines dtr. Vierprophetenbuch mit dem
Argument bestreitet, „dass keine typisch dtr. Theologumena vorliegen", dann beruht sein Urteil
auf einer zu engen Sicht dessen, was als „deuteronomistisch" zu qualifizieren ist, s. u. 15–19
[[= S. 230–235 im vorliegenden Band]].
32 Vgl. Die frühen Sammlungen, 281 f.
33 Vgl. Jeremia 1–25, 281–302; Jeremia 26–45, 93–122. Zur Forschungsgeschichte, in der das von
Thiel erreichte Ergebnis teilweise unterbewertet wurde, vgl. R. Albertz, Exilszeit, 231–236.
34 Vgl. dazu R. Albertz, Exilszeit, 236–246; s. die beiden Buchschlüsse (Jer 25,1–13abα; 45,1–5) und
die drei selbstreferentiellen editorischen Bemerkungen (Jer 25,13bα; 30,1; 45,1). |

Wie die dtr. Historiker und die VPR stellen auch die Redaktoren des ersten dtr. Jeremiabuchs (Jer 1–25*; JerD[1]R)[35] die voraufgegangene Geschichte als eine Geschichte der Treulosigkeit Israels dar. In regelrechten Frage-Antwort-Spielen hämmerten sie ihren Zeitgenossen ein, dass es der Abfall des Volkes von JHWH und der Ungehorsam gegenüber seinen Geboten waren, die an der Verwüstung des Landes und der Exilierung eines Teils der Bevölkerung schuld seien (Jer 5,19; 9,11–15; 16,10–13; vgl. 22,8 f.). Anders als die VPR, die der Exilierung durch ihre Deutung als göttliches Reinigungsgericht einen positiven Sinn abzugewinnen suchten, aber ähnlich wie die dtr. Historiker werteten auch die JerD[1]R den staatlichen Untergang als furchtbare Katastrophe. Aber wie jene und anders als diese fassten sie die Geschichte der Treulosigkeit Israels weit radikaler. Ihrer Meinung nach begann der Abfall Israels von JHWH schon am Tage des Auszugs (7,23 f.; 11,4.6–8). Er führte nur deswegen nicht gleich zur Katastrophe, weil JHWH in seiner Langmut sein Volk immer wieder gewarnt hatte (Jer 7,13; 11,7; 25,3) und fortlaufend seine Knechte, die Propheten, gesandt hatte (Jer 7,25; 25,4), um Israel zur Umkehr und zur Besserung seines Verhaltens aufzurufen (7,3; 25,5 f.). Doch fortlaufend hatte sich Israel geweigert, auf das prophetische Gotteswort zu hören (7,13; 11,8; 25,7). Als letzten in der Kette der Propheten hatte JHWH Jeremia zur Warnung seines Volkes gesandt; als sie auch auf ihn nicht hören, sondern ihn mundtot machen wollten, war der Bund endgültig gebrochen (11,10) und das Unheil unausweichlich (Jer 11–20).[36] Es gab für die JerD[1]R keine lichteren Perioden in der Geschichte Israels wie für die dtr. Historiker, sondern nur eine lange Kette verpasster Heilschancen. Auch königliche Kultreformen spielten keine Rolle; selbst die Josianische Reform wird übergangen.[37] Denn nach Ansicht der JerD[1]R waren nicht die Könige, sondern war das Volk selber für das Geschick Israels verantwortlich. Da die Judäer die letzte von Jeremia eröffnete Heilschance verworfen hatten, waren vornehmlich sie, nicht wie im DtrG der König Manasse, am staatlichen Untergang Judas schuld;[38] sie waren sehenden Auges in die Katastrophe hineingelaufen.

Es entspricht dieser aufs Volk ausgerichteten Sicht, dass die JerD[1]R einen möglichen Neuanfang allein von einer radikalen Umkehr des Volkes erwarteten,

---

35 Zu ihm gehört der Grundbestand von Jer 1,1–25,13abα, besonders ohne 1,4–10; 18; 24; vgl. im Einzelnen R. Albertz, Exilszeit, 236–242; 246–250.

36 Dass der Angriff auf den Propheten und sein Wort das Unheil unausweichlich gemacht habe, war auch ein Thema, das die VPR anhand des Amosbuches bearbeiteten (Am 2,11 f.; 7,10–17; 8,11–12).

37 Obwohl die JerD[1]R ein positives Urteil Jeremias über Josia vorfanden (Jer 22,15 f.), haben sie es nicht zum Anlass genommen, ihn für seine Kultreform zu loben.

38 Nur einmal werden die Sünden Manasses als einer der Gründe für das Gericht neben anderen erwähnt (Jer 15,4). |

nicht etwa von einer königlichen Kultreform wie dtr. Historiker. Dabei musste diese Umkehr – ganz im Sinne der Anklagen Jeremias – sowohl eine religiöse Hinkehr zu JHWH als auch eine Besserung des sozialen Verhaltens umfassen (Jer 7,3.5–7; 25,5); in dieser Hinsicht stimmten JerD¹R mit den VPR gegen die dtr. Historiker überein. Wie schon Jeremia das falsche Ver|trauen auf den Jerusalemer Tempel gegeißelt hatte (7,4), so warnten auch JerD¹R davor, – entgegen der Hoffnung der dtr. Historiker – von einem Wiederaufbau des Tempels eine Wende zum Besseren zu erwarten (7,1–15); hatte doch der Tempel dazu gedient, soziales Unrecht und religiöse Missstände zuzudecken (7,11).

Desgleichen traten die JerD¹R schroff den Hoffnungen entgegen, die sich im DtrG an die Person Jojachins geheftet hatten (2. Kön 25,27–30). Ihrer Meinung war und blieb Jojachin, wie schon Jeremia verkündet hatte, von Gott verworfen (Jer 22,24–28), und dies bedeutete für sie, dass kein einziger seiner Nachkommen jemals wieder auf dem Thron Davids sitzen und über Juda herrschen solle (V. 29–30). Die davidische Dynastie hatte nach dem Urteil der JerD¹R vollständig abgewirtschaftet; darum wollten sie ihre mögliche Restitution auf jeden Fall verhindern.[39] Die Lehre, die nach Meinung JerD¹R aus der fehlgelaufenen Geschichte Israels gezogen werden müsse, war somit, dass nicht etwa eine begrenzte königliche Kultreform von oben, wie die dtr. Historiker meinten, sondern allein eine umfassende religiöse und sittliche Erneuerung von unten zu einem Neuanfang führen könne.

In ihrer zweiten, vor allem um die Jeremiaerzählungen vermehrten Ausgabe des dtr. Jeremiabuchs (JerD²: Jer 1–45*)[40] setzten sich die Bearbeiter vor allem mit den nach ihrer Meinung für die Katastrophe Schuldigen auseinander, den Königen Jojakim und Zedekia, den national-religiös gesinnten Beamten und Militärs, die die beiden Könige zu antibabylonischen Aufständen verführt hatten (36–38), und den Priestern und Heilspropheten, die mit ihren Worten die Aufstandsbewegung geschürt hatten und gegen Jeremia vorgegangen waren (27–29). Im Kontrast dazu stellten sie heraus, dass die Beamten um die Familie Schafan den Propheten Jeremia geschützt (26,24) und versucht hatten, seiner Botschaft beim König Gehör zu verschaffen (36,10–26). Gegenüber dem DtrG, das geflissentlich die Schuld der Verantwortlichen überging (2. Kön 25,18–21a), meldeten damit die Schafaniden und ihre Anhänger ihren Anspruch auf politische und geistige Führung bei einem Neuanfang an. Die generelle Schulderkenntnis, die die JerD¹R in den Mittelpunkt ihrer früheren Ausgabe gestellt hatten, durfte nicht dazu führen,

---

39 Vgl. genauer zu diesem wichtigen Dissens Albertz, Wer waren die Deuteronomisten?, 286–288.
40 Zu ihm gehört außer JerD¹ Jer 1,4–10; 18; 26, 27* (LXX); 28; 29,1–14aα.15.21–32; 35,1–43,7; 44–45, vgl. dazu im Einzelnen R. Albertz, Exilszeit, 236–242; 250–255. |

dass die Nachfahren der persönlich Schuldigen, die deportiert worden waren, meinten, weiter Führungspositionen beanspruchen zu können wie bisher. Diese Klärung war insofern nötig, weil die JerD²R nach manchen Enttäuschungen, die die Daheimgebliebenen erlitten hatten (Jer 41–43), ihre Hoffnung erneut auf die babylonischen Exulanten setzten; sie erwarteten deren Rückkehr nach einer Periode von 70 Jahren (29,10–14aα), auf die JHWH die babylonische Weltherrschaft begrenzt habe (27,7). Die Frage des Führungsanspruches würde sich also für sie, anders als für die VPR, die die Führungseliten insgesamt abgeschrieben hatten, über kurz oder lang stellen.

Um ihre Heilshoffnungen abzustützen, entwickelten die JerD²R aus ihrem Nachdenken über die Geschichte Israels und Judas eine Regel für das göttli | che Handeln in der Geschichte, die über Israel hinaus für alle Völker und Königreiche Gültigkeit habe: Mal entschlösse sich JHWH, ein Volk oder Königreich niederzureißen, doch kündige er seine Absicht zuvor an. Wenn dann dieses Volk sich von der Unheilsbotschaft zur Umkehr bewegen lasse, würde Gott von seinen Unheilsplänen Abstand nehmen. Mal entschlösse sich Gott, ein Volk oder Königreich aufzubauen, doch wenn das Volk, das eine solche Heilsbotschaft hört, im Ungehorsam gegen Gott verharrte, dann würde Gott auch von seinen Heilsplänen wieder Abstand nehmen (Jer 18,7–10). Aufgrund einer solchen Theorie ließ sich erklären, warum dem babylonischen Reich die Weltherrschaft von JHWH für eine Weile verliehen, aber dann auch wieder genommen werden würde (27,5–7). Eine solche Theorie konnte aber auch dazu anleiten, die Heilschancen, die JHWH Israel nach dem Gericht eröffnen könnte, aufmerksam zu suchen und dann auch zu ergreifen. Damit legten die JerD²R aber die Grundlage, um – anders als das DtrG und mehr noch als das VPB – die Geschichte Israels international einzubetten. Für sie war Jeremia nicht mehr nur ein Prophet für Israel, sondern ein Prophet für die Völker gewesen, der am Niederreißen und Aufbauen der Königreiche beteiligt war (1,5.10) und mit seinen Worten die Pädagogik und die Moralität der göttlichen Weltregierung in der Geschichte aufgedeckt hatte.

Die dritte Ausgabe des Jeremiabuchs (JerD³: Jer 1–51*),[41] das sie um je eine Sammlung von Heilsworten (Jer 30–31) und Völkerworten (46–51) vermehrten, gestalteten die dtr. Redaktoren auf dieser Linie zu einem Abriss der dramatischen Geschichte des gesamten Vorderen Orients vom Niedergang Assyriens bis zum Aufstieg Persiens (ca. 640–520 v. Chr.). Der Zusammenbruch der assyrischen Weltmacht bot eine Heilschance für das ehemalige Nordreich (Jer 2,4–4,2), doch wurde sie vertan (4,10). Der Aufstieg der neubabylonischen Weltmacht führte das Gericht

---

41 Zu ihm gehört außer JerD² Jer 2,2aβ.3; 3,14 f.; 7,30–8,3; 12,14–17; 19,6–9.12–13; 23,1–4.23–32; 30,1–31,34*; 32; 34; 43,8–12; 46,2–51,64, vgl. dazu im Einzelnen R. Albertz, Exilszeit, 236–242; 255–260. |

JHWHs über Juda (4,3–28,7) herauf, traf aber auch einige seiner Nachbarn (46–49); dabei war dem König Nebukadnezar die Weltherrschaft anvertraut und diente JHWH als Gerichtswerkzeug (27,5 f.). Doch durch eine Begrenzung der babylonischen Herrschaft auf 70 Jahre (29,10 f.) erwuchs den exilierten und daheimgebliebenen Judäern eine neue Heilschance (28–32), doch auch diese wurde erst einmal vertan (34–36). So führte die frivole Zerstörung des Prophetenworts (36) Juda in den totalen Untergang (37–39). Doch JHWH eröffnete sogar noch in der Katastrophe mit Gedalja eine vielversprechende Heilsmöglichkeit, aber selbst diese wurde durch die Ermordung Gedaljas und die Abwanderung nach Ägypten verspielt (40–43). Wenn JHWH nun nach langer Zeit mit der Erweckung der Könige von Medien den Sturz des Babylonischen Weltreichs einleitete (Jer 50,2.11–13), dann sollten – so warben die JerD³R – die babylonische Gola und die daheimgebliebenen Judäer nun endlich die große Heilschance ergreifen, die Gott ihnen anbot.

So stellt JerD³ eine großangelegte Geschichtsdeutung dar, die Israel die verborgene Treue seines Gottes über die Jahrhunderte vor Augen führen wollte. Es waren, so stellten seine Redaktoren klar, nicht irgendwelche Zu | sagen, die am Königtum oder dem Tempel hingen, sondern allein die nicht enden wollende Gnade dieses universalen Weltschöpfers (Jer 32,17–19), die Israel eine neue Zukunft eröffnen würde. Er würde schließlich auch für eine radikale Erneuerung des Gottesverhältnisses sorgen, indem er den Israeliten seine Tora in ihr Inneres legen werde, um so ihren notorischen Ungehorsam zu überwinden (31,31–33). Damit fände Gottes große Pädagogik in der Geschichte in der Internalisierung der Tora durch jeden einzelnen Israeliten ihr letztes Ziel.

4 Die Geschichtsdeutung des deuteronomistischen Zweiprophetenbuchs (ZPB)

Es war schon mehrfach vermutet worden, dass auch das Buch Proto-Sacharja (Sach 1–8) eine deuteronomistische Bearbeitung erfahren hat.[42] Inzwischen hat J. Wöhrle den Umfang dieser Bearbeitungsschicht, die er „Wort-Redaktion" nennt, in einer detaillierten redaktionsgeschichtlichen Analyse des Haggai- und Protosacharjabuchs genauer bestimmen können.[43] Er hat darüber wahrscheinlich gemacht, dass diese Redaktion, dadurch dass sie das Protosacharjabuch mit einem

---

42 Vgl. H.-G. Schöttler, Gott, 438–440; R. Albertz, Religionsgeschichte II, 484; R. Lux, Zweiprophetenbuch, 212.
43 Nämlich Sach 1,1–7.14aβ–17aα; 2,10–14; 4,9b; 6,15; 7,1.7.9–14; 8,1–5.7–8.14–17.19b, vgl. Wöhrle, Die frühen Sammlungen, 362–366.

Datierungssystem versah (Sach 1,1.7; 7,1), dieses mit dem Haggaibuch, das schon zuvor chronikartig ausgestaltet worden war, zusammenschloss.[44] Da diese Redaktionsschicht ein aus Hag 1–2* und Sach 1–8* bestehendes Zweiprophetenbuch schuf, sei ihr Werk hier – in Analogie zum dtr. Vierprophetenbuch – im Folgenden ‚dtr. Zweiprophetenbuch' (ZPB) und seine Verfasser ‚Zweiprophetenbuch-Redaktoren' (ZPR) genannt. Allerdings gehört diese Redaktion, da sie die literarische Hinterlassenschaft von zwei frühnachexilischen Propheten zusammenfasst, schon in eine spätere Zeit als die bisher behandelten dtr. Werke. Man wird sie darum besser als spätdeuteronomistisch bezeichnen. Die Differenz zeigt sich auch im sprachlichen Bereich; die ZPR lehnen sich zwar häufig an dtr. Wendungen und Vorstellungen an, wandeln sie aber freier ab als ihre exilischen Kollegen.[45] |

Auch die frühnachexilischen spätdtr. Redaktoren des ZPB wollen noch eine Lehre aus der vorexilischen Geschichte ziehen: Nach ihrer Sicht hatte JHWH den Vätern schwer gezürnt (Sach 1,2); zwar hatten die früheren Propheten sie eindrücklich zur Umkehr von ihrem bösen Verhalten aufgefordert (1,4; vgl. 2. Kön 17,13; Jer 18,11; 25,5; 35,15), aber sie hatten nicht auf diese gehört, und darum hatten sie die Gerichtsworte der Propheten und die Flüche, die an den Gesetzen hingen, eingeholt (1,6a: נשׂג wie Dtn 28,15.45). Darum sollten sich die Angeredeten von ihren Vätern distanzieren (1,4) und nun die Umkehr vollziehen, was sie interessanterweise dann auch tun (Sach 1,6b). Die ZPR orientieren sich in dieser pau-

---

44 Vgl. a. a. O., 367–374; diese These erklärt sowohl die Übereinstimmungen als auch die Abweichungen der Überschriftssysteme von Haggai und Sacharja. Entscheidend dabei ist die Beobachtung, dass die Datierung von Sach 1,1 (8. Monat des 2. Jahres des Darius) vor das Datum der Tempelgründung (Hag 2,10: 24.9. des zweiten Jahres) zurückgreift; damit werden beide Bücher zeitlich ineinander verschränkt.

45 Nur ein typisches Beispiel für viele sei hier genannt: In Sach 1,6b heißt es: „Wie JHWH Zebaoth uns zu tun geplant (זמם לעשׂות) hat nach unseren Wegen und nach unseren Taten (כדרכינו וכמללינו), so hat er uns getan." Die Wendung „planen zu tun" mit göttlichem Subjekt erinnert an JerD² (Jer 18,8; 26,3; 36,3), doch dort wird regelmäßig formuliert „gedenken zu tun" (וחשׁב לעשׂות); die Wurzel זמם, die die ZPR auch noch in Sach 8,14.15 verwenden, ist dtr. ungebräuchlich und kommt zusammen mit עשׂה z. B. in Thr 2,17; Jer 51,12 vor. Doch erinnert das Nebeneinander von דרך und מעלל wieder stark an JerD (Jer 7,3.5; 18,11; 25,5; 26,13; 35,15). W. A. M. Beuken, Haggai-Sacharja, 84–138, hatte wegen solcher und anderer Abweichungen, die Schicht einer chronistischen Redaktion zuweisen wollen, doch sind die Hinweise | darauf meist wenig spezifisch, und die seltenen spezifischen übereinstimmenden Wendungen wie כתף סררת „störrische Schulter" (Sach 7,11; Neh 9,29) und רוח ביד הנביאים „mit seinem Geist durch die Propheten" (Sach 7,12; Neh 9,30 dort mit Suffixen der 2. pers. sing.) sind eher durch literarische Abhängigkeit auf Seiten des Nehemiagebets zu erklären, das sich an viele Texte anlehnt. Die eigenartige Verbindung von Geist und Propheten als göttliche Vermittlungsmedien ist wahrscheinlich durch das Reden von Gottes Geist als Wirkmacht in der vorgegebenen Tradition Hag 2,5; Sach 4,6; 6,8 veranlasst. So hat Beukens Herleitung nur wenig für sich, vgl. auch J. Wöhrle, Die frühen Sammlungen, 363 f.

schal negativen Sicht der Vergangenheit vor allem an JerD, auch in der Parallelisierung von Prophetenwort und Gesetz.[46] In einem weiteren Rückblick auf die vorexilische Geschichte (7,7–14) führen die ZPR genauer aus, welche prophetische Botschaft von den Vätern störrisch überhört worden war: Es war die soziale Mahnung, wahrhaft Recht zu üben (Ez 18,18), Treue und Barmherzigkeit untereinander walten zu lassen, Witwe, Waise und Fremdling nicht zu unterdrücken (Jer 7,6; Ez 22,7.29) und nicht heimlich das Unglück des Nächsten („Bruders") zu planen (Sach 7,9 f.). Das sind zwar nicht unbedingt typische soziale Forderungen aus dem dtr. Repertoire, doch orientieren sich die ZPR am Geist der dtn. Bruderschaftsethik (vgl. z. B. Dtn 24,7.9–11.14). Interessant ist an dieser Stelle, dass die ZPR die sozialen Forderungen ganz in den Vordergrund rücken, mehr noch als die VPR und die JerDR. Dagegen kommen die religiös-kultischen Gebote, welche die Geschichtsdarstellung des DtrG beherrschten, gar nicht mehr vor. Sie waren für die ZPR offenbar im frühnachexilischen judäischen Gemeinwesen mit seinem erneuerten Tempelkult weitgehend eingelöst.

Die Wende vom Gericht zum Heil wurde nach Ansicht der ZPR durch JHWHs freie Entscheidung in der Lenkung der Geschichte seines Volkes bewirkt (Sach 8,14 f.), nicht etwa durch den Tempelbau, wie der Prophet Haggai verkündet hatte (Hag 1,5–8; 2,15–19). Mit dieser Erklärung schlossen sich die ZPR frei der Regel an, die die JerD²R für das göttliche Geschichtshandeln formuliert hatten (Jer 18,7–10): Wie JHWH gegenüber den treulosen Vätern Böses zu tun geplant hatte, ohne es sich dessen noch einmal gereuen zu lassen, so hat er nun geplant, Jerusalem und Juda Gutes zu tun. Da die Judäer diese göttliche Entscheidung schon durch eine entsprechende Umkehr honoriert hatten, bräuchten sie sich nicht mehr zu fürchten (Sach 8,17). Doch um Gottes heilvolle Pläne voll zum Durchbruch kommen zu lassen, sollten sie nun, anders als ihre Väter, der sozialen prophetischen Botschaft folgen | (7,9–10) und eine auf Recht, Wahrhaftigkeit und Friedfertigkeit gegründete Solidargemeinschaft aufbauen (8,16–17.19b).

Mit ihrer Bearbeitung verfolgten die ZPR drei Ziele:[47] Sie wollten erstens klarstellen, dass schon die Gründung des neuen Tempels (Hag 2,10.15–19) aufgrund einer Umkehr des Volkes erfolgte (Sach 1,6).[48] Damit wollten sie das Missverständnis korrigieren, dass schon der Wiederaufbau des Tempels unter Leitung eines Davididen die Umkehr beinhalte und – quasi von alleine – eine heilvolle Entwicklung garantiere, eine Auffassung, die sich auf Haggai, aber durchaus auch auf das DtrG berufen konnte. Zweitens wollten sie deutlich machen, dass die

---

46 Vgl. Jer 11,1–14.17 u. ö. dazu R. Albertz, Religionsgeschichte II, 393. |
47 Vgl. dazu wegweisend J. Wöhrle, Die frühen Sammlungen, 362; 375–379.
48 Vgl. die Datierung dieser Umkehr durch Sach 1,1 vor die Grundsteinlegung des Tempelbaus (Hag 2,10).

schon erlebte Wende zum Heil, die erfolgte Rückkehr JHWHs zum Zion und Wiederherstellung von dessen Heiligkeit (Sach 1,15a.16; 2,14; 8,1–3) nicht auf dem Tempelbau als solchem, sondern auf der voraufgegangenen Umkehr des ganzen Volkes beruhten.[49] Mit Aufnahme dieser Heilsvorstellungen ließen sich die ZPR weit auf die einstige Jerusalemer Tempeltheologie ein, noch weiter als dies schon die dtr. Historiker getan hatten. Aber gleichzeitig suchten sie diese unkonditionierte Heiligtumstheologie – durchaus im Sinne der dtr. bearbeiteten Tempelrede Jeremias (Jer 7,1–15) – ethisch zu relativieren und neu zu fundieren. Drittens versuchten sie eine Erklärung dafür zu liefern, warum die Heilswende bisher noch so kläglich verlaufen war: Noch zwei Jahre nach Beginn des Tempelbaus (Sach 7,1) lag Jerusalem in Trümmern (Sach 1,16), litt unter Bevölkerungsarmut (8,4 f.7 f.), noch lebten viele Judäer gefährdet in Babylon und anderswo auf der Welt (2,10–12; 8,7), noch war Juda Plünderungen durch fremde Völker ausgesetzt (2,12). All diese Nöte, so gaben die ZPR zu bedenken, waren dadurch verursacht, dass das Volk den sozial-ethischen Weisungen der Propheten noch nicht gefolgt war. Dem zukünftigen Heil, das in prophetischen Hinterlassenschaft Haggais und Sacharjas aufbewahrt war, würde erst eine grundlegende soziale Umorientierung zum Durchbruch verhelfen (8,14–19). So wurde die Botschaft der beiden heilsprophetischen Bücher durchweg ethisch konditioniert.

Die ZPR stellen somit neben den dtr. Historikern, den VPR und den JerDR noch einmal einen eigenen Typ von Deuteronomisten dar; im Gegensatz zu den dtr. Bearbeitern des Vierpropheten- und des Jeremiabuches maßen sie den auf Jerusalem und seinem Tempel liegenden Verheißungen hohe Bedeutung bei; sie wollten diese trotz aller Zweifel, die dagegen erhoben wurden (Sach 2,13; 4,9; 6,15) nicht nur bewahren, sondern sie schrieben sie auch noch aktualisierend fort (1,14aβ–17aα; 2,10–14; 6,15; 8,16–17). Dennoch stellten sie all' diese Verheißungen – wiederum auf der Linie der JerDR und der VPR – generell unter eine sozialethische Bedingung. Wohl fehlte den ZPR der sozialkritische Radikalismus der VPR, aber in manchen Zügen, wie etwa dem der Wahrhaftigkeit, stimmt ihr Bild einer idealen Solidargemeinschaft auf dem Zion (Sach 8,16 f.) durchaus mit dem von den VPR entworfenen überein (Zeph 3,11–13). |

5 Deuteronomismus – ein pluralistisches Phänomen

In den oben beschriebenen Geschichtsdeutungen lassen sich durchaus eine Reihe von Gemeinsamkeiten erkennen, die durchgehende Orientierung an der Theolo-

---

49 Vgl. die Korrespondenz von der Umkehr des Volkes (1,3.6b) und der Rückkehr Gottes (1,16), beidemal ausgedrückt mit der Wurzel שוב. |

gie, Ethik und Sprache des Deuteronomiums, die Grundüberzeugung, dass Gott nicht nur die Geschichte lenkt, sondern dass er sich dabei unmittelbar vom Verhalten der Menschen beeinflussen lässt, und schließlich die Hochschätzung der Prophetie, weil diese den Menschen Gottes Geschichtspläne im Voraus offenbart und ihnen darum die Möglichkeit zur Verhaltensänderung eröffnet. Doch trotz dieser Gemeinsamkeiten, die es berechtigt, alle diese Literaturwerke als ‚deuteronomistisch' zu klassifizieren, weisen die vier verglichenen Werke sowohl in ihrer Sicht der vergangenen Geschichte als auch in ihren Optionen für die Zukunft so große Unterschiede auf, dass es unmöglich wird, sie einer einzigen und in sich geschlossenen dtr. Gruppe, Bewegung oder Schule zuzuordnen. Offenbar gab es unterschiedliche dtr. Gruppen, die trotz aller sprachlicher und theologischer Gemeinsamkeiten im kultischen, politischen und sozialen Bereich recht unterschiedliche, ja sogar gegensätzliche Ansichten und Forderungen vertraten. Und dabei ging ihr Streit vor allem um die Frage, welche Lehren aus der fehlgelaufenen Geschichte für die Bestimmung der zukünftigen Rollen von davidischem Königtum und Jerusalemer Tempel, der sozialen Gestaltung der Gesellschaft und des Einflusses der Führungseliten zu ziehen seien. D. h. trotz gemeinsamer theologischer Herkunft und ähnlicher Ausbildung konnten sich die Deuteronomisten offenbar ganz unterschiedlichen Parteien, gesellschaftlichen Gruppen oder Institutionen verpflichtet fühlen.

Um dieser Pluralität gerecht zu werden, hatte ich vorgeschlagen, den Deuteronomismus als „eine theologische Zeitströmung" des 6. und frühen 5. Jhs. v. Chr. anzusehen, „die recht unterschiedliche Gruppen erfasste".[50] Doch diese noch etwas offene Definition lässt sich nun, da eine ganze Reihe dtr. Werke miteinander verglichen werden kann, genauer fassen.

Die gemeinsame theologische, ethische und sprachliche Ausrichtung der verschiedenen dtr. Gruppen lässt sich daraus erklären, dass sie alle ihren Ursprung in der Beamtenschaft am Hof des Königs Josia haben, die u. a. maßgeblich an den Reformen dieses Königs und an der Schaffung des Deuteronomiums beteiligt gewesen waren. Aus dem Bericht von 2. Kön 22 lässt sich noch die führende Rolle des Schreibers Schafan und des Oberpriesters Hilkia erheben (V. 3.8.12).[51] Da die

---

50 Religionsgeschichte II, 391. Ich dachte damals an solche Phänomene wie den „Existentialismus" im 20. Jh.; C. Hardmeier, Prophetie im Streit, 467, sprach auf ähnliche Weise von einem „Epochenphänomen".

51 T. Römer, Deuteronomistic History, 112–117, will schon die Herkunft der Deuteronomisten selbst, die er weiter als eine Form von Schule begreift, in der josianischen Beamtenschaft ansetzen. Doch unterschätzt er dabei ein wenig die Bedeutung der Umbrüche, die diese Beamtenschaft nach Josia noch erlebt hat. Doch grundsätzlich hat er mit diesem institutionellen Ausgangspunkt recht.

Ämter am Hofe, wie gerade für diese führenden Beamtenfamilien nachweisbar,[52] vererbt wurden, können wir da|von ausgehen, dass auch die Schreiberausbildung und das damit verbundene theologische und juristische Training innerhalb dieser Familien erfolgte (Famulussystem). Dies erklärt, warum die dtn./dtr. Tradition auch nach dem Untergang des judäischen Staates nicht abbrach.

Entscheidend für die spätere Diversifizierung dtr. Gruppen war die politische Aufspaltung der königlichen Beamtenschaft nach dem Tod Josias und das damit verbundene Scheitern der Reform. In der Zeit von Josias Nachfolgern Jojakim und Zedekia stoßen wir auf zwei sich bekämpfende Parteien, eine national-religiöse Partei unter Leitung der Hilkiaden, der die Kultreform am Tempel genügte und die je länger je mehr antibabylonisch votierte, und eine Reformpartei unter Leitung der Schafaniden, die weiter an den Zielen, auch den sozialen Zielen der Josianischen Reform festhielt, das dtn. Gesetz – nun in Opposition zum Königshaus – weiter fortschrieb[53] und probabylonisch ausgerichtet war.[54] Aus dieser politischen Aufspaltung der Beamtenschaft in der spätvorexilischen Zeit erklären sich die Unterschiede zwischen der dtr. Gruppe, die hinter dem DtrG steht, und der dtr. Gruppierung, die für die drei Editionen des Jeremiabuches verantwortlich ist: Die Verfasser der Jeremiabücher lassen sich klar mit den Nachfahren der Schafaniden identifizieren, die im Lande blieben und die in Mizpa, wahrscheinlich in der dort ansässigen babylonischen Provinzverwaltung tätig waren (vgl. Gedalja und Jer 40,1–3). Die Verfasser des DtrG lassen sich wahrscheinlich mit einer Gruppierung der Nachfahren der national-religiösen Partei unter der Leitung der Hilkiaden in Verbindung bringen, die wohl im Umkreis der an den babylonischen Königshof verbrachten Familie des Königs Joja-

---

52 Zwei Söhne Schafans, Achikam (Jer 26,24) und Gemarja (36,9), waren Beamte unter Jojakim; ein weiterer Sohn, Elasa, unter Zedekia; der Enkel Schafans und Sohn Achikams, Gedalja, wurde von den Babyloniern zum Statthalter eingesetzt | (40,7). Nach 1. Chr 5,39 f.; Esr 7,1 wurde das Amt des jerusalemer Oberpriesters Hilkia an dessen Sohn Asarja und sodann an seinen Enkel Seraja vererbt, der 2. Kön 25,18 von den Babyloniern hingerichtet wurde, wahrscheinlich weil er ein führender Vertreter der antibabylonischen Partei gewesen war (vgl. vielleicht Jer 36,26). Dessen Sohn Jozadak wurde nach Babylon deportiert (1. Chr 5,41) und dessen Sohn Josua wurde der erste Hohe Priester am wiederaufgebauten Tempel (Hag 3,4; Sach 3).

53 Da sich das merkwürdige in das dtn. Königsgesetz eingeschobene Verbot, das Volk nach Ägypten zurückzuführen, um dem König Pferde für seine Streitwagen zu verschaffen (Dtn 17,16aα²bβ.b), mit einiger Wahrscheinlichkeit auf den Nubienfeldzug Psammetichs II. 593/2 v. Chr. bezieht, scheint die Fortschreibung der dtn. Gesetzgebung durch die Schafaniden in dieser Zeit weitgehend abgeschlossen gewesen zu sein, vgl. R. Albertz, Deuteronomic Legislation, 283–291.

54 Vgl. C. Hardmeier, Prophetie im Streit, 443–449; R. Albertz, Religionsgeschichte II, 360–373; ders., Wer waren die Deuteronomisten?, 292–295.

chin lebten.[55] In beiden Gruppen erfolgte die Schreiberausbildung weiter inner-familiär, so lassen sich die Ähnlichkeiten, aber auch die Entwicklung von Unterschieden im Sprachgebrauch erklären. Zeitlich ging wohl die Abfassung des DtrG, die durch die Begnadigung Jojachins durch den Sohn Nebukadnezars, Amēl-Marduk, im Jahr 562 v. Chr. veranlasst war, in den Jahren zwischen 560 und | 547 voraus;[56] die drei Editionen des Jeremiabuches folgten etwa in den Jahren 550 bis 520. So geht es diesen beiden konträren dtr. Gruppen in ihren Werken auch um den Streit um ihren jeweiligen Führungsanspruch bei einem möglichen Neuanfang.

Doch aus dieser politischen Aufspaltung der judäischen Beamtenschaft lässt sich die Existenz des dtr. VPB nicht allein erklären. Die Tatsache, dass sich hier einige Nachfahren der judäischen Führungselite voll mit den Interessen der einfachen Landbevölkerung Judas identifizierten und der Oberschicht insgesamt jegliche Führungsrolle absprachen, hat offenbar mit der Tatsache zu tun, dass durch den Untergang Judas die staatlichen Institutionen, der Hof und der Tempel, zusammengebrochen waren und sich damit auch die institutionelle Anbindung der Schreiber gelockert hatte. Es gab in Juda offensichtlich ungebundene, aber dennoch dtr. geschulte Intellektuelle, die mit der Autorität der Gerichtsprophetie im Rücken auf radikale Weise gegen die politischen Ansprüche beider dtr. Führungsgruppen opponierten und der Geschichtssicht der dtr. Historiker explizit widersprachen. Wahrscheinlich stammt diese Redaktion schon aus der Zeit nach dem Untergang des neubabylonischen Reiches, d. h. zwischen den Jahren 539–520 v. Chr., als sich die Möglichkeit eines Neuanfangs abzeichnete.[57]

Schließlich lässt die spezifische Eigenart des dtr. Haggai-Sacharja-Buches den umgekehrten Vorgang einer Re-Institutionalisierung dtr. geschulter Schreiber erkennen. Aus der Tatsache, dass sich die ZPR voll auf die Jerusalemer Heiligtumstheologie einließen, lässt sich folgern, dass sie zur Beamtenschaft des Zweiten Tempels gehörten, und zwar, da sich in ihrer Sprache nur wenige priesterliche Elemente finden,[58] wahrscheinlich zu deren laizistischem Teil. Dennoch suchten

---

55 Vgl. R. Albertz, Wer waren die Deuteronomisten?, 295–300; so ähnlich jetzt auch Römer, Deuteronomic History, 115–117. Wie die Weidner-Tafeln (ANET 308) belegen, lebte Jojachin in Babylon mit einem kleinen Hofstaat, vgl. R. Albertz, Exilszeit, 67; 87. |
56 Wieweit einzelne Passagen des DtrG erst in der persischen Zeit verfasst wurden, wie jüngst von T. Römer, Deuteronomistic History, 165–178, vertreten, bedarf noch genauerer Untersuchungen.
57 Vgl. Wöhrle, Die frühen Sammlungen, 281.
58 Vgl. vielleicht die prominente Rede vom ‚Zorn‘ bzw. ‚Zürnen‘ Gottes (קָצַף/קֶצֶף Sach 1,2.15; 7,12; vgl. 8,14), die zwar gelegentlich auch in dtn./dtr. Schriften begegnet (Dtn 9,19; 29,27), aber in priesterlichen Texten populär wird (Ex 16,20; Lev 10,6.16; Num 1,53; 16,22; 17,11; 18,5; 31,14) und auch in der Chronik häufig vorkommt (2. Chr 19,2.10; 24,18; 29,8; 32,25 f.).

diese Beamten auch in ihrer neuen Umgebung, den ethischen Anspruch der dtr. Tradition, insbesondere in sozialethischer Hinsicht, in die Tempeltheologie einzubringen.[59] Die Datierung der ZPR ist bisher noch vage; Wöhrle setzte diese Redaktion in die 1. Hälfte des 5. Jhs.[60] und brachte deren völkerfeindliche Tendenz mit Aufständen nach dem Tod des Darius im Jahr 486 v. Chr. in Verbindung, so etwa mit dem | Aufstand in Ägypten (486–484).[61] Diese Datierung lässt sich wahrscheinlich weiter präzisieren, wenn man berücksichtigt, dass die ZPR inmitten ihrer eigenen Heilsworte in Sach 2,10 f. die babylonischen Exulanten auffordern, aus Babylon zu fliehen und sich zum Zion zu retten (vgl. 6,15).[62] Diese Aufforderung lässt sich gut mit den Aufständen in Babylonien in Verbindung bringen, die für die erste Hälfte der Regierungszeit des Xerxes (486–465) belegt sind.[63] Zwar ist die Datierung der Aufstände noch nicht restlos gesichert,[64] aber wahrscheinlich erhoben sich vom Sommer bis Herbst 484 gleich zwei babylonische Usurpatoren in Zentralbabylonien, Bel-Šimanni und Šamaš-erība. Die Niederschlagung der Aufstände durch die Perser war immerhin so gewalttätig, dass in mehreren zentralbabylonischen Städten in diesem Jahr eine ganze Anzahl von Archiven abbrach, so z. B. auch das Archiv des berühmten Handelshauses Egibi in Babylon.[65] Mögli-

---

59 Wenn man bedenkt, dass sich die ZPR, obgleich sie sich stark an JerD orientierten, um das Erbe des Propheten Haggai bemühten, der, wie aus seinem Heilswort über Serubbabel (2,23) erkennbar, welches das Gerichtswort Jer 22,24–30 aufhob, in scharfer Opposition zu den Jeremia-Deuteronomisten gestanden hatte, dann könnte es sich bei ihnen um späte Nachfahren der schafanidischen Reformfraktion handeln, die von der Provinz- in die Tempelverwaltung gewechselt hatten.

60 Die frühen Sammlungen, 364; 380. |

61 Die Plünderungen, von denen in Sach 2,12 die Rede ist, könnten mit Sach- und Geldleistungen für die Kriegszüge des Xerxes zu tun haben.

62 Ein vergleichbarer Aufruf zur Flucht aus Babylon begegnet in Jes 48,20 f.; dieser hat wahrscheinlich die babylonischen Aufstände zu Beginn der Regierung des Darius 521 v. Chr. zum Hintergrund, vgl. Albertz, Exilszeit, 296–301. Für eine gefährliche politische Situation spricht die Verwendung des Terminus ישע im nif. oder hif. ‚(sich) retten' im Zusammenhang der Rückführung der Exulanten (Sach 2,11; 8,7). Da die genannten Passagen des Sacharjabuchs bisher meist dem Propheten selbst zugewiesen worden waren, wurde der hier vorgeschlagene zeitgeschichtliche Bezug bisher anscheinend übersehen, vgl. H. Graf Reventlow, Propheten, 48 f.

63 Vgl. P. Briant, From Cyrus to Alexander, 525–535.

64 F. M. T. de Liagre Böhl, Prätendenten, 110–113, denkt an zwei getrennte Aufstände in den Jahren 484 und 482 v. Chr.; P. Briant, Date, 12, präferiert dagegen die beiden Jahre 481 und 479, also unmittelbar vor und nach dem Griechenlandfeldzug (489–479 v. Chr.), zur ausgedehnten Diskussion vgl. C. Waerzeggers, Revolts, 151–156; die Ansetzung beider Usurpatoren in die Regierungszeit des Xerxes ist durch die Tafeln BM 87357 Nr. 1 und BM 96414 Nr. 4 inzwischen erwiesen.

65 So die wohlbegründete jüngste Rekonstruktion von C. Waerzeggers, Revolts, 150–162. Dagegen sind ältere Rekonstruktionen aufgrund der Nachrichten der griechisch-römischen Historiker, dass Xerxes den babylonischen Tempel Esangila zerstört und seine Marduk-Statue geraubt habe (so noch F. M. T. de Liagre Böhl, Prätendenten, 113 f.) inzwischen widerlegt, vgl. A. Kuhrt/S. Sher-

cherweise flammte der Aufstand im Jahr 479, nach den Niederlagen des Xerxes in Plataia und Mykale, erneut auf, und zwang Xerxes, seinen Griechenlandfeldzug (480–479) überraschenderweise abzubrechen.[66] Wenn diese zeitliche | Ansetzung richtig ist, dann waren es die schweren politischen Erschütterungen in Babylonien und anderen Teilen des persischen Reiches, welche die ZPR veranlassten, eine Neuedition der Haggai- und Sacharjaprophetie zu wagen und deren weitreichende Heilsperspektive mit sozialethischen Appellen zu verbinden. Nachdem die Weltgeschichte wieder in Bewegung geraten war, schien die Gelegenheit günstig, dem vollen Durchbruch des Heils durch ethische Anstrengungen nachzuhelfen.

Die Re-Integration der judäischen Beamtenschaft in die kultischen (Tempel) und zivilen Institutionen (Ältestenrat, Provinzverwaltung) der persischen Provinz Juda, führte allerdings im Laufe der Zeit dazu, dass sich die spezifischen Merkmale dtr. Literatur im 5. Jh. mehr und mehr verflüchtigten und mit andersartigen Merkmalen vermischten. Der Deuteronomismus ist somit keine generelle „theologische Zeit*strömung*", sondern war mit den Nachfahren der königlichen Beamten Josias in ihrer wechselvollen Geschichte nach dem Scheitern der Reform und dem Untergang der staatlichen Institutionen verbunden, aber er ist in sofern eine *Zeit*strömung, als er auf eine bestimmte Epoche, nämlich das 6. und frühe 5. Jh. v. Chr., beschränkt blieb.

Literatur

R. Albertz, A Possible Terminus ad Quem for the Deuteronomistic Legislation – A Fresh Look at Deut 17:16, in: G. Galil/M. Geller/A. Millard (eds.), Homeland and Exile. Biblical and Ancient Near Eastern Studies in Honour of Bustenay Oded, VT.S 130, Leiden & Boston 2009, 271–296.
R. Albertz, Die Exilszeit. 6. Jahrhundert v. Chr., BE 7, Stuttgart 2001.
R. Albertz, Intentionen und Träger des Deuteronomistischen Geschichtswerks (1989), in: ders., Geschichte und Theologie. Studien zur Exegese des Alten Testaments und zur Religionsgeschichte Israels, BZAW 326, Berlin & New York 2003, 257–277.
R. Albertz, Religionsgeschichte Israels in alttestamentlicher Zeit, Bd. II, GAT 8/2, Göttingen ²1997.

---

win-White, Destruction, 79–78; P. Briant, From Cyrus to Alexander, 543–545. Esangila war unter Artaxerxes I noch voll in Betrieb. Dennoch können ein religiöser Hintergrund des Aufstands und darum auch begrenzte kultische Strafmaßnamen des Xerxes nicht ausgeschlossen werden, vgl. die sog. Daiva-Inschrift des Xerxes (= XPh; vgl. P. Lecoq, Inscriptions, 256–258) und die Nachricht Herodots, Historien I, 183, Xerxes habe ein Standbild aus Esangila geraubt, wenn auch nicht die Mardukstatue.
66 So besonders P. Briant, From Cyrus to Alexander, 533–535, im Anschluss an griechisch-römische Historiker; er spricht in diesem Zusammenhang von der Gefahr eines Zweifrontenkriegs. Wenn in Sach 8,7f. von einer Rettung und Heimführung der Exulanten aus Ost und West die Rede ist, dann könnte das darauf hinweisen, dass das persische Reich zur Zeit der Redaktion an zwei Fronten in Aufruhr geraten war. |

R. Albertz, Wer waren die Deuteronomisten? Das historische Rätsel einer literarischen Hypothese (1997), in: ders., Geschichte und Theologie. Studien zur Exegese des Alten Testaments und zur Religionsgeschichte Israels, BZAW 326, Berlin & New York 2003, 279–301.

R. Albertz, Why a Reform like Josiah's Must have Happened, in: L. L. Grabbe (ed.), Good Kings and Bad Kings, JSOT.S 393, European Seminar in Historical Methodology 5, London & New York 2005, 27–46. [[= S. 21–43 im vorliegenden Band]]

M. Beck, Der „Tag YHWHs" im Dodekapropheton. Studien im Spannungsfeld von Traditions- und Redaktionsgeschichte, BZAW 356, Berlin & New York 2005.

P. Briant, From Cyrus to Alexander. A History of the Persian Empire, Winona Lake, IN 2002.

P. Briant, La date de révoltes Babyloniennes contre Xerxès, Studia Iranica 21 (1991), 7–20. |

W. A. M. Beuken, Haggai-Sacharja 1–8. Studien zur Überlieferungsgeschichte der frühnachexilischen Prophetie, Assen 1967.

O. Eißfeldt, Einleitung in das Alte Testament, Tübingen ⁴1976.

C. Hardmeier, Prophetie im Streit vor dem Untergang Judas. Erzählkommunikative Studien zur Entstehungssituation der Jesaja- und Jeremiaerzählungen in II Reg 18–20 und Jer 37–40, BZAW 187, Berlin & New York 1990.

Herodot, Historien. Buch I-IX, hrsg. von W. Marg, 2 Bde., Zürich & München 1991.

P. Lecoq (éd.), Les inscriptions de la Perse achéménide. Traduit du vieux perse, de l'élamite, du babylonien et de l'araméen, Paris 1997.

K. Koch, Das Profetenschweigen des deuteronomistischen Geschichtswerks, in: J. Jeremias/ L. Perlitt (Hrsg.), Die Botschaft und die Boten, FS H. W. Wolff, Neukirchen-Vluyn 1981, 115–128.

A. Kuhrt/S. Sherwin-White, Xerxes's Destruction of Babylonian Temples, in: H. Sancisi-Weerdenburg/A. Kuhrt (eds.), Archaemenid History II: The Greek Sources. Proceedings of the Groningen 1984 Achaemenid History Workshop, Leiden 1987, 69–78.

F. M. T. de Liagre Böhl, Die babylonischen Prätendenten zur Zeit des Xerxes, BiOr 19 (1962), 110–114.

R. Lux, Das Zweiprophetenbuch. Beobachtungen zu Aufbau und Struktur von Haggai und Sacharja 1–8, in: E. Zenger (Hrsg.), „Wort JHWHs, das geschah ..." (Hos 1,1). Studien zum Zwölfprophetenbuch, HBS 35, Freiburg, Wien & New York 2002, 191–217.

J. Nogalski, Literary Precursors to the Book of the Twelve, BZAW 217, Berlin & New York 1993.

J. Nogalski, Redactional Processes in the Book of the Twelve, BZAW 218, Berlin & New York 1993.

M. Noth, Könige 1. 1. Könige 1–16, BK IX/1, Neukirchen-Vluyn 1968.

M. Noth, Überlieferungsgeschichtliche Studien. Die sammelnden und bearbeitenden Geschichtswerke im Alten Testament, Tübingen ³1967.

H. Graf Reventlow, Die Propheten Haggai, Sacharja und Maleachi, ATD 25,2, Göttingen 1993.

T. Römer, The So-Called Deuteronomistic History. A Sociological, Historical and Literary Introduction, London & New York 2005; paperback 2007 = 2009.

A. Schart, Die Entstehung des Zwölfprophetenbuchs. Neubearbeitungen von Amos im Rahmen schriftenübergreifender Redaktionsprozesse, BZAW 260, Berlin & New York 1998.

H.-G. Schöttler, Gott inmitten seines Volkes. Die Neuordnung des Gottesvolks in Sach 1–6, TThSt 43, Trier 1987.

W. H. Schmidt, Die deuteronomistische Redaktion des Amosbuches. Zu den theologischen Unterschieden zwischen dem Prophetenwort und seinem Sammler, ZAW 77 (1965), 168–193.

W. Thiel, Das Jeremiabuch als Literatur, VuF 43 (1998), 76–84.

W. Thiel, Deuteronomistische Redaktionsarbeit in den Elia-Erzählungen, in: Ders., Gelebte Geschichte. Studien zur Sozialgeschichte und zur frühen | prophetischen Geschichtsdeutung Israels, Neukirchen-Vluyn 2000, 139–160.

W. Thiel, Die deuteronomistische Redaktion von Jeremia 1–25, WMANT 41, Neukirchen-Vluyn 1973.

W. Thiel, Die deuteronomistische Redaktion von Jeremia 26–45, WMANT 52, Neukirchen-Vluyn 1981.

W. Thiel, Gedeutete Geschichte. Studien zur Geschichte Israels und ihrer theologischen Interpretation im Alten Testament, BThSt 71, Neukirchen-Vluyn 2005.

W. Thiel, Grundlinien der Erforschung des „Deuteronomistischen Geschichtswerks" (2003), in: ders., Unabgeschlossene Rückschau. Aspekte alttestamentlicher Wissenschaft im 20. Jahrhundert, BThSt 80, Neukirchen-Vluyn 2007, 63–81.

W. Thiel, Könige 2, BK IX/2,1–4, 4 Lieferungen, Neukirchen-Vluyn 2000–2009.

W. Thiel, Verfehlte Geschichte im Alten Testament (1985), in: ders., Gedeutete Geschichte. Studien zur Geschichte Israels und ihrer theologischen Interpretation, BThSt 71, Neukirchen-Vluyn 2005, 64–89.

C. Waerzeggers, The Babylonian Revolts Against Xerxes and the ‚End of the Archives', in: AfO 50 (2003/04), 150–173.

J. Wöhrle, Die frühen Sammlungen des Zwölfprophetenbuches. Entstehung und Komposition, BZAW 360, Berlin & New York 2006.

How Radical Must the New Beginning Be? The Discussion between the Deutero-Isaiah and the Ezekiel School

The notion that the prophetic books, collected, revised, and edited during the period of exile, are heavily preoccupied with a theological reappraisal of Israel's disastrous history, the destruction of the Northern and Southern Kingdoms (722 and 587 BCE), has often been observed. But that they are likewise engaged in a controversial discussion of how a new beginning after the catastrophe should take place commonly goes unnoticed.[1] One of the few scholars who has recently stressed not only the proclamations of judgment, but also the promises for restoration, is Walter Brueggemann, to whom I am happy to offer my congratulations for his most impressive lifework.[2] In his commentary on the book of Jeremiah, which he regarded as primarily directed to the exiles, he emphasizes the consolatory function of chs. 30–33: 'The faithfulness and the power of Yahweh assure that in the depth of Israel's exile God will work a homecoming, in the face of Israel's death God will work new life'.[3] Fundamentally agreeing with this statement I would like to ask: How new is this 'new life' conceptualized by the prophetic books? How far is its continuity with the past broken? Should it be available to any Israelite or only to those who comply with specific criteria? To answer questions like these, I would like to consider the most prominent prophetic collections of the exilic period, the books of Deutero-Isaiah (Isa. 40–55) and Ezekiel. |

1 The Emergence and Date of the Books

The literary problems of the books of Ezekiel and Deutero-Isaiah cannot be treated here in detail. I refer to my investigations of these two works in my mono-

---

1 The most comprehensive investigation of this topic is still the old study of Siegfried Herrmann, *Die prophetischen Heilserwartungen im Alten Testament: Ursprung und Gestaltwandel* (BZAW, 85; Stuttgart: Kohlhammer, 1965), but because of its tradition-historical approach it presents a harmonizing view.
2 I met him first, when he came to Heidelberg as a research fellow and joined the doctorate group of Claus Westermann.
3 Walter Brueggemann, *A Commentary on Jeremiah: Exile and Homecoming* (Grand Rapids: Eerdmans, 1998), p. 266. |

Note: A shorter version of this article was read in the session 'The Exilic Discussion of a New Beginning', chaired by Saul Olyan, Aaron Schart, Jakob Wöhrle and myself during the EABS Meeting in Dresden, August 2005.

https://doi.org/10.1515/9783111202228-015

graph *Israel in Exile*,[4] where I have also reported the scholarly discussion in detail. The following is a summary of my results.

It is still highly probable that the book of Ezekiel goes back to the priestly prophet of that name (Ezek. 1.3; 24.24), who most probably was deported with the exiles of 598/7 and was at work in Babylonia between 594 and c. 570 BCE. Thus Ezekiel is the only prophet of doom who survived the destruction of Jerusalem in 587 and remained active for a long time. According to his book, he uttered oracles of salvation (Ezek. 34–37) already during the exilic period and toward the end of his life (in the year 574) he envisioned a new temple in the land of Israel (40.1–2).

Since Ezekiel's visions of how the glory of Yhwh, which had appeared to him in Babylonia (Ezek. 1–3), left the defiled temple of Jerusalem (chs. 8–11) and would return to the new temple (42.1–13), constitutes the structure of the whole collection, the editorial work on the book of Ezekiel could not have started before the latest temple vision which was only two to four years before the prophet died. Although the book is designed as a personal legacy of the prophet (1.1; reports in first person), most of its parts must have been written by his pupils. Because of the elaborate promises of return and reconstruction (chs. 34; 36–37) combined with the detailed nature of chs. 40–48, the whole book presupposes the possibility of a major political change, which was not imaginable before the end of Nebuchadrezzar's long reign in 562 BCE. A first glimmer of hope for a new beginning may have been fueled by the release of Jehoiachin from prison in the first year of Nebuchadrezzar's son Amel-Marduk (2 Kgs. 25.27–30). Since Amel-Marduk was murdered after two years, it remains uncertain whether or not a major change of Babylonian policy actually took place at that time. It is more likely that the reign of Nabonidus (556–539) could have raised some hope, as he attempted to provide the provinces with more support. So, the decade between 560 and 550 BCE constitutes a *terminus post quem*.[5] Since most of the detailed reform programme for the temple and the whole society in Ezek. 40–48 could not have | been carried out along the lines the prophet envisioned, it is highly improbable that the Ezekiel tradition would have developed much later than the reconstruc-

---

4 Rainer Albertz, *Israel in Exile: The History and Literature of the Sixth Century BCE* (trans. D. Green; Studies in Biblical Literature, 3; Atlanta: Society of Biblical Literature, 2003), pp. 345–433 (German 2001).

5 Here I differ from my position in Albertz, *Israel in Exile*, p. 352, and come closer to the position of Thomas Krüger, *Geschichtskonzepte im Ezechielbuch* (BZAW, 180; Berlin: de Gruyter, 1989), p. 340, who dated the 'older Ezekiel book' after 562 BCE. The fact that in the book of Ezekiel the new beginning is not connected with the rise of the Persian empire contradicts a later *terminus post quem* during the rise of Cyrus (547/6 BCE). |

tion of the Jerusalem temple in 520–515 BCE when the conditions were already established. Therefore, the book of Ezekiel was probably written between 560 and 515 BCE with chs. 40–48 being developed in detail in a final phase, perhaps by a second generation of pupils. On the basis of dating the book late in the period it is possible to consider most of it a literary unity. Only chs. 38–39 are clearly a later addition.[6] The perspectives of doom and salvation were deliberately closely intermingled[7] in order to define the criteria for a new beginning. Thus one can say: 'clearly the book of Ezekiel is to be read from the very start from the perspective of the conditions needed for a new beginning'.[8]

In contrast to the book of Ezekiel the book of Deutero-Isaiah does not stem from a date earlier than the late exilic period.[9] The anonymous prophet, who has to be considered as the master of a prophetic group (Isa. 50.4–9) most probably began his prophecy of salvation among the Babylonian exiles just after the victorious campaign of Cyrus against Lydia in the year 547/6 BCE. But only parts of the book, mainly the material collected in Isa. 41–48, came from an early phase of preaching and coincided with the time before Cyrus took Babylon in 539 (see, for example, the older composition of Isa. 42.14–44.22*). However, the original message that Yhwh has called Cyrus for Israel's sake failed (45.4) because Cyrus co-operated with the Babylonian Marduk priesthood, not with the Judaean exiles and he neither conquered nor humiliated Babylon, but instead elevated the city to the status of one of his capitals while Jerusalem lay in ruins. Thus, after 539 BCE the Deutero-Isaiah group struggled with its failure (49.4a, 6a) and reflected upon the meaning of Israel's lasting exilic existence in the first and the second Servant Songs (42.1–4; 49.1–6).

In any event, with Cambyses' campaign to Egypt (525 BCE) the political situation changed. Judah's strategic location next to the route to Egypt resulted in the elevation of its status to a more important province in the eyes of the | Persians. After the sudden death of Cambyses and Gaumata's revolt, Darius' usurpation of the Persian throne (522 BCE) granted the exiled Judaeans a new chance. During a period of instability, Babylonia revolted against Darius like other provinces in

---

6 Possible later additions are Ezek. 34.25–31; 36.33–36, 37–38. The oracles against foreign nations (chs. 25–36), however, were part of the exilic book, since their derision of the ravaged temple, city and land moved Yhwh to intervene and deliver his people (cf. 36.2, 3, 16–21; etc.), against Krüger, *Geschichtskonzepte*, pp. 317 ff.

7 A beneficial prospect can be found in the oracles of doom: Ezek. 5.3–4, 13 (?); 6.8–10; 11.14–20; 12.16; 14.11, 22–23; 16.53–58, 59–62; 17.22–24; 20.32–44; cf. 28.25–26. Elements of accusation and judgment can be found next to oracles of salvation in: 33.23–29; 34.1–10, 17–22; 36.17–19; 43.8–9; 44.6–12; 45.9.

8 See Albertz, *Israel in Exile*, p. 360.

9 For the following, see Albertz, *Israel in Exile*, pp. 393–404. |

the Eastern part of the empire and was conquered by him twice in the winter of 522 and the summer of 521 BCE. So the prophecy of the Deutero-Isaiah group started to be fulfilled. Out of concerns to secure the loyalty of the displaced Judaeans in the revolting province, Darius was prepared to resettle a major group of them as a means of stabilizing the Western part of his empire. It is possible that while negotiations with the exiles took place, the prophetic group fled from civil war in Babylonia in order to bring the salvific message to Jerusalem and to support the repatriation that had suddenly become possible (Isa. 48.20–22), and that actually took place in the year of 520 BCE under the official leadership of Zerubbabel and Joshua.

These dramatic events of the year of 522/521 probably constitute the background for the first edition of the book of Deutero-Isaiah. In the eyes of this prophetic group King Darius was carrying out what they had prophesied Cyrus would do. Thus, they supplemented their famous Cyrus oracle (Isa. 44.24–45.7) with a series of anonymous royal oracles (42.5–9; 45.11–13; 48.12–16a), which could implicitly refer to Darius without revoking the original message. On the basis of a combination of composition criticism and redaction criticism developed by Jürgen Werlitz[10] and myself,[11] we can now verify with a high degree of probability that the first edition of the book consists of most of the text of Isa. 40.1–52.12.[12] Probably this edition was composed in Judah for use in public recitation as a means of motivating the people. Thus the editing of the book of Deutero-Isaiah is directly involved in the realization of the new beginning in Judah.

2 The Concepts of the Books for a New Beginning

Since the two prophetic books and their authorial groups are so closely connected in time and place, it is no wonder that they shared similar expectations | and theological topics.[13] For both, the hope for a return of the exiles to the land of Israel is central. To give you typical examples.

---

10 Cf. Jürgen Werlitz, *Redaktion und Komposition: Zur Rückfrage hinter die Endgestalt von Jesaja 40–55* (BBB, 122; Berlin: Philo, 1999), pp. 237–82.

11 Cf. Albertz, *Israel in Exile*, pp. 391–99.

12 The thesis converges with the results of Karl Elliger, *Deuterojesaja in seinem Verhältnis zu Tritojesaja* (BWANT, 63; Stuttgart: Kohlhammer, 1933); Reinhard G. Kratz, *Kyros im Deuterojesaja-Buch* (FAT, 1; Tübingen: Mohr-Siebeck, 1991); Jürgen van Oorschot, *Von Babel zum Zion: Eine literarkritische und redaktionskritische Untersuchung* (BZAW, 206; Berlin: de Gruyter, 1993); Ulrich Berges, *Das Buch Jesaja: Komposition und Endgestalt* (HerBS, 16; Freiburg: Herder, 1998); cf. Albertz, *Israel in Exile*, pp. 385–91 and pp. 397–99 for the verses included in this edition. |

13 Cf. Dieter Baltzer, *Ezechiel und Deuterojesaja: Berührungen in der Heilserwartung der beiden großen Exilspropheten* (BZAW, 121; Berlin: de Gruyter, 1971).

Ezek. 11.17   'Say therefore', so speaks Adonay-Yhwh.
'I will gather you from the nations
and will assemble you from the countries,
over which I have scattered you.
And I will give you the soil of Israel.'

Isa. 43.5   Do not fear, for I am with you!
From the East I will bring back your offspring,
and from the West I will gather you.
6   I will say to the North: 'Give!'
and to the South: 'Do not hold back!
Bring my sons from afar,
and my daughters from the end of the earth!'

In connection with the return both prophetic groups promised the reconstruction
of the Judaean towns (Isa. 44.26; 45.13; 49.19; Ezek. 36.33) and the recultivation of
the land (Isa. 49.8; Ezek. 36.29, 34). The Ezekiel pupils placed more emphasis on
the reconstruction of the temple (Ezek. 37.26–27; 40.1–43.12) than the Deutero-
Isaiah group (Isa. 44.28; cf. 52.11). Both prophetic groups expected a similar return
of Yhwh to Zion with one anticipating the deity's return to his city Jerusalem
(Isa. 40.9–11; 52.7–8) and the other to his new temple (Ezek. 43.1–12). Both speak
of the 'glory of Yhwh' (כבוד יהוה) (Isa. 40.5; Ezek. 1.28; 3.12; 8.4; 11.22–23; 43.2;
etc.) and presuppose Zion theology (Isa. 52.1–2; Ezek. 43.7). Finally, both prophetic
groups compare the return of the exiles with the exodus from Egypt (Isa. 43.16–
17; 48.21; 52.9; Ezek. 20.5–10, 30–38). Nevertheless, a closer look at the two prophetic books reveals striking differences in the theological framework in which their
common hopes are embedded. Unfortunately, these are largely overlooked by
Dieter Baltzer.[14]

2.1 The concept of the Deutero-Isaiah group

The Deutero-Isaiah group felt instructed by God to bring a message of comfort to
Jerusalem.

Isa. 40.1   'Comfort, comfort my people!', says your God!
2   'Speak tenderly to Jerusalem, and proclaim to her.
Truly, her servitude has ended, truly, her guilt is removed,
for she has received from the hand of Yhwh double for all her sins!'

---

14 Cf. Baltzer, *Ezechiel und Deuterojesaja*, pp. 178–83. |

In its view, the period of judgment has come to an end and Jerusalem has | been punished by Yhwh more than enough during the long period of exile. Accordingly, its guilt is removed and the prophetic group proclaims to it the dawn of a new age of salvation.

According to this historic-theological concept, the present message of Deutero-Isaiah deals primarily with salvation. Its core, the oracles of salvation (Isa. 41.8–13, 14–16; 43.1–7; 44.1–5) are unconditional assurances. And the little hymns, which structure the whole book of the first edition, anticipate the divine comfort and deliverance of Israel and Jerusalem as if they had already taken place (44.23; 49.13; 52.9; cf. 48.20). However, the salvific message of Yhwh's appointment of the Persian kings Cyrus and Darius to repatriate the exiles and to reconstruct Jerusalem (45.13) was not easily accepted among the exilic and the Judaean communities. As the disputations show, the prophetic group faced many objections from their audience such as, Did Yhwh, god of this tiny ethnic group, have the power to impose his will on nations as powerful as the Persians (40.15–17)? Were their gods not more powerful (40.18–20, 25–26)? Did Yhwh actually act in history on the basis of moral categories and rational principles (40.13–14)? Was he even still interested in his people after such a long period of silence (40.12–14)? Has he not decided to get divorced from his city (50.1)? Would he be able to liberate his people (50.2)? And finally: How could Yhwh appoint a foreign king as the anointed saviour (45.1)? So, the prophetic group was confronted with scepticism, dejection, pusillanimity and theological doubts, which considerably diminished the stimulating effect of their message. If we can believe the testimony of the third Servant Song, the prophetic group was even abused and beaten by those inhabitants of Judah who were tired of all hope (50.4–6).

Thus, in spite of its unconditional message, the prophetic group had to face the problem that the majority of its people refused to trust in it. In response they started a programme of theological education in order to renew the belief of their audience. They reminded them of the old hymns where Yhwh's omnipotence as the creator of the world and the sovereign of history along with his mercy was praised (Isa. 40.12–31). They taught the deaf and the blind, who were not able to hear their message and to notice God's acts in history, that no other power than Yhwh has caused their disaster (42.18–25). Thus, for Deutero-Isaiah, the acceptance of the prophecy of doom constitutes the prerequisite of a new relationship with God. Moreover, since Yhwh had predicted the fall of Israel and Judah, he had demonstrated his purposeful governance of history down to the coming of Cyrus (41.22–23) and proved to be the only God (41.14, 28; etc.). Likewise, the prophetic group argued against the self-pity of their companions. In contradistinction to complaints that God had not honoured all the community's cultic and sacrificial efforts in the pre-exilic period, the Deutero-Isaiah group let God point out that they | had not served him, but rather burdened him with their constant sins (43.23–28). 'Only this recognition of sin and clarification of responsibility could open the way for the restoration of Israel's shattered relationship with God'.[15] According to Deutero-Isaiah, only God – not Israel – could interrupt their sinful history. The deity has, therefore, forgiven all Israel's sins for his own sake (43.25). Yhwh's merciful forgiveness of Israel's sins and the conclusion of the period of judgment constitute the secure foundation on which the new Israel can be built.

At the end of the older composition (42.14–44.23), which was so much engaged with the renewal of the people's belief, an admonition for repentance is placed strategically.

Isa. 44.21   Think of these things, Jacob,
             for you are my servant.
             I have formed you, you are my servant,
             Israel, you are not forgotten by me.
      22   I have wiped out your crimes like a cloud
             and your sins like a mist.
             Return to me! For I have redeemed you.

That means: in spite of the unconditional status of salvation, Israel's return to Yhwh is still necessary.[16] However, Israel's repentance is not a prerequisite for salvation, but rather its consequence. Yhwh's assurances to Israel of his redemption and forgiveness of sins reminds each member of the community of his honoured status as the deity's servant for which any Israelite should thankfully change his ways and thoughts in order to do justice to Yhwh's salvific plans.

---

15 See Albertz, *Israel in Exile*, p. 411.

16 Because of this apparent contradiction, Claus Westermann, *Das Buch Jesaja: Kapitel 40–66* (ATD, 19; Göttingen: Vandenhoeck & Ruprecht, 5th edn, 1986), p. 116, suggested that this admonition could not have emerged in the same situation as the oracles of salvation, but must have been spoken later by pupils of Deutero-Isaiah after their remigration. Similarly, Werlitz, *Redaktion und Komposition*, pp. 248–50, thinks of a redactional text, and Oorschot, *Von Babel zum Zion*, pp. 216–18, assigns it to his 'Naherwartungsschicht' dated in the late 6th or early 5th century. But already Hans Walter Wolff, 'Das Thema "Umkehr" in der alttestamentlichen Prophetie', in his *Gesammelte Studien zum Alten Testament* (ThB, 22; München: Kaiser, 1964), pp. 130–50 (144–45), has pointed out that the call of repentance derived from the oracle of salvation. Isa. 44.21–22 must be understood, therefore, as an attracting invitation. That the admonition constituted the target for an older collection (Isa. 42.14–44.23) was shown by Christof Hardmeier, '"Geschwiegen habe ich seit langem ... wie die Gebärende schreie ich jetzt": Zur Komposition und Geschichtstheologie von Jes 42.14–44.23*', *WuD* 20 (1989), pp. 155–79 (176–78); cf. likewise Albertz, *Israel in Exile*, pp. 411–12. |

Against the background of the dramatic political history of the Persian empire in the years of 522–521 BCE the return to Yhwh included three | conditions. First, both the golah in Babylonia and the Judaeans at home had to accept the prophetic message that Yhwh had intervened in international history in order to provide his people with a chance of salvation. This means that the capture of Babylon by Darius had to be interpreted as the very end of the period of exile (Isa. 47) and Darius's usurpation had to be viewed as Yhwh's appointment made to facilitate the repatriation of the golah and the reconstruction of Jerusalem (45.13; 48.12–16a). Second, the exiles in Babylon and elsewhere were faced with the decision about their willingness to take a chance and venture the risky enterprise of repatriation (48.20; 52.9). Third, the Judeans in Judah had to ascertain how many repatriates they were willing to accept and welcome in a friendly way (52.1–2, 11–12).

It seems that the Deutero-Isaiah group did not want to exclude anybody from the new beginning. Even the Judaeans in Egypt who had been castigated by the pupils of Jeremiah (Jer 44) were included (Isa. 48.12). They considered their main task to be the encouragement of as many Judaeans and Israelites as possible to participate in Yhwh's restoration. In their enthusiasm they sought to avert the loss of the opportunity of return to the homeland. Since the Deutero-Isaiah group was directly involved in the political enterprise of repatriation, they were not so interested in the formulation of clear theological criteria for the new society. However, only those who had participated in the repatriation or supported it would witness the saving power of Yhwh and the extension of his supreme divine sovereignty to the nations (Isa. 43.8–13; 44.6–8; 52.9–10). In contrast, those who refused repatriation excluded themselves from Yhwh's salvific plans for his people.

2.2 The concept of the Ezekiel group

Since the pupils of Ezekiel started their editorial work during the stable phase of the Babylonian empire, their reflections about a new beginning were not connected with a definite historical development like the fall of Babylon or the rise of Cyrus, but remained more theoretical.

In contrast to the Deutero-Isaiah group, the Ezekiel pupils have given much more thought about who would participate in the new beginning. According to their view, unbroken continuity between the old and the new Israel was not a possibility. They agreed with Amos that the old Israel had come to an end (Amos 8.2): it had literally died under the judgment of God (Ezek. 7). The future Israel would be a new divine creation, resurrected from a heap of dry bones with the help of the prophetic word (37.1–11). The same discontinuity is shown with regard to the Jerusalem temple. After the glory of Yhwh had left the sanctuary, it was handed over to destruction (vv. 8–11). The new temple, which would be a totally new building, could only exist after the glory of God had returned to it (43.1–12). Therefore, 'not all those whose families had survived the catastrophe should conclude that they would automatically | belong to the new Israel, not to mention enjoy their old position',[17] and no one should think that one could simply restore the pre-exilic institutions. In the new Israel the strict separation of the temple and palace, along with the consequences that such a division would entail, was a necessity!

In principle, all Israel could share the coming salvation. In contrast to K.-F. Pohlmann I would like to emphasize that no group was generally excluded.[18] For certain, the first golah of 598/7, which had experienced God's judgment already (Ezek. 11.17–20) was addressed by the promise, but the second golah of 587 would profit by it as well, after it had experienced the same fate (6.8–10; 14.22–23). Yhwh would assemble both groups from among the nations and bring them back to the land of Israel (34.12–14; 36.8, 24; 37.12–14). Those who had remained in Judah and who challenged the property-rights of the golah and continued to practice their abominations, would meet further divine judgment (33.23–29). However, this does not imply their general exclusion, as the oracles of salvation for Jerusalem show (cf. 16.53–58, 59–63). Even the Israelites of the former Northern kingdom would be included among the reunited people at the end (16.61; 37.15–19; 47.15–48.29). In contrast to the Deutero-Isaiah group, the pupils of Ezekiel do not conceive of a general absolution for all previous sins. Nonetheless, according to their opinion, every member of the community, wherever that person may live, has a chance of repentance and can be sure of God's forgiveness of the individual (18.21; cf. 33.15).

However, what is true for the ordinary people is not also true for the religious and political leaders. The pupils of Ezekiel subjected the latter to more severe criteria and a more comprehensive judgment. The false prophets, whose divinations were a lie, were definitely excluded from the house of Israel and were not allowed to enter the land of Israel (Ezek. 13.9). 'Such irresponsible prophets, who had misled the people with their constant talk of šālôm (13.10) and thus prevented them from changing their ways, were useless for the new beginning'.[19] They must be kept outside! Likewise the prophet's pupils accused those elders who outward-

---

17 See Albertz, *Israel in Exile*, pp. 362–63.
18 He postulated a golah-oriented edition, which stresses the preferential treatment of the golah from 597 BCE, while those who remained in Judah would be seen to be eliminated (cf. Ezek. 11.14–21; 33.21–33); cf. Karl-Friedrich Pohlmann, *Der Prophet Hesekiel/Ezechiel*, I (ATD, 22/1–2; Göttingen: Vandenhoeck & Ruprecht, 1996/2001), pp. 27–28.
19 See Albertz, *Israel in Exile*, p. 363. |

ly had behaved devoutly and responsibly, but continued secretly to practise idolatry in their private devotions (14.1–11). Speaking with the authority of sacral law, the Ezekiel school pronounced their exclusion from the people of Yhwh (14.8). The same verdict applied to any prophet who aided and abetted these elders with a word of God (14.9–10). Such irresponsible political and religious leaders, | who endangered the people, could no longer be tolerated in the new community. The pupils of Ezekiel brought a harsh indictment against the shepherds of Israel as well (34.1–6). All the members of the royal family and the officials who had selfishly exploited the people in the past would be removed and deprived of their power before the future salvation would happen (34.7–15). 'There could also be no continuity at the pinnacle of political authority'.[20] Only after Yhwh had created a just balance between the wealthy and the poor could a new kingdom be established there (34.16–24).

Although the prophet's pupils differed in their notion about the identity of the new king, be it a descendant of Jehoiachin (Ezek. 17.22–24), a new David (34.23–24; 37.24–25) or someone else (37.20–22), they all agreed that his power must be reduced. Therefore they called him מֶלֶךְ 'king' only twice (37.22, 24) and more frequently used the term נָשִׂיא 'prince' (34.24; 37.25; 44.3; 45.7–9; etc.). Consequently, the pupils of the second generation stripped this future petty king of all his former sacrality (46.1–10). Moreover, they sought to remove the need for any royal exploitation of the people (46.16–18) and conceptualized a new institutional order where political and religious powers would be divided strictly between the prince, the tribal leaders and the priests (45.1–8; 47.21–48.29). Likewise, those priests who had misled the people to apostasy in the past would be degraded to the minor class of Levites (44.9–14) and would have to carry their guilt (44.10, 12). Thus, those political and religious leaders who had conducted their offices irresponsibly in the past would be either excluded or have their status diminished.

With their most critical view of the new beginning, the Ezekiel school came in conflict with other late exilic groups like the Deutero-Isaiah prophets or the tradents of the Deuteronomistic History. In consequence, they felt obliged to defend their insights in the central chap. 20 of their book.[21] Since Ezekiel 20 refers to topics like the exodus (vv. 5–10, 36)[22] and the kingship of Yhwh (20.33)[23] which

---

20 See Albertz, *Israel in Exile*, p. 364.

21 Krüger, *Geschichtskonzepte*, pp. 206–14, has convincingly shown that Ezekiel 20 should be considered an original unit.

22 Cf. Isa. 43.16–17, 18–20; 48.21; 51.9–10; 52.12, although the exodus theme is not as central in Deutero-Isaiah as often believed; see Rainer Albertz, 'Loskauf umsonst? Die Befreiungsvorstellungen bei Deuterojesaja', in *Freiheit und Recht: Festschrift für Frank Crüsemann zum 65. Geburtstag* (ed. C. Hardmeier, R. Kessler and A. Ruwe; Gütersloh: Gütersloher Verlagshaus, 2003), pp. 360–79 (360–62).

23 Cf. Isa. (40.10); 41.21; 43.15; 44.6; 52.7.

are otherwise lacking in the book but of central importance in Deutero-Isaiah, we can conclude that the Ezekiel pupils entered into fierce debate with their prophetic colleagues.[24] Apart from this they referred | to Deuteronomic and Deuteronomistic topics like Israel's divine election (v. 5)[25] and God's acts with 'a strong hand and outstretched arm' (vv. 33, 36),[26] thereby showing that they wanted to dispute with the Deuteronomists, too.

What was the nature of the disagreement? If one conceptualizes the repatriation of the exiles as a 'new exodus', as the Deutero-Isaiah group had done, then all Israelites can participate, because Yhwh had brought all of Israel out of Egypt. The same inclusive view can also be inferred from the Deuteronomic topic of Israel's election. In chap. 20, however, the Ezekiel pupils wanted to disprove this argument on the basis of Israel's salvation history. They did not deny that Yhwh had elected Israel (Ezek. 20.5) and had solemnly promised the people to bring it out of Egypt into a wonderful land (v. 6). But according to the Ezekiel pupils, Israel's constant apostasy already made a farce of the exodus. Because the people were not willing to give up their Egyptian idols, Yhwh violently separated them by removing them from Egypt. In their view, then, the exodus was more a purgative judgment than a saving act (20.8b–10). They thus emphasized that it led only indirectly to the promised land by way of the wilderness (v. 10). Likewise, Israel's disobedience made a farce of the legislation on Mount Sinai which resulted in the cancellation of the divine promise of land for the generation currently in the wilderness (v. 15).[27] The Ezekelian recital of Israel's history taught that there never was an unconditional claim to enter the promised land.

According to the Ezekiel school, Yhwh made another attempt with the second generation in the wilderness, but was disappointed again. Because of their disobedience and apostasy he announced expulsion from the land while they were still in the wilderness (Ezek. 20.23).[28] Moreover, he gave them bad instructions, which

---

24 Walther Zimmerli, 'Der "neue Exodus" in der Verkündigung der beiden großen Exilspropheten', in his *Gottes Offenbarung: Gesammelte Aufsätze* (ThB, 19; München: Kaiser, 1969), pp. 192–204 (193–94), pointed out correctly that the topics of the exodus | and divine kingdom occur only in Ezek. 20. But since he presupposes an early exilic dating of the text (pp. 203–204), he cannot appreciate the reference to Deutero-Isaiah. That Ezekiel 20 should rather be regarded as a late chapter of the book is supported by Pohlmann's observation that it interrupts the close thematic connections between chap. 19 and chs. 21–22 and has a wider horizon than its context (cf. *Der Prophet Hesekiel*, II, pp. 303–304).

25 Cf. Deut. 7.6–7; 10.15; 14.2; etc.

26 Cf. Deut. 4.34; 5.15; 26.8; Jer. 21.5, and many similar expressions like Deut. 7.19; 11.2; 1 Kgs 8.42.

27 As the parallel with the Deuteronomistic History shows (Deut. 1.34–36), the reversal of the land promise is probably not generally meant, but only with respect to the first generation.

28 Here the Ezekiel pupils contradicted the view of the Deuteronomistic History in which the second generation could enter the promised land without any difficulty and in their warning that the land could be lost is uttered only after the occupation by Joshua (Josh. 23). |

would mislead them (vv. 25–26). Thus the pupils contradict the Deuteronomists and the Deutero-Isaiah group that there had ever existed any salvific phase in Israel's early history on which one could find | one's claim and from which one could draw parallels with the new beginning. Even the gift of the Mosaic law on which the Deuteronomists were based was infected by Israel's apostasy and needed a critical prophetical review.

In the eyes of the Ezekiel pupils, the exilic generation persisted also in the apostacy of their fathers who had lived in the land (Ezek. 20.27–31).[29] In contrast to the Deutero-Isaiah group the promise of return could have nothing to do with a general divine absolution. In their view, Yhwh was ready to gather the exiles from the foreign countries and to bring them out of the nations (v. 33) in order to offset the likelihood that they would become assimilated (v. 32). Moreover, this new exodus would not automatically bring the exiles into the land of Israel, but it would lead them only to the wilderness as in the previous exodus. Here, in the 'desert of the nations' (v. 34), which the Ezekiel pupils equated with the 'desert of the land of Egypt' (v. 36), Yhwh personally would sit in judgment on the exiles and would select each person, 'who revolted and rebelled against me' (v. 38) and exclude that person from coming home. Only those who passed this purgative judgment were allowed to build up the new community in the land of Israel. They would be brought back in 'the bond', that is, in 'the obligation of covenant' (v. 37), in order that they might practice the divine laws by heart.[30] In addition, according to other texts in the book of Ezekiel, the defiled land of Israel (36.17; 11.18) and the new community in the land (36.25, 29; 37.23) would require a thorough cultic purgation.

While the editor of the Book of the Four interpreted the entire exile as a judgment of purgation (Hos. 3.1–5; Amos 9.7–10; Mic. 5.9–13; Zeph. 1.4–6; 3.9–11),[31] the Ezekiel school is the only prophetic group that expected an additional purgative judgment at the end of the exile. In their eyes, it would be similar to what had occurred already in the first exodus. By formulating the return in this way – that Yahweh's judgment demonstrates his kingship over Israel (אמלוך עליכם, Ezek. 20.33) – they explicitly contradicted the message of the Deutero-Isaiah group who proclaimed that Yhwh would reveal his sovereignty through salvific actions,

---

29 The contradiction to Ezek. 20.15 verifies that the reversal of the land promise in this verse cannot generally be meant.

30 For this interpretation, see Moshe Greenberg, *Ezekiel 1–20: A New Translation with Introduction and Commentary* (AB, 22; New York, NY: Doubleday, 1983), pp. 372–73, and Krüger, *Geschichtskonzepte*, pp. 268–69. Probably, this strange little picture should be expressed with the easier metaphor of implanting a new heart and a new spirit (Ezek. 11.19; 36.26–27).

31 Cf. Albertz, *Israel in Exile*, pp. 204–37. |

the conquest of Babylon (Isa. 43.14–15) and the triumphant return (40.9–11; 52.7–9). 'Clearly they saw in the unconditional message of salvation for all the exiles the nascent danger of | cheap grace, which imperiled the new beginning they desired'.[32] Although they agreed with their prophetic colleagues that Yhwh would rescue exiled Israel for his own sake (Isa. 43.25; 48.11; Ezek. 36.22, 32), or more precisely, 'for the sake of his name, that it might not be profaned in the sight of the nations' (Ezek. 20.9, 14, 22; cf. 20.44; 36.20–23) and that divine salvation would never be dependent on Israel's conduct (20.44), they elevated individual responsibility so that the participation of each person in the restoration became contingent on that person's confession and repentance. According to Ezekelian thought, a new beginning that would correspond to God's salvific act could never take place without the feeling of shame and disgust about what was done in the past (Ezek. 6.9; 20.43; 36.31; cf. 16.53, 63).

3 Conclusion

Although the two prophetic schools mentioned above worked at a similar place – starting in Babylonia and ending in Jerusalem – and during a similar period – starting in the mid or the late exilic period and ending in early postexilic times – they developed, in spite of some material and theological convergences, two nearly opposite concepts for Israel's new beginning after the exile.

The reasons for the divergence are not easy to determine. Probably, the different concepts have to do with the different origin of the two groups. The Deutero-Isaiah group, on the one hand, derived in all probability from the former non-priestly ministers of the Jerusalem temple, primarily the temple singers[33] whose fathers had probably stood close to the nationalistic party of the late monarchic time where Isaiah was interpreted as a prophet of salvation.[34] As the universalism of Deutero-Isaiah shows, the prophetic group partly distanced itself

---

32 See Albertz, *Israel in Exile*, p. 367.
33 Cf. Albertz, *Israel in Exile*, p. 381.
34 See, mainly, the Assur-redaction from the time of Josiah, which had turned the divine judgment against the aggressor Assur; cf. Hermann Barth, *Die Jesaja-Worte in der Josiazeit: Israel und Assur als Thema einer produktiven Neuinterpretation der Jesajaüberlieferung* (WMANT, 48; Neukirchen–Vluyn: Neukirchener Verlag, 1977). Christof Hardmeier, *Prophetie im Streit vor dem Untergang Judas: Erzählkommunikative Studien zur Entstehungssituation der Jesaja- und Jeremiaerzählungen in II Reg 18–20 und Jer 37–40* (BZAW, 187; Berlin: de Gruyter, 1990), pp. 247–436, has pointed out that the original Isaiah legend (2 Kgs. 18–20*), which portrays Isaiah as a prophet of salvation, was created by a member of the nationalistic party in the dispute over alliances that occurred during the siege of Jerusalem 588 BCE. |

from the nationalistic view of its earlier environment. It is understandable, then, that they were less critical of the conflicts within the exilic Israelite community. |

The Ezekiel school, on the other hand, inherited the critical legacy of its master. Ezekiel had belonged to a priestly group, which – although Zadokite – had nothing to do with the leading Hilkiads, who had constituted the head of the nationalistic party.[35] As can be seen from Ezekiel 17 the prophet had opposed the nationalistic politics of Zedekiah and he had heavily criticized all social abuses (22.6–12, 25). In so doing, his political position was close to that of the reform party who had supported the prophet Jeremiah in Judah (Jer. 26.24; 36.9–26). It is understandable, therefore, that the pupils of Ezekiel insisted on a radical change in the future Judaean society.

In spite of being so different, both concepts turned out to be necessary for the history of early postexilic Israel. Without the emphatic preaching of the Deutero-Isaiah group far fewer exiles would have been encouraged to risk the adventure of return; and perhaps the repatriation programme itself would have failed. The emphasis on the beginning of a new era, the assurance of divine forgiveness and the unconditional promise of salvation were absolutely necessary for the motivation of as many persons as possible. Any attempt to restrict the homecomers because of their previous deeds would have been counter-productive in this situation. A little later, however, after the temple had been rebuilt, the inner organization of the new Judaean community was at stake. Now the more theoretical reflections of the Ezekiel school became important. Without their idea that the glory of God enforces the dissolution of the former amalgamation of the holy and the political realm (Ezek. 43.1–12), the separation of political and religious powers and the independence of the priests would probably never have been carried out. Of course, many other aspects of the two future prophetic concepts remained utopian. Nevertheless, both had an important impact on the future course of Israelite history.

Selected Bibliography

Albertz, R. 'Darius in the Place of Cyrus: The First Edition of Deutero-Isaiah (Isaiah 40.1–52.12) in 521 BCE', *JSOT* 27 (2003), pp. 371–83.

Albertz, R. *Die Exilszeit: 6. Jahrhundert v. Chr.* (Biblische Enzyklopädie, 7; Stuttgart: Kohlhammer, 2001).

Albertz, R. *A History of Israelite Religion in the Old Testament Period* (2 vols.; OTL; Louisville: Westminster/John Knox, 1994).

---

35 Cf. Rainer Albertz, *A History of Israelite Religion in the Old Testament Period*, I (OTL; Louisville Westminster/John Knox, 1994), pp. 232–41. |

Albertz, R. *Israel in Exile: The History and Literature of the Sixth Century B.C.E.* (trans. D. Green; Studies in Biblical Literature, 3; Atlanta: Society of Biblical Literature, 2003).

Albertz, R. 'Loskauf umsonst? Die Befreiungsvorstellungen bei Deuterojesaja', in *Freiheit und Recht: Festschrift für Frank Crüsemann zum 65. Geburtstag* (ed. C. Hardmeier, R. Kessler and A. Ruwe; Gütersloh: Gütersloher Verlagshaus, 2003), pp. 360–79. |

Baltzer, D. *Ezechiel und Deuterojesaja. Berührungen in der Heilserwartung der beiden großen Exilspropheten* (BZAW, 121; Berlin: de Gruyter, 1971).

Barth, H. *Die Jesaja-Worte in der Josiazeit: Israel und Assur als Thema einer produktiven Neuinterpretation der Jesajaüberlieferung* (WMANT, 48; Neukirchen-Vluyn: Neukirchener Verlag, 1977).

Berges, U. *Das Buch Jesaja: Komposition und Endgestalt* (HerBS, 16; Freiburg: Herder, 1998).

Brueggemann, W. *A Commentary on Jeremiah: Exile and Homecoming* (Grand Rapids: Eerdmans, 1998).

Elliger, K. *Deuterojesaja in seinem Verhältnis zu Tritojesaja* (BWANT, 63; Stuttgart: Kohlhammer, 1933).

Greenberg, M. *Ezekiel 1–20: A New Translation with Introduction and Commentary* (AB, 22; New York: Doubleday, 1983).

Hardmeier, C. '"Geschwiegen habe ich seit langem … wie die Gebärende schreie ich jetzt": Zur Komposition und Geschichtstheologie von Jes 42.14–44.23*', *WuD* 20 (1989), pp. 155–79.

Hardmeier, C. *Prophetie im Streit vor dem Untergang Judas: Erzählkommunikative Studien zur Entstehungssituation der Jesaja- und Jeremiaerzählungen in II Reg 18–20 und Jer 37–40* (BZAW, 187; Berlin: de Gruyter, 1990).

Herrmann, S. *Die prophetischen Heilserwartungen im Alten Testament: Ursprung und Gestaltwandel* (BZAW, 85; Stuttgart: Kohlhammer, 1965).

Kratz, R. G. *Kyros im Deuterojesaja-Buch* (FAT, 1; Tübingen: Mohr-Siebeck, 1991).

Krüger, T. *Geschichtskonzepte im Ezechielbuch* (BZAW, 180; Berlin: de Gruyter, 1989).

Oorschot, J. van. *Von Babel zum Zion: Eine literarkritische und redaktionsgeschichtliche Untersuchung* (BZAW, 206; Berlin: de Gruyter, 1993).

Pohlmann, K.-F. *Das Buch des Propheten Hesekiel/Ezechiel* (2 vols.; ATD, 22/1–2; Göttingen: Vandenhoeck & Ruprecht, 1996/2001).

Werlitz, J. *Redaktion und Komposition: Zur Rückfrage hinter die Endgestalt von Jes 40–55* (BBB, 122; Berlin: Philo, 1999).

Westermann, C. *Das Buch Jesaja: Kapitel 40–66* (ATD, 19; Göttingen: Vandenhoeck & Ruprecht, 5th edn, 1986).

Wolff, H. W. 'Das Thema "Umkehr" in der alttestamentlichen Prophetie', in his *Gesammelte Studien zum Alten Testament* (ThB, 22; München: Kaiser, 1964), pp. 130–50.

Zimmerli, W. 'Der "neue Exodus" in der Verkündigung der beiden großen Exilspropheten', in his *Gottes Offenbarung: Gesammelte Aufsätze* (ThB, 19; München: Kaiser, 1969), pp. 192–204.

Welche Art von Individualität förderte die altisraelitische Familienreligion?

Meine Beiträge zur alttestamentlichen Anthropologie liegen zwar schon ein halbes Menschenalter zurück,[1] doch habe ich mich vor einigen Jahren noch einmal zusammen mit Rüdiger Schmitt einer umfassenden Studie der „Family and Household Religion" im alten Israel und bei seinen Nachbarn zugewandt. Hier konnten wir erstmals die in Privathäusern gefundenen Kultobjekte und die inzwischen stattliche Anzahl epigraphisch belegter Personennamen systematisch auswerten.[2]

   Mir scheint die Themenstellung, nach den Auswirkungen der familiären Religionspraxis auf die Ausbildung von Individualität zu fragen, für die weitere Erforschung der theologischen Anthropologie ausgesprochen fruchtbar und weiterführend zu sein. In den zahlreichen anthropologischen Studien der letzten beiden Jahrzehnte konnte in einem erstaunlich breiten Konsens geklärt werden, dass das Alte Testament ein „konstellatives Menschenbild" aufweist, nach dem sich der Einzelne in vier wechselseitigen Bezügen eingebunden | findet, nämlich in einem Bezug zu sich selbst bzw. zur eigenen Leibsphäre, in einem Bezug zu Gott bzw. zu einem religiösen Symbolsystem, in einem Bezug zum Mitmenschen bzw. zu seiner Sozialsphäre, und in einem Bezug zu den Tieren bzw. zur außermenschlichen Umwelt.[3] Diese vier Konstellationen stehen nun allerdings nicht unverbunden nebeneinander. Vielmehr ist es nach der erfolgten Klärung insbesondere für eine theologische Anthropologie wichtig, genauer zu untersuchen, wie sich der Gottesbezug auf die übrigen Konstellationen auswirkt, bzw. diese auf ihn zurückwirken. Hinsichtlich der Gottesbeziehung konzentriert sich der vorliegende Band auf deren unterste Ebene, die „Persönliche Frömmigkeit" bzw. „Familienreligion". Hinsichtlich der übrigen Konstellationen beschränke ich mich im Folgenden auf den Bezug zu sich selbst und zum Mitmenschen, um die Art der Individualität, welche durch die altisraelitische Familienreligion gefördert wird, genauer zu bestimmen.

---

1 Vgl. Albertz, Weltschöpfung; Ders., Persönliche Frömmigkeit; Ders., Gebet; Ders., Mensch.
2 Vgl. Albertz/Schmitt, Religion. |
3 Vgl. vor allem Janowski, Anerkennung, S. 183–185; Ders., Mensch, S. 8–28; Ders., Anthropologie, S. 28–36, in Anlehnung an Assmann, Konstellative Anthropologie, S. 97–113; aber ähnlich auch Frevel, Person, S. 79–82; Dietrich, Sozialanthropologie, S. 224–234, u. a.

https://doi.org/10.1515/9783111202228-016

I Die Gottesbeziehung des Einzelnen: Persönliche Frömmigkeit oder Familienreligion?

Lassen Sie mich mit einem kritischen Rückblick auf meine eigenen Forschungen beginnen. Als ich Anfang der 70er Jahre des vorigen Jh.s den Begriff „persönliche Frömmigkeit" wählte, um die religiöse Praxis und Symbolwelt auf der Familienebene zu bezeichnen, die von der an den großen Heiligtümern des Landes praktizierten offiziellen Religion des alten Israel unterschieden werden könnten, wollte ich mit diesem eher an den europäischen Pietismus des späten 18. und frühen 19. Jh.s erinnernden Begriff, der gleichwohl auch schon in der Ägyptologie zur Bezeichnung einer religiösen Strömung im Neuen Reich verwendet worden war,[4] vor allem gegen die sog. Kollektivismus-These einen kräftigen Kontrapunkt setzen, welche die alttestamentliche Wissenschaft Ende des 19. und Anfang des 20. Jh.s beherrscht hatte und bis in meine eigene Studienzeit fortwirkte. Nach dieser These war der Einzelne im alten Israel so fest in die Gemeinschaft von Familie, Volk und Stamm eingebunden, dass er – zumindest in vorprophetischer Zeit – über gar keine eigene Gottesbeziehung verfügte. So konnte etwa Bernhard Stade 1887 feststellen: „Israels Religion ist Volksreligion ... nur durch seine Zugehörigkeit zu dem Volke | Israel als Cultgenossenschaft Jahwes tritt der einzelne Israelit in ein Verhältnis zu Jahwe."[5] Darum sei, wie Rudolf Smend beipflichtete,[6] mit dem Ich in den Psalmen gar kein Individuum, sondern die jüdische Gemeinde gemeint. Obwohl die These schon bald allerlei Widerspruch erfuhr, lebte sie in leicht veränderter Gestalt besonders bei Gerhard von Rad weiter. Sahen die Wellhausen-Schüler in der altisraelitischen Kollektivgesellschaft noch ein primitives, eher negativ zu bewertendes Gegenbild zum modernen Individualismus, so konnte von Rad über „die fast somatische Verbundenheit des Einzelnen mit der Gemeinschaft" beinahe schwärmen. „Es gab damals kein isoliertes und auf sich gestelltes Individuum ... es gab nur Gemeinschaften, die sich mit allen ihren Gliedern als lebendige Körper wußten."[7] Dies galt für von Rad auch und gerade in religiösen Dingen, weshalb er die Psalmen in seiner Theologie unter der Überschrift „Israel vor Jahwe (Die Antwort Israels)" stellte.[8] Die Klagen des Einzelnen,

---

4 Vgl. Brunner, Persönliche Frömmigkeit, und die Votivstelen aus *Deir el-Medine*, deren Gebete an die Danklieder des Einzelnen im Alten Testament erinnern, siehe Assmann, Hymnen, S. 351–368. |

5 So Stade, Geschichte I, S. 507.

6 Siehe Smend, Psalmen, in Aufnahme einer von den Targumim, über die mittelalterlich jüdischen Ausleger zu J. Calvin und W. M. L. de Wette laufenden Auslegungstradition.

7 So von Rad, Theologie I, S. 399.

8 A. a. O., I, S. 366.

die einen Großteil des Psalters ausmachen, sind für von Rad ein Ausdruck vom „Zerbrechen des alten patriarchalischen Glaubens".[9] In ihnen würden „die sich ihrer Eigenständigkeit bewußt gewordenen Individuen" zwar „ein sehr persönliches Verhältnis zu Jahwe" gewinnen,[10] aber nicht selten ohne Schutz der Gemeinschaft in die Krise wirklicher Gottverlassenheit geraten. War die Gottesbeziehung des Einzelnen in Israel damit eine späte Dekadenzerscheinung? Das konnte doch nicht wahr sein! Es ist ja richtig, dass die Einzelnen im alten Israel stärker in ihre jeweiligen Gemeinschaften eingebunden waren als in unseren westlichen Industriegesellschaften, was übrigens bis heute für alle vorindustriellen agrarischen Gesellschaften gilt, aber muss man ihnen deswegen ihre eigene Gottesbeziehung absprechen? Als Widerspruch gegen diese ganze, heute schon fast in Vergessenheit geratene Forschungsrichtung war mein Begriff „persönliche Frömmigkeit" gemeint.[11] Und ich denke, er hat mit zu deren Korrektur beigetragen. Ich gestand allerdings schon | damals zu: „Wenn ich von persönlicher Frömmigkeit spreche, meine ich das Geschehen zwischen Mensch und Gott, das sich im Lebensbereich der Familie abspielt. Man könnte auch von ‚Familienreligion' sprechen, doch wird durch diesen Begriff suggeriert, als müsse die Familie in jedem Fall als ganze religiös tätig werden."[12]

Heute würde ich mich eher wie Karel van der Toorn[13] für den Begriff „Familienreligion" entscheiden und die Bezeichnung „persönliche Frömmigkeit" lieber für spätere Ausformungen der Familienreligion hin zu einer persönlichen Weisheitstheologie, einer Armenfrömmigkeit oder einer Torafrömmigkeit reservieren.[14] In dem mit Rüdiger Schmitt englisch geschriebenen Buch haben wir uns für die Bezeichnung „Family and Household Religion" entschieden, um anzuzeigen, dass es um die religiösen Praktiken und Vorstellungen im Bereich des ganzen kleineren oder größeren familiären Wirtschaftsbetriebs geht, damit aber doch die Grenze zur Sippen- oder Lokalreligion deutlicher markieren wollen, als es etwa van der Toorn getan hat.[15] Drei Gründe waren für den Wechsel der Termino-

---

9 A. a. O., I, S. 406.
10 A. a. O., I, S. 410.
11 Eine Variante der Kollektivismusthese, das von H. W. Robinson 1936 entwickelte „Hebrew Concept of Corporate Personality", die von Rad nur teilweise beeinflusst hat, ist vornehmlich im englischen Sprachraum populär geworden. Sie erhebt, obwohl ebenfalls mehrfach kritisiert, erstaunlicherweise durch Vermittlung von di Vito, Anthropology, S. 221–225, heute wieder ihr Haupt. Frevel, Person, S. 78, hat recht, dass das alte Konzept bei ihm trotz vordergründiger Distanzierung (vgl. di Vito, Anthropology, S. 224–225) im Hintergrund steht. |
12 So Albertz, Persönliche Frömmigkeit, S. 11.
13 Vgl. das einflussreiche Buch von van der Toorn, Family Religion.
14 Vgl. Albertz, Religionsgeschichte II, S. 561–576; 623–633.
15 Vgl. Albertz/Schmitt, Religion, S. 41–46, zu van der Toorn, Family Religion, S. 245–255, wo der Autor auch lokale Heiligtümer einer „family or clan religion" (a. a. O., S. 246) zuordnet.

logie maßgebend: Erstens wurde mir bewusster, dass die Quellen, die ich in meiner Habilitationsschrift für die „persönliche Frömmigkeit" vornehmlich ausgewertet hatte, die Klagen und Danklieder des Einzelnen, Heilsorakel sowie die theophoren Personennamen aus dem Alten Testament, die Familienreligion nur in ihrem Krisenmodus belegen, für das Alltagsleben aber noch ganz andere Textbereiche ins Spiel kommen wie etwa die Spruchweisheit[16] oder das Familienrecht, und dazu zahlreiche Opferhandlungen und Rituale, die von der Familie zu verschiedensten Gelegenheiten, etwa auch zum Begräbnis und Totengedenken, ausgeübt wurden.[17] Einen wichtigen Platz nehmen dabei inzwischen die archäologischen Funde ein.

Durch diese breitere Hinzuziehung des Belegmaterials kommt zweitens deutlicher heraus, wie stark die religiösen Praktiken auf dieser Ebene auf den Erhalt und das Überleben der Familie abzielten. Sie sind auf alle wichtigen Grundfunktionen der Familie, nämlich Reproduktion, Sozialisation, Konsumption und Produktion, bezogen und können somit zurecht als Teile einer Familienreligion klassifiziert werden. Was die Reproduktion betrifft, so machen schon Texte aus dem Alten Testament deutlich, dass die Geburt von Kindern, die als Arbeitskräfte und für die Altersversorgung zum | Überleben der Familie benötigt wurden, eine zentrale Rolle in der familiären Religiosität zukommt, auch wenn leider keine Geburtsrituale, wie wir sie aus Mesopotamien kennen, belegt sind. Wie wichtig sie war, wird durch den archäologischen Befund unterstrichen, dass fast 30 % der epigraphisch belegten Personennamen mit dem Vorgang von Schwangerschaft und Geburt zu tun haben.[18] Die Bedeutung der Sozialisation wird durch die Spruchweisheit und etwa die Kurzgebote aus dem Dekalog unterstrichen, unter denen das Elterngebot (Ex 20,12) zur Sicherung der Solidarität zu den alten Eltern hervorsticht. Die religiöse Dimension der Konsumption wird durch den archäologischen Befund bezeugt, dass Reste von Opferschalen und Libationsgefäßen gehäuft im Umkreis der Kochstelle gefunden wurden.[19] Offensichtlich war die Essenzubereitung mit Trank- und Speiseopfern verbunden, die wahrscheinlich von der Hausmutter vollzogen wurden. Dass schließlich die ackerbäuerliche Produktion und Tierzucht durch Erstlings- und Erstgeburtsopfer gesichert werden sollte, ist breit aus dem Alten Testament belegt (Ex 22,28–29; Dtn 15,19–23; 26,1–11 u. ö.). Hinzu kamen Rituale, die den Zusammenhalt der Familie über die Generationen hinweg stärken sollten, wie das familiäre Passahmahl (Ex 12,3–11) oder das Opfermahl der Sippe beim jährlichen Totengedenken (1. Sam 20,5–6.29).

---

16 Vgl. zu einer solchen Ausweitung Albertz/Schmitt, Religion, S. 336–339.
17 Vgl. A. a. O., S. 436–473. |
18 A. a. O., S. 505; vgl. S. 269–297.
19 A. a. O., S. 224–225.

Drittens hatte ich schon in meiner Habilitationsschrift herausgearbeitet, dass sich die Vorstellungswelt der persönlichen Gottesbeziehung des Einzelnen stark an den Familienbeziehungen orientiert. Mit ihren Charakteristika einer unbedingten, normalerweise unkündbaren, lebenslangen Vertrauens- und Abhängigkeitsbeziehung entspricht sie den Erfahrungen, die ein Kleinkind idealer Weise mit seinen Eltern macht.[20] Anders als bei den Primaten bricht die Mutter-Kind-Beziehung nicht mit der Geschlechtsreife der Kinder ab, sondern hält normalerweise ein Leben lang. Es ist also gerade das ganz spezifisch familiäre „Kooperations- und Solidaritätsverhältnis(ses)", mit dem sich nach Meinung der Familiensoziologin Rosemarie Nave-Herz die Familie bei aller Wandelbarkeit „von anderen Interaktionsbeziehungen in der jeweiligen Gesellschaft abhebt",[21] was die religiöse Symbolwelt der altisraelitischen Familienreligion maßgeblich geprägt hat. Auf dieser soziologischen Differenz beruht meiner Meinung nach auch ihre Sonderstellung innerhalb der Religion Israels. „Familienreligion" ist somit eindeutig der bessere, der sachgerechtere Terminus. Doch löst sich damit die Gottesbeziehung des Einzelnen auf? |

II Ausbildung einer Individualität der Familienmitglieder durch die Gebetspraxis

Gerade wenn man erkennt, wie stark die Familienreligion auf die Familie als ganze bezogen ist, wird um so auffälliger, dass so gut wie keine Familiengebete belegt sind. Die Wir-Gebete in den Psalmen sind entweder auf das Volk oder spätere religiöse Gruppen wie die der Armen oder der Frommen bezogen. Auch in den Erzählungen des Alten Testaments werden nach meiner Kenntnis keine Familiengebete überliefert. Den einzigen Hinweis, dass es solche überhaupt gegeben haben könnte, sehe ich in dem Personennamen *ʿImmānûyāhû* „JHWH ist mit uns", der dreimal epigraphisch im 8. und 7. Jh. v. Chr. belegt ist. Hier könnte sich das pluralische Suffix auf den Kreis der Familie beziehen, während ja der entsprechende Name in Jes 7,14 einen Symbolnamen darstellt, der auf das Volk bezogen werden soll.[22] Doch auch hier ist der Name mit einem singularischen Suffix, *ʿImmadîyāhû* „Jahwe ist mit mir" oder ähnlich, deutlich geläufiger; er ist neunmal bezeugt. Dementsprechend ist es ein höchst auffälliger Befund, dass die

---

20 Vgl. Albertz, Persönliche Frömmigkeit, S. 92–94.
21 Vgl. Nave-Herz, Familiensoziologie, S. 149. |
22 Vgl. Albertz/Schmitt, Religion, S. 557; vielleicht ist der Name *Šipṭān* auf gleiche Weise als „Unsere rechtliche Stütze" zu deuten, vgl. a. a. O., S. 555.

im Rahmen der Familienreligion überlieferten Gebete durchweg in der 1. Pers. Sg. formuliert sind.

Mir scheint, dieser Befund ist für unsere Frage nach der Ausbildung von Individualität von erheblicher Bedeutung. Die uns überlieferten Gebete sind, soweit wir erkennen können, zwar keine individuellen Äußerungen, sondern literarisch stilisiert bzw. Gebetsformulare. Aus den Šu-ila-Gebeten in Mesopotamien wissen wir, dass solche individuellen Gebete dem in Not geratenen Menschen vom Liturgen, dem *āšipû*, im Rahmen einer kasuellen Ritualhandlung zeilenweise vorgesprochen und von diesem nachgebetet wurden.²³ Ähnliches ist meiner Meinung nach auch für die individuellen Klagegebete im alten Israel zu vermuten, auch wenn hier – unter schlichteren kulturellen Bedingungen – die Rolle des Liturgen wahrscheinlich meist von einem Familienmitglied, etwa dem Vater oder der Mutter des oder der Leidenden, oder rituell bewanderten Bekannten, etwa einer Hebamme, ausgeübt wurden und nur in schweren Notfällen ein professioneller Liturg, etwa ein Gottesmann, zugezogen wurde.²⁴ Die Gerätschaften, die man zur Durchführung solcher Rituale etwa am Krankenlager oder auf dem Hausdach benötigte, wie Räucherständer, Opferschalen, | Libationsgefäße, Votivfiguren und apotropäische Amulette, gehörten jedenfalls wahrscheinlich zu jedem israelitischen Haushalt.

Alle diese Gerätschaften und die dazugehörigen Gebetsformulare, die sich bei anderen Gelegenheiten bewährt hatten, sollten dem in Krankheit oder sonstige Schwierigkeiten geratenen Familienmitglied helfen, bei Gott eine Wende der Not zu bewirken. Das Gebet war auch dann, wenn man gegen Bezahlung einen auswärtigen Ritualexperten hinzuzog, ein Akt der familiären Fürsorge. Aber indem man dieses Gebet dem Leidenden in der 1. Pers. in den Mund legte, wollte man ihm selber die Möglichkeit geben, sich mit seinem Leid auseinanderzusetzen und persönlich mit Gott um die Abwendung der Not zu ringen. Meine These also lautet: So sehr auch der Einzelne in seine Familie eingebunden und von ihr fremdbestimmt sein mochte, die in den Familien übliche Gebetspraxis war geradezu eine Schulung in der Ausbildung eigener Individualität. So typisch allgemein die Klagen, Bitten und Bekenntnisse in der Gebetsvorlage auch ausformuliert waren, wurde der Leidende, indem er sich diese in der Begegnung mit Gott zu eigen machte, zu einer ganz besonderen Person, um die es jetzt allein ging. Die persönliche Gottesbeziehung, die der Leidende im Gebet aktivierte, stärkte seine Individualität.

---

23 Vgl. etwa in der Anweisung für das Šu-ila-Gebet Ištar 31,49: „Die Beschwörung ‚Ištar, Herrin der Städte' lässt du ihn rezitieren," siehe Zgoll, Kunst, S. 105.
24 Vgl. die ähnlichen Überlegungen bei Gerstenberger, Mensch, S. 134–160. |

Der Ort, an dem sich das erwachende Ich-Bewusstsein in den Klagen des Einzelnen am deutlichsten ausspricht, sind Vertrauensbekenntnis und Bekenntnis der Zuversicht. Die Vertrauensbekenntnisse sind nicht selten mit der Wendung *wa'ᵃnî* „aber ich" eingeleitet, womit sich der Betende betont als ein Ich vor Gott präsentiert. Mit dem Bekenntnis „Ich aber vertraue auf deine Güte" streckt sich etwa der Beter von Ps 13 trotz aller Klagen und allen Leides auf Gott hin aus (V. 6), im Bekenntnis „Ich aber vertraue auf dich, JHWH, ich spreche: Du bist mein Gott" (V. 15) setzt sich der Beter von Ps 31 von seinen Feindklagen ab und birgt sich in seiner persönlichen Beziehung zu Gott.[25] Das *waw-adversativum* macht es sogar grammatisch greifbar: Im alten Israel ermöglichte der Gottesbezug einem Menschen in der Krise eine Distanzierung, zuerst von sich selbst, von seinem schmerzenden Körper und seinen psychischen Leiden, sodann von den echten oder eingebildeten Angriffen der Mitmenschen, und eröffnete in der Gemeinschaft mit Gott eine Neustabilisierung seines Ichs. Dies machen von der anderen Seite her auch die Bekenntnisse der Zuversicht deutlich. So hält etwa der Beter von Ps 3 gegen den Spott seiner | Mitmenschen fest: „Aber du (*wᵉ'attāh*), JHWH, bist ein Schild um mich, meine Ehre und hebst mein Haupt empor" (V. 4).[26] Gegen die isolierende Anfechtung stärkte hier der Gottesbezug das eigene Selbstwertgefühl. Insofern kann ich die Einschätzung von Bernd Janowski nur unterstreichen, dass im alten Israel „das Gebet ein primärer Ort für die Herausbildung des Ich- oder Selbstbewusstseins" gewesen ist.[27]

Es fragt sich, worauf sich dieses enge Gottesverhältnis gründet, das in den Vertrauensbekenntnissen bzw. Bekenntnissen der Zuversicht der Klagen des Einzelnen gegen Not und Leid aktualisiert wird. Wenn es wirklich in diesen Gebeten nicht um eine Beförderung der personalen, sondern der sozialen Identität ginge, wie Alexa Wilke im Anschluss an Robert di Vito nachzuweisen sucht,[28] sollte man eigentlich erwarten, dass in diesen Bekenntnissen auf die zentralen religiösen Traditionen des Volkes Israel Bezug genommen würde. Doch ist das, wie ich schon 1978 aufgezeigt habe, so gut wie nie der Fall.[29] Die an sich naheliegende Argumen-

---

25 Vgl. Ps 5,8; 52,10; 55,24b; 71,14; 73,23.28. Die Wendung *wa'ᵃnî* kommt auch in Unschulds- (26,11; 31,7; 35,13) und Schuldbekenntnissen (30,7) vor, auf die sich Wilke, Identität, S. 98, vor allem stützt, wenn sie meint, die „identitätsbestimmende(n) Sätze" dienten meist der „Abgrenzung gegenüber anderen, ethisch disqualifizierten Gruppen." Dabei unterbewertet sie aber die Distanzierung vom eigenen Leid in den Vertrauensbekenntnissen. |

26 Siehe auch Ps 59,9; 71,7; 86,15; 142,4; vgl. 22,4.

27 So Janowski, Anthropologie, S. 535, leider nur etwas versteckt in der Anmerkung 57.

28 Vgl. Wilke, Identität, S. 89–97; 111–112.

29 Vgl. Albertz, Persönliche Frömmigkeit, S. 27–32; mögliche Ausnahmen sind nur Ps 22,4–6 und Ps 143,5; doch handelt es sich in Ps 22 sicher und in Ps 143 möglicherweise um Ergänzungen, die sich aus einer Neuverwendung des Psalms in frommen Zirkeln erklären (vgl. Ps 22,24–27.28–32). |

tation: „Du hast doch unser Volk Israel aus Ägypten befreit, so rette auch mich aus meiner Not" kommt in den individuellen Klagepsalmen nicht vor. Stattdessen rekurrieren die Klagenden, wenn sie gelegentlich nach der Begründung ihres persönlichen Gottesverhältnisses Ausschau halten, auf ihre Erschaffung durch Gott (Ps 22,10 f):

> 10 Ja, du zogst mich aus dem Mutterleib
> flößtest mir Vertrauen ein an meiner Mutter Brust.
> 11 Auf dich bin ich geworfen von Mutterleib an,
> vom Schoß meiner Mutter an bist du mein Gott.

Gott selber war es gewesen, der den Betenden zur Welt gebracht und ihm schon an seiner Mutter Brust das Gottvertrauen eingeflößt hat. Darum ist dieser seit seiner Geburt von dem Gott abhängig, der als sein Schöpfer von Geburt an zu seinem Gott geworden ist. Das lebenslange persönliche Gottesverhältnis, das durch das Gefühl des Vertrauens und der Abhängigkeit geprägt ist, beruht demnach auf der persönlichen Erschaffung eines jeden Menschen durch Gott. Mir scheint, dass diese theologische Basis menschlicher Personalität und | Individualität in der Forschung noch nicht klar genug benannt wird.[30] Dass es speziell in Ps 22,10 f um die Konstituierung einer eigenständigen Person geht, wird daran deutlich, dass aus den vielfältigen Menschenschöpfungsvorstellungen gerade diejenige der Entbindung von der Mutter herausgegriffen wird.[31] Durch Gottes Schöpfungshandeln wird der Beter von seiner Mutter getrennt; wiewohl von der Mutter geboren, ist er nicht ihr Produkt, sondern ein eigenes Geschöpf Gottes.[32] Noch deutlicher kommt der Trennungsaspekt im verwandten Bekenntnis der Zuversicht von Ps 71,5–6 zum Ausdruck, wo es im masoretischen Text heißt: „Vom Mutterschoß hast du mich abgeschnitten,"[33] gemeint ist die Durchtrennung der

---

30 Offenbar scheut man sich, die Vorgänge von Schwangerschaft und Geburt direkt als Gottes Schöpfungshandeln zu klassifizieren. Wolff, Anthropologie, S. 146, spricht zwar in Bezug auf Ps 139,13 von einer „persönliche(n) Schöpfungsgeschichte", meint aber, dass hier ein Beter nur mehr oder minder *ad hoc* den „generellen Schöpfungsglauben (Gen 1–2) auf die Geburt seiner selbst" bezogen habe (a. a. O., S. 149). Für Grohmann, Fruchtbarkeit, S. 37, wird hier „die Entstehung des Menschen im Mutterleib ... eng mit dem Schöpfungshandeln Gottes in Verbindung gebracht." Nach Janowski, Anthropologie, S. 59, ist „der Beginn des Lebens ... auf Gottes schöpferische Kraft zurückzuführen."
31 Diese kommt einige Male auch mit Bezug auf die Weltschöpfung vor, vgl. Hi 38,29; Ps 90,2; vgl. Gen 1,11.24.
32 Dies gilt auch, wenn in anderen Zusammenhängen die Würde der Frau und Mutter als Mitschöpferin Gottes hervorgehoben wird, vgl. Gen 4,1.
33 Gegenüber der LXX und Hieronymus stellt die Lesung *gôzî* „ein mich Abschneidender" von MT nicht nur, wie Grohmann, Fruchtbarkeit, S. 58–59, richtig feststellt, die *lectio difficilior* dar, sie wird auch durch den Kurznamen *Gāzā'* „Er (Gott) hat abgeschnitten" (vgl. Albertz/Schmitt, Religion, S. 591), gestützt.

Nabelschnur. Die Individualität des Menschen beruht somit auf Gottes Schöpfungshandeln. Dass dieses nach alttestamentlicher Vorstellung keineswegs nur in der Urzeit geschah, sondern sich auch in der Gegenwart bei der Zeugung und Geburt eines jeden Menschen vollzieht, macht das ausführliche Bekenntnis der Zuversicht aus der Klage Hiobs in Hi 10,8–12 deutlich, in dem Hiob Gott vorhält, ihn nicht nur wie den ersten Menschen (Gen 2,7) aus Ton geschaffen (Hi 10,8–9), sondern ihn auch als Embryo kunstvoll gestaltet zu haben (V. 10–11). Auch in dem späten, sowohl Unschulds- als auch Vertrauensbekenntnis ausbauenden Psalm 139 sieht sich der Beter von Gott im Leib seiner Mutter geschaffen, wie ein kunstvolles Gewebe gewirkt (V. 13). Gegenüber einer zu engen motivlichen Differenzierung[34] ist somit festzuhalten: urzeitliche und gegenwärtige | Menschenschöpfung sind nicht klar voneinander zu scheiden (vgl. Gen 4,1); letztere vollzieht sich im Mutterleib (vgl. auch Jer 1,5; Hi 31,15; Jes 49,1.5) und umfasst den gesamten Vorgang von Zeugung, Empfängnis, Schwangerschaft und Geburt.

Es ist zuweilen eingewandt worden, die Rückbezüge auf die eigene Erschaffung in Klagen des Einzelnen seien zu marginal, um etwas darauf bauen zu können.[35] Ich hatte den nicht allzu üppigen Befund von 4–5 Psalmenbelegen[36] damit erklärt, dass die im späteren Psalter gesammelten Psalmen die Gebete der Familienreligion nicht eins zu eins abbilden, war aber auch etwas irritiert, dass sich im Alten Testament nur 9 Personennamen finden, die mit Schöpfungsverben gebildet sind.[37] Inzwischen hat sich die Evidenz dank der epigraphisch belegten Personennamen allerdings erheblich zum Besseren verschoben. In dem von mir untersuchten Sample von 675 Personennamen findet sich die stattliche Anzahl von 39 verschiedenen Schöpfungsnamen, die immerhin 148-mal belegt sind.[38] Sie bilden das Herzstück der 192 Geburtsnamen, die den ganzen Prozess von Zeugung, Empfängnis, Schwangerschaft, Geburt und Eingliederung des Neugeborenen auf ein

---

34 So will etwa Grohmann, Fruchtbarkeit, S. 66, Ps 22,10; 71,6 nicht als Schöpfungsaussagen gelten lassen: „Nicht die Schöpfung ist hier Thema, sondern Mithilfe bei der Geburt," obwohl der Hebammendienst etwa im *Atramḫasîs*-Epos sogar bei der urzeitlichen Menschenschöpfung bedacht wird (Z. I,277–295; TUAT III, S. 625) und die hebräischen Geburtsnamen selbstverständlich auch die Entbindung auf Gott zurückführen, vgl. Albertz/Schmitt, Religion, S. 590–591. |
35 So etwa Spieckermann, Heilsgegenwart, S. 74–76, und Grohmann, Fruchtbarkeit, S. 27. Ersterer will sogar Ps 22,10–11 als sekundär aus dem Psalm aussondern; vgl. Heilsgegenwart, S. 242.
36 Vgl. noch Ps 119,73. Dichter wird die Bezeugung allerdings, wenn man der These folgt, dass das Heilsorakel ursprünglich die göttliche Antwort auf die Klage des Einzelnen darstellte und darum die dort verorteten Belege bei Deuterojesaja, die von einer persönlichen Erschaffung Israels bzw. des Gottesknechtes sprechen, hinzugenommen werden dürfen, vgl. Jes 43,1.7; 44,2.24; 49,5; 54,5, vgl. Albertz, Weltschöpfung, S. 26–35.
37 Vgl. a. a. O., S. 155–156.
38 Vgl. Albertz/Schmitt, Religion, S. 277–281; 587–590.

Wirken Gottes zurückführen. Wenn aber rund 5 % von knapp 3000 untersuchten Personen Schöpfungsnamen tragen wie *Miqneyāhû* „Geschöpf JHWHs" (Arad), *Yau'āsāh* „JHWH hat (das Kind/mich) geschaffen" (Kuntillet Aǧrud) oder *S^ebakyāhû* „JHWH hat (das Kind/mich im Mutterleib) gewebt" (Lachisch, vgl. Ps 139,13), welche sie als leibhaftige Geschöpfe Gottes ausweisen, dann kann man den Glauben an die eigene Erschaffung nicht mehr als marginal oder elitär bezeichnen; es handelt sich vielmehr um einen allgemein verbreiteten und zentralen Glaubensinhalt der altisraelitischen Familienreligion.[39]

Eine wesentliche Funktion des Glaubens an die eigene Erschaffung zeigt sich nun gerade in den Klagegebeten des Einzelnen (Ps 22,10–11; 71,5–6; | Hi 10,8–12):[40] Indem sich hier die Leidenden in ihrer Not auf ihre Erschaffung durch Gott beriefen, gewannen sie ein starkes Argument, um Gott dazu zu bewegen, sich seinem bedrohten Geschöpf erneut zuzuwenden. Am schärfsten wird dieses in der Klage Hiobs (Hi 10,8–12) formuliert: Wenn du, Gott, mich so liebevoll im Mutterleib geschaffen hast, wie kannst du mich dann jetzt so herzlos umbringen? Das heißt: Die eigene Geburt, als Schöpfung Gottes verstanden, wird zu einem starken Argument gegen den Tod. Der Glaube, selber von Gott geschaffen worden zu sein, ist ein direkter Ausdruck des Lebenswillens eines Individuums. Dass ein Mensch trotz aller Todesbedrohung leben will und um die Erhaltung und Entfaltung seines Lebens kämpft, ist in seiner persönlichen Erschaffung durch Gott begründet.[41] Die Gegenprobe bestätigt dies: Wo der Lebenswille zerbrochen ist, wo verzweifelte Menschen nur noch sterben wollen, tritt an die Stelle der Rückerinnerung an die eigene Erschaffung die Verfluchung des Tages der Geburt, so anfangs bei Hiob (Hi 3) und schließlich beim Propheten Jeremia (Jer 20,14–18). Ohne Bezug auf Gott wird die Geburt zum bloßen Beginn eines elenden und sinnlosen Lebens, erst dann, wenn sie als Schöpfungshandeln Gottes verstanden wird, erhält sie die Qualität eines heilvollen Urdatums, auf das sich ein bejahtes,

---

39 Die Einschätzung Spieckermanns, Heilsgegenwart, S. 84, Anm. 33, dass das Menschenschöpfungsmotiv zwar in vorexilischer Zeit bekannt, aber ohne theologische Relevanz war, ist damit wohl endgültig widerlegt. |

40 Ps 139,13–16 ist aus formkritischen Gründen von den genannten Belegen zu trennen! Die thematisch motivierte Einbindung dieses Psalms hat in der Vergangenheit zu Unklarheiten bei der Bestimmung der Pragmatik der Rückbezüge auf die eigene Erschaffung in den Psalmen geführt. Bei Wolff, Anthropologie, S. 149, geht es um den Ausschluss jeden Mitspracherechts des Menschen, bei Grohmann, Anfang, S. 395, um das Bewusstsein der „Abhängigkeit seiner Existenz von Gott", bei Janowski, Anthropologie, S. 61, um eine emphatische „Bejahung der Verbindung von Schöpfer und Geschöpf."

41 Hier berührt sich das zum Glauben an die eigene Erschaffung Gesagte mit der eigentümlichen anthropologischen Vorstellung einer Intentionalität menschlichen Lebens, wie es Janowski, Mensch, S. 13–17, und andere herausgearbeitet haben; vgl. schon Albertz, Mensch, S. 466.

hoffnungsvolles Leben gründen lässt. So ist der Glaube, ganz persönlich von Gott geschaffen und damit von ihm gewollt zu sein, für die Stärkung des Selbstwertgefühls und der Ausbildung einer lebensbejahenden Individualität der einzelnen Familienmitglieder kaum zu überschätzen.

Es fragt sich, ab wann wir mit einer solchen Gebetspraxis und dem genannten Glaubensinhalt in den altisraelitischen Familien rechnen können. Die Klagen und Danklieder des Einzelnen des Psalters lassen sich schwer datieren. Zudem müssen wir damit rechnen, dass sie in ihrem Wortlaut nachträglich überarbeitet wurden.[42] In seinem neuesten Buch rechnet Bernd Janowski zwar mit einigen älteren Klagen und Dankliedern des Einzelnen aus dem 8.–7. Jh. v. Chr., weist aber offenbar die Masse der Texte und ausdrücklich das Motiv | der „Geschöpflichkeit" der exilisch-nachexilischen Epoche zu.[43] Das ist eine verbreitete Ansicht, doch scheint mir die hohe Zahl von 283 epigraphischen Dank- und Bekenntnisnamen, deren Vokabular eine hohe Affinität zu den individuellen Klage- und Dankpsalmen aufweist, in eine andere Richtung zu weisen:[44] Die Masse der Belege stammt aus dem 8. und 7. Jh. v. Chr., als Namenssiegel üblich wurden, einzelne Funde stammen aber auch schon aus dem 9. Jh., wie etwa der Dankname *Šᵉmaʿjau* „JHWH hat (mich) erhört" auf einer Steinschale aus Kuntillet Aǧrud.[45] Unter den Bekenntnisnamen, die dem für die Identitätsbildung so wichtigen Bekenntnis der Zuversicht in den Klagen des Einzelnen entsprechen, fanden sich etwa in der Grabung von Tel Dan aus der 1. Hälfte des 8. Jh. drei identische Krugstempel mit dem Namen *ʿImmādîyau* „Mit mir ist JHWH". Ein *plene* geschriebener Bekenntnisname, der explizit eine persönliche Gottesbeziehung ausdrückt, nämlich *ʾElîṣūr* „Mein Gott ist (mein) Fels", gehört in die 2. Hälfte des 8. Jh., stammt allerdings aus dem Antikenhandel. Ähnliches gilt für vier Bullen mit dem Namen *Mibṭaḥyāhû* „(Mein) Vertrauen(sgrund) ist JHWH", der genau dem Vertrauensbekenntnis von Ps 71,5 entspricht.[46] So ist es doch sehr wahrscheinlich, dass schon im 9. und 8. Jh. v. Chr., wenn nicht sogar schon eher, in den israelitischen und judäischen Familien Gebete gesprochen wurden, die den Psalmengebeten ziemlich ähnlich waren. Der gleiche Befund ergibt sich für den Glauben an die eigene Erschaffung; einer der Namen, der ihn bezeugt, *Yauʿaśāh* „JHWH hat (mich) geschaffen" stammt aus dem 9. Jh. und wurde in Kuntillet Aǧrud gefunden, die übrigen verteilen sich über das 8.–6. Jh. v. Chr.[47] Die Hebräische Bibel überliefert Schöpfungsna-

---

42 Vgl. etwa die Überarbeitung von Ps 22,4–6.24–27 im Sinne einer Armenfrömmigkeit. |

43 Vgl. Janowski, Anthropologie, S. 531–533.

44 Vgl. dazu die Aufstellung bei Albertz/Schmitt, Religion, S. 534–570.

45 Siehe a. a. O., S. 535, KAgr(9):4.

46 A. a. O., S. 562–563. Auf einem Ostrakon aus Lachisch ist der Name noch einmal für das frühe 6. Jh. v. Chr. belegt, Lak(6).1.1,4.

47 A. a. O., S. 587–590, insbesondere KAgr(9).8:1. |

men auch schon für das 10. Jh., aus dem wir kaum Inschriften haben, so *'Ælqānāh* „Gott hat (mich) geschaffen" für den Vater Samuels (1. Sam 1,1) oder *Beⁿāyāh* „JHWH hat (mich) gebaut" für einen der Heerführer Davids (2. Sam 20,23). So spricht einiges dafür, dass der Glaube an die eigene Erschaffung schon während der vorexilischen Zeit sowohl in den israelitischen als auch in den judäischen Familien geläufig war. Auch wenn es dann durch die Gerichtsprophetie ab der zweiten Hälfte des 8. Jh., durch den Verlust der Staatlichkeit Judas im 6. Jh. v. Chr. und die soziale Krise des 5. Jh.s noch einmal drei nachweisbare, deutliche Individualisierungsschübe in der altisraelitischen Gesellschaft gegeben hat, so hatte wahrscheinlich schon | zuvor die familiäre Gebetspraxis für eine Stärkung des Ich- und Selbstbewusstseins vieler ihrer Mitglieder gesorgt.[48]

III Die familiäre Einbindung der persönlichen Gottesbeziehung

Spielte die besonders in Lebenskrisen revitalisierte persönliche Gottesbeziehung einschließlich des Glaubens, ein eigenes Geschöpf Gottes zu sein, für die Ausbildung der Individualität der Familienmitglieder eine wichtige Rolle, so stellte diese im alten Israel nur in Ausnahmefällen eine völlig individualisierte Frömmigkeit dar, sondern war fast immer in die Familienreligion eingebunden. Aus dem Zweistromland der altbabylonischen Zeit wissen wir, dass der persönliche Schutzgott von den Familienmitgliedern nicht individuell gewählt, sondern vom Vater oder Großvater ererbt wurde. Soweit aus den Siegellegenden erkennbar, bezeichneten sich alle Familienmitglieder als Verehrer des gleichen Gottes, der darum als Familiengott charakterisiert werden kann, auch wenn meist nur einer der Söhne nach diesem benannt ist.[49] Darauf dass auch in Israel, zumindest in älterer Zeit, der persönliche Gott vom Vater und Vorvater ererbt wurde, weist die Bezeichnung „Gott meines/deines Vaters" in den Genesistexten hin.[50] Offenbar konnten bis in die Zeit Jeremias hinein in den Familien noch andere Gottheiten als JHWH als Familiengott verehrt werden (Jer 2,27–28). Doch zeigt der erhebliche Anteil JHWH-

---

48 Dafür spricht auch, dass die Frömmigkeit in den prophetischen Oppositionszirkeln, wie sie etwa am Ende der Jesaja-Denkschrift (Jes 8,16–18) und in den Klagen Jeremias erkennbar wird, eine solche Gebetspraxis voraussetzen.

49 Vgl. Charpin, Divinités, S. 61–71. Dabei scheint die Wahl eines Gottes zum Familiengott mit dessen Verehrung in einer Region zusammenzuhängen und beim Umzug beibehalten oder verändert werden zu können (a. a. O., S. 75–78).

50 Vgl. Gen 31,5.42; 32,10; 46,3; 50,17; u. ä. und 26,24; 28,13, dazu Albertz, Religionsgeschichte I, S. 53–57.

haltiger epigraphischer Personennamen von 67 Prozent, dass JHWH im 8. und 7. Jh. v. Chr. für einen Großteil der Bevölkerung auch in die Rolle des Familiengottes eingerückt war. JHWH bot sich auch deswegen als Familiengott an, weil ihm auch schon – und dies ist eine Besonderheit! – auf der staatlichen Ebene eine personale Beziehung zu einer Großgruppe eignete.[51] Dies mag ein Grund sein, warum die persönliche Gottesbeziehung in den Klage- und Dankliedern des Einzelnen aus Israel meist intensiver ausgestaltet ist als in den Gebeten aus Mesopotamien.[52] Es war nicht zuletzt die ausgeprägte Personhaftigkeit des | göttlichen Gegenübers, welche in den israelitischen Familien je länger je mehr auf die Ausbildung menschlicher Personalität zurückwirkte.[53]

Die Personennamen stellen, wie Bernd Janowski zurecht herausgearbeitet hat,[54] einen wesentlichen *identity marker* dar, mit dem ein bestimmter Menschen gerufen und von anderen unterschieden werden kann. Dabei lassen gerade die profanen Personennamen mit ihrer Bezeichnung physischer und mentaler Besonderheiten des Namensträgers und ihren zahlreichen Tier- und Pflanzenvergleichen eine Fülle individueller Persönlichkeitsmerkmale erkennen.[55] Die theophoren Namen weisen auf verschiedenste Weise auf die persönliche Gottesbeziehung des Namensträgers zurück, aber es handelt sich zumeist um vielfältige religiöse Erfahrungen der Eltern, oft der Mütter, die mit der Benennung des Kindes an die nächste Generation weitergegeben wurden. Egal ob die Kinder diese religiösen Erfahrungen der Eltern auch für ihr Leben übernahmen oder nicht, sie werden allein schon über ihre individuelle Benennung in den Rahmen der Familienreligion eingebunden.

Die theophoren Personennamen lassen zudem erkennen, dass Gott den einzelnen Menschen nicht nur erschafft, sondern auch dafür sorgt, dass sein neues kleines Geschöpf in die Familie integriert wird. Diese Integration fand bei Jungen

51 Vgl. a. a. O., I, S. 99–100.
52 Zgoll, Mensch, S. 126, hat gezeigt, dass die Šu-ila-Gebete mit ihren langen Lobeinleitungen nach dem Muster einer Audienz aufgebaut sind, in der sich der Mensch „der Gottheit | als einer hierarchisch höherrangigen Person nähert", was bei aller Vertrauensbildung eher „auf eine bewußte, starke Zurückdrängung des Ich" deute (a. a. O., S. 132). In den individuellen Klagen der Psalmen spricht der Beter dagegen Gott ohne Vorrede direkt an und beruft sich auf sein persönliches Vertrauensverhältnis zu ihm. So beobachtet Zernecke, Gott, S. 364–365, im Vergleich zu den Šu-ila-Gebeten eine „offensichtlich größere Gottesnähe" und ein „wesentlich engeres Gottesverhältnis" in den Psalmen.
53 So ist es wohl kein Zufall, wenn Martin Buber als jüdischer Religionsphilosoph „aller Menschen Personsein" von der „Personhaftigkeit" des ihnen begegnenden Gottes ableitet, vgl. Buber, Prinzip, S. 134.
54 Vgl. Janowski, Persönlichkeitszeichen, S. 319–326.
55 Vgl. Albertz/Schmitt, Religion, S. 605–609.

am 8. und bei Mädchen am 15. Tag beim Fest der Namengebung statt, das den Geburtsvorgang abschloss. Beginnend im 7. und dann generell im 6. Jh. v. Chr. kam zu ihm noch der Ritus der Beschneidung hinzu (vgl. Gen 17,12; Lk 1,59–66; 2,21). Die Personennamen, die diesen Integrationsakt widerspiegeln, gehören zu den bekanntesten überhaupt, etwa *Yᵉhônātān* „JHWH hat (das Kind) geschenkt" oder *Mattanyāhû* „Geschenk JHWHs"; Namen dieses Typs begegnen in meinem Sample über 150-mal.[56] Ein Gottesgeschenk kann man nicht ablehnen! Mit solchen Namen erkannten die Eltern, auch wenn möglicherweise der Vater leise Zweifel an seiner Vaterschaft gehegt hatte, dankbar an, dass ihnen Gott dieses Kind geschenkt und ihrer Fürsorge anvertraut hat. Die elterliche Fürsorge, die für das Überleben des Neugeborenen | absolut nötig ist, spiegelt sich etwa in dem Namen 'Amasyāhû „JHWH hat (das Kind) auf dem Arm getragen". Aus dem 7. Jh. ist bisher viermal der Name *Malyāhû* belegt, der sogar den aufkommenden Integrationsritus an Säuglingen auf Gott zurückführt. Denn er lässt sich wohl nur mit „JHWH hat (das Kind) beschnitten" übersetzen.[57] Gott selber ist daran interessiert, dass das von ihm geschaffene kleine Individuum in soziale Organisationsformen, in erster Linie in die der Familie und in zweiter dann in das Volk, eingebunden wird, ohne die es nicht überleben kann.

Dass diese Integration des Individuums in die Familie tiefer reichte als wir das in Westeuropa heutzutage gewohnt sind, verdeutlicht schließlich eine letzte Untergruppe der Geburtsnamen, nämlich die „Ersatznamen", die mit der hohen Rate der Kindersterblichkeit im alten Israel zusammenhängen.[58] In ihrer Trauer um das früh verstorbene Kind benannten Eltern das als nächstes geborene gerne mit einem solchen Ersatznamen, wie es ja auch David nach dem Tod des ersten Kindes, das ihm Bathseba geboren hatte, tat (2. Sam 12,24): *Šᵉlomoh*, besser *Šall-umoh* „sein Ersatz". D. h. Eltern fanden nichts dabei, ein nachgeborenes Kind als Ersatz für das verstorbene anzusehen und diesem zuzumuten, ein Leben lang mit einem Namen zu leben, der ihn als Stellvertreter einer anderen Person auswies. Auch diese innerfamiliäre Stellvertretung wurde auf Gott zurückgeführt: *Šellemyāhû* „JHWH hat (das verstorbene Kind) ersetzt"; sie wurde als Mittel angesehen, mit dem JHWH die trauernde Familie tröstet: *Neḥemyāhû* „JHWH hat (mit der Geburt eines neuen Kindes) getröstet". Die Ersetzung eines Individuums durch ein anderes hatte somit keinen negativen Klang. Im Gegenteil, dem Ersatz-Kind kam die Rolle des von Gott geschenkten Trösters der Familie zu, wie der häufige Personenname *Menaḥem* „Tröster" belegt. Aber die Identifizierung ging

---

56 Vgl. a. a. O., S. 593–595. |
57 Ein Bezug auf die spät-dtn. Vorstellung einer „Herzensbeschneidung" (Dtn 10,16; 30,6; Jer 4,4), wie er zuweilen erwogen wird, ist ja wohl kaum möglich, vgl. a. a. O., S. 291–292; 598.
58 Vgl. a. a. O., S. 599–601.

sogar noch weiter: Der Name *'Elyāšīb* „Gott hat zurückgebracht" bezeugt die Vorstellung, dass Gott mit der Geburt des nachgeborenen Kindes, das diesen Namen trägt, das zuvor verstorbene Kind wieder in die Familie zurückgebracht hat, im Geschwisterkind hat quasi wiederauferstehen lassen. Da dieser Name inzwischen 14-mal bezeugt ist,[59] kann man davon ausgehen, dass die Betroffenen es damals nicht als Zumutung, sondern als Ehre betrachteten, mit der Identität eines anderen Familienmitglieds zu leben. Es ist im alten Israel somit eine stark auf | die Bedürfnisse der Familie bezogene Individualität, die durch die personale Gottesbeziehung gestärkt wird.

IV Bruderkonflikte und starke Persönlichkeiten – ein Ausfluss intensiver Gottesbeziehung?

Dass im alten Israel eine solche familiär eingebundene Individualität keineswegs die Ausbildung starker Persönlichkeiten verhindert hat, machen die alttestamentlichen Texte deutlich, welche die Menschheits- und Volksgeschichte als Familiengeschichte erzählen. Wohl handelt es sich hierbei um literarische Stilisierungen, deren sozialer, moralischer und theologischer Horizont weit über die Lebenswirklichkeit der gewöhnlichen israelitischen Familie hinausreicht; aber diese Erzählungen wären wohl kaum populär geworden, wenn sie nicht doch auch an den dort möglichen Lebenserfahrungen angeknüpft hätten. Hier ist es nun ein auffälliges Merkmal, wie häufig und wie drastisch in solchen alttestamentlichen Erzählungen Konflikte zwischen Brüdern in den Mittelpunkt gestellt werden, man denke nur an die Geschichten von Kain und Abel (Gen 4,2–16), Jakob und Esau (25,21–34; 27,1–33,17*), an die Josephsnovelle (37–50) und darüber hinaus.[60] Frederick E. Greenspahn hat die Bedeutung dieses Merkmals mit dem Hinweis erhöht, dass vergleichbare Erzählungen aus der Umwelt weitaus stärker den Ton auf die Solidarität und die Harmonie zwischen Brüdern legen.[61] Während etwa im ägyptischen „Brüdermärchen" die Brüder Anubis und Bata in gegenseitiger Solidarität – nur kurzzeitig durch die Lüge einer untreuen Frau in Konflikt geraten – alle Bedrohungen überstehen und in höchste Ämter aufsteigen,[62] sind es in den genannten hebräischen Erzählungen die jüngeren Brüder wie Jakob oder Joseph,

---

59 Da der Name aus einem Ostrakon aus Arad schon für das 8. Jh. v. Chr. bezeugt ist, kann er sich nicht auf die Rückführung aus dem Exil beziehen, vgl. a. a. O., S. 267–268; 600. |

60 Etwa Ri 11; 1. Sam 16–17; 2. Sam 13–14; 2. Kön 1–2.

61 Siehe Greenspahn, Brothers, S. 3–7; er verweist etwa auf die griechische Beschreibung von Castor und Pollux.

62 Vgl. die Übersetzung bei Brunner-Traut, Märchen, S. 28–40. |

die gegen alle familiäre Rangordnung ihren Führungsanspruch erheben und teilweise sogar mit unlauteren Mitteln durchkämpfen. Sie werden dabei als eigenständige, durchsetzungsstarke Persönlichkeiten gezeichnet, die nach ihrem Erfolg allerdings bereit sind, sich entweder wie Jakob mit seinem benachteiligten älteren Bruder zu versöhnen oder wie Joseph aufgrund seiner erlangten Machtposition für seine ganze Familie zu sorgen. Alexandra Grund-Wittenberg spricht zurecht von einer „nahezu antikonformistische(n) Tendenz vieler alttestamentlicher Erzählungen, die verantwortliches Handeln Einzelner *coram* | *deo* wertschätzend herausstellen."[63] Es fällt nun auf, dass die Bruderkonflikte in der biblischen Darstellung nur vordergründig durch eine Ungleichbehandlung der Kinder durch ihre Eltern hervorgerufen werden (Gen 25,27–28; 37,3), die bis heute den häufigsten Grund dafür bildet, sondern dass letztlich Gott die Konflikte durch Orakel (25,23) und Träume (37,5–11) selber aus dem Hintergrund heraus induziert. Der Konflikt des ersten Bruderpaars wird sogar direkt durch Gottes willkürliche Bevorzugung des Erstlingsopfers Abels gegenüber dem seines Bruders vom Zaun gebrochen (4,4–5). Das lässt vermuten, dass die „antikonformistische Tendenz" dieser Erzählungen etwas mit der eigentümlichen Gottesbeziehung Israels zu tun hat. Deren Autoren waren offenbar darum bemüht, JHWHs Handeln gerade in den zwischenmenschlichen Beziehungen aufzuspüren, und sie beobachteten es vor allem dort, wo die normale menschliche Ordnung durchbrochen, ja, sogar auf den Kopf gestellt wurde. Deswegen wurden ihnen Bruderkonflikte, welche die Familienordnung durchbrachen und dadurch Gelegenheit boten, die individuelle Persönlichkeit der Konfliktbeteiligten, vor allem des jüngeren Bruders, herauszuarbeiten, so wichtig, weil sie daran das in Freiheit erwählende Handeln JHWHs aufzeigen konnten, auf dem die Existenz Israels letztlich beruhte. Es scheint mir darum die besonders intensive personale Gottesbeziehung Israels – sowohl auf familiärer als auch auf gesamtgesellschaftlicher Ebene – zu sein, die trotz aller Traditions- und Sozialbindung in vorindustriellen Agrargesellschaften, der auch das alte Israel unterlag, hier die Ausbildung selbstbewusster und facettenreicher Individuen nachhaltig förderte.

Literatur

Albertz, R., Art. Gebet. II. Altes Testament, TRE 12 (1983) S. 34–42

Albertz, R., Art. Mensch. II. Altes Testament, TRE 22 (1993) S. 464–474

Albertz, R., Persönliche Frömmigkeit und offizielle Religion. Religionsinterner Pluralismus in Israel und Babylon (CThM A9), Stuttgart 1978

Albertz, R., Religionsgeschichte Israels in alttestamentlicher Zeit, 2 Bde. (GAT 8,1-2), Göttingen ²1996/1997

---

63 So Grund-Wittenberg, Kulturanthropologie, Sp. 884. |

Albertz, R., Weltschöpfung und Menschenschöpfung. Untersucht bei Deuterojesaja, Hiob und in den Psalmen (CThM A3), Stuttgart 1974

Albertz, R./Schmitt, R., Family and Household Religion in Ancient Israel and the Levant, Winona Lake, IN 2012 |

Assmann, J., Ägyptische Hymnen und Gebete (Die Bibliothek der Alten Welt), Zürich/München 1975

Assmann, J., Konstellative Anthropologie. Zum Bild des Menschen in Ägypten, in: B. Janowski/ K. Liess (Hg.), Der Mensch im Alten Israel. Neue Forschungen zur alttestamentlichen Anthropologie (HBS 59), Freiburg u. a. 2009, S. 95–120

Brunner, H., Art. Persönliche Frömmigkeit, LÄ IV (1982) S. 951–963

Brunner-Traut, E., Altägyptische Märchen, Düsseldorf/Köln ⁴1976, S. 28–40

Buber, M., Das Dialogische Prinzip, Heidelberg 1962

Charpin, D., Les divinités familiales des Babyloniens d'après les légendes de leurs sceaux-cylindres, in: De la Babylonie à la Syrie, en passant par Mari (FS J.-R. Kupper), hg. v. Ö. Tunca, Liège 1990, S. 59–78

Dietrich, J., Sozialanthropologie des Alten Testaments. Grundfragen zur Relationalität und Sozialität des Menschen im Alten Israel, ZAW 127 (2015) S. 224–243

Frevel, C., Person – Identität – Selbst. Eine Problemanzeige aus alttestamentlicher Perspektive, in: A. Wagner/J. van Oorschot (Hg.), Individualität und Selbstreflexion in den Literaturen des Alten Testaments (VWGTh 48), Leipzig 2017, S. 65–90

Gerstenberger, E. S., Der bittende Mensch. Bittritual und Klagelied des Einzelnen im Alten Testament (WMANT 51), Neukirchen-Vluyn 1980

Greenspahn, F. E., When Brothers Dwell Together. The Preeminence of Younger Siblings in the Hebrew Bible, Oxford 1994

Grohmann, M., Der Anfang des Lebens. Anthropologische Aspekte der Rede von Geburt im Alten Testament, in: B. Janowski/K. Liess (Hg.), Der Mensch im Alten Israel. Neue Forschungen zur alttestamentlichen Anthropologie (HBS 59), Freiburg u. a. 2009, S. 365–399

Grohmann, M., Fruchtbarkeit und Geburt in den Psalmen (FAT 53), Tübingen 2007

Grund-Wittenberg, A., Kulturanthropologie und Altes Testament, ThLZ 141 (2016) S. 873–888

Janowski, B., Anerkennung und Gegenseitigkeit. Zum konstellativen Personbegriff im Alten Testament, in: ders./K. Liess (Hg.), Der Mensch im Alten Israel. Neue Forschungen zur alttestamentlichen Anthropologie (HBS 59), Freiburg u. a. 2009, S. 181–211

Janowski, B., Anthropologie des Alten Testaments. Grundfragen – Kontexte – Themenfelder. Mit einem Quellenanhang und zahlreichen Abbildungen, Tübingen 2019

Janowski, B., Der ganze Mensch im Alten Israel. Zu den Koordinaten der alttestamentlichen Anthropologie, in: ders., Das hörende Herz. Beiträge zur Theologie und Anthropologie des Alten Testaments 6, Göttingen 2018, S. 3–30

Janowski, B., Persönlichkeitszeichen. Ein Beitrag zum Personenverständnis des Alten Testaments, in: A. Wagner/J. van Oorschot (Hg.), Individualität und Selbstreflexion in den Literaturen des Alten Testaments (VWGTh 48), Leipzig 2017, S. 315–340 |

Nave-Herz, R., Art. Familiensoziologie, in: G. Endruweit/G. Trommersdorff (Hg.), Wörterbuch der Soziologie (UTB 2232), Stuttgart ²2002, S. 148–152

Rad, G. von, Theologie des Alten Testaments, 2 Bde., München ⁴1962/³1960

Robinson, H. W., The Hebrew Concept of Corporate Personality, in: J. Hempel (Hg.), Werden und Wesen des Alten Testaments (BZAW 66), Berlin 1936, S. 49–52

Smend, R., Über das Ich in den Psalmen, ZAW 8 (1888) S. 49–147

Spieckermann, H., Heilsgegenwart. Eine Theologie der Psalmen (FRLANT 148), Göttingen 1989

Stade, B., Geschichte des Volkes Israels, 2 Bde., Berlin 1887/88

Toorn, K. van der, Family Religion in Babylonia, Syria and Israel. Studies in the History and Culture of the Ancient Near East 7, Leiden/New York/Köln 1996

Vito, R. A. di, Old Testament Anthropology and the Construction of Personal Identity, in: CBQ 61 (1999) S. 217–238

Wilke, A. F., „Ich aber!" – Identität und Sprache im Gebet des Psalters, in: F. Wilk (Hg.), Identität und Sprache. Prozesse jüdischer und christlicher Identitätsbildung im Rahmen der Antike (BThSt 174), Göttingen 2018, S. 89–113

Wolff, H. W., Anthropologie des Alten Testaments, München [3]1977

Zernecke, A. E., Gott und Mensch in den Klagepsalmen. Die Handerhebungsgebete Ištar 2 und Ištar 10 und die Klagepsalmen Ps 38 und Ps 22 im Vergleich (AOAT 387), Münster 2011

Zgoll, A., Der betende Mensch. Zur Anthropologie in Mesopotamien, in: B. Janowski/K. Liess (Hg.), Der Mensch im Alten Israel. Neue Forschungen zur alttestamentlichen Anthropologie (HBS 59), Freiburg u. a. 2009, S. 121–140

Zgoll, A., Die Kunst des Betens. Form und Funktion, Theologie und Psychagogik in babylonisch-assyrischen Handerhebungsgebeten an Ištar (AOAT 308), Münster 2003

4 Anthropologie

Einführung

Als Schüler von Claus Westermann, der mit seinen zahlreichen Arbeiten über die Urgeschichte, die Psalmen und die Weisheit zu den Pionieren einer Alttestamentlichen Anthropologie gehört,[1] habe ich mich natürlich in der Vergangenheit immer wieder auch mit anthropologischen Fragestellungen beschäftigt.[2] Die in diesem Kapitel aufgenommenen neueren Beiträge zu anthropologischen Themen verdanken sich allerdings eher thematischen Vorgaben, die ambitionierte Herausgeber und Herausgeberinnen gemacht haben, um den von ihnen betreuten Festschriften ein interessantes einheitliches Outfit zu verleihen. Nun gut, es gibt die verschiedensten Möglichkeiten, wie man dazu gebracht werden kann, sich neu oder noch einmal intensiver mit Themen zu beschäftigen, auf die man von alleine nicht gekommen wäre.

Dies gilt insbesondere für die soziale, psychologische und religiöse Bedeutung, die der Mahlzeit in der Bibel neben ihrer biologischen Funktion der Nahrungsaufnahme zukommt. Deren Untersuchung ist in der bisherigen Forschungsgeschichte ziemlich vernachlässigt worden. Mein Beitrag „Die soziale und rituelle Bedeutung von Essen und Trinken in der Jakoberzählung" stößt auf die bisher übersehene Einsicht, dass die gesamte Jakob-Esau-Komposition durch eine ganze Abfolge von Mahlzeit-Erzählungen, beginnend mit der Anekdote vom „Linsengericht Esaus" (Gen 25,29–34), fortgeführt durch die ausführliche Schilderung von Isaaks rituellem Segensmahl (Gen 27) und endend mit dem Bericht vom feierlichen Vertrags- und Opfermahl Jakobs und Labans (Gen 31,43–32,1a), strukturiert wird. Dabei wird aufgezeigt, wie der konfliktreiche Kampf Jakobs um sein Lebensrecht die soziale und religiöse Bedeutung der Mahlzeit schwer beschädigt und erst gegen Ende ihre normale, Gemeinschaft stiftende Funktion möglich wird.

Bekanntlich gehört zum „konstellativen Menschenbild" der Hebräischen Bibel neben dem Bezug des Menschen zu sich selber und zu anderen Menschen auch die Beziehung zu Gott konstitutiv hinzu. So brachte mich die Vorgabe des herausfordernden Titels der Festschrift für Jürgen Ebach „Fragen wider die Ant-

---

1 Ihm wird darum auch in dem von Bernd Janowski, Alexandra Grund-Wittenberg, Jan Dietrich und Ute Neumann-Gorsolke herausgegebenen „Handbuch der alttestamentlichen Anthropologie" (HAA), das bald erscheinen wird, ein eigener Artikel gewidmet sein.
2 Man vergleiche etwa R. Albertz, Art. Mensch II. Altes Testament, in: TRE XXII (1993), 464–474, oder die ersten sieben Beiträge zum altisraelitischen und babylonischen Menschenbild in dem ersten Band meiner gesammelten Aufsätze: R. Albertz, Geschichte und Theologie. Studien zur Exegese des Alten Testaments und zur Religionsgeschichte Israels, hrsg. von Ingo Kottsieper und Jakob Wöhrle (BZAW 326), Berlin/New York 2003, 1–156.

https://doi.org/10.1515/9783111202228-017

worten" dazu, angesichts der jüngeren Diskussion über die alttestamentlichen Klagepsalmen genauer über die in diesen Psalmen an Gott gerichteten anklagenden Fragen nachzudenken. Der zweite Beitrag dieses Kapitels „Warum ‚Wozu'? Zur Pragmatik der an Gott gerichteten Fragen in den Klagegebeten der Hebräischen Bibel" führt zu dem Ergebnis, dass die „Warum"-Fragen in den Klagepsalmen keineswegs, wie zuweilen unterstellt, auf eine Antwort über den Grund des Leids abzielen, sondern vielmehr als harte Vorwürfe anzusehen sind, die Gott zu einer Änderung seines unverständlichen und inakzeptablen Verhaltens bewegen wollen. Von daher erweist sich deren neuerdings aufgrund etymologischer Erwägungen vorgeschlagene Verständnis als „Wozu"-Fragen, die auf den Zweck und Sinn des göttlichen Handelns abzielten, als fraglich, der von Claus Westermann in den Schrecken der Nazi-Zeit und des Zweiten Weltkriegs wiederentdeckte Protestcharakter vieler alttestamentlicher Klagegebete dagegen als zutreffend.[3]

Der dritte Beitrag „Erotik und Sexualität in den Gesetzen der Torah. Nicht nur ein Störfaktor, sondern auch ein Menschenrecht" ist ein Unikum. Er verdankt sich allein dem besonderen Thema, das für die Festschrift meines Freundes Manfred Oeming ausgewählt wurde. Ich selber hatte mich bisher noch nie – abgesehen von der Auslegung der wenigen einschlägigen Passagen in meinem Exoduskommentar[4] – grundlegend wissenschaftlich zu dieser Thematik geäußert. Ich war somit stark gefordert. Die Untersuchung hat zu dem auch für mich erstaunlichen Ergebnis geführt, dass die Gesetze der Tora, obgleich sie sich vornehmlich mit der Aufgabe beschäftigen, das gesellschaftlich und familiär gefährliche Potential von Eros und Sexualität einzudämmen, daneben auch darum besorgt sind, insbesondere jungen und sozial schwachen Menschen, etwa Sklavinnen und weiblichen Kriegsgefangenen, ein Recht auf Erotik und Sexualität zuzubilligen.

Die Einladung, einen Aufsatz zur Festschrift meines Freundes Saul Olyan beizusteuern, von dem ich viel über eine ethnologisch, soziologisch und psychologisch fundierte „Social Anthropology" gelernt habe,[5] brachte mich auf die Idee, dessen schöne Monographie zur Freundschaft in der Hebräischen Bibel[6] durch eine Untersuchung der Geschwister-, insbesondere der Bruder-Beziehungen zu komplimentieren, da letztere häufig einen wichtigen Referenzpunkt für erstere bilden. So steht der vierte und letzte Beitrag in diesem Kapitel unter dem Titel

---

3 Vgl. dazu auch meinen Aufsatz „The Legacy of Claus Westermann for Theology and Church", S. 355–367 im vorliegenden Band.

4 Vgl. zu Ex 21,2–11 und 22,15–16 R. Albertz, Exodus, Bd. 2: Ex 19–40 (ZBK.AT 2.2), Zürich 2015, 88–89.100–101.

5 Vgl. hierzu meinen Aufsatz „Ethnische und kultische Konzepte in der Politik Nehemias", S. 45–62 im vorliegenden Band.

6 S. S. M. Olyan, Friendship in the Hebrew Bible (AYBRL), New Haven/London 2017.

„Ambivalent Relations between Brothers in the Hebrew Bible"; auch dieses eine bisher eher unterbelichtete Thematik in der Biblischen Anthropologie. Eine Besonderheit der Hebräischen Bibel scheint mir dabei zu sein, dass sie, obwohl sie das in der antiken Welt weit verbreitete Ideal brüderlicher Solidarität und Hilfsbereitschaft teilt und in der deuteronomischen Bruderschaftsethik sogar über die Familienbande hinaus auf die ganze judäische Gesellschaft ausweitet, die Konflikte zwischen Brüdern so realistisch und brutal wie sonst nirgends in vielen ihrer Erzählungen ausmalt.

Die soziale und rituelle Bedeutung von Essen und Trinken in der Jakoberzählung

Rainer Kessler gehört zu den wenigen alttestamentlichen Forschern, die auf vorbildliche Weise eine intensive und theoretisch fundierte sozialgeschichtliche Forschung mit einer detailgenauen philologischen Exegese und einer tiefgehenden theologischen Reflexion verbunden haben. Darum möchte ich dem Freund und Namensvetter aus alten Heidelberger Tagen, von dessen Arbeit ich viel gelernt habe, einen kleinen Beitrag widmen, der anhand der Jakob-Esau-Erzählung einige Winkel sowohl der sozialen als auch der religiösen Funktionen des Essens und Trinkens in der Hebräischen Bibel auszuleuchten sucht. Möge er ihm beim literarischen Festmahl, das ihm seine Freunde und Kollegen bereitet haben, so gut munden wie die ‚Leckerbissen' (מטעמים *mat'amim*),[1] die Jakob alias Esau seinem Vater durch die Kochkunst seiner Mutter zubereitet hat!

1 Befund und Fragestellung

In den wenigen Arbeiten zu Essen und Trinken im Alten Testament[2] ist es bisher nicht aufgefallen, dass in der Jakoberzählung (Gen 25,19–33,17*) gleich mehrfach von Mahlzeiten die Rede ist: Gleich am Anfang, nach der einleiten|den Exposition (25,21–26a.27 f.) steht die eigentümliche Anekdote, wie Jakob seinem Bruder Esau für ein Linsengericht sein Erstgeburtsrecht abkauft (25,29–34). Es folgt dann – nach dem erst nachträglich eingeschobenen Kapitel 26 – in Gen 27 sogleich die

---

1 Vgl. Gen 27,4.7.9.14.17.(31). Im positiven Sinne kommt dieses Wort in der Hebräischen Bibel überhaupt nur in der Jakob-Esau-Erzählung vor. In der Weisheit wird dagegen vor den feinen und leckeren Speisen der Oberschicht gewarnt: Spr 23,3.6; Sir 31,21; 37,29.
2 S. Rudolf Smend, Essen und Trinken – ein Stück Weltlichkeit des Alten Testaments, in: Herbert Donner u. a. (Hg.), Beiträge zur alttestamentlichen Theologie. FS W. Zimmerli, Göttingen 1977, 446–459, und Eleonore Schmitt, Das Essen in der Bibel. Literaturethnologische Aspekte des Alltäglichen, Studien zur Kulturanthropologie 2, Münster 1994. Smend erwähnt Gen 25,34 als ein Beispiel dafür, „daß ‚Essen und Trinken' nicht nur eine gute Normalität, sondern auch ungute und gefährliche Zustände bezeichnen kann" (450) und Gen 31,43–54 als ein Beispiel für die Zusammengehörigkeit von Vertrag und gemeinsamer Mahlzeit (455). Letzteres erwähnt auch Schmitt (134), sie übergeht aber die Erzählung vom Linsengericht. Von beiden nicht gewürdigt wird das rituelle Segensmahl von Gen 27. Noch weniger bekommt die neueste Untersuchung von Nathan MacDonald, Not Bread Alone. | The Uses of Food in the Old Testament, Oxford 2008, die Jakoberzählung in den Blick, die den Anspruch erhebt, das lange vernachlässigte Thema endlich umfassend zu behandeln (vii; 2). Gen 25,29 f. und 31,43–54 werden nur *en passant* erwähnt (95, Anm. 68; 143; 193), Gen 27 wird gar nicht beachtet.

https://doi.org/10.1515/9783111202228-018

detailliert gestaltete Erzählung, wie Jakob seinen Bruder Esau um den väterlichen Segen betrügt. Die rituelle Segenshandlung ist dabei mit einem besonderen Festmahl für den Vater Isaak verbunden, dessen – manipulierte – Zubereitung und Durchführung im Einzelnen geschildert werden (V. 4–17.24–29.31–33). Am Ende der Erzählungen von Jakobs Aufenthalt bei seinem Onkel Laban steht schließlich ein feierliches Mahl (31,46) bzw. Opfermahl (V. 54) der beiden Parteien, das deren Konflikt durch einen Vertrag beilegt (31,43–32,2a). Dagegen fehlt ein vergleichbares Mahl bei der Aussöhnung Jakobs mit Esau am Ende der Komposition (33,1–17).

Eleonore Schmitt hat in ihrer literaturethnologischen Studie darauf aufmerksam gemacht, dass die Verfasser der biblischen Texte das Motiv von Essen und Trinken nicht einfach wahllos verwenden, sondern dort einsetzen, „wo sie entweder wirklichkeitsgetreu oder verfremdet Situationen kennzeichnen, Personen charakterisieren, Handlungsabschnitte einleiten oder beenden, Textteile miteinander verknüpfen, Themen motivisch ausgestalten, Erwartungshaltungen über den weiteren Textfortgang erzeugen, Bewertungen und Interpretationen initiieren".[3] So machte sie etwa auf die strukturierende und die Handlung vorantreibende Funktion des Motivs in der Hannaerzählung (1 Sam 1,7.9.14), der Erzählung von Nabots Weinberg (1 Kön 21,4.7) und im Buch Rut (1,3.6; 2.9.14; 3,7.15.17; 4,16) aufmerksam.[4] Es stellt sich somit die Frage, ob der Verfasser, der die Jakoberzählung – wie Erhard Blum gezeigt hat[5] – zwar teilweise unter Verwendung älteren Materials, aber doch als ein literarisch einheitliches Werk geschaffen hat, ebenfalls mit der Gestaltung und Anordnung seiner Mahlszenen eine erkennbare Absicht verfolgte. Damit beschränke ich mich auf die erste Ausgabe der Jakoberzählung Gen 25,21–33,17*, wie sie Blum überzeugend rekonstruiert hat.[6] |

---

3 Schmitt, Essen, 7.

4 Vgl. Schmitt, Essen, 139–142.

5 S. Erhard Blum, Die Komposition der Vätergeschichte, WMANT 57, Neukirchen-Vluyn 1984, 202 f.

6 S. Blum, Komposition, 7–203. Diese Analyse ist von Johannes Taschner, Verheißung und Erfüllung in der Jakoberzählung (Gen 25,19–33,17). Eine Analyse ihres Spannungsbogens, HBS 27, Freiburg u. a. 2000, zwar an einigen Stellen variiert, aber nicht grundsätzlich in Frage gestellt worden. Im Einzelnen rechne ich dieser Kom|position zu: Gen 25,21–26a.27–30a.31–34; 27,1–40a.41–44.45aα²βb; 28,10–13aα.16–21a.22; 29,1–30,20.22–43; 31,1–2.4–16.19–21aα.b.22–46.48–53aα.b.54; 32,1–9.14–32; 33,1–17. Ihr Anfang ist durch die sog. „Priesterschrift", die im Bereich der Jakoberzählung eindeutig eine Bearbeitung darstellt (Gen 25,19 f.26b; 26,34 f.; 27,46–28,9; 31,17 f.), verdrängt worden. Vorpriesterliche Ergänzungen im o. g. Textbereich sind meiner Meinung nach: 1. Eine Einfügung der Überlieferung von weiteren Jakobsöhnen: Gen 30,21 als Verklammerung der Dina-Erzählung (Gen 34,1–31); 2. Die Verklammerung von Abrahams- und Jakobsgeschichte in der ersten Ausgabe der exilischen Vätergeschichte (VG¹): Gen 28,13aβb.14; 26,1–3aα.6–23.25–33. Hinzu kommt 3. Eine spätdeuteronomistische Bearbeitung: Gen 26,3aβ–5.24; 28,15.21b; 31,3; 32,10–

2 Das im Konkurrenzkampf der Brüder depravierte Mahl

Nachdem der Erzähler schon in der Einleitung seiner Komposition dargestellt hatte, wie sich die Zwillinge im Mutterleib streiten und bei ihrer Geburt um ihren Vorrang kämpfen (Gen 25,21–26a), typisiert er in seiner Exposition (V. 27 f.) die beiden durch gegensätzliche Berufe und Lebensweisen: Esau, der Erstgeborene, entwickelt sich zum kundigen Jäger, der auf dem freien Feld herumstreift, um seines Wildbrets vom Vater geliebt; Jakob, der Zweitgeborene, wird dagegen ein gesitteter Mann, der sich lieber zuhause umtut und von der Mutter ins Herz geschlossen wird.

Die Fortsetzung des Konkurrenzkampfes der ungleichen Brüder schildert der Erzähler unter Aufnahme einer kleinen Anekdote (Gen 25,29–34) an einem sehr ungewöhnlichen Verlauf einer Mahlzeit: Jakob hatte gerade ein Gericht zubereitet, als Esau total erschöpft vom freien Feld heimkam und in wilder Gier zu essen begehrte: „Lass mich doch fressen[7] von dem Roten, dem | Roten da, denn ich bin (so) erschöpft!" (V. 30a).[8] Sein Heißhunger fegt alle Esskultur hinweg, er reduziert das Essen auf eine quasi animalische Nahrungsaufnahme. Doch auch Jakob, so

---

13, die, nachdem deutlich geworden ist, dass erst P den Übergang zum Exodusbuch geschaffen hat (vgl. Konrad Schmid, Erzväter und Exodus. Untersuchungen zur doppelten Begründung der Ursprünge Israels innerhalb der Geschichtsbücher des Alten Testaments, WMANT 81, Neukirchen-Vluyn 1999, 152 f.; Jan Christian Gertz, Tradition und Redaktion in der Exoduserzählung. Untersuchungen zur Endredaktion des Pentateuch, FRLANT 186, Göttingen 2000, 352–366; akzeptiert von Erhard Blum, Die literarische Verbindung von Erzvätern und Exodus. Ein Gespräch mit neueren Endredaktionshypothesen, in: Jan Christian Gertz u. a., Abschied vom Jahwisten. Die Komposition des Hexateuch in der jüngsten Diskussion, BZAW 315, Berlin u. a. 2002, 119–156, bes. 145–151), nachpriesterlich eingeordnet werden muss. Aus noch späterer Zeit stammen 4. Die Ergänzungen der Hexateuchredaktion: Gen 31,21aβ; 33,19; 35,1–4. Vereinzelte Glossen und Ergänzungen finden sich in Gen 25,30b; 27,40b.45aα[1]; 31,47.53aβ; 32,33.

7 Das nur hier vorkommende Verb לעט *l't* hat wahrscheinlich wie להט *lht* die Bedeutung „verschlingen" (Ps 57,5), vgl. die mhe. Bedeutungen „verschlucken, füttern" und syr. *lū'aṭā* „Kinnlade". Mit Recht betont Benno Jacob, Das Buch Genesis, Berlin 1934; Nachdruck Stuttgart 2000, 545, die animalische Konnotation des Verbs. Wenn Taschner, Verheißung, 33, meint, das seltene Verb sei nur wegen seiner Ähnlichkeit | zu מטעמים *mat'amim* ‚Leckerbissen' in Gen 27,4 u. ö. gewählt und bedeute im Hif. nur „essen lassen", dann wird das der emotionalen Sprache des Verses nicht gerecht. Erst die LXX gibt Esaus derben Ausruf in Hochsprache wieder: „Lass mich kosten von diesem roten Gekochten."

8 Die Nebenbemerkung V. 30b „deswegen nennt man ihn Edom", die Esaus Bezeichnung des Linsengerichts explizit auf den Volksnamen ausdeutet und den Dialog unterbricht, ist wohl eine erklärende Glosse, so Hermann Gunkel, Genesis, HK I/1, Göttingen ³1910; Nachdruck ⁷1966, 297; Claus Westermann, Genesis. 2. Teilband: Genesis 12–36, BK I/2, Neukirchen-Vluyn 1981, 508; Horst Seebass, Genesis II/2: Vätergeschichte II (23,1–36,43), Neukirchen-Vluyn 1999, 273; nicht ganz sicher ist sich Blum, Komposition, 73.

verdeutlicht der Erzähler, machte noch nicht einmal den Versuch, Esau zu brem-
sen und seine Essgier in gesittetere Bahnen zu lenken, sondern er nutzte eiskalt
die momentane Schwäche Esaus aus, um ihm für das heißbegehrte Essen sein
Erstgeburtsrecht abzukaufen (V. 31). Wenn Esau auf diesen überraschenden Vor-
schlag seines Bruders erwiderte: „Siehe, ich bin dabei zu sterben,[9] was soll mir
da das Erstgeburtsrecht?" (V. 32), dann ist damit wahrscheinlich nicht ein Hinweis
auf sein späteres Todesschicksal,[10] sondern auf seine akute Notlage gemeint.[11]
Es war nicht purer Leichtsinn, der ihn bewog, auf die eigentlich unverschämte
Forderung seines Bruders einzugehen, sondern seine momentane Erschöpfung
erschien ihm so lebensbedrohlich, dass ihm darüber sein Status in der Zukunft
egal war. Doch auch diese dumpfe Klage seines Bruders bewog Jakob nicht, ihm
endlich etwas zu essen zu geben. In kluger Voraussicht, dass Esau seine Zustimmung schnell wieder abstreiten könnte, wenn er erst einmal wieder zu Kräften
käme, ließ Jakob seinen Bruder schwören, um dem erpressten Handel Gültigkeit
zu verleihen. Erst dann tischte Jakob Esau das Linsengericht[12] auf. Befriedigt über
seinen Sieg spendierte er seinem unterlegenen Bruder sogar noch Brot und etwas
zu trinken (V. 34a). Wenn es vom eigent|lichen Mahl nur heißt: „Da aß er und
trank, stand auf und ging fort", dann zeichnet das weniger „karikierend den
stumpfen, rohen Jäger",[13] sondern das Elend eines Essens in zerrütteter Gemeinschaft, das ohne Gespräche, ohne Freude und gegenseitige Anteilnahme zur bloßen Einverleibung von Nahrung verkommen ist.

Man ermisst das ganze Ausmaß der Depravation, wenn man die Schilderung
von Gen 25,29–34 auf den Hintergrund der Erkenntnisse der Soziologie des Essens
stellt.[14] Diese betont, dass das menschliche Essen im Unterschied zum animali-

---

9 Vgl. zur Konstruktion des *Ptz. akt.* von הלך *hlk* „gehen" mit *Inf. cons.* +ל Gen 25,32; Ri 14,3; 17,9; Jes 30,2.
10 So Gunkel, Genesis, 298. Wendungen mit הלך *hlk*, die das allgemeine Todesschicksal um-
schreiben, lauten anders: „den Weg aller Welt gehen" (Jos 23,14; 1 Kön 2,2) o.ä.
11 So richtig Gerhard von Rad, Das erste Buch Mose. Genesis, ATD 2/4, Göttingen [7]1964, 232;
Westermann, Genesis, 510; ersterer gibt den Ausdruck mit „Ich sterbe ja vor Hunger", letzterer
mit „Ich sterbe fast vor Hunger" wieder.
12 Die Linse gehört zu den ältesten Kulturpflanzen im Vorderen Orient, vgl. Michael Zohary,
Pflanzen der Bibel, Stuttgart 1983, 82. Die nahrhafte Hülsenfrucht konnte in gekochter Form für
Suppen und Breie verwendet werden, oder ihr gemahlenes Mehl zusammen mit dem aus ande-
ren Getreidekörnern zum Backen von Kuchen. |
13 So Westermann, Genesis, 511.
14 Vgl. Georg Simmel, Soziologie der Mahlzeit, in: ders., Brücke und Tür. Essays des Philosophen
zur Geschichte, Religion, Kunst und Gesellschaft, hg. von Michael Landmann/Margarete Sus-
mann, Stuttgart 1957, 243–250; Mary Douglas, Deciphering a Meal, in: dies., Implicit Meanings.
Essays in Anthropology, London u. a. 1975 [= 1984], 249–275, bes. 254–260; dies., Standard Social
Uses of Food. Introduction, in: dies. (Hg.), Food in the Social Order. Studies of Food and Festivities
in the Three American Communities, New York 1984, 1–39, bes. 7–25; und umfassend: Eva Barlösius,

schen Fressen mehr als eine bloße Einverleibung von Nahrung darstellt. Vielmehr ist der für das Überleben notwendige biologische Vorgang von Essen und Trinken kulturell überformt. In der Mahlzeit wird einerseits die Relation des Menschen zur Speise und anderseits die Relation der Tischgenossen untereinander aufwendig gestaltet. „Beim Gastmahl wird die Nahrungsaufnahme zum bloßen Mittel der Realisierung intersubjektiver Beziehungen".[15] Darum ist das Essen für die personale Identitätsbildung konstitutiv. Die Inszenierung des Essens in der Mahlzeit ist zugleich Ausdruck personaler und kultureller Identität. Darum hat die menschliche Mahlzeit über die biologische Funktion hinaus normalerweise immer auch kulturelle, psychologische und soziale Funktionen.[16]

Was für die Mahlzeiten im Allgemeinen gilt, ist erst recht gültig für die Mahlzeiten in der Familie; lässt sich doch der familiäre Haushalt als Wohn- und Konsumtionsgemeinschaft definieren.[17] „Es kennzeichnet die häuslichen Lebensgemeinschaften aller Kulturen und Epochen, daß sie den Alltag durch Mahlzeiten gliedern. Dadurch werden die dort stattfindenden Mahlzeiten wie kaum eine andere Einrichtung des menschlichen Zusammenlebens zu einer mit größter Regelmäßigkeit wiederkehrenden, somit erwartbaren Situation | der Teilhabe und des Austauschs unter *Verschiedenen* (Männern und Frauen, Eltern und Kindern, Älteren und Jüngeren, Gleich- und Minderberechtigten, Höher- und Niedriggestellten usw.). Die Mahlzeit der häuslichen Lebensgemeinschaft ist somit wie keine andere menschliche Einrichtung der Ort, an dem das Individuum das, was es ‚ist‘, in der Differenz zu anderen erfährt und bestätigt bekommt und an dem ihm zugleich sein Wert als Person verdeutlicht wird."[18]

Zwar wird Gen 25,29–34 nicht als eine der regelmäßigen Familienmahlzeiten geschildert, aber eben doch als eine Mahlzeit im Raum der Familie. Auch diese außergewöhnliche Mahlzeit hätte zu einer Situation der Teilhabe und des Austauschs der unterschiedlichen Brüder werden können, wenn sie denn gewollt hätten. Aber indem Esau die Mahlzeit in seiner Gier auf ihre bloße biologische Funktion reduzierte (V. 30) und Jakob seine Verfügung über die von ihm zubereitete Speise als Waffe im Kampf gegen seine Benachteiligung missbrauchte (V. 31),

---

Soziologie des Essens. Eine Sozial- und kulturwissenschaftliche Einführung in die Ernährungsforschung, Weinheim/München 1999, 25–47; 168–198.

15 Ferdinand Fellmann, Kulturelle und personale Identität, in: Hans Jürgen Teuteberg u. a. (Hg.), Essen und kulturelle Identität. Europäische Perspektiven, Kulturthema Essen Bd. 2, Berlin 1997, 27–36, 35.

16 S. Schmitt, Essen, 7.

17 Vgl. David I. Kertzer, Household History and Sociological Theory, ARS 17 (1991), 155–179, bes. 156. |

18 Arnold Zingerle, Identitätsbildung bei Tische. Theoretische Vorüberlegungen aus kultursoziologischer Sicht, in: Teuteberg, Essen, 69–86, bes. 80 f.

anstatt sie mit seinem Bruder gemeinsam zu verzehren, brachen die soziale und psychologische Funktion des Mahles vollständig weg. Dieses verkam zu einem dumpfen Fressen.[19]

Nun wollte der biblische Verfasser, wie aus dem Wortanklang zwischen der roten Speise (אָדֹם) und Edom (אֱדֹם) in Gen 25,30 deutlich wird, nicht bloß familiäre, sondern auch politische Verhältnisse darstellen. Aber indem er den Aufstieg Israels über das ältere Edom auf die familiäre Ebene projiziert, zeigt er anhand des depravierten Mahles, wie verletzlich die kulturellen Institutionen menschlichen Zusammenlebens sind. Zwar kann er am Ende der Erzählung nur seine Verwunderung über die Leichtfertigkeit Esaus ausdrücken, mit der dieser aus einer augenblicklichen Not heraus seine Zukunftsansprüche preisgab (V. 34b). Aber er weist auch auf, dass Jakobs allzu clevere und unsolidarische Aufstiegsambitionen wesentliche Errungenschaften menschlicher Kultur, wie sie in der kulturellen Überformung des Essens und Trinkens greifbar sind, zu beschädigen drohen. So habe ich meine Zweifel, ob Gunkel die Intention der Anekdote richtig bestimmt hat, wenn er sagt: „Die Sage lacht den dummen Esau aus, der seine ganze Zukunft um ein Linsengericht verkauft hat, und jubelt über den klugen Jaqob, in dem die Erzähler ihr eigenes Bild wiedererkennen."[20] Ich meine, der Erzähler ist hier am Anfang seiner Erzähl|komposition durchaus selbstkritischer: Selbst wenn man sich über den Aufstieg Israels freuen mag, bleibt einem doch der Jubel angesichts der tief gestörten familiären Mahlgemeinschaft am Ende im Halse stecken.

3 Das im Konkurrenzkampf der Brüder manipulierte rituelle Segensmahl

Die ausgeführte Erzählung Gen 27 stellt im Aufbau der Jakobkomposition eine Parallele zur kurzen Anekdote 25,29–34 dar, insofern sich Jakob hier sein Vorrecht gegenüber seinem Bruder durch die Erschleichung des väterlichen Segens sichert. Doch hinsichtlich der in diesem Kapitel geschilderten Mahlzeiten könnten die Unterschiede kaum größer sei: An die Stelle einer schlichten *ad hoc* Mahlzeit (Gen 25) tritt hier ein aufwendiges Festmahl aus Anlass einer besonderen familiären Segenszeremonie; statt einer zur ungeordneten Fresserei depravierten Mahl-

---

19 Simmel, Soziologie, 244, hat treffend das erstaunliche Paradoxon beschrieben, dass – normalerweise – in der menschlichen Mahlzeit ausgerechnet „an die exklusive Selbstsucht des Essens eine Häufigkeit des Zusammenseins, eine Gewöhnung an das Vereinigtsein" geknüpft ist. Gen 25,29–34 beschreibt, wie zerbrechlich diese Verknüpfung ist.
20 Gunkel, Genesis, 299. |

zeit wird hier eine rituell geordnete Speisung des alten Vaters inszeniert; und während in Gen 25 die Mahlzeit auf die bloße Nahrungsaufnahme reduziert war, werden in Gen 27 die sozialen, psychologischen und religiösen Funktionen des Essens regelrecht zelebriert.

Es gibt wohl kaum einen anderen Text in der Hebräischen Bibel, in dem die einzelnen Phasen des Essens, welche die Soziologen herausgearbeitet haben,[21] das Beschaffen der Nahrung (V. 3.9.14.20), das Zubereiten (עשׂה: V. 4.7.9.14.31) und die Verteilung (בוא Hif.: V. 4.7.10.25.33) der Speise sowie der Verzehr der Mahlzeit (אכל: V. 4.7.10.19.25a.25b.31.33) in dieser Detaillierung erwähnt werden.

Unter Rückgriff auf die schon in Gen 25,27 f. angeordnete Exposition, die von der unterschiedlichen Vorliebe der Eltern für ihre ungleichen Söhne berichtete, setzt der Erzähler in Gen 27 damit ein, dass der alt und blind gewordene Isaak dem von ihm bevorzugten größeren Sohn Esau den Auftrag erteilte, ihm sein geliebtes Wildbret zu jagen, um ihm davon einen Leckerbissen zuzubereiten, den er essen wolle, um ihm vor seinem Tod den väterlichen Segen zu erteilen (V. 1–4). Doch zur vollen Ausführung dieses Auftrages kommt es nicht. Rebekka griff in die Vorbereitung des Segensmahles ein, indem sie den von ihr geliebten kleineren Sohn anstiftete, sich den väterlichen Segen zu erschleichen und ihn dabei mit ihrem klugen Rat und ihren guten | Kochkünsten unterstützte (V. 5–17). Mit den von der Mutter zubereiteten Leckerbissen von der heimischen Weide ausgestattet und mit den Festkleidern Esaus und Fellauflagen verkleidet, gelang es Jakob, seinen blinden, aber durchaus misstrauischen alten Vater zu täuschen (V. 18–23), sodass er das Segensritual an seinem jüngeren Sohn vollzog.[22] Dieses begann mit einer förmlichen Identifikation des zu Segnenden (V. 24). Darauf folgte das Segensmahl Isaaks als des Segensspenders (V. 25). Dessen Besonderheit besteht darin, dass der Vater es allein in der trauten Gegenwart seines Sohnes einnahm. Auf seine Aufforderung hin war Jakob nah an ihn herangetreten, hatte ihm die so geliebte leckere Fleischspeise vorgelegt und ihn auf eigenen Antrieb hin mit Wein bedient (V. 25). Es ist wohl davon auszugehen, dass Jakob während der ganzen Mahlzeit schweig- und aufmerksam bei seinem genüsslich speisenden Vater verharrte und ihm immer wieder auflegte und einschenkte. Die große Intimität,

---

21 Jack Goody, Cooking, Cuisine, and Class. A Study in Comparative Sociology, Cambridge 1982 [= 1996], 37, unterschied die Phasen: *production, distribution, preparation, consumption* und *disposal*. Bis auf die Abfallbeseitigung sind in Gen 27 alle Phasen erwähnt. |

22 V. 23 ist, wie schon Westermann, Genesis, 535, gezeigt hat, keine Doublette zu V. 27, sondern resümiert das folgende Geschehen, das dann in V. 24 mit dem förmlichen Ritual einsetzt; ähnlich Blum, Komposition, 83 f.; Martin Leuenberger, Segen und Segenstheologien im alten Israel. Untersuchungen zu ihren religionsgeschichtlichen und theologiegeschichtlichen Konstellationen und Transformationen, AThANT 90, Zürich 2008, 231, gegen Seebass, Genesis, 301; 307, der den Vers nach wie vor „verquer im Kontext" stehen sieht.

die sich während der Dauer des Segensmahls zwischen Vater und Sohn aufgebaut hatte, fand schließlich darin ihren körperlichen Ausdruck, dass Isaak seinen Sohn nach dem Mahl noch näher zu sich heranbat und zum Kuss aufforderte (V. 26). Aus dieser intimen körperlichen Berührung heraus, die so eng war, dass Isaak vom Geruch der Kleider seines Sohnes umhüllt und inspiriert wurde, erging dann der väterliche Segensspruch (V. 27). Mit ihm wünschte der alte Isaak auf seinen Sohn, den er für Esau hielt, Gottes überreiche Segensgaben und die Herrschaft über Völker und Brüder herab (V. 28 f.).[23]

In der Forschung ist umstritten, wie in dem oben nachgezeichneten Ritus Mahlzeit und Segnung näherhin zusammenhängen.[24] Auf der einen Seite stehen Forscher, die einen sozial-psychologischen Zusammenhang annehmen wollen. Ihn beschreibt etwa Benno Jacob mit den Worten: „Zum Segnen gehört eine Hochstimmung der Seele ... Dies wird bei dem engen Zusammen | hang zwischen Leib und Seele gefördert durch körperliches Wohlbehagen, das hervorgerufen wird von den wohltuenden Reizungen durch Essen, Trinken und Wohlgeruch, um so mehr, wenn sie von dem zu Segnenden kommen und für ihn einnehmen."[25] Ähnlich heißt es bei Christopher W. Mitchell, der allerdings die soziale Seite noch etwas stärker herausstreicht: „Isaac simply wants a delicious meal from Esau so that he will be full and content, in a good mood to give a benediction ... Isaac asks Esau to show his gratitude for obtaining the blessing by once again giving his father pleasure."[26] Danach dient das gute Mahl dazu, den Segensspender zu beflügeln und das soziale Band zwischen ihm und dem Segensempfänger zu festigen.

Auf der anderen Seite haben Forscher im Gefolge des religionspsychologischen Ansatzes von Johannes Pedersen[27] einen magischen Zusammenhang konstruieren wollen: So schreibt etwa Claus Westermann: „Das ‚magische' Verständ-

---

23 Die Erwähnung von weiteren ‚Brüdern' Jakobs, die es in der Familie Isaaks gar nicht gibt, ist der völkergeschichtlichen Perspektive des Erzählers geschuldet, die er hier bewusst in seiner Familienerzählung durchscheinen lassen wollte. Sie wird in Gen 27,37 explizit auf Esau appliziert. Somit liegt kein literarkritisch auswertbarer Widerspruch vor; gegen Westermann, Genesis, 531; 536 f.; vgl. Blum, Komposition, 69–79.

24 Zum Zusammenhang von Essen und Segnen vgl. auch den Beitrag von Michaela Geiger in diesem Band (Abschnitt 3). [[= Geiger, M., Erinnerungen an das Schlaraffenland. Dtn 8 als Theologie des Essens, in: dies./Maier, Chr./Schmidt, U. (Hg.), Essen und Trinken in der Bibel. Ein literarisches Festmahl für Rainer Kessler zum 65. Geburtstag, Gütersloh: Gütersloher Verlagshaus, 2009, 15–32.]] |

25 Jacob, Genesis, 561.

26 Christopher Wright Mitchell, The meaning of *BRK* „To Bless" in the Old Testament, SBL.DS 95, Atlanta, 1987, 82.

27 Vgl. Johannes Pedersen, Israel. Its Life and Its Culture I–II, London/Copenhagen 1926 [= 1959], 198–200.

nis des Segens zeigt sich daran, daß sich der Segnende, der im Segen seine Lebenskraft an den Sohn weitergibt, durch eine Mahlzeit dafür stärken muß.«[28] Und jüngst ist diese Sicht von Martin Leuenberger noch einmal kräftig unterstrichen worden, wenn er ausführt: „Dieser Konnex (sc. zwischen Essen und Segensvollzug) lässt sich nach wie vor am einfachsten plausibel machen ..., wenn das Essen bzw. näherhin Wildbret und Wein (V. 25) Isaak leib-seelisch stärken und insofern (für moderne Verhältnisse) ‚magisch' seine Segenskraft mehren, die seine נֶפֶשׁ sodann auf Jakob übertragen kann."[29] Insbesondere die Irreversibilität und Einmaligkeit des von Isaak erteilten Segens verweisen für Leuenberger auf dessen „magisch-selbstwirksame Funktionsweise"[30] und die „magische Funktion des Mahls".[31] Nach diesem Verständnis hätte das Mahl die Funktion, die Segenskraft (נֶפֶשׁ) des Segensspenders zu stärken, damit diese im Ritual durch wirkmächtige Handlung (Körperkontakt im Sinne kontagiöser Magie) und wirkmächtiges Wort (Segensspruch) auf den Segensempfänger übertragen werden kann. |

Auch ich habe früher einer solchen „magischen" Interpretation des Segensmahles von Gen 27 angehangen.[32] Aber ich habe inzwischen Zweifel, ob sie dem Text gerecht wird. Sie ist konsequent nur möglich, wenn man, wie Westermann[33] und teilweise Leuenberger,[34] all die Verse, die den Segen auf Gott beziehen (V. 7.27.28), als nachträgliche Theologisierungen aus der ursprünglichen Erzählung ausscheidet. Doch wäre erstens eine Segenserzählung ohne erhaltene Segenssprüche ausgesprochen misslich, weswegen denn auch Leuenberger zumindest V. 28 (und 39) in der ältesten Textform halten will. Damit handelt er sich allerdings das Problem ein, dass durch diesen an Gott gerichteten Segenswunsch seine Vorstellung von einer „magisch-selbstwirksame[n] Funktionsweise von Segen"[35] ein gutes Stück weit relativiert wird.[36] Zweitens setzt der Fortgang der Erzählung in den Versen 37 und 39–40a die Segenssprüche V. 28 f. einschließlich

---

28 Westermann, Genesis, 536; vgl. Claus Westermann, Der Segen in der Bibel und im Handeln der Kirche, München 1968, 56 f.
29 Leuenberger, Segen, 239.
30 A. a. O., 240.
31 A. a. O., 241. |
32 Rainer Albertz, Segen Gottes. Wo ist er erfahrbar? Wie gehen wir damit um?, in: ders., Zorn über das Unrecht. Vom Glauben, der verändern will, Neukirchen-Vluyn 1996, 85–113, bes. 95.
33 Westermann, Genesis, 531, hält die gesamten Segenssprüche V. 27–29 und 39–40 für sekundär, weil sie mit ihrer völkergeschichtlichen Perspektive den familiären Horizont der Erzählung sprengen, auch לפני יהוה „vor JHWH" in V. 7 hält er für einen Einschub.
34 Leuenberger, Segen, 234, streicht לפני יהוה „vor JHWH" in V. 7 und V. 27bβ.29a.40a.
35 A. a. O., 239.
36 Leuenberger, Segen, 237, gesteht ein: „gleichwohl zeigt V. 28, dass man sich vor einseitigen Verabsolutierungen hüten sollte".

des theologisch formulierten Fruchtbarkeitssegens ausdrücklich voraus.[37] Das bedeutet, die Erzählung hat in ihrer vorliegenden Form nie ohne die besagten Sprüche existiert.[38]

Zudem hat Rüdiger Schmitt in seiner umfassenden Untersuchung zur Magie
im Alten Testament inzwischen nachgewiesen, dass im gesamten Vorderen Orient
die Durchführung und Wirkung ‚magischer' Rituale immer mit dem Handeln der
Götter in Verbindung gebracht wurde.[39] Damit sind aber Deutungsmuster, die auf
animistischen, dynamistischen oder anderen Vor|stellungen von der Selbstwirk-
samkeit der Magie beruhen, äußerst fraglich geworden. Magie ist nach Schmitt
vielmehr als eine „ritualsymbolische Handlung" zu verstehen, „die eine göttliche
Intervention antizipiert".[40] So ist es nach Schmitts Einsichten überhaupt nicht
auffällig, dass in Gen 27,7.27.28 das göttliche Wirken im menschlichen Segensritual angesprochen wird.

Folgt man diesem veränderten Magieverständnis, dann lässt sich auch das in
Gen 27 geschilderte familiäre Segensritual als eine „ritualsymbolische Handlung"
verstehen, welche die „göttliche Intervention antizipiert": Durch den performati-
ven Akt des Rituals wird der göttliche Segen für den Sohn, der sich erst in der
Zukunft realisieren wird (V. 28 f.), vertrauensvoll in die Gegenwart hineingezogen
und schon jetzt eine Situationsveränderung (Autoritätsdelegation) herbeigeführt.[41] Aus diesem antizipatorischen Akt wird auch verständlich, warum dieser
Segen irreversibel ist und nicht einfach durch einen weiteren Segen ergänzt werden kann: Dies hat nicht etwa damit zu tun, dass „die gesamte väterliche Segenspotenz" erschöpft wäre,[42] sondern erklärt sich schlicht daraus, dass mit dem Vollzug des Rituals schon eine Applikation des zukünftigen Segenswirkens Gottes auf
den gesegneten Sohn stattgefunden hat. Die Selbstbindung Gottes an Jakob, die im
Ritualvollzug vertrauensvoll antizipiert wurde, ließ sich menschlicherseits nicht
einfach wieder rückgängig machen, wollte man nicht jegliches Vertrauen darauf
zerstören, dass Rituale auf Gott Einfluss zu nehmen vermögen. Darum verweist

---

37 Dies erkennt in Bezug auf V. 37 auch schon Taschner, Verheißung, 44; deswegen auch V. 37
zusammen mit V. 36 ebenfalls auszusondern, wie Leuenberger, Segen, 233 f., vorschlägt, geht nicht
an.

38 Nachträglich zugefügt ist wahrscheinlich nur die prosaisch formulierte Ankündigung einer
späteren Befreiung Edoms von der israelitischen Vorherrschaft in Gen 27,40b, vgl. Gunkel, Genesis, 314; Westermann, Genesis, 537; Seebass, Genesis, 301; Taschner, Verheißung, 48. Dagegen stellt
der häufig als sekundär verdächtigte Versteil 36a eine kompositorische Klammer des Verfassers
der Jakoberzählung dar, vgl. Blum, Komposition, 85.

39 Rüdiger Schmitt, Magie im Alten Testament, AOAT 313, Münster 2004, 67–106. |

40 A. a. O., 395.

41 Vgl. Schmitt, Magie, 134 f.

42 So Leuenberger, Segen, 240.

Isaak im Fortgang von Gen 27, als der Schwindel herausgekommen ist, nicht etwa auf seine erschöpfte Segenspotenz, sondern einfach auf den geschehenen Vollzug des Segensrituals (V. 37), den auch er zu akzeptieren hat (V. 33).

Ist damit die Wirkweise des Gesamtrituals geklärt, stellt sich die Frage, welche Funktion der Beköstigung des Vaters darin zukommt. Dass diese die Funktion haben sollte, die Segenskraft des alten Vaters zu stärken, ist schon deswegen relativ unwahrscheinlich, weil der Begriff נֶפֶשׁ, der für diese in Anspruch genommen wird, in Gen 27 keineswegs durchgängig gebraucht wird, sondern nur an ganz wenigen, ausgesuchten Stellen vorkommt: Die נֶפֶשׁ erscheint nur dort als Subjekt der Segensübermittlung, wo Segensspender und Segensempfänger mit Bezug auf das Segensritual in direkter Anrede unmittelbar miteinander kommunizieren (V. 4.19.25.31). Wo eine andere Person oder der Erzähler über den Vorgang berichten, ist durchgängig Isaak selber Subjekt der Segensübermittlung (V. 7.10.23.27.30).[43] Dieser bisher nicht beachtete | Befund legt es nahe, dass נֶפֶשׁ an den besagten Stellen die emotionale Bindung des Segensspenders an den Segensempfänger hervorkehren will, etwa in dem Sinne, dass die Segenshandlung des alten Vaters „aus dem Innersten heraus" oder „von ganzem Herzen" erfolgen soll.[44]

Dass die emotionale Beziehung zwischen Vater und Sohn im Segensmahl eine wesentliche Rolle spielt, macht eine zweite, wenig angestellte Beobachtung deutlich: Dort, wo Esau dem Vater – verspätet – die zubereiteten Speisen bringt (V. 31), spricht er ihm gegenüber vom „Wildbret seines Sohnes" (צֵיד בְּנוֹ); zuvor hatte Jakob an entsprechender Stelle – etwas weniger vollmundig – von „meinem Wildbret" (צֵידִי) geredet (V. 19).[45] Doch nimmt dies Isaak dort, wo er das Segensmahl einleitet, erneut mit der volltönenden Formulierung auf, indem er in Anrede Jakobs von dem „Wildbret meines Sohnes" (צֵיד בְּנִי) spricht (V. 25),[46] das er nun verzehren wolle, um ihn dann „von ganzem Herzen" zu segnen. Das heißt, es geht im Segensmahl nicht um irgendein Essen, das den Vater stärken und ihm Freude bereiten könnte, sondern um ein ganz besonderes Mahl. Es ist ein Mahl, das der zu segnende Sohn, einmal abgesehen von der Manipulation Rebekkas, in allen seinen Phasen selber für den Vater hergestellt hat: Er hat die Nahrung besorgt (V. 4.30b), er hat sie zu einer besonders leckeren Speise zubereitet

---

43 In der Anrede erscheint der Vater als Subjekt der Segensübermittlung nur in Gen 27,34.38, aber hier außerhalb des geordneten Rituals. |

44 Vgl. schon ähnlich Mitchell, Meaning, 82, mit Verweis auf Ps 103,1.2.22; 104,1.35.

45 Diese Abweichung hängt damit zusammen, dass Jakob seine Speise ja nicht selber zubereitet hat.

46 Jacob, Genesis, 565 f., hält dies für eine zärtliche Redeweise, die nachträglich das נפשׁי von Gen 27,4.19.31 erläutere.

(מַטְעַמִּים: V. 4.31; vgl. 7.9.14.17), wie sie der Vater besonders liebt (אָהֵב: V. 4.9.14), er hat sie selber aufgetragen (בוא *Hif.:* V. 31; vgl. 4.7.10.25.33) und – wie oben beschrieben – den Vater bei ihrem Verzehr aufmerksam bedient und liebevoll umsorgt. Es handelt sich somit um eine „Speise des Sohnes" im vollen Sinne des Wortes.

Geht man davon aus, dass es normalerweise der älteste Sohn ist, der dem alten Vater kurz vor seinem Tode dieses Mahl zubereitet, dann muss man berücksichtigen, dass sowieso insbesondere der Erstgeborene die Pflicht hatte, die alt gewordenen Eltern bis zu ihrem Tode mit Nahrung und Kleidung zu versorgen.[47] Unter dieser Perspektive erscheint das Segensmahl als ein besonderer Akt letzter großer Fürsorge für den Vater. Dieser wird noch einmal im vollen Sinne „geehrt", wie es das Elterngebot vorschreibt (Ex 20,12; Lev 19,3a). Das Segensmahl symbolisiert somit zugleich die hohe Verantwortungsbereitschaft und die große emotionale Zuneigung des Erstgeborenen | gegenüber seinem auf den Tod zugehenden Vater; jener demonstriert mit dieser letzten aufwendigen Beköstigung des Vaters, dass er als zukünftiges Familienhaupt auch für den Bestand der Familie sorgen wird. Und deswegen kann der so umsorgte alte Vater, physisch und emotional gestärkt, die Verantwortung getrost in die Hände seines Sohnes legen und steht ihm dadurch bei, dass er ihn für die Zeit, wenn er nicht mehr sein wird, des Segens Gottes rituell versichert und seine Führungsposition durch seine Segenshandlung religiös abstützt. Das Segensmahl hat somit die Funktion, die sozialen und emotionalen Bindungen zwischen dem Vater und seinem ältesten Sohn über den Tod hinaus zu festigen. So gesehen, passt es voll in das oben beschriebene Segensritual hinein, das sich durch eine hohe Intimität zwischen Vater und Sohn auszeichnete.

Durch den Konflikt zwischen Jakob und Esau, so stellt der Verfasser der Jakoberzählung unter Aufnahme einer vorgegebenen Überlieferung dar, werden zwar auch der Segensritus und das in ihm enthaltene Segensmahl manipuliert und beschädigt, aber ihre religiösen und sozialen Funktionen bleiben doch intakt. Die Antizipierung des göttlichen Segens veranlasst Gott, sich an Jakob zu binden, und die Intimität des Segensmahls veranlasst Isaak, seinen Zweitgeborenen als seinen Nachfolger anzuerkennen. Indem der Verfasser der Jakoberzählung zwei gegensätzliche Mahlgeschichten miteinander kombinierte, wollte er wahrscheinlich darstellen, wie der erpresste Führungsanspruch Jakobs, der mit einer Zerstörung menschlicher Esskultur einherging, im Rahmen eines kulturell verfeinerten und

---

47 Vgl. Rainer Albertz, Hintergrund und Bedeutung des Elterngebots im Dekalog (1978), in: ders., Geschichte und Theologie. Studien zur Exegese des Alten Testaments und zur Religionsgeschichte Israels, hg. v. Ingo Kottsieper u. a., BZAW 326, Berlin u. a. 2003, 157–207. Hinzu kommt die Verpflichtung, für eine würdige Bestattung zu sorgen. |

rituell geordneten Mahls die nötige väterliche und göttliche Sanktionierung erhielt.

4 Das konfliktschlichtende Vertrags- und Opfermahl

Schließlich erwähnt der Verfasser der Jakoberzählung ein Mahl am Ende von Jakobs Aufenthalt bei seinem Onkel Laban in Syrien (Gen 31,43–32,1a). Nachdem Jakob vor der Rache Esaus zu seinem Onkel hatte fliehen müssen (27,41–45) und er in der Fremde trotz aller Betrügereien Labans großen Reichtum erlangt hatte (V. 29–30), kam es zwischen den neidischen Verwandten zu einem lebensbedrohenden Konflikt: Jakob wollte ihm ausweichen, indem er mit seinen Frauen, Kindern und Herden die Flucht ergriff (31,1–21*), er wurde aber von Laban und seinen Leuten gestellt und des Diebstahls angeklagt (V. 22–42). Doch schließlich fanden sich beide Parteien bereit, den Konflikt durch einen Vertrag beizulegen (V. 43 ff.). Die Erzählung ist an dieser Stelle etwas kompliziert, da der Erzähler hier offenbar eine ältere Tradition von einem Grenzvertrag zwischen den Aramäern und Israeliten (V. 46.51–|53aα.b)[48] in seine Darstellung integrieren wollte.[49] Nach dieser ging die Initiative möglicherweise von Jakob[50] aus: Jakob ließ seine Leute einen Steinhaufen aufschichten, der von nun an die Grenze zwischen den Lebensräumen beider Gruppen markieren sollte (V. 46a). Das Mahl der beiden Parteien fand auf dieser Grenzmarkierung statt (V. 46b). Es ist ein typisches Vertragsmahl, das über dessen sozial verbindende Funktion hinaus auch eine religiöse Dimension umfasst, insofern die Vertragspartner ihre jeweiligen Familiengötter für den Fall des Vertragsbruchs zum Richter anriefen und Jakob bei dem פחד[51] seines Vaters schwor (V. 53*). Nach der Sicht des Erzählers wurde daneben noch ein Familienvertrag geschlossen, mit dem Laban die Rechte seiner Töchter in der Fremde sichern wollte (V. 50). Die Initiative dazu ging eindeutig von Laban aus (V. 43 f.); sie wurde von Jakob aber damit beantwortet, dass er seine Verwandten zu einem Opfermahl (זבח) auf dem Berg einlud (V. 54). Auch dieses Mahl hat neben der sozialen, die Vertragsparteien verbindende auch eine religiöse Funk-

---

48 Der Versteil Gen 31,53aβ „der Gott ihres Vaters" ist eine nachträgliche Zusammenfassung der beiden zuvor genannten Vätergötter.

49 Vgl. dazu Blum, Komposition, 132–140.

50 So der masoretische Text; allerdings nimmt Laban in V. 51 das Aufschichten des Haufens für sich in Anspruch. Aber nur die Vetus Latina überliefert in V. 46a ‚Laban', was eine Erleichterung des schwierigen Textes sein könnte; vgl. zum Problem Blum, Komposition, 133 f.

51 Die Deutung des Begriffs ist nach wie vor unsicher, vgl. Rainer Albertz, Religionsgeschichte Israels in alttestamentlicher Zeit, GAT 8,1–2, Göttingen ²1996/97, I, 54; Seebass, Genesis, 368.

tion. Die Mahlgemeinschaft wurde unter Beteiligung JHWHs vollzogen, der als Späher über die Einhaltung des Vertrages wachen sollte (V. 49). Das זבח war ein Kultmahl, mit dem typischerweise die Familien ihre Freude vor Gott brachten und damit ihren sozialen Zusammenhalt und ihre religiöse Identität stärkten.[52] Hier wird es auf die entfernteren Verwandten ausgeweitet und erhält damit eine Gruppen übergreifende, Frieden stiftende Funktion. In diesem Falle dauerte der freudige Festschmaus bis in die Nacht hinein. Wohlgesättigt von der leckeren Fleischspeise, übernachteten die ehemals verfeindeten Verwandten miteinander auf demselben Berg (V. 54b) und trennten sich erst am nächsten Morgen friedlich voneinander. Der Konflikt war somit wirklich beigelegt, die Frieden stiftende Funktion des Opfermahles voll zum Zuge gekommen. |

5 Schlussüberlegungen

Das religiös konnotierte Vertragsmahl von Gen 31 ist die erste Mahlzeit innerhalb der Jakoberzählung, an der – wie es normalerweise üblich ist – mehrere Personen teilnahmen.[53] Es ist auch die erste und einzige, die nicht beschädigt und manipuliert wurde, sondern einen ungestörten und kultivierten Verlauf nehmen konnte. Wenn der Verfasser der Jakoberzählung in seine Komposition, die mit durch den Konflikt der Brüder depravierten und manipulierten Mahlzeiten begann, gegen Ende eine Mahlzeit einordnete, die nicht nur ungestört in den traditionellen Bahnen ablief, sondern auch den Konflikt zwischen Jakob und seinem Onkel Laban beizulegen vermochte, dann hat er damit wahrscheinlich eine Absicht verfolgt: Er wollte wohl zeigen, dass Jakob inzwischen gelernt hatte, in seinem Kampf um sein Lebensrecht nicht länger die Grundlagen menschlicher Zivilisation, wie sie u. a. in der kulturellen Überformung von Essen und Trinken niedergelegt sind, einfach über Bord zu werfen oder zu beschädigen, sondern sie pfleglich zu behandeln und positiv zur Beilegung von Konflikten zu nutzen.

Damit stellt sich natürlich die Frage, warum der Verfasser nicht auch ganz am Ende der Komposition, dort wo Jakob und Esau wieder aufeinander treffen und ihren Konflikt beilegen, von einem gemeinsamen Mahl berichtet hat. Wäre dies nicht ein schönes Ende einer Geschichte gewesen, die mit einer zerstörten Mahlgemeinschaft begann? Der Erzähler entschied sich jedoch an dieser Stelle für einen anderen Versöhnungsritus: Nach ihm musste sich Jakob, der mit großer

---

52 Vgl. Albertz, Religionsgeschichte I, 154 f. |
53 Während Gen 25,29–34 und Gen 27,1–45 sehr außergewöhnliche Formen der Mahlzeit darstellten, stellt das Vertrags- und Friedensmahl von Gen 31 einen weitverbreiteten Typ innerhalb der außerhäuslichen Mahlzeiten dar, vgl. Barlösius, Soziologie, 194–196. |

Familie und Herdenreichtum Gesegnete, tief vor seinem um sein Glück geprellten Bruder erniedrigen und ihm generös von seinem großen Reichtum abgeben, um eine Versöhnung zu ermöglichen (Gen 33,1–11). Nur so konnte er den drohenden Racheakt des militärisch überlegenen Esau abwenden. Die bloße Einladung zu einem Essen hätte Esau in dieser Lage wohl kaum besänftigt. Es bedurfte nach Meinung des Erzählers einer außergewöhnlichen diplomatischen Aktion, um das aufgestaute Drohpotential abzuwenden. Ein Vertragsmahl wäre hier deplatziert gewesen.

So macht das überraschend gestaltete Ende der Jakobkomposition darauf aufmerksam, dass die sozialen und friedensstiftenden Funktionen, die das gemeinsame Essen entfaltet, auch an Grenzen stoßen. Wohl war ein Versöhnungsmahl in der Lage, rechtliche Konflikte zwischen zwei etwa gleich starken | Parteien beizulegen, doch bei asymmetrischen Konflikten, noch dazu wenn sie mit der Drohung militärischer Gewalt einhergehen, ist es offenbar nicht das probate Mittel.

Warum ‚Wozu'? Zur Pragmatik der an Gott gerichteten Fragen in den Klagegebeten der Hebräischen Bibel

Jürgen Ebach, dem ich zu seinem 65. Geburtstag herzlich gratulieren möchte, hat immer wieder nachdrücklich auf die theologische Bedeutung der harten an Gott gerichteten Fragen in der Hebräischen Bibel hingewiesen. So schrieb er zu der scharfen Anklage, die Mose nach dem Scheitern der Verhandlungen mit Pharao vor JHWH erhob (Ex 5,22): „JHWH, warum handelst du böse an diesem Volk, warum hast du mich gesandt?" „Mose erfaßt das Scheitern als Element des Handelns Gottes und bringt es vor Gott als den einzig möglichen Adressaten [...] Die Anklage vor Gott ist [...] der Ausdruck des Festhaltens an der Berufung im Augenblick des Scheiterns. Weil Mose nicht vor der Übermacht der Verhältnisse kapituliert, bringt er sein Scheitern klagend und anklagend vor Gott."[1] Und er resümiert: „Bezeugt das Lob die Schöpfung der Welt und des Menschen, so beharrt die Klage und noch die Anklage Gottes auf der Erlösungsbedürftigkeit des Menschen und der Welt. Die Frage nach dem ‚Warum?' wird im Gebet zur Frage: ‚Wie lange noch, Herr?!'".[2] So weisen die anklagenden Fragen in den Gebeten der Hebräischen Bibel für Ebach auf ein Wesensmerkmal menschlicher Existenz vor Gott in einer noch von Unterdrückung, Unrecht, Leid und Zerstörung gezeichneten Welt hin, das nicht übersprungen werden kann.[3]

1 Die forschungsgeschichtliche Problemlage

Für einen, der wie ich vor langer Zeit einmal im Bereich der Psalmen geforscht hatte[4] und der nun nach längerer Abstinenz wieder einmal zu diesem | Gebiet

---

1 J. Ebach, „Herr, warum handelst du böse an diesem Volk?". Klage vor Gott und Anklage Gottes in der Erfahrung des Scheiterns, in: ders., Hiobs Post. Gesammelte Aufsätze zum Hiobbuch, zu Themen biblischer Theologie und zur Methodik der Exegese, Neukirchen-Vluyn 1995, 73–83, hier 79.
2 A. a. O., 82.
3 Vgl. J. Ebach, Streiten mit Gott. Hiob, 2 Bde., Neukirchen-Vluyn 1996, z. B. I, 54 f., u. ö.
4 Vgl. R. Albertz, Weltschöpfung und Menschenschöpfung in den Psalmen. Unter|sucht bei Deuterojesaja, Hiob und in den Psalmen (CThM A3), Stuttgart 1974; ders., Persönliche Frömmigkeit und offizielle Religion. Religionsinterner Pluralismus in Israel und Babylon (CThM A9), Stuttgart 1978; ders., Art. Gebet, in: TRE XII, 34–42. Zu den Klagen des Volkes und den Threni habe ich mich später noch einmal geäußert: ders., Die Exilszeit. 6. Jahrhundert v. Chr. (BE 7), Stuttgart 2001, 117–135.

https://doi.org/10.1515/9783111202228-019

zurückkehrt, stellt sich die gegenwärtige Forschungslage zu den Klagen merkwürdig widersprüchlich dar.

1.1 Die Anklage Gottes in der gegenwärtigen Diskussion

Auf der einen Seite werde ich – als Schüler Claus Westermanns mit Freuden – gewahr, wie der Aufsatz Westermanns „Struktur und Geschichte der Klage" aus dem Jahr 1954,[5] in dem Westermann nicht nur die Bedeutung der Klage in ihrer dreifachen Grundstruktur von Anklage Gottes, Wir-/Ich-Klage und Feindklage für die Geschichte des Gebets im alten Israel herausgestellt, sondern auch auf das merkwürdige Verstummen der Klage, insbesondere der Anklage Gottes, in den Gebeten des frühen Judentums und Christentums hingewiesen hatte, eine ganz erstaunliche Fernwirkung entfaltet hat. Fast fünfzig Jahre nach seinem Erscheinen sind um die Jahrtausendwende zwei gewichtige Sammelbände erschienen, die beide von der Absicht geleitet sind, das Element der Klage alttestamentlicher Gebete erneut zu einer Dimension des christlichen Gebets zu machen. So sucht der von Georg Steins herausgegebene Band „Schweigen wäre gotteslästerlich. Die heilende Kraft der Klage" die theologische Legitimität selbst harter Anklagen Gottes herauszuarbeiten: „Die Not in der Klage herauszuschreien, ja Gott an seine guten Absichten zu erinnern, bedeutet nicht die Krise oder das Ende der Gottesbeziehung, sondern ist eine Intensivform des Glaubens";[6] ja, der Band will der Klage sogar eine heilende, gleichsam therapeutische Funktion zubilligen.[7] Noch | programmatischer will der von Ottmar Fuchs und Bernd Janowski verantwortete Band „Klage" die „Klagespiritualität" der Hebräischen Bibel für heutige Christinnen und Christen zurückgewinnen angesichts erschütternder Katastrophen wie

---

5 Wiederabgedruckt in ders., Lob und Klage in den Psalmen, Göttingen 1974, 125–194.

6 Würzburg 2000, 10, in der Einleitung des Herausgebers.

7 So besonders in dem Beitrag des Moraltheologen und Psychotherapeuten Georg Beier, Die heilende Kraft der Klage, a. a. O., 16–41. Beier kann die „Klage als heilsame Wirklichkeitserfahrung", „als heilende Enttäuschung", als „befreiende Erinnerung", „als kathartischer Weg der Heilung", „als Arbeit am / mit Leid" und „als heilende Annahme seiner selbst" (20–29) bezeichnen, manchmal so, als ginge die heilende Wirkung von der Klage als solcher und nicht von Gott aus. Wenn er schreibt: „Klage ist nicht psychische Verinnerlichung des Leids, nicht passive Duldung und fromme Hingabe, sondern Schrei des Protestes und Widerstandes, anklagendes Einfordern von Hilfe, Aufsprengen des In-sich-Verkrampftseins im Leid, Zerbrechen des duldenden Nach-Innen" (20), dann wird er der Schärfe alttestamentlicher Klagen | durchaus gerecht. Doch wenn er der Meinung ist „Klage geht nie zu weit" (20), dann ist er sich offensichtlich der Tatsache, dass schon im Hiobbuch um die rechte Form des Betens heftig gestritten wird, nicht bewusst, vgl. Ijob 5; 22; 35,8–16.

die des Terroranschlags vom 11. September 2001.[8] Er sucht nicht nur ein exegetisches Fundament zu legen, sondern geht auch der von Westermann nur angedeuteten Frage im Einzelnen nach, wie es zum Verstummen der Klage in der Alten Kirche bis hin zu ihrer „Kriminalisierung" in der Frömmigkeitsliteratur des 19. Jhs. kam.

Auf der anderen Seite beobachte ich bei einigen Autoren, z. T. bei den gleichen, die sich um eine Rehabilitierung der Klage als Teil des Gebets bemühen, eine mehr oder minder starke Tendenz, die Klagegebete des Alten Testaments theologisch zu domestizieren und ihre Härte z. T. unter Einsatz philologischer Mittel abzumildern. Nach Bernd Janowski ist gar nicht die Klage, sondern „das Vertrauensmotiv das Basismotiv des Klageliedes".[9] Indem er in Ps 13 schon die bloße Anrede JHWHs in V. 2 und seine Prädizierung als persönlicher Gott des Beters in V. 4a als Ausdruck des Vertrauens wertet, wird in seiner Sicht die gesamte Klage dazwischen (VV. 2 f.) schon vom Gottvertrauen getragen und läuft darum konsequent auf das Bekenntnis der Zuversicht und die Gewissheit der Erhörung am Ende des Psalms hinaus (V. 6).[10] Entsprechend kann Janowski an anderer Stelle die alttestamentlichen Klagepsalmen in Aufnahme eines Begriffs von Christoph Markschies[11] als ein „zielgerichtetes Vertrauensparadigma" bezeichnen, die „*indem* sie gesprochen werden, einen Vorschuß an Vertrauen zu Gott enthalten. [...] Sie sind zwar in der Situation der Gottverlassenheit bzw. der Gottesferne gesprochen, aber doch in der Hoffnung, daß Gott gerade *in* dieser Not nahe ist."[12] Es fragt sich, | ob bei einer solchen Sicht die Gestörtheit der Gottesbeziehung und die Verzweiflung, die sich in vielen Klagen der Psalmen ausspricht, voll in den Blick kommen. Auch Westermann konnte davon sprechen, dass in fast allen Kla-

---

8 S. M. Ebner u. a. (Hg.), Klage (JBTh 16), Neukirchen-Vluyn 2001. Von katholischer Seite hatte Ottmar Fuchs schon 1987 ein in ähnliche Richtung gehendes Plädoyer vorgelegt, s. ders., Klage. Eine vergessene Gebetsform, in: H. Becker u. a. (Hg.), Im Angesicht des Todes (Pietas Liturgica 3/4), St. Ottilien 1987, 939–1024.
9 B. Janowski, Das verborgene Angesicht Gottes. Psalm 13 als Muster eines Klageliedes des einzelnen, in: M. Ebner u. a. (Hg.), Klage (JBTh 16), Neukirchen-Vluyn 2001, 25–23, hier 50.
10 Vgl. a. a. O., 50–53.
11 C. Markschies, „Ich aber vertraue auf dich, Herr!" – Vertrauensäußerung als Grundmotiv in den Klageliedern des Einzelnen, in: ZAW 103 (1991), 386–398, hier 397 f.
12 Konfliktgespräche mit Gott. Eine Anthropologie der Psalmen, Neukirchen-Vluyn 2003, 77. Janowski leitet hier den „Vertrauensvorschuß" schon aus der Tatsache ab, dass der Leidende überhaupt das Klagegebet an Gott richtet. Da nun jedes Klagegebet, wie man weiß, zugleich zu und gegen Gott gesprochen ist, verliert damit aber | die Kategorie des ‚Vertrauens' ihre analytische und differenzierende Kraft. Problematisch erscheint mir im Zitat vor allem die Formulierung „daß Gott gerade *in* dieser Not nahe ist"; dies scheint mir ein Eintrag aus der christlichen Theologie zu sein.

geliedern eine Bewegung vom Flehen zum Loben erkennbar sei.[13] Aber er hat doch den Gegensatz, der zwischen den verzweifelten Klagen und den vertrauensvollen Bekenntnissen besteht, hervorgehoben.[14]

Eine etwas anders geartete Entschärfung der Klage, die nun auch das Verständnis der an Gott gerichteten Fragen betrifft, lässt sich im Beitrag von Christoph Dohmen zu dem von Georg Steins edierten Sammelband beobachten.[15] Im Anschluss an Diethelm Michel[16] möchte Dohmen die mit dem hebräischen Interrogativadverb *lāmmāh* eingeleiteten Anklagen Gottes nicht mehr als ‚Warum‘-, sondern als ‚Wozu‘-Fragen verstehen.[17] Es werde in ihnen somit nicht nach dem Grund, sondern nach der Intention oder dem Sinn des göttlichen Handelns gefragt. Damit wandelt sich aber für Dohmen die Zielrichtung der Klagegebete erheblich: „Das Klagegebet, das an Gott die Frage nach dem Wozu des Leidens richtet, durchbricht den Teufelskreis, der immer dann entsteht, wenn Menschen angesichts der Leiden anderer nach dem Grund dieses Leidens fragen."[18] Die ‚Wozu‘-Fragen der Klage bedeuteten nach Dohmen nun sogar eine Befreiung von solchen zermürbenden Fragen; sie würden Gott gar nicht mehr die Unverständlichkeit seines Handelns vorwerfen, „sondern im Vertrauen und Hoffnung auf Gott nach dem Sinn und Ziel"[19] seines Handelns fragen. Wenn Dohmen die Antwort auf solche Fragen bei Elihu findet, der das Leid als Erziehungsmaßnahme Gottes verstehen will (Ijob 33,14–22), dann erhebt sich für mich der Einwand, ob durch solche ra|tionalisierenden Antworten die verzweifelten Fragen, die Hiob und viele andere Leidenden in der Hebräischen Bibel Gott entgegengeschleudert haben, nicht doch vorschnell entschärft werden. So hat es fast den Anschein, dass die Entschärfung der Klagegebete, bediene sie sich nun theologischer oder philologischer Mittel, zuweilen der Preis für ihre christliche Rezeption sei.

---

13 Vgl. C. Westermann, Loben Gottes in den Psalmen, Göttingen ³1963, 55 f.

14 Vgl. das häufige *waw-adversativum* zur Einleitung der Bekenntnisse der Zuversicht, a. a. O., 52 f. Westermann spricht ausdrücklich von „Entgegensetzung" (53).

15 Vgl. C. Dohmen, Wozu, Gott? Biblische Klagen gegen die ‚Warum‘-Frage im Leid, in: G. Steins (Hg.), Schweigen wäre gotteslästerlich. Die heilende Kraft der Klage, Würzburg 2000, 113–125.

16 Vgl. D. Michel, „Warum" und „Wozu"? Eine bisher übersehene Eigentümlichkeit des Hebräischen und ihre Konsequenzen für das alttestamentliche Geschichtsverständnis (1988), in: ders., Studien zur Überlieferungsgeschichte alttestamentlicher Texte (ThB 93), Gütersloh 1993, 13–34, hier 21–28.

17 Auch Janowski hat sich Michels semantischer Analyse angeschlossen, s. Konfliktgespräche, 78.360, Anm. 56.

18 So Dohmen, Wozu, Gott?, 120.

19 A. a. O., 123. |

1.2 Die Einschätzung der Anklage Gottes seit Hermann Gunkel

In diesem Zusammenhang ist es nicht uninteressant daran zu erinnern, dass auch
schon Hermann Gunkel, dem wir die formkritische Klassifizierung der Gattungen
„Klagelieder des Volkes" und „Klagelieder des Einzelnen" verdanken, seine Schwierigkeiten mit einer angemessenen Würdigung ihrer Klage-Elemente, insbesondere
der Anklage Gottes hatte. Klage ist für ihn primär Leidklage, wie es dem deutschen
Sprachgebrauch entspricht (‚sich beklagen').[20] Die auf Gott bezogene Dimension
der Klage in den Klageliedern des Volkes kommt bei ihm nur unter dem Aspekt
in den Blick, dass „die politischen Mißgeschicke zugleich als Nöte der Religion
aufgefaßt" würden: „Das, was man jetzt erleben muß, widerspricht dem, was man
sonst von dem Gotte zuversichtlich geglaubt hat, aufs furchtbarste; daher das be-
ständige verzweifelte ‚Warum', das für die Klagelieder [...] bezeichnend ist. [...]
Neben diesem ‚Warum' der Verzweiflung steht das ‚Wie lange' der Ungeduld."[21]
Auch wenn die Funktion der an Gott gerichteten Fragen gut erfasst ist, kommt die
zentrale Bedeutung der Anklagen Gottes für diese Gattung, die später Westermann
feststellen sollte,[22] nicht heraus.

Den Terminus ‚Anklage' benutzen Gunkel/Begrich erstmals in Blick auf die
Klagelieder des Einzelnen, und zwar eher negativ.[23] Hier wird die gegen Gott
gerichtete Klage über die „leidenschaftliche Aufwallung des Betenden" begründet,
insbesondere da, wo sie sich in der Form der Frage äußert: „Ja der Beter schleu-
dert Jahve selbst die ungeduldige Frage ins Gesicht: ‚Warum, Jahve, stehst du
ferne ...?'" (Ps 10,1). „Man sucht Aufklärung für das, was einen betroffen hat."
Aber ein solches Beten scheint Gunkel/Begrich nicht ganz geheuer zu sein; sie
schreiben: „Man empfindet, daß die erregten Klagen der im | Innersten erschüt-
terten Menschen zuweilen den Abstand zwischen Gott und Mensch vergessen.
Aus der Klage wird gelegentlich eine Anklage gegen ihn." Und sie meinen, dass
schon einige Psalmisten „an solchen Klagen Anstoß genommen" hätten, weswegen die Klage in einigen Psalmen dieser Gattung zurückträte. Und es scheint fast
so, als würden sie ihre eigenen theologischen Vorbehalte formulieren, wenn sie
unterstellen: „Die feinere Frömmigkeit dieser Dichter hat instinktiv empfunden,
daß die lauten, lärmenden, wilden Klagen zu weit gehen. Sie haben ein Gefühl
dafür, daß das stürmische Dringen in Jahve, das Murren und Grollen gegen ihn

20 S. H. Gunkel/J. Begrich, Einleitung in die Psalmen. Die Gattungen der religiösen Lyrik Israels
(1933; HK, Ergänzungsband zur II. Abteilung), Göttingen ²1966, 125 f., in Bezug auf die Klagelieder
des Volkes, und 214–216, in Bezug auf die Klagelieder des Einzelnen.
21 A. a. O., 127.
22 Vgl. Westermann, Struktur und Geschichte der Klage, 136.
23 Vgl. Gunkel/Begrich, Einleitung, 217. Von hier stammen auch die weiteren Zitate. |

leicht zur Vermessenheit führt."[24] An anderer Stelle versteigen sich Gunkel/Begrich sogar zu dem Urteil, dass die vorwurfsvollen Fragen in der Klage „eigentlich mehr von menschlichem Egoismus zeugen als von dem Gottesglauben." Dabei legen sie offen, dass hinter ihren Vorbehalten das Vorbild des stillen, gottergebenen Gebets Jesu im Garten Gethsemane steht (Mk 14,36).[25] Interessant ist, dass Gunkel/Begrich zwar die Anklagen des Volkes Israel – gleichsam aus der Distanz – sachlich referieren konnten, aber bei solchen einzelner Menschen, die auch von Christen direkt rezipiert werden können, ihre frommen Bedenken nicht zurückzuhalten vermochten.

Es war erst Claus Westermann, der nach den Erfahrungen der Schrecken der Nazi-Zeit und des Zweiten Weltkriegs, in denen gerade die Klagepsalmen für viele Mitglieder der Bekennenden Kirche in ihren Nöten eine große Hilfe geworden waren, die theologische und seelsorgerliche Bedeutung der Klage, insbesondere der Anklage Gottes, aufdeckte und ohne jede Vorbehalte in den theologischen Diskurs einbrachte. Er entdeckte nicht nur die drei Subjekte der Klage (Gott, Ich/ Wir, die Feinde), welche die Klage als ein Wortgeschehen erkennen ließen, das sowohl das Verhältnis zu Gott, zur eigenen Person als auch zum sozialen Umfeld betrifft.[26] Sondern Westermann hat auch die sich in den Klagen ausdrückende Verzweiflung und Orientierungslosigkeit ohne jede Beschönigung beschrieben. So charakterisierte er 1954 die Anklage:

> Der Klagende hat in dem Schlag, der ihn traf, erfahren: Gott hat versagt. Diese Erfahrung ist ihm ein gänzlich Unheimliches, Unverständliches. Die Warum-Frage ist wie das Tappen eines, der im Dunkel nicht mehr weiter weiß. Sie hat den Sinn des | Sich-Zurechtfindens; dabei ist vorausgesetzt, daß der erfahrene Schlag in der Abwendung Gottes begründet ist.[27]

---

24 Gunkel/Begrich sehen sich durch Ps 39,2 bestätigt, wo ein Beter beschließt, seinen Mund angesichts der Frevler im Zaum zu halten, vgl. die Auslegung von H. Gunkel, Die Psalmen (HK II/ 2), Göttingen [5]1968, 164. Dass Gunkel/Begrich hier die gleichen Vorbehalte erheben wie Eliphas gegenüber den Klagen Hiobs (Ijob 5; 22), scheint ihnen nicht bewusst geworden zu sein.
25 Gunkel/Begrich, Einleitung, 231.
26 So schon Westermann, Loben Gottes, 48 f., dann ders., Struktur und Geschichte, 108 f. |
27 Westermann, Struktur und Geschichte, 135. In seinem Aufsatz „Die Rolle der Klage in der Theologie des Alten Testaments" (in: ders., Forschung am Alten Testament. Gesammelte Studien II [ThB 55], München 1974, 250–268), konnte Westermann formulieren: „Da es in der Klage [...] immer um das Leben geht, spricht sich in den drei Aspekten der Klage das Menschsein als Ganzes aus. Für den Klagenden ist von der andrängenden Macht des Todes, die er im Leiden erfährt, nicht nur das isolierte Ich bedroht; bedroht ist zugleich sein Stehen in der Gemeinschaft. [...] Bedroht ist aber auch die Gottesbeziehung und mit ihr der Sinn seines Daseins; denn nach ihm fragt die Warum-Frage der Gottklage" (257). Zur ‚Warum'-Frage in der Volksklage schreibt er: „Die gegenwärtige Not erfährt das Volk als das Widersinnige, wie es die Warum-Frage an Gott zum Ausdruck bringt. Wie kann Gott so schweres Leid über sein Volk bringen, wenn es doch sein Volk ist, an dem er früher Großes getan hat? Sofern das Widersinnige Gott vorgewor-

Diese Charakterisierung der Anklage Gottes ist radikal und nur schwer zu ertragen. Und so verwundert es nicht, dass gut drei Jahrzehnte später die Kritik von Diethelm Michel gerade hier ansetzte. Michel stimmt Westermann in soweit zu, als es auch nach seinem Verständnis in der *lāmmāh*-Frage um ein Sich-Zurechtfinden der Beter geht. Doch habe Westermann dieses nicht hinreichend charakterisiert. So fügt er hinzu:

> Neben der Feststellung, daß der erfahrene Schlag in der Abwendung Gottes begründet sei, wäre als Voraussetzung der Frage unbedingt noch zu betonen, daß trotz aller Ratlosigkeit die Beter mit der *lama*-Frage daran festhalten, daß Gott einen Sinn und ein Ziel bei seinem Handeln hat, auch wenn die Beter diese im Augenblick nicht erfassen. Nur weil Westermann dies nicht erkennt, kann er die *lama*-Frage als eine ‚Anklage Gottes' deuten.[28]

Hintergrund dieser Kritik ist, dass Michel – wie schon erwähnt – die Bedeutung des hebräischen Fragewortes *lāmmāh* auf ‚Wozu?' anstelle von ‚Warum?' festlegen möchte. Beruht damit Westermanns Charakterisierung der am häufigsten an Gott gerichteten Frage auf einem semantischen Missverständnis? Mehr noch, ist die Kategorie ‚Anklage Gottes' damit generell hinfällig?

Ausgangspunkt der etymologischen und semantischen Untersuchung von Michel ist die Existenz zweier ähnlicher Frageadverbien im Hebräischen, *lāmmāh* und *maddūǎ'*, deren Bedeutung Michel neu abzugrenzen sucht. Schon die Etymologie spricht nach Michel für einen klaren Bedeutungsunter|schied: *maddūǎ'* lasse sich aus *māh* + *yadūǎ'* ‚was gewusst?' ableiten, *lāmmāh* dagegen aus *lě* + *māh* ‚zu was?'. Daraus legt sich für Michel „die Vermutung nahe, *maddu*ᵃ' frage nach einem vorfindlichen Grund, *lama* dagegen nach einer intendierten Absicht, die als Grund für etwas angesehen wird."[29] Michel überprüft diese Vermutung an einigen ausgesuchten Bibelstellen und kommt zu dem Ergebnis: „*maddu*ᵃ' fragt nach einer vorfindlichen, objektiven Begründung für ein Geschehen, *lama* fragt nach dem bei einem Geschehen intendierten oder immanenten Sinn. *maddu*ᵃ' fragt nach der Vergangenheit, *lama* nach der Zukunft."[30] Diese semantische Differenzierung wendet Michel sodann auf die an Gott gerichteten Fragen an. So wendet er sich gegen die traditionelle Übersetzung von Ps 22,2: „Mein Gott, mein Gott, warum hast Du mich verlassen?" mit der Begründung:

---

fen wird, enthält die Volksklage ein Moment des Protestes, des Protestes einer Gruppe gegen das, was ihr angetan wird. Der Protest richtet sich zwar an Gott; aber er ist doch Protest, der das Widersinnige nicht demütig und geduldig hinnimmt, sondern der sich als Protest äußert", a. a. O., 259.

28 Michel, „Warum" und „Wozu", 24. |
29 A. a. O., 14.
30 A. a. O., 21.

... für deutsches Sprachempfinden wirkt die Frage ‚warum hast du mich verlassen?‘ als rückwärtsgewandte Frage nach einer Information über einen vorliegenden Sachverhalt. Die Antwort könnte sein: ‚weil du dich nicht entsprechend meinen Forderungen verhalten hast‘ oder ‚weil ich mich in meinem Verhalten dir gegenüber geändert habe‘. Wir hatten aber gesehen, daß die *lama*-Frage gerade nicht in dieser Weise in der Vergangenheit bohrt und nach einem aufweisbaren Grund fragt. Adäquater wäre die paraphrasierende Wiedergabe: ‚W o z u hast du mich verlassen?‘, ‚Was hast du dir dabei gedacht, daß du mich verlassen hast?‘ Damit aber ergeht diese Frage von einer anderen Haltung aus als die Frage nach einem aufweisbaren Grund. Der Beter setzt voraus, dass Jahwe bei seinem Handeln, auch wenn der Mensch es als ein Verlassen empfindet und keinen Sinn erkennen kann, doch einen Sinn hat, ein Ziel, auf das hin er handelt und das man erfragen kann. Kurz: die *lama*-Frage verläßt nicht den Boden des Glaubens.[31]

Bei diesen Ausführungen Michels fragt man sich unwillkürlich, ob hier eine semantische Analyse – einmal ihre Richtigkeit unterstellt – nicht doch damit überfordert wird, solche weitgehenden theologischen Aussagen zu machen. Dennoch werden sie etwa von Janowski und Dohmen zustimmend aufgegriffen, weil sie offenbar zu ihrer Konzeption des Klageliedes passen.[32] Allerdings ist festzuhalten: Die Annahme Michels, dass die israelitischen Beter in der *lāmmāh*-Frage immer schon die Sinnhaftigkeit göttlichen Handelns trotz erfahrener Verlassenheit voraussetzen, wird in den Klagepsalmen der Hebräischen Bibel nirgends explizit bestätigt;[33] und auch Michels Vermutung, dass | die *lāmmāh*-Frage „typisch israelitisch" sei,[34] lässt sich eindeutig widerlegen. Es gibt – wenn auch relativ selten – mit einem ganz entsprechend gebildeten Interrogativadverb (*ammīni* aus *ana* + *mīni* ‚zu was?‘) Klagen in den akkadischen Gebeten. [35]

Und schließlich: Stimmt die Annahme Michels, dass die in der Klage an Gott gerichtete *lāmmāh*-Frage überhaupt auf eine Antwort abzielt? Zielt sie auf einen aufweisbaren Grund des Leides oder auf Sinn und Ziel göttlichen Handelns, das den Klagenden in sein Leid gestürzt hat? Was soll denn die Antwort auf die ‚Wozu‘-Frage sein, abgesehen von den rationalisierenden Erklärungen (Strafe, Prüfung, Erziehung), welche fromme Theologen seit den Freunden Hiobs den Leidenden feilbieten? Schon Thomas Hieke hat auf die Problematik der „Lösung"

---

31 A.a.O., 22.
32 S. Janowski, Konfliktgespräche, 360, Anm. 65, und Dohmen, Wozu, Gott?, 120–123.
33 Auch aus dem „Vorschuss an Vertrauen" (Konfliktgespräche, 77) ist eine solche Voraussetzung des Beters nicht mit Sicherheit ableitbar. Abgesehen von den Vertrauenspsalmen bleibt die Sinnhaftigkeit göttlichen Tuns in den Klagen gerade strittig. |
34 S. Michel, „Warum" und „Wozu", 31.
35 So in einem altbabylonischen Gottesbrief an den persönlichen Gott „Warum hast du mich vernachlässigt?" (s. bei J. J. Stamm, Akkadische Namengebung, Darmstadt 1968, 54 f., Z. 4), oder einer neuassyrischen *Šigû-Klage*: „Warum sind Krankheit, Herzeleid, Verstörtheit und Verlust an mich gebunden?" (SAHG, 269, Z. 4).

Michels und Dohmens aufmerksam gemacht: „Vielleicht hilft es, statt mit ‚warum'
mit ‚wozu' zu übersetzen, wobei aber wieder dieses ‚Wozu' als Ausdruck der klagenden Verständnis- und Orientierungslosigkeit zu verstehen ist. Die ‚Wozu-Frage'
der Klagepsalmen wäre aber wiederum missverstanden, wenn man dahinter die
Frage nach einem ‚pädagogischen Konzept' Gottes vermuten würde."[36]

Methodisch krankt die Untersuchung Michels daran, dass sie zu schnell von
der Etymologie auf die Semantik schließt[37] und die Pragmatik, d. h. die Funktionen der mit den Adverbien *lāmmāh* und *maddūăʿ* eingeleiteten Fragen kaum in
den Blick nimmt. Dies soll darum hier nachgeholt werden. |

2 ‚Warum?' oder ‚Wozu?' Zur Pragmatik der hebräischen ‚Warum'-Fragen

In der neueren Linguistik ist längst geklärt, dass der Fragesatz in einer Kommunikationssituation vielfältige Funktionen übernehmen kann. Neben den „echten"
Fragen, die auf den Erhalt einer Information aus sind, gibt es in Frageform formulierte höfliche Bitten, Vorwürfe, Vorschläge, Ratschläge und Warnungen.[38] Dabei
bildet die reine Informationsfrage nur einen Typ unter vielen. Einen zweiten Typ
stellen solche Fragen dar, die einen verminderten Informationsanspruch aufweisen wie Versicherungsfragen, Bestätigungsfragen, Behauptungsfragen, Erlaubnis-
fragen und direktive Fragen. Einen dritten Typ bilden schließlich Fragen mit
anderen illokutionären Funktionen wie Fragen, die zu einer anschließenden
sprachlichen Handlung auffordern, metakommunikative Fragen und interaktions-
relevante Fragen.[39] Ein wichtiger Untertyp der letzteren ist die Vorwurfsfrage; in
ihr überlagert der Vorwurf gleichsam das Informationsersuchen; an die Stelle der
Antwort tritt hier die Rechtfertigung, die aber auch ausbleiben kann. Dabei „wer-

---

36 T. Hieke, Schweigen wäre gotteslästerlich. Klagegebete – Auswege aus dem verzweifelten
Verstummen, in: G. Steins (Hg.), Schweigen wäre gotteslästerlich. Die heilende Kraft der Klage,
Würzburg 2000, 45–68, hier 54.
37 Dabei ist sich Michel durchaus der Warnungen von J. Barr, Bibelexegese und moderne Semantik. Theologische und linguistische Methode in der Bibelwissenschaft, München 1965, 111–115,
bewusst, die Ergebnisse der Etymologie zu direkt für eine Analyse des aktuellen Sprachgebrauchs
auszuwerten, doch lässt er sich bei seiner semantischen Analyse schon stark von seinem etymo-
logisch gewonnenen Vorverständnis leiten. |
38 Vgl. W. Frier, Zur linguistischen Beschreibung von Frage-Antwort-Zusammenhängen, in: ders.
(Hg.), Pragmatik. Theorie und Praxis (Amsterdamer Beiträge zur Neuen Grammatik 13), Amster-
dam 1981, 41–91, hier 56–59.
39 Vgl. a. a. O., 63–66.

den Vorwürfe gern in Form von warum-Fragen geäußert."[40] Man hat solche Fragen, die nicht auf eine informative Antwort abzielen, gemeinhin als „rhetorische
Fragen" bezeichnet. Aber dieser Begriff ist viel zu pauschal und muss der genaue-
ren pragmatischen Analyse weichen. Wolfgang Frier betont in diesem Zusammenhang, dass auch solche sog. „rhetorischen Fragen" durchaus Reaktionen beim
Kommunikationspartner auslösen wollen.[41] Allerdings müssen diese nicht verba-
ler Natur sein.

2.1 Fragen mit dem Interrogativadverb *maddūă'*

Betrachtet man nach diesen Vorklärungen den Befund in der Hebräischen Bibel,
so zeigt sich, dass die mit dem Fragewort *maddūă'* eingeleiteten Sätze zu einem
erheblichen Anteil Informationsfragen darstellen. Von den 71 *maddūă'*-Sätzen (72-
maliges Vorkommen des Adverbs) sind 43 oder 60,5 % auf die Erlangung einer
Information aus, und immerhin 28 (39,4 %) erhalten in narrativen Zusammenhän-
gen eine direkte und weitere zehn eine indirekte | Antwort (insgesamt 53,5 %).
Dabei geht es aber weniger um „objektive Sachfragen" (eigentlich nur in Ex 3,3),
sondern meist um das Verhalten des Kommunikationspartners (53,5 %), das eigene Ergehen (12,7 %) oder das Verhalten oder Ergehen Dritter (33,8 %). Oft ist die
Frage emotional gefärbt, es geht um die anteilnehmende Erkundigung (Gen 40,7;
Neh 2,2 f.), die erschrockene (1 Sam 21,2), besorgte (2 Sam 11,10; 13,4), erstaunte[42]
oder enttäuschte Frage (Jes 5,4). Ex 1,18 kommt einem Verhör nahe; in weiteren
Fällen haben die Fragen einen vorwurfsvollen Unterton.[43] Das heißt, eine Festlegung der *maddūă'*-Fragen auf eine einzige Gefühlslage des Sprechers, das Erstau-
nen, wie sie von Alfred Jepsen vorgeschlagen worden war,[44] ist nicht möglich.
      Interessant ist, dass sich zwar einige dieser auf Information ausgerichteten
maddūă'-Fragen klar auf einen ‚vorfindlichen Grund' beziehen, wie es Michel
dargestellt hat,[45] dass aber häufig schon hier nicht mehr zwischen einem solchen
‚vorfindlichen Grund' und einer ‚intendierten Absicht' unterschieden werden
kann. In Gen 26,27, wo Isaak den Philisterkönig Abimelech und seine Begleitung

---

40 A. a. O., 58.
41 Vgl. a. a. O., 61 f. |
42 So in Gen 26,27; Ex 2,18; 18,14; 2 Sam 18,11; 19,42; 24,21; 1 Kön 1,13; 2 Kön 4,23; 8,12; Neh 13,11.
43 So in Lev 10,17; Jos 17,14; Ri 11,7; 12,1; 2 Sam 3,7; 11,20; 2 Kön 12,8; 2 Chr 24,6.
44 So A. Jepsen, Warum? Eine lexikalische und theologische Studie, in: F. Maas (Hg.), Das ferne
und das nahe Wort, FS Leonard Rost (BZAW 105), Berlin/New York 1967, 106–113, hier 106 f. In 1
Sam 21,2 wird das Erschrecken explizit erwähnt.
45 So in Gen 40,7; Ex 2,18; 2 Sam 13,4; 1 Kön 1,41; 2 Kön 8,12, vgl. Michel, „Warum" und „Wozu",
16 f.

fragt: „Warum kommt ihr zu mir? Hasst ihr mich doch und habt mich von euch vertrieben", kann sich die Frage sowohl auf den Grund, den die Philister zu ihrem überraschenden Kommen veranlasste, als auch auf die Absicht, die sie bei ihrem Besuch hegen, beziehen. Und ähnliches gilt für Ex 18,14; Lev 10,17; Ri 11,7; 12,1; Rut 2,10; 2 Sam 3,7; 18,11 und öfter. Das heißt, Michels Differenzierung erscheint schon hier eher künstlich und nicht dem hebräischen Sprachgebrauch angemessen.

Hinzu kommt, dass auch schon mit dem Interrogativadverb *maddūā'* Vorwürfe (Ri 11,26; 2 Sam 19,44; Ijob 33,13; Jes 50,2), Beschuldigungen[46] und eine Warnung (Neh 13,21) eingeleitet werden, die nicht mehr auf eine verbale Antwort zielen. Sie wollen, wie auch die zur Verantwortung ziehende Frage „Warum tust du das?" (2 Sam 16,10; 1 Kön 1,6), dass der Angesprochene in sich geht und sein Fehlverhalten einsieht. Die Stellen mit dieser pragmatischen Ausrichtung machen etwa 22 % der *maddūā'*-Fragen aus. Es wird sich zeigen, dass die *lāmmāh*-Fragen in solcher Pragmatik ihren Schwerpunkt haben (46 %). Doch sind inhaltliche Differenzen zwischen beiden Fragewörtern in dieser Hinsicht kaum noch zu erkennen. Die mit *maddūā'* formulier|ten Vorwürfe und Beschuldigungen können sich sowohl auf die externen Gründe (Ex 5,14) als auch auf die Intentionen (Num 16,3) oder auch beides beziehen (Num 12,8). Tendenziell lässt sich sagen, dass sich die *maddūā'*-Beschuldigungen konkreter auf bestimmte Handlungen beziehen; hier wirkt noch der Schwerpunkt in der Informationsfrage nach. Dagegen weiten sich die mit *lāmmāh* formulierten Vorwürfe und Beschuldigungen gerne ins mehr Grundsätzliche aus (z. B. Gen 44,4).

Diese Differenz mag damit zu tun haben, dass *maddūā'* nur ein einziges Mal in der Anklage Gottes vorkommt, in der es um die Gottesbeziehung und damit um die ganze Existenz geht. Sie steht in dem Zitat eines Volksklageliedes in Jer 14,19–22:

Jer 14,19	Hast du denn Juda ganz verworfen,
	oder hast du Zion verabscheut in deinem Innern?
	Warum (*maddūā'*) hast du uns so geschlagen,
	dass es keine Heilung mehr gibt?
	Hoffen auf Frieden, aber da ist nichts Gutes,
	auf eine Zeit der Heilung, aber siehe da: Schrecken.

Wie der unmittelbare Kontext zeigt, drückt die Anklage gegen Gott die ganze Enttäuschung und Fassungslosigkeit der Sprechenden aus. Der hier mit einer *maddūā'*-Frage erhobene Vorwurf ist genauso umfassend wie die mit *lāmmāh* formulierten Anklagen in der benachbarten Volksklage Jer 14,1–9:

---

46 So in Ex 5,14; Num 12,8; 16,3; 2 Sam 12,9; 1 Kön 2,43; Jer 26,9; 32,3; 36,29; Est 3,3. |

Jer 14,8 Warum (*lāmmāh*) wandelst du dich zu einem Fremden im Lande,
zu einem Wanderer, der (nur) zum Übernachten einkehrt?

Jer 14,9 Warum (*lāmmāh*) wandelst du dich zu einem hilflosen Mann,
zu einem Helden, der nicht mehr retten kann?

Michels Erklärung, dass die *maddūă'*-Anklage in Jer 14,19 auf einen vorfindlichen Grund, nämlich das menschliche Fehlverhalten, ziele, weil in V. 20 ein Sündenbekenntnis folgt,[47] überzeugt nicht, weil dieses nicht als Antwort auf die Frage von V. 19 formuliert ist. Daneben begegnen im Jeremiabuch noch klagende Fragen Zions oder des Propheten (Jer 13,22; 30,6; 46,5.15), die der Wir- oder Ich-Klage nahe kommen. Der Gebrauch des Interrogativadverbs *maddūă'* an diesen Stellen lässt sich hier dadurch erklären, dass die Klagen in ein kleines Frage-Antwort-Spiel eingebettet sind. Eigentümlicherweise sind auch die Klagen Gottes über Israels Verhalten oder Schicksal im Jeremiabuch als *maddūă'*-Fragen formuliert (Jer 2,14.31; 8,5.19), obgleich sie von Gottes | Seite her die ganze Fassungslosigkeit über das Geschehen ausdrücken.[48] Wenn die Klagen des lebensmüden Hiob einmal mit *maddūă'* (Ijob 3,12) und einmal mit *lāmmāh* (3,11) gestellt werden, dann ist keinerlei Unterschied zwischen den beiden Fragepartikeln mehr zu erkennen.[49] Dagegen lässt sich der Umstand, dass die Frage nach dem Glück der Frevler und damit die Theodizee-Frage (Jer 12,1; Ijob 21,7) mit dem Adverb *maddūă'* formuliert ist, vielleicht so erklären, dass die Frage noch auf eine Antwort aus ist, auch wenn diese nicht gegeben werden kann. So zeigt das Fragewort *maddūă'* sehr wohl einen eigentümlichen Schwerpunkt in der Informationsfrage; aber es kann auch mit anderen illokutionären Funktionen verwendet werden und überschneidet sich dabei mehr oder minder mit dem zweiten Fragewort *lāmmāh*.

2.2 Fragen mit dem Interrogativadverb *lāmmāh*

Das Interrogativadverb *lāmmāh* begegnet deutlich häufiger als *maddūă'* in der Hebräischen Bibel, insgesamt 178-mal, verteilt auf 169 Verse.[50] Zieht man solche

---

47 Vgl. Michel, „Warum" und „Wozu", 25. |

48 Vgl. auch die klagenden Fragen bezüglich Jojachins (Jer 22,28) und des Landverlustes (49,1), die nicht klar einem bestimmten Sprecher zugeordnet werden können.

49 Diese wird auch von Michel, „Warum" und „Wozu", 25, Anm. 15, zugestanden.

50 Zweifach begegnet das Fragewort in Gen 4,6; Ex 5,22; Num 11,11; 1 Sam 19,17; 1 Chr 21,3; Ps 42,10; 43,2; dreifach in 1 Sam 1,8, aber nur in 1 Sam 19,9; Ps 42,10; 43,2 liegen funktional differente Fragesätze vor.

Belege ab, in denen der Text schadhaft[51] oder doublettenhaft[52] ist oder das Fragewort schon zur bloßen Konjunktion ‚dass nicht‘ abgeblasst ist,[53] so kommt man
auf 161 Vorkommen. Ein erster deutlicher Unterschied zu *maddūaʿ* zeigt sich darin, dass in den narrativen Texten nur in 17 Fällen (10,5 %) eine Antwort auf eine
lāmmāh-Frage überliefert wird. Auch wenn man berücksichtigt, dass es sich nicht
um Wiedergaben echter Gespräche, sondern um literarische Stilisierungen handelt, kann man daraus folgern, dass *lāmmāh* seinen Schwerpunkt nicht bei den
Informationsfragen hat, sondern bei den Fragen mit „anderen illokutionären
Funktionen".[54] Dem entspricht, dass 70 % der *lāmmāh*-Fragen in der 2. Person
ergehen, also unmittelbar auf den Kommunikationspartner ausgerichtet sind,
während Fragen in der 3. Person nur 17 % ausmachen. Bei den *maddūaʿ*-Fragen
waren die entsprechenden Anteile 53 % und 34 % gewesen. So sind die *lāmmāh*-
Fragen | noch stärker im personalen Kommunikationsprozess verankert, sie
scheinen ihren Schwerpunkt in den „interaktionsrelevanten Fragen" zu haben,
um erneut eine Kategorie von Wolfgang Frier aufzunehmen.[55]

In etwa 11 % der Fälle zielen die *lāmmāh*-Fragen auf eine Information und
sind hier von den *maddūaʿ*-Fragen nicht zu unterscheiden. Sie bilden Erkundigun-
gen mit einem etwas vorwurfsvollen (Num 22,37; Ri 15,10) oder besorgten (1 Sam
1,8) Unterton; sie stellen verwunderte oder erstaunte Fragen dar,[56] genauso wie
die mit *maddūaʿ* formulierten. Auch eine höhnisch herausfordernde Frage (1 Sam
17,8) und eine Verhörfrage (2 Sam 19,26) sind darunter. So ist eine Festlegung auf
die vorwurfsvolle Frage, die Jepsen vorschlug,[57] nicht möglich.

Aber auch Michels Klassifizierung erweist sich schon hier, wo meist Antworten überliefert sind, als fragwürdig. Wenn der moabitische König Balak den Seher
Bileam fragt: „Habe ich nicht zu dir gesandt, um dich zu rufen? Warum bist du
nicht zu mir gekommen? Sollte ich dich nicht tatsächlich ehren können?"
(Num 22,37), dann zielt die *lāmmāh*-Frage auf die Erkundung eines vorgegebenen
Hinderungsgrundes, mag er nun ‚objektiv‘ oder – aus Balaks Sicht – eingebildet
sein. Wie die nachgeschobene Frage verdeutlicht, vermutet Balak, dass Bileam
die Bezahlung, die er ihm angeboten hatte (22,7), nicht ausgereicht habe. Doch in
seiner Antwort übergeht Bileam dergleichen niedere Unterstellungen. Eine Über-

---

51 Dazu rechne ich Ps 68,17.
52 So in 1 Chr 17,6; 21,3; 2 Chr 25,19; dazu die funktional ähnlichen Doppel- oder Dreifachfragen
Gen 4,6; Ex 5,22; Num 11,11; 1 Sam 1,8.
53 So in Hld 1,7; Koh 7,16.17; Dan 1,10; Neh 6,3; 2 Chr 32,4.
54 So in der Typologie von Frier, Pragmatik, 64 f. |
55 Vgl. a. a. O., 65.
56 So in Gen 18,13; 1 Sam 9,21; 28,16; 2 Sam 15,19; 16,17; 18,22; 2 Kön 5,8; Jes 40,27; 55,2; Mi 4,9;
Ps 2,1.
57 Vgl. Jepsen, Warum?, 107 f. |

setzung: „Wozu bist du nicht zu mir gekommen?" wäre geradezu unsinnig; selbst wenn Bileam seine Weigerung zu kommen mit einer Absicht verbunden hätte, wovon nichts berichtet wird, hätte Balak an dieser Stelle der Erzählung, wo er ihm noch gute Absichten unterstellt, gar keinen Anlass dazu gehabt, sie zu erfragen. Auf einen vorfindlichen Grund zielt auch die indirekte Frage in 1 Sam 6,3.

In der Mehrzahl der Fälle, etwa dort, wo der Pharao Abraham befragt, warum er seine Frau als Schwester ausgegeben habe (Gen 12,18), lässt sich allerdings gar nicht unterscheiden, ob die *lāmmāh*-Frage auf einen vorfindlichen Grund oder eine intendierte Absicht hinzielt. Es ist schlicht beides gemeint. Wenn Abraham die Antwort nicht verweigert hätte, hätte er vielleicht gesagt: „Ich hatte Angst vor Ägypten und wollte mein Leben retten" (vgl. VV. 11–13). Da auch das deutsche Interrogativadverb ‚Warum?', sofern es sich auf Personen bezieht, nicht nur äußere Gründe, die sie zu einem Verhalten veranlassten, sondern immer auch Motivationen, Absichten und Ziele bei | ihrem Verhalten mit umgreift, ist die Übersetzung mit ‚warum' für *lāmmāh* beizubehalten.

Der Schwerpunkt der Verwendung des hebräischen Interrogativadverbs *lāmmāh* liegt allerdings in einem Bereich, in dem es kaum oder gar nicht um die Gewinnung von Information geht, sondern um eine Auseinandersetzung zwischen zwei Gesprächspartnern. In 31 Fällen werden mit den von ihm eingeleiteten Sätzen Vorwürfe gegen den Gesprächspartner erhoben,[58] das sind fast 20 % aller Vorkommen. In 16 weiteren Fällen werden Beschuldigungen gegen ihn ausgesprochen,[59] in 14 weiteren an das Verantwortungsgefühl des Gegenübers appelliert.[60] Hinzu kommen Warnungen in 13 Fällen.[61] Zählt man alle diese Fälle zusammen, die fast nur die zwischenmenschlichen Auseinandersetzungen betreffen, dann kommt man auf einen stattlichen Anteil von 46 Prozent.

Obgleich solche vorwurfsvollen und beschuldigenden Fragen, Appelle und Warnungen nicht auf eine informative Antwort abzielen, wollen sie dennoch beim Gesprächspartner etwas bewirken. Diese These, die Frier in Bezug auf die sog. „rhetorischen Fragen" aufgestellt hat,[62] bewährt sich auch an den narrativen Texten der Hebräischen Bibel, die in etwa der Hälfte der Fälle verbale und non-

---

58 So in Gen 12,18.19; Ex 2,20; 17,3; Num 20,4.5; Ri 5,16.17; 12,3; 1 Sam 6,6; 17,28; 21,15; 22,13; 24,10; 26,18; 28,9.12.15; 2 Sam 3,24; 11,21; 19,12.13.43; 1 Kön 2,22; 14,6; Jer 29,27; Ijob 19,22; 27,12. Vorwürfe Gottes stellen Jer 2,29; 44,7 dar.

59 So in Gen 29,25; 31,27.30; 43,6; 44,4; Ex 2,13; 5,4; Jos 9,22; 1 Sam 2,23.29; 15,19; 19,17; 26,15; 2 Sam 14,31; 2 Chr 24,20; 25,15.

60 So in Gen 42,1; 44,7; 47,15.19; Ex 5,15; Num 32,7; Jos 7,10; 1 Sam 19,5; 20,8.32; 2 Sam 14,13; 19,11; 20,19; Spr 5,20.

61 So in Gen 4,6; Num 14,41; 1 Sam 19,17; 2 Sam 2,22; 24,3; 2 Kön 14,10; Jer 27,13.17; 40,15; Ez 18,31; 33,11; Spr 22,27; Koh 5,5; 2 Chr 25,16.

62 Vgl. Frier, Pragmatik, 61. |

verbale Reaktionen des Gesprächspartners berichten: So kann Davids Vorwurf gegen Saul, der ihn verfolgt (1 Sam 24,10; 26,18), diesen zur Reue bewegen (24,17 ff.; 26,21 ff.), Labans Beschuldigungen gegen Jakob (Gen 31,27.30) fordern diesen zur Verteidigung heraus (V. 31). Der Appell Jonathans an Sauls Verantwortung in 1 Sam 19,5 zeigt Wirkung; Saul lässt von seinen Mordplänen gegen David vorläufig ab. Aber ein Vorwurf kann auch die gegenteilige Wirkung haben: Mose wird, als er einem Hebräer vorwirft, seinen Nächsten zu schlagen, von diesem mit einem empörten Gegenvorwurf bedacht (Ex 2,13 f.). Jonathans zweiter Appell an Saul (1 Sam 20,32) ruft einen Mordanschlag seines Vaters hervor (V. 33) und eine Warnung des Königs von Israel vor Hybris (2 Kön 14,9–10) wird von Ahasja in den Wind geschlagen (V. 11). So kann man mit einigem Recht postulieren: Auch dort wo auf solche als *lāmmāh*-Fragen formulierten Vorwürfe, Beschuldigungen und | Appelle keine Reaktionen berichtet werden, zielen sie doch darauf ab, dass der damit Angesprochene irgendeine Reaktion zeigt; etwa dass er in sich geht, beschämt wird, einen Rechtfertigungsdruck verspürt oder Verantwortung zeigt und möglicherweise sein Verhalten ändert. Wegen dieser starken illokutionären Wirkabsicht haben die *lāmmāh*-Vorwürfe einen sich leicht ins Grundsätzliche ausweitenden Charakter.

Es ist schon häufig notiert worden, dass die an Gott gerichteten ,Warum'-Fragen der Gebetssprache fast ausschließlich mit dem Frageadverb *lāmmāh* eingeleitet werden.[63] Von solchen begegnen allein 24 als Du-Anklage gegen Gott,[64] 7 als Ich- oder Wir-Klagen,[65] 4 als Feindklagen[66] und 3 als Anklagen Gottes in der 3. Person,[67] das sind insgesamt 26 % aller Fälle. Grundsätzlich gehören auch diese an Gott gerichteten *lāmmāh*-Fragen in die große Gruppe der Vorwürfe, Beschuldigungen und Appelle an die Verantwortung hinein. Allerdings handelt es sich um eine gespaltene Kommunikationssituation. Gott ist nicht da, wo der leidende Mensch oder die in Not geratene Gruppe ist.[68] Schon aus diesem Grund kann es im Regelfall gar keine direkten Antworten geben.[69] Aber, wie schon bei Betrach-

---

63 Vgl. Jepsen, Warum?, 108 ff.; Michel, „Warum" und „Wozu", 21 ff., u. ö.

64 So in Ex 5,22; 32,11; Num 11,11; 21,5; Jos 7,7; Jes 63,17; Jer 14,8.9; Hab 1,3.13; Ps 10,1; 22,2; 42,10; 43,2; 44,24.25; 74,1.11; 80,13; 88,15; Ijob 7,20; 10,18; 13,24; Klgl 5,20.

65 So in Num 11,20; Ri 6,13; 21,3; Jes 58,3; Jer 15,18; Ps 42,10; 43,2.

66 So in Ex 32,12; Ps 79,10; 115,2; Joel 2,17.

67 So in Num 14,3; 1 Sam 4,3; Ijob 3,20.

68 Aus diesem Grunde würde ich zögern, das Klagegebet ein „Konfliktgespräch mit Gott" zu nennen, wie es O. Fuchs, Die Klage als Gebet. Eine theologische Besinnung am Beispiel des Psalms 22, München 1982, 159, und Janowski, Das verborgene Angesicht, 53; ders., Konfliktgespräche, passim, tun. Ich würde das Gebet als eine Rede zu Gott bezeichnen.

69 Diese Feststellung schließt Antworten Gottes an die Führer der Vergangenheit nicht aus, vgl. Ex 6,1; Num 11,16 ff.; 14,11 ff.; Jos 7,7 ff. Daneben existierte das Heilsorakel, das in besonderen Fällen auf die Klage des Einzelnen hin erteilt werden konnte, vgl. Albertz, Exilszeit, 137–140.

tung der zwischenmenschlichen Kommunikationssituationen deutlich wurde, sind solche mit *lāmmāh* formulierten Vorwürfe auch gar nicht mehr auf direkte Antworten aus. Dennoch wollen auch diese an Gott gerichteten ‚Warum'-Fragen etwas bei ihm bewirken, sie wollen, dass Gott in sich geht, sein Verhalten gegenüber den Klagenden überdenkt und möglichst bald ändert. Was schon Gunkel/ Begrich als Ziel des gesamten Klageliedes bestimmten, gilt für die an Gott gerichteten ‚Warum'-Fragen in besonderem Maße: Der Beter ist mit ihnen bestrebt, „das Herz seines Gottes zu bewegen."[70] |

In die Nähe des Gebets gehören noch solche ‚Warum'-Klagen, in denen die Sinnhaftigkeit des eigenen Lebens in Frage gestellt wird (Gen 25,22; 27,45.46; Jer 20,18; Ijob 3,11). Hier wird Gott nicht angeredet, aber gerade deswegen spricht sich in ihnen eine tiefe Verzweiflung und Orientierungslosigkeit aus. Wie man an dem Klagetyp ‚Verfluchung des Tages der Geburt' in Jer 20,14–18 und Ijob 3,1–19 zeigen kann, verschwindet Gott aus dem Blickfeld des Menschen, wenn der Lebenswille erlöscht; umgekehrt hängt, wie das Hiobbuch zeigt, die Hinwendung zu Gott mit dem Erwachen des Lebenswillens zusammen.

Mehr in das Selbstgespräch hinein gehört die ‚Warum'-Frage, die den Wert des eigenen Status (Gen 25,32) oder die Sinnhaftigkeit des eigenen Verhaltens negiert (2 Sam 12,23; 14,32; Ijob 9,29; Koh 2,15). Aber auch eine Selbstvergewisserung kann im Gebet als ‚Warum'-Frage an sich selber ausgedrückt werden (Ps 49,6: „‚Warum' sollte ich mich fürchten in bösen Tagen?"). Auch im Selbstgespräch kann die Frage einen umorientierenden Effekt entwickeln (2 Sam 12,23).

In der normalen Kommunikationssituation kann die *lāmmāh*-Frage einen Protest ausdrücken; ein bestimmtes Ergehen (Dtn 5,25: Tod) oder ein bestimmtes Verhalten (2 Sam 16,9: Verfluchung des Königs) werden durch sie als inakzeptabel bezeichnet. In die Nähe gehören die Zurückweisung eines Verhaltens (Rut 1,11.21; 2 Sam 7,7) oder die Ablehnung eines Angebots (Gen 33,15; 1 Sam 27,5; 2 Sam 19,36 f.); mit der gleichen Frageform lehnt Gott Opfergaben ab (Jer 6,20). In den metakommunikativen Bereich gehören solche ‚Warum'-Fragen, die eine Verweigerung der Antwort bedeuten (Gen 32,30; Ri 13,18) oder den Abbruch der Kommunikation vollziehen (2 Sam 19,30).

Überblickt man diese weit gefächerte Pragmatik der untersuchten hebräischen Fragesätze, dann wird deutlich, dass diejenigen, die mit *lāmmāh* eingeleitet sind, noch weit weniger als solche, die mit *maddūaʿ* formuliert waren, auf eine Beantwortung abzielen.[71] Dies bedeutet aber: Wenn sowohl Michel als auch Doh-

70 Gunkel/Begrich, Einleitung, 231. |
71 So schon mit Recht H. Irsigler in seiner Sprechaktanalyse zu Psalm 13, s. ders., Psalm-Rede als Handlungs-, Wirk- und Aussageprozeß. Sprechaktanalyse und Psalmeninterpretation am Beispiel von Psalm 13, in: K. Seybold/E. Zenger (Hg.), Neue Wege der Psalmenexegese, FS Walter Beyerlin (HBS 1), Freiburg u. a. ²1995, 63–104, hier 77 f.

men scheinbar selbstverständlich annehmen, dass die *lāmmāh*-Frage in der Klage auf eine Antwort ziele, zwar nicht in der Vergangenheit nach einem Grund für das Leid bohren, aber doch Gott auf ein Ziel seines Handelns hin befragen wolle, dann gehen sie von einer falschen Voraussetzung aus.[72] Damit ist aber auch das theologische Anliegen Dohmens, | das hinter einer Ersetzung des Interrogativums ‚Warum?' durch das Frageadverb ‚Wozu?' stand, gegenstandslos.

3 Die an Gott gerichteten Fragen in den Klagegebeten

Die meisten Fragen, die in den Klagegebeten an Gott gerichtet werden, gehören den drei Teilen der Klage, der Anklage Gottes, der Ich-/Wir-Klage oder der Feind-klage an. Fragen an Gott, die sein Tun betreffen, gehören zur Anklage; hier stellen die genannten mit *lāmmāh* eingeleiteten Fragesätze den häufigsten Typ dar. Diese begegnen fast regelmäßig in den wenigen überlieferten Volksklageliedern (Ps 44,24.25; 74,1.11; 80,13; Klgl 5,20; Jes 63,17; Jer 14,8.9), dazu einmal gleichbedeu-tend mit dem Interrogativadverb *maddūä'* (Jer 14,19). Seltener sind die *lāmmāh*-Anklagen in den weitaus häufiger belegten Klageliedern des Einzelnen (Ps 10,1; 22,2; 42,10; 43,2; 88,15; vgl. Hab 1,3.13).[73] Wie oben schon gezeigt, haben diese ‚Warum'-Fragen die Funktion von Vorwürfen an Gott, mit denen die Klagenden ihm ihr ganzes Unverständnis für sein Verhalten ihnen gegenüber ausdrücken und zum Einlenken bewegen wollen. Neben der ‚Warum'- stellt die ‚Wie lange'-Frage den zweithäufigsten Typ der Anklagefragen dar, sie begegnet in der Volks-klage mit dem Frageadverb *'ad-māh* („bis was?') in Ps 74,9; 79,5; 89,47, mit dem Adverb *'ad-mātay* („bis wann?') in Ps 80,5: „JHWH, Gott-Zebaoth, wie lange willst du zürnen beim Gebet deines Volkes?" In der Klage des Einzelnen begegnet sie mit den Frageadverbien *'ad-mātay* (Ps 6,4), *'ad-'ānāh* („bis wohin?'; Ps 13,2) und *kāmāh* („wie was', ‚wie oft?'; Ps 35,17; vgl. Ps 119,84; Ijob 7,19).[74] In den ‚Wie lange'-Fragen drückt sich die Ungeduld der Klagenden angesichts des anhaltenden Leids aus.[75] Unter den Anklagen der Volksklagelieder findet sich auch die ‚Wo'-Frage (*'ayyēh*; Ps 89,50; Jes 63,15: „Wo sind dein Eifer und deine Heldenkraft, das Aufwal-len deiner Gefühle und dein Erbarmen?"), die Gott mit dem Ausbleiben seiner früheren Gnadentaten bzw. Machterweise konfrontiert. Hinzu kommen einige Satz-Fragen, eingeleitet mit der hebräischen Partikel *hä*, die ungläubiges Un-

---

72 So Michel, „Warum" und „Wozu", 22; Dohmen, Wozu, Gott?, 120. |

73 In Ijob 7,21; 10,2 werden ‚Warum'-Fragen mit dem Adverb *māh* (eigentlich: ‚was?') eingeleitet.

74 Eine ähnliche Funktion haben die ‚Wann'-Fragen (*mātay*) in Ps 119,82.84.

75 Die ‚Wie lange'-Anklagen sind ebenfalls in den babylonischen Gebeten belegt, vgl. etwa das *Eršaḫunga-Gebet*, SAHG, 225–228, Z. 47–50, oder das *Šigû-Gebet*, SAHG, 269 f., Z. 14. |

verständnis gegenüber Gottes Verhalten gegenüber seinem Volk ausdrücken (Ps 60,12; Jes 64,11; Jer 14,19aα: „Hast du | Juda ganz verworfen, bist du Zions überdrüssig geworden?"). In den Klagen des Einzelnen fehlen, soweit ich sehe, solche anklagenden Satzfragen; sie begegnen aber massiv in den Klagen Hiobs (z. B. Ijob 10,3–5).

Fragen an Gott, die das Elend des oder der Klagenden betreffen, sind demgegenüber deutlich seltener. In den eigentlichen Klageliedern des Volkes fehlen sie ganz, hier herrschen Elendsschilderungen vor, mit denen man Gott rühren will (z. B. Klgl 5,2–5.8–16a). Innerhalb der Abwandlungen könnte man allerdings die ‚Warum'-Frage Jes 58,3 und die ‚Wie lange'-Frage Jer 12,4 (*ʿad-mātay*) nennen. In den Klagen des Einzelnen sind die Belege etwas zahlreicher, so begegnet die ‚Warum'-Frage in Ps 42,10; 43,2 (vgl. Jer 15,18) und die ‚Wie lange'-Frage in Ps 13,3a: „Wie lange (*ʿad-ʾānāh*) soll ich Sorgen in meinem Innern tragen, Kummer in meinem Herzen Tag für Tag?" Mit diesen Fragen soll Gott die Sinnlosigkeit und die unerträgliche Dauer des Leidens vorgehalten werden.

Auch die Fragen an Gott, die das Treiben der Feinde betreffen, sind in den Volksklagen eher selten. Eine ‚Warum'-Frage begegnet in Ps 79,10a: „Warum sollen die Völker sagen: ‚Wo ist nun ihr Gott?'" (vgl. Ps 115,2), eine ‚Wie lange'-Frage in Ps 74,10: „Wie lange (*ʿad-mātay*), Gott, soll der Widersacher noch schmähen und der Feind deinen Namen immerfort lästern?" Gott wird vorgehalten, ob oder wie lange er das gegen ihn selbst gerichtete Treiben noch hinnehmen will. In den Klagen des Einzelnen, in denen die Feindklage sowieso eine größere Rolle spielt, sind solche die Feinde betreffenden Fragen etwas dichter gesät. Eine ‚Warum'-Frage mit dem seltenen Frageadverb *ʿal-māh* (‚wegen was?') begegnet in Ps 10,13: „Warum darf der Frevler Gott verachten und in seinem Herzen sprechen: ‚Du greifst nicht ein'?" ‚Wie lange'-Fragen mit dem Adverb *ʿad-ʾānāh* tauchen in Ps 13,36 und Ps 94,3 auf; sie wollen Gott animieren, dem unerträglichen Triumph der Feinde bzw. der Frevler endlich ein Ende zu machen.[76] In einem mit dem Fragewort *māh* (eigentlich ‚was?') formulierten Ausruf hält der Beter in Ps 3,2 Gott die ungeheure Zahl seiner Feinde vor Augen: „JHWH, wie sind meine Feinde so zahlreich ... ?!" In Ps 94,20 stellt der Beter JHWH die in der Tat beunruhigende Satzfrage, ob sich „der Thron des Frevels" mit Gott verbrüdern dürfe, obgleich er Unrecht gegen das Gesetz schaffe. Und Jeremia fragt Gott in seinem Gebet noch grundsätzlicher, warum (*maddūăʿ*) die Frevler so erfolgreich sind (Jer 12,1). Schließlich ist wahrscheinlich der textlich nicht ganz sichere Versteil, Ps 56,8a, trotz fehlender Fragepartikel als Satzfrage aufzufassen, ob es für die Feinde trotz

---

76 Eine ‚Wie lange'-Feindklage begegnet z. B. im *Šuila-Gebet* an Ishtar, SAHG, 238–333, Z. 56–59.

des – von ihnen angerichteten – Unheils ein Entkommen geben soll.[77] | So beinhalten die Feindklagefragen nicht nur den Vorwurf an Gott, warum er die Frevler gewähren lässt, sondern auch einen Protest gegen die ungerechten gesellschaftlichen Zustände.

Abgesehen von der dreiteiligen Klage kommen an Gott gerichtete Fragen in den Klagegebeten nur sporadisch vor. Diejenigen, die Gottes eigenes Tun betreffen, sind *māh*- oder *mī*-Fragen, die lobend die Wunderbarkeit (Ps 31,20: „Wie groß ist deine Güte!") oder die Unvergleichlichkeit JHWHs (Ps 35,10; 71,19: „Wer ist dir gleich?"; vgl. Ps 89,9) festhalten wollen. Sie sind als staunende Ausrufe bzw. rhetorische Fragen im engeren Sinn zu bestimmen. Auch die ausführlichen Fragen an JHWH, ob er an den Toten Wunder tun kann und darum sein Lob in der Unterwelt gesungen wird (Ps 88,11–13), wurden bislang meist als rhetorische Fragen auf der Linie des Motivs „die Toten loben Gott nicht" (Ps 6,6; 30,10) verstanden, doch hat Frank Crüsemann einige Gründe dafür geltend gemacht, dass es sich um echte Fragen handelt.[78] Zu den Fragen an Gott, die die eigene Person des Beters betreffen, gehört die *mī*-Frage von Ps 6,6 „Wer wird im Totenreich dich preisen?"; sie dient der Motivation der Bitte des Beters, der Gott damit vorhält, dass er im Falle seines Todes einen Verehrer verlieren und sich somit selber schaden würde.[79] In Ps 130,3 gehört die *mī*-Frage: „Wenn du die Sünden anrechnest, JHWH, Herr, wer könnte bestehen?" in eine staunende Reflexion über das Sündenbekenntnis. Beide Fragen sind rhetorisch, die Antwort wäre: Niemand! Dagegen ist die *māh*-Frage Ps 39,8a „Doch nun, was habe ich zu hoffen, Herr?" als echte Frage in einem Frage-Antwort-Spiel zu werten, denn der Beter gibt Gott sogleich die Antwort in V. 8b: „Meine Hoffnung ist allein bei dir!" Die Funktion dieser Frage ist die der Selbstvergewisserung in einer Abwandlung des Bekenntnisses der Zuversicht.

Der Überblick macht deutlich, dass die Fragen, die an Gott in den Klagegebeten gerichtet sind, sich in hohem Maße auf das Klage-Element konzentrieren, in der Klage des Volkes insbesondere auf die Anklage Gottes, in der Klage des Einzelnen in geringerer Konzentration auf die Anklage, die Feindklage und die Ich-Klage verteilen. Es stellt sich die Frage, warum gerade in diesem Element der

---

77 Während K. Seybold, Die Psalmen (HAT 1/15), Tübingen 1996, 226, den Versteil für | zerstört hält, haben sich F.-L. Hossfeld/E. Zenger, Psalmen 51–100 (HThK.AT), Freiburg u. a. 2000, 105–108, für sein Verständnis als rhetorische Frage ausgesprochen.

78 Vgl. F. Crüsemann, Rhetorische Fragen? Eine Aufkündigung des Konsenses über Psalm 88,11–13 und seine Bedeutung für das alttestamentliche Reden von Gott und Tod, in: Biblical Interpretation 11 (2003), 345–360.

79 Vgl. zum gesamten Motiv C. Hardmeier, „Denn im Tod ist kein Gedenken an Dich" (Ps 6,6): Der Tod des Menschen – Gottes Tod?, in: EvTh 48 (1988), 292–311. |

Klagepsalmen neben den hier vorherrschenden Aussagesätzen doch so relativ zahlreiche Fragesätze vorkommen. Worin liegt die be|sondere Funktion der klagenden Fragen in Bezug auf die klagenden Aussagen und das gesamte Klagegebet?

Untersucht man die Stellung der Klagen in Frageform in den Klagegebeten, so lassen sich einige Muster erkennen. In einer Reihe von Klagepsalmen bilden die ‚Warum'- oder ‚Wie lange'-Klagen den kraftvollen Auftakt des ganzen Klagepsalms (Ps 13,2–3; 22,2; 74,1; vgl. Hab 1,2);[80] selbst die Anrede Gottes ist in die Klage integriert. Schon diese Beobachtung spricht gegen die Annahme von Janowski, die ‚Wie lange'-Frage in Ps 13 wollte „den Vorwurf an Gott und die Hoffnung auf die Wende der Not" ausdrücken.[81] Die Vertrauens- oder Hoffnungsbasis ist ja noch gar nicht verbalisiert, selbst die vertrauensvolle Anrede „mein Gott, mein Gott" in Ps 22 reißt ja nur den schmerzlichen Widerspruch zur beklagten Erfahrung der Verlassenheit von Gott noch weiter auf. Die einleitenden gegen Gott gerichteten Vorwürfe in Frageform sind darauf aus, den abgewandten oder erzürnten Gott zu einer Verhaltensänderung zu bewegen; aber ob dies gelingt, ist noch völlig offen.

In weiteren Klagepsalmen steht die an Gott gerichtete Frage hinter der Anrede und der einleitenden Bitte und leitet zugleich einen längeren Klageteil mit Aussagesätzen ein (Ps 9,20 f.; 10,1.2–11; 80,2–3.5.6–8; 94,1–2.3.4–7). Diese hervorgehobene Spitzenstellung der ‚Warum'- und ‚Wie lange'-Fragen weist auf ihre pragmatische Funktion, Gott für das Anhören der folgenden Klage bereiter zu machen. Daneben gibt es auch den umgekehrten Fall, in dem die an Gott gerichtete Frage einen Klageteil in Aussagesätzen abschließt und dabei meist zur Bitte überleitet (Ps 6,3b–4a.4b.5; 35,11–16.17aα.17aβ.b; 79,1–4.5.6–7; 89,39–46.47.48–49; 89,50.51 f.).[82] Hier fassen die ‚Wie lange'-Klagen die zuvorigen Klageschilderungen zusammen und wollen Gott dazu anstacheln, endlich einzugreifen. Als Motivationen zum Eingreifen werden die klagenden Fragen in Ps 44,24–27; Jes 63,15 direkt in die Bitten eingestreut.

Von den eben genannten Stellen ist die folgende Konstellation zu unterscheiden, in der eine an Gott gerichtete Klage zwar ebenfalls zur Bitte überleitet, davor jedoch ein Rückblick auf Gottes früheres Heilshandeln (Ps 80,9–12.13–14.15–18), ein

---

80 In Ps 88,15 steht die ‚Warum'-Anklage immerhin am Anfang eines mit der Schilderung des Klagens erneut eingeleiteten Klageteils.
81 So in Janowski, Das verborgene Angesicht Gottes, 30.
82 Auch in Psalm 74,9–11 wird eine lange schildernde Feindklage (VV. 4–8) durch gleich drei an Gott gerichtete Fragen abgeschlossen, es folgt aber erst einmal ein Rückblick auf Gottes mächtiges Urzeithandeln (VV. 12–17), bevor die Bitten einsetzen (VV. 18–23). Auch in der prophetisch stilisierten Klage Jer 14,17–22 fassen die Satz- und *maddûā'-Frage* in V. 19a die klagende Schilderung des Propheten (VV. 17–19) zusammen und führen nach einem Sündenbekenntnis (V. 20) zur Bitte (V. 21). |

Bekenntnis der Zuversicht (Ps 43,2aα.2aβ.b.3; Jes 63,16.17.18) oder ein hymnisches Bekenntnis (Klgl 5,19.20.21–22) platziert | ist.[83] Sie stehen darum eher im hinteren Teil des Klagegebets. Wie insbesondere aus den Volksklagen Ps 80 und Jes 63,7–64,11 erkennbar wird, zielt diese Konstellation darauf, die Wucht des Vorwurfs gegen Gott noch zu verstärken: Wie kann JHWH, der mit so viel Mühe und Sorgfalt den Weinstock Israel gepflanzt und gehegt hat, plötzlich die Mauern des Weinbergs zerbrechen, sodass die wilden Tiere ihn ungehindert verwüsten können (80,9–14)? Das heißt, es wird Gott in der ‚Warum'-Frage von V. 13 die geradezu skandalöse Widersprüchlichkeit seines Verhaltens vor Augen gestellt. Ähnliches gilt auch noch für die exilische Volksklage Jes 63,16–17: Wie kann JHWH, der doch Israels Vater ist, seine Kinder so in die Irre laufen lassen? In den Volksklagen Klgl 5 und Jer 14,1–9 hat man dagegen den Eindruck, dass die exilischen Volksklagen in heilsarmer Zeit die Bekenntnisse zu dem Zweck verwenden, eine Vertrauensbasis für ihre anklagenden Fragen an Gott zu gewinnen. Ähnliches gilt auch für Ps 42/43, der schon Züge eines gegen die Anfechtung formulierten Vertrauenspsalms zeigt. Das heißt aber, nur für diese drei letztgenannten Fälle gilt nun wirklich die von Bernd Janowski vertretene Sicht, dass die anklagenden Fragen vom Gottvertrauen getragen sind; nur ist die Aktualisierung des Vertrauensverhältnis zu Gott als Basis für die Anklage gegen ihn die Ausnahme.

Einen letzten Sonderfall stellt Jes 64,11 dar. Es handelt sich um eine Gott anklagende Satzfrage, die offenbar bewusst an das Ende dieser exilischen Volksklage gestellt worden ist: Nachdem die Betenden JHWH klagend die Verwüstung Judas, Jerusalems und des Tempels geschildert haben (V. 9–10), fügen sie eine abschließende Frage an ihn an: „Kannst Du dich bei all dem zurückhalten, schweigen und uns noch mehr niederdrücken?" Diese anklagende Frage soll offenbar den letzten Versuch unternehmen, JHWH doch noch zu einer Reaktion zu bewegen. Hier ist von Vertrauen nichts zu spüren. Hier herrscht blanke Verzweiflung.

Die an Gott gerichteten Fragen haben also eine herausragende Stellung in den Klagen der Klagegebete, die auf der ihnen innewohnenden illokutionären Kraft beruht. Sie zielen nicht auf Antworten, aber sie wollen Gott zu einer Reaktion provozieren. Sie wollen erreichen, dass er sich für die geschilderte Notlage interessiert; sie wollen ihm den schreienden Widerspruch zwischen seinem früheren und jetzigen Verhalten vorhalten, ihn bei der Ehre packen. | Sie wollen an

---

83 In Ps 42,10 ist zwar eine ‚Warum'-Anklage und -Ich-Klage durch vertrauensvolle Gottesprädikation eingeleitet, doch leiten die Fragen hier eine kurze Ich- und Feindklage in Aussageform ein. Die Bitte erfolgt hier erst nach einer Selbstvergewisserung (V. 12) in 43,1. In Jer 14,8.9 ist die Warum-Anklage in VV. 8b.9a geradezu von Bekenntnissen der Zuversicht umgeben (VV. 8a.9bα), erst darauf folgt die Bitte (V. 9bβ). |

seine Verantwortung appellieren, sie wollen, dass er in sich geht und sein jetziges Verhalten überdenkt. Sie wollen schließlich, dass er sich endlich dazu durchringt, zugunsten der Klagenden einzugreifen und ihre Not zu wenden.

4 Theologische Schlussbemerkung

Jürgen Ebach schreibt in dem schon am Anfang zitierten Aufsatz: „In der Anklage vor Gott [...] hält der Glaubende an beidem fest: daran, daß die ganze Welt die Welt Gottes ist, und daran, daß die vorfindliche Welt nicht das letzte Wort Gottes ist."[84] Ich möchte die beiden Teile dieser Feststellung abschließend unterstreichen und ein wenig ergänzen: Auch Leid, Scheitern, Unterdrückung, Unrecht und Zerstörung gehören zur Welt Gottes. Ja, die Klagegebete der Hebräischen Bibel, insbesondere deren Anklagen, bringen diese Schattenseiten der Welt mit Gott direkt in Verbindung und behaften ihn persönlich damit; Gott lässt die Not nicht nur zu, etwa das Unrecht, was die Frevler bewirken, sondern bewirkt sie sogar selber. Dadurch gerät das Gottesbild in eine nicht ungefährliche Spannung, die Hiob anfangs in die Richtung auflöst, dass Gott ein willkürlicher Machtpopanz sei, den niemand zur Verantwortung ziehen könne: „Wer könnte zu ihm sagen, was tust du da?" (9,12), um ihn dann später doch vor die Schranken des Gerichts zu fordern. Die an Gott gerichteten Fragen in den Klagegebeten halten demgegenüber eine Mittellinie ein, sie machen Gott schwere Vorwürfe, aber sie halten daran fest, dass man an Gottes Verantwortlichkeit, seine Ehre, seine Menschlichkeit, sein Gerechtigkeitsempfinden und sein Mitleid appellieren kann. Diese vorwurfsvollen Fragen wollen Gott bewegen, sein wahres Gesicht zu zeigen, aber sie lassen ihm auch den Spielraum dazu. Sie nageln Gott nicht auf die Position eines zynischen Potentaten fest, sondern kämpfen darum, dass sich das von Gott bewirkte Leid oder das von ihm zugelassene Unrecht „nicht [als] das letzte Wort Gottes" erweisen. Insofern arbeiten die klagenden Fragen im Gebet, die Gott mit dem ganzen Elend und Unrecht konfrontieren, gerade weil sie offene Fragen bleiben, auf eine Humanisierung des Gottes- und Weltbildes hin; sie verhindern, dass für den Leidenden beide, Gott und seine Welt, in Verzweiflung oder Zynismus versinken.

---

84 Ebach, „Herr, warum handelst du böse an diesem Volk?", 82.

Erotik und Sexualität in den Gesetzen der Torah: Nicht nur ein Störfaktor, sondern auch ein Menschenrecht

Nachdem ich im Alter aus dem Münsterland wieder nach Heidelberg umgezogen bin, habe ich Manfred Oeming, den ich mit diesem Beitrag als versierten Theologen und Archäologen ehren möchte, als einen ausgesprochen liebenswürdigen und großzügigen Freund kennengelernt. Ich hätte ihm gerne mit einem Beitrag über die großzügige Liebe Gottes gedankt, der seine Freiheit, die er gegenüber Mose in seinem berühmten Statement „Ich werde sein, der ich sein werde" (Ex 3,14) betont, dazu verwendet, dass er gegenüber Israel, als dieses ihm untreu geworden und zum Goldenen Kalb abgefallen ist, mit den Worten „Ich bin gnädig, wem ich gnädig bin, und erbarme mich dessen, wessen ich mich erbarme" (33,19) Gnade vor Recht ergehen lässt und es nicht vernichtet, wie er eigentlich nach seinem eigenen Gesetz hätte tun müssen (22,19).[1] Von dieser großzügigen Freiheit der Liebe Gottes leben auch wir Christen. Die Herausgeber dieser Festschrift, die mir ebenfalls wert sind, wollten allerdings, dass ich mich mit den Aspekten der menschlichen Liebe in den Gesetzen der Torah beschäftige. Das ist für mich ein eher ungewohntes Terrain; und ich bitte alle, auch Manfred Oeming, die darauf intensiver gearbeitet haben als ich, schon jetzt um Nachsicht. Die zuvor erwähnte großzügige Liebe Gottes ist aber auch bei allen Sexual- und Ehegesetzen der Torah,[2] die in seinem Namen erlassen wurden und die in unseren Ohren zuweilen schroff und unbarmherzig klingen, im Hintergrund immer mitzuhören. |

1 Begriffe für Erotik und Sexualität in den Gesetzen der Torah

Da es Gesetzgeber generell vor allem mit den Taten und weniger mit den Gefühlen von Menschen zu tun haben, spielt auch die Erotik in den Gesetzen der Torah

---

1 Der enge sachliche Zusammenhang, der zwischen diesen beiden Selbstaussagen Gottes in *idem-per-idem*-Formulierung nicht nur auf theologischer, sondern auch auf literarischer Ebene besteht, ist mir leider erst bei der Ausarbeitung des zweiten Bandes meines Exoduskommentars aufgegangen, vgl. Rainer Albertz: Exodus, Band I: Ex 1–18, ZBK.AT 2.1, Zürich 2012, 84–87, und Rainer Albertz: Exodus, Band II: Ex 19–40, ZBK.AT 2.2, Zürich 2015, 298–300. Ich weise hier beide Passagen der relativ späten Hexateuchredaktion (HexR) zu.
2 Berücksichtigt werden im Folgenden: Ex 20,14; 21,2–6.7–11; 22,15–16; Lev 18,6–23; 19,20–22.29; 20,7–21; 21,7–8.9.13–15; Num 5,11–31; Dtn 5,18; 20,7; 21,10–14.15–17; 22,13–21.22.23–24.25–27.28–29; 24,1–4.5; 25,5–10. |

https://doi.org/10.1515/9783111202228-020

kaum eine Rolle. Im ausdrücklichen Sinne ist es nur ein einziges Mal der Fall (Dtn 21,11), wo davon gesprochen wird, dass ein Israelit nach einem erfolgreichen Feldzug unter den Kriegsgefangenen eine Frau von schöner Gestalt (יפת־תאר *ypt-t'r*) sieht und sich von ihr so angezogen fühlt, dass er sich an sie hängt (חשק *ḥšq*), d. h. sich in sie verliebt (vgl. Gen 34,8). Der Eros stellt eine spontane Macht dar, die selbst wildfremde Menschen zusammenbringt, ob es einem passt oder nicht; deswegen müssen selbst die Gesetzgeber ihn manchmal berücksichtigen. Von der Liebe im weiteren Sinn (אהב *'hb*) ist in den Gesetzen nur die Rede, wo ein Schuldsklave seinen Herrn, seine Frau und Kinder so gern hat, dass er auf seine Freilassung verzichtet (Ex 21,5), oder wo ein Mann in polygamer Ehe seine eine Frau mehr liebt als seine andere (Dtn 21,15–16). Eher haben die Gesetzgeber damit zu tun, wenn das Gefallen an der Frau erstorben ist (לא חפץ *l' ḥpṣ*, 21,14; 25,7.8; vgl. Ex 21,8) oder gar in Abneigung oder Hass umschlägt (שנא *śn'*, Dtn 21,15–17; 22,13.16; 24,3), was meist zur Scheidung führt. Das Gefühl der Eifersucht, das sich bei dem Verdacht fremder sexueller Beziehungen der Frau beim Ehemann einstellt (קנא *qn'*), ist so stark, dass es bei den priesterlichen Gesetzgebern sogar auf einen „Geist der Eifersucht" zurückgeführt wird (רוח־קנאה *rwḥ-qn'h*, Num 5,14[2×].30). So sind es weniger die anziehenden als die abstoßenden Emotionen zwischen Mann und Frau, die in den Gesetzen zur Sprache kommen.

Weitaus häufiger als von Erotik ist in den Gesetzen von dem Akt der sexuellen Vereinigung die Rede. Meist wird er mit dem Euphemismus „liegen bei" (שכב עם *škb 'm*)[3] oder „liegen mit" (שכב את *škb 't*)[4] einer Frau ausgedrückt, von dem auch die nominalen Ausdrücke מִשְׁכָּב *miškāv* (Lev 18,22; 20,13), שְׁכָבָה *šikhbâ* (19,20; Num 5,13) und שְׁכֹבֶת *šəkhovæt* (Lev 18,20.23; 20,15; Num 5,20) für „Beischlaf", zum Teil mit dem Attribut זֶרַע *zr'* „Samen(erguss)" ergänzt, in den priesterlichen Gesetzen abgeleitet sind. Der unerlaubte sexuelle Verkehr mit weiblichen Verwandten wird dort meist mit dem ebenfalls euphemistischen Ausdruck גלה ערות *glh 'rwt* pi. „die Blöße von jemandem aufdecken" bezeichnet.[5] Seltener wird der in der Erzählliteratur geläufige Ausdruck בוא אל *bw' 'l* „eingehen in" die Frau für den Koitus verwendet (Dtn 21,13; 22,13). In allen diesen Wendungen wird sexuelle Vereinigung vom Manne aus gedacht. Er ist es, von dem sie ausgeht; die Frau ist nur empfangender Partner oder Opfer. Unter den Ausdrücken für illegitimen Sexualverkehr gilt dies auch für den Ehebruch. Das Verb נאף *n'p* „ehebrechen" bezeichnet speziell den Einbruch des Mannes in eine fremde Ehe (Ex 20,14; Dtn 5,18; Lev 20,10[4×]). Doch ist für die | Gesetzgeber immerhin im Blick, dass die Frau durch illegitimen und in besonderen Fällen auch legitimen

---

3 Ex 22,15; Dtn 22,22(2×).23.25(2×).28.29; vgl. Ex 22,18; Lev 15,33.
4 Lev 19,20; 20,12.13.18.20; Num 5,13.19; vgl. Lev 15,18.24.
5 Lev 18,6.7.8.9.10.11.12.13.14.15(2×).16.17(2×).18.19; 20,11.17.18.19.20.21. |

Sexualverkehr psychisch-physische Gewalt und soziale Erniedrigung erfahren kann, wofür sie entschädigt werden muss. Dies wird mit dem Verb עִנָּה *'nh* pi. „Gewalt antun, vergewaltigen" ausgedrückt (Dtn 21,14; 22,24.29), das keineswegs, wie zuweilen gemeint,[6] den normalen Geschlechtsverkehr bezeichnet. Sexuelle Seitensprünge der Ehefrau werden mit dem komplizierten Ausdruck שָׂטֹה תַחַת אִישׁ *śṭh tḥt 'yš* „auf Abwege anstelle ihres Mannes geraten" ausgedrückt (Num 5,19.20.29) und als Treulosigkeit gegenüber ihrem Ehemann gewertet (מָעַל בָּ *m'l ma'al bə*, 5,12.27). Nur bei der gesellschaftlich geächteten Promiskuität bzw. gewerbliche Hurerei steht die weibliche Aktivität im Vordergrund (זנה *znh*, Lev 19,29; 21,9; Dtn 21,21). Für die sexuellen Kontakte von Frauen mit Tieren wird das spezielle Verb רבע *rb'* verwendet (Lev 18,23; 20,16), das sonst das Begatten von Tieren bezeichnet (19,19). Ausgespart wird in den Gesetzen dagegen völlig das Verb שָׁגַל *šgl* „beschlafen", das offenbar einen so obszönen Klang hatte, dass es überall, wo es sonst im hebräischen Text vorkommt, abgeändert wurde.[7] So wird in den Gesetzen fast die ganze Bandbreite aller nur möglichen Spiel- und Abarten der Sexualität berücksichtigt.

2 Sexualität als Störfaktor für die sozialen Beziehungen der Gesellschaft

Eros und Sexualität bilden zwar ein starkes Bindemittel in der Gesellschaft, weil sie Männer und Frauen über die Familiengrenzen hinweg miteinander vereinen, die wiederum neue Familien gründen, aus denen eine neue Generation von Männern und Frauen hervorgeht, dennoch tauchen sie in den Gesetzen der Torah vornehmlich als Störfaktoren auf, welche die bestehenden sozialen Beziehungen der Gesellschaft bedrohen oder sogar ernsthaft gefährden. Die Ambivalenz von Eros und Sexualität wird schon in der Schöpfungserzählung Gen 2 bedacht, wenn hier einerseits die Anziehungskraft zwischen den Geschlechtern auf einen Schöpfergott zurückgeführt wird, der dem Menschen eine ideal zu ihm passende Partnerin schuf (V. 22–23), jedoch andererseits dieser Kraft für die Zukunft eine derart eruptive Wirkung zugeschrieben wird, dass „ein Mann seinen Vater und seine Mutter verlässt und an seiner Frau klebt" (V. 24).[8] Das geht nun gegen alle Kon-

---

6 So etwa Moshe Weinfeld: Deuteronomy and the Deuteronomic School, Oxford 1972, 286; Eckart Otto: Deuteronomium 12–34. Erster Teilband: 12,1–23,15, HThK.AT, Freiburg/Basel/Wien, 2016, 1618, in der Übersetzung von Dtn 21,14; anders allerdings in der Auslegung, a. a. O., 1650.

7 Vgl. Dtn 28,30; Jes 13,16; Jer 3,2; Sach 14,2.

8 Mit dem Zusammenhang von Schöpfungstheologie und Sexualität befassen sich auch Fischer, Zur sexuellen Aktivität erschaffen; Schmid, Das Patriarchat als Strafe (beide in diesem Band) [die Hrsg.] [[= Fischer, I., Zur sexuellen Aktivität erschaffen – zur sexuellen Inaktivität verurteilt?,

vention der patriarchalischen israelitischen Gesellschaft, in der die junge Frau ihre Familie zu verlassen hat, um ihrem Mann in dessen | Familie zu folgen.[9] Die Gesetzgeber sehen sich darum vornehmlich vor die Aufgabe gestellt, diese nie völlig kontrollierbare eruptive Kraft von Eros und Sexualität in einigermaßen geordnete Bahnen zu lenken, damit die sozialen Strukturen der Gesellschaft nicht beschädigt werden.

Ein Gesetz, das noch am ehesten das erotische Liebesspiel berücksichtigt, ist zugleich das älteste und steht vereinzelt im Bundesbuch aus der 2. Hälfte des 8. Jhs. v. Chr.:

> Ex 22,15 Und wenn ein Mann eine Jungfrau, die (noch) nicht verlobt ist, verführt und Beischlaf mit ihr hält, muss er sie sich zum vollen Brautpreis zur Frau nehmen.
> 16 Falls sich aber ihr Vater entschieden weigert, sie ihm zu geben, soll er Silber abwiegen entsprechend dem Brautpreis für Jungfrauen.

Ein Mann hat eine junge Frau,[10] die noch keinem anderen Mann durch einen Ehevertrag versprochen worden ist und die somit noch – vor sexuellen Kontakten weitgehend geschützt – im Hause ihres Vaters lebt, verführt (פתה *pth*), d. h. ihr schöne Augen gemacht und sie so sehr mit Komplimenten und kleinen Liebesbe-zeugungen und Zärtlichkeiten überhäuft, dass sie sich zur sexuellen Vereinigung bereit gefunden hat. Die Gesetzgeber bestimmen, dass der Liebhaber seine Gelieb-te nach einem solchen Akt nun nicht etwa im Stich lassen darf, sondern heiraten muss und zwar zum vollen Brautpreis, den er hätte zahlen müssen, wenn er zuvor um die Hand der jungen Frau bei deren Vater angehalten hätte. Der Mann wird mit der Verantwortung behaftet, die seinem erotischen Werben innewohnt; die Frau wird vor dem sexuellen Missbrauch geschützt. Doch eigentlich geht es den Gesetzgebern weniger um die junge Frau, nach deren Zustimmung zur Ehe gar nicht gefragt wird, als um die Besitzrechte des Vaters, warum das Gesetz auch unter die Eigentumsdelikte des Bundesbuches eingereiht steht (Ex 21,37–22,16).[11]

---

in: Bindrim, D./Grunert, V./Kloß, C. (Hg.), Erotik und Ethik in der Bibel. Festschrift für Manfred Oeming zum 65. Geburtstag, ABIG 68, Leipzig: Evangelische Verlagsanstalt, 2021, 21–30; Schmid, K., Das Patriarchat als Strafe. Überlegungen zu Genesis 3,16 und seinen Auslegungen, in: a. a. O., 31–40]]. |

9 Es ist darum erstaunlich, dass Gen 2,24 heute von Juden und Christen als Begründung der Ehe verstanden wird; vom Text her ist eher das rechtlich ungebundene Liebesleben im Blick, das im Hohen Lied besungen wird.

10 Zur Problematik der „Jungfräulichkeit" vgl. auch Grunert/Kloß, Virgo intacta (in diesem Band) [die Hrsg.] [[= Grunert, V./Kloß, C., Virgo intacta? Moderne Medizin, antike Statistiken und die Frage, wie voreheliche Sexualität in der Hebräischen Bibel bewertet wird, in: Bindrim u. a. (Hg.), Erotik und Ethik in der Bibel, 201–227]].

11 Vgl. Albertz, Exodus II (wie Anm. 1), 83–84. |

Er droht durch das erfolgreiche Liebesspiel des Mannes um die Zahlung des Brautpreises für seine Tochter betrogen zu werden. Ihm wird darum von den Gesetzgebern ausdrücklich die Entscheidung überlassen, ob er seine Tochter an den jungen Mann verheiraten will oder nicht lieber auf eine ihm günstiger erscheinende Gelegenheit wartet. Aber auch für den Fall, dass der Vater sein Veto einlegt, muss der Liebhaber den vollen Brautpreis für Jungfrauen zahlen. Denn aufgrund ihrer sexuellen Affäre würde jener für seine Tochter bei einer späteren Eheschließung wahrscheinlich nur noch ein geringeren oder gar keinen Brautpreis mehr erzielen. In keinem Fall soll der Vater durch den erotischen Vorfall nach Willen der Gesetzgeber in seinen Eigentumsrechten beschnitten werden. |

Diente schon der Brauch der Zahlung eines Brautpreises in patriarchalischen Gesellschaften der Stärkung der Kontrolle des Vaters über die Sexualität seiner Töchter,[12] weil sich deren Erziehung zu einer vorehelichen Keuschheit für ihn in barer Münze auszahlte, so wollen auch die Gesetzgeber des Bundesbuches den vorehelichen Sexualverkehr dadurch begrenzen, dass sie diesen so weit wie möglich in die Rechtsform der Ehe überführen, ihn aber in jedem Fall mit der Zahlung des höchstmöglichen Brautpreises belegen, egal ob die Ehe zustande kommt oder nicht.

Etwa ein Jahrhundert später gehen die Gesetzgeber des Deuteronomiums auf diesem Weg noch einen Schritt in dieselbe Richtung voran. Sie dekretieren in einem vergleichbaren Fall:

Dtn 22,28 Wenn ein Mann eine junge Frau, eine Jungfrau, trifft, die (noch) nicht verlobt ist, und er sie ergreift und Beischlaf mit ihr hält, und sie ertappt werden,

29 dann soll der Mann, der mit ihr Beischlaf gehalten hat, dem Vater der jungen Frau 50 (Schekel) Silber zahlen, und sie soll seine Frau werden, dafür dass er ihr Gewalt angetan hat. Er darf sie sein Leben lang nicht verstoßen.

Die Exegeten sind sich uneinig, ob es sich bei diesem Text nur um eine Variante von Ex 22,15–16 oder um einen anderen Fall handelt.[13] Eindeutig geht es in ihm

---

12 So mit Recht Tikva Frymer-Kenski, Virginity in the Bible, in: Victor H. Matthews/Bernhard M. Levinson/Dies. (Hrsg.), Gender and Law in the Hebrew Bible and the Ancient Near East, JSOT.S 262, Sheffield 1998, 79–96; hier 84–85; aufgenommen von Aaron Koller, Sex or Power? The Crime of the Bride in Deuteronomy 22*, in: ZAR 16, 2010, 279–296, 287–288.
13 Zwei verschiedene, ja, sogar komplementäre Fälle von Verführung und Vergewaltigung sehen z.B. Cynthia Edenburg, Ideology and Social Context of the Deuteronomic Women's Sex Laws (Deuteronomy 22:13–19), in: JBL 128, 2009, 43–60, 55–57; Adele Berlin, Sex and the Single Girl in Deuteronomy 22, in: Nili Sacher Fox u.a. (Hrsg.), Mishneh Todah. Studies in Deuteronomy and Its Cultural Environment. FS J. H. Tigay, Winona Lake, IN 2009, 95–112, hier 104–105, ähnlich auch Albertz, Exodus II (wie Anm. 1), 100–101. Als Varianten ein und desselben Falls beurteilen z.B. Weinfeld, Deuteronomy (wie Anm. 6), 286–287; Carolyn Pressler, The View of Women Found in the Deuteronomic Family Laws, BZAW 216, Berlin/New York 1993, 36–37; Robert S. Kawashima,

härter zu. Der Mann verführt die junge Frau nicht bloß mit schönen Worten wie | in Ex 22,15, sondern ergreift (תפש *tpś*) sie,[14] als er auf sie trifft, drängt sie also auch unter Einsatz von körperlicher Gewalt zum Sexualverkehr. Auf Gewaltanwendung könnte auch die Strafbegründung in Dtn 22,29 hindeuten, dass der Mann die junge Frau heiraten muss und sich nie von ihr scheiden lassen darf, „dafür dass er ihr Gewalt angetan hat". Das verwendete Verb ענה *'nh* pi. kann durchaus die Vergewaltigung einer Frau bezeichnen (Gen 34,2; 2Sam 13,12.14 u. ö.), doch könnte hier auch oder sogar eher die soziale Degradierung der jungen Frau gemeint sein, die dadurch zustande kommt, dass sie in der Öffentlichkeit im vorehelichen Beischlaf mit einem Mann ertappt wurde. Nach Willen der deuteronomischen Gesetzgeber soll somit ein Mann, der eine unverheiratete und noch keinem anderen Mann versprochene Frau unter Einsatz von körperlicher Gewalt in der Öffentlichkeit zum Sexualverkehr nötigt, deutlich schärfer als in Ex 22,15–16 bestraft werden: Er muss erstens an den Vater unverhandelbar die feste Summe von 50 Schekel Silber zahlen, d. h. den vollen Brautpreis inklusive einer Entschädigung, Und er muss die sexuell Genötigte in jedem Fall heiraten und verliert ihr gegenüber lebenslänglich das Scheidungsrecht. Der voreheliche Sexualverkehr wird damit für die Männer deutlich risikoreicher.

Gegenüber Ex 22,16 fällt auf, dass ein Entscheidungsrecht des Vaters, ob er seine Tochter dem draufgängerischen Liebhaber zur Frau geben will, nicht mehr erwähnt wird. J. G. Tigay ergänzt ein solches im Gefolge der jüdischen Tradition mit der Begründung: „It is inconceivable that he [e.g. the father] would be forced to give his daughter to her rapist".[15] Hier liegt in der Tat – zumindest nach unseren Maßstäben – eine schwer verständliche Härte des dtn. Gesetzes vor. Wenn dies so gemeint ist, wie es dasteht, wofür einiges spricht,[16] schließt es jeden Spielraum aus, den der Vater, der ja auch um das Wohl seiner Tochter besorgt ist, zu

---

Could a Woman Say „No" in Biblical Israel? On the Genealogy of Legal Status in Biblical Law and Literature, in: Association for Jewish Studies Review 35.1 (2011), 1–22, 17–18, die Texte. Otto, Deuteronomium III/1 (wie Anm. 6), 1724, sieht die Unterschiede zwischen Merkmalen der Verführung und Vergewaltigung, aber weniger klar differenziert als etwa im Mittelassyrischen Gesetz § 55 und 56. Robert J. V. Hiebert, Deuteronomy 22:28–29 and Its Premishnaic Interpretation, in: CBQ 1994, 203–220, hat gezeigt, dass zwar die Mischna (Ketubot 3,4) klar zwischen beidem unterscheidet, aber schon in der frühjüdischen Tradition Ex 22,15–16 und Dtn 22,28–29 miteinander kombiniert werden konnten, so in der Tempelrolle (11QT[b] 66,8–11), von Josephus (Ant. 4.252) und Philo (Spec. 3.65–71). |

14 Beim Verb תפש *tpś*, das in Bezug auf Personen „ergreifen, gefangen nehmen" bedeutet, ist immer ein Stück körperlicher Zwang im Spiel, vgl. Gen 39,12, 1Kön 13,4; 2Kön 10,14; Jer 37,13–14.
15 Jeffrey H. Tigay: דברים, Deuteronomy, JPS Torah Commentary 5, Philadelphia/Jerusalem 1996, 208.
16 Etwa dass das Deuteronomium auch sonst die elterlichen Rechte über ihre Kinder beschneidet, vgl. Dtn 21,18–21.

ihren Gunsten in die eine oder andere Richtung entscheiden könnte. E. Otto möchte im Ausschluss des Interventionsrechts des Vaters „a fundamental improvement of the status of women" sehen,[17] doch auch bei Aussicht auf eine lebenslange Versorgung bleibt für die Frau die Perspektive, ihren Vergewaltiger heiraten zu müssen, eine Zumutung. Offensichtlich nehmen die Gesetzgeber diese Härte bewusst in Kauf, um deutlich zu machen, dass selbst im Fall, dass eine unverheiratete Frau mit Gewalt zum Sexualverkehr genötigt wurde, diese so schnell wie möglich in eine unkündbare Ehe mit ihrem Sexualpartner gebracht werden muss, ohne dass noch jemand dagegen | Einspruch erheben kann. A. Berlin trifft meiner Meinung nach das Anliegen der deuteronomischen Gesetzgeber genau, wenn sie formuliert: „Because this case of premarital sex is a social offense, not a moral one, the law seeks to ›anul‹ it, or neutralize it, as it were, to normalize the woman's situation by quickly marrying her off to the man with whom she had sex".[18]

Die soziale Bedrohung, welche vom vorehelichen Sex nach Sicht der deuteronomischen Gesetzgeber ausgeht, wird deutlich an dem ersten Rechtsfall (Dtn 22,13–21), mit dem sie ihre kleine Komposition von Sexualgesetzen in 22,13–23,1 einleiten.[19] In einer ausführlichen Musterprozessordnung 22,13–19 stellen sie dar, dass der Vorfall, dass ein frischgebackener Ehemann, wohl vom ersten Sexualverkehr mit seiner Frischvermählten enttäuscht, den Vorwurf fehlender Jungfräulichkeit gegen sie erhebt, in einem öffentlichen Verfahren vor den Ältesten der Stadt gerichtlich geklärt werden muss. Ein solcher Verdacht darf nicht mehr zwischen den beteiligten Familien verhandelt und irgendwie vertuscht werden, sodass möglicherweise die Gerüchteküche weiter schwelt. An einer Klarstellung besteht ein öffentliches Interesse.

Man hat den Eindruck, dass die Gesetzgeber die jung Verheiratete und ihre Familie so gut wie möglich vor der sie alle kompromittierenden Anklage des Ehemanns schützen wollen. Es wird den Eltern leicht gemacht, irgendein Beweisstück für die Jungfräulichkeit ihrer Tochter herbeizuschaffen. Denn normalerweise wird das Bettzeug der Hochzeitsnacht beim Ehemann und dessen Familie ver-

---

17 Siehe Eckart Otto, False Weights in the Scales of Biblical Justice? Different Views of Women from Patriarchal Hierarchy to Religious Equality in the Book of Deuteronomy, in: Victor H. Matthews/Bernhard M. Levinson/Tikva Frymer-Kenski (Hrsg.), Gender and Law in the Hebrew Bible and the Ancient Near East, JSOT.S 262, Sheffield 1998, 128–146, 133. |
18 Siehe Berlin, Sex (wie Anm. 13), 106.
19 Otto, Deuteronomium III/1 (wie Anm. 6), 1713–1714, hat überzeugend gezeigt, dass die breite Fallschilderung Dtn 22,13–19 über die knappe ergänzte Strafbestimmung in V. 20–21 in die Abfolge von Sexualgesetze V. 22–29 einbezogen wurde.

wahrt.[20] Gefälscht oder nicht,[21] es geht den Gesetzgebern nur um eine öffentliche Demonstration eines Beweisstückes durch den Vater der Frau, das zugleich der ganzen Stadtgesellschaft beweist, dass sich die Eltern vor ihrer aller Augen voll und ganz mit ihrer in Verruf gebrachten Tochter solidarisieren. Je nach gesellschaftlichem Ansehen der Familie der Frau wird dies seinen | Eindruck nicht verfehlt haben. Jedenfalls wird als Regelfall in der Musterprozessordnung angenommen, dass der Ehemann der falschen Anklage überführt wird. Er wird durch Schläge öffentlich gedemütigt, muss noch einmal das Doppelte des Brautpreises plus Strafgebühren an den Brautvater zahlen, muss die Ehe mit der nunmehr öffentlich rehabilitierten Ehefrau fortführen und verliert ihr gegenüber das Scheidungsrecht (Dtn 22,18–19). All diese Strafen treffen ihn, „weil er eine Jungfrau Israels in schlechten Ruf gebracht hat" (V. 19). Die Keuschheit der jungen Frauen ist für die deuteronomischen Gesetzgeber nicht mehr nur ein familiärer Wert, der sich in der Höhe des Brautpreises materialisiert, sondern ein nationaler Wert, den es öffentlich zu verteidigen gilt. Bei derart drastischen Strafen sollte sich jeder Ehemann dreimal überlegen, ob er eine ihm unlieb gewordene Braut öffentlich der Unkeuschheit bezichtigen sollte, um sie nicht nur loszuwerden, sondern auch noch seinen Brautpreis zurückzubekommen. Ein solches Vorgehen, das die soziale Ordnung einer Stadt erschüttert, könnte leicht doppelt und dreifach auf ihn zurückfallen.

An die ausführliche Prozessordnung haben die Gesetzgeber noch eine knappe Strafregelung angehängt für den Fall, dass sich die Anklage des Ehemanns als wahr erweist (Dtn 22,20–21), um das Ganze in die folgende Sexualgesetzgebung einzuordnen. Das Problem ist, dass sie in diesem Fall auf alle Angaben zur Beweisführung und Näherbestimmung der Straftat verzichten, so dass wir auf Vermutungen angewiesen sind. Es mag sein, dass im Prozess Zeugen aufgetreten

---

20 Darauf macht mit Recht Frymer-Kenski, Virginity (wie Anm. 12), 95, aufmerksam. Doch die Lösung für diese Schwierigkeit, die Jonathan P. Burnside, The Signs of Sin. Seriousness of Offence in Biblical Law, JSOT.S 364, Sheffield 2003, 143–147, im Anschluss an Gordon J. Wenham, B^etûlāh ‚A Girl of Marriageable Age', in VT 22, 1972, 326–348, 330–336, anbietet, dass sich der Prozess nicht um einen Nachweis der Jungfräulichkeit, sondern der Schwangerschaft der Frau zur Zeit der Eheschließung dreht, bei dem die Eltern ein Kleidungsstück der Tochter mit Menstruationsblut vorweisen, hat den semantischen Befund gegen sich, dass בתולה btwlh zumindest in Rechtstexten oft eindeutig die Bedeutung „Jungfrau" hat, vgl. Clemens Locher, Die Ehre einer Frau in Israel. Exegetische und rechtsvergleichende Studie zu Deuteronomium 22,13–21, OBO 70, Fribourg/Göttingen 1986, 176–192. Zu den eindeutigen Stellen gehört nach Matitiahu Tsevat, ThWAT I, 875, auch Dtn 21,19.

21 Frymer-Kenski, Virginity (wie Anm. 12), 93, übertreibt vielleicht die Leichtigkeit, mit der unter den damaligen diagnostischen Mitteln eine Fälschung hergestellt werden konnte. Aber möglicherweise wollten die Gesetzgeber den vorzeigbaren Gegenbeweis so leicht wie möglich machen. |

sind, welche die Anklage des Ehemannes stützten, möglich ist aber auch, dass die Eltern der Braut über den verheimlichten vorehelichen Sexualverkehr ihrer Tochter so sehr verärgert waren, dass sie nicht mehr öffentlich für sie einstehen wollten. Immerhin hatte jene auch sie in Verruf gebracht. E. Otto meint, die drastische Strafe einer öffentlichen Steinigung der Frau deute darauf hin, dass die Gesetzgeber den Fall im Sinne von V. 23–24 als Ehebruch der „inchoativ verheirateten Ehefrau"[22] verstanden wissen wollten. Dann hätte der außereheliche Sexualverkehr der Braut in der Zeit stattgefunden haben müssen, als sie schon durch Ehevertrag an ihren künftigen Ehemann gebunden war, aber noch im elterlichen Haus lebte. Das ist ein mögliches Verständnis; sein Problem liegt nur darin, dass in V. 20–21 der Zeitpunkt des Sexualverkehrs nicht spezifiziert wird, und ein solcher vor der „Verlobung" nach V. 28–29 nicht mit dem Tode bestraft worden wäre.[23] Warum sehen die deuteronomischen Gesetzgeber für die Frau, deren Sexualverkehr vor oder nach der Verlobung erst kurz nach der Heirat aufgedeckt wird, eine derart drastische Strafe wie die öffentliche Steinigung am Haus ihrer Eltern vor? In V. 21 begründen sie | diese damit, dass die Frau eine Schandtat (נבלה *nblh*) in Israel begangen hat, indem sie im Haus ihres Vaters Hurerei (זנה *znh*) getrieben habe. Letzteres ist kaum im wörtlichen Sinne zu verstehen,[24] da sich ein solches sexuelles Treiben, gewerblich ausgeübt oder nicht, wohl kaum verheimlichen ließe. Vielmehr wird mit diesem Ausdruck auf drastische Weise der schwere Vertrauensbruch beschrieben, den die junge Frau gegenüber ihren Eltern, die den Ehevertrag aufsetzten, und gegenüber ihrem Ehemann, der sie im guten Glauben zur Frau nahm, begangen hat. In der Prophetie Hoseas war schon im 8. Jh. v.Chr. das Wort זנה *znh* „huren" zur beherrschenden Metapher für den Vertrauensbruch und die Untreue Israels gegenüber seinem Gott JHWH geworden,[25] hatte dieser Prophet doch das Verhältnis der beiden als exklusives Liebesverhältnis vorgestellt, in der Gott den Ehemann und Israel seine Ehefrau verkörpert.[26] Mir scheint, dass nun hier bei den Deuteronomikern, die auch sonst viel von Hosea gelernt haben, die religiöse Metapher wiederum auf ihre Einschätzung

---

22 So Otto, Deuteronomium III/1 (wie Anm. 6), 1713.

23 Alexander Rofé, Family and Sex Laws in Deuteronomy and the Book of the Covenant, in: Ders., Deuteronomy. Issues and Interpretation, Edinburgh/New York 2002, 169–192, 178–179, hatte aus der Tatsache, „that Deut 22.20–21 is in conflict with the other biblical sex laws", gefolgert, die Verse müssten von einem späteren Redaktor stammen, der von den scharfen Idolatrie-Gesetzen (Dtn 13,2–19; 17,2–7) beeinflusst sei. Doch haben diese sich inzwischen teilweise als ein Kern der dtn. Gesetzgebung herausgestellt. |

24 So Burnside, Signs (wie Anm. 20), 134, unter Einbeziehung von Lev 19,29.

25 Vgl. Hos 1,2; 2,7; 3,3; 4,12; 5,3; 9,1.

26 Vgl. Hos 1,2–3; 2,4–14.21–22; 3,1–4.

des Sexualverhaltens abfärbt.[27] Ein Sexualverhalten der jungen Frau, das die Exklusivität, die jeder erotischen Beziehung innewohnt, schlichtweg leugnet und nichts dabei findet, den künftigen Ehepartner an der Nase herumzuführen und damit tief zu kränken, ist für die deuteronomischen Gesetzgeber „eine Schandtat in Israel",[28] eine Untat von nationalem Ausmaß, die an den Grundwerten der Gesellschaft rüttelt und darum nicht akzeptiert werden kann. Das sich darin manifestierende Böse soll darum aus ihrer Mitte ausgerottet werden. Und dabei sollen wohl mit der Lokalisierung der Steinigung am väterlichen Haus auch die Eltern mit bestraft werden, die bei der Erziehung ihrer Tochter so schmählich versagt hatten.

Wenn man bedenkt, welche hohe Bedeutung die deuteronomischen Gesetzgeber der Unbescholtenheit und Vertrauenswürdigkeit der Frauen bei ihrer Eheschließung beimessen, wird auch verständlich, warum sie so sehr daran interessiert sind, jeden vorehelichen Sexualverkehr, der öffentlich aufgedeckt wurde, selbst dann, wenn er mit einer Nötigung der Frau einher gegangen war, sofort in die Rechtsform der Ehe zu überführen (Dtn 22,28–29). Sie wollten damit möglichst verhindern, dass es überhaupt zu solchen unschönen und die Öffentlichkeit erregenden Prozessen kommt, wie sie in der Musterordnung von V. 13–21 geschildert werden. Dass den deuteronomischen Gesetzgebern besonders am Herzen lag, insbesondere Vertrauensbrüche zwischen jungen Leuten zu verhindern, machen auch die übrigen Sexualgesetze der Komposition deutlich. Während sie den Ehebruch, den ein Mann mit einer schon verheirateten Frau begeht, relativ knapp abhandeln und für die auf frischer Tat Ertappten nur | die gewöhnliche Todesstrafe vorsehen, welche das Eindringen eines fremden Mannes in einen Familienbetrieb und die Geburt eines illegitimen Erben in jedem Fall verhindern soll (V. 22), behandeln die Gesetzgeber den Ehebruch mit einer verlobten, d. h. durch Ehevertrag einem Mann erst versprochenen jungen Frau, in aller Ausführlichkeit (V. 23–27) und sehen für den Fall, dass von einer Mitschuld der Frau ausgegangen werden muss,[29] die öffentliche Steinigung beider am Stadttor vor (V. 24), was eine besonders degradierende und exkludierende Form der Todesstrafe darstellt.[30]

---

27 Schon Hosea hatte den Konnex zwischen der religiösen Untreue Israels und dem sexuellen Fehlverhalten von Frauen und Männern in Israel hergestellt (vgl. Hos 4,12–14).
28 Locher, Ehre (wie Anm. 20), 237, spricht hier zutreffend von der Verknüpfung von individueller und nationaler Ehre. |
29 Sie wird darin gesehen, dass die Frau sich nicht gegen den Geschlechtsverkehr in der Stadt, wo man sie hätte hören können, durch Hilfeschreie gewehrt hat. Die Misshandlung der Frau (עִנָּה *'nh* pi.), die dem Mann in Dtn 22,24 zur Last gelegt wird, kann in diesem Fall nicht die körperliche Vergewaltigung meinen, sondern die soziale Entehrung, weil sie einem anderen Mann versprochen war.
30 Auf diese Differenz hat vor allem Tikva Frymer-Kensky, Law and Philosophy. The Case of Sex and the Bible, in: Semeia 45, 1989, 89–102, 93, aufmerksam gemacht.

Nur dann, wenn davon ausgegangen werden muss, dass die junge Frau in den illegalen Sexualverkehr nicht eingewilligt hat, sondern Opfer einer Vergewaltigung wurde, wird allein der Ehebrecher gesteinigt (V. 25), während sie straffrei bleibt (V. 26–27). Der Einbruch eines fremden Mannes in eine gerade erst entstehende Paarbeziehung bzw. die mögliche Treulosigkeit einer jungen Frau gegen ihren Verlobten waren für die deuteronomischen Gesetzgeber ganz besonders verwerflich und mussten deswegen öffentlich scharf gebrandmarkt werden.

Aber auch dem sexuellen Verhalten älterer Eheleute legen die deuteronomischen Gesetzgeber strengere Regeln auf. Gerade weil eine Scheidung zumindest für einen begüterten Ehemann relativ einfach zu bewerkstelligen war, verbieten die Gesetzgeber ihm, seine geschiedene Frau nach deren zweiter Ehe erneut zu heiraten (Dtn 24,1–4). Die neue intime sexuelle Vertrauensbeziehung hat seine ehemalige Frau für ihn tabuisiert (V. 4);[31] diese ist ihm gegenüber ohne jede Verpflichtungen und darf sich frei neu orientieren. Die rasche Abfolge von Heiraten und Scheidungen und erneuten Heiraten darf nicht zu einer treulosen Promiskuität unter dem Deckmantel des Eherechts missbraucht werden. Eine solche wäre für die Gesetzgeber ein Gräuel für JHWH, die das ganze Land in Schuld bringt (V. 4). Hier wird somit auch einmal dem sexuellen Begehren des Mannes eine harte Schranke aufgerichtet. Erneut wird deutlich, wie eine Nationalisierung und religiöse Aufladung des Sexualrechts die Ansprüche an ein dem Partner angemessenes Sexualverhalten in die Höhe treibt. |

3 Sexualität als Störfaktor für die innerfamiliären Beziehungen

Die Ambivalenz von Eros und Sexualität zeigt sich innerfamiliär noch drastischer als bei den sozialen Beziehungen in der Gesellschaft. Auf der einen Seite entsteht die Familie erst durch Eros und Sexualität, auf der anderen Seite kann sie durch beide schwer beschädigt oder gar zerstört werden. Gerade in einer Gesellschaft, in der – wie wir aus archäologischen Funden aus dem alten Israel abschätzen können – Kernfamilien, oft durch vereinzelte Verwandte erweitert, in den Stadthäusern von 30–70 m² zu 5–7 Personen auf engsten Raum nebeneinander über-

---

31 Zur Forschungsgeschichte dieses schwer zu interpretierenden Gesetzes siehe Eckart Otto, Deuteronomium 12–34. Zweiter Teilband: 23,16–34,12, HThK.AT, Freiburg/Basel/Wien, 2017, 1801–1806. Sein Vorschlag, הֻטַּמָּאָה *huṭṭammā'ā* in Dtn 24,4 deklarativ im Sinne von „nachdem sie für unrein erklärt worden ist" auf die Scheidungserklärung des ersten Ehemannes zu beziehen, hat die Schwierigkeit, dass er nicht erklärt, warum erst die zweite durchlebte Ehe die Frau seinen sexuellen Wünschen entzieht. |

nachten mussten und selbst die größeren Häuser von 120–130 m^2 auf dem Land den Großfamilien, die aus ca. 15 Personen und meist aus mehreren verheirateten Paaren bestanden, nur wenige Rückzugsmöglichkeiten boten,[32] ist es nötig, die möglichen erotischen Beziehungen und sexuellen Kontakte klar auf die dazu berechtigten Personen zu beschränken. Die Sexualität ist, wie es E. Gerstenberger formuliert, „– auch und gerade im engsten Familienkreis – eine bedrohliche, unberechenbare Macht ..., die es zu kontrollieren gilt".[33] Warum Letzteres so wichtig ist, machen Einsichten der modernen Familiensoziologie verständlich. Nach R. Nave-Herz ist die Familie in ihrer „biologisch-sozialen Doppelnatur", aus der sich ihre grundlegende Reproduktions- und Sozialisationsfunktion ergibt, u. a. notwendig durch eine Generationsdifferenz und „durch eine bestimmte Rollenstruktur (Mutter/Vater/Tochter/Sohn/Enkel/Schwester usw.)" gekennzeichnet.[34] Diese für den Bestand der Familie konstitutiven Elemente würden nun aber völlig durcheinandergebracht, wenn etwa durch Sexualverkehr des Sohnes mit seiner Mutter jener in die Vaterrolle hineinrückte oder durch Sexualverkehr des Vaters mit seiner Tochter diese in die Mutterrolle erhoben würde. Schwere emotionale Konflikte und tiefe seelische Verletzungen wären die Folge. Es ist deswegen kein Zufall, dass mit der fast weltweiten Verbreitung der Familie auch die Inzestvermeidung ein universales menschliches Kulturgut darstellt.[35]

Eine Besonderheit Israels besteht darin, dass die priesterlichen Gesetzgeber – wohl in der 1. Hälfte des 5. Jhs. v. Chr. – eine lange Reihe von regelrechten Inzestverboten im Namen Gottes veröffentlichten (Lev 18,6–16). Verboten wird hier der sexuelle Verkehr mit der leiblichen Mutter, der Stiefmutter, der Voll- und Halbschwester, der Enkelin, den Tanten mütterlicher- und väterlicherseits, der Frau des Onkels sowie der Schwiegertochter und Schwägerin, d. h. den | weiblichen Mitgliedern der Kern- und Großfamilie plus einigen weiblichen Verwandten (wie etwa der Schwester der Mutter), die in Ausnahmefällen bei ihr wohnen konnten. Auffällig ist nur das Fehlen der Tochter, die nach unseren Erfahrungen eigentlich besonderen Schutzes bedurft hätte. Sie ist entweder unter den in V. 6 angesprochenen unmittelbar Blutsverwandten („alles Fleisch seines Fleisches") mit gemeint[36] oder war vielleicht zu diesen Zeiten noch durch den Brautpreis, dessen

---

32 Vgl. dazu Rainer Albertz/Rüdiger Schmitt, Family and Household Religion in Ancient Israel and the Levant, Winona Lake, IN 2012, 26–41.

33 Siehe Erhard Gerstenberger, Das 3. Buch Mose. Leviticus, ATD 6, Göttingen 1993, 228–229.

34 Siehe Rosemarie Nave-Herz, Familiensoziologie, in: Günter Endruweit/Gisela Tromms-Dorf (Hrsg.), Wörterbuch der Soziologie, UTB 2232, Stuttgart 2002, 148–152, 149.

35 Vgl. Christoph Antweiler: Was ist den Menschen gemeinsam? Über Kultur und Kulturen, Darmstadt 2007, 252–255. |

36 So etwa Susan Rattray, Marriage Rules, Kinship Terms, and Family Structure in the Bible, in: Seminar Papers 26, 1987, 537–544, 542.

der Vater bei einem sexuellen Übergriff auf sie verlustig ging, genügend geschützt. Als besonders bedroht sahen die Gesetzgeber offenbar die Mutter oder die oft jüngere Stiefmutter durch den herangewachsenen Sohn und die Schwiegertochter durch den alternden Vater an.[37] Auffällig ist, dass die Gesetzgeber zur Begründung der Inzestverbote bei leiblichen Verwandten auf die sozialen Rollen verweisen, welche die Frauen innehaben („deine Mutter/Schwester ist sie" V. 7.11) bzw. deren Männer spielen („dein Onkel ist er" V. 14; „Frau deines Sohnes ist sie" V. 15), die auch in der Soziologie als so wichtig erachtet werden. Der Hinweis soll die familiäre Solidarität und Verantwortung stärken. Bei entfernteren Verwandten, etwa Tanten, wird das Verwandtschaftsverhältnis („Fleisch") zu näher Verwandten (Vater, Mutter) hervorgehoben (V. 12.13). Bei den nicht leiblich verwandten Familienmitgliedern machen die Gesetzgeber darauf aufmerksam, dass mit dem „Aufdecken der Blöße" der Stiefmutter, Enkelin oder Schwägerin auch „Blöße", d. h. der Intimbereich der zugehörigen leiblichen Verwandten verletzt wird (18,8.10.16; vgl. 20,11.20).

Das besondere Anliegen der priesterlichen Gesetzgeber wird nun darin erkennbar, dass sie den keineswegs außergewöhnlichen Inzestverboten eine kultische Qualität zuschreiben. Mit ihrer Übertretung würden sich nicht nur die Täter selbst kultisch verunreinigen (Lev 18,24[2×].30), sondern auch – bei entsprechender Häufung – das ganze Land unrein machen (V. 27.28; vgl. 25), so dass dieses die Israeliten ausspeien könnte wie schon seine Vorbewohner zuvor (V. 24.25.28). D. h. die Kategorie der kultischen Unreinheit, die traditionell nur mit ganz bestimmten Formen sexueller Unzucht verbunden war, wie dem Beischlaf mit einer Menstruierenden (V. 20) oder der Begattung durch ein Tier (V. 23), wird auf alle Arten inzestuösen Sexualverhaltens ausgedehnt, um dieses damit zusätzlich auch noch religiös zu tabuisieren.[38]

Das Mittel der religiösen Tabuisierung illegitimen Geschlechtsverkehrs durchzieht dann auch die übrige priesterliche Sexual- und Heiratsgesetz | gebung: Am besonderen Fall der Verführung einer verlobten, aber noch nicht freigekauften Schuldsklavin (Lev 19,20–22) machten die Gesetzgeber klar, dass selbst dann, wenn ein solcher Einbruch in eine inchoative Ehe nach Dtn 22,23–27 nicht gericht-

---

37 Vgl. die verdoppelte Verbotsformulierung für die Mutter und die Schwiegertochter in Lev 18,7.15; und die Aufnahme des Verkehrs mit der Stiefmutter und der Schwiegertochter unter die todeswürdigen Verbrechen in Lev 20,11.12.

38 Im wohl später anzusetzenden priesterlichen Eifersuchtsritual Num 5,11–31 ist die Formulierung „sich verunreinigen" (טמא *ṭm'* ni.) zur gängigen Bezeichnung des illegitimen Sexualverkehrs der Ehefrau geworden (vgl. V. 13.14[2×].20.27.28.29). Doch immerhin schaffen die Priester damit gegenüber dem harten Gesetz Dtn 22,22 ein kultisches Mittel, mit dem die Frau ihre mögliche Unschuld beweisen kann. |

lich zu ahnden war, weil der Sklavin die nötige Rechtsfähigkeit fehlte, er doch eine Sünde gegenüber Gott darstellte, die von dem Verführer mit einem Schuldopfer gesühnt werden müsste.[39] Wenn die priesterlichen Gesetzgeber das generelle Verbot, die eigene Tochter zur Hurerei anzuhalten (Lev 19,29), was in bitterer Not vielleicht von manchen armen Familien als letzter Rettungsanker angesehen wurde, mit den Worten formulierten: „Du sollst deine Tochter nicht entweihen!" (חלל ḥll pi.),[40] dann schrieben sie der weiblichen Keuschheit eine quasi sakrale Qualität zu, die durch gewerblichen Sex zerstört würde. In gleicher Weise wird davor gewarnt, dass sich die Tochter eines Priesters durch häufig wechselnden Geschlechtsverkehr so sehr entweihen könnte (חלל ḥll ni.), dass sie auch den geweihten Status ihres Vaters in Mitleidenschaft ziehen würde (21,9). Eine solche Bedrohung der kultischen Ordnung war nicht hinnehmbar; die Tochter müsse in einen schlimmen Feuertod sichtbar ausgemerzt werden wie der Mann, der zugleich eine Frau und deren Mutter heiratet (20,14). Auf den geweihten Status der Priester nehmen auch die Heiratsgesetze für sie Bezug. Der gewöhnliche Priester darf keine Hure, Entehrte[41] oder Geschiedene heiraten, „da er heilig für seinen Gott ist" (21,7). Der Hohe Priester darf darüber hinaus keine Witwe heiraten, sondern nur „eine Jungfrau aus seiner Sippe, damit er seine Nachkommen in seiner Sippe nicht entweihe" (חלל ḥll pi.) (V. 14–15). Alles andere als die quasi sakrale Keuschheit einer Jungfrau aus seiner weiteren Verwandtschaft würde die geforderte Heiligkeit des Hohen Priesters beeinträchtigen. Mit der sakralen Überhöhung der weiblichen Keuschheit und der religiösen Tabuisierung illegitimer Sexualkontakte möchten die Schöpfer des Heiligkeitsgesetzes dazu beitragen, dass sich die judäische Gesellschaft ein Stück weit an die Heiligkeit ihres Gottes annähert. Dieser göttlichen Heiligkeit kann nach ihrer Ansicht nur eine strengstens regulierte Sexualität entsprechen. |

4 Ein kleiner rechtlicher Schutzraum für die bedrohte Erotik und Sexualität

Obwohl für die Gesetzgeber der Torah die Eindämmung der die gesellschaftlichen und familiären Beziehungen störenden oder sogar zerstörenden Kräfte von Eros

39 Vgl. Jacob Milgrom: Leviticus 17–22. A New Translation and Commentary, AB 3A, New York u. a. 2000, 1674–1675.
40 Zur Deutung dieser Stelle vgl. auch Grunert/Kloß, Virgo intacta (in diesem Band) [die Hrsg.] [[= Grunert/Kloß, Virgo intacta, in: Bindrim u. a. (Hg.), Erotik und Ethik in der Bibel, 201–227]].
41 Da die in Lev 21,7.14 eng bei der Hure (זֹנָה zōnā) stehende „Entehrte, Entweihte" (חֲלָלָה ḥalālā) – in V. 14 sogar ohne Kopula – bei den Priestern und dem Hohen Priester genauso ausgeschlossen ist, kann der Begriff kaum, wie Wenham, Girl (wie Anm. 20), 336–337, behauptet, „a

und Sexualität stark im Vordergrund stehen, versuchen sie ihnen an einigen Stellen einen rechtlichen Schutzraum zu gewähren. Das ist um so erstaunlicher, weil Eros und Sexualität unter normalen Umständen stark genug sind, um sich in den menschlichen Beziehungen alleine genügend Raum zu verschaffen. Es sind darum rechtliche Regelungen zum Schutz von Personen minderen Rechts oder Regulierungen für die Ausnahmesituation des Krieges, mit denen die Gesetzgeber den Betroffenen ausdrücklich ein Recht auf Eros und Sexualität einräumen.

Als die Gesetzgeber des Bundesbuches daran gingen, die sich in der sozialen Krise des 8. Jhs. v. Chr. ausweitende Schuldsklaverei auf maximal sechs Jahre zu begrenzen (Ex 21,2–6),[42] dachten sie darüber nach, unter welchen Umständen möglicherweise ein Schuldsklave auf seine Entlassung verzichten könnte. Dies sahen sie höchstens dann als gegeben an, wenn sein Herr ihm eine Frau gegeben und ihm so ermöglicht habe, mit ihr eine Familie zu gründen (V. 4). Denn weil Frau und Kinder weiter im Besitz seines Herrn blieben, wäre der Schuldsklave gezwungen, sich bei seiner Entlassung von seiner Familie zu trennen. Sofern der Schuldsklave ausdrücklich erklärt, dass er seine Frau und Kinder sowie seinen Herrn, der ihm die Familiengründung ermöglichte, so sehr liebt, dass er nicht freigelassen werden will (V. 5), waren die Gesetzgeber bereit, eine rituell und religiös abgestützte Zeremonie zuzulassen, durch welche die begrenzte Schuldsklaverei ausnahmsweise in eine Dauersklaverei umgewandelt werden konnte (V. 6). Sie waren bereit, ihr wichtiges soziales Reformprojekt einzuschränken, um im Einzelfall die eheliche Liebesbeziehung des Sklaven nicht zu beschädigen.

Der Verkauf von Töchtern in die Schuldsklaverei (Ex 21,7–11) war ein Kreditgeschäft auf den Brautpreis, bei dem der Kreditgeber dem verarmten Vater schon vorab die Summe zahlte, die er später beim Heranwachsen des Mädchens als Brautpreis zu entrichten hätte.[43] Da es um eheähnliche Verhältnisse ging, war normalerweise keine Entlassung der Schuldsklavin vorgesehen. Dennoch bemühten sich die Gesetzgeber des Bundesbuches die Stellung der jungen Frau im Hause ihres Herrn soweit zu stärken, dass sie nicht als Familienhure missbraucht wurde (V. 9 gegen Am 2,7). Darum sahen sie für den Fall, dass der Kreditgeber kein Gefallen mehr an ihr fand, ein Rückkaufrecht vor und verboten ausdrücklich den Verkauf an eine fremde Sippe mit der Begründung: „weil | er treulos an ihr

---

woman who has been defiled" bedeuten, da dann unverständlich wäre, warum beim Hohen Priester der jungfräuliche Status der Heiratskandidatin so stark hervorgekehrt wird. Es muss sich vielmehr um eine Frau, deren mehrfache und vielleicht auch wechselnde Sexualkontakte bekannt sind, handeln. |

42 Vgl. ausführlicher bei Albertz, Exodus II (wie Anm. 1), 86–88.
43 Vgl. dazu Albertz, Exodus II (wie Anm. 1), 88–89. |

gehandelt hat" (Ex 21,8).[44] Das Nicht-Einhalten des Eheversprechens gegenüber der jungen Sklavin wurde von den Gesetzgebern als Vertrauensbruch angesehen, für das der Kreditgeber mit einer Einschränkung seiner Besitzrechte büßen muss-te. Sofern der Kreditgeber die Schuldsklavin zwar heiratete, sich aber bald noch eine andere Frau hinzu nahm, bestimmten die Gesetzgeber, dass er ihren Anteil an „Festspeisen, Kleidung und an Beischlaf nicht kürzen dürfe" (V. 10). Die Bedeu-tung des letztgenannten hebräischen Wortes עֹנָה ‘ōnā ist zwar etymologisch nicht gesichert, doch zielen die Versionen in die besagte Richtung.[45] Wenn damit das Richtige getroffen ist, dann wird der eher ungeliebten Schuldsklavin ausdrücklich ein Recht auf sexuellen Verkehr zugesprochen. Andernfalls muss sie nach dem Willen der Gesetzgeber unentgeltlich in die Freiheit entlassen werden (V. 11).

Billigten schon die Verfasser des Bundesbuches den hebräischen Schuldsklavinnen ein Recht auf Sexualität zu, so gingen die Gesetzgeber des Deuteronomiums sogar so weit, weiblichen Kriegsgefangenen aus anderen Völkern einen rechtlichen Weg in eine geordnete Ehe zu bahnen (Dtn 21,10–14). Wie leider bis heute waren auch in den antiken Kriegen die Frauen des Feindes häufig sexuelles Freiwild; sie wurden von den siegreichen Soldaten erbeutet und vergewaltigt (Ri 5,30). Obgleich die deuteronomischen Gesetzgeber Mischehen mit Ausländerinnen eher kritisch bis ablehnend gegenüberstanden, waren sie gewillt ein solches schändliches sexuelles Treiben in Israel so weit wie möglich zu unterbinden. Darum gestanden sie einem judäischen Mann, der sich in eine hübsche Kriegsgefangene verliebt hatte, ausdrücklich zu, diese zu heiraten (Dtn 21,11). Doch legten sie ihm erst einmal eine einmonatige Periode der Enthaltsamkeit auf, in der die junge Frau sich in seinem Hause vom Schmutz der Kriegswirren reinigen und gebührend von ihrer Vergangenheit, etwa von ihren im Krieg umgekommenen Eltern, Abschied nehmen konnte (V. 12–13a).[46] Erst dann durfte er Sexualverkehr mit ihr aufnehmen und so die Ehe zwischen ihnen besiegeln (V. 13b). E. Otto geht vielleicht ein bisschen zu weit, wenn er diese Bestimmungen als „a moral revolution on the long road towards equal | dignity and rights of men and women"

---

44 Das Verb בגד *bgd* „treulos handeln", das nur hier im Pentateuch vorkommt, wird zwar bei Hosea (5,7; 6,7) und Jeremia (3,8.11.20; 5,11) für die religiöse Untreue Israels gegenüber JHWH verwendet, scheint aber hier im Bundesbuch noch ohne religiösen Nebensinn gebraucht zu sein. Eine Parallelisierung beider Sinnebenen ist erst in Mal 2,14–16 belegt.
45 Vgl. die LXX ὁμιλία *homilía* „Gemeinschaft, Umgang, sinnlicher Verkehr", die Vulgata *pretium pudicitiae* „Preis der Keuschheit" und William C. Propp, Exodus 19–40. A New Translation with Introduction and Commentary, AB 2A, New York/London u. a. 2006, 202–203. Auch der Talmud betont das Recht der Ehefrau auf sexuelle Befriedigung, vgl. Mischna Ketubot 5,6 u. ö.
46 Dass die lange Zeitdauer auch dazu dienen sollte zu überprüfen, ob die junge Frau ihre Regel bekam oder schwanger war, wie Ulrike Bechmann, Die kriegsgefangene Frau (Dtn 21,10–14), in: BiKi 60, 2005, 200–204, 202, vermutet, ist damit nicht ausgeschlossen. |

bezeichnet,[47] da die Frau um ihr Einverständnis zur Ehe nicht gefragt wird. Aber es ist doch deutlich ein Bemühen der Gesetzgeber zu erkennen, die Würde der jungen Ausländerin in ihrer elenden Zwangslage soweit aufzubauen, dass die erotischen Beziehungen zwischen ihrem judäischen Ehemann und ihr zur Erfüllung kommen konnten. Für den Fall, dass dies nicht gelingen sollte, sondern der Ehemann über die Zeit sein Gefallen an ihr verlor, ordneten die Gesetzgeber die völlige Freilassung der Frau an. Der Ehemann darf sie weder als Sklavin verkaufen noch sie irgendwie sonst ihrer Freiheit berauben, „dafür dass er ihr Gewalt (עָנָה *'nh* pi.) angetan hat" (V. 14).[48] Die Gewalt gegenüber der Frau besteht hier darin, dass der Judäer ihre Zwangslage als erbeutete Gefangene ausgenutzt hat. Darum sollte die ehemals kriegsgefangene Ausländerin aufgrund ihrer geschiedenen Zwangsehe immerhin ihre persönlichen Freiheitsrechte erhalten.

Waren die deuteronomischen Gesetzgeber schon darum bemüht, das Kriegsrecht soweit zu zivilisieren, dass erotische Beziehungen zwischen Siegern und Besiegten eine Chance auf eine dauerhafte Verwirklichung erhielten, so räumten sie auch gegenüber ihrer eigenen Bevölkerung ein Recht auf Sexualität am deutlichsten ausgerechnet in ihren Kriegsgesetzen ein. Einem Mann, der sich gerade mit einer Frau verlobt, aber noch nicht die Heirat sexuell vollzogen hat, soll bei der Mobilmachung erlaubt werden, nachhause zurückzukehren (Dtn 20,7), damit sich an ihm nicht der tragische Fluch ereignet (28,30), dass er in der Schlacht fällt und ein anderer Mann die Frau heiratet, die er geliebt hat. Ebenso soll ein Jungvermählter für ein Jahr von allem Kriegsdienst und staatlichem Frondienst[49] befreit werden, damit er seine junge Ehefrau – wie es im masoretischen Text heißt – „erfreuen" (שִׂמַּח *śmḥ* pi.) kann (24,5). Auch ein Verständnis „sich mit" oder „an ihr freuen" (שָׂמַח *śmḥ* q.) ist möglich.[50] Eros und Sexualität werden hier als ein selbstverständlicher Teil der Lebensfreude angesehen, auf den jeder Mann und jede Frau ein Anrecht haben. Nach Meinung der Gesetzgeber ist es für ein geordnetes Gemeinwesen wichtig, dass auch in besonderen Ausnahmesituationen, wo ein Krieg das Leben eines Mannes auslöschen oder ein gefährlicher Einsatz z.B. im Steinbruch seinen Körper verstümmeln könnte, die Verlobten und Jungvermählten die Chance erhalten, den Anfang ihres Liebeslebens in aller Fröhlichkeit auch sexuell auszukosten. Da Eros und Sexualität nach Auffassung der

---

47 Siehe Otto, Weights (wie Anm. 17), 145.
48 Die Gewaltanwendung kann kaum darin bestehen, dass der Israelit die Erwartungen der Kriegsgefangenen auf eine Heirat enttäuscht habe, wie Frymer-Kensky, Law (wie Anm. 30), 100 Anm. 9, erwägt, da die syntaktische Einleitung des Verses Dtn 21,14 mit וְהָיָה אִם *whyh 'm* auf einen gewissen Zeitraum zwischen Heirat und Scheidung hinweist (vgl. 24,1).
49 So vor allem Otto, Deuteronomium III/2 (wie Anm. 31), 1806.
50 So das Targum Pseudo-Jonathan, die Syrische Bibel und die Vulgata. |

Gesetzgeber zum gelingenden, | d. h. von Gott gesegneten Leben dazugehört,[51] scheuen sie sich nicht – für uns in der Moderne fast unvorstellbar –, das Verfügungsrecht des Staates über die jungen Männer auf Freiersfüßen ganz erheblich einzuschränken.

5 Abschließende Bemerkungen

Wie in den Gesetzen zu Ausnahmesituationen erkennbar, billigten die Gesetzgeber hinter der mosaischen Torah besonders den jungen Menschen durchaus ein Recht auf Eros und Sexualität zu. Dennoch suchten sie vor allem die vor- und außereheliche Sexualität, die sie als schwere Bedrohung der gesellschaftlichen Ordnung ansahen, möglichst weit einzudämmen und so schnell wie möglich durch die vertraglich geregelte Institution der Ehe zu kanalisieren. Das mag in einer Zeit, die sich rühmt, Eros und Sexualität von allen Begrenzungen und Kriminalisierungen befreit zu haben, als altbacken und völlig überholt erscheinen. Doch bleibt die Frage, wie die auf Exklusivität drängende erotische und sexuelle Intimbeziehung zwischen zwei Menschen soweit geschützt werden muss, dass sie zur Erfüllung kommen kann und nicht von außen beschädigt oder von innen missbraucht wird, auch uns heute aufgegeben. Der Weg der religiösen und kultischen Aufladung des sexuellen Verhaltens, den die Gesetzgeber zu dessen Zügelung je länger je mehr beschritten, hat sich meiner Meinung nach, insbesondere wenn man seine christliche Fortsetzung mit bedenkt, als problematisch erwiesen.[52] Die eheliche Treue an der Treue zu Gott zu messen und die sexuelle Keuschheit an der Heiligkeit der Priester zu orientieren, stellt eine Überforderung dar, zumal solche religiösen Idealisierungen meist zu Lasten der Frau gehen. Weiterführender scheint mir der Ansatz der alttestamentlichen Gesetzgeber zu sein, im komplexen Beziehungsgeflecht von Eros und Sexualität an das Verantwortungsgefühl der Beteiligten zu appellieren (Ex 22,15–16; Lev 19,7.8.11.15 u. ö.) und die Würde des schwächeren Partners zu stärken (Ex 21,7–11; Dtn 21,10–14), damit bei allem erotischen Überschwang die Frauen vor der Ausbeutung ihrer Sexualität durch die Männer geschützt werden.

---

51 Vgl. auch Fischer, Zur sexuellen Aktivität erschaffen (in diesem Band) [die Hrsg.] [[= Fischer, Zur sexuellen Aktivität erschaffen, in: Bindrim u. a. (Hg.), Erotik und Ethik in der Bibel, 21–30]].
52 In der christlich katholischen Tradition führt etwa die Sakralisierung der Ehe in Analogie zur Liebesbeziehung Christi zur Kirche (Eph 5,25–33) zu einem derart starren Postulat ihrer Unkündbarkeit, dass Ehescheidung und Wiederverheiratung zu Sünden werden, die kirchlich nicht mehr vergeben werden können.

Ambivalent Relations between Brothers in the Hebrew Bible

1 Brothers, Somewhat Neglected Figures in Biblical Studies

Of course, famous brothers such as Cain and Abel, Jacob and Esau, Joseph and his brothers, or David's sons are often treated in commentaries or other studies. More systematic studies on the family in ancient Israel, however, are almost always focused on the vertical relations between father or mother and their children, while neglecting the horizontal relations between the siblings.[1] To my knowledge, there are only a few studies that are concerned with brother relations especially.[2] A nice exception | comes – not by chance – from Saul Olyan. Comparing the characteristics of friendship in the Hebrew Bible, he elaborates some important features of brother relations, being characterized by love, reliability, loyalty, and fraternal support including some special obligations of serving as levir or redeemer, revenging bloodshed, or celebrating funerals.[3] Olyan shows that it is always the fraternal solidarity that constitutes the example for good

---

1 See, e.g., Leo Perdue et al., *Families in Ancient Israel* (Louisville: Westminster John Knox, 1997), where the dimension of sibling relations is nearly completely overlooked, or my own investigations on family religion, although we mentioned that אָח, "brother," next to אָב, "father," plays an important role as a divine designation. See Rainer Albertz and Rüdiger Schmitt, *Family and Household Religion in Ancient Israel and the Levant* (Winona Lake, IN: Eisenbrauns, 2012), 350–53.

2 For example, Frederick E. Greenspahn, *When Brothers Dwell Together: Preeminence of Younger Siblings in the Hebrew Bible* (Oxford: Oxford University Press, 1994); Johanna Erzberger, "Brüderpaare," in *Esau – Bruder und Feind*, ed. Gerhard Langer (Göttingen: Vandenhoeck & Ruprecht, 2009), 115–21; Kathleen Rochester, | "The Missing Brother in Psalm 133," *ExpTim* 122.8 (2011): 380–82; Matthias Millard, "Die Konflikte zwischen Brüdern in der Genesis – typisch männliche Konflikte?," in *Männerbeziehungen: Männerspezifische Bibelauslegung* (Göttingen: Vandenhoeck & Ruprecht, 2015), 2:15–29.

3 See Saul M. Olyan, *Friendship in the Hebrew Bible*, AYBRL (New Haven: Yale University Press, 2017), 11–37.

Note: Saul Olyan, a friend of mine, to whom I would like to send my warmest greetings with this paper, impressed me over the years by his outstanding ability to use insights from sociological, psychological, and anthropological studies for analyzing societal structures, political and cultic institutions, and collective constructions of self- and worldviews in the Hebrew Bible. We have him to thank for books with titles such as *Rites and Rank*, *Disability in the Hebrew Bible*, and *Friendship in the Hebrew Bible*, which became classic investigations in the field. Therefore, I want to honor and please him by dealing with a basic anthropological topic, the sibling, specifically brother relations in the Hebrew Bible.

https://doi.org/10.1515/9783111202228-021

friendship, never the other way around,[4] thus demonstrating the basic anchoring of the familial concept. The idea that relations between brothers should be governed by reliability and solidarity, however, is proven to be an idealistic concept by many biblical texts, which tell that brothers compete with, fight against, cheat, hate, and even kill each other. Frederick Greenspahn has pointed out that biblical narrative traditions are not so much interested in brotherly harmony but rather focus on brotherly conflicts more than any other comparable literature.[5] Nevertheless, important biblical legal traditions increase the ideal of fraternal solidarity to the point that it even includes people beyond family bonds. Thus, we may ask: How is it possible that in the Hebrew Bible the ambivalence of brotherhood embraces such an extremely wide range?

2 Sibling Relations in View of Modern Empirical Research

In modern empirical sciences as well, be it psychiatry, psychology, sociology, or modern history, the significance of sibling relations was detected rather late.[6] Not until 1982 did psychologists Stephen Bank and Michael Kahn write their famous book *The Sibling Bonds*, showing that these bonds constitute one of the most durable and influential relations of human life.[7] | The relations between siblings, like those of children to their parents, are not created by choice but predetermined by birth; they are not conditional and normally cannot be divorced. Longer than the relations to one's parents, they often last one's entire lifetime. Empirical studies show that sibling relations are very close and emotional during childhood and early youth; they subside during the phase when each of the siblings establishes his or her own family but often see a revival in older age, when the parents have to be cared for and buried.[8] After the death of parents, siblings become the only emotional link to one's youth.[9]

From their very start relations between siblings are determined by both love and rivalry.[10] As small children, siblings compete for the love of their parents,

---

4 See Olyan, *Friendship in the Hebrew Bible*, 12, 25.

5 See Greenspahn, *When Brothers Dwell Together*, 3–5, 137–38.

6 An overview on the research history can be found in Leonore Davidoff, *Thicker Than Water: Siblings and Their Relations; 1780–1920* (Oxford: Oxford University Press, 2012), 29–45.

7 See in the German translation Stephen P. Bank and Michael D. Kahn, *Geschwister-Bindung*, RIPH 44 (Paderborn: Junfermann, 1989), 8–9. |

8 See Bank and Kahn, *Geschwister-Bindung*, 22; Ann Goetting, "The Developmental Tasks of Siblingship over the Life Cycle," *JMF* 48 (November 1986): 703–14.

9 See Hartmut Kasten, *Geschwisterbeziehung* (Göttingen: Hogrefe, 1993), 1:161.

10 See the title from an influential book in Germany: Horst Petri, *Geschwister – Liebe und Rivalität: Die längste Beziehung unseres Lebens* (Zürich: Kreuz 1994).

later on for their talents, their attractiveness, their success in their professions, and in old days for their parental inheritance. Sigmund Freud's theory of an initial deep trauma to the older sibling, evoked by the birth of the younger one and producing wishes to annihilate the latter, is only valid under pathologic circumstances. In normal cases, where parents show love to all of their children, the older siblings are able to rearrange their position in the family and to build up a positive relationship to the new family member, which becomes more and more constituted by closeness and intimacy.[11] Rivalry and fights between siblings, which are stronger between brothers of similar ages than between those of more different ages or between brothers and sisters, have the positive effects of mastering one's own aggressions and of building up one's own identity. In contrast to the hierarchical relation to parents, siblings regard their relations among themselves as principally egalitarian, although the older ones are considered to have some more strength and authority. Thus, they very sensitively react to any kind of unequal treatment and injustice. According to psychotherapist Horst Petri, it is not so much the order of birth, as thought by Alfred Adler, that can evoke heavy, even destructive conflicts between siblings, but much more the experienced or assumed injustice between them.[12] During childhood and early youth, unequal treatment | by the parents stands at the fore, which is often regarded as unjust, even if the parents try to avoid preferential treatment. Typically those siblings who felt at loss do not direct their hate and aggression towards their parents but against the favorite sibling.[13] In later stages of their life, siblings more often experience unequal treatment caused by different societal forces or unfortunate circumstances. But even for that, they might blame the luckier brother or sister. Nevertheless, the sibling who has problems normally expects some help from his brothers or sisters in many cases. Mutual psychical and physical solidarity and support is a primary characteristic of sibling relations even in industrial societies and has been even more important in preindustrial countries, where there are many more large families and less public welfare.[14] Of course, not all of these empirical insights taken from modern Western societies can be easily transferred to ancient Near Eastern societies. Nonetheless, there seems to be a stock of anthropological patterns that appears similar to those in the Hebrew Bible, as will be shown, although it mostly focuses on male siblings, the relation between brothers.

---

11 See the observations of Petri, *Geschwister – Liebe und Rivalität*, 116–21.
12 See Petri, *Geschwister – Liebe und Rivalität*, 140–48. |
13 See Martina Stotz and Sabine Walper, "'Lieblings- oder Schattenkind': Bedeutung und Entstehungshintergründe elterlicher Ungleichbehandlung," in *Bruderheld und Schwesterherz: Geschwister als Ressource*, ed. Inés Brock (Gießen: Psychosozial-Verlag, 2015), 135–60, esp. 138.
14 Kasten points out that in developing countries the elder siblings often take over completely the care for their younger siblings (*Geschwisterbeziehung*, 47).

3 Common Ideals of Brotherhood in the Hebrew Bible and Other Literature

The Hebrew Bible shares many concepts concerning brotherhood with the literature of the surrounding cultures and beyond. To start with linguistic usage: אָח, "brother," is the second most frequent kinship term in the Hebrew Bible. It occurs 629 times, about half as much as אָב, "father," and two times more than אֵם, "mother." According to Lev 21:2, one's brother belongs to one's closest kin, on the same level as one's father, mother, sons, and unmarried daughters. If one's brother has not only the same father but also the same mother, he is regarded as a very close intimate (Deut 13:7). Like *aḫu* in the Akkadian language,[15] however, the Hebrew אָח can denote not only a natural brother but other kinds of relatives such | as nephews (Gen 13:8), cousins (2 Sam 20:9), or clan members (1 Sam 20:29); it embraces even unrelated colleagues (Neh 3:1; see *KAI* 200:10–11) and political allies (1 Kgs 9:13), but normally not friends, as Olyan has pointed out.[16]

As Olyan has already shown, according to the ideal of brotherhood in the Hebrew Bible brothers should live together in harmony (Ps 133:1), should be loyal and honest to each other (Jer 12:6; Job 6:15), should show sympathy with their brother's sorrow (Ps 35:13–14) and should care for him in his need (Prov 17:17). In reality there are limits of support, for example, when one's brother has fallen into longer poverty (Prov 19:7; 27:10), or when the brother, from whom help is expected, was deceived before (Prov 18:19). In exceptional cases a friend can be more loyal than a brother (Prov 18:24) or a close neighbor more helpful than a far brother (Prov 27:10).[17] But when it happens that brothers generally have become unreliable and unfaithful (Jer 9:3), the order of society has broken down. A similar picture is drawn in omen and incantation texts from Babylonia.[18]

While the faithful cooperation of brothers is only touched on in biblical narratives (e.g., Gen 9:23; 34), the ideal of harmonious brotherhood is much more enfolded in narratives of Israel's Near Eastern environment. From Egypt of the late second millennium BCE survives a longer narrative called the Story of Brothers or *Brüdermärchen*.[19] Here it is told that an older married brother, Anubis,

---

15 See the article *aḫu* A in *CAD* 1.1:195–205. |
16 See Olyan, *Friendship in the Hebrew Bible*, 29. When David denotes Jonathan as "his brother" in 2 Sam 1:26, it may have to do with the generalizing language of funeral laments, where every deceased one seems to be seen as a brother of the living. See 1 Kgs 13:30; Jer 22:18.
17 Prov 18:24 belongs to יֵשׁ proverbs, which denote exceptions from the normal order; 27:10b belongs to the טוֹב מִן proverbs, which revalue the normal preference.
18 See *CAD* 1.1:196–97.
19 An abridged English version is given in *ANET*, 23–25. A complete German translation can be found in Emma Brunner-Traut, *Altägyptische Märchen*, 4th ed. (Düsseldorf: Diederichs, 1976), 28–40. |

lives on a farm together with his younger unmarried brother, Bata, in full harmony. Bata is serving his elder brother and his wife with pleasure, making their clothes, cultivating his fields, and driving his cattle. The harmonious relation between the brothers is destroyed by the deceitful wife, who tries to seduce Bata. After being rejected by him, she accuses Bata of trying to rape her, as Potiphar's wife did with Joseph. Anubis becomes furious with his brother and | wants to kill him; but, warned by his cattle, Bata is able to flee.[20] Separated by a dangerous waterway, the two brothers meet again. Bata, reminding Anubis that he is his younger brother and of their former familial harmony, is able to convince him of his innocence, emphasized by cutting off his phallus. Becoming weak from his self-mutilation, Bata asks his brother for future help after he goes away to the magic Valley of Cedar. Anubis feels pity for his brother and weeps aloud but cannot help him immediately. He goes home, kills his treacherous wife, and mourns for his lost brother. Much later, when Bata has come to death in the Valley of Cedar, Anubis fulfills the demand of his brother. He goes to the magic valley, searches for many days for his lost heart, finally finds it, and is able to revive his brother. After this, the two brothers come to the court of Pharaoh and together defend themselves against additional nasty attacks by another woman. Finally, Bata becomes the new Pharaoh, and Anubis follows him on the throne. Thus, the miraculous story impressively shows how mutual solidarity of brothers overcomes all dangers and leads to the highest success.

The ideal of mutual solidarity and support between brothers is even more explicitly stressed in the Aramaic Ahiqar story from the late seventh or early sixth century BCE.[21] The former wise counselor reminds the high official Nabusumiskun, who was sent by king Esarhaddon to kill him, that he brought him to his own house, sustained (סבל *pael*) him there "as a man deals with his brother," and hid him from Sennacherib as long as the king was angry.[22] Thus, Ahiqar expects the same brotherly behavior from Nabusumiskun, who fulfills his expectations. In his inscription from northern Syria of the late ninth century BCE, King Kilamuwa praises himself that he provided a neglected part of his people with goods and care like a father, mother, and brother.[23] Greenspahn points also to the Greek depiction of the Dioscuri Castor and Polydeuces (Pollux), whose "harmony became legend ... So intense was their unity that in the face of Castor's death

---

20 Prov 6:19 states that God hates those who are telling a pack of lies and stir up quarrels between brothers.

21 See *ANET*, 427–30; *TAD* 3:25–57 (C1.1); *TUAT* 3.2:320–47.

22 See *TAD* C1.1.III–IV:46–52; *ANET*, 428; *TUAT* 3.2:344–45. The latter edition suggests that the narrative frames the proverbs and assigns the passage to XVII:15–XVIII:4.

23 See *ANET*, 654; *KAI* 24:10–13. |

Polydeuces rejected Zeus's offer of immortality" with the words: "Bid me die, O |
King, with my brother."[24] One can also refer to the German tale "The Three Brothers,"[25] who compete heavily against each other for the inheritance of their father's house but in the end decide to live together because they love each other
and can successfully do their different trades side by side.

The participation of ancient Israelites in an idealized concept of brother relations known in the Levant and beyond is also verified by Israelite personal
names, where the kinship term אח, "brother" – next to "father," "mother," "uncle,"
and "father-in-law" – constitutes a divinized designation for the family god.[26]
Similar names occur in the Aramaic, Phoenician, Ammonite, and Moabite ono-
mastica; they are also found in Mesopotamia. The divinized brother designation
seems to have been quite popular. From a sample of about 3,000 epigraphically
attested Hebrew names, of which nearly 2,000 are theophoric, 155 or 7.8 percent
are formed with the element אח, even more than those names with the element
אב, "father."[27] This popularity might be explained by the fact that in preindustrial
societies often the eldest brother took over the care for the younger siblings when
the parents became ill or died early. The predicates of these names show similar
characteristics with those containing other divine elements. However, names such
as 'Aḥî'ezer, "my divine brother is help," or 'Aḥîsāmāk, "my divine brother has
supported," attested in the Bible (Exod 31:6), fit well with experiences among
human brothers. Thus, there is a wide range, in which the Hebrew Bible shares
common ideals of brotherhood with other cultures.

4 Where the Hebrew Bible Goes beyond the Common Ideals

In the face of this extensive agreement, it is all the more surprising that the
Hebrew Bible diverges from the common background in two directions: First, in
a very realistic manner it stresses the conflicts and rivalry between brothers in
a number of dramatic narratives, especially in the book of Genesis (Gen 4; 25–33;
37–50) but also in the historical books (Judg 11; 1 Sam 17; 2 Sam 13–14; 1 Kgs 1–2).
This rivalry often has to do with the | preeminence of the younger or youngest
brother, typically conceded in the Hebrew Bible.[28] Second, several legal passages

---

24 See Greenspahn, *When Brothers Dwell Together*, 4, with sources and literature.
25 Heinz Rölleke, ed., *Grimms Märchen: Text und Kommentar*, 2nd ed. (Frankfurt: Deutscher
Klassikerverlag, 2015), 518–20 (no. 124).
26 See Albertz and Schmitt, *Family and Household Religion*, 350–53, 534–609, and the index, 668–
69.
27 See Albertz and Schmitt, *Family and Household Religion*, 508–13. |
28 See the comprehensive study of Greenspahn, *When Brothers Dwell Together*, 111–40.

of the Hebrew Bible, especially in the book of Deuteronomy (Deut 15–25) but also in the book of Leviticus (Lev 25), develop from the common ideal of brotherhood a specific ethic, where the traditional solidarity and responsibility between brothers was expanded beyond the family bonds in order to oblige wealthy citizens to support poor people within Israelite society.[29]

4.1 Stressing Conflicts between Brothers and Showing Their Solutions

The Bible's first story dealing with brothers (Gen 4:2–16) is short and brutal.[30] Born and raised by the same parents, Cain, the elder brother, becomes a tiller of the soil, while Abel, the younger one, becomes a shepherd. It is not the division of labor as such, however, that creates competition between the brothers. According to the story, it is God who induces the conflict. When each of the brothers offers their sacrifice from the goods of their work, which have to be understood as firstling offerings, which should secure divine blessing for one's work in the future, God prefers Abel's and neglects Cain's offering. This means that Abel's herd breeding becomes much more successful than Cain's tilling the soil. That his younger and weaker brother has more success with his work than he himself seems to be unbearable for Cain; he feels at a loss and begins to hate his brother. The solidarity between the brothers breaks down. Many theologians have racked their brains regarding the reason for God's unjust decision, which induces such a heavy conflict between brothers who insist on being equal. One may refer to the fact that the biblical God often sides with the weaker partner. The story, however, deliberately does not provide any divine motivation. It intends to confront the reader and Cain with the fact that there are fateful disadvantages that are totally unexplainable. Cain is not able to bear his discrimination and tolerate the | preferential treatment of his brother. Although warned by God, he lures Abel to the open country and beats his brother to death. In his view, the injustice done to him can only be abolished by eliminating his privileged brother. As is typical, he does not accuse the person responsible for his unjust treatment but thinks that he must punish his innocent brother for his misfortune.

Only God's questioning after the fratricide brings Cain back to a better perspective. Asked by God, "Where is your brother Abel?" he is reminded of his

---

29 See Eckart Otto, *Theologische Ethik des Alten Testaments*, TW 3.2 (Stuttgart: Kohlhammer, 1994), 186–92.
30 See especially the interpretations of Claus Westermann, *Genesis* (Neukirchen-Vluyn: Neukirchener Verlag, 1974–1982), 1:381–435; Jan Christian Gertz, *Das erste Buch Mose: Genesis; Die Urgeschichte Gen 1–11*, ATD 1 (Göttingen: Vandenhoeck & Ruprecht, 2018), 150–74. |

fraternal responsibility. His mocking answer, "Am I my brother's keeper?" (Gen 4:9), does reject God's question as an unreasonable demand, but against his own intention Cain guesses what real brotherly relationship should have entailed.[31] Thus, the ideal of solidarity between brothers is not absent from the conflict.[32] The murderer of his brother is driven from the soil to outside the human community by God's punishment. But now, complaining to God, Cain is not totally banned but protected by him from arbitrary attacks. He gets the chance for a new beginning. According to the primeval history of the Hebrew Bible,[33] with worldwide scope, brotherhood was especially threatened by the experience of unexplainable preference and discrimination by an unjust destiny.

The long Jacob composite, comprising Gen 25:21–34; 27:1–33:17* in its original form,[34] draws a much more complex picture of the conflict between two brothers. It already starts before and during birth, when the two twins press hard on each other in their mother's womb, and the second born, Jacob, grasps the heel of the firstborn, Esau, with his hand (Gen 25:22, 26). The competition between the two is settled when they grow up and develop different characters and skills: Esau loves the open plain and becomes a skillful hunter, while Jacob is well-behaved and prefers to | stay at home (v. 27). In contrast to Cain and Abel, the conflict between Jacob and Esau is triggered not by God but by the parents. They do not treat their sons equally, but Isaac favors his firstborn, Esau, because of his venison, while Rebecca prefers her second born, Jacob (v. 28). According to the story, however, God is not uninvolved. He induces the conflict in the background and uses it for his plan to make Jacob, the younger one, the blessed ancestor of his chosen people, superior to Esau and his descendants, as the birth oracle already indicated (v. 23), the blessing ritual will show (Gen 27:27–29), and later theophanies will make clear (Gen 28:18–22; 33:23–33).

Under hidden divine protection, Jacob develops into a real careerist, who fights for his advantage against his brother and does not shrink from even tricks and frauds. Cold and calculating, he takes advantage of Esau's ravenous hunger and forces him into selling his rights as the firstborn, just for a lentil meal

---

31 Unless otherwise indicated, all biblical translations are mine.

32 See the frequent epithet "[my, your, or his] brother," which occurs no less than seven times in Gen 4:2–11.

33 The story belongs to the non-Priestly primeval history (Gen 2:4b–8:22*) from the late eighth or early seventh century, which according to my view was integrated into the Priestly one by a post-Priestly redactor. See Rainer Albertz, *Pentateuchstudien*, FAT 117 (Tübingen: Mohr Siebeck, 2018), 477.

34 Here I follow the influential literary reconstruction of Erhard Blum. See Blum, *Die Komposition der Vätergeschichte*, WMANT 57 (Neukirchen-Vluyn: Neukirchener Verlag, 1984), 7–203. It was probably formed by using some older material during the ninth century BCE. |

(Gen 25:29–34). The narrator of this little anecdote intends to show that all solidarity and emotional relationship between the two brothers has disappeared. No further word is exchanged during the meal; even the term *brother* is no longer used.

Driven and supported by his mother, Jacob purloins from his brother Esau the paternal blessing (Gen 27:1–45). Feeling the end of his life, Isaac orders his elder son to prepare the ritual farewell meal, receive his blessing, and thus become his follower (vv. 1–4). But his wife, Rebecca, revolts against this normal order; she wants to promote her beloved younger son to highest rank in the family. In the face of this chance, Jacob does not refuse to cheat his old blind father and supplant his brother. Funnily dressed as Esau, he celebrates the ritual meal cooked by his mother; and his father, although having some doubts, solemnly bestows God's blessing on him, which not only includes fertility but also power above his brother and his descendants (vv. 27–29). The narrator depicts Esau's reaction with some sympathy: when the latter discovers that he had been deceived so badly by his brother, he cries and begs his father for some kind of second blessing. But Isaac cannot cancel God's ritually assured bonds to Jacob. Thus, Esau turns all his aggression against his brother; he insults him as a born cheater, alluding to a possible meaning of the name Jacob (v. 36a), becomes hostile to him, and plans to kill him as soon as possible (v. 41). Although blessed, Jacob has to flee from Esau's revenge. His and Rebecca's ambitions result in the destruction of their family (vv. 43–45).

It is impressive to see how realistically the rivalry between brothers is depicted here, and it is astonishing how self-critically the career of Israel's | own ancestor is evaluated in this story.[35] But the narrator of the Jacob composite does not end with the hostility and separation of the two brothers. He wants to show the ideal of brotherhood in his composition, too. Thus, he narrates that Jacob, after having become a blessed and rich man in the land of his flight, comes home and meets his brother once more (Gen 32–33). Esau, still angered, confronts him with four hundred men, and Jacob fears an attack. The reconciliation of the brothers, however, becomes possible because Jacob, as the favorite brother, deeply humiliates himself before his deprived brother and presents him a lot of the goods that

---

35 This aspect is especially emphasized by Greenspahn, *When Brothers Dwell Together*, 125–35. That such a realistic depiction of the conflict was no longer borne in later times becomes apparent in the book of Jubilees, where, in spite of Jacob's tricks, both brothers are obliged by Rebecca (Jub 35.1–26) and Isaac (36.1–17) to keep fraternal love; the conflict between the two is much later induced by the sons of Esau (37–38). See Gerhard Langer, "Esau im Buch der Jubiläen," in Langer, *Esau – Bruder und Feind*, 55–61.

he earned from God's blessings (Gen 33:1–11).[36] Prior to this, he learned through a divine attack at night that he must wrestle with God for his blessing rather than compete with other people (Gen 32:23–33). As the elect one who is ready to reconcile with his disadvantaged brother, Jacob becomes the true ancestor of Israel.

The Joseph novella (Gen 37:3–50:22a*) deals not with relations between two but among twelve brothers, from which the three oldest, Reuben, Simeon, and Judah, and the two youngest, Joseph, of course, and Benjamin play a major role. Even more than the Jacob composite, the Joseph novella is interested in the topic of reconciliation.[37] The conflict between Joseph and his brothers is also caused by the preference of their father. Jacob loves Joseph, the child of his old age, more than all his sons, and expresses his love with a special robe for him; therefore, his brothers hate him (Gen 37:3–4). It seems as if Jacob is forced to repeat the faults of his own parents.[38] The father's preference, however, is only one reason | for conflict between Joseph and his brothers. Their hate and jealousy are increased by Joseph's ambitious dreams, which indicate his claim to rule his brothers and the entire family (vv. 5–11). Thus, again, the divine world triggers the conflict in a mysterious way. While young Joseph still shows fraternal solidarity, his elder brothers seize the next opportunity to eliminate him. First, they want to kill him in a pit; only Reuben, the eldest, takes some responsibility for his younger brother. Then, Judah proposes to sell him as a slave abroad, referring to their bonds of blood with him. After having disposed of Joseph, the brothers soak the sleeved robe, the symbol of his preference, with the blood of a goat, in order to feign an accident for their father, Jacob. His inconsolable mourning for his beloved son shows the collapse of familial confidence (vv. 17–35).

After this short depiction of a drastic conflict between brothers, the narrator of the Joseph story gives an exhaustive account about how the familial confidence is rebuilt such that a reconciliation of the brothers becomes possible. Once Joseph becomes a governor of all Egypt and meets his brothers among the petitioners who want to buy some corn in the drought, he does not give up his anonymity but subjects them to a hard test to determine whether they have learned to keep fraternal solidarity. He accuses them of being spies and takes Simeon to prison

---

36 The act of reconciliation is not questioned by the final separation of the brothers (*pace* Millard, "Konflikte zwischen Brüdern," 19).

37 It contains even two scenes of reconciliation (Gen 45; 50), which may point to a later extension. In its extended form the novella seems to come from the eighth century BCE (see Albertz, *Pentateuchstudien*, 63–68).

38 A force of repetition between generations is observed by psychologists (see Petri, *Geschwister – Liebe und Rivalität*, 145). Although the Jacob and Joseph stories were originally independent, their different authors might have known about it. |

as hostage (Gen 42:5–25) in order to test whether they will give him up as lost or redeem him. He demands that they bring their youngest brother, Benjamin, with them on their next journey, in order to test whether they will be able to overcome the mistrust of their father and guarantee Benjamin's security. Finally, he accuses Benjamin of having stolen his silver goblet (Gen 44:1–12) in order to test whether the elder brothers will give up the younger one as lost once more or will take responsibility for him. Only after the brothers have confessed their earlier guilt (Gen 42:21–22; 44:16) and Judah states that he vouches for Benjamin, despite his being preferred by their father, as was Joseph earlier (v. 20), and that he will be willing to assume the punishment instead of him (vv. 32–34) is Joseph ready to become reconciled with his brothers (Gen 45:1–15). By his political advancement, he regards himself as being commissioned by God to care for his brothers and all the family. Having tight emotional bonds to his brothers, especially to Benjamin, he refuses the subjugation of his brothers but renews his promise of fraternal care for them after their father's death (Gen 50:16–21). At the end, Joseph personifies the ideal of solidarity and responsibility that should govern the relations between brothers. |

Thus, from the most prominent brother stories of the Hebrew Bible, which depict the rivalry and conflict between brothers in an extraordinarily realistic way, the ideal of solidarity between them is not completely absent. The Cain and Abel story hints at it briefly (Gen 4:9), the Jacob story profoundly deals with it in its final chapters (Gen 32–33), and the Joseph story reflects on its prerequisites and benefits in great detail (Gen 42–45; 50).

4.2 Promoting Brotherly Solidarity beyond Family Bonds

The Joseph story celebrates solidarity among brothers, which can even – combined with political influence – overcome catastrophes such as a heavy drought. Such an innerfamilial solidarity, however, has its strict limits. It focuses all one's emotional empathy and social responsibility on related people and excludes all unrelated people. Normally, in ancient societies these limits of fraternal solidarity were regarded as natural and were unquestioned. In the Hebrew Bible, however, an extraordinary development concerning the concept of brotherhood can be observed. Probably induced by a longer social crisis, in which many small landowners had lost their soil and more and more impoverished people were no longer supported by their familial social network,[39] some influential Judean

---

39 For the sociohistorical background of the brother ethic, see Otto, *Ethik*, 192.

scribes of the late seventh and early sixth centuries BCE, who were responsible for the law code of the book of Deuteronomy (Deut 12–26), looked for new religious and social concepts that would help to strengthen the sense of togetherness of their society. Apart from the centralization of all sacrificial cult in Jerusalem, they found that the new idea that all male members of the society are to be regarded as brothers was the most powerful. Lothar Perlitt has pointed out that this idea cannot be derived from the old model of blood relations between the tribes, nor from examples of Israel's environment. It does not have any ethnic or nationalistic intention, but it aims at the consolidation of humanity.[40]

The intention of the legislators can well be observed in the law of the remission of debts (Deut 15:1–3, 7–11), where the term אח, "brother," is used no less than six times. When the reformers order that in every sev|enth year no creditor should collect the debts from "his neighbor" (רעהו) but release them and modify the term "his neighbor" with "his brother" (ואחיו), they intend to provide their law with a strong emotional motivation. Every wealthy citizen should regard his debtor as his own brother, for whom he is responsible in some way. He should show fraternal solidarity with him and should be ready to renounce his right and to go without his money in favor of him. From verses 7, 9, and 11, where the legislators speak of "your poor brother," it becomes clear that these acts of solidarity should be done especially in favor of poor countrymen. Thus, the ideal of brotherly care is evoked and extended beyond family bonds in order to create a societal responsibility for needy but unrelated people. Similarly, the legislators demand for fair treatment of debt slaves by calling them "your Hebrew brother" (Deut 15:12) and forbid charging interest from "your brother" (Deut 23:20–21). In public punishments, "your brother" must not be beaten in a degrading way (Deut 25:3). Even the resident alien should profit from this new societal solidarity (Deut 24:14); only independent foreigners are excluded from the brotherly community (Deut 15:3; 23:21).

Among the ideals of familial brotherhood, apart from solidarity and help, honest behavior was also important. Thus, beyond family bonds too, no one of the Judean society should give false witness against "his brother" (Deut 19:18–19), and anybody who finds someone's lost animals or clothes should not secretly take possession of them but should care for them in order to bring them back to "your brother," even if one does not know or like him (Deut 22:1–4). Thus, the new brother ethic of Deuteronomy already comes close to the commandment of compassion, for the first time formulated in the Holiness Code (Lev 19:17,

---

40 See Lothar Perlitt, "'Ein einzig Volk von Brüdern': Zur deuteronomischen Herkunft der biblischen Bezeichnung 'Bruder,'" in *Deuteronomium-Studien*, FAT 8 (Tübingen: Mohr-Siebeck 1994), 50–73, esp. 57–72. |

34).[41] The theological ground for this demanding extension of brotherhood can be seen in the belief that YHWH has redeemed all the Israelites, even those now blessed and wealthy, from slavery in Egypt (Deut 15:15) and will honor the unselfish solidarity between them with his further blessings (vv. 10, 18).

5 Concluding Remarks

The reason why the ambivalence of brother relations covers such an extraordinarily wide range in the Hebrew Bible, from realistic depictions of drastic | conflicts between brothers in Genesis and elsewhere to fastidious demands in Deuteronomy of realizing fraternal solidarity even beyond family bonds, has to be sought – according to my view – in Israel's especially intensive relation to its God. On the one hand, the biblical narrators seem to be very sensitive in sensing God's acting in human affairs. They observe it especially where the normal human order is turned upside down, for example, when the younger brother becomes more important or successful than the older one. Thus, in all cases discussed above, God is seen to be responsible for inducing the conflict between brothers, more or less. Therefore, rivalry and conflict between brothers became important; they have to do with God and testify his challenging or electing acts in some way. They must not be concealed but can realistically be depicted. The weakness of the involved parents and brothers, their preferences, their jealousy, their faults and sins are not justified by the divine actions behind them, but the biblical narrators do not shrink from depicting them, because they want to show how they deal with divine challenges.

On the other hand, the Deuteronomic legislators are convinced that YHWH has special demands on his chosen people. In their view, he is no longer satisfied by the normal fraternal solidarity within family bonds. Since all Israelite families can no longer support their impoverished members, brother relations must be extended to the entire society, because God has redeemed all his people from slavery. As Perlitt has formulated it: "As a brother, an Israelite demands greater, even the greatest, attention from a fellow Israelite."[42] One may ask whether such an immense extension of fraternal responsibility does not overtax many individuals, but it can be stated that the demanding brother ideal developed by the Deuteronomic legislators shows such an influence that human charity beyond family bonds became an attractive trademark of later Judaism and early Christianity in the ancient world.

---

41 See the other later adoptions of the brother ethic in Lev 25:25, 35–47; Zech 7:9–10. |
42 See Perlitt, "Ein einzig Volk," 64: "Als Bruder verlangt der Israelit vom Mitisraeliten höhere, ja höchste Aufmerksamkeit."

5 Theologie

Einführung

Es mag die eine oder den anderen vielleicht verwundern, dass ein Autor, der in jüngeren Jahren einmal dafür plädiert hat, die „Theologie des Alten Testaments" durch eine „Religionsgeschichte Israels" zu ersetzen,[1] im Alter den zweiten Band seiner gesammelten Aufsätze mit sechs bibeltheologischen Beiträgen abschließt. Mein Anliegen von damals ist allerdings häufig missverstanden worden. Es war nie meine Absicht, die Theologie durch die Religionswissenschaft abzulösen. Ich hielt nur den Vorlesungstyp „Religionsgeschichte Israels" für geeigneter als den der „Theologie des Alten Testaments", um den religiösen und theologischen Gehalt der Hebräischen Bibel in all seiner Vielgestaltigkeit und geschichtlichen Entwicklung für das Theologiestudium zusammenzufassen. Dabei habe ich schon in der damaligen Kontroverse erklärt, dass ich mir sehr wohl einen theologischen Umgang mit dem Alten Testament vorstellen kann, nämlich einen, der klar von gegenwärtigen theologischen Fragestellungen bzw. Herausforderungen der Kirche ausgeht und die dafür relevanten Einzelthemen der biblischen Überlieferung historisch-kritisch und theologisch aufbereitet.[2] Eben solche bibeltheologischen Studien zu konkreten Themen und Aufgaben, die für die heutige christliche Theologie und Kirche von Bedeutung sind, finden sich im letzten Kapitel dieses Aufsatzbandes versammelt.

Bevor ich allerdings zu meinen eigenen bibeltheologischen Studien komme, ist es mir ein Anliegen, erst noch einmal an die wichtigen bibeltheologischen Impulse zu erinnern, die aus meiner Sicht mein Lehrer Claus Westermann für Theologie und Kirche gesetzt hat. Der erste Beitrag im Kapitel „Theologie" lautet darum „The Legacy of Claus Westermann for Theology and Church". Er geht auf einen Vortrag zurück, den ich in einer akademischen Feierstunde der Theologischen Fakultät Heidelberg, an der Westermann von 1958 bis 1978 lehrte, zum Gedenken an die 100. Wiederkehr seines Geburtstags im Jahr 2009 gehalten habe. So scheinen mir der allumfassende Horizont der Theologie Westermanns, seine universal-menschheitsgeschichtliche Auslegung der Biblischen Urgeschichte, seine Aufwertung des Segenshandelns Gottes und seine Wiederentdeckung der alttestamentlichen Klagepsalmen als Möglichkeit christlichen Gebets bis heute wichtig zu sein. Westermanns weitgefächerte bibeltheologische Arbeit hat mein Denken tief beeinflusst, auch mit der Einsicht, dass natürlich zwischen den bibli-

---

1 Vgl. R. Albertz, Religionsgeschichte Israels statt Theologie des Alten Testament! Ein Plädoyer für eine forschungsgeschichtliche Umorientierung, in: B. Janowski/N. Lohfink u. a. (Hg.), Religionsgeschichte Israels oder Theologie des Alten Testaments (JBTh 10), Neukirchen-Vluyn 1995, 3–24.
2 Vgl. R. Albertz, Hat die Theologie des Alten Testaments doch noch eine Chance?, ebd., 177–187.

https://doi.org/10.1515/9783111202228-022

schen Erkenntnissen und ihrer Aufnahme in der Gegenwart immer noch hermeneutische Überlegungen und Gesichtspunkte anderer theologischer Disziplinen
bedacht sein müssen. Dennoch stellen sie – insbesondere in den reformatorischen
Kirchen – wichtige Impulse zur Erneuerung der Theologie und der Reform der
kirchlichen Praxis dar.

Das Thema des zweiten Beitrags „Der Auszug Israels aus Ägypten und das
christliche Freiheitsverständnis" wurde mir, der ich gerade einen Exoduskommentar abgeschlossen hatte,[3] vom Leiter der Konferenz der Reformierten Hoch-
schullehrer im Jahr 2018 vorgegeben und zeigt damit einen aktuell bestehenden
theologischen Klärungsbedarf an. Es stellt sich nämlich heraus, dass der systematisch-theologische Freiheitsdiskurs seltsamerweise weitgehend an der biblischen
Exodustradition vorbei geführt wird, obwohl diese von der grundlegenden Befrei-
ungstat Gottes berichtet, welche die gesamte biblische Heilsgeschichte in Gang
setzt und in Jesus Christus ihren Höhepunkt findet.[4] Der Artikel plädiert für eine
substantielle Einbeziehung der Exodus- und Sinai-Überlieferung in den Diskurs
über das christliche Freiheitsverständnis, um so dessen individualistische Ver-
engung und zu starke geistige Sublimierung zu überwinden.

Der dritte Beitrag „Biblische Perspektiven zur Wirtschaftsethik" entsprang
der Mitarbeit in der Projektgruppe „Religion und Wirtschaft" innerhalb des
Münsteraner Exzellenzclusters „Religion und Politik in den Kulturen der Vormo-
derne und der Moderne". Er konnte zwar nicht direkt etwas zu dem dort im Kreis
von Wirtschaftsjuristen und Sozialethikern diskutierten Thema der christlichen
Kapitalismuskritik in der Weimarer Republik und der Frühzeit der Bundesrepublik Deutschland beitragen, wohl aber aufzeigen, wie schwierig es schon auf der
Stufe der agrarischen Subsistenzwirtschaft des Alten Israel war, die eigenständige
ökonomische Rationalität wirtschaftlichen Handelns durch eine religiös begründete Gesetzgebung in ihren zerstörerischen Auswirkungen einzugrenzen und hu-
manisierend aufzubrechen. Dazu wurden frühere Erkenntnisse zur Theologisierung des Rechts im Alten Israel aufgegriffen.[5]

Im Gefolge der erschreckenden religiös motivierten Gewalttaten, die in der
jüngeren Vergangenheit die Welt erschütterten, wurde insbesondere von Jan Ass-

---

3 Vgl. R. Albertz, Exodus, Bd. 1: Ex 1–18 (ZBK.AT 2.1), Zürich [2]2017; Ders., Exodus, Bd. 2: Ex 19–40
(ZBK.AT 2.2), Zürich 2015.
4 Nach Sicht des Autors des Judasbriefes war Jesus sogar schon bei der Herausführung des
Volkes aus Ägypten und bei der Bestrafung von dessen Ungläubigen in der Wüste selber am
Werk! Vgl. die jetzt in der 28. Auflage des Nestle-Aland vollzogene textkritische Entscheidung für
die Lesart des Vaticanus u. a. von Jud 5.
5 Vgl. R. Albertz, Geschichte und Theologie. Studien zur Exegese des Alten Testaments und zur
Religionsgeschichte Israels, hrsg. von Ingo Kottsieper und Jakob Wöhrle (BZAW 326), Berlin/New
York 2003, 187–207.

mann die provokante These vorgetragen, dass dem monotheistischen Gottes-
glaube im Judentum, Christentum und Islam ein gefährliches Gewaltpotential in-
newohne. In dieser Debatte versucht der vierte Beitrag „Muss die exklusive
Gottesverehrung gewalttätig sein? Israels steiniger Weg zum Monotheismus", unter Aufnahme früherer religionsgeschichtlicher Erkenntnisse[6] einige klare Kriterien für einen theologisch verantwortlichen Umgang mit dem Monotheismus der
eigenen jüdisch-christlichen Tradition zu formulieren.[7]

Verortet in einer interdisziplinären Debatte um die Auswirkungen des theokratischen Arguments in der europäischen Geistes- und Gesellschaftsgeschichte,
bringt der fünfte Beitrag unter dem Titel „Theokratie und Gewaltenteilung: Der
sogenannte Verfassungsentwurf des Ezechiel (Ez 40–48)" den visionären Verfassungsentwurf des Ezechielbuches in Erinnerung.[8] Er führt aus, wie hier schon im
6. Jh. v. Chr. aus einer durch das Exil stärker sensibilisierten Erkenntnis der Heiligkeit Gottes heraus die bis dahin übliche enge Verbindung von Thron und Altar
zerschnitten und eine Teilung der Gewalten zwischen den Institutionen von Tempel, Palast und Hauptstadt propagiert wurde. Wäre dieses Konzept in der christlichen Kirchengeschichte stärker wirksam geworden, hätte man sich die Irrwege
des „Caesaropapismus" oder des „Landesherrlichen Kirchenregiments" ersparen
können.

Der sechste und letzte Beitrag dieses Kapitels und des gesamten Bandes „Eine
himmlische UNO: Religiös fundierte Friedensvermittlung nach Jes 2,2–5" ent-
stammt der ersten Ringvorlesung, die das Münsteraner Exzellenzcluster „Religion
und Politik" im Wintersemester 2008/09 für alle Mitglieder der Universität sowie
die interessierten Bürgerinnen und Bürger der Stadt unter dem Titel „Mediation"
veranstaltet hat.[9] Anlass für diese Thematik war die Verleihung des Westfälischen
Friedenspreises an den ehemaligen Generalsekretär der Vereinten Nationen, Kofi
Anan, am 11. 10. 2008 in Münster. Die entscheidenden exegetischen Beobachtungen zur berühmten Friedensvision von Jes 2,2–5, die auch die Gründung der irdi-
schen UNO mit beeinflusst hat, hatte ich schon im Rahmen von zahlreichen Ge-
meindevorträgen im Rahmen der Friedensbewegung der 80er Jahre des vorigen
Jahrhunderts gemacht, z. B. dass Israel keinerlei eigenen Vorteil aus dem konflikt-

---

6 Vgl. Albertz, ebd., 359–378.

7 Die Fassung eines ähnlichen Beitrags in englischer Sprache findet sich unter dem Titel „Monotheism and Violence in Ancient Israel", in: J. van Ruiten/C. de Vos, The Land of Israel in the
Bible. History and Theology. Studies in Honor of Ed Noort (VT.S 124), Leiden 2009, 372–387.

8 Vgl. die historisch-kritische Untersuchung in R. Albertz, Die Exilszeit. 6. Jahrhundert v. Chr.
(BE 7), Stuttgart 2001, 276–283.

9 Alle Vorträge wurden von dem Mittelalterhistoriker Gerd Althoff unter dem Titel „Frieden
stiften. Vermittlung und Konfliktlösung vom Mittelalter bis heute" (Darmstadt 2011) herausgegeben.

schlichtenden Handeln seines Gottes zwischen den Völkern zieht.[10] Im öffentlichen Vortrag – übrigens dem ersten nach meiner Pensionierung – habe ich diese Einsichten nach allen Regeln der exegetischen Kunst, in philologischer, historischer, traditionsgeschichtlicher und theologischer Hinsicht detailliert entfaltet, um dem großen, vornehmlich aus Nicht-Theologen bestehenden Publikum zu demonstrieren, dass auch die akademische Theologie substantielle Beiträge zu wichtigen aktuellen gesellschaftspolitischen Debatten leisten kann.

Es war mir bei meinen interdisziplinären Engagements neben dem fruchtbaren fachlichen Austausch immer auch ein Anliegen, das Ansehen der Theologie, besonders meines Faches „Altes Testament", bei den Vertretern der nicht-theologischen Nachbardisziplinen der Universität zu stärken. Ich kann nur hoffen, dass ein solches Unterfangen auch in Zukunft gelingen möge, wenn die christlichen Kirchen in Deutschland mehr und mehr in eine gesellschaftliche Minderheitenposition geraten.

---

10 Vgl. R. Albertz, Konfliktschlichtung durch Machtverzicht – Jes 2,2–5 auf dem Hintergrund der alttestamentlichen Kriegs- und Friedenstraditionen, in: Ders., Der Mensch als Hüter seiner Welt. Alttestamentliche Bibelarbeiten zu den Themen des Konziliaren Prozesses, Stuttgart 1990, 114–131.

The Legacy of Claus Westermann for Theology and Church

John Barton, to whom I would like to pass my warmest congratulations and compliments, is one of the outstanding biblical scholars of the world, who endeavours to elaborate the significance of the Hebrew Bible with regard to the development of Christian thought. I still remember his deep philosophical and theological reflections in a session that took place in Louvain in 1994, when we discussed the theological impact of summarizing the beliefs and practices of ancient Israel either in the way of an Old Testament Theology or alternatively under the perspective of a History of Israelite Religion (Barton 1995: 24–34). Although I pleaded for the latter alternative in this case (Albertz 1995b: 4–34), I admire John Barton's emphatic theological approach, because I have learned from my teacher Claus Westermann the importance of transferring insights from Biblical Studies into the realm of the other theological disciplines, such as Church History, Systematic and Practical Theology, and even into the realm of the beliefs and practices of the Churches (Albertz 1995a: 181–4). Therefore, I would like to honour John Barton by presenting some reflections on the legacy of Claus Westermann from my perspective, which may be of some interest for him.[1]

In the year 1977 the former philosopher of the Theological Faculty of Heidelberg, Georg Pitch, challenged his colleagues to answer the fundamental question, 'Theology, what is that?' Westermann, who was then working on his 'Theology of the Old Testament', did not hesitate to accept this challenge. | His contribution to the volume started with the following fundamental statement (1984b: 9):

> Von Gott reden heißt vom Ganzen reden. Eine Eigenart des Alten Testaments besteht darin, daß sein Reden das Ganze umfaßt. Es setzt mit dem Beginn von Welt und Menschheit in der Schöpfung ein, und es kündigt in den Apokalypsen das Ende der Welt und das Ende der Menschheit an. Es umfaßt Anfang und Ende; es redet von Gott, indem es vom Ganzen redet.
>
> Das Alte Testament umfaßt zwischen Anfang und Ende alles, was die Welt und was in der Welt ist; es umfaßt die ganze Menschheit und den ganzen Menschen in seinem Daseinsbogen von der Geburt bis zum Tod. Es redet von Himmel, Erde und Gestirnen, von Blumen und Bäumen, von Strömen und Bächen, von Tieren aller Art, von Meeren und Wüsten. Es redet von der Menschheit in allen Völkern und in allen Rassen; nahe beieinander stehen die alle damals bekannten Völker umfassende Völkertafel und die Verheißung an Abraham:

---

1 This chapter is derived from a lecture I gave at the Theological Faculty of the University of Heidelberg on 14 October 2009 to celebrate the one hundredth birthday of Claus Westermann. He worked at the university for thirty years. The German lecture has only been published internally so far; see Albertz 2009–10: 55–69. |

https://doi.org/10.1515/9783111202228-023

In dir sollen sich segnen alle Geschlechter der Erde. Es redet vom einzelnen Menschen in
seinem ganzen Daseinsbogen: die ganz kleinen Kinder und die ganz alten Leute gehören
dazu, die Kranken und die Gesunden, die Freien und die Gefangenen, die Könige und die
Hausfrauen.
Indem das Alte Testament von diesem großen Ganzen redet, redet es von Gott. Es könnte
nicht von Gott reden, würde es nicht von diesem großen Ganzen reden. Gott hat zu allem,
was es gibt, eine Beziehung; alles, was es gibt, hat eine Beziehung zu Gott, denn alles, was
es gibt, ist Gottes Schöpfung.

These sentences are of monumental simplicity, which was typical of Claus Westermann. If you read them aloud, they can take your breath away. In a carefree
manner, Westermann lets Theology and Church know what theologians have to
deal with if they want to speak of God; it is no less than talking about 'the whole'.
First, 'the whole' spans the entire time of the world, from its beginning, the creation of the world, until the end of the world, because God is the first and the last
(Isa. 41:4), the Alpha and Omega (Rev. 21:6; 22:13), embracing the entire world
time. Second, 'the whole' includes the entire reality between the beginning and
the end during the course of time, all non-human creatures, all the nations, all
men and women in their different social classes and ranks, the entire human
being on its journey through life, from birth to death, because the divine creator
has established a relationship with all these creatures (Gen. 1; Ps. 104; 148). Third,
to 'the whole' – only indicated here, but elaborated later (1984b: 14) – the specific
history belongs, which God started with Abraham and continued with the people
of Israel. Through Jesus Christ, God has extended this history to the heathens by
incorporating them into the history of the Church, which has endured until the
present time and will continue until the final return of Christ. This important
part of divine activity, too, gets its true meaning only from God's relationship to
'the whole' (1984b: 14–18). If theology did not talk comprehensively about this
entire reality, it would fail its subject. It would not really speak of God, at least,
not of that God on whom the Bible reports. |

Thus, according to Westermann, theology is not allowed to restrict itself to
parts of the events that are happening between God and the world or God and
man, for example to the justification of the sinner or the salvation of the individual's soul, as important as these topics may be in the dogmatic tradition. Likewise,
the Church is not allowed to limit itself to looking after its members only. In
the Hebrew Bible, which Westermann always integrated into an entire biblical
perspective, the relationships that God has established with his non-human and
human creatures are much wider and varied: God deals not only with various
individuals, but also with families, tribes, peoples, nations, and religious communities, all of whom develop their specific relationship with the divine. He does
not restrict himself only to those who believe in him, but also includes all other
people in his agenda. He does not only care for his human creatures, but also

looks after the animals, plants, stones, planets, and galaxies, as it is told by the Primeval History (Gen. 1–11), the Patriarchal Story (Gen. 12–50), the Psalms, and the book of Job, which have all been studied by Westermann in great detail. In this connection, Westermann views as especially important Psalm 148, where all creatures are called to praise God, beginning from the stars, clouds, and winds, down to the mountains, trees, and animals, and ending with the kings and the young women. Westermann, in a reformatory gesture, transfers these biblical insights directly to the present institutions of Theology and Church and asks that they be considered seriously: although all modern sciences and humanities are specializing themselves to a higher and higher degree, Theology is not allowed to do so, because of the nature of the matter to which it is committed. Political parties or trade unions may confine themselves to the interests of their members, but the churches must not do that for the sake of the message they have to preach. Of course, Westermann knows that theology is forced to specialize itself to some degree, too, because of the growing amount of knowledge in its disciplines; he knows, of course, that the purview of churches is rather limited, simply for financial reasons. Even so, he urges that these constraints be resisted and encourages Theology and Church to develop counter-strategies.

Apart from the biblical insights, Westermann has another reason for why Theology and Church should endeavour to include the entire reality in their focus and avoid the insidious loss of reality in their doctrine. These are the more and more globalized challenges with which mankind will be confronted in the future. Far-sightedly, in 1981, in an article about the future tasks of a Biblical Theology, he wrote:

> In einer Zeit, in der die Gefahren und die Bedrohungen, die am Horizont heraufziehen, die Menschheit als ganze und die Welt als ganze betreffen, sollte die Aufgabe der Kirchen und ihres Redens von Gott, ihrer Botschaft und ihrer Theologie, sich bewußter und entschlossener der Menschheit als ganzer und der | Welt als ganzer zuwenden. Daß die Kirche eine Aufgabe am Ganzen hat, ist in ihrem Wesen begründet; von Gott reden heißt vom Ganzen reden.[2]

In this article, Westermann intended to emphasize the unity of the theological disciplines on the basis of a Biblical Theology which, in his opinion, should become fundamental for the self-understanding of the entire theological scholarship. Thus, Westermann connected his biblical theological insights with the practical endeavour for a reform of academic theology facing the challenges of a globalized world to come.

---

2 Westermann (1984a: 203). The German title reads: 'Aufgaben einer zukünftigen biblischen Theologie'.

It is not possible to deal in this chapter with all the stimuli that Westermann has given to Theology and Church. Some of them have already been considered before.[3] Here, I would like to mention only three of his important topics: first, the universalism and particularism of divine activity; second, the blessing activity of God; and third, the complaint of man.

1 The Universalism and Particularism of Divine Activity

In my view, it is one of Westermann's most important achievements that he has laid the biblical foundations for distinguishing the universal and particular activity of God more clearly. In the beginning (Gen. 1–11), God's universal activity is predominately focused on the entire world and all mankind. In the middle, however, God's particular activity is in the foreground, his history with his people, be it Israel or the Church. At the end, the divine activity adopts universal dimensions again. Interestingly enough, God's particular activity for his people remains always related to his universal one. One example is the promise of blessing at the beginning of the Abraham story (Gen. 12:1–3), which should radiate over all families of the world. Another is God's saving act in Jesus Christ, which is meant for all mankind, but founded the particular history of Christian churches up until now, though spread over many nations (cf. Westermann 1984b: 14).

This clear and relatively simple model that Westermann developed was blocked as long as the dogmatic tradition – following Paul in Romans 5 – directly related the first three chapters of the Primeval History, understood as the creation and fall of mankind, to the salvation of Jesus Christ, and regarded them as a primarily negative backdrop for divine salvation. By this procedure the universality of the salvation of Christ could be clearly | established, but at the expense of narrowing God's universal activity as creator, if not monopolizing it in a Christian manner. Westermann, however, has shown exegetically that Genesis chs. 1–3 cannot be separated from the rest of the Primeval History. Chapter 4, for example, intentionally tells the story of Cain's offence against his human brother in parallel to the narrative in ch. 3, which tells of how Adam and Eve committed an offence against God. Moreover, Westermann could show that the biblical Primeval History constituted by the contrast of creation and flood does not intend to describe a one-sided negative picture of a world and mankind fallen in sin, but to expound – like the Atrahasis epic – the ambivalent basic conditions of the world and mankind, which are not only determined by the transgression and endangering of

---

3 See Oeming (2003) with contributions by Westermann, Albertz, H.-P. Müller, J. Kegler, and K. Meyer zu Utrup. |

man, but also by the positive forces of the divine creator. Finally, Westermann clarified that the Primeval History does not belong to God's *Heilsgeschichte* with his people. The name 'Israel' is not mentioned in these first eleven chapters of the Bible at all. Instead, the term אדם ('man, mankind') is frequently mentioned, no less than thirty-three times. That means the Primeval History simply has a different subject than that of other parts of the Pentateuch; it deals with the world and the common ancestry shared by the forefathers of many nations, including Israel. Thus, Westermann has clarified that the biblical Primeval History constitutes a universal introduction to Yhwh's particular history with Israel, which does not start before Abraham in Genesis 12. In contrast to a narrowed Christian understanding of Genesis 1–11, Westermann elaborated a much wider interpretation of these chapters looking at the history of mankind. He supported this meaning by showing that these eleven chapters have a higher number of parallels with the ancient Near East and other parts of the world than any other part of the Hebrew Bible. Thus, according to Westermann, the biblical Primeval History can be read by Christians from at least two directions: in a direction towards Jesus Christ with a narrowing tendency, and in a direction from Jesus Christ towards the world and all mankind with a broadening tendency. Concerning the second case, he ascribed to it 'eine verbindende, überbrückende Funktion' (1974b: 90). Westermann was aware of the high significance of such a bridging function which this part of the Jewish-Christian Bible could obtain for the dialogue with other religions, especially about inter-religious strategies for coping with the global threats of the present time.

I would like to suggest here that the range of the universal activity of God attested in the Hebrew Bible can be considerably extended beyond that which Westermann has mentioned. Following the dogmatic tradition, Westermann rightly pointed out that the creation activity constitutes the centre of God's universal engagement: 'mit dem Reden vom Schöpfer [ist] notwendig ein Universalismus verbunden' (1978: 87). He is probably also right to suggest: 'Im Reden von der Schöpfung hat der Mensch zum ersten mal "den Menschen" und "die Welt" als ganze gedacht' (1984b: 12). Beyond the dogmatic tradition | Westermann also included the blessing in God's universal activity. With regard to Gen. 1:28 he stated: 'Im Segen wirkt der Schöpfer, darum ist der Segen universal, er gilt allen Lebewesen' (1978: 88). I will return to this later. Astonishingly enough, however, Westermann exclusively assigned the divine activity of saving and judging to Yhwh's particular engagement with Israel. This assignment becomes questionable already in the Primeval History. Here God saved Noah, his family, and all the animals through the flood (Genesis 6–9) and here he passed his judgement on the inhabitants of the world, who were exerting themselves in building a high tower in Babel (Gen. 11:1–9). The Psalms and the Prophets also mention the judgement and salvation of other nations, for example in the praise of the lord of history (Ps. 33:10–11) or in the oracles concerning foreign nations (Isa. 19:1–25). Amos 9:7 even claims that Yhwh has provided the Philistines and the Arameans with an exodus, too. It is true that Yhwh, who according to Deut. 10:14 possesses 'the heaven and the highest of heaven, the earth and everything in it', has chosen in his groundless love just the small people of Israel from all other nations (10:15; cf. 7:6–7), but it seems to be likewise true that he has also varied his relationships with other nations, although they are only mentioned sporadically in the Bible. This would mean that not only at the beginning and the end of history, but also during the long history in between, God's universal activity remains present. According to the testimony of the Bible, the activity of the universal God far exceeds the particular history of his adherents.

Claus Westermann was a practical person and he thought about how his insight into the high significance of the universal activity of God could be better learned by Christians in a way that would shape their beliefs and determine their deeds. This was one of the reasons why he took the churches and their modes of worship so seriously. It is not surprising, therefore, that he concluded his article on the future tasks of Biblical Theology with a critical remark that the *Confessio Augustana* does not contain an article on 'creation', and the festival calendar of the churches – apart from the harvest festival – does not know any feast where the divine creator and his creation can be considered. For Westermann, the harvest festival alone is insufficient because it does not focus on all divine creatures, regardless of whether human beings receive benefit in them. According to Psalm 148, however, all of them should be included in the praise of God, their creator. Thus, Westermann made the suggestion, 'daß der Sonntag Jubilate als Sonntag der Schöpfung gefeiert wird mit dem Text der Schöpfungsgeschichte' (1984a: 210). I do not know whether this has yet been taken up anywhere.[4] In any case, it belongs to the legacy of this famous biblical scholar. |

2 The Blessing Activity of God

There is probably no work of Claus Westermann that has become as influential as his small book *Der Segen in der Bibel und im Handeln der Kirche* from 1968. It was taken up, for example, by Magdalene Frettlöh (2005 [1998], 5th edn.), who studied the blessing not only in its biblical context, but also in its dogmatic and practical theological context. The biblical part was elaborated, for example, by

---

4 In Germany, there is some effort to make the first Friday in September 'a day of creation'. |

Martin Leuenberger (2008), who also included the epigraphical material in his study. In his little book, Westermann was successful in rediscovering the peculiarity and theological significance of the divine blessing activity, which had long been covered by the general category of 'God's saving acts' and was often marginalized because of rational and theological reservations against alleged 'magical' rituals. From the present perspective, it is almost impossible to realize that in the period in which this book was written, the topic of blessing was regarded as so strange and arbitrary that the first publisher to whom Westermann offered the manuscript rejected it. I still remember how delighted Westermann was when he found in Christian Kaiser a publisher who was willing to print this book.

According to Westermann, blessing in its primary sense is the power of fertility which the creator presented to all living things (Gen. 1:22, 28). God's blessing caused growing and flourishing, and it also included the success of labour, wealth, and richness (Deut. 28:3–5). Or, to cite Westermann himself (1968: 13): 'Es ist die segnende Kraft Gottes, die das Kind zum Mann und zur Frau wachsen und reifen läßt; es ist die segnende Kraft, die den Menschen in seinem Werden auf vielfältige Weise begabt und die ihn aus allen möglichen Quellen körperlicher und geistiger Nahrung speist.' Therefore, God's blessing causes the individual differences between human beings. Again, you can observe Westermann's interest in bringing the entire reality of human being into the theological field of view. In his Theology of the Old Testament he summarizes (1978: 97):

> Das Reden vom Segen im Alten Testament bedeutet, daß die Gottesbeziehung den Menschen in seinem ganzen Lebensbogen von der Geburt bis zum Tod umfaßt. Sie schließt das Wachsen und Reifen, Zunehmen und Abnehmen der Kräfte, das Genesen und Erholen, das Hungern und Sättigen ein. Weiter meint es den Menschen in der Gemeinschaft, von Ehe und Familie bis in alle Differenzierungen des Gemeinschaftslebens hinein, den Menschen in seiner Arbeit, im Wirtschaftsleben mit allen Problemen ... Das Anerkennen der Besonderheit des segnenden Wirkens Gottes bedeutet, daß es Gott nicht nur um das 'Heil' des Menschen geht, sondern um den Menschen in der ganzen Fülle seiner Möglichkeiten und Bedürfnisse, um den Menschen als eine Kreatur unter Kreaturen.

I still remember a conversation with Westermann, when I drove him in my little car from his home in St Leon to Heidelberg. He thought that there must | be something wrong with the doctrine of justification if it has been able to ignore the matter of whether those sinners who have been justified by God are men or women, children or seniors, homeless people or factory owners, elementary pupils or professors. According to this doctrine, all these people would be equally *simul iustus et peccator*. Westermann insisted that actual differences between them should be taken into consideration not only in the context of spiritual welfare, but also by New Testament and Systematic Theology. By appreciating the blessing activity of God, he intended to contribute a possible solution.

On the one hand, Westermann sharply distinguished between God's blessing activity, which he characterized as 'ein stilles, stetiges, unmerklich fließendes Handeln' (1978: 88), and God's saving activity, which would be experienced in concrete events. This contrast was often criticized, for example, by Frettlöh (2005: 54), on the grounds that it would tear apart the realms of nature and history. On the other hand, Westermann was interested to show that Israel's history did not only consist of 'God's great saving acts', but also of steady processes, both of which were closely intermingled (1968: 12). For him, the basis of all history is constituted by the steady sequence of birth, marriage, procreation, and death in the chain of generations, as it is shown by the genealogies of the Bible (1974b: 470–71). God's contingent saving and judging interventions can be seen as an addition to this basic biological process, and presuppose it. Nevertheless, there are also material intersections between the blessing and saving activity of God, for example in the healing of illness. And finally, there are kinds of divine activity that do not fit well with Westermann's binary division. For example, God's attendance (being 'with' somebody), support, and protection are located somewhere in between steady processes and distinguishable actions. In my view, it is still meaningful to distinguish a specific blessing activity of God and to emphasize its significance, but it should be integrated into a broader range of different kinds of divine activity. At this point, I see Westermann's legacy in the commitment to elaborate the dogmatic topics of the *providentia Dei, gubernatio Dei,* and *concursus Dei* in much more detail than has been done in our theological tradition up to now.

More than Westermann, I would emphasize today that the blessing should be regarded as an ambivalent gift of God, which can cause hot disputes and severe conflicts as can be shown by the Jacob and Esau stories (Gen. 25–33). Thus whoever who has been bestowed by God with a bigger portion of blessing is especially obligated to handle it with care and responsibility. The divine blessing contains an ethical obligation (cf. Deuteronomy 15).[5] In the case of Jacob, the conflict with his brother Esau could only be settled when the more | blessed brother was ready to share some of his wealth with the brother who was less blessed (Gen. 33:8–11).

3 The Complaint of Man

Ever since his attendance at the Predigerseminar at Naumburg in 1934, Westermann occupied himself with the Psalms. As a young curate of the Confessing

---

5 See for more details Albertz (1996: 101–09). |

Church he was suddenly confronted with the challenge to defend the Old Testament against the attacks and denigrations by those Christians who aligned themselves with the ideology of the German National Socialists (so-called 'Deutsche Christen'). In this period, editions of the Bible containing just the New Testament were common, to which only the Psalms were attached. Thus, the book of the Psalms was the best known part of the Old Testament for German Christians. This was the outer reason why Westermann turned his attention to the Psalms.[6]

More important, however, was the inner reason. As a dissident pastor under the Nazi dictatorship, a simple soldier during the Second World War, and a prisoner of war in Russia, Westermann got into many dangerous and often life-threatening situations. Through this experience he found a specific existential approach to the Psalms, which developed independently of academic exegesis. He used the laments practically in his distress, and expressed his relief with the psalms of thanksgiving. Thus he was not influenced by the theological reservations that Gunkel, Begrich, and others had expressed against the individual laments of the Hebrew Bible.[7]

Under these specific conditions, Westermann discovered that prayers in the Old Testament are *reactio* and not *actio*; that is, not pious work that I carry out, but a reaction which is evoked 'durch ein Geschehen, ein Widerfahrnis' (1984b: 22). According to him, this occurrence is part of the dialogical events between God and the human being. Prayers are the answers of man to God's judging and saving acts. Since these events are not constant but vary, the human answer to God cannot always be the same, but must also vary between complaint and praise in accordance with what has happened (1984b: 22):

> Ein ... Kennzeichen des Gebets in den Psalmen ist, daß die Reaktion des Antwortens polar ist, bestimmt von den beiden Polen der Klage und des Lobes; in der zu Gott gerichteten Antwort kommen Klage und Lob zu Wort. Dieser polare Charakter ergibt sich notwendig daraus, daß das Gebet im Alten Testament Reaktion auf Erfahrenes, Geschehenes ist. Diese Reaktion kann nicht immer die | gleiche sein, das wäre nicht mehr menschlich, denn die menschliche Erfahrung ist von Freude und Leid bestimmt. Es zeigt sich hier ein Menschenverständnis, nach dem das Menschsein eine Bewegung ist, und zwar eine vom Ganzen des Menschseins bestimmte Bewegung von der Geburt zum Tod.

Westermann's insights concerning prayers again correspond to his view of 'the whole of human existence'. Westermann sees some connections with the philosophy of Martin Heidegger, who described human existence as temporal existence.

---

6 Cf. Westermann's own description of the situation in Oeming (2003: 19–21).
7 See Gunkel and Begrich (1966: 127, 217). According to them, the severe accusations of these complaints testify 'mehr von menschlichem Egoismus ... als vom Gottesglauben' (1966: 231). |

While Heidegger, however, defined human existence as 'Sein zum Tode' and there-fore determined by worries, Westermann regarded it as stamped by contrasting experiences – birth and death or joy and sorrow – during the entire lifetime. In his work on the Psalms, too, Westermann intended to make sure that the entire human being is allowed to talk through with God all the experiences of his life.

Although Westermann's first academic study, which he published in 1953 af-ter the long years of war, is called *Das Loben Gottes in den Psalmen* (1963), his real credit is the fact that he rediscovered – on the background of his experiences in war and resistance – the high theological significance of the lament psalms in the Hebrew Bible. In this respect, his article on 'Struktur und Geschichte der Klage in den Psalmen' from 1954 became seminal. Here, he not only clearly de-scribes the tripartite structure of the complaint – the accusation against God, the lament about one's own distress (I- or We-complaint), and the complaint about the enemies of the sufferer – but also elaborates in detail how lament was elimi-nated from prayers in late texts of the Old Testament and Apocrypha, but then reappeared as secular protests, which were no longer directed to God (1954: 51–66, 75–9). Westermann notices that Christianity also shared the suppression of laments in early Judaism; in the prayers of the New Testament, even in the Lord's Prayer, the element of complaint is lacking, and they consist only of petitions, thanksgivings, and praise.

In his article from 1977, Westermann connected this process of suppression with a timeless understanding of the human being, which has led to the opinion that human prayers could be always the same, regardless of the situation in which they are said (1984b: 23):

> Nach der traditionellen Auffassung bedeutet das, daß ein Christ eigentlich immer zu danken hat und deshalb nie zu klagen. Das Gebet ist von der Situation des Menschen weitgehend abgelöst, es ist nicht mehr polar von Klage und Lob bestimmt. Die Klage wurde deshalb aus dem christlichen Gebet ausgeschieden. Erst in jüngster Zeit, verursacht durch die Welt-kriege und vor allem durch die jungen Völker und die amerikanischen Neger, ist die Klage als ein auch für den Christen unter Umständen notwendiges Rufen zu Gott wieder durchge-brochen. Die Frage aber, ob dies der Botschaft von Christus entspricht, ob die Klage legi-times christliches Gebet sein kann, ist noch nicht beantwortet. |

The last sentence reveals that Westermann was not sure whether his rediscovery of the complaint would be appreciated by Theology and Church. With some delay, however, his stimulus was widely accepted, for example by the Catholic practical theologian Ottmar Fuchs (1982, 1987), by the authors of the volume edited by Georg Steins (2000), and by the lengthy 'Jahrbuch der Theologie' volume on com-plaint (Ebner *et al.* 2001), to which no less than eighteen Protestant and Catholic biblical scholars, church historians, systematic and practical theologians, and literary specialists contributed. All these works intend to regain the complaint as a lost dimension of addressing God for Christian prayer.

As praiseworthy as this endeavour is, it seems to have a problem: some of the authors, who intend to integrate the element of complaint into the Christian faith, are inclined to moderate the harshness of the individual lament prayers of the Psalms and to domesticate them in a theological manner. According to Bernd Janowski, for example, the basic motif of the lament prayer is no longer the complaint, but the expression of trust (2001: 50). Already, the fact that the sufferer in his distress turns towards God, shows that the lament psalms, '*indem* sie ge-sprochen werden, einen Vorschuß an Vertrauen zu Gott enthalten ... Sie sind zwar aus der Gottverlassenheit bzw. der Gottesferne gesprochen, aber doch in der Hoffnung, daß Gott gerade *in* dieser Not nahe ist' (Janowski 2003: 77). The psalms of lament would be, as Christoph Markschies put it years ago, 'ein zielge-richtetes Vertrauensparadigma' (Markschies 1991: 397).

Admittedly, Claus Westermann himself noticed that nearly all psalms of la-ment show a dynamic from complaint to praise, from petition to the confession of confidence (1963: 52–6), but he always emphasized that there is a sharp con-trast between the despairing complaints and the trustful confessions of confi-dence, which is expressed on the grammatical level by a *waw-adversativum*. In his early work, he characterized the accusation against God, expressed in Lam. 5:20 for example by the words 'Why will you quite forget us and forsake us these many days?', without any glossing over (1954: 52–3):

> Der Klagende hat in dem Schlag, der ihn traf, erfahren: Gott hat versagt. Diese Erfahrung ist ihm ein gänzlich Unheimliches, Unverständliches. Die Warum-Frage ist wie das Tappen eines, der im Dunkel nicht mehr weiter weiß. Sie hat den Sinn des Sich-Zurechtfindens; dabei ist vorausgesetzt, daß der erfahrene Schlag in der Abwendung Gottes begründet ist.

Two decades later, he addressed the matter of what is expressed by the 'why-questions' in the collective lament psalms with the following words (Westermann 1974a: 259):

> Die gegenwärtige Not erfährt das Volk als das Widersinnige, wie es die Warum-Frage an Gott zum Ausdruck bringt. Wie kann Gott so schweres Leid über sein Volk bringen, wenn es doch sein Volk ist, an dem er früher Großes getan hat? Sofern das Widersinnige Gott vorgeworfen wird, enthält die Volksklage einen | Moment des Protestes, des Protestes einer Gruppe gegen das, was ihr geschieht oder angetan wird. Der Protest richtet sich zwar an Gott; aber er ist doch Protest, der das Widersinnige nicht demütig und geduldig hinnimmt, sondern der sich als Protest äußert.

According to Westermann the complaint is the human reaction to an eerie and incomprehensible blow. It is a protest against what God has done to his people or his adherents. Of course, the protest aims at persuading God to make a concession. Whether it is successful or not, however, is an open question during the prayer. Thus, the laments of the Psalms are clearly distinguished from the humble and trustful prayer, which is transmitted from Jesus in the garden of Gethsemane: 'Take the cup away from me. Yet not what I will, but what you will' (Mk 14:36). This prayer, which leaves it up to God to decide what to do, is often taken as an example of the attitude a Christian should adopt in prayer. I think that Westermann expects us to cope with these differences; one should not try to level them, for example through inserting New Testament concepts into the Psalms, such as that of the closeness of God even in distress, or others. According to Westermann it is important that all kinds of complaint, even the furious protest of a despairing human being, can be uttered towards God without any limitations and preconditions. For this purpose, the lament psalms lend us the language. For the theological justification Westermann refers to the fact that – according to the Evangelists – Jesus Christ himself has taken up Psalm 22 in the pain of his crucifixion and complained to God: 'My God, my God, why have you forsaken me?' (Mk 15:34; Mt 27:46). He commented on this passage in the following way (1987: 200):

> Jesus nimmt in dieser Klage die Sprache des Leides auf, die das Leid vieler Menschen in seinem Volk in vielen Generationen geprägt hat. Er ist einer von ihnen. Er ist nicht nur für die Sünder, er ist auch für die Leidenden gestorben. Sein Wirken bis in diesen Abgrund der Sinnlosigkeit hinein geschah auch für das Leiden der Menschheit.

In my opinion, this positive theological appreciation of the complaints is another important part of the legacy that Claus Westermann left to Theology and Church, a part which we should keep carefully and – if necessary – defend.[8]

Bibliography

Albertz, R. (1995a), 'Hat die Theologie des Alten Testaments noch eine Chance? Abschließende Stellungnahme', in B. Janowski and N. Lohfink (eds), *Religionsgeschichte | Israels oder Theologie des Alten Testaments* (JBTh, 10; Neukirchen-Vluyn: Neukirchener Verlag), 177–87.
Albertz, R. (1995b), 'Religionsgeschichte Israels statt Theologie des Alten Testaments: Plädoyer für eine forschungsgeschichtliche Umorientierung', in B. Janowski and N. Lohfink (eds), *Religionsgeschichte Israels oder Theologie des Alten Testaments* (JBTh, 10; Neukirchen-Vluyn: Neukirchener Verlag), 3–24.
Albertz, R. (1996), 'Der Segen Gottes. Wo ist er erfahrbar? Wie gehen wir damit um?', in *Zorn über das Unrecht: Vom Glauben, der verändern will* (Neukirchen-Vluyn: Neukirchener Verlag), 85–113.
Albertz, R. (2009–10), '"Von Gott Reden, heißt vom Ganzen Reden ...": Ein Vermächtnis von Claus Westermann an Theologie und Kirche', *JTFUH* 5: 55–69.
Albertz, R. (2010), 'Warum "Wozu"? Zur Pragmatik der an Gott gerichteten Fragen in den Klagegebeten der Hebräischen Bibel', in K. Schiffner, S. Leibold, M. Frettlöh, J.-D. Döhling, and

---

8 For an attempt to defend it see Albertz (2010: 318–40) [[= p. 295–316 in the present volume]]. |

U. Bail (eds), *Fragen wider die Antworten* (*Festschrift* for J. Ebach; Gütersloh: Gütersloher Verlagshaus), 318–40. [[= p. 295–316 in the present volume]]

Barton, J. (1995), 'Alttestamentliche Theologie nach Albertz?', in B. Janowski and N. Lohfink (eds), *Religionsgeschichte Israels oder Theologie des Alten Testaments* (JBTh, 10; Neukirchen-Vluyn: Neukirchener Verlag), 25–34.

Ebner, M., I. Fischer, J. Frey, O. Fuchs, B. Hamm, B. Janowski, R. Koerrenz, C. Markschies, D. Sattler, W. H. Schmidt, G. Stemberger, S. Vollenweider, M.-T. Wacker, M. Welker, R. Weth, M. Wolter, and E. Zenger. (eds) (2001), *Klage* (JBTh, 16; Neukirchen-Vluyn: Neukirchener Verlag).

Frettlöh, M. (2005[1998]), *Theologie des Segens: Biblische und dogmatische Wahrnehmungen* (Gütersloh: Gütersloher Verlagshaus; 5th edn).

Fuchs, O. (1982), *Die Klage als Gebet: Eine theologische Besinnung am Beispiel des Psalms 22* (Munich: Kösel).

Fuchs, O. (1987), 'Die Klage: Eine vergessene Gebetsform', in H. Becker, B. Einig, and P.-O. Ullrich (eds), *Im Angesicht des Todes* (PiLi, 3/4; St. Ottilien: EOS), 987–1024.

Gunkel, H. and J. Begrich (1966[1933]), *Einleitung in die Psalmen. Die Gattungen der religiösen Lyrik Israels* (HKE; Göttingen: Vandenhoeck & Ruprecht; 2nd edn).

Janowski, B. (2001), 'Das verborgene Angesicht Gottes: Ps 13 als Muster eines Klageliedes des einzelnen', in M. Ebner et al. (eds), *Klage* (JBTh, 16; Neukirchen-Vluyn: Neukirchener Verlag), 25–72.

Janowski, B. (2003), *Konfliktgespräche mit Gott: Eine Anthropologie der Psalmen* (Neukirchen-Vluyn: Neukirchener Verlag).

Leuenberger, M. (2008), *Segen und Segenstheologien im Alten Israel* (AThANT, 90; Zürich: Theologischer Verlag).

Markschies, C. (1991), '"Ich vertraue auf dich, Herr!" – Vertrauensäußerungen als Grundmotiv in den Klageliedern des Einzelnen', *ZAW* 103: 386–98.

Oeming, M. (2003), Claus Westermann: *Leben – Werk – Wirkung* (BzVB, 2; Münster: LIT).

Steins, G. (ed.) (2000), *Schweigen wäre gotteslästerlich: Die heilende Kraft der Klage* (Würzburg: Echter).

Westermann, C. (1954), 'Struktur und Geschichte der Klage im Alten Testament', *ZAW* 66: 44–80 = Westermann (1964): 266–305 = Westermann (1977), 125–64. |

Westermann, C. (1963), *Das Loben Gottes in den Psalmen* (Göttingen: Vandenhoeck & Ruprecht; 3rd edn) = Westermann (1977), 11–124.

Westermann, C. (1964), *Forschungen am Alten Testament: Gesammelte Studien* I (TB, 24; Munich: Kaiser).

Westermann, C. (1968), *Der Segen in der Bibel und im Handeln der Kirche* (Munich: Kaiser).

Westermann, C. (1974a), 'Die Rolle der Klage in der Theologie des Alten Testaments', in *Forschungen am Alten Testament: Gesammelte Studien* II (TB, 55; Munich: Kaiser), 250–68.

Westermann, C. (1974b), *Genesis: 1. Teilband: Genesis 1-11* (BKAT, I/1; Neukirchen-Vluyn: Neukirchener Verlag).

Westermann, C. (1977), *Lob und Klage in den Psalmen* (Göttingen: Vandenhoeck & Ruprecht).

Westermann, C. (1978), *Theologie des Alten Testaments in Grundzügen* (ATD Ergänzungsreihe, 6; Göttingen: Vandenhoeck & Ruprecht).

Westermann, C. (1984a), 'Aufgaben einer zukünftigen biblischen Theologie' [*Deutsches Pfarrerblatt* 1 (1981): 2–6], in *Erträge der Forschung am Alten Testament: Gesammelte Studien* III (TB, 73; Munich: Kaiser), 203–12.

Westermann, C. (1984b), 'Das Alte Testament und die Theologie', [in G. Picht and E. Rudolph (eds), *Theologie, was ist das?* (Stuttgart: Kreuz, 1977), 49–66] in Westermann, *Erträge der Forschung am Alten Testament: Gesammelte Studien* III (TB, 73; Munich: Kaiser), 9–26.

Der Auszug Israels aus Ägypten und das christliche Freiheitsverständnis

Als Mitherausgeber des Zürcher Kommentars hat Thomas Krüger wesentlich dazu beigetragen, dass mir die Abfassung zweier Bände zum Buch Exodus übertragen wurde. Das war für mich eine Herausforderung, aber auch ein Geschenk, das mein theologisches Forschen und Denken in den letzten 20 Jahren bereicherte, wofür ich Thomas Krüger dankbar bin. Da er selber gerne altorientalische und alttestamentliche Themen über die Fächergrenzen hinaus bearbeitet, hoffe ich, ihm mit dieser alttestamentlich-systematisch-theologischen Studie[1] eine kleine Freude zu bereiten.

1 Persönliche Vorbemerkungen

Einige persönliche Erfahrungen aus meinem Leben lassen die ganze Bandbreite der Probleme der christlichen Exodus-Rezeption aufscheinen: Als ich in den 80er Jahren des vorigen Jahrhunderts in Siegen Religionslehrer ausbildete und wir gehalten waren, unseren Unterricht ein Stück weit an den Lehrplänen des Landes Nordrhein-Westfalen auszurichten, musste ich zu meiner Überraschung feststellen, dass der Auszug Israels aus Ägypten dort nur als religionskundliches Thema in den Schulen vorgesehen war: Es sollte die Schüler darüber informieren, was im Zentrum des jüdischen Passahfestes steht.

Als ich Mitte der 90er Jahren frisch an die Universität Münster berufen worden war, steckte mir ein ausgewiesener Kenner der Reformationsgeschichte einen Sonderdruck zu, in dem er nachwies, dass Luthers Verständnis von Freiheit, die Befreiung von Sünde, Tod und Teufel, nicht das Geringste mit den Vorstellungen von politischer Freiheit in der Moderne zu tun habe. Als sich bei einer nachfolgenden Einladung ein neutestamentlicher Kollege zu der Ansicht verstieg, christliche Freiheit lasse sich im Gegenteil am klarsten im Gefängnis bezeugen, war das selbst dem Kirchengeschichtler zu viel, denn er kämpfte gerade für den Erhalt des Buß- und Bettages als gesetzlichem Feiertag. Einen gewissen politischen Freiraum brauche die Kirche schon, um das Evangelium nicht nur zu predigen, sondern auch mit Leben zu füllen. |

Nach meiner Pensionierung bin ich durch die vorzügliche Kantorin meiner Heidelberger Kirchengemeinde in die kirchenmusikalische Arbeit hineingeraten.

---

[1] Den Ausführungen liegt ein Vortrag zugrunde, den ich am 12. 10. 2019 an der Konferenz der Reformierten Hochschullehrer in Wuppertal gehalten habe. |

https://doi.org/10.1515/9783111202228-024

Sie führte mich zu einer intensiven Beschäftigung mit dem Oratorium „Messiah" von Georg Friedrich Händel, das am Ersten Advent 2019 in der Universitätskirche aufgeführt werden sollte und zu dem ich zwei Vorträge hielt. Das Oratorium, das die gesamte Geschichte des Messias von seiner Ankündigung bis zu seiner Wiederkunft darstellen will, beginnt zwar nicht mit dem Exodus aus Ägypten, wohl aber mit dem zweiten Exodus aus der babylonischen Gefangenschaft. Und indem es die Geschichte von Jesus Christus in die große Befreiungsgeschichte Gottes, die hier mit dem „Tröstet, tröstet mein Volk!" (Jes 40,1) anhebt, hineinstellt und mit der Aufrichtung der Königsherrschaft Gottes in der Welt durch die Predigt des Evangeliums weiterführt (vgl. das „Halleluja"), vermittelt es auch dem Sieg Jesu über Sünde und Tod in seinem Leiden und seiner Auferstehung und Verherrlichung im Himmel, eine weltgeschichtliche Weite, an der der Einzelne im Glauben wohl Anteil erhält, die aber keineswegs im individuellen Glauben aufgeht.

Zwei Jahre zuvor hatte ich aus dem gleichen Grund mit dem Oratorium „Das befreite Israel" von Georg Friedrich Telemann zu tun, das 1759 in Hamburg uraufgeführt wurde. Dieses besingt die Rettung Israels am Schilfmeer und seine Hoffnung auf ein Leben in Freiheit im verheißenen Lande (Ex 14–15), in die sich der christliche Chor fürbittend einschließt. Dabei habe ich mich gefragt: Wie kommt es, dass dieses Telemann-Oratorium in Deutschland fast vergessen ist, während das 20 Jahre früher von Händel komponierte Oratorium „Israel in Egypt" in England wahre Triumphe feierte. Hängt es damit zusammen, dass in der Anglikanischen Kirche – wie schon in der Alten Kirche – Israels Auszug aus Ägypten noch immer den Subtext zu Jesu Leiden und Auferstehung bildete? Die gesamte Exodusgeschichte wurde in England während der Passionszeit in den Früh- und Abendgottesdiensten verlesen, was wohl auch ein Grund dafür gewesen ist, dass sich die Puritaner ein Stück weit mit dem Alten Israel identifizierten.[2] Warum ging dieser gute liturgische Brauch, der teilweise auch noch in der Katholischen Kirche fortlebt (Ex 15 in der Osternacht), in den Kirchen der Reformation auf dem Kontinent – soweit ich weiß – völlig verloren? |

2 Ein Exodusschweigen in der deutschen systematischen Theologie?

Als ich versuchte, mich ein wenig kundig zu machen, ob und wieweit die Exodustradition im Freiheitsdiskurs der neueren deutschen systematischen Theologie

---

2 Vgl. dazu erhellend Assmann, Oratorium, 220–245. |

eine Rolle spielt, führte meine Suche zu einem weitgehend negativen Ergebnis.[3] Eine substantielle Rolle spielt der Exodus eigentlich nur bei Jürgen Moltmann, und zwar noch nicht in seiner „Theologie der Hoffnung" (1964), wo er sich zwar auf die Exodusverheißung als Strukturprinzip bezieht, aber diese ihres konkreten Befreiungsimpulses weitgehend entkleidet hat,[4] sondern erst in seinem späteren Buch „Der Geist des Lebens" von 1991, in dem er sich von der lateinamerikanischen Befreiungstheologie hat beeinflussen lassen.[5] Nicht die Befreiung Israels aus der ägyptischen Fron selbst, aber immerhin die davon beeinflussten „Erbarmensgesetze" zum Schutz der Fremdlinge und Schwachen (Ex 22,20–23,9 u. a.) aus dem Bundesbuch und Deuteronomium haben für Michael Welker eine auch für Christen bleibende Bedeutung.[6] Doch in einschlägigen neueren Werken zum christlichen Freiheitsverständnis, sei es von Wolfgang Huber, von Jörg Hübner oder Martin Laube, fand ich so gut wie nichts.[7] Sollte es wirklich der Fall sein, dass in der deutschen Theologie der Freiheitsdiskurs weitgehend an der biblischen Exodustradition vorbei geführt wird? Und ist es ein Zufall, dass in dem neusten theologischen Sammelband zum Thema Freiheit aus dem Jahr 2014, in dem sich auch das Fach Altes Testament äußern darf, ausgerechnet mit Uwe Becker ein Kollege zu Worte kommt, der den Exodus nicht nur historisch, sondern auch in seiner sozialpolitischen Bedeutung weitgehend in Frage stellt?[8] Mir scheint, dass es bis heute fast nur die amerikanischen Befreiungstheologen sind, wie Gustavo Gutiérrez und Clodovis Boff in Lateinamerika oder Peter C. Hodgson aus den USA, welche den Auszug Israels aus Ägypten in eine große Befreiungsgeschichte Gottes einordnen, die für alle Völker in Jesus Christus ihr Ziel findet.[9] Doch wegen der da|malig turbulenten politischen Verhältnisse in einigen lateinamerikanischen Ländern, manchen bedenklichen Instrumentalisierungen z. B. durch James H. Cone etwa im Kampf der Schwarzen um Bürgerrechte in den

---

3 Das hat sicher mit meinem beschränkten Fachhorizont zu tun; aber auch der Systematiker Jörg Lauster aus München, mit dem ich mich in der Sache austauschte, kam zu einem ähnlichen Resultat.

4 Vgl. Moltmann, Theologie, 85–112.

5 Vgl. Moltmann, Geist, 111–135.

6 Vgl. Welker, Gottes Geist, 27–30.

7 Vgl. die Spuren bei Huber, Freiheit, 151–152; Laube, Tendenzen, 260. Hübner, Ethik der Freiheit, 36–58, beschränkt sich ganz auf das Neue Testament.

8 Vgl. Becker, Befreiung, 26–32; auf S. 28–29 versteht er etwa den Exodus als Chiffre für das *extra nos* des Heils.

9 Vgl. Gutiérrez, Theologie der Befreiung, 205–242; Boff/Pixley, Option für die Armen, 35–38; Hodgson, Birth of Freedom, 290–321. Die Prägung des Terminus „Theology of Liberation" geht übrigens auf den brasilianischen Presbyterianer Rubem Alves im Jahr 1968 zurück; zum Exodus vgl. Alves, Hope, 89–91. |

USA[10] und einer Furcht vor marxistischer Unterwanderung des Christentums wurde die Befreiungstheologie in Europa nicht nur auf katholischer Seite von höchster Stelle scharf verurteilt, sondern auch von protestantischer Seite mehrheitlich abgelehnt. Sie fand auf beiden Seiten nur ganz wenige prominente Unterstützer, die kritisch beäugt wurden und werden (Johann Baptist Metz, Jürgen Moltmann, Ulrich Duchrow). Vielleicht hat ja die Scheu, die Exodusthematik im gegenwärtigen theologischen Freiheitsdiskurs erneut aufzugreifen, immer noch mit dieser Aversion gegen die Befreiungstheologie zu tun. Doch nach dem politischen Zusammenbruch des Marxismus besteht ja zumindest die Furcht vor einer Unterwanderung von dieser Seite aus nicht mehr. Ich war nie ein großer Freund der Befreiungstheologie, dazu schien sie mir zu sehr auf einen für Mitteleuropa fremden gesellschaftlichen Kontext bezogen. Doch wenn ich heute, da sich der Staub des Kampfgetümmels gelegt hat, die Bücher von Gutiérrez oder Hodgson lese, finde ich darin viel Bedenkenswertes, was auch für uns in Europa wichtig werden könnte. Selbst Papst Franziskus nimmt ja inzwischen manche ihrer Einsichten auf.

Wenn nun Wolfgang Huber sich der Meinung anschließt, „die christliche Freiheit muss politische Konsequenzen haben; sonst wird sie zum egoistischen Trost des Einzelnen,"[11] und wenn Martin Laube am Ende seiner Untersuchung feststellt: „Ein angemessenes christliches Freiheitsverständnis widerspricht damit allen Tendenzen, die Freiheit nur zu einer bloß innerlichen Haltung zu verflüchtigen,"[12] dann scheint es ein wesentliches Problem im heutigen protestantischen Freiheitsdiskurs zu sein, wie es gelingt, die individualistische Verengung und die zu starke geistige Sublimierung im christlichen Verständnis von Freiheit zu überwinden. Und so lautet meine schlichte Frage: Könnte nicht dabei gerade ein stärkerer Rückbezug auf die Herausführung des Volkes Israel aus dem ägyptischen Sklavenhaus, die in unserer Bibel als erste große Befreiungstat unseres Gottes erzählt wird, eine ganz wesentliche Hilfe sein? Denn dass es sich hier um einen überindividuellen, sozialen, ja politischen Befreiungsprozess mit realen Auswirkungen handelt, dürfte außer Frage stehen. |

---

10 Vgl. Cone, God of the Oppressed, 204–220, wo er die Anwendung von Gewalt im Befreiungskampf von Schwarzen gegen Weiße direkt mit dem Exodusgeschehen rechtfertigt.
11 Huber, Freiheit, 22.
12 Laube, Dialektik, 186. |

3 Die Herausführung aus Ägypten als Befreiung aus einer totalitären und menschenverachtenden Willkürherrschaft

Nach der Darstellung der ersten 15 Kapitel des Buches Exodus geht es bei dem politischen Befreiungsprozess, den Gott in Ägypten in Gang setzt, nicht um ein Weniger oder Mehr an Wahlfreiheit oder Selbstbestimmung, sondern viel grundsätzlicher um die Rettung aus einem mörderischen Unterdrückungssystem, um das nackte Überleben.[13] Als ein echter Demagoge schürt der Pharao den Fremdenhass gegen eine ethnische Minorität in seinem Lande, indem er behauptet, sie würde bald die eigene Bevölkerung an Zahl überflügeln und im Kriegsfall mit den Feinden paktieren (Ex 1,9–10). Die staatliche Fronarbeit, mit der er die Israeliten planvoll unterdrücken will, soll zu ihrer Dezimierung führen. Vernichtung durch Arbeit (V. 11–12)! Und als dies nicht recht funktioniert, beschließt er, alle männlichen hebräischen Säuglinge gleich bei ihrer Geburt durch ägyptische Hebammen heimlich umbringen zu lassen (V. 15–16), bzw. wo man sie findet, in den Nil zu werfen (V. 22). Das zielt auf biologische Ausrottung! Auf fatale Weise erinnern diese willkürlichen und menschenverachtenden staatlichen Unterdrückungsmaßnahmen an die Nazizeit. Es geht bei dem, was der Pharao in Ex 1 anordnet, um nichts weniger als das, was wir heute als „Verbrechen gegen die Menschlichkeit" und als „Genozid" bezeichnen.[14]

Der menschenverachtende Zynismus und der Totalitätsanspruch der Herrschaft, unter der die hebräischen Fronarbeiter zu leiden hatten, wird insbesondere in Ex 5 geschildert. Als Mose und Aaron um Urlaub für das Volk bitten, um einen Gottesdienst für JHWH in der nahen Wüste zu feiern (Ex 5,3), nimmt der Pharao dies zum Anlass, auf schikanöse Weise das Arbeitssoll der Arbeiter zu erhöhen. Sie müssen sich bei der Lehmziegelherstellung künftig das Stroh selber von den Stoppeln der Äcker zusammensuchen, aber trotzdem denselben Tagessoll an Ziegeln abliefern wie zuvor (V. 6–10). Eine Arbeitsunterbrechung für einen Gottesdienst ist für den Pharao nur ein Zeichen von Faulheit; der Gottesdienst bildet für ihn nur eine gefährliche Gelegenheit, „nach Lügenworten Ausschau zu halten" (V. 9). Die ununterbrochene Monotonie der Arbeit unter den Schlägen der Aufseher soll den Israeliten jeden Lebensmut nehmen. Auch hier drängt sich der

---

13 Zum Folgenden vgl. Albertz, Exodus 1–18, 39–255.
14 Es waren übrigens zwei jüdische Juristen aus Lemberg, Hersch Lauterpacht und Raphael Lemkin, die während des zweiten Weltkriegs die Straftatbestände des Verbrechens gegen die Menschlichkeit und des Genozids in das internationale Strafrecht einführten. Beide haben ihre Familie im Naziterror verloren, vgl. Sands, Rückkehr, 201–266.431–497. |

Vergleich mit moderner Zwangsarbeit auf, sei es nun in den KZs oder den Gulags des 20. Jahrhunderts. |

Der maßlose Vernichtungswille des Gewaltherrschers wird dann noch einmal am Schilfmeer geschildert. Selbst nachdem der unter dem Druck der göttlichen Sanktionen eingewilligt hat, die hebräischen Fronarbeiter aus seinem Herrschaftsbereich zu entlassen, setzt er seine ganze Streitwagentruppe in Gang, um die unbewaffnete Menschengruppe wieder einzufangen (Ex 14,5–6). Lieber sie alle umbringen, als auf ihre Ausbeutung zu verzichten! Das ist so, als würde man heute mit Panzern auf einen Flüchtlingstreck schießen. Allein schon aus dem Grund, sich als Theologe zu vergegenwärtigen, was alles passiert, wenn sich menschliche Hybris, Bosheit, Lüge und Sünde mit politischer Macht verbinden, ist eine aufmerksame Lektüre der Exodusgeschichte überaus lehrreich.

Angesichts der gewaltigen Unterdrückungsmacht stellt sich die Befreiung durch Gott in Ex 1–15 als ein langwieriger, schwieriger politischer Befreiungsprozess dar, der immer wieder zu scheitern droht. Als der junge Mose von sich aus einen Aufstandsversuch startet, indem er einen ägyptischen Aufseher, der einen der hebräischen Fronarbeiter quält, spontan erschlägt und im Sand verscharrt, wird das von seinen Landsleuten keineswegs als Fanal zum Widerstand verstanden. Sie sind durch die Zwangsarbeit derart entsolidarisiert, dass sie die erfahrene Gewalt untereinander weitergeben und sich jedes schlichtende Einschreiten des Mose verbitten. Mose wird von den eigenen Leuten denunziert und muss vor der Strafverfolgung des Pharao ins Ausland fliehen (Ex 2,11–15).

Das Exodusbuch stellt es so dar, dass erst da, als menschlicherseits keinerlei Hoffnung mehr auf Besserung der Lage bestand, Gott in das Geschehen eingriff, indem er Mose in Midian, fernab des Geschehens, offenbarte, dass er sich des Leides der unterdrückten Fronarbeiter in Ägypten annehmen werde:

Ex 3,7	Ich habe das Elend meines Volkes gesehen, das in Ägypten ist. Und ihr Geschrei vor seinen Antreibern habe ich gehört. Ja, ich kenne seine Schmerzen.
8	Darum bin ich herabgestiegen, um es zu retten aus der Hand Ägyptens und es heraufzuführen aus diesem Land in ein gutes und weites Land, ein Land, in dem Milch und Honig fließt, an den Ort der Kanaanäer, der Hethiter, Amoriter, Peresiter, Hiwiter und Jebusiter.
9	Doch nun, siehe das Wehgeschrei der Israeliten ist zu mir gedrungen, und ich habe auch die Unterdrückung gesehen, mit der sie die Ägypter bedrücken.
10	Doch nun, geh, ich will dich zum Pharao senden, und führe mein Volk, die Israeliten, aus Ägypten heraus!	

Damit, dass Gott sich vom Wehgeschrei der gequälten Israeliten hat rühren lassen, beginnt er sein großes Befreiungswerk. Er solidarisiert sich einseitig mit den Geschundenen und Entwürdigten. Er will sich um sie kümmern, sie aus dem Herrschaftsbereich Ägyptens hinausführen in ein gutes und weites Land, wo sie sich frei entfalten können. Und er beauftragt Mose, die Verhandlungen mit Pharao zu führen und die Herausführung in die Wege zu leiten.

Erstaunlicherweise hören die Israeliten diesmal auf Mose, als er ihnen nach seiner Rückkehr aus Midian die göttliche Befreiungsbotschaft ausrichtet. Sie lassen sich einhellig trotz aller Risiken im Glauben auf das göttliche Verheißungswort ein (Ex 4,31). Als dann aber die ersten Verhandlungen mit Pharao um eine Erleichterung der Fronarbeit scheitern, überschütten die israelitischen Vorarbeiter, die für die Nichteinhaltung der verschärften Normen von ihren ägyptischen Vorgesetzten verprügelt worden waren, Mose mit schweren Vorwürfen (5,20–21), sodass dieser nur noch seine verzweifelten Klagen an Gott richten kann:

Ex 5,22 Herr, warum hast du so übel an diesem Volk gehandelt und warum hast du mich denn gesandt?

23 Seit ich zum Pharao hineingegangen bin, um in deinem Namen zu reden, hat der übel an diesem Volk gehandelt und du hast dein Volk überhaupt nicht gerettet.

Das Befreiungswerk scheint, kaum begonnen, schon wieder gescheitert zu sein. Mose sieht sich durch Gott regelrecht düpiert. Der göttliche Befreiungsauftrag an ihn hat die Lage des Volkes nur noch verschlimmert. Erst diese tiefe Krise bringt Gott dazu, nun direkt in die Auseinandersetzung mit dem Pharao einzugreifen, um ihn mit seinen göttlichen Sanktionen zur Freilassung Israels zu zwingen (Ex 6,1). Nach Vorstellung des priesterlichen Bearbeiters ist in dieser Krise sogar eine nochmalige Berufung des Mose nötig, in der Gott eine noch profundere, auf den Abrahambund gestützte Befreiungsverheißung gibt (V. 2–8). Aber auch diese kann das Vertrauen der Israeliten nicht zurückgewinnen: „sie hörten nicht auf Mose aus Kleinmut und wegen der harten Arbeit" (V. 9). Doch Gott ist dies inzwischen nach priesterlicher Sicht völlig egal. Er stattet Mose und Aaron mit Wunderkräften aus, mit denen sie den Pharao und seine Magier beeindrucken sollen, während sich Gott nach älterer Sicht sehr eng an Mose bindet, so dass er auf dessen Ankündigung hin seine Plagegeister, die Frösche, Bremsen und Heuschrecken, auf wunderbare Weise gegen den mächtigen Pharao mobilisiert. Immer wieder schickt er Mose zum Pharao, um den selbstherrlichen Potentaten mit seiner göttlichen Freilassforderung zu konfrontieren: „Lass mein Volk frei, dass es mir in der Wüste diene!" (Ex 7,16 u. ö.). Dem Sklavendienst stellt Gott den Gottesdienst gegenüber. Dieser, den | der Pharao den Fronarbeitern als Arbeitsunterbrechung versagt hat, wird damit von Gott zum Kennzeichen einer von Unterdrückung befreiten, einer menschenwürdigen Existenz erklärt. Als gewiefter Machtmensch reagiert der Pharao scheinheilig auf die göttlichen Sanktionen. Unter ihrem Druck macht er Zugeständnisse, zieht sie aber, sobald die Plage vorbei ist, schnell wieder zurück: Wie wär's mit einem Gottesdienst im Lande (Ex 8,21–

24)? Ja, ihr dürft außer Landes ziehen, aber die Kinder müssen hierbleiben (Ex 10,8–11). Doch bleibt Mose in den sich hinziehenden Verhandlungen beharrlich bei seiner Forderung, dass das ganze Volk freigelassen werden muss. Er lässt sich nicht auseinanderdividieren. Nach der Heuschrecken- und Finsternisplage ist man sich fast einig, es geht nur noch um die Mitnahme des Viehs. Erst als der Pharao die Verhandlungen wütend abbricht, weil sein Plan nicht aufgeht, aus der Gefangenenbefreiung wenigstens noch einen kleinen Reibach zu machen (Ex 10,24–29), kündigt Mose die Tötung der Erstgeborenen an (Ex 11,4–6). Erst jetzt, als die göttliche Sanktion das Liebste trifft, was der Pharao und die Ägypter haben, erfolgt der Durchbruch. Der mächtige Potentat gibt sich geschlagen, er erlaubt den Auszug seiner Fronarbeiter und den Gottesdienst für JHWH, den er ihnen so lange versagt hat; er bittet nur, dabei auch seiner segnend zu gedenken (Ex 12,31–32). Auch die politische Befreiung, von der das Exodusbuch erzählt, ist – trotz aller menschlichen Beteiligung – von Gott geschenkte, ist verdankte Freiheit.

Doch diese Entlassung der Zwangsarbeiter aus dem ägyptischen Herrschaftsbereich bedeutet nun keineswegs die Erlösung von allen Nöten. Das befreite Israel findet sich in der Wüste mit ihren vielen Gefahren vor. Schlimmer noch, der wankelmütige Potentat verfolgt mit einer gewaltigen Streitmacht die Freigelassenen und stellt sie am Schilfmeer (Ex 14,1–10). Noch ein weiteres Mal droht das Befreiungswerk Gottes dramatisch zu scheitern. Angesichts der militärischen Übermacht beschimpfen die gerade erst Befreiten Mose, sie hintergangen zu haben, und wünschen sich in die Unfreiheit zurück:

> Ex 14,11 Gab es denn keine Gräber in Ägypten, dass du uns genommen hast, damit wir in der Wüste sterben? Was hast du uns angetan, dass du uns aus Ägypten herausgeführt hast?
>
> 12 War das nicht das Wort, das wir zu dir in Ägypten gesprochen haben: „Lass uns in Ruhe! Wir wollen den Ägyptern dienen!" Denn es ist besser für uns, den Ägyptern zu dienen als in der Wüste zu sterben.

In ihrer gegenwärtigen Angst lügen sich die Israeliten ihre frühere Not einfach hinweg. Und weil im politischen Befreiungsprozess Gott immer auch auf menschliche Kooperation angewiesen ist, besteht die einfache Möglichkeit, dem Beauftragten Gottes die Schuld in die Schuhe zu schieben. Nur unter Auf|bietung seines ganzen Gottvertrauens gelingt es Mose, eine Panik unter seinen Leuten zu verhindern. Er stellt ihnen in Aussicht, dass Gott diesmal ganz allein für ihr Überleben kämpfen wird (Ex 14,13–14). Und Gott lässt Mose nicht im Stich. Er erfüllt die Erwartung seines Beauftragten und vernichtet das ägyptische Heer auf wunderbare Weise. Erst nach dieser Erfahrung einer erneuten befreienden Rettung findet das Volk wieder zu dem Glauben zurück (Ex 14,31), der am Anfang des Befreiungswerkes Gottes gestanden hatte (Ex 4,31). Erst wenn man das, was man

„Israels Auszug aus Ägypten" nennt, in seinen Einzelheiten wahrnimmt, kann man ermessen, was alles an konkreten Realitätsbezügen in den christlichen Freiheitsdiskurs gelangen könnte, wenn man die Exodusüberlieferung stärker in ihn einbeziehen würde. Dies könnte neben der Erweiterung auf den größeren sozialen und politischen Horizont dem theologischen Freiheitsdiskurs auch einen Schutz vor schleichendem Realitätsverlust vermitteln.

4 Die Ausgestaltung der verdankten Freiheit am Sinai

Mit der Herausführung aus Ägypten ist allerdings der Befreiungsprozess Israels noch längst nicht zu Ende. Es gehört mindestens noch die Offenbarung Gottes am Sinai dazu, bei der sich Gott aus den befreiten Fronarbeitern sein erstes Gottesvolk Israel erschuf, indem er ihm Regeln an die Hand gab, wie sie ihre geschenkte Freiheit bewahren und ihn, ihren göttlichen Befreier, verehren könnten.[15] Schon in der vorpriesterlichen Exoduserzählung hat Gott Israel deswegen aus der Gewalt des Pharaos befreit, um es „auf Adlersflügeln", d. h. so schnell wie möglich, zu sich an den Sinai zu holen, damit er mit ihm einen Bund schließen kann (Ex 19,4–8). Nach Sicht des ersten priesterlichen Bearbeiters entsprang die Herausführung der Israeliten aus Ägypten letztlich dem Wunsch Gottes, „in ihrer Mitte zu wohnen", d. h. in einem Heiligtum ganz nah bei ihnen präsent zu sein (Ex 29,46). Diese enge Verbindung von Exodus und Sinai im Exodusbuch wurde auch in der alttestamentlichen Forschung nicht immer genügend gewürdigt.[16] Erst beim Schreiben meines zweiten Kommentarbandes wurde mir deutlich, dass die im Exodusbuch erkennbare Struktur genau dem Aufbau des Heidelberger Katechismus entspricht: Seine ersten 15 Kapitel, die von der Unterdrückung Israels in Ägypten und seiner Befreiung handeln, entsprechen den ersten beiden Teilen des Katechismus „Von des Menschen Elend" und „Von des Menschen Erlösung". Die Kapitel 18–40, die | von der Gabe der Gebote und des Heiligtums an das befreite Israel handeln, entsprechen dem dritten Teil des Katechismus „Von der Dankbarkeit", der ebenfalls die Gebote Gottes und das Gebet zu Gott zum Inhalt hat. Am Sinai legt Gott die Grundlagen für die dankbare Reaktion der Befreiten auf die ihnen geschenkte Befreiung. In ihrer Verpflichtung auf Gottes Gebote und seine gottesdienstlichen Ordnungen können sie ihren Befreier dankbar ehren und zugleich die ihnen geschenkte Freiheit gesellschaftlich ausgestalten.

---

15 Zum Folgenden vgl. Albertz, Exodus 1–18, 296–314; idem, Exodus 19–40, 27–228.
16 Vgl. nur die einflussreiche These Gerhard von Rads, dass die Sinaitradition eine eigenständige Größe war, die erst sekundär und spät mit der Exodus-Landnahme-Tradition verbunden wurde, so von Rad, Problem, 15–33. |

Kommen wir zuerst zum Gottesdienst, dessen wichtige Rolle für eine freiheitliche Gesellschaftsordnung häufig übersehen wird. Der Kampf um Gewährung des Freiraums für einen Gottesdienst spielte schon im Befreiungsprozess selber, wie wir gesehen haben, eine wichtige Rolle (Ex 5,1.3; 7,16 u. ö.). Er sollte nicht zu einem trickreichen Vorwand für eine heimliche Flucht kleingeredet werden,[17] denn von einer solchen Flucht ist in der vorherrschenden Darstellung des Exodusbuches nicht die Rede; ein winziger Rest einer solchen Vorstellung findet sich einzig in Ex 14,5a. Nein, der Gottesdienst ist ein Freiheitsfanal gegen Ausbeutung und Tyrannei, er dient – noch ganz abgesehen davon, was in ihm geschieht – der Humanisierung einer totalisierten Arbeitswelt und Begrenzung eines totalitären politischen Herrschaftsanspruchs. Am Sinai bekommt der Gottesdienst dann seine inhaltliche Füllung: Im ersten Gottesdienst, der in Ex 18 am Sinai gefeiert wird, übrigens auf Anregung des midianitischen Schwiegervaters des Mose, steht das Gotteslob für die erfahrene Befreiung aus der Gewalt des Pharao im Zentrum (V. 10–12). Der Gottesdienst ist der Ort, wo die Dankbarkeit gegenüber Gott eingeübt wird, wo bewusst gemacht wird, dass die Freiheit keineswegs selbstverständlich, sondern eine geschenkte Freiheit ist und bleibt. Der zweite Gottesdienst am Sinai besiegelt den Bund mit dem göttlichen Befreier, in den die Israeliten aus freien Stücken eintreten (Ex 19,8). Einerseits räumt ihnen JHWH eine privilegierte Gottesnähe ein („Königreich von Priestern"), andererseits verpflichten sich die Israeliten, den Geboten und Gesetzen, die Gott ihnen zum Aufbau einer gerechten und solidarischen Gesellschaft offenbart hat, Folge zu leisten (Ex 19,6; 24,4–8). Der Gottesdienst zielt darauf ab, im dankbaren Gehorsam gegenüber Gott den Schritt von der „Freiheit von" zur „Freiheit zu" einzuüben. Und schließlich dient der Bau des gottgewollten Heiligtums dem Ziel, Gott inmitten des Volkes einen Raum zu schaffen, an dem man ihm gefahrlos regelmäßig begegnen kann (Ex 29,42–46). Dabei sollen die darin gefeierten Gottesdienste nach priesterlicher Vorstellung nicht nur ermöglichen, dem göttlichen Befreier Dankopfer darzubringen (Lev 7,11–16), sondern auch durch seine Präsenz Befreiung von der Sündenlast zu erlangen (Lev 16), wenn sich die Israeliten gegen Gottes Willen vergangen haben sollten. |

Ebenso wichtig ist sodann der Gehorsam gegenüber Gottes Geboten und Gesetzen, den man auch als „Gottesdienst im Alltag" bezeichnen kann. Er wurde von den Tradenten des Exodusbuches sogar an die erste Stelle der Sinaioffenbarung gerückt (Ex 19–23). Es wäre nun völlig falsch, den Gebotsgehorsam als einen Zwang zu bezeichnen, welcher dem Zwang des Pharao nicht unähnlich sei, weil er die Selbstbestimmung zur Fremdbestimmung verkehre. Denn erstens entschei-

---

17 So Baentsch, Exodus, 26, u. a. |

den sich die Israeliten mehrfach freiwillig dazu, ihre Verpflichtungen in dem von Gott angebotenen Bund zu übernehmen (Ex 19,8; 24,3), das letzte Mal, nachdem ihnen Mose die ihm geoffenbarten Gebote und Gesetze im Einzelnen vorgelesen hat: „Alles, was JHWH geredet hat, wollen wir tun und hören!" (Ex 24,7). Sie wollen nicht nur ihr alltägliches Handeln nach Gottes Geboten ausrichten, sondern sich sogar immer wieder über das darin Gemeinte belehren lassen.

Zweitens ist es darüber hinaus, wie es der allen weiteren Gesetzesoffenbarungen vorangestellte Dekalog ausdrücklich feststellt, der Gott, der sie aus dem ägyptischen Sklavenhaus befreit hat, der ihnen nun gebietet (Ex 20,2). Alles, was JHWH gebietet, soll damit zu ihrem Besten dienen, soll ihnen helfen, ihre gewonnene Freiheit zu bewahren. Diese Zielrichtung lässt sich, wie Frank Crüsemann schon vor vielen Jahren herausgearbeitet hat,[18] an den einzelnen Dekaloggeboten aufzeigen: Fremdgötter und Bilderverbot schützen nicht nur das intime Gottesverhältnis Israels zu JHWH, sondern auch vor Vergötzung von Geld und politischer Macht.[19] Das Sabbatgebot räumt ausdrücklich auch den abhängigen Arbeitern eine wöchentliche Arbeitsruhe ein. Das Elterngebot schützt das Überleben der alten, arbeitsunfähig gewordenen Eltern, das Ehebruchsverbot den familiären Wirtschaftbetrieb vor dem Eindringen eines fremden Chefs. Das Verleumdungsverbot sichert den gesellschaftlichen Frieden und das Funktionieren der Rechtsprechung. Das Diebstahlverbot schützt zwar das persönliche Eigentum als eine Voraussetzung für Freiheit, doch der Gier nach Ausweitung des eigenen Eigentums auf Kosten anderer wird im 10. Gebot eine klare Absage erteilt. Hätte Luther nicht den Rückbezug auf die Befreiung aus Ägypten aus der Dekalogeinleitung herausgestrichen und hätten nicht auch die übrigen Reformatoren den Dekalog ständig auf das sog. „Naturrecht" reduziert,[20] wäre der Befreiungsimpuls, der den Dekalog durchzieht, in der christlichen Ethik stärker bewahrt worden.[21] Vielleicht wären uns dann auch regel|recht repressive Gehorsamsforderungen, wie der Bezug des Elterngebots auf die elterliche Autorität (leider schon in Eph 6,1) oder sogar die der staatlichen Obrigkeit (Luthers großer Katechismus) erspart geblieben. Wie dem auch sei, eindeutig belegt der Dekalog jedenfalls, dass die Befreiung

---

18 Vgl. Crüsemann, Bewahrung der Freiheit, 36–78.
19 Vgl. die Kritik an der Vergötzung des Geldes in Ps 52,9; 62,11; Hi 31,24–25 und der Staatsmacht in Dan 3; 6.
20 Zur hohen Bedeutung des Naturrechts bei den Reformatoren vgl. Strohm, Melanchthon, 476–482.
21 Der Freiheitsimpuls des Dekalogs wurde schon in der frühjüdischen Überlieferung hervorgehoben. Pirqe Abot 6,2 berichtet, dass Rabbi Joshua ben Levi in Ex 32,16 nicht lesen wollte, der Dekalog sei „in Gottesschrift geschrieben, eingegraben (ḥārût) auf die Tafeln", sondern er sei | „Gottesschrift, Freiheit (ḥērût) auf den Tafeln", „denn ein Freier ist nur der, der sich mit Gesetzeslehre befasst."

der Verpflichtung nicht nur zeitlich, sondern auch sachlich vorangeht. Der Heidelberger Katechismus hat recht: Die freiwillige Verpflichtung auf Gottes Gebote
geschieht aus Dankbarkeit aufgrund der von Gott her erfahrenen geschenkten
Befreiung. Wenn man zumindest den Dekalog in seiner ursprünglichen biblischen
Fassung wieder stärker in die Bemühungen um eine christliche Freiheitsethik
einbinden könnte – eine solche fehlt z. B. völlig in der „Ethik der Freiheit" von
Jörg Hübner –, wäre meiner Meinung nach schon einiges für deren konkretere
gesellschaftliche Orientierung gewonnen.

Aber unser gütiger Gott hat den von ihm Befreiten auf dem Sinai in seiner
Tora noch über den Dekalog hinaus sehr viel mehr Orientierung zum Aufbau
einer gerechten, solidarischen und freiheitlichen Gesellschaft vermittelt. Ich sehe
eine gewisse Tragik darin, dass Luther sich in seiner Auseinandersetzung mit
Karlstadt, den Schwärmern und den Bauern, die sich auf Elemente der mosaischen Gesetzgebung beriefen, dazu hat hinreißen lassen, die von Gott auf dem
Sinai geoffenbarte Tora als „der Juden Sachsenspiegel" herabzustufen und damit
alles – abgesehen vom Dekalog – als irrelevant für die christliche Ethik zu erklären, obgleich er hier durchaus einiges besser geregelt fand als im Römischen
Recht.[22] Ob die Reformierten in Genf, Zürich oder anderswo mehr von der sozialen Gesetzgebung des Alten Testamentes positiv aufgenommen haben, bin ich mir
nicht sicher. Hier stand wohl eher die Kirchenzucht im Vordergrund. Seltsamerweise griffen im vom Calvinismus geprägten Raum eher die Juristen und religiöse
Dissidenten im 17. Jh. auf die herrschaftskritischen Regelungen der „Hebräischen
Republik" zurück, wie sie das durch die Sinaigesetzgebung verfasste Gemeinwesen nannten.[23] Möglicherweise war der Befreiungsimpuls der alttestamentlichen
Tora den gesellschaftlichen Verhältnissen im Europa des 16. Jhs. zu weit voraus.

Aber vielleicht wäre es im 21. Jh. an der Zeit, die Entscheidungen der Refor-
mation zur alttestamentlichen Tora neu zu überdenken. Immerhin handelt es |
sich am Sinai um eine ausdrückliche Offenbarung des biblischen Gottes, ja, die
zentralste im ganzen Ersten Testament. Dabei geht es nicht gleich um die Frage,
ob auch die Christen als das zweite Gottesvolk die gesamte Sinaitora übernehmen,
die dem ersten Gottesvolk gegeben wurde. Die kultischen und rituellen Vorschrif-
ten bleiben sowieso außen vor. Aber es könnte sich doch lohnen, ernsthaft zu

---

22 Vgl. dazu Strohm, Melanchthon, 469; Bubenheimer, Consonantia, 243–250.
23 Vgl. dazu das sehr interessante Buch von Nelson, Hebrew Republic, 23–139. Einer der berühm-
testen Dissidenten war Roger Williams, der sich von den Puritanern in Massachusetts trennte,
um in Rhode Island eine neue Republik zu gründen, in der Glaubens- und Gewissenfreiheit
herrschen sollten. Allerdings bezog sich Williams zur Rechtfertigung mehr auf das Neue Testament, etwa das Gleichnis vom Unkraut unter dem Weizen (Mt 13,36–38), da das Alte Testament
von seinen puritanischen Gegnern zur Legitimation ihrer Religionskontrolle benutzt wurde, vgl.
Davies, Religious Liberty, 86.140–149. |

fragen, ob wir nicht all solche Regelungen zum Schutze und zur Hilfe für die sozial Schwachen und Ausgegrenzten, die am deutlichsten den Befreiungsimpuls aus der Exodusgeschichte atmen, zumindest für die ethische Urteilsbildung berücksichtigen sollten, wie es ansatzweise Michael Welker getan hat.[24] Da diese von Welker so genannten „Erbarmensgesetze" schon für die Israeliten eine nicht unerhebliche Beschneidung ihrer Freiheitsrechte zugunsten der sozial und rechtlich Benachteiligten bedeuteten, wurden sie nicht selten ausdrücklich mit einem Hinweis auf die von ihnen erfahrene Befreiung aus Ägypten begründet. Nur drei dieser göttlichen Gebote seien hier zitiert:

Ex 22,20	Einen Fremdling sollst du nicht bedrücken und ihn nicht unterdrücken, denn ihr seid Fremdlinge im Land Ägypten gewesen [...]
22	Falls du ihn tatsächlich erniedrigst, wenn er dann laut zu mir schreit, werde ich sein Geschrei ganz bestimmt erhören.
Lev 25,35	Wenn dein Bruder verarmt und sich nicht mehr halten kann neben dir, sollst du ihn unterstützen [...]
37	Du sollst von ihm keinen Zins oder Zuschlag verlangen, wenn du ihm Geld oder Nahrung gibst.
38	Ich bin JHWH, euer Gott, der euch herausgeführt hat aus dem Land Ägypten, euch das Land Kanaan zu geben, um euer Gott zu sein.
Dtn 24,21	Wenn du in deinem Weinberg Lese hältst, sollst du keine Nachlese halten. Dem Fremden, der Witwe und Waise soll es gehören.
22	Und du sollst daran denken, dass du Sklave gewesen bist in Ägypten; darum gebiete ich dir, dass du so handelst.

Dass ein solidarisches Verhalten so direkt aus der Dankbarkeit über die eigene Befreiung entspringen soll und dass sich Gott im Konfliktfall genauso mit den Schwachen und Unterdrückten identifiziert, wie er es damals mit den unterdrückten Fronarbeitern in Ägypten getan hat, das scheint mir eine so schlichte, aber deswegen eine um so eindrucksvollere theologische Argumentation zu sein, die wir vielleicht auch für unsere christliche Ethik zurückgewinnen könnten, wenn wir uns auch als Christen auf die Exodustradition zurückbeziehen. Denn die Befreiungsgeschichte Gottes, die für uns Christen in Tod und Auferstehung ihren Höhepunkt erhielt, hat mit der Befreiung Israels aus Ägypten | begonnen. Jedenfalls sollte die Verpflichtung, die wir Christen aus der Dankbarkeit für unsere Befreiung aus der Macht der Sünde und des Todes durch Jesus Christus auf uns nehmen, nicht hinter der Tora Gottes vom Sinai zurückbleiben. In der neuen Perikopenordnung der Evangelischen Kirchen in Deutschland wurde unter die für den Ostersonntag vorgeschlagenen Predigttexte erstmals auch die Schilfmeerer-

---

24 Welker, Gottes Geist, 27–30. |

zählung (in Auszügen) und das Mirjamlied (Ex 14; 15,20–21) aufgenommen. So soll zumindest alle sechs Jahre am Fest der Auferstehung Jesu Christi auch der Befreiung Israels aus Ägypten gedacht werden. Ostern 2021 war dies in vielen Kirchen Deutschlands zum ersten Mal der Fall. Ein erster wichtiger Schritt!

Literaturverzeichnis

Albertz, Rainer, Exodus 1–18 (ZBK.AT 2/1), Zürich [2]2017.

Albertz, Rainer, Exodus 19–40 (ZBK.AT 2/2), Zürich 2015.

Alves, Rubem A., A Theology of Human Hope, St. Meinard [3]1975 (= Toward a Theology of Liberation, Diss.theol. Princeton 1968).

Assmann, Jan, Das Oratorium Israel in Egypt von Georg Friedrich Händel (Bibel und Musik), Stuttgart 2015.

Baentsch, Bruno, Exodus–Leviticus–Numeri (HK 1/2), Göttingen 1903.

Becker, Uwe, Zwischen Befreiung und Autonomie. Freiheitsvorstellungen im Alten Testament, in: Martin Laube (Hg.), Freiheit (TdT 7; UTB 3771), Tübingen 2014, 21–37.

Boff, Clodovis/Pixley, Jorge, Die Option für die Armen, Düsseldorf 1987.

Bubenheimer, Ulrich, Consonantia Theologiae et Iurisprudenciae. Andreas Bodenstein von Karlstadt als Theologe und Jurist zwischen Scholastik und Reformation (JusEcc 24), Tübingen 1977.

Cone, James H., God of the Oppressed, New York [2]1997.

Crüsemann, Frank, Bewahrung der Freiheit. Das Thema des Dekalogs in sozialgeschichtlicher Perspektive (KT 78), München 1983.

Davies, James Calvin, On Religious Liberty. Selections of Works of Roger Williams, Cambridge/London 2008.

Gutiérrez, Gustavo, Theologie der Befreiung, Mainz [10]1992.

Hodgson, Peter C., New Birth of Freedom. A Theology of Bondage and Liberation, Philadelphia 1976.

Huber, Wolfgang, Von der Freiheit. Perspektiven für eine solidarische Welt, München 2012.

Hübner, Jörg, Ethik der Freiheit. Grundlegung der Handlungsfelder einer globalen Ethik in christlicher Perspektive, Stuttgart 2012.

Laube, Martin, Die Dialektik der Freiheit. Systematisch-theologische Perspektiven, in: idem (Hg.), Freiheit (TdT 7; UTB 3771), Tübingen 2014, 119–191.

Laube, Martin, Tendenzen und Motive im Verständnis von Freiheit, in: idem (Hg.), Freiheit (TdT 7; UTB 3771), Tübingen 2014, 255–267. |

Moltmann, Jürgen, Der Geist des Lebens. Eine ganzheitliche Pneumatologie, München 1991.

Moltmann, Jürgen, Theologie der Hoffnung. Untersuchungen zur Begründung und zu den Konsequenzen einer christlichen Eschatologie, München [12]1985.

Nelson, Eric, The Hebrew Republic. Jewish Sources and the Transformation of European Political Thought, Cambridge/London 2010.

Rad, Gerhard von, Das formgeschichtliche Problem des Hexateuch, in: idem, Gesammelte Studien zum Alten Testament (ThB 8), München [2]1961, 9–86.

Sands, Philippe, Rückkehr nach Lemberg. Über die Ursprünge von Genozid und Verbrechen gegen die Menschlichkeit. Eine persönliche Geschichte, Frankfurt a. M. 2018.

Strohm, Christoph, Melanchthon et l'éthique réformée. Le probleme du statut du droit naturel, in: Maria-Christina Pitassi/Daniela Solfaroli Camillocci (Hg.), Crossing Traditions. Essays on the Reformation and Intellectual History. FS Irena Backus, Leiden/Boston 2018, 467–491.

Welker, Michael, Gottes Geist. Theologie des Heiligen Geistes, Neukirchen-Vluyn [3]2005.

Biblische Perspektiven zur Wirtschaftsethik

Einleitung

Biblische Vorstellungen und Regelungen zur Wirtschaft sind bisher nur selten zur Ausbildung einer materialen Wirtschaftsethik herangezogen worden. Was das Neue Testament betrifft, hängt dies damit zusammen, dass dessen Zentralforderung der Gottes- und Menschenliebe (Matth 22,34–40 par.) sehr allgemein bleibt und gemeinhin nur auf den individuellen Lebensbereich bezogen wird. Zudem wurden die radikalen Vorstellungen des Neuen Testaments zu wirtschaftlichen Themen, etwa der totale Besitzverzicht, der dem reichen Jüngling von Jesus abgefordert wird (Mark 10,17–27), oder die Gütergemeinschaft der Apostel (Apg 2,42 ff.), meistens als zu weit von der eigenen ökonomischen Realität entfernt empfunden.

Aber auch dem oft „realitätsnäheren" Alte Testament erging es nicht besser. Die Zehn Gebote sprechen den wirtschaftlichen Bereich direkt nur im Diebstahlverbot an („Du sollst nicht stehlen!" Ex 20,15), während dem abschließenden Begehrensverbot („Du sollst nicht das Haus bzw. die Frau deines Nächsten begehren!" V. 17) bisher nur selten wirtschaftliche Relevanz zugebilligt wurde. Auch die arbeitsrechtliche Dimension des Sabbatgebotes (V. 8–11) wurde kaum ausgewertet, da es nicht zur zweiten Tafel gehört, dessen Gebote als Maxime einer allgemein gültigen Sittlichkeit, auf katholischer Seite sogar als Ausdruck des Naturrechts angesehen wurden. Noch weniger wurden die vielen Gesetze und Gebote zum Wirtschaftsbereich, die das Alte Testament jenseits des Dekalogs enthält, zur sozialethischen Urteilsbildung herangezogen, da man diesen gesamten Bereich alttestamtlicher Gesetzgebung als „der Juden Sachsenspiegel" (so Luther) abqualifizierte, der für Christen keinerlei Gültigkeit mehr habe.[1] |

Umso erstaunlicher ist es, dass im politischen Diskurs der Gegenwart seit einigen Jahrzehnten plötzlich alttestamentliche Konzepte zur materialen Wirtschaftsethik eine aktuelle Bedeutung gewinnen, so etwa als sich Bürgerinitiativen

---

[1] Selbst in der ersten ausführlichen *Evangelischen Wirtschaftsethik* von Georg Wünsch spielt die Bibel nur eine geringe Rolle. Zum Thema Eigentum etwa beschränkt er sich für das Alte Testament auf das Diebstahlverbot im Dekalog (Ex 20,15), dem er nur noch Ex | 21,18–22,15 als Erläuterung zuzieht. Aus dem Neuen Testament geht er etwas ausführlicher auf Luk 3,11, Matth 10,1–15 und Apg 2,42–47 ein, um nachzuweisen, dass es trotz der hier vorherrschenden kritischen Sicht des Eigentums „nirgends das Gebot eines radikalen Kommunismus" gibt (vgl. Wünsch, *Wirtschaftsethik*, S. 662 f.). Aber immerhin leitet er aus der biblischen und kirchlichen Tradition die Haltung eines „Gesinnungssozialismus" ab, der „über die gegebene private Eigentumsordnung hinausstrebt" (ebd., S. 689).

https://doi.org/10.1515/9783111202228-025

ab dem Ende der 80er Jahre des vorigen Jahrhunderts angesichts der massiven
Schuldenkrise in einigen Ländern Afrikas und Lateinamerikas auf die Gesetze im
Alten Testament zum Schuldenerlass beriefen (Dtn 15,1–11; Lev 25; Sabbat- bzw.
Jobeljahr). Die öffentliche Debatte führte wirklich dazu, dass im Jahr 2005 die G8-
Staaten und der Internationale Währungsfonds einen Schuldenerlass für 19 der
20 ärmsten Staaten der Welt beschlossen. Noch heute prangt der Satz aus
Lev 25,10 („Heiligt das fünfzigste Jahr und verkündet Freiheit für alle Bewohner.
Ein Erlassjahr soll es für euch sein") auf der Internetseite der Initiative „Erlass-
jahr e. V.".[2]

Ökonomische Rationalität im Alten Israel

Die Ökonomie des Alten Israel der vorstaatlichen und frühköniglichen Zeit (11.–
9. Jh. v. Chr.) lässt sich als agrarische Subsistenzwirtschaft klassifizieren. Innerhalb einer verwandtschaftlich basierten Gesellschaft verfügten die Familien über
Grundeigentum und Viehbesitz und versorgten sich mit dem, was sie durch
Ackerbau und Viehzucht produzierten, weitgehend selbst. Es gab, abgesehen vom
Fernhandel mit Luxusgütern für einige Wohlhabende, nur einen gering entwickelten lokalen Handel (meist Tauschhandel) mit agrarischen Produkten, Tieren
und Handwerksgütern. Da die Familien mit ihren eigenen Angehörigen bzw. näheren Verwandten produzierten, existierte kaum abhängige Lohnarbeit; dafür
gab es einige | Sklaven und Gastarbeiter („Fremdlinge"), die innerhalb der Famili-
en beschäftigt und versorgt wurden.[3]

Obwohl die Ökonomie des frühen alten Israel nur wenig entwickelt war, verfügte sie dennoch schon über ihre eigene Rationalität. Es galt unter den prekären
ökologischen Bedingungen des Regenfeldbaus im Vorderen Orient durch Fleiß
und Geschick möglichst so viel zu produzieren, dass es zum Überleben der Familie reichte. Überschüsse wurden eingetauscht oder verkauft, aber es wurde nicht
für einen Markt produziert. Während der Handel mit Grundstücken stark eingeschränkt war, galt für den Handel mit Lebensgütern ein ungeschriebenes Kauf-
und Vertragsrecht, das auf einen Interessenausgleich zwischen den Handelspart-

2 Siehe http://www.erlassjahr.de/ueber-uns/ (Abruf am 30. 1. 2014). Prominente Unterstützer sind
nicht etwa Theologen, sondern Personen des öffentlichen Lebens wie Wim Wenders und Smudo. |
3 Eine Wirtschaftsgeschichte des Alten Israel ist noch nicht geschrieben. Einen Überblick über
die Sozialgeschichte gibt Kessler, *Sozialgeschichte*, S. 57–113; vgl. ansonsten Albertz, *Religionsgeschichte I*, S. 112–117, 160–172.

nern hinauslief. Soweit wir erkennen können, unterlag dieser gesamte Bereich wirtschaftlichen Handelns in der Frühzeit keiner religiösen Normierung.

Die frühen Gesetze zur Regelung des wirtschaftlichen Handelns, die in die Rechtssammlung des sogenannten „Bundesbuches" (Ex 20,22–23,19) aus dem späten 8. Jahrhundert v. Chr. aufgenommen sind, aber selber wohl aus dem 9. Jahrhundert stammen, sind rein profan.[4] Sie lassen noch eine Balance zwischen dem Verfügungsrecht des Eigentümers über sein Eigentum und der Verpflichtung des Eigentümers gegenüber seinen Mitbürgern erkennen (Sinaga 2013, S. 53–146). Dass die Gesetzgeber der königlichen Rechtsschule ein weitgehend unbegrenztes Verfügungsrecht des Eigentümers über sein Eigentum anerkennen, wird z. B. aus dem in Ex 21,20–21 abgehandelten Fall erkennbar, dass ein Mann seinen Sklaven mit einem Stock züchtigt. Hier unterliegt der Mann nur dann einer Strafverfolgung, wenn der Sklave noch unter den Schlägen stirbt und damit der Verdacht eines vorsätzlichen Totschlags im Raum steht. Sofern der Sklave aber noch mindestens 24 Stunden überlebt, geht der Mann straffrei aus, | und zwar mit der Begründung, dass der Sklave „sein Geld", also sein Eigentum sei. Der Herr hat sich nach dieser Logik mit der Todesfolge seiner harten Züchtigung selber einen wirtschaftlichen Verlust zugefügt.

Es ist darum nur folgerichtig, dass die Gesetzgeber auf der einen Seite das Eigentum des Eigentümers zu schützen trachten. So wird in Ex 21,37–22,3 der Diebstahl von Vieh hart bestraft: Sofern der Dieb das gestohlene Vieh schon geschlachtet oder weiterverkauft hat, muss er vierfachen Ersatz zahlen. Falls er dazu nicht in der Lage ist, wird er in die Fremdsklaverei verkauft. Nur für den Fall, dass die Tiere noch lebend bei ihm gefunden werden, reduziert sich die Strafe auf doppelten Ersatz. Wird der Dieb auf frischer Tat während der Nacht vom Geschädigten erschlagen, gilt dies als Notwehr. Das Strafmaß vom zweifachen Ersatz gilt z. B. auch bei Veruntreuung von anvertrautem Gut (22,6–8).

Auf der anderen Seite unterwerfen die Gesetzgeber den Eigentümer der Verpflichtung, für jene Schäden, die auf seinem Eigentum oder durch sein Eigentum an anderen entstehen, zu haften. Wenn er etwa eine Zisterne auf seinem Grundbesitz offenstehen lässt oder beim Bau nicht abdeckt und das Rind oder der Esel

---

4 Früher hat man das Bundesbuch in der vorstaatlichen Zeit angesetzt, da der König nicht oder nur andeutend erwähnt ist (vgl. Ex 22,27). Weil es jedoch schon auf Konflikte einer entstehenden Klassengesellschaft reagiert, wird es zunehmend in das ausgehende 8. Jahrhundert v. Chr. datiert. Vgl. Otto, *Wandel der Rechtsbegründungen*, S. 45–56; Schwienhorst-Schönberger, *Das Bundesbuch*, S. 285; Osumi, *Kompositionsgeschichte*, S. 220; Crüsemann, *Tora*, S. 132–138; Albertz, *Religionsgeschichte I*, S. 283–285, wobei der Teil Ex 21,12.15–22,16, der noch ganz untheologische kasuistische Rechtssätze enthält, wahrscheinlich älter ist. Detaillierte inhaltliche Auslegungen des Bundesbuches finden sich bei Crüsemann, *Tora*, S. 132–234; und Otto, *Wandel der Rechtsbegründungen*, S. 18–116; sowie zuletzt in Albertz, *Exodus II*, S. 78–130. |

eines anderen hineinstürzt, so muss er dem Geschädigten einfachen Ersatz leisten, darf aber das tote Tier behalten (Ex 21,33–34). Dass hinter einer solchen Schadensregulierung keinerlei Einsichten aus dem JHWH-Glauben Israels stehen, wird dadurch deutlich, dass jene fast gleichlautend auch im mesopotamischen Recht tausend Jahre früher belegt ist.[5] Es geht einfach um einen vernünftigen wirtschaftlichen Interessenausgleich. Ein ähnlicher Schadensausgleich gilt auch für den Fall, in dem weidende Tiere eines Eigentümers das Feld oder den Weinberg eines Nachbarn abweiden (Ex 22,4–5).

Erst später kommt es zu der Entwicklung, dass unter dem Einfluss religiöser Normierung das Verfügungsrecht über das Eigentum immer weiter zugunsten zunehmender Verpflichtungen des Eigentümers eingeschränkt wird. |

Prophetische Kritik an den Wirtschaftspraktiken einer entstehenden Klassengesellschaft

Für die Entwicklung einer Wirtschaftsethik ist und bleibt es wichtig, dass im Alten Israel erst im Verlauf einer schweren sozialen Krise, welche durch die Herausbildung einer antiken Klassengesellschaft ausgelöst wurde, der Bereich wirtschaftlichen Handelns in den Fokus ethischer und religiöser Diskurse und Reflexionen geriet. In Israel und Juda hatte sich während des 8. Jahrhunderts v. Chr. eine neue Klasse von wohlhabenden königlichen Beamten, Militärs und Kaufleuten gebildet, welche ihren Grundbesitz immer stärker und zum Teil aggressiv auf Kosten der traditionellen Kleinbauern ausweiteten. Handhabe gab ihnen dazu das antike Schuldrecht, das nicht nur eine Pfändung des gesamten mobilen und immobilen Eigentums des säumigen Schuldners, sondern auch die Pfändung seiner Person und seiner Familienmitglieder, also deren Degradierung zu Schuldsklaven, vorsah. War ein Kleinbauer erst einmal in wirtschaftliche Schwierigkeiten geraten, nahm der Großgrundbesitzer, der als dessen Kreditgeber auftrat, seine Chance wahr, diesen immer weiter in die Verschuldung und Abhängigkeit zu treiben, um damit seinen Grundbesitz zu erweitern und abhängige Arbeitskräfte zu gewinnen. Zwar arbeiteten so die ehemaligen Kleinbauern oft noch auf ihrem Acker, aber faktisch hatten sie ihr Verfügungsrecht darüber verloren und produzierten als abhängige Arbeitskräfte minderen Rechts für ihren Schuldherrn. Mit ihren Betrieben produzierten die Großgrundbesitzer über ihren Bedarf hinaus für einen Markt in den Städten, in denen sie residierten. Aus den Kleinbauern, die im Verschuldungsprozess ihren Grundbesitz vollständig verloren hatten,

---

5 So im Kodex Eschnunna § 53 aus dem 19. Jahrhundert v. Chr., vgl. Kaiser, *Texte*, Bd. I, S. 38. |

entstand im 7. Jahrhundert die neue Gruppe der Tagelöhner (*śākîr*, Dtn 24,14), die ihre Arbeitskraft auf der Straße für Stunden oder Tage anboten.[6]

Solche wirtschaftlichen Entwicklungen zur Klassengesellschaft hat es in vielen antiken Kulturen gegeben. Das Besondere an Israel und Juda ist der Umstand, dass hier ab der Mitte des 8. Jahrhunderts v. Chr. Propheten auftraten, die im Namen des Nationalgottes JHWH gegen den wirtschaftlichen Verdrängungsprozess und die damit verbundenen Wirtschaftspraktiken öffentlich Protest einlegten. So geißelt etwa der Prophet Jesaja in Juda | den Expansionsdrang der Großgrundbesitzer und kündigt ihnen das Gericht JHWHs an:

Tab. 1: Prophetische Sozialkritik aus dem 8. Jahrhundert v. Chr.

Jes 5,8	Wehe denen, die Haus an Haus reihen, die Feld an Feld rücken, bis kein Platz mehr da ist und ihr nur noch allein inmitten des Landes wohnt.
9	In meinen Ohren ist ein Schwur JHWH Zebaoths: Wahrhaftig, viele Häuser werden verheert werden, große und schöne, dass niemand mehr darin wohnen kann.
10	10 *Zemed* Reben (ca. 20.000 qm) wird ein *Bat* bringen (ca. 40 l) und ein *Homer* Aussaat (ca. 400 l) wird ein *Epha* bringen (ca. 40 l).

Statt eines Wirtschaftsaufschwungs, dessen Dynamik die Großgrundbesitzer mit der Expansion ihrer Güter meinten freisetzen zu können, wird es nach Jesaja eine desaströse Missernte geben. Statt einer Verdoppelung oder gar Verdreifachung des eingesetzten Saatgutes werden sich die Ernteerträge dezimieren.

Und der Prophet Micha deckt etwas später die psychologischen Triebkräfte hinter dem wirtschaftlichen Handeln der Oberschichtsangehörigen auf:

Tab. 2: Prophetische Sozialkritik aus dem späten 8. Jahrhundert v. Chr.

Mi 2,1	Wehe denen, die auf ihren Lagern Unheil planen und böse Taten! Bei Morgenanbruch führen sie es aus, weil es in ihrer Macht steht:
2	Sie gieren (*ḥāmad*) nach Äckern und rauben sie, nach Häusern und nehmen sie weg. Damit unterdrücken sie (das Prinzip): ein Mann und sein Haus, einen Mann und sein Erbbesitz.

---

6 Zur sozialen Krise, deren Gründe und Mechanismen im Einzelnen etwas unterschiedlich dargestellt werden, vgl. Albertz, *Religionsgeschichte I*, S. 248–255; und Kessler, *Sozialgeschichte*, S. 114–126. |

Tab. 2 (fortgesetzt)

3	Darum, so spricht JHWH: Seht, gegen diese Sippe plane ich Unheil, aus dem ihr euren Hals nicht herausziehen werdet, und ihr werdet nicht (mehr) aufrecht herumstolzieren, denn es ist eine böse Zeit.

Hinter dem Verdrängungsprozess steht nach Micha eine unbändige Gier der wirtschaftlich Mächtigen nach dem Eigentum des wirtschaftlich Schwächeren. Dasselbe Verb *ḥāmad* („begehren, gieren") begegnet uns | übrigens auch im 10. Gebot des Dekalogs. Die clevere Anwendung des scheinbar legalen Schuldrechts ist nach Micha nichts anderes als Raub, mit dem das Prinzip der kleinbäuerlichen Gesellschaft, dass jedem Familienoberhaupt ein Acker und ein Haus zustehe, mit Füßen getreten wird.

Die zu Unrecht pervertierten rechtlichen Mechanismen, deren sich die Oberschichtsangehörigen bedienten, hatte als erster der Prophet Amos im Nordreich Israel offengelegt:

Tab. 3: Prophetische Sozialkritik aus der Mitte des 8. Jahrhunderts v. Chr.

Am 2,6	So spricht JHWH: Wegen drei Vergehen Israels oder wegen der vier nehme ich (mein Gericht) nicht zurück: weil sie den Gerechten für Geld verkaufen und den Armen für (die Schuld im Wert von) ein Paar Sandalen.
7	In den Staub treten sie den Kopf der Bedürftigen und weisen (den Rechtsweg) der Elenden ab. Ein Mann und sein Vater gehen zum selben Mädchen, um meinen heiligen Namen zu entweihen.

Nach dem Urteil Gottes, das Amos verkündet, wird der „Gerechte", d. h. der ohne Schuld in wirtschaftliche Not Geratene, sogleich seiner Freiheitsrechte beraubt und als Schuldsklave sogar an andere weiterverhökert, auch dann wenn die Schuldsumme nur den lächerlichen Gegenwert von ein Paar Sandalen ausmacht (V. 6b). Will sich ein so Misshandelter vor Gericht wehren, wird er vor dem örtlichen Laiengericht, in dem die Angehörigen der Oberschicht den Ton angaben, fertig gemacht und sein Rechtsbegehren abgeschmettert (V. 7a). Und diese setzen der Perversion von Recht und Moral die Krone auf, indem sie attraktive Schuldsklavinnen nicht etwa als Nebenfrauen ehelichen, sondern quasi als Familiennutten zwischen Vater und Sohn hin- und herschieben.

Die Propheten scheuten sich nicht, das wirtschaftliche Handeln der Oberklasse, das die Lebensmöglichkeit der wirtschaftlich und sozial Schwachen rücksichtslos zerstört, als Sünde gegen Gott zu brandmarken. Nach ihrer Verkündigung würde Gott ein solches Verhalten nicht mehr länger hinnehmen, sondern eine solche ungerechte Gesellschaft dem Untergang weihen. |

Religiös begründetes Recht zur sozialen Verpflichtung der Eigentümer und zum Schutz der wirtschaftlich Schwachen

Während die Propheten des 8. Jahrhunderts auftraten, haben nur ganz wenige Zeitgenossen ihre theologische Verurteilung bestimmter wirtschaftlicher Verhaltensmuster ernst genommen. Meist wurden sie als Verrückte verlacht (Hos 9,7) oder als Aufrührer vertrieben (Am 7,10–17). Doch als das Nordreich Israel 722 v. Chr. wirklich unterging, haben einige Verantwortliche in Juda darüber nachgedacht, wie die von den Propheten als Sünde benannten sozialen und wirtschaftlichen Missstände einzudämmen seien, um ihrem Staat ein ähnliches Schicksal zu ersparen. Unter dem König Hiskia am Ende des 8. Jahrhunderts kam es zu einer noch relativ beschränkten, unter dem König Josia im letzten Drittel des 7. Jahrhunderts v. Chr. zu einer breiten Reformbewegung.[7] Ihr Ziel war eine religiöse, soziale und nationale Erneuerung der judäischen Gesellschaft. Ihr Mittel war eine Reformgesetzgebung, die unmittelbar auf Gott zurückgeführt wurde, um sie mit höchster Autorität auszustatten. Mit dieser Theologisierung des Rechts ging eine Ethisierung des Rechts einher.[8] Jeder judäische Bürger sollte sich direkt von JHWH angesprochen wissen, um sich von ihm zu einer Besserung seines Verhaltens motivieren zu lassen. Insbesondere den Wohlhabenden redete Gott direkt

---

7 Näheres dazu siehe Albertz, *Religionsgeschichte I*, S. 280–290 und 304–360.

8 Mit der durch die Propheten angestoßenen Theologisierung und Ethisierung des Rechts beschritt Israel einen Sonderweg, auf dem es sich immer weiter von der altorientalischen Rechtskultur entfernte. In den altorientalischen Kulturen galten zwar die Götter generell als Hüter von Recht und Gerechtigkeit, überließen es aber dem König bzw. dessen Rechtsschulen und Richtern, als Sachwalter des Rechts zu fungieren. In den jüngeren Partien des Bundesbuches und dann im Deuteronomium wurde jedoch der Gott JHWH selber zur Rechtsquelle erhoben, wobei im Letzteren Mose als Rechtsmittler an die Stelle des Königs trat. Vgl. zu diesem wichtigen Prozess Otto, *Theologische Ethik*, S. 111–116; und Albertz, Theologisierung, S. 187–207. |

ins Gewissen und erlegte ihnen eine Fülle von Verzichtsleistungen und Verpflichtungen auf.

Zuerst ging es den Reformgesetzgebern in den jüngeren Passagen des Bundesbuches nur darum, die schlimmsten Auswüchse der wirtschaftlichen Entwicklung zur Klassengesellschaft zu begrenzen. So wurde das Kredit- und Pfandrecht eingeschränkt: |

Tab. 4: Sozialgesetzgebung aus dem Ende des 8. Jahrhunderts v. Chr.

Ex 22,24	Falls du [meinem Volk] dem Armen bei dir Geld leihst, so sollst du ihm gegenüber nicht wie ein Pfandleiher auftreten. Ihr sollt auf ihn keinen Zins legen.
25	Falls du überhaupt den Mantel deines Nächsten pfändest, sollst du ihm diesen bis zum Untergang der Sonne zurückgeben.
26	Denn er ist seine einzige Zudecke, er ist die Hülle für seine (nackte) Haut. Worin soll er schlafen? Wenn er zu mir schreit, werde ich (es) hören. Denn ich bin gnädig (ḥannûn ʿᵃnî).

Die Reformgesetzgeber warben im Namen Gottes dafür, die Armen, d. h. die verarmten Kleinbauern, aus dem üblichen Kreditgeschäft herauszunehmen. Von ihnen sollten keine Sicherheitspfänder genommen, ihnen sollte kein Zins auferlegt werden. Erst später wurde die Regel, die tief in das übliche wirtschaftliche Handeln eingriff, auf das ganze Gottesvolk ausgeweitet.

Sollte es bei einem völlig Verarmten dennoch zur Pfändung seines Mantels kommen, um ihn zur Rückzahlung seiner Schulden zu bewegen, dann sollte diesem das Pfandstück am Abend wieder zurückgegeben werden, damit er sich darin beim Schlaf in der kühlen Nacht einhüllen konnte. Interessant ist die ethische Argumentation innerhalb des Gesetzes: Auf der einen Seite wird rational an die Einsicht und an das Verantwortungsgefühl des Kreditgebers appelliert: Der Mantel ist für den Verarmten, der sonst keine wärmenden Kleidungsstücke besitzt, schon aus rein kreatürlichen Gründen überlebenswichtig. Auf der anderen Seite wird vor einer möglichen göttlichen Strafe gewarnt. Sollte der Arme im Falle einer Misshandlung zu Gott schreien, würde dieser seinen Hilferuf sicher erhören und sich gegen den unbarmherzigen Kreditgeber wenden. JHWH würde parteilich zugunsten des sozial Schwachen in den ökonomischen Konflikt eingreifen, weil er ein gnädiger (ḥannûn) Gott ist.

Einen Schritt weiter gingen die Reformgesetzgeber mit ihrer Novellierung des Schuldsklavenrechtes (Ex 21,1–11), indem sie die zerstörerischen Auswirkungen von Wirtschaftsstrukturen abzumildern suchten: Die Dauer der Schuldsklaverei wurde – ganz gleich wie viele Schulden sich in den vorangegangenen Kreditgeschäften angesammelt hatten – auf sechs Jahre begrenzt (V. 2). Damit wurde dem Kreditgeber die Möglichkeit genommen, nachträglich immer weitere Forderungen nachzuschieben, um die Arbeitskraft verarmter Kleinbauern möglichst lange wirtschaftlich nutzen zu können. Eine dauerhafte Verwendung des Schuldsklaven sollte nur | noch dann möglich sein, wenn dieser ausdrücklich und unter öffentlicher Kontrolle auf seine Entlassung verzichtete und durch einen rituellen Akt als Dauersklave markiert wurde (V.5–6). Darüber hinaus versuchten die Gesetzgeber auch das Los der Schuldsklavinnen zu bessern, indem sie auf eine klare eheliche Zuordnung zum Kreditgeber oder dessen Sohn drangen (V. 7–9). Sollte dies nicht möglich sein, so war die Schuldsklavin wieder zum Loskauf freizugeben (V. 8). Wurde sie als Nebenfrau völlig vernachlässigt und so ihrer Rechte beraubt, war sie unentgeltlich freizulassen (V. 10 f.).

Die nochmalige Novellierung des Schuldsklavenrechtes im Deuteronomium (Dtn 15,12–18) ist ein gutes Beispiel dafür, wie die Gesetzgeber der Josianischen Reform im 7. Jahrhundert dazu übergingen, die zerstörerischen Auswirkungen der ökonomischen Rationalität aus religiösen Gründen nicht nur zu begrenzen, sondern auch in Richtung auf eine Humanisierung zu transformieren.[9] Sie forderten nämlich von den Kreditgebern, dass sie bei der Entlassung dem Schuldsklaven ein Startkapital zu zahlen hätten:

Tab. 5: Sozialgesetzgebung aus dem letzten Drittel des 7. Jahrhunderts v. Chr.

Dtn 15,12	Wenn sich dir dein Bruder verkauft, ein Hebräer oder eine Hebräerin, dann soll er dir sechs Jahre dienen, doch im siebten Jahr sollst du ihn entlassen, frei von dir.
13	Wenn du ihn von dir freilässt, sollst du ihn nicht leer entlassen.
14	Du sollst ihm reichlich aufladen, von deinem Kleinvieh, von deiner Tenne und von deiner Kelter. Womit JHWH, dein Gott, dich gesegnet hat, davon sollst du ihm geben.
15	Dabei sollst du daran denken, dass du Sklave gewesen bist im Lande Ägypten und dass dich JHWH, dein Gott, losgekauft hat. Deswegen gebiete ich dir heute diese Sache. [...]
18	Es soll in deinen Augen nicht hart erscheinen, wenn du ihn von dir freilässt. Denn für das Äquivalent des Lohnes eines Lohnarbeiters hat er dir sechs Jahre gedient. So wird dich JHWH, dein Gott, segnen, bei allem, was du tust.	

---

9 Zur grundlagenkritischen Wirtschaftsethik, die auf eine Transformation der ökonomischen Vernunft zielt, siehe Robra, *Evangelisches Kirchenlexikon*, S. 1305. |

Die ökonomische Rationalität der Schuldsklaverei bestand darin, dass der zahlungsunfähige Schuldner seine Schulden durch seiner Hände Arbeit abarbeite-te. Nach den sechs Jahren waren Kreditgeber und Kreditnehmer quitt. Wenn die Reformgesetzgeber dem Kreditgeber nun auch noch eine Vergütung bei der Entlassung des Schuldsklaven auferlegten, dann durchbrachen sie diese Logik, wahrscheinlich weil sie inzwischen die Erfahrung gemacht hatten, dass die Klein-bauern auch nach dem Abarbeiten ihrer Schulden nur schwer wieder auf die Beine kamen. Sie benötigten Saatgut, einen kleinen Viehbestand und ein paar Reben, um einen wirtschaftlichen Neustart durchzustehen. Diesen nicht unerheb-lichen Eingriff in die Besitzrechte der Wohlhabenden begründeten die Gesetzge-ber gleich vierfach: *erstens* rational damit, dass der Großgrundbesitzer mit dem Schuldsklaven ein relativ gutes Geschäft gemacht hatte. Er hat für dessen Versor-gung – einschließlich des Startkapitals – nicht mehr ausgegeben als für einen Lohnarbeiter (V. 18), dafür jedoch eine verlässliche Arbeitskraft gehabt. *Zweitens* begründeten sie es in religiöser Hinsicht damit, dass der Wohlstand, von dem der Grundbesitzer etwas für das Startkapital seines Schuldsklaven abzweigen solle, ein Ausfluss des Segen Gottes sei (V. 14). Sein Wohlstand und Besitz war ein Ge-schenk Gottes an ihn, deswegen sollte es ihm nicht hart ankommen, davon etwas herzuschenken. *Drittens* erinnerten die Gesetzgeber den Kreditgeber an das theo-logische Grunddatum Israels (V. 15). Ganz Israel, und damit auch der Sklavenhal-ter, war selbst einmal Sklave in Ägypten gewesen und war von JHWH aus der Sklaverei losgekauft worden. Darum sollte er sich in die Bedürfnisse der Schuld-sklaven hineinversetzen können und sich dessen Freilassung – Gottes Beispiel folgend – etwas kosten lassen. Das Startkapital für den Schuldsklaven war ein Ausdruck der Dankbarkeit gegenüber Gott, dass er in Freiheit und Sicherheit leben durfte. *Viertens* verbanden die Gesetzgeber ihre Reform mit einer aus-drücklichen Segensverheißung: Die Hingabe von Eigentum würde JHWH mit neu-em Segen belohnen. Da der Erfolg wirtschaftlichen Handelns menschlicherseits letztlich unverfügbar war, sollte der Großgrundbesitzer darauf aus sein, sich Got-tes Wohlwollen dafür zu sichern, dass sein Wohlstand in Zukunft Bestand haben würde. Auffällig ist, dass die Gesetzgeber keine Vorschriften über die Höhe des Startkapitals machten. Sie waren sich offenbar bewusst, dass sie bei ihrem Ein-griff in die Eigentumsrechte auf die bessere Einsicht und Zustimmung der Wohl-habenden angewiesen waren. Es ging ihnen um eine Erziehung weg von der Gier hin zur Großzügigkeit. |

Drastischer griffen die josianischen Reformgesetzgeber in die Struktur der Wirtschaftsordnung ihrer Zeit ein, als sie einen Schuldenerlass alle sieben Jahre verordneten:

Tab. 6: Reform des Schuldrechts aus dem letzten Drittel des 7. Jahrhunderts v. Chr.

Dtn 15,1	Nach Ablauf von 7 Jahren sollst du eine Loslassung (*š^emiṭṭâ*) durchführen:
2	Und dies ist der Inhalt der Loslassung: Loslassen soll jeder ‚Kreditgeber‘[10] seinen Schuldanspruch. Was immer er seinem Nächsten geliehen hat, soll er bei seinem Nächsten und Bruder nicht eintreiben. Denn man hat eine Loslassung für JHWH ausgerufen.
3	Bei einem Fremden darfst du eintreiben, doch was dir bei deinem Bruder gehört, sollst du loslassen.

Schuldenerlasse kannte man im alten Mesopotamien und auch im Alten Israel bis dahin nur als Gnadenrecht, das ein Herrscher – etwa bei Regierungsantritt oder in einer besonderen Krisenlage – huldvoll gewährte, um der Überschuldung größerer Teile der Bevölkerung Herr zu werden.[11] Den Reformgesetzgebern ging es darum, den notorischen Verarmungsprozess der Kleinbauern in der judäischen Klassengesellschaft dadurch abzustoppen, dass sie einen regelmäßigen Schuldenerlass einführten, der vom Wohlwollen des Herrschers unabhängig war. Dabei knüpften sie an den Tabubrauch der Ackerbrache an, der für jedes Feld alle sieben Jahre durchgeführt wurde (Ex 23,10–11). So wie der Landwirt seinen Acker brach liegen lassen und damit auf seinen Ertrag verzichten sollte (*šāmaṭ* = „loslassen"), um Gottes Segenskräfte nicht überzustrapazieren, so sollte jeder Kreditgeber alle sieben Jahre auf die Eintreibung der Kredite verzichten, die er bis dahin einem seiner Mitbürger ausgeliehen hatte. Dabei ging | es (wie V. 7 und 9 verdeutlichen) um Kredite an arme Mitbürger, nicht um Geschäftskredite zwischen den Wohlhabenden. Ausgenommen sind ausdrücklich Kreditgeschäfte mit Ausländern (Dtn 15,3). Letztere stehen außerhalb der Solidargemeinschaft aus „Brüdern", deren Zerfall die Gesetzgeber durch den regelmäßigen Schuldenerlass verhindern wollten. Darum war es den Reformern auch wichtig, dass der Schuldenerlass als ein öffentlicher Akt „für JHWH", d. h. zur Ehre des gemeinsamen Gottes der ar-

---

10 Lies *ba'al maśśœh*, wörtlich „Herr des Darlehens" anstelle der freien Wiedergabe bei Luther „wenn einer seinem Nächsten etwas geborgt hat". Das Wort *maśśœh* („Schulden, Darlehen") ist im hebräischen Text einmal infolge von Haplographie ausgefallen; vgl. Nielsen, *Deuteronomium*, S. 158; und Nelson, *Deuteronomy*, S. 187–189.
11 Vgl. zu den *andurāru-*, *mīšaru-* und *šubarû-*Edikten der babylonischen und assyrischen Könige, etwa dem berühmten *mīšarum-*Edikt des altbabylonischen Königs Ammiṣaduqa, bei Pritchard, *Ancient Near Eastern Texts*, S. 526–528. Das hebräische Wort *d^erôr* „Freilassung" (Jes 61,1; Jer 34,8.15.17), das im Jobeljahrgesetz aus dem frühen 5. Jahrhundert v. Chr. für die allgemeine Lastenbefreiung von Menschen und Grundeigentum alle 50 Jahre verwendet wird, erinnert noch daran. |

men und reichen Judäer, vollzogen wurde. In diesem siebten Jahr sollte die zerstörerische Logik des Kreditrechts feierlich außer Kraft gesetzt werden. Damit räumten die judäischen Gesetzgeber mit Gottes Autorität im Rücken erstmals den Armen ein Recht auf eine periodische Löschung ihrer Schulden ein.[12]

Die Gesetzgeber waren sich allerdings der Risiken ihrer Wirtschaftsreform bewusst. Weil die Wohlhabenden ihre Kredite notfalls verloren geben mussten, konnte dies zur Konsequenz haben, dass gar keine Kredite an Arme mehr vergeben wurden. Darum schlossen sie an ihr Gesetz eine ernste Ermahnung an:

Tab. 7: Grenzen der Schuldrechtsreform

Dtn 15,9	Hüte dich, dass nicht ein nichtswürdiger Gedanke in deinem Herzen aufsteigt: „Das siebte Jahr, das Jahr der Loslassung, ist nahe" und dein Auge böse auf deinen armen Bruder schaut, und du ihm nichts gibst, so dass er über dich zu JHWH schreit und eine Sünde auf dir liegt.
10	Reichlich sollst du ihm geben, und dein Herz soll nicht böse sein, wenn du ihm gibst. Denn um der Sache willen wird JHWH, dein Gott, dich segnen bei allen deinem Tun und bei allen deinen Unternehmungen.

Die Gewinn- und Verlustkalkulation in den Bahnen ökonomischer Rationalität wird im Fall des Kreditgeschäfts mit armen Mitbürgern als ein „unnützer" bzw. „nichtswürdiger Gedanke" disqualifiziert, weil er die Solidarität zum armen Bruder zerstört und sich sogar, weil Gott im Konfliktfall für den Armen Partei ergreift, zu einer Sünde auswachsen kann, welche die Gottesbeziehung des Reichen belastet. Nach dem Gesetzgeber sollten die | Wohlhabenden lieber nicht das Gesetz zu umgehen versuchen. Wenn sie bereit wären, generös auf einen Teil ihrer Gewinne zugunsten der Armen zu verzichten, würde sie Gott mit Glück und Erfolg bei ihren zukünftigen wirtschaftlichen Unternehmungen belohnen.

Alle weiteren sozialen Schutzgesetze und die erstaunlichen Ansätze zu einer regelrechten Armenversorgung werden hier übergangen,[13] um stattdessen abschließend zu den wirtschaftsethischen Grundprinzipien zu kommen, die diese Reformgesetzgebung bestimmten.

---

12 Die utopische Verheißung in Dtn 15,4–6, dass es in Israel gar keine Armen mehr geben werde, wenn das Volk wirklich auf die Stimme Gottes hört, ist ein frommer Zusatz. |
13 Vgl. etwa das Nachleseverbot in Dtn 24,18–22 zugunsten der wirtschaftlich schwachen Bevölkerungsgruppen oder den Armenzehnt in Dtn 14,28–29, der in jedem dritten Jahr zur Speisung der Bedürftigen vor Ort verwendet werden soll. |

Theologische Konzepte zur Transformation der ökonomischen Vernunft

1. Ein wichtiges theologisches Konzept, das besonders die deuteronomischen Reformgesetzgeber in die wirtschaftsethische Urteilsbildung einfließen ließen, ist die Vorstellung, dass wirtschaftlicher Gewinn und Erfolg nicht nur Ergebnis menschlicher Arbeit und Klugheit sind, sondern letztlich Ausdruck des Segens Gottes (Prov 10,22: „JHWHs Segen, der macht reich, und nichts fügt hinzu die Mühe neben ihm"; vgl. 16,3; Ps 127,1; Dtn 28,3–5). Einerseits werden damit Profit und Reichtum eindeutig positiv gewertet, andererseits schränkt das theologische Konzept die Verfügungsgewalt des Menschen über sein Eigentum ein. Profit und Reichtum sind ein Geschenk Gottes, dessen man sich würdig erweisen muss. In Dankbarkeit und Verantwortung Gott gegenüber ist der reich Gesegnete verpflichtet, dem weniger Gesegneten etwas von seinem Geschenk abzugeben (Dtn 15,14; vgl. Gen 33,8–11). Nur so kann er verhindern, dass der Segen Gottes in Fluch umschlägt und künftiger Wohlstand einigermaßen gesichert ist (Dtn 15,10.18). Dieses theologische Konzept klingt auch heute noch in der Bestimmung des Grundgesetzes zur Sozialpflichtigkeit des Eigentums im säkularen Gewande nach.

2. Schon die Reformgesetzgeber des Bundesbuches übernahmen von den Propheten die theologische Einsicht, dass sich Gott im Fall extrem asymmetrischer wirtschaftlicher Konflikte offen auf die Seite der Armen stellt. Seine Barmherzigkeit gilt in diesen Fall nur ihnen, während die Rei|chen, welche die Armen unterdrücken, von seinem Gericht bedroht werden (Ex 22,20–26). Mit diesem theologischen Konzept richten die Gesetzgeber eine klare Grenze für wirtschaftliches Handeln und ökonomische Rationalität auf, die sich danach definiert, dass die Lebensmöglichkeit und die Würde der sozial Schwachen nicht zerstört werden. Mit der persönlichen Applikation der religiösen Tradition, dass Gott die Israeliten aus der ägyptischen Sklaverei befreit habe (Dtn 15,15), schufen die Gesetzgeber daneben für die Wohlhabenden ein starkes Motivationspotential, sich mit ihren Sklaven und Schuldnern zu solidarisieren und sich ihnen gegenüber generös zu verhalten.

3. Im Kontrast zu ihrer Anklage, dass die Großgrundbesitzer die Kleinbauern rücksichtslos in die Schuldenfalle treiben, formulierten die Propheten ein besonderes Konzept von Recht und Gerechtigkeit. Im Unterschied zum griechisch-römischen Konzept des *suum cuique* definieren sie Gerechtigkeit von den Lebensmöglichkeiten der sozial Schwachen her. „Recht und Gerechtigkeit" (*mišpāṭ ûṣedāqâ*, Am 5,7.24; 6,12; vgl. Jes 5,7) sind nur dann gewahrt, wenn die fundamentalen Lebensrechte der Verlierer einer wirtschaftlichen Entwicklung noch gewahrt sind, gleichgültig wie legal die Mittel sind, die zu deren Verdrängung eingesetzt wurden.

4. Die alttestamentlichen Propheten- und Rechtstexte belegen eindeutig, dass auch und gerade das wirtschaftliche Handeln und die konkreten Wirtschaftsordnungen vor Gott verantwortet werden müssen. Wiewohl legal und rechtlich legitimiert, können doch beide von Gott als Sünde disqualifiziert und seinem Gericht unterworfen werden (Am 2,6; Dtn 15,9). Das bedeutet, dass auch das Nächstenliebegebot des Neuen Testaments nicht nur im privaten Lebensbereich, sondern auch im Bereich der Ökonomie Gültigkeit hat. Der „Nächste" ist im Konfliktfall nicht der wohlhabende Geschäftspartner, sondern wie im Gesetz zum Schuldenerlass (Dtn 15,2.7.9) der „arme Bruder" (parallel zum „Nächsten"), das heißt, die möglichen Opfer bzw. Kritiker meiner wirtschaftlichen Entscheidungen. Dies gilt umso mehr, als auch das Neue Testament mit dem Alten Testament die Einsicht in die Parteilichkeit Gottes mit den Armen teilt (Luk 4,18–19; 6,20–26 u. ö.).[14] Wie die biblische Perspektive eines Vorrangs der Armen vor Gott mit der heutigen ökonomischen und politischen Rationalität vermittelt werden kann, gehört gegenwärtig immer noch zu den wichtigs|ten Fragen einer christlichen Wirtschaftsethik (Bedford-Strohm 1993; Robra 1996, S. 1305).

Literatur

Albertz, Rainer, „Die ‚Antrittspredigt' Jesu im Lukasevangelium auf ihrem alttestamentlichen Hintergrund", in: *Zeitschrift für die neutestamentliche Wissenschaft und die Kunde der älteren Kirche* 74 (1983), S. 182–206.

Albertz, Rainer, *Religionsgeschichte Israels in alttestamentlicher Zeit*, 2., durchges. und verbesserte Auflage, Göttingen 1996/1997 (Grundrisse zum Alten Testament, Bd. 8,1–2).

Albertz, Rainer, „Die Theologisierung des Rechts im Alten Israel", in: Ders. (Hg.), *Geschichte und Theologie. Studien zur Exegese des Alten Testaments und zur Religionsgeschichte Israels*, Berlin/New York 2003 (Beihefte zur Zeitschrift für die alttestamentliche Wissenschaft, Bd. 326), S. 187–207.

Albertz, Rainer, *Exodus*, Bd. II: *Ex 19–40*, Zürich 2015 (Zürcher Bibelkommentare. Altes Testament, Bd. 2.2).

Bedford-Strohm, Heinrich, *Vorrang für die Armen. Auf dem Weg zu einer theologischen Theorie der Gerechtigkeit*, Gütersloh 1993.

Crüsemann, Frank, *Die Tora. Theologie und Sozialgeschichte des alttestamentlichen Gesetzes*, München 1992.

Kaiser, Otto (Hg.), *Texte aus der Umwelt des Alten Testaments*, 3 Bde., Gütersloh 1982–2001.

Kessler, Rainer, *Sozialgeschichte des Alten Israel. Eine Einführung*, Darmstadt 2006.

Nelson, Richard D., *Deuteronomy. A Commentary*, Louisville/London 2002 (The Old Testament Library).

Nielsen, Eduard, *Deuteronomium*, Tübingen 1995 (Handbuch zum Alten Testament, Bd. I/6).

---

14 Vgl. zur breiten und teilweise kontrovers geführten Diskussion darüber nur Schottroff/Stegemann, *Jesus von Nazareth*; Theißen, *Religion der ersten Christen*, S. 101–167; und Albertz, „Antrittspredigt". |

Osumi, Yuichi, *Die Kompositionsgeschichte des Bundesbuches Exodus 20,22b–23,33*, Fribourg/Göttingen 1991 (Orbis Biblicus et Orientalis, Bd. 103).

Otto, Eckart, *Wandel der Rechtsbegründungen in der Gesellschaftsgeschichte des antiken Israel. Eine Rechtsgeschichte des „Bundesbuches", Ex XX 22–XIII 13*, Leiden 1988.

Otto, Eckart, *Theologische Ethik des Alten Testaments*, Stuttgart 1994.

Pritchard, James B., *Ancient Near Eastern Texts Relating to the Old Testament*, Princeton (NJ) [3]1969.

Robra, Martin, „Wirtschaftsethik", in: *Evangelisches Kirchenlexikon*, Bd. 4, Göttingen 1996, S. 1298–1308.

Schottroff, Luise/Stegemann, Wolfgang, *Jesus von Nazareth – Hoffnung der Armen*, Stuttgart [2]1981. |

Schwienhorst-Schönberger, Ludger, *Das Bundesbuch. Studien zu seiner Entstehung und Theologie*, Berlin/New York 1990 (Beihefte zur Zeitschrift für die alttestamentliche Wissenschaft, Bd. 188).

Sinaga, Hulman, *Eigentumsrecht nach den Regelungen der altisraelitischen Rechtssammlungen des Pentateuchs und nach der Adat der Toba-Bataks Indonesiens. Eine biblisch-exegetische Untersuchung zu Möglichkeiten und Grenzen kulturvergleichender kontextueller Bibelauslegung*, Aachen 2013.

Theißen, Gerd, *Die Religion der ersten Christen. Eine Theorie des Urchristentums*, Gütersloh 2000.

Wünsch, Georg, *Evangelische Wirtschaftsethik*, Tübingen 1927.

Muss die exklusive Gottesverehrung gewalttätig sein? Israels steiniger Weg zum Monotheismus

Seit dem 11. September 2001 ist es allen Menschen innerhalb und außerhalb Amerikas klar geworden, dass der religiös motivierte Fanatismus und die religiös begründete Gewalt eine gefährliche Bedrohung aller menschlicher Zivilisation darstellt. Angesichts dieser alarmierenden Erfahrung, die keineswegs auf den Bereich der islamischen Religion beschränkt werden kann, sind alle Theologen gefordert, das gewalttätige Potenzial ihrer eigenen religiösen Tradition zu überprüfen. Oft werden die drei monotheistischen Religionen, das Judentum, das Christentum und der Islam, verdächtigt, besonders aggressiv und gewalttätig zu sein. Darum möchte ich als christlicher Theologe die selbstkritische Frage stellen: Muss unsere exklusive Gottesverehrung, die wir vom alten Israel ererbten, gewalttätig sein?

Im letzten Jahrzehnt wurde diese Frage oft bejaht. In den USA schrieb 1997 Regina Schwartz ihr anklagendes Buch mit dem Titel *The Curse of Cain: The Violent Legacy of Monotheism*.[1] In Deutschland war es besonders der Ägyptologe Jan Assmann, der mit seinen Büchern *Moses der Ägypter: Entzifferung einer Gedächtnisspur*[2] und *Die mosaische Unterscheidung oder der Preis des Monotheismus*[3] eine breite Debatte über das Gewaltpotenzial entfachte. Während christliche und jüdische Theologen gerne den Monotheismus als den Höhepunkt der religionsgeschichtlichen Entwicklung bewerten, hat Jan Assmann eine Gegenrechnung aufgemacht: Nachdem ,den antiken Polytheismen ... der Begriff einer unwahren Religion vollkommen fremd' gewesen sei, habe die „Mosaische Unterscheidung" von wahrer und falscher Religion, die alle anderen Religionen als „Heidentum" ausgrenze, die Welt radikal und gefährlich verändert.[4] Dies lasse sich an den Durchbrüchen zum Monotheismus belegen: ,Echnatons monotheistische Revolution war nicht nur der erste, sondern auch der radikalste und gewaltsamste | Ausbruch einer Gegenreligion in der Menschheitsgeschichte. Die Tempel wurden geschlossen, die Götterbilder zerstört, ihre Namen ausgehackt und ihre Kulte abgebrochen. Je tiefer man in die altägyptische Welt eindringt, desto klarer läßt sich nachvollziehen, was für ein furchtbarer Schock dieser Göttersturz gewesen sein muß ...'.[5] Aber nicht nur Echnatons exklusive Verehrung des Gottes Aton zeitigte

---

1 Chicago: Chicago University Press, 1997.
2 München: Carl Hanser, 1998.
3 München: Carl Hanser, 2003.
4 Assmann, *Moses*, 19–20. |
5 Assmann, *Moses*, 49.

https://doi.org/10.1515/9783111202228-026

solche gewalttätigen Konsequenzen. Auch Israels Weg zum Monotheismus, den Assmann auf eigentümliche Weise wirkungsgeschichtlich mit Echnatons Revolution verschlungen sieht, hinterließ eine breite Blutspur: ‚Der Monotheismus erzählt die Geschichte seiner Durchsetzung als eine Geschichte der Gewalt in einer Serie von Massakern. Ich denke, um nur einige Beispiele zu nennen, an das Massaker im Anschluß an die Szene mit dem Goldenen Kalb (Ex 32–34), das Massaker an den Baalspriestern im Anschluß an den Opferwettstreit mit Elias (1 Kg 18), an gewaltsame Durchsetzung der Josianischen Reform (2 Kg 23. 1–27) und an die Zwangsscheidung der Mischehen (Esra 9. 1–4; 10. 1–17). Diese und andere Stellen sind der biblischen Religion seit den Tagen der Aufklärung immer wieder von ihren Kritikern als Beweis für die inhärente Gewalttätigkeit und Intoleranz des Monotheismus vorgehalten worden'.[6] Dabei ist es nach Assmanns Meinung unwichtig, ob sich alle diese Ereignisse realgeschichtlich zugetragen haben, was er keineswegs behaupten wolle, erschreckend sei vielmehr, dass im Alten Testament die Durchsetzung des Monotheismus ‚in allen Registern der Gewaltsamkeit erzählt' werde.[7] Unleugbar sei die ‚den biblischen Texten eingeschriebene Semantik der Gewalt',[8] die wiederum historisch schlimme Wirkung gezeigt habe.

Assmann räumt dann zwar ein, dass sich im Judentum diese religiöse Aggression mehr nach innen, gegen den ‚Heiden im eigenen Herzen' gerichtet habe, er beharrt aber darauf, dass sie bei den Christen und Moslems zu einer politischen Theologie umgesetzt wurde, welche die ‚Unterdrückung der Heiden ringsum auf ihre Fahnen geschrieben' habe. ‚Die Gewalt ihres Gottes gegen die anderen Götter gibt ihnen das Recht, Gewalt gegen Menschen zu üben, die in ihren Augen anderen Göttern anhängen'.[9] So kann Jan Assmann allen christlichen Theologen und allen muslimischen Rechtsgelehrten ins Stammbuch schreiben: ‚In dieser Tradition offenbarungstheologischer Gewaltbereitschaft ... liegt m. E. das eigentliche „politische | Problem" des Monotheismus. Wenn man die monotheistische Idee retten will, dann muß man sie ihrer inhärenten Gewalttätigkeit entkleiden'.[10]

Ich möchte diese Provokation Assmanns aufnehmen und die Frage stellen, ob Israels monotheistischer Glaube notwendigerweise zu gewalttätigen Konsequenzen führte und wie wir mit diesem gefährlichen Potenzial auf theologisch verantwortliche Weise umgehen können.

---

6 Assmann, *Unterscheidung*, 36; ähnlich Jan Assmann, *Herrschaft und Heil: Politische Theologie in Altägypten, Israel und Europa* (München: Carl Hanser, 2000), 263–64.
7 Assmann, *Unterscheidung*, 36.
8 Assmann, *Unterscheidung*, 37.
9 Assmann, *Herrschaft*, 263. |
10 Assmann, *Herrschaft*, 264.

1 Die Herkunft des israelitischen Monotheismus

Nach der Sicht der biblischen Tradition entstand der Monotheismus schon in den Anfängen Israels, kurz nachdem JHWH das Volk aus Ägypten befreit hatte. Am Berg Sinai offenbarte JHWH Mose alle Regelungen für das religiöse und soziale Leben Israels, darunter an erster Stelle die Verbote, irgendwelche anderen Götter oder Götterbilder zu verehren (Exod. 20.2–4). Allerdings wird dann berichtet, dass Israel schon am Sinai von JHWH abfiel und ein goldenes Kalb anbetete (32). Und erst recht, nachdem es in das gelobte Land gelangt war, wandte es sich immer wieder fremden Göttern zu (Num. 25; Judg. 2), bis erst unter dem König Josia, fast am Ende der vorexilischen Zeit, die alleinige JHWH-Verehrung öffentlich durchgesetzt werden konnte.

Diese biblische Sicht eines mosaischen Ursprungs des israelitischen Monotheismus, der nur längere Zeit von einer synkretistischen Götterverehrung verdeckt gewesen sei, wurde von vielen älteren Exegeten wie Gerhard von Rad[11] oder Werner H. Schmidt[12] geteilt. Erst seit etwa 30 Jahren meldeten sich mehr und mehr Exegeten wie Bernhard Lang,[13] Herrmann Vorländer,[14] Manfred Weippert[15] oder Robert Karl Gnuse[16] zu Wort, welche | die biblische Sicht weitgehend destruierten: Ihrer Meinung nach war die Religion Israels in vorexilischer Zeit eine polytheistische Religion, die erst in der späten Königszeit und in der Exilszeit von einer radikalen Minderheit in Richtung Monotheismus gedrängt wurde.[17]

Ausgelöst wurde diese Debatte von drei verschiedenen Faktoren: Erstens wurde neues archäologisches Material gefunden, das eine Verehrung anderer

11 *Theologie des Alten Testaments*, 2 vols. (I 4th ed., II 3rd ed.; München: Kaiser, 1962), 39.

12 „Jahwe und …"', in *Die hebräische Bibel und ihre zweifache Nachgeschichte*, FS R. Rendtorff (eds. E. Blum, C. Macholz und E. W. Stegemann; Neukirchen: Neukirchener Verlag, 1990), 437–47 (442 ff).

13 Bernhard Lang, ‚Die Jahwe-allein-Bewegung', in *Der einzige Gott: Die Geburt des biblischen Monotheismus* (ed. B. Lang; München: Kösel, 1981), 47–83 (53).

14 ‚Der Monotheismus Israels als Antwort auf die Krise des Exils', in *Der einzige Gott: Die Geburt des biblischen Monotheismus* (ed. B. Lang; München: Kösel, 1981), 84–113 (98 ff).

15 ‚Synkretismus und Monotheismus. Religionsinterne Konfliktbewältigung im alten Israel', in *Kultur und Konflikt* (ed J. Assmann und D. Harth; Edition Suhrkamp, 1612; Frankfurt am Main: Suhrkamp, 1990), 143–79 (i.b. 151) = M. Weippert, *Jahwe und die anderen Götter: Studien zur Religionsgeschichte des antiken Israel in ihrem syrisch-palästinischen Kontext* (FAT, 18; Tübingen: Mohr Siebeck, 1997), 1–24 (10). |

16 *No Other Gods. Emergent Monotheism in Israel* (JSOT.S, 241; Sheffield: Sheffield Academic Press, 1997), 177 ff.

17 Eine gute Übersicht über die Debatte und ihre forschungsgeschichtlichen Hintergründe gibt M. Köckert, ‚Von einem zum einzigen Gott: Zur Diskussion der Religionsgeschichte Israels', *Berliner Theologische Zeitschrift* 15 (1998), 137–75.

Gottheiten neben JHWH im vorexilischen Israel mehr oder minder sicher belegt: Zu nennen sind hier vor allem die Aufsehen erregenden Inschriften aus *Kuntillet Ajrud* und *Chirbet el-Qôm*,[18] die *'Ašerāh* JHWHs Begleiterin nennen, dazu neue Personennamen auf Siegeln bzw. Siegelabdrücken,[19] neue Auswertungen der Ikonographie auf Siegeln und Kleinfunden[20] und ebenso der Frauen- und Tierterrakotten mit möglichem religiös-kultischem Hintergrund.[21] Hinzu kam zweitens eine sich langsam durchsetzende Bereitschaft, viele Texte, die man bislang für die vorstaatliche bzw. frühe staatliche Zeit in Anspruch genommen hatte, später zu datieren. Erhebliche Konsequenzen für die Rekonstruktion der Gesamtentwicklung hatte z. B. die Bestreitung eines frühen Jahwisten[22] und die inzwischen mehrfach vertretene | Umdatierung des Bundesbuches – und mit ihm des ältesten Belegs für das Fremdgötterverbot (Exod. 22.19; vgl. 20.24; 23.13) – von der

---

18 Die ersten Publikationen dieser Inschriften veranlassten den Sammelband von O. Keel (ed.), *Monotheismus im Alten Israel und seiner Umwelt* (Biblische Beiträge, 14; Fribourg: Schweizer Katholisches Bibelwerk, 1980); vgl. J. Renz und W. Röllig, *Handbuch der althebräischen Epigraphik*, 4 vols. (Darmstadt: Wissenschaftliche Buchgesellschaft, 1995), I, 56–64; 202–11. Ich verstehe ולאשרתה „und durch seine *'Ašerāh*" trotz des ungewöhnlichen Suffix als Namen der Göttin; zur Begründung vgl. R. Albertz, *Religionsgeschichte Israels in alttestamentlicher Zeit*, vol. I: Von den Anfängen bis zur Königszeit; vol. II: Vom Exil bis zu den Makkabäern (Grundrisse zum Alten Testament, 8/1–2; Göttingen: Vandenhoeck & Ruprecht [²1996; ²1997; English 1994]), I, 132–33.
19 Renz, *Handbuch*, II/1: 55–87; 2003 II/2: 116–438.
20 Vgl. O. Keel – Ch. Uehlinger, *Göttinnen, Götter und Gottessymbole. Neue Erkenntnisse zur Religionsgeschichte Kanaans und Israels aufgrund bislang unerschlossener ikonographischer Quellen* (Quaestiones disputatae, 134; Freiburg, Basel und Wien: Herder, ⁴1999); H. Weippert, *Palästina in vorhellenistischer Zeit* (Handbuch der Archäologie: Vorderasien, II,1; München: C. H. Beck, 1988), 627–28.
21 Vgl. U. Winter, *Frau und Göttin: Exegetische und ikonographische Studien zum weiblichen Gottesbild im Alten Testament und dessen Umwelt* (OBO, 53; Fribourg und Göttingen: Universitätsverlag und Vandenhoeck & Ruprecht, 1983); S. Schroer, *In Israel gab es Bilder: Nachrichten von darstellender Kunst im Alten Testament* (OBO, 74; Fribourg und Göttingen: Universitätsverlag und Vandenhoeck & Ruprecht, 1987); Weippert, *Palästina*, 629–31.
22 Vgl. etwa die wichtige Rolle, die E. Zenger, ‚Das jahwistische Werk – ein Wegbereiter des jahwistischen Monotheismus', in *Gott, der Einzige: Zur Entstehung | des Monotheismus in Israel* (ed. H. Haag; Quaestiones disputatae 104; Freiburg, Basel und Wien: Herder, 1985), 26–53 (44; 55), und F.-L. Hossfeld, ‚Einheit und Einzigkeit Gottes im frühen Jahwismus', in *Im Gespräch mit dem dreieinen Gott: Elemente einer trinitarischen Theologie*, FS W. Breuning (ed. M. Böhnke und H. Heinz; Düsseldorf: Patmos, 1985), 57–74 (62–68), dem Jahwisten für die Entwicklung zubilligen; ihre vielseits begrüßte These des Übergangs von einer integrierenden zu einer intoleranten Monolatrie ab dem 9.Jh. beruht auf dieser fraglich gewordenen literarischen Basis des Jahwisten. Das gleiche gilt für die von B. Halpern, „Brisker Pipes than Poetry": The Development of Israelite Monotheism', in *Judaic Perspectives on Ancient Israel* (ed. J. Neusner, B. A. Levine und E. S. Frerichs; Philadelphia: Fortress Press, 1987), 77–115 (101–103), vorgeschlagene Entwicklung von einem „unbewußten" zu einem „bewußten" Monotheismus.

vorstaatlichen Zeit in das ausgehende 8. oder in das 7. Jh.[23] Drittens lässt sich heute auf dem Feld der Religionsgeschichte generell die Tendenz erkennen, über die von der Dialektischen Theologie geprägte Forschergeneration hinweg auf die Position Julius Wellhausens[24] zurückzugreifen, dass die israelitische Religion – entgegen der biblischen Präsentation – nicht schon von Anfang an „fertig" ausgebildet war, sondern ‚sich aus dem Heidentum erst allmählich emporgearbeitet' habe.

So gut begründet die neue Position zu sein scheint, so birgt sie doch ein Problem in sich, das oft übersehen wird. Wenn Israels Religion von Haus aus ein Polytheismus wie jeder andere gewesen ist, wie konnte es dann überhaupt in dieser Religion zu einer monotheistischen Sonderentwicklung kommen? Warum protestierte Elia gegen die Verehrung des phönizischen Baal an der Seite JHWHs, wenn ein solcher diplomatischer Synkretismus sonst allseits akzeptiert war? Und wie konnte ein solcher exklusiv monotheistischer | Glaube überhaupt in der jüdischen Bevölkerung durchgesetzt werden, wenn so mächtige Menschen wie der ägyptische Pharao Echnaton oder der babylonische König Nabonid bei viel bescheideneren Bestrebungen in dieser Richtung kläglich scheiterten?

Will man nicht mit unerklärlichen „Mutationen" in der kulturellen Evolution der Menschheit rechnen, wie Robert Karl Gnuse[25] es tat, muss man nach Anlagen in der Religion Israels suchen, die diese erstaunliche Sonderentwicklung erklärbar machen. Ganz zweifellos trug die vorexilische Religion Israels deutliche polytheistische Züge, aber vielleicht war sie doch nicht ein Polytheismus wie jeder andere. Der Begriff Polytheismus, der als polemischer Gegenbegriff zum Monotheismus gebildet wurde, ist viel zu unspezifisch, die Besonderheiten und Unterschiede nicht-monotheistischer Religionen zu beschreiben.[26]

---

23 So unabhängig voneinander F. Crüsemann, *Die Tora: Theologie und Sozialgeschichte des alttestamentlichen Gesetzes* (München: Kaiser, 1992), 133–35, und Albertz, *Religionsgeschichte*, I, 283–85. Noch keinerlei Konsens ist hinsichtlich der Datierung von Exod. 34.11–27 zu erkennen mit seinem breiten Bündnis- und Fremdgötterverbot (V.11b–16). Während immer noch viele mit J. Halbe, *Das Privilegrecht Jahwes Ex 34,10–26: Gestalt und Wesen, Herkunft und Wirken in vordeuteronomischer Zeit* (FRLANT, 114; Göttingen: Vandenhoeck & Ruprecht, 1975), 96–160, hier vorstaatliches „Privilegrecht" finden wollen (vgl. etwa N. Lohfink, ‚Zur Geschichte der Diskussion über den Monotheismus im Alten Israel', in Haag, *Gott*, 9–25 (24); F. Crüsemann, *Tora*, 138–70), wird der Text immer häufiger vordtn. (z. B. Hossfeld, ‚Einheit', 69: JE) oder gar in spätdtr. Zeit (E. Blum, *Studien zur Komposition des Pentateuch* [BZAW, 189; Berlin und New York: de Gruyter, 1990], 365–75: nachexilische Mal'ak-Redaktion) hinabdatiert. Da nach Halbes Datierung Exod. 34 der einzige Text wäre, der ein militant-exklusives Gottesverhältnis Israels in der Frühzeit belegen würde, ist sie nach heutiger Sicht kaum noch zu halten (vgl. Köckert, ‚Diskussion', 167–68).

24 Julius Wellhausen, *Israelitische und jüdische Geschichte* (Berlin und New York: de Gruyter, 2004⁹), 32. |

25 Gnuse, *No Other Gods*, 174–75.

26 Vgl. die kritischen Bemerkungen von G. Ahn, „„Monotheismus" – „Polytheismus": Grenzen und Möglichkeiten einer Klassifikation von Gottesvorstellungen', in *Mesopotamica – Ugaritica –*

Es sind nach meiner Sicht vor allem zwei Merkmale der Religion Israels, welche die Möglichkeit einer späteren Entwicklung zum Monotheismus in sich bargen:[27] Das erste hängt mit dem Gott JHWH selber zusammen: Von seinem Ursprung her als ein Gott der nordarabischen Bergwüste, war JHWH solitär;[28] es ermangelte ihm einer göttlichen Familie, er war nicht fest in ein Pantheon eingefügt. Dies hatte zur Folge, dass er selbst dann, als er zuerst als Gott der israelitischen Stämme dem Götterkönig El untergeordnet (Deut. 32.8–9) und spätestens als Gott des Davidischen Großreiches mit diesem gleichgesetzt wurde und von ihm dessen Frau 'Ašerāh und dessen himmlischen Hofstaat erbte, immer doch eine gewisse Sonderstellung behielt. Das Pantheon, dem er vorstand, war nur wenig differenziert; nur wenige individuelle Göttergestalten, wie *Ba'al, Šamš, Šalem, Ṣedeq, Môt* und *'Ašerāh*, lassen sich identifizieren. Meist bleibt der Hofstaat JHWHs namenlos und wird pauschal mit dem Terminus *Zebaoth* „Heerscharen" bezeichnet (Isa. | 6.5 u. ö.). JHWH hatte einen Großteil der göttlichen Personalität der ihm zugeordneten Götter quasi in sich aufgesogen.[29] Nie werden die Götter des Pantheons „Söhne JHWHs" genannt, sie blieben Söhne Els bzw. Eljons (Ps. 29.1; 82.6); d. h. die ursprüngliche Kinderlosigkeit JHWHs wirkte nach, auch nachdem er mit El identifiziert worden war. Diese nie vergessene solitäre Stellung aus der Frühzeit ermöglichte es, JHWH in der späten Königszeit wieder aus seinem polytheistischen Rahmen herauszuheben, ohne ihm etwas von seiner Majestät zu nehmen, die ihm als König eines himmlischen Pantheons zugewachsen war.

Das zweite Merkmal hängt mit einer Eigentümlichkeit des israelitischen Gottesverhältnisses zusammen. Anders als in den anderen vorderorientalischen Religionen steht im Zentrum der Religion Israels ein personal strukturiertes Gottesverhältnis zu einer Großgruppe. JHWHs häufigstes Epitheton lautet „Gott Israels" (202-mal vom alten Deboralied Judg. 5.3, 5 bis hin zu Mal. 2.16), das heißt, er

---

Biblica, FS K. Bergerhof (ed. M. Dietrich und O. Loretz; AOAT, 232; Kevelaer und Neukirchen: Butzon & Bercker und Neukirchener Verlag, 1993), 1–24 zum Begriff des Polytheismus.

27 Vgl. R. Albertz, ‚Der Ort des Monotheismus in der israelitischen Religionsgeschichte', in *Ein Gott allein?: JHWH-Verehrung und biblischer Monotheismus im Kontext der israelitischen und altorientalischen Religionsgeschichte* (ed. W. Dietrich und M. A. Klopfenstein; OBO, 139; Fribourg und Göttingen: Universitätsverlag und Vandenhoeck & Ruprecht, 1993), 77–96; R. Albertz, ‚Das Rätsel des israelitischen Monotheismus', *Welt und Umwelt der Bibel* 11 (1999), 3–5; und R. Albertz, ‚Jahwe allein! Israels Weg zum Monotheismus und dessen theologische Bedeutung', in *Geschichte und Theologie. Studien zur Exegese des Alten Testaments und zur Religionsgeschichte Israels* (ed. I. Kottsieper und J. Wöhrle; BZAW, 326; Berlin und New York: de Gruyter, 2003), 359–82.

28 Vgl. Lang, ‚Jahwe-allein-Bewegung', 60–61. |

29 Vgl. Klaus Koch, ‚Die hebräische Sprache zwischen Polytheismus und Monotheismus', in *Spuren hebräischen Denkens: Beiträge zur alttestamentlichen Theologie* (ed. K. Koch; Gesammelte Aufsätze, Bd. 1; Neukirchen: Neukirchener Verlag), 25–64 (37–57).

wurde über die Menschengruppe, einen Stämmeverband, bzw. ein Volk, zu dem er in einer Beziehung stand, definiert. Ein personales Gottesverhältnis kannten die übrigen vorderorientalischen Religionen nur in Bezug auf Kleingruppen (Familiengott) oder das Königshaus (Dynastiegott). Im politischen Bereich waren die Götter auf bestimmte Städte und Länder bezogen; vorherrschend war hier ein Sachbezug, der allerdings über den Personalbezug des Königs vermittelt wurde.[30] Diese Differenz gilt übrigens auch für die sog. syrisch-palästinischen „Nationalgötter" des 1. Jts., die gerne mit JHWH verglichen werden:[31] So heißt es in der Stele des moabitischen Königs Mescha bezeichnenderweise: ‚Kamosch zürnte seinem Land',[32] während JHWHs Zorn regelmäßig gegen sein Volk entflammt (Num. 11.1, 11 u. ö.).

Dieses personale Gottesverhältnis einer Großgruppe ist nach meiner Meinung in der Ausnahmesituation eines revolutionären Befreiungsprozesses entstanden, der hinter der Tradition vom Exodus aus Ägypten anzunehmen ist.[33] Insofern bildet der Exodus eine Grundlage, die später eine monotheistische Entwicklung ermöglichte. Denn dem personalen Gottes|verhältnis einer Großgruppe wohnt wie allen personalen Beziehungen strukturell die Tendenz zur gruppeninternen Solidarisierung und gruppenexternen Abgrenzung, d. h. zu einer gewissen Exklusivität inne. Genau durch diese beiden Funktionen wurde der JHWH im Aufstand der „Hebräer" gegen die ägyptische Fron politisch wirksam. Doch hatte diese spezifische Strukturierung des Gottesverhältnisses Israels lange Zeit noch nichts mit Monotheismus zu tun. Sie äußerte sich, soweit wir erkennen können, in der Frühzeit weniger in religiöser als in politisch-militärischer Hinsicht.[34] JHWH sicherte in den Kriegen der vorstaatlichen Epoche Israels Existenz gegen seine Feinde nach außen und solidarisierte die Stämme zur freiwilligen Heerfolge unter-

---

30 R. Albertz, *Persönliche Frömmigkeit und offizielle Religion: Religionsinterner Pluralismus in Israel und Babylon* (Calwer Theologische Monographien, A9; Stuttgart: Calwer Verlag, 1978 [repr. Atlanta: Society of Biblical Literature, 2006]), 161–63.

31 Vgl. Lang, ‚Jahwe-allein-Bewegung', 54; Weippert, ‚Synkretismus', 151.

32 H. Donner und W. Röllig, *Kanaanäische und aramäische Inschriften* (vol. I–III, Wiesbaden: Harrassowitz, 1973–79) (= KAI), 181, Z. 5 f.

33 Vgl. Albertz, *Religionsgeschichte*, I, 68–104. Dass die Exodustradition zumindest im Nordreich des ausgehenden 10. Jhs. bekannt war, belegt 1 Kgs 12.28 f. |

34 Vgl. Fritz Stolz, ‚Monotheismus in Israel', in Keel, *Monotheismus*, 143–89 (163–65). Religiös ist die vorstaatliche Zeit durch ein unkontrolliertes Nebeneinander verschiedener lokaler El- und Baal-Gottheiten unterhalb der Ebene von El/JHWH charakterisiert. Auch *'Ašerāh* könnte schon in dieser Zeit von der Symbolik der „Höhenheiligtümer" her (Mazzeben und Ascherim) JHWH als Begleiterin zugeordnet worden sein. Hinzu kamen die Familiengötter und vergöttlichten Ahnen; vgl. Albertz, *Religionsgeschichte*, I, 117–39, und K. van der Toorn, *Family Religion in Babylonia, Syria and Israel: Continuity and Change in the Forms of Religious Life* (Studies in the History and Culture of the Ancient Near East, 7; Leiden, New York und Köln: Brill, 1996), 236–65.

einander (Judg. 5); zugleich verhinderte er die Ausbildung stetiger Herrschaft im
Innern (8.22–23). Aber damit war die Möglichkeit zu einer späteren religiösen
Sonderentwicklung angelegt.

2 Synkretistischer Ausbau der JHWH-Religion und gewaltsame Gegenreaktionen

Die veränderten gesellschaftlichen Bedingungen seit der Etablierung des Königtums drängten auf einen synkretistisch-polytheistischen Ausbau der JHWH-Religion. Entsprechend der Ausdifferenzierung der Gesellschaft wurde JHWH in Jerusalem König eines Pantheons. Die Jerusalemer Königstheologie rückte die personale
Beziehung JHWHs zum Herrscher in den Vordergrund und drückte die traditionelle Bindung JHWHs an das ganze Volk beiseite. Die Jerusalemer Tempeltheologie stellte – wie im Vorderen Orient üblich – die lokale Bindung JHWHs an seine
Stadt in den Mittelpunkt. Wie sehr dieser die ursprüngliche Struktur verändernde
Umbau der israelitischen Religion echten gesellschaftlichen Bedürfnissen entsprach, wird daran erkennbar, dass diese frühen staatlichen Synkretismen gelangen und auch in der Folgezeit nicht mehr grundsätzlich in Frage gestellt wurden.[35]

Im Zuge der Großreichsbildung und der diplomatischen Verflechtungen wur-
den JHWH Götter anderer Staaten unter- und zugeordnet ('*Aštarte*, | *Milkom*,
Kamoš, *Ba'al*).[36] Die unter Aufnahme von El- und Baaltraditionen vollzogene Erhe-
bung des „Gottes Israels" zum König der Götter und der Völker (Ps. 47.9; 95.3) und
seine in der Depotenzierung aller übrigen Götter nachwirkende Einzelstellung
gaben der israelitischen Staatstheologie einen verschärften imperialistischen Charakter. Dennoch ist sie unverzichtbare Voraussetzung für die spätere Ausformulie-
rung eines universalen Monotheismus.

Wenn diese „ganz normale" religionsgeschichtliche Entwicklung nicht in einem Polytheismus endete, so deswegen, weil sich in Israel Oppositionsgruppen
gegen desintegrative gesellschaftliche und assimilierende religionspolitische Er-
scheinungen auf die alten, nie ganz in Vergessenheit geratenen, nach innen soli-
darisierenden und nach außen abgrenzenden, religiösen Befreiungstraditionen
berufen konnten.

Dies geschah erstmals historisch nachweisbar in der Jehu-Revolution in der
Mitte des 9. Jhs., in der sich der religiöse Protest mit großer Grausamkeit entlud.

---

35 Albertz, *Religionsgeschichte*, I, 200–12. |
36 Vgl. 1 Kgs 11.5, 7, 33; 2 Kgs 23.13; 1 Kgs 16.32; 2 Kgs 10.18–27.

Darum sei auf diesen Fall, der in 2 Kgs 9–10 ausführlich geschildert wird,[37] genauer eingegangen. Zunächst zur Vorgeschichte: Der König Omri hatte als Usurpator
das junge Nordreich aus der innenpolitischen Destabilisierung und der außenpo-
litischen Isolierung herausgeführt, indem er mit Samaria eine neue Hauptstadt
gründete und Bündnisse mit den umliegenden Staaten Juda, Phönizien und Aram
schloss. Deutlichster Ausdruck dieser neuen diplomatischen Einbindung war die
Verheiratung seines Sohnes Ahab mit der phönizischen Königstochter Isebel
(1 Kgs 16.31). Die militärischen und kulturellen Erfolge dieser neuen Politik waren
beeindruckend: Ahab konnte in der Schlacht von Qarqar 853 BCE 2000 Streitwagen gegen die Assyrer aufbieten, mehr als alle seine Bündnispartner; und seine
Palast- und Festungsbauten in Samaria, Megiddo, Jesreel und Hazor zeugen von
einem enormen wirtschaftlichen und kulturellen Aufstieg.

Mit dem ökonomischen Aufstieg war zugleich ein tiefer sozialer Umbruch
verbunden. Die traditionellen Kleinbauern kamen unter den Druck einer wach-
senden Klasse von Beamten, Militärs und Kaufleuten, die zu Großgrundbesitzern
aufstiegen (2 Kgs 4.1). Bauern wie Naboth, die gegen die Ausweitung königlicher
Ländereien demonstrierten, wurden aus dem Wege geräumt, auch um den Preis
von Justizmorden (1 Kgs 21.1–20). Im Klima eines solchen sozialen Konfliktes wurde der JHWH-Baal-Synkretismus, den Ahab vornehmlich aus diplomatischen
Gründen eingeführt hatte, | zu einem Symbol der modernen gesellschaftlichen
Entwicklung des Nordreichs und seiner internationalen Integration, das von deren Gewinnern befürwortet, von deren Opfern jedoch abgelehnt wurde.

Es ist sehr unwahrscheinlich, dass Ahab den JHWH-Kult zugunsten Baals reduzieren oder gar abschaffen wollte. Soweit wir erkennen können, strebte er
einen offiziellen Dyotheismus an (1 Kgs 18.21), bei dem JHWH Nationalgott blieb,
aber nun von Baal, dem Gott des phönizischen Verbündeten, begleitet werden
sollte. Wenn wir der späteren Elia-Tradition (1 Kgs 17–18) glauben können, erhoffte sich der König von der Einbeziehung dieses alten syro-palästinischen Wetter-
gottes in die israelitische Staatsreligion eine Förderung des Ackerbaus in seinem
Land. JHWH blieb gleichfalls auf der Ebene der königlichen Familienreligion der
wichtigste Gott; Ahab entschied, dass alle seine Kinder, die ihm seine phönizische
Frau gebar, nach JHWH benannt wurden (Ataliah, Ahaziah, Joram). Doch in den
Augen der sozialen Opfer und konservativen Gegner der gesellschaftlichen Ent-

---

37 Vgl. dazu die eingehende Untersuchung von S. Otto, *Jehu, Elia und Elisa: Die Erzählungen
von der Jehu-Revolution und die Komposition der Elia–Elisa-Erzählungen* (BWANT, 152; Stuttgart:
Kohlhammer, 2001), 29–111. Nach Otto ist die Erzählung unter Jerobeam II. im Umkreis und
zur Legitimation der Jehuiden verfasst worden, darum sehr parteilich, aber weniger als ein
Jahrhundert von den Ereignissen getrennt. |

wicklung konnte es so aussehen, als sei der König unter den schlechten Einfluss seiner ausländischen Frau geraten und bereit, die Identität Israels preiszugeben.[38]

Nach meiner Sicht war es somit das Zusammentreffen eines sozialen Konfliktes und eines klar erkennbar fremden religiösen Imports, das in Israel den Protest gegen den offiziellen JHWH-Baal-Synkretismus der omridischen Dynastie in Gang brachte. Nicht zufällig stammten seine Wortführer, Elia und Elisa, aus der östlichen Peripherie des Reiches, in der wahrscheinlich eine noch weniger entwickelte Form der JHWH-Religion überlebt hatte. Hier wurde JHWHs persönliche Beziehung zu seinem Volk und seine ursprünglich solitäre Stellung noch lebendiger erinnert als in der Hauptstadt. Aus dieser Erinnerung heraus konnten Elia und Elisa JHWH zu einem Symbol für den konservativen Widerstand gegen die königliche Religions- und Gesellschaftspolitik aufbauen. Die Opposition gegen alles, was als Unrecht und als fremdländischer Einfluss verstanden wurde, konnte so als Kampf für die Alleinverehrung JHWHs interpretiert werden.

Solange Ahab fest im Sattel saß, war der Einfluss der konservativen Opposition begrenzt; der Prophet Elia konnte nur kleinere Konflikte mit dem Königshaus wagen (1 Kgs 17–18). Doch sobald Ahabs Sohn Joram militärische Schwäche gegen die Aramäer im Ostjordanland zeigte (2 Kgs 8.28–29), setzte Elisa einen gewaltsamen Aufstand gegen die Omriden in Gang. Er schickte einen seiner Prophetenschüler an die Front, um im Heerlager den Offizier Jehu heimlich zum Gegenkönig zu salben (1 Kgs 9.1–6, 10b). Mit dieser religiösen Legitimation im Rücken, gewann Jehu Unterstützung unter seinen Mitoffizieren und jagte in wilder Fahrt von der Front in die königliche Residenz Jesreel, wo sich Joram nach einer Verletzung zur | Heilung aufhielt. Als der König Jehu mit seinem Streitwagen heranstürmen sah, fuhr er ihm besorgt, aber arglos entgegen. Doch kaltblütig schoss Jehu seinen Herrn und König regelrecht ab (9.24). Vor der Residenz angekommen, befahl er den Höflingen, Isebel, die ihn mit stolzem Sarkasmus als Mörder begrüßte, aus dem Fenster des Turms herabzustürzen (v. 32). Das Blut der verhassten Königinmutter, die als der Grund allen Übels angesehen wurde, spritzte über das Pflaster, während Pferde ihren Leichnam zertrampelten (v. 33). Diese brutalen Morde schüchterten die Aristokraten von Samaria derart ein, dass sie auf Befehl Jehus die gesamte omridische Königsfamilie umbrachten, immerhin 70 Personen, einschließlich aller Kinder (10.1–9).

Doch die Ausrottung der Omri-Dynastie war noch nicht das Endziel der blutigen Revolte. Sie zielte letztlich auf die Vernichtung des Baaltempels in Samaria.[39]

---

38 Wie sehr sich der ganze Hass der Aufständischen auf Isebel konzentrieren konnte, zeigt die wüste Anklage Jehus in 2 Kgs 9.22. |

39 Otto, *Jehu*, 64–111, hat überzeugend gezeigt, dass 2 Kgs 10.15–27 ursprünglich zur Jehu-Erzählung hinzugehört. Die Sicht von E. Würthwein, *Die Bücher der Könige: 1. Kön. 17–2. Kön. 25* (ATD, 11.2; Göttingen: Vandenhoeck & Ruprecht, 1984), 324–42, dass die religiösen Passagen (9.1–6; 10.12–

Kaum in der Hauptstadt angekommen, lud Jehu alle Baalpriester und Baalverehrer unter dem Vorwand in den Baaltempel ein, mit ihnen ein großes Fest zu
Ehren ihres Gottes feiern zu wollen (2 Kgs 10.18–20). Doch während der Gottesdienst im Gange war, ließ Jehu den Tempel von seinen Soldaten stürmen, alle
Baalverehrer niedermetzeln (v. 25), die Gebäude zerstören und in Latrinen um-
wandeln (v. 27).

Zweifellos ist die Jehu-Revolution ein erschütterndes Zeugnis religiös moti-
vierter Gewalt. Zum ersten Mal zeigte die inhärent exklusive Tendenz der israelitischen Gottesbeziehung intolerante und fanatische Konsequenzen. In Verbindung
mit politischer Macht konnte sie sich sogar in einem brutalen Massaker entladen.
Der diplomatische Synkretismus zwischen JHWH und Baal, wurde, da ihn die
konservativen JHWH-Verehrer als ein Symbol des Unrechts und der kulturellen
Überfremdung ansahen, gewaltsam wieder aufgelöst. Allerdings hatte der Sieg
der radikalen Opposition einen hohen Preis: Das Nordreich geriet erneut in die
politische Isolation. Jehu war gezwungen, sich freiwillig den Assyrern zu unterwerfen, um ihre Unterstützung gegen seine irritierten Nachbarn zu gewinnen,
wie auf dem berühmten Schwarzen Obelisken Salamanassars III. ersichtlich wird.
Dennoch war Israel den Angriffen der Aramäer in den nächsten 50 Jahren schutz-
los ausgeliefert. So mündete der erste Versuch, in Israel unter den Bedingungen
der Staatlichkeit eine exklusive JHWH-Verehrung durchzusetzen in ein außenpoli-
tisches Desaster. Auch innenpolitisch blieb er umstritten: Während | ihn die Jehu-
Dynastie und die Schüler Elias zu verteidigen suchten (1 Kgs 18.40; 2 Kgs 9–10),
verurteilte ihn der Prophet Hosea ein Jahrhundert später als ‚Blutbad von Jesreel'
(Hos. 1.1–4), obwohl er ebenfalls gegen den „Baalskult" stritt. Der gewalttätige
Kampf für die alleinige Verehrung JHWHs war somit selbst unter radikalen Oppositionsgruppen nicht unumstritten.

3 Die alleinige JHWH-Verehrung als Umerziehungsprogramm

Soweit wir erkennen können, verlief die religiöse Auseinandersetzung im 8. und
7. Jh. weniger gewalttätig. In den letzten Jahrzehnten des Nordreiches kämpfte
der Prophet Hosea mit dem bloßen Wort gegen religiöse und kultische Missstände. Er konzipierte dabei erstmals die personale Beziehung Israels zu seinem Gott
als ein enges, geschichtlich begründetes Liebesverhältnis, das ebenso wie menschliche Liebesverhältnisse einen exklusiven Charakter habe. Jede Verehrung ande-

---

27) der ursprünglich profanen Erzählung zugefügt seien, entspringt einer sympathischen Scheu,
die JHWH-Religion mit solchen grausamen Gewalttaten in Zusammenhang zu bringen (339), doch
lässt sie sich weder literarisch noch religionsgeschichtlich halten. |

rer Götter wurde von ihm damit als JHWH kränkende Untreue, als unwürdige Hurerei disqualifiziert (Hos. 1.2; 2.4–15; 3.1–4; 5.4 u. ö.). Damit wurden erstmals auch die Gottesbilder als störende Eindringlinge, die Israel von seinem Gott ablenkten, grundsätzlich abgelehnt (4.17; 8.4–6; 10.5; 11.2; 13.2). Dabei wurde der Gottesname „Baal" von Hosea als Chiffre für alles benutzt, was er als unvereinbar mit der von ihm als „wahr" erkannten JHWH-Verehrung ansah. Es waren somit israelitische religiöse Anschauungen und kultische Gegenstände, die nun als „fremde kanaanäische" Einflüsse abgestempelt und ausgegrenzt wurden.[40] Angesichts der sich auflösenden staatlichen und gesellschaftlichen Einheit des Nordreiches bot Hosea seinen Zeitgenossen die Möglichkeit an, die Identität Israels in Zukunft über seinen einen, unverwechselbaren Gott auf neue Weise religiös zu definieren.

Hoseas Predigt wäre wohl folgenlos verhallt, wenn das Nordreich nicht 722 BCE untergegangen wäre. Da sich aber seine Botschaft bewahrheitet hatte, dass die Verehrung anderer Götter neben JHWH in den Untergang führe, versuchten einflussreiche Kreise im Umkreis Hiskias, das Südreich vor dem gleichen Schicksal zu bewahren. Darum schufen sie das neue Instrument der religiösen Gesetzgebung, um mit ihrer Hilfe einer stärker monolatrischen Form der JHWH-Verehrung gesellschaftliche Geltung zu verschaffen. Der erste Schritt vollzog sich in der sog. „Hiskianischen Reform" am Ende des 8. Jhs. Ihr fiel ein altes JHWH-Symbol, die Schlange Nehuschtan, zum Opfer (2 Kgs 18.4). Wahrscheinlich diente das sog. „Bundesbuch" (Exod. 20.23–23.19) als rechtliche Basis der Reform.[41] Es | war für die Verlesung im Gottesdienst konzipiert und wollte, indem es Gott selber die Reformgesetze in den Mund legte, die Gemeinde zu einem neuen Verständnis der eigenen Religion und einem angemesseneren rituellen und ethischen Verhalten erziehen.[42] Der Opferkult für andere Götter wurde mit Todesstrafe und Einziehung des Vermögens bedroht (22.19). Schon das Aussprechen der Namen anderer Götter im JHWH-Kult wurde untersagt (23.13) und der Gottesdienst auf ausgewiesene JHWH-Heiligtümer eingeschränkt (20.24). So streng die angedrohten Sanktionen auch waren, so wurde doch das Gewaltpotenzial der exklusiven Gottesverehrung durch das Recht sublimiert und in eine Form religiöser Erziehung verwandelt.

---

40 Vgl. Albertz, *Religionsgeschichte*, I, 271–72.

41 Vgl. Albertz, *Religionsgeschichte*, I, 280–90. |

42 Vgl. R. Albertz, ‚Die Theologisierung des Rechts im Alten Israel', in *Religion und Gesellschaft: Studien zu ihrer Wechselbeziehung in den Kulturen des Antiken Vorderen Orients* (ed. R. Albertz in cooperation with S. Otto; AOAT, 249 = Veröffentlichungen des Arbeitskreises zur Erforschung der Religions- und Kulturgeschichte des Antiken Vorderen Orients [AZERKAVO], 1; Münster: Ugarit-Verlag), 115–32 (120–24).

Die königliche Reform hatte wahrscheinlich nur geringe Auswirkungen, weil Hiskias Aufstandspolitik gegen den assyrischen Hegemon im Jahr 701 scheiterte. Stattdessen strömten während der langen Regierungszeit Manasses, der ein treuer Vasall Assyriens blieb, eine Fülle an religiösen Symbolen und kultischen Praktiken aus Syrien und Mesopotamien nach Juda ein, die offenbar von großen Teilen der judäischen Bevölkerung begierig aufgegriffen wurden. Neue Praktiken wie Gestirnsverehrung und Moloch-Kult und neue Götter wie Schamasch, Adad-Milki und die Himmelskönigin Ischtar machten sich breit.[43]

Als das assyrische Reich in der zweiten Hälfte des 7. Jhs. in sich zusammenbrach und Juda langsam frei wurde, nutzte eine breite Koalition unter dem König Josia diese historische Chance zu einer erneuten Reform.[44] Auch die Josianische Reform verwendete erneut und noch konsequenter das Mittel des Rechts, um das monolatrische Ideal durchzusetzen. Rechtliche Basis bildete das Deuteronomische Gesetz (Deut. 12–26). Es legitimierte sich abermals als göttliches Recht, war aber diesmal durch Mose vermittelt, der anstelle des Königs die legislative Gewalt übernahm. Ihm entsprach in der Realität ein Obergericht aus Priestern und Laienrichtern, dessen Weisungen auch der König unterworfen war. Dieses sollte über die Einhaltung der Reformgesetze wachen. Ziel der Gesetzgebung war die Durchsetzung und Kontrolle der exklusiven JHWH-Verehrung in der judäischen Gesellschaft und ihre Reinigung von all solchen Elementen, die als fremde Einflüsse angesehen wurden. Um die exklusive JHWH-Verehrung besser überwachen zu können, wurde der offizielle JHWH-Kult | auf den Jerusalemer Tempel konzentriert; dagegen wurden die kleineren Heiligtümer aller anderen Orte stillgelegt.

Die Josianische Reform wurde zweifellos mit staatlichen Machtmitteln durchgeführt: Priester anderer Götter und Göttinnen wurden entlassen und vertrieben (2 Kgs 23.5, 7), falsche Kultinstallationen wurden abgerissen und entweiht (23.4, 6, 11–12). Aber es fand kein Gemetzel statt. Brutaler ging es nur bei der Zerstörung des Konkurrenzheiligtums von Bethel zu (23.15–18). Sie bildet den Hintergrund für die abschreckende Beispielerzählung von der Zerstörung des Goldenen Kalbes und der Tötung seiner Verehrer in Exod. 32, die allerdings erst aus der Exilszeit stammt.[45] Wenn es in 2 Kgs 23.20 pauschal heißt, Josia habe die Priester aller übrigen Nordreichheiligtümer auf den Altären geschlachtet, dann handelt es sich eher um eine Reminiszenz an Jehus Bluttaten als um eine historische Nachricht.

43 Vgl. 2 Kgs 21.5; 23.11–12; 16.3; 17.17, 31; 23.11; 17.31; Jer. 7.18; 44.15–19 und Albertz, *Religionsgeschichte*, I, 291–304.
44 Vgl. Albertz, *Religionsgeschichte*, I, 307–60; Albertz, ‚Theologisierung‘, 124–30. |
45 J. C. Gertz, ‚Beobachtungen zu Komposition und Redaktion von Exodus 32–34‘, in *Gottes Volk am Sinai: Untersuchungen zu Ex 32–34 und Dtn 9–10* (ed. M. Köckert und E. Blum; Veröffentlichungen der Wissenschaftlichen Gesellschaft für Theologie, 18; Gütersloh: Kaiser/Gütersloher Verlagshaus), 88–106 (97–102).

Die religiösen Zwangsmaßnahmen waren in der Josianischen Reform vornehmlich nach innen gerichtet. So wird z. B. in Deut. 13 jeder mit der Todesstrafe bedroht, der aufgrund irgendwelcher Vorzeichen oder Nöte einen Mitmenschen oder gar einen ganzen Ort zur Verehrung eines anderen Gottes als JHWH verführte. Bei heimlicher Verehrung anderer Götter waren die Familienmitglieder gegenseitig anzeigepflichtig (v. 7–12). Das wirkt auf uns heute als unerträgliche Glaubensschnüffelei, die an die kirchliche Inquisition erinnert.[46] Doch wenn man der Überzeugung ist, dass jeder Synkretismus, und sei er noch so privat, den Staat als Ganzes gefährden kann, dann ist ein solcher Rigorismus durchaus verständlich. Der Gefahr der Denunziation in religiösen Dingen versuchten die Gesetzgeber durch die Einführung einer Zwei-Zeugen-Regelung zu entgehen (17.2–7).

Auch die deuteronomische Gesetzgebung hat eine starke pädagogische Komponente. Die Reformer schufen im Dekalog einen regelrechten kleinen Katechismus, mit dessen Hilfe ein jeder israelitischer Hausvater die für ihn entscheidenden religiösen und ethischen Forderungen an den zehn Fingern seiner Hand memorieren konnte. Mit der öffentlichen Rezitation des Bekenntnisses *Šěma' Jiśrā'el* (Deut. 6.4–5), sollte jeder Israelit in das exklusive, ganz persönliche Gottesverhältnis emotional eingeübt werden.[47] Die Reformer wollten mit diesem „gepredigten Gesetz" ganz Israel zu einem | „heiligen Volk" umerziehen, das freiwillig Gottes Willen tut. Darum führten sie nach dem Modell der assyrischen Vasallenverträge die neue Idee eines Bundes zwischen JHWH und Israel ein, in dem sich beide Seiten zur gegenseitigen Treue verpflichteten (Deut. 26.16–19). Indem die Reformer das Verhältnis zwischen JHWH und Israel auf eine solche quasi juristische Weise interpretierten, schufen sie ein wichtiges neues Instrument der religiösen Verpflichtung: Jeder, der dem Bund angehörte, verpflichtete sich selbst, sein Leben freiwillig nach der Tora des Mose auszurichten. Auf diese Weise wurde die religiöse Kontrolle zu einem guten Teil verinnerlicht. So suchten die Träger der Josianischen Reform die monolatrische Verehrung JHWHs keineswegs nur durch die Androhung äußerer Sanktionen, sondern je länger je mehr auf der Grundlage innerer Überzeugung durchzusetzen.

Wir können damit festhalten, dass im alten Israel der gewalttätige Kampf gegen den Synkretismus und für die exklusive JHWH-Verehrung, wie er noch in der Jehu-Revolution stattgefunden hatte, Schritt für Schritt mithilfe des Rechts, der Erziehung und der Selbstverpflichtung sublimiert und internalisiert wurde. Meiner Meinung nach stellt dies Israels wichtigsten Fortschritt auf seinem Weg

---

46 B. Lang, ‚Segregation and Intolerance', in *What the Bible Really Says* (ed. M. Smith und R. J. Hoffmann; Buffalo: Prometheus Books, 1989), 115–35.
47 Köckert, ‚Diskussion', 174 will erst in Deut. 6.4b das früheste Zeugnis einer „exklusiv-polemischen Jahweverehrung" sehen; doch übersieht er in seiner Darstellung 2 Kgs 9–10. |

in Richtung Monotheismus dar. Ich würde sagen: Die ausschließliche Gottesverehrung hätte sich in Israel nicht ganz ohne die Anwendung von Gewalt entwickelt; aber Monolatrie und später Monotheismus wären in Israel nie erfolgreich gewesen, wenn es nicht gelungen wäre, die äußeren politischen und militärischen Zwangsmittel durch die Mittel einer individuellen Selbstverpflichtung und einer inneren Glaubensüberzeugung abzulösen.

Allerdings hatte die Josianische Reform eine politische Konsequenz, die nur deswegen nicht zum Problem wurde, weil sie mit Josias plötzlichem Tod im Jahr 609 schon nach 12 Jahren zum Erliegen kam. Mit ihrer schroff abgrenzenden Tendenz verlangte sie von Juda eine außenpolitische Isolation, die in einer polytheistischen Umwelt nur schwer ohne Kompromisse durchhaltbar gewesen wäre.

4 Der Durchbruch zum Monotheismus

Angesichts des unauflösbaren Widerspruchs von Weltherrschaftsansprüchen und Isolationismus, in den die aus der vorstaatlichen Zeit ererbte Sonderstellung JHWHs Israel unter den Bedingungen der Staatlichkeit trieb, verwundert es nicht, dass die monotheistische Tendenz der JHWH-Religion erst nach dem Zusammenbruch des Staates voll zum Durchbruch kommen konnte. Ohne den Verlust der Staatlichkeit, der die Israeliten direkt unter die Abhängigkeit fremder Götter brachte, wäre die JHWH-Religion wahrscheinlich bei der Monolatrie stehengeblieben. Nun aber bekam die Behauptung der alleinigen universalen Geschichtsmächtigkeit JHWHs und der | Nichtigkeit aller übrigen Götter, die Deuterojesaja im Exil verkündete, für die ohnmächtigen Exulantengruppen in ihrer fremdreligiösen Umwelt eine neue befreiende Funktion.[48] Mit der Potenzierung JHWHs zum einzigen Gott der Welt war allerdings kein Machtzuwachs Israels mehr verbunden, wohl aber eine Depotenzierung des Unterdrückers Babylon (Isa. 46.1–2; 47). Der behauptete universale Monotheismus hob die exklusive Gottesbeziehung Israels nicht auf, gab ihr aber eine dienende Aufgabe für alle Völker (42.1–4; 49.1–6).[49]

---

48 Das ist die rhetorische Funktion der sog. Gerichtsreden gegen die Völker (Isa. 41.1–5, 21–29; 43.8–13; 44.6–8; 45.20–25), in denen der Monotheismus nicht „nüchtern gelehrt", sondern die Aufdeckung der Nichtigkeit der anderen Götter immer wieder „nacherlebbar" vollzogen wird.
49 Genauer in Albertz, *Religionsgeschichte*, II, 431–46; und R. Albertz, *Die Exilszeit: 6. Jahrhundert v. Chr.* (Biblische Enzyklopädie, 7; Stuttgart: Kohlhammer, 2001 [English 2003]), 301–17. |

5 Verantwortlicher Umgang mit dem monotheistischen Bekenntnis

Die religionshistorische Nachfrage hat zwar zu dem Ergebnis geführt, dass der Weg Israels zum Monotheismus nicht derart mit Gewalttaten gepflastert war, wie Jan Assmann es unterstellt hatte. Dennoch lässt sich nicht leugnen, dass die exklusive Gottesverehrung in der Tat ein Gewaltpotenzial in sich birgt, das es theologisch zu bändigen gilt. Darum möchte ich eine theologische Reflexion über einen verantwortlichen Umgang mit dem monotheistischen Bekenntnis anschließen.

Wie die religionsgeschichtliche Entwicklung im 9. Jh. krass verdeutlicht, birgt die exklusive Verehrung eines Gottes in Verbindung mit politisch-militärischer Macht in der Tat die Gefahr einer gewalttätigen religiösen Intoleranz in sich, die sich leicht in fanatischen und blutigen Massakern entladen kann. Hinzu kommt unter den Bedingungen der Staatlichkeit das Problem des Isolationismus. Die exklusive Verehrung eines Gottes erschwert erheblich die Bündnisse mit Staaten und Völkern, die andere Götter verehren, jedenfalls solange der ganze Bereich der Politik, auch der internationalen Politik, von Religion durchtränkt ist. In einer solchen multireligiösen Welt gestattet der Polytheismus, der eine Integration der Hauptgötter des Bündnispartners in das eigene Pantheon ermöglicht, eine einfachere Gestaltung von politischen Beziehungen. Allerdings darf man die Differenz auch nicht übertreiben: Auch polytheistische Staaten pflegen Weltherrschaftsträume und wollen, wenn sich die Gelegenheit ergibt, ihren Einflussbereich vergrößern und ihren Hauptgöttern die Welt unterwerfen (vgl. Assyrien und auch Ägypten). Dagegen gehörte Echnaton mit seinem | königlichen Monotheismus zu den Pharaonen, die außenpolitisch am wenigsten aggressiv waren; und Israel und Juda sind trotz sich ausbildender Monolatrie auch nicht kriegerischer als ihre Nachbarn gewesen. Wiederum üben auch polytheistische Staaten eine religiöse Kontrolle aus, welche Kulte sie in ihrem Herrschaftsbereich zulassen und welche nicht (Athen, Rom).

Dennoch bleibt es eine Tatsache, dass insbesondere christliche und muslimische Staaten ihre weltweiten Eroberungskriegszüge nicht selten unter der Ägide des monotheistischen Bekenntnisses geführt und es zur Rechtfertigung der schonungslosen Abschlachtung Andersgläubiger gebraucht haben. Hierzu bleibt dreierlei zu bedenken:

Erstens: Überblickt man die Entwicklung des monotheistischen Bekenntnisses Israels im Ganzen, dann wird deutlich, dass der entscheidende Kampf um die alleinige Verehrung JHWHs durch Israel geführt worden ist, nicht um die Leugnung anderer Götter oder Religionen. Dem entspricht auch eine theologische Gewichtung in der Hebräischen Bibel selber: Nur die monolatrische Verehrung JHWHs steht im Zentrum der Tora, mit einem kleinen monotheistischen Ausblick in Deut. 4.35, 39. Die Götzenpolemiken Deuterojesajas dagegen sind nicht in die Sinaioffenbarung aufgenommen worden. D.h. es geht im Kern des monotheistischen Bekenntnisses um die ausschließliche existenzielle Bindung des ganzen Gottesvolkes an den einen Gott, die der besonderen personalen Bindung JHWHs an sein Volk angemessen ist. So muss es meiner Meinung nach auch den christlichen Kirchen heute primär darum gehen, wie der ungeteilten personalen Bindung der gesamten Christenheit an den einen dreieinigen Gott angesichts der theologischen, politischen und ökonomischen Gespaltenheit der Christenheit glaubwürdig Ausdruck verschafft werden kann. Eine herabsetzende Polemik gegen andere Religionen oder gar ein Kampf der Kulturen lässt sich aus dem monotheistischen Bekenntnis, wenn es richtig verstanden wird, nicht ableiten.

Zweitens: Es ist richtig, dass der exklusiven Gottesverehrung ein intolerantes und aggressives Potenzial innewohnt, das leicht in Gewalt gegen all die umschlagen kann, die diese Exklusivität verletzen. Doch bleibt zu beachten, dass sich in Israel diese Gewalt primär nach innen, gegen die eigenen Verehrer anderer Götter richtete und gegen Ausländer nur, sofern sie fremde Kulte offensiv in der israelitischen Gesellschaft förderten. Von großer Wichtigkeit scheint mir nun hier die Beobachtung zu sein, dass in Israel der Kampf um die Monolatrie schon recht bald nicht mehr gewalttätig, sondern mit den Mitteln des Rechts, der Erziehung und der religiösen Selbstverpflichtung ausgefochten wurde. Auch heute muss es deswegen darum gehen, dass den monotheistischen Religionen inhärente Gewaltpotenzial durch einen verbindlichen Rechtsrahmen von außen und religiöse Erziehung von innen zu sublimieren. |

Drittens: Es bleibt von zentraler Bedeutung, dass Israel zum strengen monotheistischen Bekenntnis, das den Göttern der Völker jegliche Existenz bestreitet, erst im Exil, d.h. in einer tiefen Ohnmachtssituation durchgestoßen ist. Das heißt eine politische Vereinnahmung des zum einzigen Schöpfer und Weltherrscher aufgestiegenen Gottes für eigene Weltherrschaftsansprüche war absolut ausgeschlossen. Das über die Welt zerstreute Israel erhält nun zwar die Aufgabe, die einzigartige Rettermacht seines Gottes vor allen Völkern zu bezeugen. Aber dieses Zeugenamt geschieht allein mit dem ohnmächtigen Wort; ob die Angehörigen der Völker darauf hören und der Einladung, sich dem einzigen Gott zuzuwenden, folgen, bleibt deren freiwillige Entscheidung und darf unter keinen Umständen erzwungen werden.

Es war und ist ein unzulässiger theologischer Kurzschluss, aus der Allmacht des als einzig erkannten Gottes einen universalen Machtanspruch seiner Verehrer ableiten zu wollen. Der eine Gott ist größer und weiter als ihn sich Menschen je werden vorstellen können. Nur da, wo die Allmacht des einzigen Gottes bewusst von jeder politischen Macht seines Volkes, sei es nun Israel, die Kirche oder die 'Umma sorgsam getrennt wird, nur da, wo die Unverfügbarkeit dieses universalen

Gottes gegen alle Versuche der politischen Instrumentalisierung sichergestellt ist, bleibt die theologische Legitimität des monotheistischen Bekenntnisses gewahrt. Wo dies nicht geschieht, rutscht das Bekenntnis in reine Ideologie ab, die eigene Machtinteressen nur religiös überhöhen will. Damit aber pervertiert das monotheistische Bekenntnis, das eigentlich Götzendienst verhindern soll, selber zum Götzendienst.

Ich habe Ida Fröhlich im Jahr 2006, als sie der European Association of Biblical Studies (EABS) an Ihrer Hochschule in Piliscsaba großzügig Gastfreundschaft gewährte, als eine Kollegin kennengelernt, welche die Einzelergebnisse ihrer Forschungen zu biblischen und frühjüdischen Themen immer in einen größeren kulturellen Horizont einzuordnen sucht. Darum möchte ich sie mit diesen grundsätzlicheren Überlegungen zum Monotheismus im alten Israel herzlich grüßen und die Hoffnung verbinden, damit vielleicht auch Ihre Anliegen zu treffen.

Theokratie und Gewaltenteilung: Der sogenannte Verfassungsentwurf des Ezechiel (Ez 40–48)

Die Hebräische Bibel enthält an etwas verborgener Stelle in ihrem Prophetenkanon eine interessante theokratisch begründete Teilung zwischen der Macht der drei staatlichen Institutionen des alten Israel, des Tempels, des Palastes und der Hauptstadt, die in der Folgezeit, als es auch unter dem Banner des Christentums zu mehr oder minder engen und lang anhaltenden Verbindungen von Thron und Altar kam, weitgehend in Vergessenheit geraten ist: im sogenannten Verfassungsentwurf des Ezechiel, der sich in den Schlusskapiteln 40–48 des gleichnamigen Prophetenbuches findet. Hier beschreiben wahrscheinlich die Schüler des 597 v. Chr. nach Babylon deportieren Priesterpropheten gegen Ende des 6. Jahrhunderts ein detailliertes visionäres Programm für eine kultische, politische und gesellschaftliche Neuordnung Israels für die Zeit nach der Rückkehr aus dem Exil. Und da Ezechiel und seine Schüler das babylonische Exil als ein hartes Gericht Gottes über die Missstände im vorexilischen Juda deuten, stellen sie diese Neuordnung als einen radikalen Bruch mit den früheren gesellschaftlichen Zuständen dar, der von Gott selber gewollt sei. Um das Revolutionäre dieses Verfassungsentwurfs zu verdeutlichen, soll hier kurz auf die Zuordnung der religiösen und politischen Institutionen im vorexilischen Staat Juda eingegangen werden.

I „Caesaropapismus" im vorexilischen Staat Juda

Nach der Sicht der offiziellen Jerusalemer Theologie, die vor allem in den vorexilischen Königs- und Zionspsalmen zutage tritt,[1] war der davidische | König Sohn Gottes (Ps 2,7; 89,28; vgl. 2. Sam 7,14), der als solcher die Herrschaft JHWHs auf Erden ausführt; außenpolitisch hatte er die Völker für JHWH zu unterwerfen und damit die Völkerwelt zu bändigen (Ps 2), innenpolitisch hatte er seinen Untertanen den Segen und die Gerechtigkeit von Gott her zu vermitteln (Ps 72) und für sie fürbittend vor Gott einzutreten (1. Kön 8). Seine repräsentative Mittlerstellung zwischen Gott und Mensch verlieh dem König Sakralität; als „Gesalbter Jahwes" war er nicht nur gegenüber politischen Gegnern sakrosankt (2. Sam 1,14.16 u. ö.), sondern auch mit der höchsten Priesterwürde ausgestattet. Ähnlich wie etwa in Ägypten und Assyrien, aber im Unterschied etwa zum Nordreich Israel und zu

---

1 Hier kann nur ein kurzer Abriss der rekonstruierbaren Jerusalemer Königs- und Tempeltheologie geboten werden, für eine ausführlichere Darstellung vgl. Rainer Albertz, Religionsgeschichte Israels in alttestamentlicher Zeit (GAT 8,1–2), 2 Bde., 2. Aufl., Göttingen 1996/1997, Bd. I, 173–212. |

https://doi.org/10.1515/9783111202228-027

Babylonien, übten die judäischen Könige ihr priesterliches Amt wirklich aus. Bei besonderen Anlässen opferten sie selber (1. Kön 8,62–64), sprachen Fürbitten (V. 31 ff.) und teilten den gottesdienstlichen Segen aus (V. 14.55). Ebenso wurden für die Könige lange Fürbitten im Gottesdienst gesprochen (Ps 20; 72). Sogar divinatorische Funktionen als Offenbarungsmittler wurden ihnen zuerkannt (2. Sam 23,2 f.; Prov 16,10).

Der engen Verbindung von politischer und religiöser Sphäre in der Gestalt des Königs (*mælæk*) entsprach in Jerusalem eine enge bauliche Zuordnung von Tempel und Palast auf dem Zionberg (1. Kön 7,12; 2. Kön 11,13; 16,18; Jer 36,20; vgl. Abb. 1). JHWH wurde in der Jerusalemer Tempeltheologie selber als König vorgestellt, der inmitten seines Hofstaates in und über seinem Heiligtum thront (Jes 6,1–3); das Allerheiligste war mit einem riesigen Kerubenthron aus vergoldetem Olivenholz ausgefüllt. Himmlischer und irdischer König thronten und regierten damit auch räumlich eng beieinander. Wie die babylonischen Könige, so waren auch die judäischen Monarchen Erbauer und Versorger des Heiligtums. Salomo baute den Jerusalemer Tempel prächtig aus (1. Kön 6–8), dessen Opferkult ganz wesentlich mit dem Vieh aus den königlichen Domänen unterhalten wurde (vgl. 1. Chr 27,29–31). Die Könige spendeten dem Tempel kostbare Beutestücke aus ihren Kriegszügen (2. Kön 11,10) und kontrollierten die Finanzen zu seiner Renovierung (12,5–7). So war der Jerusalemer Tempel zugleich Reichsheiligtum und königliche Kapelle (vgl. Am 7,13). Sogar der Kern der Hauptstadt galt als königlicher Besitz („Davids Stadt": 2. Sam 5,7.9 u. ö.).

Was für die bauliche und rechtliche Stellung des Tempels galt, spiegelt sich genauso in der Stellung des Kultpersonals. Die Jerusalemer Priester waren weisungsgebundene königliche Beamte (2. Sam 8,17), z. T. auch Mitglieder der königlichen Familie (V. 18) oder doch mit ihr verwandt (2. Kön 11,2); der König konnte sie bestellen, aber auch nach Gutdünken entlassen (1. Kön 2,26 f.). So ist es denn auch kein Wunder, dass die königlichen Hoftheologen, zu denen neben den Priestern auch Hofpropheten (Nathan, Gad) und Schreiber gehörten, den Davididen treu ergeben waren. |

Sie gingen sogar so weit, nicht nur dem jeweils regierenden König und der Institution des Königtums als solcher die göttliche Legitimation zu verleihen, wie dies etwa in Ägypten und Babylonien geschah, sondern sogar speziell der davidischen Dynastie eine unbefristete göttliche Bestandsgarantie zu verschaffen (2. Sam 7,11b–16).

Gegen den politischen und religiösen Monopolanspruch des davidischen Königtums und seiner Theologen erhob sich allerdings in Israel schon früh Protest. Die tribalen Führer versuchten in mehreren Aufstandsbewegungen eine stärkere Partizipation an der politischen Macht durchzusetzen (2. Sam 15–17; 20; 1. Kön 1), was aber nicht gelang und schließlich zur Trennung der mittel- und nordisraeli-

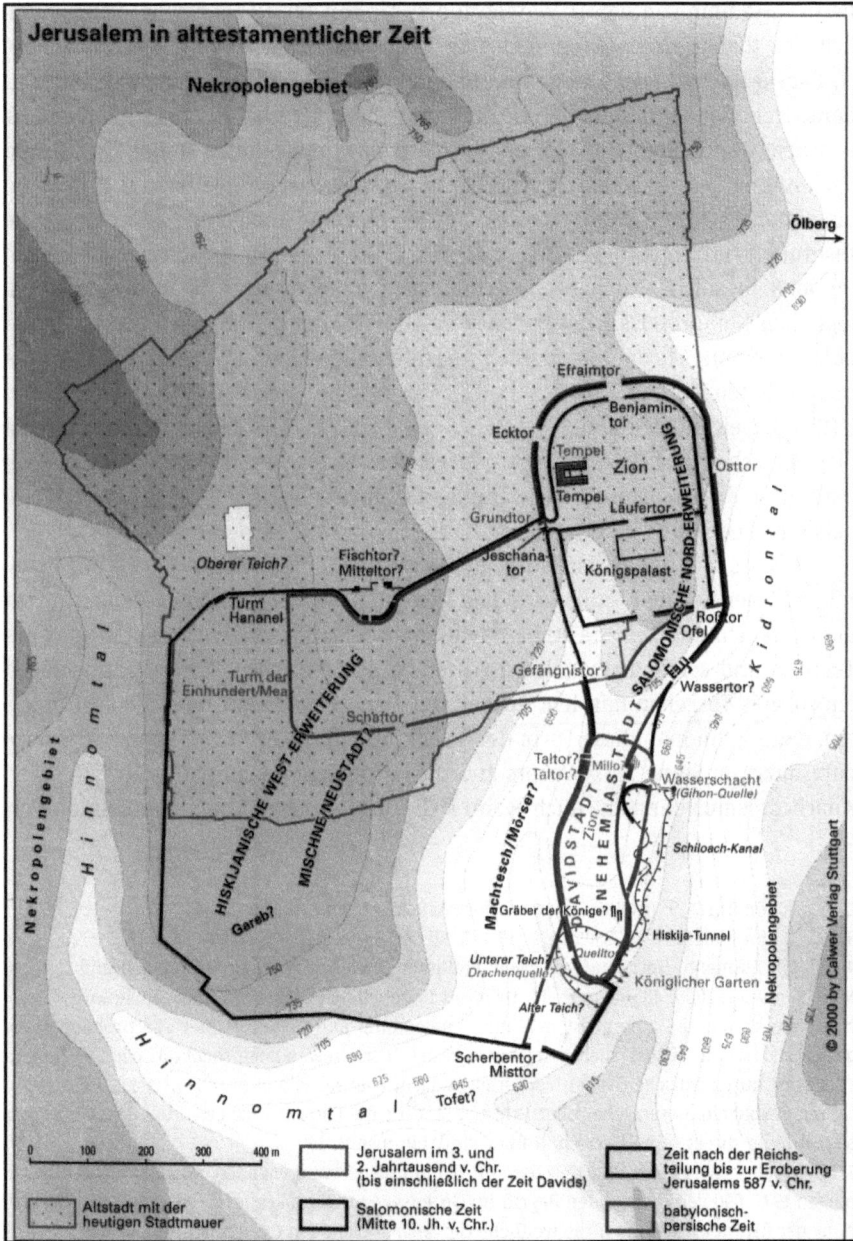

Abb. 1: Ungefähre Zuordnung von Tempel und Palast auf dem Zionberg in vorexilischer Zeit (aus Wolfgang Zwickel, Calwer Bibelatlas [Calwer Verlag], Stuttgart 2000, 41) |

tischen Stämme von den Davididen führte (1. Kön 12). Dabei spielte wahrscheinlich das theokratische Argument eine Rolle, dass JHWH König über Israel sei
(1. Sam 8,7; 12,12). Nach alter Anschauung, die sich noch in vorstaatlicher Zeit
herausgebildet hatte, stand JHWH in unmittelbarem Verhältnis zu seinem Volk, er
war der „Gott Israels" (Ri 5,3.5) und bedurfte darum eigentlich keiner königlichen
Vermittlung. So ist es kein Wunder, dass sich in Israel von Seiten der Propheten
eine immer schärfer werdende Kritik gegen einzelne Könige und sogar gegen die
Institution des Königtums als ganze erhob.[2] Die davidischen Hoftheologen suchten im 8. Jh. solche prophetische Kritik dadurch aufzufangen, dass sie einen theologischen Kompromiss anboten, nach dem JHWH mit den Königen nur einen *na-
gîd*, d. h. einen „Thronprätendenten", berufen habe, um sein Volk Israel zu retten
und zu leiten (1. Sam 9,16; 2. Sam 5,2; 7,8); dies ließ der Vorstellung Raum, dass
JHWH der eigentliche König Israels sei (vgl. Ps 80,2: „Hirte Israels"). Doch hielten
die judäischen Hoftheologen selbst nach dem Untergang des Staates Juda noch
daran fest, dass die göttliche Erwählung der Davididen und des Jerusalemer Tempels ihre Bedeutung nicht verloren hätten.[3]

So lässt sich das vorexilische Juda als eine „repräsentative Theokratie" cha-
rakterisieren in dem Sinne, wie Jan Assmann den Begriff definiert hat.[4] Stellt
man in Rechnung, wie stark die davidischen Könige in die Angelegenheiten des
Tempels und seines Personals eingriffen und wie offensiv | ihre Hoftheologen
ein solches Vorgehen mit dem Ausbau der Königs- und Zionstheologie legitimier-
ten, dann kann man diese Form der Theokratie durchaus dem Typ des „Caesaropapismus" im Sinne Max Webers zuordnen,[5] obwohl der Begriff natürlich einen
Anachronismus darstellt. Auch wenn sich in Israel gegen die monarchische Ver-

---

2 Vgl. 1. Kön 21,17–19; Jes 7,10–17; 11,1–5; Jer 22,18–23.24–30; Hos 13,9–11 u. ö.
3 Vgl. 1. Kön 8,16; 11,11–13.32.36; 14,21; 15,4; 2. Kön 8,19; 19,32–34; 25,27–30.
4 Vgl. Jan Assmann, Herrschaft und Heil. Politische Theologie in Altägypten, Israel und Europa,
München/Wien 2000, 48, dazu 42–44. Dagegen halte ich seinen Begriff einer „identitären Theokratie" (ebd., 44, 48), zumindest in seiner Anwendung auf das alte Israel, für problematisch,
da die Herrschaft JHWHs auch beim herrschaftskritisch gewendeten theokratischen Argument
allermeist durch irdische Größen vermittelt gedacht war, sei es nun durch charismatische Heer-
führer, Propheten, Gesetzgeber oder Priester. Erst für die Endzeit wird erwartet, dass Gott mehr
oder minder direkt seine Herrschaft über die Welt ausübt. |
5 Max Weber, Wirtschaft und Gesellschaft. Grundriss der verstehenden Soziologie, 5. Aufl., Tübingen 1972, 690 verwendete den Begriff im Gegensatz zur Hierokratie, als „die völlige Unterord-
nung der priesterlichen unter die weltliche Gewalt"; er sieht den Caeseropapismus zwar in „ganz
reiner Form" historisch nirgends verwirklicht, aber doch von den ägyptischen Pharaonen, den
indischen, chinesischen, byzantinischen Monarchen und den *summi episcopi* anglikanischer und
protestantischer Prägung angestrebt. In die Kette der Beispiele ließen sich durchaus auch die
judäischen Monarchen einordnen. Erst ab dem Ende des 8. Jh. v. Chr. lässt sich hier eine gewisse
Einschränkung ihrer religiös-kultischen Kompetenzen erkennen. |

einahmung des Kultes und gegen die monarchische Monopolisierung der Gottesbeziehung z. T. heftige Kritik erhob und einige Kompromisse erzwungen wurden,
ist das Konzept eines vom König dominierten Staatskultes von Seiten der Hoftheologen nie in Frage gestellt worden.

II Die theokratisch motivierte „Gewaltenteilung" im sog. Verfassungsentwurf des Ezechiel

Ezechiel war wahrscheinlich priesterlicher Herkunft und gehörte damit wohl
auch ins Umfeld der Jerusalemer Hoftheologie; jedenfalls vertritt er teilweise
durchaus traditionelle Ansichten der Zionstheologie, wie etwa die Vorstellung
vom Jerusalemer Tempel als Thronsitz JHWHs. Dennoch hat er sich aufgrund
seiner prophetischen Erfahrungen weit von diesem Umfeld distanziert: Folgt man
der Darstellung des Buches, so erschien dem Propheten bei seiner Berufung im
Jahr 594 v. Chr. JHWH in seiner ganzen Majestät auf seinem – nunmehr beräder-
ten – Thronsitz in Babylonien am Fluss Kebar (Ez 1–3). Daraus erkannte Ezechiel,
dass der Gott Israels wegen des Götzendienstes der Laien (Ez 8) und der Schlam-
pigkeit der Priester, die nicht mehr klar zwischen heilig und profan unterschieden
hatten (22,26), sein Jerusalemer Heiligtum verlassen hatte und es der Zerstörung
preisgeben würde (10,1–11,24). Nachdem sich seine Unheilsprophetie mit dem Untergang Judas und der Zerstörung des Tempels 587 v. Chr. bewahrheitet hatte, begann Ezechiel langsam mit einer Heilsverkündigung für sein geschlagenes Volk.
Kurz vor seinem Tod um das Jahr 570 v. Chr. schaute der alte Prophet 574 in einer
Vision den Jerusalemer Tempel „wie den Bau einer Stadt" auf einem hohen Berg
liegen (40,2). Seine solitäre Lage und sein festungsartiges Aussehen implizierten
dabei schon im Kern | die ganze Reformidee, die seine Schüler sukzessiv in der
späten Exilszeit ausarbeiteten: die bauliche, territoriale und organisatorische Verselbständigung des neuen Jerusalemer Tempels (40,5–43,12) und damit den Bruch
mit der staatskultischen Tradition (44–46).[6]

---

6 Auch Bernhard Lang, Theokratie, in: Handbuch religionswissenschaftlicher Grundbegriffe, Bd. V,
Stuttgart 2001, 178–189, 182 führt in seinem Überblicksartikel den sog. „Verfassungsentwurf des Ezechiel" (Ez 40–48) ausdrücklich als ein wichtiges jüdisches Beispiel für ein vom theokratischen Gedan-
ken geleitetes Gesellschaftsmodell an. Im Einzelnen vgl. dazu die Arbeiten von Hartmut Gese, Der
Verfassungsentwurf des Ezechiel (Kap. 40–48). Traditionsgeschichtlich untersucht (BHTh 25), Tübingen 1957; Jürgen Ebach, Kritik und Utopie. Untersuchungen zum Verhältnis von Volk und Herrscher
im Verfassungsentwurf des Ezechiel (Kap. 40–48), Hamburg 1972; Moshe Greenberg, The Design and
Themes of Ezekiel's Program of Restoration, in: Interpretation 38 (1964), 181–208. Gegenüber der lite-
rarkritischen Aufteilung der Texte auf eine Vielzahl von Schichten durch Thilo Rudnig, Heilig und
Profan. Redaktionsgeschichtliche Studien zu Ez 40–48 (BZAW 287), Berlin/New York 2000, und ders.

Diese radikale Neuerung begründeten die Prophetenschüler durch eine Offenbarung Ezechiels, in der die Heimkehr der Herrlichkeit JHWHs zum neuen Tempel visionär geschildert wird:

43,1 Dann führte er (sc. der Engel) mich zum Tor, das nach Osten schaut.

2 Und siehe, die Herrlichkeit des Gottes Israels kam von Osten her,
und ihr Geräusch war wie das Rauschen großer Wasser,
und die Erde leuchtete auf von ihrem Glanz.

3 Und die Erscheinung, die ich sah, war ganz wie die Erscheinung, die ich gesehen hatte, als ‚er' kam, um die Stadt zu vernichten „...', und wie die Erscheinung, die ich am Fluss Kebar gesehen hatte.
Darauf fiel ich auf mein Angesicht.

4 Währenddessen war die Herrlichkeit in den Tempel hineingegangen durch ‚das'[7] Tor, das nach Osten schaut.

5 Da erhob mich der Geist und trug mich in den inneren Vorhof.
Und siehe, der Tempel war ganz von der Herrlichkeit JHWHs angefüllt.

6 Da hörte ich aus dem Tempel zu mir reden, während der Mann neben mir stand. |

7 Da sprach er zu mir:
„Menschensohn, dies ist der Ort meines Thrones und dies ist der Ort meiner Fußsohlen, wo ich unter den Israeliten auf ewig wohnen will.
Nicht mehr soll das Haus Israel meinen heiligen Namen verunreinigen, sie und ihre Könige, durch ihre Hurerei und durch die Totenopfer ihrer Könige ‚bei deren Tod',[8]

8 dadurch dass sie ihre Schwelle neben meine Schwelle setzten
und ihren Türpfosten neben meinen Türpfosten
und (nur) eine Wand zwischen mir und ihnen war,
und so meinen heiligen Namen verunreinigten durch die Gräuel, die sie taten, sodass ich sie in meinem Grimm verzehrte.

9 Nun (aber) mögen sie ihre Hurerei und die Totenopfer ihrer Könige von mir fernhalten, so dass ich auf ewig in ihrer Mitte wohne."

bei Karl-Friedrich Pohlmann, Der Prophet Hesekiel/Ezechiel (ATD 22,1–2), 2 Bde., Göttingen 1996/2001, Bd. II, 527–630 lässt sich der gesamte Verfassungsentwurf als eine – wiewohl gewachsene – kompositionelle Einheit verstehen, die denselben theokratischen Grundgedanken immer weiter entfaltet, vgl. dazu Albertz, Religionsgeschichte (Anm. 1), Bd. II, 446–459; Rainer Albertz, Die Exilszeit. 6. Jahrhundert v. Chr. (BE 7), Stuttgart 2001, 276–283; Ders., Heiligkeit Gottes im Raum. Rituelle Grenzziehungen und territoriale Gewaltenteilung im Reformkonzept des Ezechielbuches, in: Räume und Grenzen. Topologische Konzepte in den antiken Kulturen des östlichen Mittelmeerraums (Quellen und Forschungen zur Antiken Welt 52), hrsg. v. dems./Anke Blöbaum/Peter Funke, München 2007, 123–143, bes. 127–141.
7 Ergänze den Artikel mit wenigen hebräischen Handschriften und den alten Übersetzungen. |
8 Lies statt MT *bamotam* „(auf) ihren Höhen" mit einigen hebräischen Handschriften, Theodotion und Targumeditionen *bĕ-motam* „bei ihrem Tod".

Auch der neue Tempel soll, so erklärt JHWH bei seinem Einzug, der Ort seines Thrones sein, an dem er in seiner ganzen Majestät unter seinem Volke wohnen wolle. Aber dieser neue Tempel muss viel höheren Heiligkeitskriterien genügen als der alte: Gott führt bittere Klage darüber, dass sein heiliger Name in der Vergangenheit verunreinigt wurde; und zwar nicht nur durch den Götzendienst der Israeliten, sondern insbesondere durch die Totenopfer,[9] welche die Könige im Tempelareal dargebracht hatten (Ez 43,7). Diese hatten ihm sogar zugemutet, Tür an Tür und Wand an Wand mit ihnen zu wohnen (V. 8), darum hatte JHWH sie in seinem Grimm verzehrt. In Zukunft, so verfügt Gott, sollen dergleichen Missstände unbedingt abgestellt werden; alle Unreinheit müsse unbedingt vom Tempel ferngehalten werden.

Die Prophetenschüler wollen mit dieser Vision aufdecken, dass die frühere bauliche und organisatorische Verquickung von Tempel und Palast den himmlischen Herrscher in seiner Heiligkeit verletzt und in seiner Göttlichkeit beschädigt hat. Doch Gott hatte sich von dieser politischen Vereinnahmung distanziert und den königlichen Tempel zerstört. Der neue Tempel muss darum von den politischen Machtträgern klar geschieden sein, um den hohen Ansprüchen des himmlischen Herrschers zu genügen. |

Um den Tempel in Zukunft vor jeder Art von Verunreinigung und das heißt auch vor politischen Übergriffen zu schützen, wurde die Tempelanlage als ein durch starke Umfassungsmauern klar abgegrenzter heiliger Bezirk von 500 Ellen Kantenlänge (ca. 260 Metern) konzipiert, der mit keinem anderen Gebäude mehr in Verbindung stand (s. Abb. 2). Ein unbebauter Grünstreifen von 50 Ellen rundherum sollte die Geschiedenheit der Anlage von ihrem Umland nochmals unterstreichen (Ez 45,2). Von außen bot der Tempel den Eindruck einer Festung. Die drei gewaltigen Tore, die mit Ausmaßen von 26 mal 13 Metern die Größe der gewaltigen Tore in den Festungen Hazor, Megiddo und Gezer noch übertreffen,[10] sollten den Tempel vor jedem, selbst jedem bewaffneten Eindringling schützen und dem Tempelpersonal die Kontrolle des Zutritts auch ohne staatliche Hilfe ermöglichen.

Im quadratischen Tempelareal sollte das eigentliche Tempelgebäude nochmals mehrfach vor Entweihung geschützt sein. Eine massive Mauer mit nochmals

---

9 Die Deutung des hebräischen Wortes *pægær* ist unsicher; meist bedeutet es „Leichnam", doch ist es unwahrscheinlich, dass die judäischen Könige im Tempelbereich begraben wurden. Vom Ugaritischen her hat man die Bedeutung „Stele" annehmen wollen, doch bleibt sie unsicher. Allerdings kann *pagrûm* in Mari und wahrscheinlich auch *PGR* im Ugaritischen ein Opfer bezeichnen, das wohl mit dem Totenkult zu tun hat, vgl. Jürgen Ebach, *PGR* = (Toten-)Opfer? Ein Vorschlag zum Verständnis von Ez 43,7.9, in: UF 3 (1971), 365–368. |
10 Das eisenzeitliche Stadttor von Hazor misst 20,3 mal 18 Meter, das von Megiddo 20,3 mal 17,5 Meter und das von Gezer 19 mal 16,2 Meter. |

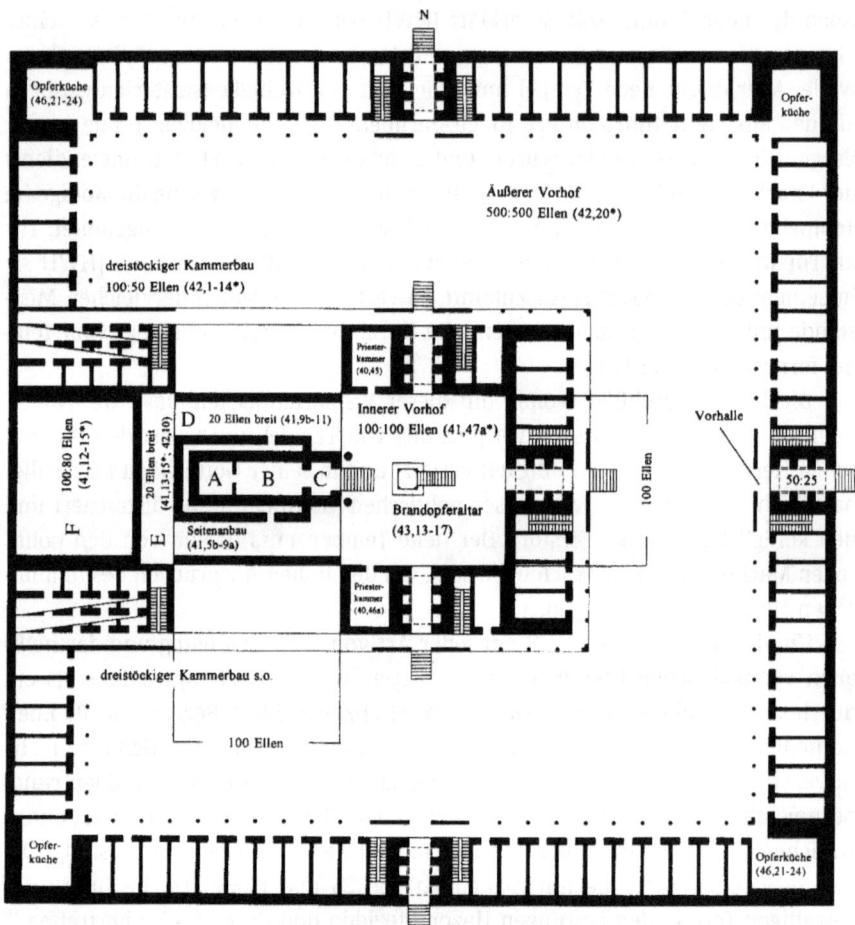

Abb. 2: Der visionär konzipierte Tempel bei Ezechiel (aus Pohlmann, Ezechiel II [Anm. 6], 631)

A Allerheiliges (*qodœš haqqodašîm*) des Tempelgebäudes
B Heilige Haupthalle (*hêkal*) des Tempelgebäudes
C Vorhalle (*'ulam*) des Tempelgebäudes
D „Freigelassenes"
E Sperrplatz
F (leerer) Bau (*binjân*) zur Abschottung des Allerheiligen |

drei gewaltigen Toren sollte den inneren Vorhof, in dem die Priester die Opfer auf dem Brandopferaltar darbrachten, vom äußeren Vorhof, zu dem die Laien Zutritt hatten, abriegeln. Der Langhaustempel sollte wie schon sein Jerusalemer Vorgänger nochmals drei Räume mit gestufter Heiligkeit aufweisen, eine Vorhalle (*'ulam*), die Haupthalle (*hêkal*) und das Allerheiligste (*qodœš haqqodašîm*). Um das Allerheiligste auch von hinten her vor jeder Kontaminierung zu schützen, sollte ein großes leeres Gebäude (*binjân*; 52 mal 41 Meter) ihm gegenüber in die Außenmauer eingefügt werden. Auf diese Weise sollte mithilfe der priesterlichen Logik der räumlichen Trennung von Heiligem und Profanem die bauliche Grundlage für eine institutionelle Verselbständigung des Tempels gegenüber der politischen Macht gelegt werden.

Die massive bauliche Absicherung der Heiligkeit des im Tempel thronenden Gottes hatte nun eine Reihe wichtiger politischer Konsequenzen: Die erste Konsequenz bestand in einer Entsakralisierung und Depotenzierung des Königs. Da nur die Priester aufgrund gründlicher Reinigungsriten den inneren Vorhof betreten durften, wurde dem König von den Prophetenschülern sein traditionelles Recht, Opfer darzubringen, entzogen (Ez 46,2); ja, selbst der Zutritt zum inneren Vorhof wurde ihm ausdrücklich untersagt (V. 2.8). Zwar räumten die Prophetenschüler ihm beim Gottesdienst noch gewisse Privilegien ein, die noch von Ferne an seine frühere Sakralität erinnern: Er durfte seine privaten Opfermahlzeiten im zugemauerten östlichen Vorhoftor einnehmen, durch das die Herrlichkeit Gottes eingezogen war (44,3). Es wurde ihm erlaubt, von der Schwelle des östli | chen Tores des inneren Vorhofs den offiziellen Opferzeremonien der Priester zuzusehen (46,2). Dies änderte aber nichts daran, dass der Herrscher kultrechtlich den Laien zugerechnet wurde. Der zukünftige König sollte nicht mehr Kultmittler, sondern nur noch vornehmster Repräsentant der Laiengemeinde sein (46,10). Er war auch nicht mehr Versorger des Heiligtums, sondern hatte nur noch die Aufgabe, die – relativ geringe – Opfersteuer, die dem Volk auferlegt wurde (45,13–15), einzusammeln und an den Tempel weiterzuleiten (V. 16–17). Träger des Tempelkultes sollte in Zukunft das Volk sein; der König sollte dabei nur noch als *primus inter pares* der Laiengemeinde fungieren. Es ist deswegen kein Zufall, dass die Verfasser des Verfassungsentwurfs den so seiner früheren Sakralität Entkleideten gar nicht mehr mit dem Königstitel (*mælœk*) bezeichneten, sondern schlicht *nasî* „Fürst" nannten (44,3; 45,7–9.16 f.22 u. ö.). Er bekleidete damit nur noch ein deutlich reduziertes politisches Amt. So hat nach der prophetischen Konzeption der Ezechielschüler die Heiligkeit und Majestät des himmlischen Herrschers eine Entsakralisierung und Depotenzierung des irdischen Herrschers zur Folge.

Die Beschränkung der kultischen Funktionen des Fürsten auf ein Minimum eröffnete den Schülern des Priesterpropheten den Freiraum, der nötig war, um die priesterlichen Belange neu und besser zu regeln: Die Priester sollten in Zukunft nicht mehr wie zuvor dem König unterstehen, sondern völlig unabhängig von ihm den Tempel eigenständig verwalten und die kultischen Dinge selbstverantwortlich regeln. Dabei verlangten die strengen Heiligkeitsregeln eine Neuorganisation des Kultpersonals. Da sich die Priester, die den Opferdienst versahen, penibler Reinheitsrituale unterziehen mussten, waren sie gar nicht in der Lage, weltliche und schmutzigere Aufgaben bei der Verwaltung und Pflege des Tempels zu übernehmen. Es bedurfte dafür einer niedrigeren Priesterklasse, der Leviten. Diese sollten etwa die polizeiliche Aufgabe des Bewachens der Tempeltore übernehmen, für die man früher häufig ausländische Tempelsklaven verwendet hatte, aber auch niedere Priesterdienste wie das Schlachten der Laienopfer im äußeren Vorhof leisten (Ez 44,4–14); von der Darbringung der Opfer, die allein den zadokidischen Priestern vorbehalten war, sollten sie dagegen ausgeschlossen sein (V. 13). Die Schaffung eines *clerus minor* hat vermutlich mit internen priesterlichen Rivalitäten zu tun. Grundsätzlich ist sie jedoch eine notwendige Konsequenz aus dem Vorhaben, den Tempel und das Tempelpersonal institutionell zu verselbständigen.

Die Selbständigkeit der Priester und Leviten konnte nun allerdings erst dann als dauerhaft gewährleistet gelten, wenn für deren wirtschaftliche Existenzsicherung eine Lösung gefunden wurde, welche in der Lage war, die ehemals staatliche Versorgung zu ersetzen. Die Prophetenschüler sahen durchaus realistisch, dass zu einem solchen Zweck die traditionell den | Priestern zustehenden Opferanteile nicht ausreichten, selbst wenn man diese etwas vermehrte (Ez 44,28–31). Darum konzipierten sie eine völlig neue Form priesterlicher und levitischer Selbstversorgung als Teil einer großen Bodenreform: Wenn den Stämmen das Land neu ausgeteilt werden würde, sodass jeder – sogar der Fremdling – einen gerechten Bodenanteil bekam (47,13–48,29), dann sollten die Stämme einen Landstreifen mit einer Länge vom Mittelmeer bis zum Jordan und einer Breite von 25.000 Ellen (ca. 13 km) als eine Art „Weihgabe" (*tĕrumah*) spenden (s. Abb. 3).[11] Aus diesem Landstreifen sollte ein Gebiet von je zweimal 25.000 mal 10.000 Ellen als „heilige Weihgabe" (*tĕrumah haqqodœš*) für die Priester und Leviten gestiftet werden (45,1–8; 48,8–14). Die Priester sollten auf ihrem Anteil, der auch *tĕrumijjah*, vielleicht „Sonderabgabe", genannt wird (48,12), siedeln und Vieh halten dürfen (45,4); die Leviten sollten innerhalb ihres Gebiets sogar festen Bodenbesitz erhalten und damit Ackerbau treiben dürfen (V. 5). Diese praktische Lösung des Versorgungsproblems, welche die Ezechielschüler hier für die Priesterversorgung propagierten, widersprach nun allerdings diametral der alten „Levitenregel" von der Besitzlosigkeit der Priester (Dtn 18,1 f.), die noch aus der Zeit der wandernden

---

11 Der Bergriff *tĕrumah* meint eigentlich eine kultische Abgabe, der eine gewisse Freiwilligkeit zukommt, vgl. Dtn 12,6.11.17; Ez 20,40; Lev 22,12 u. ö. Nur in Prov 29,4 kann er eine königliche Steuer bezeichnen.

Priestergenossenschaften stammte. Die neu geschaffene Regelung erschien manchen als so anstößig, dass sie sogar spätere Eingriffe in den hebräischen Text
provozierte.[12] Doch die Prophetenschüler nahmen – gedeckt durch ihre charismatische Autorität – den Bruch mit der Tradition bewusst in Kauf, weil sie erkannten, dass nur die Einführung des neuen Prinzips einer weitgehenden Selbstversorgung der Priester und Leviten dem Kultpersonal seine wirtschaftliche
Unabhängigkeit gegenüber staatlichen Stellen dauerhaft garantieren würde und
gleichzeitig die Belastung für die Gesamtbevölkerung so niedrig wie möglich hielt.
Bei einer Gesamtfläche von immerhin 134 km^2 konnte sich aus dem Areal durchaus eine stattliche Anzahl von Tempelbediensteten ernähren. |

Innerhalb des Priestergebietes sollte auch der Tempel situiert werden;[13] er
war damit auch räumlich dem Eingriff des Fürsten entzogen, dessen Land sich
rechts und links an die „heilige Weihgabe" anschloss. Auch dadurch erhielt die
eigenständige Tempelverwaltung der Priester und Leviten noch einmal sinnenfälligen Ausdruck.

Vom ausgesonderten Quadrat sollte der Rest von 25.000 mal 5.000 Ellen der
Hauptstadt gehören, die damit ebenfalls außerhalb vom Land des Fürsten platziert wurde. Sie sollte darum nicht mehr dem König, sondern den Stämmen gehören und von diesen gemeinsam verwaltet werden (Ez 45,5; 48,15–18). Dabei sollte
das Umland der Stadt den Bediensteten der Stämme zur Selbstversorgung zur
Verfügung stehen (48,18), sodass keine Steuern für die staatliche Verwaltung anfielen. In Differenz zum historischen Jerusalem sollte der Tempel nicht mehr Teil
der Hauptstadt sein; vielmehr lagen beide nach dem Entwurf ca. 10 km voneinander entfernt.[14]

---

12 Der Versteil Ez 45,4bβ „und ein Heiligtum für das Heiligtum" gibt keinen Sinn; er wurde
offenbar in der masoretischen Texttradition bewusst verstümmelt. Lies mit der Septuaginta und
Jos 14,4: *u-migraš lĕ-miqnœh* „und Weideplatz für das Vieh". Auch der Satz Ez 45,5 „ihnen soll es
als Eigentum gehören, für zwanzig Kammern" ist im masoretischen Text verstümmelt; die zweite
Sequenz ist mit der Septuaginta zu lesen: *'arîm la-šœbœt* „als Städte zum Wohnen". |
13 Wenn man die Aussage von Ez 48,8.21, dass das Heiligtum in der Mitte (*bĕtoko*) der *tĕrumah*
liegt, auf die geometrische Mitte des ganzen Quadrats bezieht, dann müsste das Priestergebiet
nach 45,3 ebenfalls in die Mitte platziert werden, so Walther Zimmerli, Ezechiel (BK XIII,1–2),
2. Aufl., Neukirchen-Vluyn 1979, Bd. II, 1222–1224; Hans Ferdinand Fuhs, Ezechiel II: 25–48
(NEB 22), Würzburg 1988, 271; Rudnig bei Pohlmann, Ezechiel (Anm. 6), Bd. II, 625 f. Doch hat
Georg Christian Macholz, Noch einmal: Die Planungen für den Wiederaufbau nach der Katastrophe von 587. Erwägungen zum Schlussteil des sog. „Verfassungsentwurfs des Hesekiel", in: VT 19
(1969), 322–352, bes. 333–336 gute Gründe dafür beigebracht, dass an eine nord-südliche Abfolge
Priester-, Leviten- und Stadtgebiet gedacht ist (s. Abb. 3). Der hebräische Ausdruck *bĕtok* braucht
nicht die exakte Mitte, sondern kann auch einfach eine Ortslage „inmitten" eines Gebiets bezeichnen.
14 Sofern man der obigen Rekonstruktion folgt, dass der Tempel im nördlich gelegenen Priestergebiet lag und von der Stadt noch einmal durch das Levitengebiet getrennt war. |

Judah

Terumah
Weihgabe

25.000

Priester	
Terumijjah Sonderweihgabe	Tempel
	Terumah
Leviten	*haq-qodœš*
Besitz der Leviten	

10.000

10.000

Fürst

Fürst

„heilige Weihgabe"

25.000

Bedienstete	Stadt	**der Stadt**

5.000

„Besitz der Stadt"

Benjamin

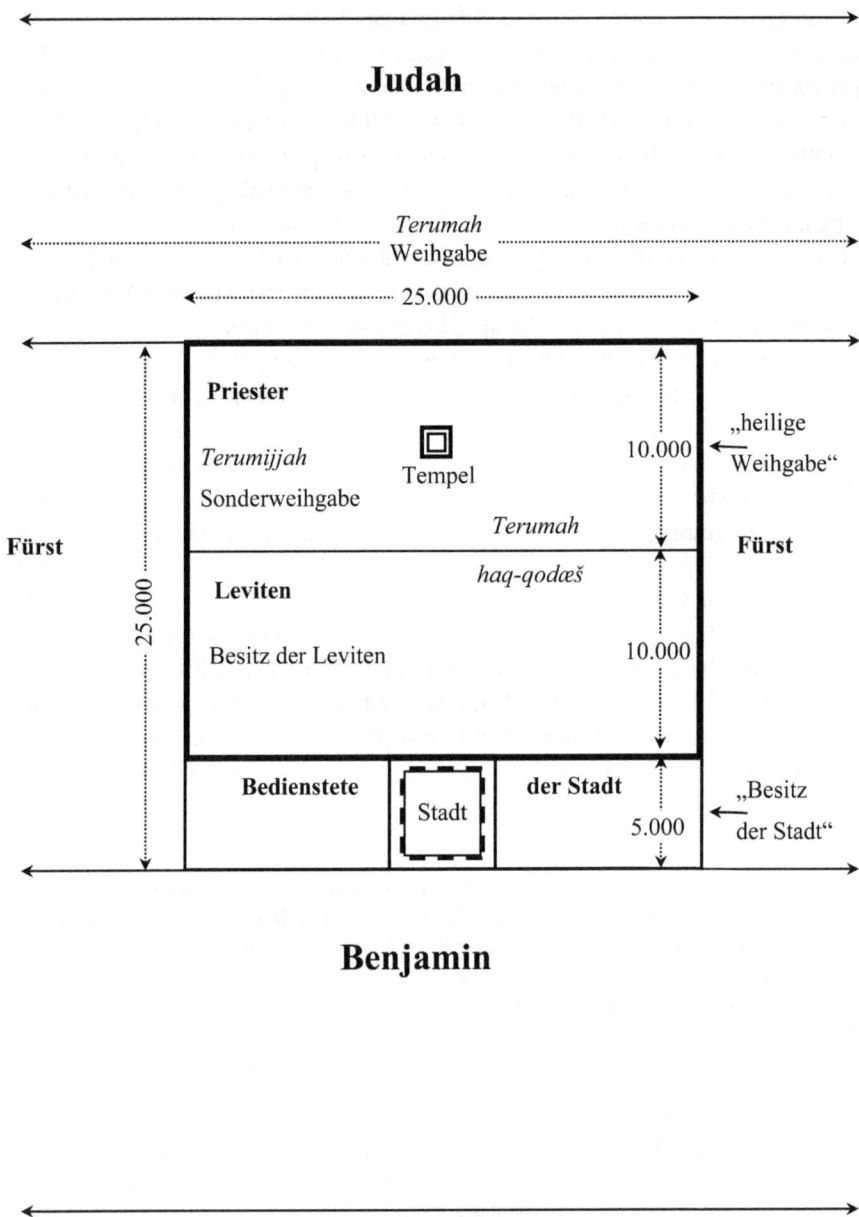

Abb. 3: Die neue Zuordnung von Tempel, Hauptstadt und Fürstenland nach Ez 45,1–8 und 48,8–22 (eigene Zeichnung, vgl. Albertz, Heiligkeit [Anm. 6], 136) |

Rechts und links vom Besitz der Stadt und dem Priester- und Levitenland
sollte dem Fürsten der gesamte übrige Landstreifen zur Versorgung seiner Familie und seiner Bediensteten zur Verfügung stehen, was eine Königsteuer überflüs-
sig machte. Doch durfte der Fürst von dem Land nur seinen Familienangehörigen
etwas dauerhaft vererben. Landschenkungen an Bedienstete sollten dagegen
nach deren Tod wieder an den Fürsten fallen (Ez 46,16–18). Damit sollte verhindert werden, dass erneut ein ständig steigender Landbedarf der Krone wie in
vorexilischer Zeit die normale Landbevölkerung von ihren Äckern vertrieb. Die
Eingrenzung des Fürsten auf das ihm zugewiesene Land sollte die verheerenden
wirtschaftlichen und sozialen Entwicklungen, die Israel im Gefolge der Einführung der Monarchie gemacht hatte, in Zukunft schon im Keim ersticken. Die
Depotenzierung des Königs hatte somit auch eine soziale Zielsetzung. |

Die sich aus dem verschärften göttlichen Heiligkeitsanspruch ergebene He-
rauslösung des Tempels aus der königlichen Herrschaft und institutionelle und
ökonomische Verselbständigung der Priesterschaft hatte somit für die Prophetenschüler weitreichende politische und wirtschaftliche Konsequenzen. Die drei
staatlichen Institutionen Tempel, Palast und Hauptstadt, die vorexilisch in der
Verfügungsgewalt des sakralen Königs zusammengebunden waren, wurden terri-
torial und organisatorisch entflochten; dessen Gewalt wurde auf die Träger der
drei Institutionen, die Priester bzw. Leviten, die tribalen Autoritäten und den
Fürsten aufgeteilt. Dies bedeutete eine Entsakralisierung und Depotenzierung des
Königs; die Funktion des Fürsten wurde auf mehr repräsentative Aufgaben beschränkt. Es bedeutete eine Stärkung der tribalen Autoritäten, die durch das Königtum entmachtet worden waren. Und es bedeutete eine erhebliche Stärkung
der Priesterschaft; sie übernahm neben ihren spezifischen priesterlichen Aufgaben alle sakralen Funktionen des Königs, zuvorderst die Mittlerschaft zwischen
Gott und dem Volk, und die administrative Verwaltung des Tempels. Die verschärften Heiligkeitsanforderungen Gottes erzwangen also nicht nur eine Gewaltenteilung unter den drei menschlichen Funktionsträgern, sondern auch eine
klare institutionelle Trennung zwischen einem religiös-kultischen und einem
weltlich-politischen Bereich.

Versucht man das „theokratische Argument" der Ezechiel-Schüler mit dem
Fragenkatalog dieser Tagung aufzuschlüsseln, dann lässt sich folgendes zusammenfassend festhalten:

1. Die Ezechielschüler führen ihren Bruch mit der Staatskulttradition des vorexilischen Juda ausdrücklich auf eine göttliche Offenbarung zurück, die ihrem
prophetischen Meister widerfuhr (Ez 40,1–4). Sie arbeiteten die kultischen, politischen und wirtschaftlichen Implikationen dieser Offenbarung bis ins Einzelne
schriftlich aus, um damit die Überzeugungskraft ihrer Botschaft zu stärken.

2. Träger der „theokratischen Argumentation" ist eine kleine Gruppe prophetisch orientierter Reformpriester im babylonischen Exil, die wohl einer der

führenden Linien innerhalb der ehemaligen Jerusalemer Priesterschaft, der Zadokiden, nahestand,[15] aber offensichtlich im Streit mit den Priestern und Hoftheologen lag, die zur Entourage des exilierten Königs Jojachin und seiner Familie gehörten.[16] |

3. Die politischen Rahmenbedingungen der Auseinandersetzung sind gekennzeichnet durch den erfolgten Zusammenbruch des Staates Judas aufgrund der neubabylonischen Eroberungen in den Jahren 597 und 587 v. Chr. Die davidische Monarchie musste abdanken, der letzte überlebende König Jojachin lebte als Geisel am babylonischen Hof;[17] der Tempel war von Nebukadnezar nach einigem Zögern auch deswegen so brutal zerstört worden, weil er die religiöse Keimzelle der antibabylonischen Rebellionen gewesen war.[18] Die Reformpriester um den Propheten Ezechiel wollten die Zerstörung der staatlichen und kultischen Institution nutzen, um einen radikalen Neubeginn zu propagieren. Hinsichtlich ihres Ziels einer Verselbständigung von Tempel und Tempelpersonal waren sie vielleicht von babylonischen Vorbildern beeinflusst, da in Babylonien die Tempel als große Wirtschaftsbetriebe traditionell mehr Eigenständigkeit gegenüber der Krone bewahren konnten.

4. Die Prophetenschüler suchen mit ihrem Verfassungsentwurf die als falsch erkannte „repräsentative Theokratie", die im sakralen Königtum der Daviden institutionalisiert war, durch die neue Form einer institutionalisierten Theokratie zu ersetzen, in der die göttliche Herrschaft kritisch die Aufteilung und Begrenzung irdischer Macht erzwingt, die Funktion der Repräsentanz göttlicher Herrschaft auf den Tempel und die Priesterschaft beschränkt und dafür die politische Herrschaft von Fürst und Stammesführern verweltlicht.[19]

---

15 Vgl. die Sicherung der exklusiven Ansprüche der Zadokiden auf den Altardienst in Ez 40,46; 43,19; 44,15 f.; 48,11.
16 Vgl. Albertz, Exilszeit (Anm. 6), 89–91, 105–112. Letztere stehen wahrscheinlich hinter dem sog. „Deuteronomistischen Geschichtswerk" (Dtn 1–2. Kön 25*), das einen Neubeginn unter Führung eines Davididen befürwortete, vgl. Albertz, ebd., 216 f., 229–231. |
17 Vgl. 2. Kön 24,15; 25,27–30 und Albertz, Exilszeit (Anm. 6), 87–91.
18 Vgl. Rainer Albertz, Die Zerstörung des Jerusalemer Tempels 587 v. Chr. Historische Einordnung und religionspolitische Bedeutung, in: Zerstörungen des Jerusalemer Tempels, hrsg. v. Johannes Hahn (WUNT 147), Tübingen 2002, 23–39, bes. 32–38.
19 Auch diese neue Konzeption der Theokratie lässt sich, obwohl sie kritisch gegen die Vorstellung einer „repräsentativen Theokratie" gerichtet war, nicht als „identitäre Theokratie" im Sinne Assmanns, Herrschaft (Anm. 4), 48 f. bezeichnen, da weiter menschliche Funktionsträger die Herrschaft Gottes repräsentieren; jedoch wird die Repräsentation auf den kultischen Bereich eingeschränkt und dafür die politische Herrschaft säkularisiert. Mit Recht streicht Lang, Theokratie (Anm. 6), 182 heraus, dass der Verfassungsentwurf des Ezechiel eine typisch jüdische Ausformung des Theokratie-Gedankens darstellt; allerdings wird in seiner Darstellung nicht ganz klar,

5. Innerhalb des Buches Ezechiel haben die Prophetenschüler ihren Verfassungsentwurf ausführlich geschichtstheologisch begründet: Ein wesentlicher Grund für die Katastrophe war die Entweihung des Jerusalemer Tempels durch die Bevölkerung und die Könige gewesen; darum muss der neue Tempel nachhaltig gegen jegliche Art von Verunreinigung geschützt | werden. Da die schlimmste Verunreinigung die enge Verquickung von Thron und Altar darstellte, muss diese in Zukunft aufgelöst werden.

6. Die priesterlich orientierten Prophetenschüler vertreten einen Monopolanspruch nur bei der Regelung des kultischen Bereichs und beim Bau und der Verwaltung des Tempels. Über diesen Bereich hinaus will ihr theokratisch fundiertes Reformprogramm nur eine Rahmenordnung für die Gesellschaft und ihre Institutionen festschreiben. Innerhalb dieses Rahmens bleibt den politischen Funktionsträgern weitgehende Handlungsfreiheit. Im spätexilischen Diskurs, in dem um den möglichen Neuanfang Judas ausnahmslos mit „theokratischen Argumenten" gestritten wurde, waren die Ezechielschüler nur eine Stimme unter anderen.[20]

7. Mit ihrem „theokratischen Argument" greifen die Ezechielschüler tief in die Regelung des Kultes und die Organisation des Tempels ein und setzen in anderen Bereichen gewisse Standards, z. B. Gerechtigkeit bei der Landverteilung oder Beschränkung der Steuerlast. Indem sie die Repräsentation des Göttlichen auf den Bereich des Kultes beschränken, schaffen sie erstmals so etwas wie weltliche „Reservatsfelder".

8. Der prophetische Verfassungsentwurf will durch Worte überzeugen, er ist kein „Beitrag zur Militanz". Das schließt nicht aus, dass die Hoftheologen um Jojachin und seine Nachkommen den Text als unverschämten Angriff auf ihre Grundpositionen verstanden haben.

III Die Folgen: Grundlegung für ein königsloses Gemeinwesen mit Tempel und die Entwicklung zu einer „Hierokratie"

Natürlich konnte nur ein geringer Teil dieses radikalen prophetischen Verfassungsentwurfs in der nachexilischen Zeit verwirklicht werden; für eine vollstän-

---

dass nicht nur die königliche Macht stark eingeschränkt, sondern auch der priesterliche Einfluss begrenzt wird. Die Entwicklung zur Hierokratie in der hellenistischen Zeit ist als eine Abkehr vom Theokratie-Modell der Ezechielschule zu bewerten. |

20 Neben der prophetischen Deuterojesaja-Gruppe (Jes 40–55), den Hoftheologen hinter dem Deuteronomistischen Geschichtswerk (DtrG), den Reformbeamten hinter dem Deuteronomistischen Jeremiabuch (JerD) und den Sympathisanten der armen Landbevölkerung Judas hinter

dige Umsetzung hatte er eine ganze Reihe zu utopischer Züge, etwa den Plan einer gerechten Neuverteilung von Grund und Boden oder die Verlegung der Hauptstadt 10 km südlich vom Tempelberg. Außerdem hätten für den Bau einer so gewaltigen Tempelanlage, wie sie die Ezechielschüler visionär konzipiert hatten, im engen und ärmlichen Jerusalem der persischen Zeit schlicht der Platz und das Geld gefehlt.[21] |

Im Jahrzehnt nach der Rückkehr einer ersten Gruppe von Exilierten im Jahr 520 v. Chr. hatten erst einmal die Promotoren des alten staatskultischen Modells das Sagen; der Wiederaufbau des Tempels wurde auf Initiative des Jojachin-Enkels, Serubbabel, und des Enkels des letzten Jerusalemer Oberpriesters, Josua, die beide die Rückkehrergruppe angeführt hatten, in sehr viel bescheideneren Ausmaßen in Angriff genommen (Hag 1–2). Der Prophet Haggai hoffte sogar auf eine Wiedererrichtung der davidischen Monarchie unter Serubbabel (Hag 2,20–23).[22] Doch als dieses nationale Projekt scheiterte und Serubbabel – möglicherweise durch eine Intervention der Perser – von der politischen Bühne verschwand, schlug die Stunde der Reformpriester in der Nachfolge Ezechiels. Sie, die sowieso der Monarchie kritisch gegenüberstanden, nutzten das entstandene Machtvakuum und setzten die eigenständige Verwaltung des Tempels durch die Priesterschaft durch. Der noch aus dem Kreis der Hoftheologen stammende Hohepriester Josua wurde – offenbar weil er sich nicht den strikten Reinheitsregeln der Reformer anpassen wollte – unter Anklage gestellt und bald durch die zadokidischen Reformpriester verdrängt.[23] Dies wird aus den priesterlichen Texten des Pentateuchs erkennbar, die zwar im Einzelnen viele Dinge anders regeln, als von den

---

dem Deuteronomistischen Vierprophetenbuch (Hos, Am, Mi, Zeph), vgl. Albertz, Exilszeit (Anm. 6), 296–301, 216 f., 242–246, 184 f.

21 Zur historischen und sozialgeschichtlichen Rekonstruktion der frühnachexilischen Zeit s. genauer Albertz, Religionsgeschichte (Anm. 1), Bd. II, 468–495; Ders., Exilszeit (Anm. 6), 97–112. |

22 Dabei sah sich Haggai gezwungen, die göttliche Verwerfung Jojachins und seiner Nachkommen, die im Deuteronomistischen Jeremiabuchbuch ausgesprochen war (Jer 22,24–40), im Namen Gottes ausdrücklich aufzuheben.

23 Dies scheint hinter der visionären Szene von Sach 3,1–8 zu stehen, in der „der Satan", der hier zum ersten Mal als himmlischer Ankläger auftaucht, den Hohenpriester Josua bezichtigt, woraufhin dieser jedoch von Gott unter bestimmten Auflagen im Amt bestätigt wird. Dabei spielt die Reinheit seiner Kleidung und die gewissenhafte Aufsicht über den Tempel eine Rolle (V. 4 f.7). Der Text, der einen Einschub in die Nachtgesichte Sacharjas darstellt, stammt wohl aus dem Ende des 6. Jh. v. Chr., vgl. Jakob Wöhrle, Die frühen Sammlungen des Zwölfprophetenbuches. Entstehung und Komposition (BZAW 360), Berlin/New York 2006, 360 f. Er wurde wahrscheinlich von einem Anhänger der hoftheologischen Richtung formuliert, der nach dem Scheitern Serubbabels seine Hoffnung auf den Hohen Priester als Platzhalter für einen künftigen Davididen setzte (Sach 3,8). Doch haben sich diese Hoffnungen nicht erfüllt; die Davididen bleiben von der politischen Macht ausgeschlossen.

Ezechielschülern vorgesehen, zum Beispiel eine Versorgung der Priester und Levi-ten durch Steuern und Abgaben statt durch Selbstversorgung,[24] aber in wesentli-chen Positionen, etwa in der Ablehnung der staatskultischen Option, voll mit ihnen übereinstimmen.[25]

Zusammen mit den Reformbeamten, die hinter dem Deuteronomistischen Je-remiabuch standen und eine Wiedererrichtung der davidischen Dynastie aufs Schärfste ablehnten (Jer 22,24–30), bauten die Reformpries|ter in Juda ein sub-staatliches Gemeinwesen unter persischer Oberhoheit auf. Dieses bestand un-terhalb des persischen Statthalters und seiner Provinzverwaltung aus zwei judäischen Führungsgremien: dem laizistischen Ältestenrat und dem Priesterkol-legium.[26] In ihrer Differenzierung und gleichgewichtigen Zuordnung sind diese beiden Gremien durchaus mit dem Nebeneinander von Stammesführern und Priestern im Verfassungsentwurf der Ezechielschüler vergleichbar. Nur der „Fürst" war entfallen, bzw. wurde durch den persischen Statthalter ersetzt. Unter-halb der beiden judäischen Führungsgremien gab es noch eine Volksversamm-lung, die allerdings nur wenig Einfluss hatte. Die Gewaltenteilung zwischen laizis-tischen und priesterlichen Führungskräften, die der Verfassungsentwurf der Ezechielschüler vorgesehen hatte, wurde somit in der Provinz Juda des 5. Jhs. v. Chr. großteils verwirklicht.

Erst in spätpersischer und dann in hellenistischer Zeit, als der Tempel von Jerusalem zum ideellen und kultischen Mittelpunkt eines erstarkenden und welt-weit verbreiteten Judentums immer mehr wirtschaftliche Macht erhielt, überflü-gelte die Jerusalemer Priesterschaft den Ältestenrat an politischem Einfluss.[27] Da die Ptolemäer noch dazu darauf verzichteten, eigene Statthalter in der Provinz Juda einzusetzen, sondern dem Hohenpriester die Finanzhoheit übertrugen, ent-wickelte sich hier in hellenistischer Zeit erstmals so etwas wie eine „Hierokratie", in der die Jerusalemer Priesterschaft unter Leitung des Hohenpriesters neben ihren priesterlichen Pflichten auch administrative, wirtschaftliche und politische

---

24 Vgl. Ex 30,11–16; Lev 7,8.14.31–36; 22,1–16; Num 3,44–31; 18.
25 Vgl. Albertz, Religionsgeschichte (Anm. 1), Bd. II, 523–526. |
26 Vgl. schon Kurt Galling, Studien zur Geschichte Israels, Tübingen 1964, 162 f. zu den in einem Brief aus der jüdischen Garnison in Elephantine genannten Adressaten in Jerusalem; dazu Al-bertz, Religionsgeschichte (Anm. 1), Bd. II, 472 f.
27 In diese Richtung kann man eine Silbermünze mit der Legende „Joḥanan, der Priester" inter-pretieren, die aus den letzten Jahren des Persischen Reiches stammt, auch wenn unsicher bleibt, ob es sich dabei um den Hohepriester handelt, der damit über das Prägerecht verfügt hätte, vgl. Deborah W. Rooke, Zadok's Heirs. The Role and Development of the High Priesthood in Ancient Israel, Oxford 2000, 219–237, und Albertz, Religionsgeschichte (Anm. 1), Bd. II, 592–594. Mit Recht schließt Rooke die Existenz einer Hierokratie für den größten Teil der persischen Zeit aus (ebd., 218).

Aufgaben in der Provinzregierung übernahm (JesSir 50,2–4). Erst damit, dass nun die Priester den politischen Bereich usurpierten und der Hohepriester zu einer Art Vasallenkönig aufstieg, wurde die Selbstbeschränkung der priesterlichen Gewalt, die den Verfassungsentwurf des Ezechielbuches gekennzeichnet hatte, fallengelassen. Wenn der verweltlichte Priesterspross Josephus diese Priesterherrschaft im hellenistischen Juda mit dem von ihm neu geschaffenen Begriff „Theokratie" belegt,[28] dann redet er damit eine Verquickung | von geistlicher und politischer Herrschaft schön, die in der prophetischen Tradition des Judentums eigentlich schon längst überwunden gewesen war.

---

28 So Contra Apionem 2.164–165, in Anlehnung an die klassisch griechische Staatsformlehre, welche die Herrschaftsformen Monarchie, Demokratie und Aristokratie unterschied.

Eine himmlische UNO: Religiös fundierte Friedensvermittlung nach Jes 2,2–5

Nachdem dem ehemaligen Generalsekretär der UNO, Kofi Annan, vor zwei Wochen der Westfälische Friedenspreis im Rathaus von Münster verliehen wurde, soll in dieser Ringvorlesung ein Text aus der Hebräischen Bibel erneut ins Gespräch gebracht werden, dessen visionäre Aussage, dass einst die Völker ihre Waffen zu Pflugscharen und Winzermessern umschmieden und das Kriegshandwerk nicht mehr lernen werden (Jes 2,4), die Bemühungen um den Aufbau einer internationalen Friedensvermittlung, welche kriegerische Konflikte verhindert bzw. beilegt, seit den Haager Friedenskonferenzen 1899/1907, der Gründung des Völkerbundes im Jahre 1919 bis hin zur Gründung der UNO im Jahr 1945 beeinflusst hat.[1] Sinnfälligen Ausdruck bekam dieser Einfluss dadurch, dass die Sowjetunion der UNO im Jahr 1959 eine Bronzeskulptur von Jewgeni Wutschetitsch schenkte, welche – in der Manier des sozialistischen Realismus – einen Mann darstellt, der unter gewaltigen Hammerschlägen das Umschmieden eines Schwertes in Angriff nimmt und damit die prophetische Vision zu realisieren beginnt. Die Skulptur wurde trotz des damaligen Kalten Krieges im Garten der UNO am East River in New York aufgestellt, wo sie bis heute steht. Und nicht zufällig wählte die Friedensbewegung in der DDR in den 70er und 80er Jahren des vorigen Jahrhunderts gerade diese Skulptur, die den ‚offiziellen' Friedenswillen der Sowjetunion dokumentierte, zum Emblem für Ihren Widerstand gegen die Militarisierung der DDR. Der an das alttestamentliche Prophetenwort angelehnte Slogan ‚Schwerter zu Pflugscharen' wurde zur Parole der kirchlichen und politischen Friedensbewegung in Ost- und Westdeutschland gegen die Aufrüstung Europas mit atomaren Mittelstreckenraketen in den 80er Jahren;[2] und er ist es bis heute

---

1 Auch wenn sich ein direkter Einfluss in offiziellen Verlautbarungen der genannten Organisationen nicht nachweisen lässt, weist doch die Tatsache, dass selbst politikwissenschaftliche Publikationen über die UNO, ihre Vorgeschichte und ihre Zukunft das Motto ‚Swords into Plowshares' im Titel führen (Inis L. Claude, Swords into Plowshares. The Problems and Process of International Organization, New York [4]1971; Roy S. Lee (Hg.), Swords into Plowshares. Building Peace through the United Nations (Nijhof Law Specials 65), Leiden – New York 2006) auf einen untergründigen Zusammenhang.

2 In diesem Kontext gehören auch meine früheren Arbeiten zu diesem Text, s. Rainer Albertz, Shalom und Versöhnung. Alttestamentliche Kriegs- und Friedenstraditionen, in: Theodor Strohm – Bernhard Moltmann – Christoph Meier (Hgg.), Friede ist der „Weg zum Frieden". Dienst und Versöhnung im Auftrag der christlichen Gemeinde (Theologia Practica 18), München 1983, S. 16–29; Ders., Konfliktschlichtung durch Machtverzicht – Jesaja 2,2–5 auf dem Hintergrund der alttestamentlichen Kriegs- und Friedenstraditionen, in: Ders., Der Mensch als Hüter seiner Welt. Alttestamentliche Bibelarbeiten zu den Themen des konziliaren Prozesses, Stuttgart 1990, S. 114–131.

https://doi.org/10.1515/9783111202228-028

in der amerikanischen Friedensbewegung („Swords into Plowshares') gegen den von Präsident Bush und seiner Regierung initiierten Irak-Krieg.

Um zu erkunden, ob der Rückbezug auf den an die 2500 Jahre alten Text aus der Hebräischen Bibel im politischen Diskurs um die internationale Friedensvermittlung überhaupt sachgemäß ist, soll erstens sein richtiges Verständnis abgesichert werden. Um diesen kurzen Text genauer zu verstehen, wird zweitens sein traditionsgeschichtlicher Hintergrund ausgeleuchtet. Drittens wird versucht den möglichen geschichtlichen Hintergrund des Textes zu erkunden. Viertens soll seine kontextuelle Einbettung untersucht werden, um | damit etwas über die Rahmenbedingungen für das im Text geschilderte göttliche Friedenshandeln herauszubekommen. Und schließlich sollen wichtige Merkmale der göttlichen Friedensvermittlung herausgearbeitet werden, um damit Einsichten zur Mediation in internationalen Konflikten zu gewinnen, und zwar auch und gerade für deren religiöse Dimension. Dabei soll es auch um die Frage gehen, die Joachim Gauck letzte Woche aufgeworfen hat, ob Wahrheit und Versöhnung konkurrierende Ziele oder gar Gegensätze bei der Bearbeitung von Konflikten darstellen oder nicht doch bei jeder wirklich gelungenen Mediation zusammenkommen müssen.

1 Absicherung des Textverständnisses

Die prophetische Heilsschilderung Jes 2,2–5 kommt in ihrem Kern fast wortgleich noch einmal in Mi 4,1–5 vor. Nur die abschließenden Applikationen weichen ab. Heißt es in Jes 2,4: ‚Haus Jakobs, kommt, lasst uns gehen im Lichte JHWHs!', so werden in Mi 4,4–5 die Friedensfolgen und die Konsequenzen für die Zionsgemeinde weiter ausgemalt:

Mi 4,4a	Dann wird ein jeder unter seinem Weinstock
	und unter seinem Feigenbaum sitzen,
	und keiner wird da sein, der sie aufschreckt.
4b	Denn der Mund JHWHs hat es gesprochen.
5	Wenn auch alle Völker (ihren Weg) gehen,
	ein jeder im Namen seines Gottes,
	so wollen wir doch (unseren Weg) im Namen JHWHs, unseres Gottes,
	gehen, auf immer und ewig.

Deutlich wird aus diesen Abweichungen am Ende, dass sich das eigentliche Prophetenwort auf die ersten drei Verse beschränkt (Jes 2,2–4 // Mi 4,1–3). Es gibt in der alttestamentlichen Wissenschaft eine lange Debatte über die Frage, ob der Jesaja- vom Michatext oder umgekehrt der Micha- vom Jesajatext abhängt, bzw. beide Fassungen auf eine gemeinsame Quelle zurückgehen, die uns nicht mehr erhalten ist.[3] Die Streitfrage ist mit zusätzlichen, sich aus der Redaktionsgeschichte des Michabuches ergebenden Argumenten von Jakob Wöhrle[4] in seiner gerade veröffentlichten Habilitationsschrift in der Richtung entschieden worden, dass der Jesaja-Text die ältere Textform darstellt. Ich möchte mich darum auf diese beschränken.

Liest man Jes 2,2–4 in der Übersetzung Martin Luthers in der Weimariana von 1534, die bis in die Lutherbibeln vor der Revision von 1975 – abgesehen von orthographischen Angleichungen – fast wörtlich durchgehalten wurde, dann scheint die prophetische Heilsschilderung kaum etwas mit Friedensvermittlung zu tun zu haben. Sie lautet:[5] |

Jes 2,2a	Es wird zur letzten zeit der berg da des HERRN haus ist /
	zugericht werden / höher denn alle berge/
	und uber alle hügel erhaben werden /
2b	Und werden alle Heiden dazu lauffen /
3a	und viel völcker hingehen / und sagen /
	Kompt, last uns auff den berg des HERRN gehen /
	zum hause des Gottes Jacob /
3b	das er uns lere seine wege / und wir wandeln auf seinen steigen /
	Denn von Zion wird das Gesetz ausgehen /
	und des HERRN wort von Jerusalem /
4	Und er wird richten unter den Heiden / und straffen viel völcker /
	da werden sie jre schwerter zu pflugscharen /
	und jre spiesse zu sicheln machen /
	Denn es wird kein volck wider das ander ein schwerd auffheben /
	und werden fort nicht mehr kriegen lernen /

Die ganze prophetische Schilderung handelt nach Luthers Lesart von der letzten Zeit, der Endzeit. Die Heiden kommen nach Jerusalem, um über Gottes Wege belehrt zu werden, d.h. über die von Gott geforderten Verhaltensweisen, wie sie in dem Gesetz,[6] d.h. dem mosaischen Gesetz, niedergelegt sind. Darauf wird Gott die Heiden einem strafenden Völkergericht unterziehen. Es geht also nicht um irgendeine Art von göttlicher Mediation, sondern um den Vorgang einer Bekeh-

---

3 Zur Diskussion vgl. Otto Kaiser, Das Buch des Propheten Jesaja. Kapitel 1–12 (ATD 17), Göttingen ⁵1981, S. 63, insbes. Anm. 14; dazu Jakob Wöhrle, Die frühen Sammlungen des Zwölfprophetenbuches. Entstehung und Komposition (BZAW 360), Berlin – New York 2006, S. 156–158.
4 Vgl. Jakob Wöhrle, Der Abschluss des Zwölfprophetenbuches. Buchübergreifende Redaktionsprozesse in den späten Sammlungen (BZAW 389), Berlin – New York 2008, S. 346–350.
5 S. Die Luther-Bibel von 1534. Vollständiger Nachdruck, 2 Bde., Köln 2002, Bd. 2: II. Hinzugefügt wurde die Zählung der Verse, die es zu Luthers Zeiten noch nicht gab. Die Schreibung der Umlaute wurde dem heutigen Gebrauch angepasst.
6 Luther setzte hier den Artikel, der im hebräischen Original nicht steht!

rung und Bestrafung der Völker. Und nur weil die Heiden sich zum Judentum bzw. Christentum bekehrt und das göttliche Gericht erfahren haben, sind sie bereit, auf ihre Waffen zu verzichten. In diesem Sinne deutete noch Otto Kaiser 1978 den Text, wenn er schreibt, Gott werde „einst in der Vollendung der wirren Weltgeschichte als der erscheinen, der allein seiner Menschheit durch sein richtendes und den Menschen seiner Sünde überführendes Wort dauernden Frieden geben kann"[7]. Auch er versteht den Text ausdrücklich als „eschatologisch"[8].[9]

Doch dieses Textverständnis hat erstens sachliche Schwierigkeiten: Es kann nicht erklären, warum das göttliche Strafgericht der freiwilligen Bekehrung der Völker noch folgen sollte. Kaisers Erklärungsversuch: „Sie wissen, dass sie nur dort Anleitung für ein Leben finden können, mit dem sie vor dem Gericht Gottes bestehen"[10] ist einigermaßen künstlich und würde ja bedeuten, dass das göttliche Gericht nur noch eine reine Formsache darstellt. Auch ist nicht verständlich, warum die Völker mit so betonter Freiwilligkeit zu ihrem Strafgericht auf dem Zionberg erscheinen sollten. Und schließlich bleibt unverständlich, warum Bekehrung und Gericht ausgerechnet eine allgemeine Abrüstung zur Folge haben sollte. Im Gesetz des Mose wird der Krieg zwar eingeschränkt (Dtn 20), aber nicht verboten.[11]

Zweitens stößt ein solches Textverständnis auf erhebliche philologische Schwierigkeiten: Das gilt besonders für den zentralen Vers 4a, den Luther auf das Endgericht Gottes bezog: Wo Luther unscharf übersetzte ‚Und er wird *richten unter* den Heiden ...‘[12] steht im hebräischen Text וְשָׁפַט בֵּין הַגּוֹיִם *wešāfaṭ | bēn haggōjīm* ‚er wird richten zwischen den Heiden‘, oder besser ‚den Völkern‘. Die hebräische Präposition בֵּין *bēn* heißt ‚zwischen‘ und nicht ‚unter‘; und an den

---

7 Otto Kaiser, Der Prophet Jesaja. Kapitel 1–12 (ATD 17), Göttingen ⁴1978, S. 22.

8 Kaiser, Jesaja (wie Anm. 7), S. 23.

9 Die willige Unterwerfung der Völker unter Gottes Schiedsspruch führt Kaiser, Jesaja (wie Anm. 7), S. 22 dementsprechend auf deren „Neuschöpfung" zurück, von der allerdings im Text nichts steht. In der stark umgearbeiteten fünften Auflage seines Kommentars löst sich Kaiser ein Stück weit von der durch Luther vorgegebenen Sicht, hält aber daran fest, dass das mosaische Gesetz im Hintergrund der prophetischen Konfliktschlichtung steht. Er spricht zwar nicht mehr von einer „Bekehrung der Völker" (ebd., S. 22), aber von einer „Einbeziehung aller Völker in die Jerusalemer Theokratie", Kaiser, Buch Jesaja (wie Anm. 3), S. 65.

10 Kaiser, Jesaja (wie Anm. 7), S. 21.

11 Dies ist ein klares sachliches Argument gegen neuere, aus übergreifenden theologischen Anliegen gespeiste Versuche, die Tora vom Zion doch wieder mit der Tora vom Sinai gleichzusetzen (Ludger Schwienhorst-Schönberger, Zion – Ort der Tora. Überlegungen zu Mi 4,1–3, in: Ferdinand Hahn u. a. (Hgg.), Zion – Ort der Begegnung. FS L. Klein (BBB 90), Bodenheim 1993, S. 107–125, S. 117–121; Irmtraud Fischer, Tora für Israel – Tora für die Völker. Das Konzept des Jesajabuches (SBS 164), Stuttgart 1995, S. 122).

12 Ähnlich auch die King James Version von 1611/1769: „he shall judge among the nations ...".

14 Stellen, wo sie mit dem Verb שָׁפַט *šāfaṭ* ‚richten' verbunden steht, ist gemeint, dass Gott oder ein Mensch zwischen den konkurrierenden Rechtsansprüchen zweier Personen oder Gruppen entscheidet und damit einen rechtlichen Ausgleich zwischen diesen herbeiführt.[13] Das heißt, es geht in Jes 2,4a nicht um ein göttliches Gericht an den Völkern, sondern um ein göttliches Schiedsgericht zwischen den Völkern. Dann kann aber auch im parallelen Versteil kein Strafgericht gemeint sein, so wie Luther übersetzte ‚er wird *strafen* viele Völker'. Zwar hat das verwendete hebräische Verb הוֹכִיחַ *hōkīaḥ* (יכח *jākaḥ* im *Hif'il*) ein weites Bedeutungsspektrum, das von ‚zurechtweisen' (Gen 21,25; Hi 5,17; 6,26 u. ö.), ‚tadeln' (Hi 6,25), ‚richten' (Gen 31,37[ebenfalls mit בֵּין].42; Jes 11,3), ‚rechten' (Hi 9,33), ‚beweisen' (Hi 19,5) bis hin zu ‚zur Rechenschaft ziehen' (2. Kön 19,4; Prov 30,6), ‚züchtigen' (Ps 6,2; 38,2) und ‚strafen' (2. Sam 7,14; Jer 2,19) reicht und damit auf der Grenze zwischen pädagogischer und juristischer Semantik angesiedelt ist. Doch mit der Präposition לְ *lě* ‚für', die in Jes 2,4 verwendet wird, legt sich die Bedeutung ‚jemandem Recht verschaffen' nahe (vgl. Jes 11,4; Hi 16,21).[14] Und dabei kann das Partizip des Verbs, מוֹכִיחַ *mōkīaḥ*, mehrfach den ‚Schiedsrichter' bezeichnen, der zwischen zwei Personen oder Parteien (Hi 9,33; Ez 3,26[15]), insbesondere im örtlichen Torgericht (Am 5,10; Jes 29,21) einen gerechten Ausgleich zu erreichen sucht und damit der schwächeren Partei gegen die stärkere ihr Recht verschafft. Auch in diesem zweiten Stichos geht es also um einen rechtlichen Ausgleich zwischen den Völkern, der auch durch Einsatz pädagogischer Mittel erreicht werden kann. Damit hat unser prophetischer Text in der Tat mit Mediation zu tun.

Diese philologische Klarstellung, die schon Hans Wildberger[16] in seinem Jesajakommentar vorgenommen hat, ist heute fast allgemein akzeptiert[17] und ist in

---

13 Außer in Jes 2,4 und Mi 4,3 noch in Gen 16,5; 31,53; Ex 18,16; Num 35,24; Dtn 1,16; Ri 11,27; 1. Sam 24,13.16; Jes 5,3; Ez 34,17.20.22; in Ex 18,16; Num 35,24. Dtn 1,16 wird dabei mit der Wendung ausdrücklich das Wirken menschlicher Richter im zivilen und sakralen Rechtsverfahren bezeichnet.

14 Sonst wird die Präposition nur noch wenige Male verwendet, wo vom ‚Zurechtweisen' einer Person die Rede ist (Prov 9,7.8; 15,12); in den meisten Fällen wird bei dieser Bedeutung das Verb mit dem Akkusativ konstruiert (Gen 21,25; Lev 19,17; Hos 4,4; Ps 50,8.21; 105,14; 141,5; Hi 5,17; 6,26; 13,10; 22,4; 40,2). Mit לְ *lě* und Akkusativ hat das Verb in Gen 24,14.44 die Sonderbedeutung ‚jemandem jemand zuweisen'.

15 In Ez 3,26 ist dabei sogar mehr an einen Anwalt gedacht, der für Israel bei Gott eintritt. Um dem Propheten Ezechiel diese Funktion zu versagen, wird er bis zur Erfüllung seiner Gerichtsbotschaft mit Stummheit geschlagen; vgl. Rainer Albertz, Die Exilszeit. 6. Jahrhundert v. Chr. (BE 7), Stuttgart 2001, S. 267.

16 Hans Wildberger, Jesaja (BK X/1), Neukirchen-Vluyn 1972, S. 83–86.

17 Vgl. etwa Peter Höffken, Das Buch Jesaja. Kapitel 1–39 (NSKAT 18/1), Stuttgart 1993, S. 47 f.; John T. Willis, Isaiah 2:2–5 and the Psalms of Zion, in: Craig C. Broyles – Craig A. Evans (Hgg.),

die neuen Bibelübersetzungen übernommen worden.[18] Durch sie erhält der Text
nach hinten einen klaren Zusammenhang: Weil Gott auf dem Zion den Völkern
ihre Konflikte geschlichtet hat, können sie auf ihre Waffen verzichten (Jes 2,4b).
Aber auch nach vorne hin zu Vers 3 wird nun ein Zusammenhang erkennbar:
Mit der Tora und dem Wort JHWHs, das von Jerusalem ausgeht, ist nicht das
Gesetz des Mose, sondern eben die konfliktschlichtende Weisung Gottes gemeint,
die den Zion für die Völker so anziehend macht. „Tora" hat in der hebräischen
Bibel ein weites Bedeutungsspektrum: Es kann die Weisung der Mutter an ihren
Sohn (Prov 1,8), die Weisung eines Priesters an die Laien (Hag 2,10 ff.), das (deute-
ronomische) Gesetz des Mose (2. Kön 23,24) oder aber als zusammenfassender
Begriff die Gesetze und Verheißungen der Fünf Bücher Mose (Pentateuch) bezeichnen (Mal 3,22). Hier im Jesajabuch meint der hebräische Begriff תורה *tōrāh*
‚Weisung' neben דבר *dābār* ‚Wort' eindeutig das weisende und klärende Prophetenwort im Namen Gottes (Jes 1,10; 5,24; 30,9; vgl. 8,16). Mit der Wahl dieser Begrif-
fe wird angedeutet, | an welche Art der Vermittlung bei der Mediation hier ge-
dacht ist.[19] Damit sind aber mit den ‚Wegen' und ‚Pfaden' Gottes in V. 3a, auf
denen die Völker wandeln wollen, nicht die gottgewollten Wege der Frommen
(Ps 1,6), sondern schlicht die Wege gemeint, die Gottes konfliktschlichtende Weisung eröffnet. Es geht in V. 3 also gar nicht um eine Bekehrung der Völker.[20] Die
Völker erklären nur, dass sie die konfliktschlichtenden Weisungen dieses Gottes
auf dem Zion akzeptieren wollen, mehr nicht.

Bleibt damit die Zukunftsschau von Jes 2 noch relativ nah an der geschichtlichen Realität einer in politischen Konflikten und religiös gespaltenen Völkerwelt,
so will sie darum wahrscheinlich gar nicht von einer Endzeit reden, die jenseits

---

Writing and Reading the Scroll of Isaiah. Studies of an Interpretive Tradition (VT.S 70/1), Leiden
u. a. 1997, S. 295–316, S. 303 f.; Ulrich Berges, Das Buch Jesaja. Komposition und Endgestalt
(HBS 16), Freiburg u. a. 1998, S. 74 f.; Baruch J. Schwartz, Torah from Zion. Isaiah's Temple Vision
(Isaiah 2,1–4), in: Alberdina Houtman (Hg.), Sanctity of Time and Space (JChPS 1), Leiden u. a.
1998, S. 11–26, S. 17; Helmut Utzschneider, Michas Reise in die Zeit. Studien zum Drama als Genre
prophetischer Literatur des Alten Testaments (SBS 180), Stuttgart 1999, S. 157 f.; Willem A. M.
Beuken, Jesaja 1–12 (HThKAT), Freiburg u. a. 2003, S. 92–94.

18 So etwa die revidierte Elberfelder Bibel 1993 und die Neue Zürcher Bibel 2007. Die Einheits-
übersetzung bietet: ‚Er spricht Recht im Streit der Völker, / er weist viele Nationen zurecht'; im
ersten Stichos ist sie sehr frei, trifft aber sachlich ungefähr das Richtige. Durch die Wortwahl
und den zweiten Stichos wird allerdings die hoheitlich tadelnde Seite des göttlichen Schlichtens
problematisch hervorgekehrt.

19 Dazu s. unten vor Fußnote 45.

20 Wo eine solche in den Texten der Hebräischen Bibel erwartet wird, wird eine völlig abwei-
chende Terminologie verwendet: לוה *lāwāh nifal* ‚sich anschließen' (Sach 2,15; vgl. Jes 56,3.6); mit
Ausdrücken des Anbetens und Verehrens (1. Kön 8,41–43; Jes 45,23; Zeph 2,11; 3,9 f.; Sach 8,20–22;
Ps 86,9; 102,23) oder mit Ausdrücken Sich-Bekehrens Jer 3,17; 16,19–21; Ps 22,28.

der Geschichte liegt. Die hebräische Wendung באחרית הימים *bĕ'aḥarīt hajjāmīm* in Jes 2,2 heißt zwar wörtlich ‚am Ende der Tage‘, und konnte auch in späten Texten in eben diesem Sinne verstanden werden (Ez 38,16; Dan 10,14). Doch bevor diese apokalyptische Konzeption einer Endzeit ausgebildet wurde, bezeichnet sie meistens wie auch die parallele babylonische Wendung *ina aḥrat ūmi* einfach eine fernere, noch unbestimmte Zukunft (Gen 49,1; Num 24,14 u. ö.).[21]

Damit sind die philologischen und sachlichen Probleme von Jes 2,2–4 soweit geklärt, dass der Text – sachgerechter als durch Luther geschehen – folgendermaßen übersetzt werden kann:

Jes 2,2a	Es wird geschehen in zukünftigen Tagen,
	da wird fest gegründet sein der Berg des Hauses JHWHs
	an der Spitze der Berge
	und wird überragen die Hügel.
2b	Dann werden zu ihm alle Völker strömen,[22]
3a	und viele Nationen werden hinziehen und sprechen:
	„Auf, wir wollen zum Berg JHWHs hinaufziehen,
	zum Haus des Gottes Jakobs!
3b	Dass er uns belehre über seine Wege
	und wir auf seinen Pfaden wandeln.
	Denn vom Zion geht Weisung aus
	und das Wort JHWHs von Jerusalem."
4a	Dann wird er Recht sprechen zwischen den Völkern
	und Recht schaffen (als Schlichter auftreten) für viele Nationen.
4b	Dann werden sie ihre Schwerter zu Pflugscharen umschmieden
	und ihre Speere zu Winzermessern.
	Kein Volk wird mehr gegen ein anderes das Schwert erheben,
	und sie werden nicht mehr das Kriegshandwerk lernen.

---

21 So mit Recht erneut auch Schwartz, Torah from Zion (wie Anm. 17), S. 13 f.
22 Ebd., S. 14 f. und Beuken, Jesaja (wie Anm. 17), S. 88 plädieren wegen der Ungewöhnlichkeit der Vorstellung, dass die Völker wie ein Fluss strömen werden (ונהרו *nāharū*) dafür, das Verb nicht von נהר I ‚Strom‘, sondern von נהר II ‚strahlen‘ abzuleiten. Doch wirkt die Übersetzung Beukens ‚Alle Nationen starren strahlend auf ihn‘ gekünstelt, und die Übersetzung von Schwartz ‚so that all nations will see it‘ hat sich schon weit von der Wurzelbedeutung entfernt. Schwartz’ Bedenken gegen die traditionelle Übersetzung ist von dem berechtigten Vorbehalt gegen die Auffassung getragen (Schwartz, Torah from Zion (wie Anm. 17), S. 16 f.), dass in Jes 2 von einer Bekehrung aller Völker die Rede sei. Aber deswegen braucht man nicht die Anknüpfung an das Motiv der Völkerwallfahrt zu leugnen (vgl. die Entsprechung zwischen Jes 2,3a und Ps 122,1). Für die traditionelle Übersetzung spricht der Parallelismus zwischen Jes 2,2b und 3a und die Parallele Jer 51,44.

Nach dieser korrigierten Lesart wird in einer fernen Zukunft der Zion, der Jerusalemer Tempelberg, zum höchsten Berg der Region erhöht werden.[23] Dann werden alle Völker zu diesem weithin sichtbaren Markierungspunkt der Welt herbeiströmen, um sich dort ihre Konflikte schlichten zu lassen. Und dabei üben die konfliktschlichtenden Weisungen des dort anwesenden | Gottes eine solche Attraktivität aus, dass die Völker freiwillig kommen und die göttlichen Schiedssprüche wie selbstverständlich akzeptieren. Darum werden sie – nach Hause zurückgekehrt – selber ihre überflüssig gewordenen Waffen zerstören und die in ihnen gebundenen Rohstoffe in nützlicheres Ackergerät umwandeln. So wird die kriegerische Austragung der Konflikte aufhören und das Kriegshandwerk vergessen werden wie andere überflüssig gewordene Kulturtechniken auch. Der Text handelt also in der Tat von einer wunderbaren göttlichen Friedensvermittlung, einer Art himmlischer UNO in Jerusalem, die mit ihrer gelingenden Mediation alle Schwierigkeiten und Misserfolge unserer irdischen UNO weit hinter sich lässt.

2 Traditionsgeschichtlicher Hintergrund

Die Besonderheiten dieses nur knapp skizzierten prophetischen Konzeptes einer göttlichen Friedensvermittlung in der Stadt Jerusalem werden erst erkennbar, wenn man sie auf ihrem traditionsgeschichtlichen Hintergrund betrachtet. Obwohl das semitische Wort für Friede *salīmu, salām, šalōm* o.ä. in ihrem Namen anklingt, war der Stadt Jerusalem die zugedachte Rolle eines Zentrums für göttliche Friedensvermittlung nicht in die Wiege gelegt. Jerusalem war nie überregionales Heiligtum wie etwa Delphi gewesen, zu dessen Rolle die politische Konfliktschlichtung von alters gehört hätte. In israelitischer Zeit war es vielmehr Staatstempel und königliche Kapelle zuerst des vereinten Davidisch-Salomonischen Reiches und dann des judäischen Königreichs gewesen und darum institutionell und ideologisch fest in diesen Staat eingebunden. Bis zur Zerstörung des ersten Jerusalemer Tempels im Jahr 587 v. Chr. waren dessen Priester königliche Beamte. Und die Jerusalemer Königs- und Tempeltheologie diente – in Anlehnung an vorderorientalische Vorbilder[24] – primär der Legitimation und Absicherung der davidischen Dynastie und ihres Herrschaftsbereichs.[25]

---

23 Dies ist das einzige Element der Heilsschilderung, das die vorfindliche Realität völlig sprengt. Der Jerusalemer Tempelberg ist mit seinen 734 m über N.N. ein Stück niedriger als der Ölberg im Osten (810 m) und der Südwesthügel (765 m).

24 Zur vorderorientalischen Kriegs- und Friedenstheologie vgl. den Überblick von Eckart Otto, Krieg und Frieden in der Hebräischen Bibel und im Alten Orient. Aspekte für eine Friedensordnung in der Moderne (Theologie und Frieden 18), Stuttgart 1999, S. 13–75.

25 Zur Jerusalemer Königs- und Tempeltheologie vgl. zusammenfassend Rainer Albertz, Religionsgeschichte Israels in alttestamentlicher Zeit, 2 Bde. (GAT 8/1–2), Göttingen ²1996/97, S. 172–210;

Charakteristisch für die ältere Jerusalemer Königs- und Tempeltheologie, die uns vor allem in den Königs- und Zionspsalmen überliefert ist, ist eine fast vollständige Identifizierung JHWHs mit der politischen Herrschaft des Königs. Nach Ps 2,1–6 bändigt und regiert JHWH die aufbegehrende Völkerwelt mit Hilfe des davidischen Königs; und der davidische König führt mit seinen Eroberungskriegen JHWHs Auftrag aus:

Ps 2,8	Erbitte von mir, dann will ich dir Völker zum Erbe geben
	und zum Besitz die Enden der Welt.
9	Du sollst sie zerschmettern mit eisernem Stab
	wie Töpfergeschirr sie zertrümmern.

In Erfüllung dieses göttlichen Auftrages setzt der König zugleich die Anerkennung JHWHs in der Welt durch: |

Ps 2,10	Doch nun, ihr Könige, werdet klug,
	lasst euch warnen, ihr Herrscher der Erde!
11a	Dienet JHWH mit Furcht,
11b.12aα	,mit Zittern küsst seine Füße'!
12aβ	Dass er nicht in Zorn gerät
	und ihr umkommt auf (eurem) Weg,
	denn leicht kann entbrennen sein Zorn.[26]

Die Bändigung der Völkerwelt war nach dieser Theologie nur in der Weise einer militärischen Unterwerfung vorstellbar.

Weil nun die göttliche Herrschaft über die Welt universale Züge trägt, wurde in der Jerusalemer Königstheologie auch die Herrschaft des davidischen Königs universal konzipiert, wie die Königsfürbitte Ps 72 verdeutlicht:

Ps 72,8	Er möge herrschen von Meer zu Meer,
	vom Strom bis an die Enden der Erde!
9	Vor ihm mögen knien Wüstenbewohner,
	und seine Feinde mögen Staub lecken!
10	Die Könige von Tarsis und die Inseln mögen Gaben bringen,
	die Könige von Scheba und Saba mögen Tribut entrichten!

Othmar Keel, Die Geschichte Jerusalems und die Entstehung des Monotheismus, 2 Bde. (Orte und Landschaften der Bibel IV,1–2), Göttingen 2007, S. 733–740.

26 In Vers 11b und 12aα ist der hebräische Text gestört; die beiden Satzteile müssen zusammengezogen werden. Vers 12b ist eine spätere Ergänzung des Königspsalms aus der Zeit, als er schon messianisch verstanden wurde.

11   So mögen sich ihm unterwerfen alle Könige,
        alle Völker mögen ihm dienen.[27]

Auch wenn die judäischen Könige nur wenig Gelegenheit hatten, eine solche Weltherrschaft auch nur ansatzweise zu realisieren, ließ sich von der Jerusalemer
Königstheologie her jeder nur mögliche Angriffskrieg legitimieren.

Auch die Jerusalemer Tempeltheologie trug universale Züge: Der Jerusalemer
Tempelberg wird hier als Weltmittelpunkt angesehen und mit dem mythischen
Götterberg im Norden gleichgesetzt, der als Weltachse die ganze Erde trägt:

Ps 48,2   Groß ist JHWH und sehr zu preisen in der Stadt unseres Gottes,
           sein heiliger Berg,
3   der schöne Hügel, die Wonne der ganzen Welt,
           der Berg Zion im äußersten Norden,
           die Stadt eines großen Königs.

Weil JHWH in der Gottesstadt Jerusalem als unmittelbar anwesend gedacht wird,
erscheint diese als unzerstörbar gegenüber den gegen sie anbrausenden Chaos-
wassern (Ps 46,2–4) und als unzerstörbar gegenüber den gegen sie anstürmenden
Völkern:

Ps 46,5   Eines Stromes Arme erfreuen die Gottesstadt,
           die heiligste der Wohnungen Eljons.
6   Gott ist in ihrer Mitte, so wankt sie nicht,
           es hilft ihr Gott beim Anbruch des Morgens. |

---

27 In jüngster Zeit mehren sich die Stimmen, die dafür plädieren, Ps 72,8–11 einschließlich V. 15
und V. 17 ayb, die ebenfalls die Weltherrschaft des Königs im Auge haben, für eine spätere
Ergänzung zu betrachten (Erich Zenger, „Es sollen sich niederwerfen vor ihm alle Könige"
(Ps 72,11). Redaktionsgeschichtliche Beobachtungen zu Ps 72 und zum Programm des messianischen Psalters Ps 2–89, in: Eckart Otto – Ders. (Hgg.), „Mein Sohn bist du" (Ps 2,7). Studien zu
den Königspsalmen (SBS 192), Stuttgart 2002, S. 66–93, S. 66–69; Bernd Janowski, Die Frucht der
Gerechtigkeit. Psalm 72 und die judäische Königstheologie, in: ebd., S. 66–134, S. 101–105; Martin
Arneth, Psalm 72 in seinen altorientalischen Kontexten, in: ebd., S. 135–172, S. 150–154). Doch sind
die dafür vorgebrachten sachlichen und kompositionellen Argumente keineswegs zwingend; und
die Kontextbezüge lassen sich in verschiedene Richtungen interpretieren. Doch selbst wenn sie
Bestand hätten, ist die Zugehörigkeit der Weltherrschaftskonzeption zur judäischen Königstheo-
logie durch Ps 2,8–12a und 89,26.28 gesichert. Eine Ansetzung von Ps 72,8–11 nach dem Untergang
des davidischen Königtums bleibt auch nach Zengers Versuch einer messianischen Deutung
(S. 80–91) schwierig, da der Text die Ausübung der Weltherrschaft in aller Drastik schildert, ohne
dass eine kritische Distanz sichtbar würde. Für die nachexilische Zeit ist eher eine kritische
Brechung der Jerusalemer Königstheologie typisch, vgl. Sach 9,9 f. und Wöhrle, Abschluss des
Zwölfprophetenbuches (wie Anm. 4), S. 174–189. Zur kritischen Brechung der Jerusalemer Tempeltheologie s. unten nach Fußnote 31.

> 7   Es mögen brausen die Völker, es mögen schwanken die Königreiche.
>   Er donnert drein, da wogt die Erde.
> 8   JHWH-Zebaoth ist mit uns,
>   eine Zuflucht für uns ist der Gott Jakobs.

Auch wenn hier JHWH fast vollständig mit Jerusalem identifiziert wird, hat die Zionstheologie einen etwas defensiveren Charakter als die Königstheologie, sie zielt vornehmlich auf eine Absicherung der Hauptstadt. Dabei strahlt, wie die letzte Strophe von Ps 46 deutlich macht, Gottes machtvoller Einsatz für seine Stadt auch befriedend auf die ganze Welt aus:

> Ps 46,9   Auf, schaut die Werke JHWHs,
>   der Entsetzen verbreitet auf Erden.
> 10   Der den Kriegen ein Ende macht bis an das Ende der Erde,
>   den Bogen zerbricht und den Speer zerschlägt,
>   die Schilde verbrennt im Feuer.
> 11   „Lasst ab und erkennt, dass ich Gott bin,
>   dass ich erhaben bin über die Völker,
>   erhaben auf Erden!"

Allerdings unterscheidet sich dieses universale Frieden stiftende Handeln Gottes deutlich von dem in Jes 2.[28] Das Zerbrechen der Waffen ist, wie die assyrischen Parallelen belegen,[29] eine demütigende Siegerpose, die den schon besiegten und am Boden liegenden Feind noch zusätzlich demütigt. Das Friedensreich der ursprünglichen Zionstheologie beruht somit nicht auf Mediation, sondern – ähnlich wie die Königstheologie – auf einer Unterwerfung und Entmachtung der Völker. Es ist ein Friede unter israelitischer bzw. judäischer Vorherrschaft, der *pax assyri-*

---

28 Weil es beide Male Gott ist, der den Frieden schafft, werden diese Differenzen bei Willis, Isaiah (wie Anm. 17), S. 305 f.; Otto, Krieg und Frieden (wie Anm. 24), S. 116 f.; Beuken, Jesaja (wie Anm. 17), S. 93; Erich Zenger, „Erhebe dich doch als Hilfe für uns!". Die Komposition Ps 42–44; 46–48 als theologische Auseinandersetzung mit dem Exil, in: Ingo Kottsieper – Rüdiger Schmitt – Jakob Wöhrle (Hgg.), Berührungspunkte. Studien zur Sozial- und Religionsgeschichte Israels und seiner Umwelt. FS R. Albertz (AOAT 350), Münster 2008, S. 295–316, S. 312 f. eingeebnet. Die Verwandtschaft, in die damit Ps 46,9–12 zu Jes 2,2–4 gerät, ist dabei für Otto und Zenger ein wesentlicher Grund, in diesen Versen eine spätere Ergänzung zu Ps 46,2–8 zu sehen, die erst aus der Exilszeit stamme.

29 S. Wolfram von Soden, Akkadisches Handwörterbuch, Bd. 3, Wiesbaden 1981, Sp. 1206, s. v. *šebēru* ‚zerbrechen'; vgl. die Darstellung auf einem Relief Assurbanipals aus Ninive bei Ottmar Keel, Die Welt der altorientalischen Bildsymbolik und das Alte Testament am Beispiel der Psalmen, Zürich – Neukirchen-Vluyn 1972, S. 220, Nr. 328. Eine ähnliche Symbolik kannte auch Ägypten, vgl. ebd., S. 91. Das Zerbrechen des Bogens ist auch in Hos 1,5; Jer 49,35 Symbol für die totale Niederlage, die JHWH einem Volk beibringt.

ca oder der *pax romana* vergleichbar. Angriffe auf Jerusalem wie auch mögliche Konflikte zwischen den Völkern werden durch das Eingreifen einer überlegenen militärischen Macht einfach erstickt.[30]

Zu dieser Interpretation passt, dass in dem ältesten Beleg für die Vorstellung, dass sich Völker in friedlicher Absicht in Jerusalem versammeln, es sich um die Abgesandten der unterworfenen Vasallen handelt:

Ps 47,9   König wurde ‚JHWH' über die Völker,
          ‚JHWH' hat Platz genommen auf seinem heiligen Thron.
       10 Die Edlen der Völker sind versammelt,
          ‚mit'[31] dem Volk des Gottes Abrahams.
       11 Denn ‚JHWH' gehören die Schilde der Erde,
          hoch erhaben ist er.

Die Königsherrschaft JHWHs über die Völker und seine militärische Überlegenheit werden daran sichtbar, dass neben seinem eigenen Volk auch die Gesandten der von ihm unterworfenen Völker ihm die Reverenz erweisen.

Diese imperiale Jerusalemer Staatstheologie, die sich eigene Herrschaftssicherung nur mit dem Mittel der kriegerischen Unterwerfung anderer Völker | vorstellen konnte, hat schon in der fortgeschrittenen monarchischen Epoche von einigen Propheten scharfe Kritik erfahren. Im 8. Jh. kritisierte etwa Micha das illusionäre Vertrauen auf die Unverletzlichkeit Jerusalems, das ihre Einwohner völlig unsensibel für das in ihr geschehene Unrecht gemacht habe, und sagte der Stadt darum die völlige Verwüstung an (Mi 3,11 f.); und Jesaja geißelte unter anderem das Vertrauen auf Waffen als Sünde gegen Gott (Jes 7,4; 30,1–5.15–20; 31,1–3), der Assyrien als „Zornesrute" gegen sein eigenes Volk herbeigerufen habe (5,25–29; 10,5 ff.). Den künftigen König entkleidete er von allen Weltherrschaftsgelüsten (11,1–5).

So verwundert es nicht, dass nach dem Zusammenbruch des judäischen Staates, bei dem auch Jerusalem und sein Tempel in Flammen aufgingen (587 v. Chr.), die Zionstheologie abgewandelt und zunehmend ihrer imperialistischen Spitze beraubt wurde. Auf ein Eingreifen JHWHs in der Geschichte hin, so erwarteten exilische und nachexilische Propheten, würden die Völker in einer Art „Völkerwallfahrt" freiwillig zum Zion kommen, um etwa die exilierten Judäer zurückzubringen (Jes 43,6; 49,22; 60,4.9), um ihre Schätze nach Jerusalem zu schleppen und damit den Wiederaufbau von Stadt und Tempel zu ermögli-

---

30 Vgl. das Zusammenbrechen des syrisch-ephraimitischen Angriffs auf Jerusalem im Jahr 733 v. Chr. durch das Eingreifen der von Ahab zu Hilfe gerufenen Assyrer (1. Kön 16,5–9).
31 Im Hebräischen Text fehlt die Präposition, sie ist aber wahrscheinlich durch Haplographie ausgefallen.

chen (60,5–9.11.16 f.; Hag 2,7–9) und um JHWH und sein Heiligtum zu verherrlichen (Jes 60,6 f.9b.13 f.).[32] Ja, die Völker würden Israel dadurch dienen, dass sie für es, das als Priestervolk die religiösen Angelegenheiten regeln werde, die landwirtschaftlichen Tätigkeiten übernähmen (61,5 f.). An die Stelle der durch Waffengewalt erzwungenen Tribute und politischer Unterwerfung treten hier die freiwillige Gabe und religiöse Verehrung.

In die Tradition dieses Völkerwallfahrtsmotivs gehört auch Jes 2,2–4 hinein (vgl. Ps 122,1). Nur ist es hier noch konsequenter aller Weltherrschafts- und wirtschaftlicher Retributionsvorstellungen entkleidet. Die Völker kommen in Jes 2 nicht als Vasallen, sie kommen nicht, um ihre Schätze zu bringen und Israel zu dienen, sie kommen noch nicht einmal, um die Herrlichkeit JHWHs und seines Tempels zu mehren. Die Völker kommen überhaupt nicht, um etwas zu bringen, sondern sie kommen, um sich vom Zion etwas zu holen: die konfliktschlichtende Weisung des dort anwesenden Gottes.

3 Historischer Hintergrund

Schon die motivgeschichtliche Einordnung macht es unwahrscheinlich, dass die prophetische Heilsschilderung Jes 2,2–4 vom Propheten Jesaja aus dem 8. Jh. v. Chr. stammt, wie dies etwa noch von Hans Wildberger[33] vertreten wurde. Sie setzt nicht nur die Kritik Jesajas an der Rüstungs- und Bündnispolitik der Könige Ahas und Hiskia voraus (Jes 7,1–9; 30,1–5.15–20; 31,1–3), sondern auch die Reflexionen der Deuterojesajagruppe über die neue Rolle, die JHWH seinem Volk durch dessen Exilierung bei seiner Weltregierung zugedacht habe. So kommt sie etwa zu dem Schluss, dass Israel als JHWHs | Knecht, nun, da es über keine politische Macht mehr verfügt, das Recht (מִשְׁפָּט) zu den Völkern hinausbringen solle, und zwar nicht das Recht des Stärkeren, sondern ein solches, das den Schwachen aufhilft (Jes 42,1–4). Wenn es dabei heißt, dass ‚auf seine Weisung (תורה) die Inseln harren‘, dann klingt dies schon an die attraktive Weisung von Jes 2,4 an. Desgleichen sieht sich die Prophetengruppe als Vorreiter Israels von Gott beauftragt, ‚Licht für die Völker zu sein, damit meine Rettung bis an die Enden der Erde gelange‘ (49,6). JHWHs heilvolles Handeln, so erkennen diese exilischen Propheten, lässt sich nicht mehr auf sein Volk Israel beschränken, sondern zielt auf die ganze Welt; und Israel kommt innerhalb dieser universalen Weltregierung erstmals eine eminent positive orientierende Funktion für die Völkerwelt zu deren eigenem Wohl zu. Auch in seiner eigenen Weltregierung will Gott, so erkennt

---

32 Vgl. Claus Westermann, Das Buch Jesaja. Kapitel 40–66 (ATD 16), Göttingen ⁵1986, S. 280–290.
33 Vgl. Wildberger, Jesaja (wie Anm. 16), S. 80.

die Prophetengruppe, dem hilfreichen Recht anstelle der bloßen Gewalt eine zentrale Rolle einräumen:

> Jes 51,4 Habt acht auf mich, mein Volk,
> und hört auf mich, meine Nation!
> Denn Weisung geht von mir aus
> und mein Recht als Licht für die Völker.
>
> 5 ‚Im Nu lasse ich nahen‘[34] mein Heil,
> und meine Hilfe zieht aus,
> und meine Arme werden den Völkern Recht schaffen.
> Auf mich harren die Inseln,
> auf meinen Arm warten sie.

Abgesehen von der fehlenden Bindung an den Zion, kommt dieser Deuterojesaja-Text dem in Jes 2 avisierten schiedsrichterlichen Wirken Gottes für die Völkerwelt recht nah. Doch gegen Ende der zweiten Edition des Buches wird dann auch der Zion in die heilvolle Mittlerrolle Israels für die Völker eingebunden:

> Jes 55,5 Siehe ein Volk, das du nicht kennst, wirst du rufen,
> und Völker, die dich nicht kannten, werden zu dir laufen,
> um JHWH, deines Gottes willen, des Heiligen Israels,
> denn er hat dich (e.g. Zion)[35] verherrlicht.

Alle diese Elemente werden in der Heilsschilderung Jes 2,2–4 vorausgesetzt. Damit bildet das Deuterojesajabuch in seinen beiden Editionen einen klaren *terminus a quo*. Die erste Edition lässt sich gut in die Anfangszeit des Perserkönigs Darius datieren, kurz bevor die erste große Rückwanderung der Exilierten einsetzte (521 v. Chr.).[36] Möglicherweise ist die Betonung des Rechts als Basis der Politik gegenüber den Völkern des Perserreichs dabei schon eine Replik auf die Propaganda des Darius bei der Niederschlagung der Aufstände, die seine Usurpation 522 hervorrief.[37] Die zweite Edition lässt sich weniger klar datieren, gehört aber wohl ans Ende des 6. oder den Anfang des 5. Jhs.[38] |

---

34 Das letzte Verb von V. 4 ist mit V. 5 zu verbinden, vgl. die Septuaginta.

35 Das Suffix ist weiblich und bezieht sich damit auf eine Ortsbezeichnung.

36 Vgl. Albertz, Exilszeit (wie Anm. 15), S. 296–301.

37 Vgl. die programmatische Verwendung des persischen Begriffs *dāta* bzw. des aramäischen דת *dāt* ‚Recht Wahrheit‘ schon in der Behistun-Inschrift § 8 (Otto Kaiser (Hg.), Texte aus der Umwelt des Alten Testaments, Bd. 1/4: Historisch-chronologische Texte 1, Gütersloh 1985, S. 424) und in den weiteren Inschriften des Darius DNa § 3 (Pierre Lecoq, Les inscriptions de la Perse achéménide, Paris 1997, S. 220), DNb §§ 2–3 (ebd., S. 222), DSe §§ 3–4 (ebd., S. 233) und Xerxes XPh § 3 (ebd., S. 257); XPl §§ 2–3 (ebd., S. 260); dazu auch S. 167.

38 Vgl. Albertz, Exilszeit (wie Anm. 15), S. 319–323.

Terminus ad quem bildet die ironische Aufnahme von Jes 2,4b in Joel 4,10:

Joel 4,9   Ruft dies aus unter den Völkern:
            Heiligt (euch für) den Krieg! Setzt die Helden in Bewegung!
            Herkommen, heraufkommen sollen alle Kriegsleute!
       10   Schmiedet eure Pflugscharen zu Schwertern
            und eure Winzermesser zu Lanzen!
            Der Schwächling sage: Ich bin ein Held!

Hier werden die Völker aufgerufen, sich zum großen Völkergericht JHWHs zu rüsten und dabei wird ihnen – in ironischer Verkehrung von Jes 2,4 – geraten, auch noch ihre Ackergeräte in Waffen umzuschmieden. Dabei ist von vornherein klar, dass sie gar keine Chance zu ihrer Verteidigung haben. Wöhrle[39] datiert die Redaktion des Zwölfprophetenbuches, dem Joel 4,1–3.9–17 angehört („Fremdvölkerschicht I"), mit guten Gründen gegen Ende des 5. Jhs.[40] Weil sich in der zweiten Hälfte des 5. Jhs. aufgrund der Abgrenzungspolitik Nehemias die offene Einstellung gegenüber den Völkern völlig verkehrte, gehört Jes 2,2–4 eher in dessen erste Hälfte. So könnte Ulrich Berges[41] mit seiner These recht haben, dass die prophetische Friedensschau aus den Anfangsjahren der Regierung des Perserkönigs Xerxes stammt (486–465 v. Chr.). Bevor Xerxes 480 zu seiner großen Strafexpedition gegen Griechenland aufbrach, hatte er noch Aufstände in Ägypten und Babylonien niederzuwerfen. Berges hebt darauf ab, dass nur noch in Jer 51,44 der eigentümliche Sprachgebrauch begegnet, dass ‚Völker strömen' (נהרו גוים) vgl. Jes 2,2); dort wird allerdings angekündigt, dass mit der Eroberung Babylons keine Völker mehr in diese Metropole und zu seinem Gott Bel strömen werden. So könnte es gut sein, dass die Eroberung Babylons durch Xerxes im Jahr 482 v. Chr., der Stadt, die seit der Zerstörung Jerusalems durch die Neubabylonier als die Konkurrentin zu Jerusalem angesehen wurde (Jes 47; Jer 50 f.), den Anlass zu der Hoffnung geliefert hat, dass nun Jerusalem, das zu dieser Zeit bis auf den Tempelbezirk noch in Schutt und Asche lag, zu einem anerkannten Weltmittelpunkt erhöht werden werde (Jes 2,2). Aber diese erhoffte Erhöhung Jerusalems war nun nicht mehr mit Weltherrschaftsträumen verbunden, sondern mit der Vorstellung, dass in den Kriegswirren, die seit dem Ende der Regierungszeit des

---

39 Vgl. Wöhrle, Abschluss des Zwölfprophetenbuches (wie Anm. 4), S. 162.
40 Ab dem letzten Jahrzehnt des 5. Jhs. v. Chr. kommt es im Zuge der Loslösung Ägyptens aus dem persischen Reich zu einer verschärften Kontrolle der Perser über Samaria und Juda, die sich u. a. in einer Reihe von Festungsbauten dokumentiert. In diesen Zusammenhang gehört wahrscheinlich auch die siebenjährige Strafsteuer, die der persische Statthalter Bagoses nach dem Bericht des Josephus (Ant. XI, 297–303) der Provinz Juda und dem Jerusalemer Tempel auferlegt.
41 Vgl. Berges, Jesaja (wie Anm. 17), S. 75 f.

Darius im Perserreich und in der Konfrontation mit den griechischen Staaten aufgeflammt waren, der Welt ein Zentrum für eine Friedensvermittlung zur Verfügung gestellt werde, das der Völkerwelt helfen könnte, die nicht enden wollenden Kriege zu überwinden.

4 Kontextuelle Einbettung

An ein prophetisches Zukunftskonzept göttlicher Friedensvermittlung lässt sich die Frage nach den politischen und institutionellen Rahmenbedingungen | der Mediation nicht direkt richten. Wohl aber lässt sich klären, welche Voraussetzungen der nachexilische Redaktor, der Jes 2,2–5 an die jetzige Stelle des Jesajabuches einfügte, für notwendig ansah, damit Jerusalem die Rolle eines Zentrums göttlicher Friedensvermittlung übernehmen könnte. Diese werden an der kontextuellen Einbettung der Heilsschilderung erkennbar. Wir können hier auf die komplizierte Frage der Redaktion und Komposition des Jesajabuches nicht eingehen. Doch hinsichtlich seines Anfangs haben jüngst Ulrich Berges[42] und Willem A. M. Beuken[43] gezeigt, dass die Eingangskapitel Jes 1,2–4,6 eine zweiteilige Ouvertüre des Jesajabuches bilden und dass hierin unser Text Jes 2,1–5 den Abschluss und Höhepunkt deren ersten Teils darstellt.[44]

Der erste Teil der Ouvertüre beginnt damit, dass JHWH verzweifelt über seine missratenen Söhne klagt (1,2–3). Sie waren so unbelehrbar, dass unter seinen Schlägen am Ende nur noch der Zion als ‚eine Hütte im Weinberg und ein Unterstand im Melonenfeld übrig blieb‘ (1,8). Damit wird deutlich auf die Zerstörung Jerusalems in der Exilskatastrophe angespielt. Doch Gott hatte einige aus der Katastrophe entrinnen lassen. An diese, die despektierlich Sodomsfürsten und

---

42 Ebd., S. 56–76.

43 Vgl. Beuken, Jesaja (wie Anm. 17), S. 60–96.

44 Diese Sicht ist nur möglich, weil Berges, Jesaja (wie Anm. 17), S. 72 f. zeigen konnte, dass nicht nur Jes 1,29–31, sondern auch die neue Überschrift Jes 2,1, die jetzt den Zusammenhang mit Kap. 1 verdunkeln, nochmals spätere Einschübe darstellen. Demgegenüber ist die Alternative, Jes 2,2–4 im Kontext der Kapitel 2–4 zu interpretieren, wie sie Marvin A. Sweeney, Micah's Debate with Isaiah, in: JSOT 93, 2001, S. 111–124 erneut vorgelegt hat, weniger aussagekräftig, weil sie zwar auch die weltweite göttliche Konfliktschlichtung mit einem Jerusalem betreffenden Reinigungsgericht in Verbindung bringen kann, aber doch nicht klar als deren Voraussetzung. Außerdem steht in Jes 2 f. stärker der Hochmut und weniger das Unrecht im Zentrum der Anklage und des Gerichts. Die Stichworte, die Jes 2,2–4 und Jes 1 miteinander verbinden (תורה ‚Weisung‘: 1,10; 2,3; דבר ‚Wort‘: 1,10; 2,[1].3; שפט ‚Recht sprechen‘: 1,17.23.26; 2,4; יכח ‚zurechtweisen, schlichten‘: 1,18; 2,4; משפט ‚Recht‘: 1,17.21.27; צדק/צדקה ‚Gerechtigkeit‘: 1,26.27), fehlen in Jes 2,5–4,4 fast völlig. Nur in Jes 3,2 wird das Partizip von שפט im Sinne von ‚Richter‘ unter anderen Ämtern und in Jes 3,14; 4,4 משפט zur Bezeichnung des göttlichen Gerichtes verwendet.

Volk von Gomorra genannt werden, richtet sich nun JHWHs Wort und Weisung (1,10). Hierbei werden dieselben Begriffe דבר *dābār* und תורה *tōrāh* verwendet wie später in Jes 2,3 an die Völker. Nur hier, an Israel gerichtet, bezeichnen sie eine scharfe prophetische Anklage, welche die Wahrheit schonungslos aufdeckt: Die Judäer haben versucht, das von ihnen verursachte soziale Unrecht mit erhöhter Kultobservanz zuzudecken. Doch ihre Hände sind voll Blut. Darum ergeht an sie die scharfe Mahnung:

Jes 1,16a	Wascht euch! Reinigt euch!
	Entfernt das Böse von euren Taten! Mir aus den Augen!
16b.17	Steht ab vom Bösen, lernt Gutes tun.
	Suchet das Recht, tadelt den Unterdrücker!
	Schafft Recht der Waise,
	führt den Rechtsstreit der Witwe!

Im Folgenden wird nun gezeigt, dass nur diejenigen, die bereit sind umzukehren (1,17–19) und der Mahnung Jesajas entsprechend für Recht und Gerechtigkeit in Jerusalem sorgen (1,27), dem Reinigungsgericht Gottes über Jerusalem (1,21–26) entgehen (1,27), während die anderen umkommen (1,28). Erst die von Gott tief gedemütigte und dann von allen Unterdrückern gereinigte Stadt, die wieder von Recht und Gerechtigkeit wie in der Frühzeit erfüllt sein wird, kann nach Meinung des nachexilischen Jesaja-Redaktors zum Hort eines vertrauenswürdigen Schiedsgerichts für die Völker werden. Erst die Einwohner Jerusalems, welche nach dem Untergang des eigenen Staates vom Propheten gelernt haben, ein soziales und gerechtes substaatliches Gemeinwesen aufzubauen, sind zu einer gerechten und damit wirklich Frieden stiftenden Konfliktschlichtung in der Lage. Konzeptionell ist damit die ‚himmlische UNO' von Jes 2,2–4 post-staatlich. Sie setzt die Erfahrung, dass der eigene | Staat aufgrund von militärischer Hybris und sozialem Unrecht zusammengebrochen ist, voraus, und liegt jenseits der etablierten Herrschaftssysteme.

5 Merkmale der religiös fundierten Friedensvermittlung von Jes 2,2–4

Versucht man, das in Jes 2 entworfene Konzept einer göttlichen Friedensvermittlung für das Thema Mediation auszuwerten, dann ist es ratsam, dies auf die menschliche Ebene herunterzubrechen. Göttliches Handeln entzieht sich *per se* dem Vergleich mit menschlichem Handeln. Doch die bloße Einsicht, dass göttliche Mediation im Unterschied zur menschlichen eben erfolgreich sei, führt nicht recht weiter.

Da nun im Jesajabuch selber die Begriffe „Weisung und Wort JHWHs", die in Jes 2,3 f. die Schlichtung in den Konflikten der Völker herbeiführen, zur Bezeichnung des prophetisch vermittelten Gotteswortes verwendet werden (Jes 1,10; 5,24; 30,9), sind wir meiner Meinung nach berechtigt, auch in Jes 2 von einer prophetischen Vermittlung der göttlichen Konfliktschlichtung auszugehen. Dabei kann man sich die prophetischen Mediatoren durchaus auch in der Rolle der treuen ‚Richter' (שֹׁפְטִים) und ‚Ratgeber' (יֹעֲצִים) vorstellen, die Gott in der Sicht von Jes 1,26 nach dem großen Reinigungsgericht erneut in Jerusalem installieren will. Welchen Anforderungen müssen nun diese prophetischen Mediatoren genügen? Welche Merkmale weist die von ihnen geleistete religiös fundierte Mediation auf?

5.1 Integrität der Mediatoren

Voraussetzung für die religiös fundierte internationale Konfliktschlichtung ist die absolute Integrität der auf dem Zion in Gottes Auftrag tätigen Mediatoren. Sie verfügen selber über keinerlei politische Macht; sie wirken allein durch das an sich ohnmächtige Wort. Sie verfügen allerdings über ein tiefes Gespür für Gerechtigkeit, weil sie aus der eigenen leidvollen Geschichte gelernt haben, dass nur ein solches Recht, das den Schwächeren schützt und den Stärkeren in die Schranken verweist, ein gedeihliches und friedliches Zusammenleben ermöglicht. Als solche sind sie unbestechlich und weichen – wie schon der Prophet Jesaja – vor äußerem Druck nicht zurück.

5.2 Absehen von allen eigenen politischen Interessen

Es ist ein oft übersehener Befund, dass Israel in dem Szenario der Frieden stiftenden Konfliktschlichtung zwischen den Völkern selber gar nicht vorkommt. Es begegnet nur indirekt in der Bezeichnung „Gott Jakobs" (Jes 2,3) und ist implizit darin vorausgesetzt, dass Jerusalem seine Hauptstadt darstellt. | Es liefert damit sozusagen den Völkern den Gott und den Ort der Friedensmediation, hat aber selber von der Konfliktschlichtung zwischen den Völkern keinen eigenen Vorteil mehr. Hierin unterschied sich Jes 2,2–4 ja gerade von allen anderen Texten, die eine Völkerwallfahrt zum Zion ausmalen, in denen Israel zumindest wirtschaftlich und in seiner religiösen Ehrenstellung vom Kommen der Völker profitiert (Jes 60; Hag 2,7 f.; Sach 14,16–19). Die Konfliktschlichtung in Jes 2 ist noch nicht einmal mit Bekehrung der Völker zum Gott Israels verbunden. D.h. aber: Die Mediatoren, die auf dem Zion im Namen JHWHs die Konflikte zwischen den Völkern schlichten sollen, haben gelernt, dass sie bei ihrer Arbeit keinerlei Rücksicht auf die Interessenlage ihres Volkes nehmen dürfen. Die Glaubwürdigkeit und Wirkungskraft ihres religiös fundierten friedensstiftenden Handelns zwischen den Völkern beruht darauf, dass es ihnen gelingt, sich völlig von den Interessen ihres Volkes zu distanzieren. Oder theologisch gesprochen: Nur weil sich JHWH in der leidvollen Geschichte Israels von der machtpolitischen Vereinnahmung durch sein eigenes Volk distanziert hat, kann er nun zu einem Frieden stiftenden Gott für die Völker werden, dessen Weisung von allen als gerechter Interessenausgleich anerkannt wird. Die totale Unabhängigkeit der in der internationalen Konfliktschlichtung tätigen Mediatoren von allen etablierten Herrschaftssystemen scheint mir ein ganz wesentliches Merkmal der religiös fundierten Friedensvermittlung zu sein.

5.3 Politische Ohnmacht und überzeugende Autorität

In Jes 2,4 wird die Mediation als ein schiedsgerichtliches Verfahren dargestellt, wobei auch belehrende und erzieherische Elemente dazu kommen können: Die sich streitenden Völker kommen freiwillig nach Jerusalem, tragen vor den prophetischen Richtern ihre Klagen vor, erhalten von ihnen Weisung und Belehrung und akzeptieren – ebenso freiwillig – das von den Richtern in ihrem Rechtsstreit gefundene Urteil. Die Mediatoren haben somit eine richterliche Befugnis; sie bringen die sich streitenden Parteien nicht nur dazu, selber eine Konfliktlösung zu finden. Aber sie verfügen offenbar über keinerlei Zwangsmittel, ihr Urteil gegen den Willen der Parteien durchzusetzen.

Bei einem solchen Mediationsverfahren orientierte sich der Autor von Jes 2,2–4 offenbar an der typischen zivilen Rechtsprechung im Israel der vorstaatlichen und frühen staatlichen Zeit, dem sog. ‚Torgericht'.[45] Auf die Klage eines

---

45 Vgl. die Verwendung der gleichen Wendung שׁפט בין *šafaṭ bēn* ‚richten zwischen' von Jes 2,4a für die Tätigkeit der Richter in zivilen Prozessen (Ex 18,16; Dtn 1,16) und den Ausdruck מוכיח בשׁער *mōkīaḥ bĕša'ar* ‚der im Tor zurechtweist' in Jes 29,21 und Am 5,21 (hier in umgekehrter Wortfolge) für den Schiedsrichter im Tor. Schwartz, Torah from Zion (wie Anm. 17), S. 18–22 möchte dagegen das Obergericht in Jerusalem, das in Dtn 17,8–13 eingeführt wird, als Vergleichsmodell erweisen. Doch bis auf die Parallele, dass auch die Entscheidungen des Obergerichts in Dtn 17,10.11 als דבר *dābār* und תורה *tōrāh* bezeichnet werden, überwiegen die Differenzen: Die Anweisungen des Obergerichts, das in schwierigen Fällen eine Legalinterpretation für die Ortsgerichte vornahm (vgl. dazu Georg Macholz, Zur Geschichte der Justizorganisation in Juda, in: ZAW 84, 1972, S. 314–340, S. 324–330; Eckart Otto, Tendenzen der Geschichte des Rechts in der Hebräischen Bibel, in: Ders., Altorientalische und biblische Rechtsgeschichte. Gesammelte Studien, Wiesbaden 2008, S. 1–56, S. 21 f.), sind wortwörtlich zu befolgen und Zuwiderhandeln wird mit dem Tod bestraft (V. 10–13). Die Entscheidungen des Obergerichts waren somit im Gegensatz zu den Urteilen der prophetischen Schlichter von Jes 2 strafbewehrt.

Geschädigten trafen hier die sich streitenden Familien im Tor der Ortschaft zusammen und die als Richter fungierenden Ältesten fällten nach Anhörung der Parteien einen Schiedsspruch, bei dem es sich mehr um einen Streitbeendigungsvorschlag handelte, der auf die Akzeptanz durch die Betroffenen angewiesen war.[46] Auch hier verfügten die Richter über keine Zwangsmittel, ihr Urteil durchzusetzen. Seine Geltung beruhte auf der Güte des gefundenen | rechtlichen Ausgleichs, der Autorität der Richter und dem Gruppendruck der Öffentlichkeit.

Beim prophetischen Konzept schiedsgerichtlicher Schlichtung internationaler Konflikte von Jes 2 sind es grundsätzlich die gleichen Mechanismen, die dem auf dem Zion gesprochenen Urteil Geltung verschaffen, nur nehmen hier die prophetischen Richter zusätzlich die göttliche Autorität für sich in Anspruch. Dieses Vorgehen kann allerdings nur deswegen dem sofortigen Verdacht einer bloßen ideologischen Verbrämung eigener Interessen entgehen, weil diese Mediatoren aus einer bewusst eingenommenen Ohnmachts- und Außenseiterposition heraus handeln, die ihre absolute Überparteilichkeit in dem verhandelten Konflikt glaubwürdig macht. Oder anders herum: Die religiöse Überhöhung des Mediationsvorganges sichert die Exterritorialität der Mediatoren im Konfliktfeld und stattet sie trotz notwendiger politischer Ohnmacht mit einer ‚außerweltlichen‘, einer geistlichen Autorität aus.

5.4 Hat Friedensvermittlung notwendig immer auch eine religiöse Dimension?

In der berühmten Heilsschilderung aus dem Jesajabuch wird eine Form der Friedensvermittlung beschrieben, die durch und durch religiös imprägniert ist. Es mag sein, dass Mediationen in überschaubaren Konflikten im privaten oder auch wirtschaftlichen Bereich allein mit dem persönlichen Geschick eines Mediators auskommen. Doch je weitreichender die Konflikte werden und je fraglicher es

---

46 Vgl. Gerhard Liedke, Gestalt und Bezeichnung alttestamentlicher Rechtssätze. Eine formgeschichtlich-terminologische Studie (WMANT 39), Neukirchen-Vluyn 1971, S. 40–48; S. 88–92; sie betreffen das kasuistische Recht; daneben belegen apodiktische Rechtssätze wie Ex 21,12–17 die Existenz autoritärer Urteile, die durch den Vater, den König oder ein sakrales Gericht ausgesprochen werden konnten (ebd., S. 130–135). Ab dem 8. Jh. v. Chr. sind auch staatliche Richter belegt (Jes 1,26; 10,1; vgl. Macholz, Justizorganisation (wie Anm. 45), S. 314–318). Das Dtn aus dem 7. Jh. bezeugt dann eine Bürokratisierung der Ortsgerichte durch Einsetzung von Richtern und Gerichtssekretären, vgl. Jan Christian Gertz, Die Gerichtsorganisation Israels im deuteronomischen Gesetz (FRLANT 165), Göttingen 1994, S. 226–228. Zum ganzen vgl. auch Hermann M. Niehr, Rechtsprechung in Israel. Untersuchungen zur Geschichte der Gerichtsorganisation im Alten Testament (SBS 130), Stuttgart 1987, S. 39–76; Otto, Geschichte des Rechts (wie Anm. 45), S. 16–23.

wird, ob die Mediatoren nicht selber Partei im Konflikt sind und einen wirklich unabhängigen Standort für den gerechten Ausgleich einnehmen können, kommt meiner Meinung nach eine religiöse Dimension der Konfliktschlichtung ins Spiel. In der UNO, die eine rein politische Organisation sein will, besteht ja bei vielen guten Ansätzen und einzelnen gelungenen Missionen der Friedenssicherung das Hauptproblem darin, dass besonders die Vertreter der großen Nationen im Sicherheitsrat, der die Rolle eines internationalen Schiedsgerichts übernehmen sollte, nicht genügend bereit oder in der Lage sind, sich von den Interessen ihrer Staaten zu distanzieren, sondern die UNO mehr oder minder verdeckt dazu missbrauchen, die kurzfristigen weltpolitischen Interessen ihrer Staaten durchzusetzen.[47] Bedürfte es nicht auch hier einer religiösen Dimension, um zumindest soweit von den mehr oder minder egoistischen Partikularinteressen Abstand zu gewinnen, damit die längerfristigen Ziele, die dem Allgemeinwohl der Weltgemeinschaft dienen, verfolgt werden können?

Bei der Wahl der Generalsekretäre der UNO wird dies immerhin ansatzweise sichtbar. Bevorzugt werden Angehörige kleiner Staaten, die keine eigenen weltpolitischen Ambitionen haben, aber viele dieser Personen haben oder entwickeln bei ihren Friedensvermittlungen ein ausgesprochenes Charisma. Wenn Sie die Rede von Kofi Annan bei der Verleihung des Friedenspreises im Fernsehen gesehen oder im Internet nachgelesen haben, dann werden Sie viel|leicht gespürt haben, hier redet einer von einer Position jenseits des politischen Interessenkampfes, fast so wie ein Pfarrer von der Kanzel. Er redet den Politikern und uns allen ins Gewissen und strahlt dabei ein Charisma aus, das erst einmal überzeugt. Bedarf also damit ein international tätiger Mediator der Religion, nicht nur um andere von seinem Vermittlungsvorschlag zu überzeugen, sondern auch um seine Überparteilichkeit durchzuhalten und sich gegen alle nur möglichen Verdächtigungen zu erwehren?

---

47 Das Problem wird auch von UNO-Experten durchaus gesehen, vgl. die Ausführungen des langjährigen Botschafters Sloweniens bei der UNO und jetzigen slowenischen Staatspräsidenten Danilo Türk, Improving Decision-Making in the UN Security Council, in: Lee (Hg.), Swords into Plowshares (wie Anm. 1), S. 1–9, der zwar die Erwartung „that states serving on the Security Council will forsake their immediate national interest for enlightened self-interest or altruism" in den Bereich der Utopie verweist (ebd., S. 2), aber anmahnt, dass die Entscheidungen des Sicherheitsrates mehr „credible, predictable and reliable" werden müssten: „The Council needs to act in a consistant manner and avoid the impression of applying double standards" (ebd., S. 9). Es ist sicher kein Zufall, wenn Newton Bowles, Will the UN Hope survive, in: Lee (Hg.), Swords into Plowshares (wie Anm. 1), S. 167–174, S. 174, langjähriger kanadischer UNO-Diplomat und jetziger ‚senior adviser to UNICEF', seine Hoffnung auf eine Zukunft der UNO gerade in der verstärkten Zusammenarbeit mit Nicht-Regierungsorganisationen (NGOs) begründet sieht, die ihre Arbeitsziele bewusst jenseits nationaler Interessen liegend definieren.

Kofi Annan, protestantischer Christ, antwortete 2003 auf eine Frage von Hans Küng, aus welcher Quelle er seine persönliche Kraft beziehe, unter anderem: „In Zeiten der Krise muss man tief in sich hineingehen, um Stärke und Mut zu finden, weiterzumachen ... Und natürlich hilft mir auch mein Glaube."

Abkürzungsverzeichnis

AASF	Annales Academiae Scientiarum Fennicae
AB	Anchor Bible
ABIG	Arbeiten zur Bibel und ihrer Geschichte
ABS	Archaeology and Biblical Studies
AfO	Archiv für Orientforschung
AIL	Ancient Israel and its Literature
AJSL	American Journal of Semitic Languages and Literatures
ALASPM	Abhandlungen zur Literatur Alt-Syrien-Palästinas und Mesopotamiens
ANET	Pritchard, J. B. (Hg.), Ancient Near Eastern Texts Relating to the Old Testament, Princeton: Princeton Univ. Press, ^{3}1969
AOAT	Alter Orient und Altes Testament
ARS	Annual Review of Sociology
ATD	Das Alte Testament Deutsch
AThANT	Abhandlungen zur Theologie des Alten und Neuen Testaments
AYBRL	Anchor Yale Bible Reference Library
BA	Biblical Archaeologist
BASOR	Bulletin of the American Schools of Oriental Research
BBB	Bonner Biblische Beiträge
BE	Biblische Enzyklopädie
BEAT	Beiträge zur Erforschung des Alten Testaments und des antiken Judentums
BEThL	Bibliotheca Ephemeridum theologicarum Lovaniensium
BETL	→ BEThL
BHTh	Beiträge zur historischen Theologie
Bib.	Biblica
BibInt	Biblical Interpretation
BiKi	Bibel und Kirche
BiOr	Bibliotheca orientalis
BK	Biblischer Kommentar. Altes Testament
BKAT	→ BK
BN	Biblische Notitzen
BThSt	Biblisch-Theologische Studien
BWANT	Beiträge zur Wissenschaft vom Alten und Neuen Testament
BZAR	Beihefte zur Zeitschrift für Altorientalische und Biblische Rechtsgeschichte
BZAW	Beihefte zur Zeitschrift für die alttestamentliche Wissenschaft
BzVB	Beiträge zum Verstehen der Bibel
CAD	The Assyrian Dictionary of the Oriental Institute of the University of Chicago
CB.OT	Coniectanea biblica. Old Testament Series
CBQ	Catholic Biblical Quarterly
CIS	Copenhagen International Seminar
CThM	Calwer Theologische Monographien
DBAT	Dielheimer Blätter zum Alten Testament
EdF	Erträge der Forschung
EHS	Europäische Hochschulschriften
ESHM	European Seminar in Historical Methodology
ÉTR	Études théologiques et religieuses

https://doi.org/10.1515/9783111202228-029

EvTh	Evangelische Theologie
ExpTim	Expository Times
FAT	Forschungen zum Alten Testament
FRLANT	Forschungen zur Religion und Literatur des Alten und Neuen Testaments
fzb	Forschung zur Bibel
GAT	Grundrisse zum Alten Testament
GK	Gesenius, W./Kautzsch, E., Hebräische Grammatik, Hildesheim u. a.: Georg Olms, ^{28}1909.
HAT	Handbuch zum Alten Testament
HBM	Hebrew Bible Monographs
HBS	Herders Biblische Studien
HerBS	→ HBS
HK	Handkommentar zum Alten Testament
HKAT	→ HK
HKE	Handkommentar zum Alten Testament. Ergänzungsband
HThKAT	Herders Theologischer Kommentar zum Alten Testament
HThK.AT	→ HThKAT
HUCA	Hebrew Union College Annual
IEJ	Israel Exploration Journal
INJ	Israel Numismatic Journal
JBL	Journal of Biblical Literature
JBTh	Jahrbuch für Biblische Theologie
JChPS	Jewish and Christian Perspectives Series
JMF	Journal of Marriage and Family
JNSL	Journal of Northwest Semitic Languages
JQR	Jewish Quarterly Review
JSJ	Journal for the Study of Judaism in the Persian, Hellenistic, and Roman Periods
JSOT	Journal for the Study of the Old Testament
JSOT.S	Journal for the Study of the Old Testament. Supplement Series
JSOTSup	→ JSOT.S
JTFUH	Jahresheft der Theologischen Fakultät der Universität Heidelberg
JusEcc	Jus ecclesiasticum
KAI	Donner, H./Röllig, W., Kanaanäische und aramäische Inschriften, Wiesbaden: Harrassowitz, ^{3}1971–1976
KAT	Kommentar zum Alten Testament
KT	Kaiser-Taschenbücher
LÄ	Lexikon der Ägyptologie
LHBOTS	Library of Hebrew Bible/Old Testament Studies
NEA	Near Eastern Archaeology
NEB	Neue Echter Bibel
NSKAT	Neuer Stuttgarter Kommentar. Altes Testament
OBO	Orbis Biblicus et Orientalis
OTL	Old Testament Library
OTS	Oudtestamentische Studiën
PiLi	Pietas liturgica
RB	Revue biblique
RIPH	Reihe Innovative Psychotherapie und Humanwissenschaften
RLA	Reallexikon der Assyriologie

SAHG	Falkenstein, A./von Soden, W., Sumerische und akkadische Hymnen und Gebete, Bibliothek der Alten Welt. Alter Orient, Zürich/Stuttgart 1953
SBL.DS	Society of Biblical Literature. Dissertation Series
SBL.SS	Society of Biblical Literature. Symposium Series
SBS	Stuttgarter Bibelstudien
SHANE	Studies in the History of the Ancient Near East
STAR	Studies in Theology and Religion
TA	Tel Aviv
TAD	Porten, B./Yardeni, A., Textbook of Aramaic Documents from Ancient Egypt, Jerusalem: Hebrew University, 1986–1999
TB	Theologische Bücherei
TdT	Themen der Theologie
TGI	Galling, K. (Hg.), Textbuch zur Geschichte Israels, Tübingen: Mohr Siebeck, ³1979
ThB	→ TB
ThLZ	Theologische Literaturzeitung
ThQ	Theologische Quartalschrift
ThR	Theologische Rundschau
ThRv	Theologische Revue
ThW	Theologische Wissenschaft
ThWAT	Theologisches Wörterbuch zum Alten Testament
ThZ	Theologische Zeitschrift
TRE	Theologische Realenzyklopädie
TThSt	Trierer Theologische Studien
TUAT	Texte aus der Umwelt des Alten Testaments
TW	→ ThW
TynB	Tyndale Bulletin
UF	Ugarit-Forschungen
UTB	Uni-Taschenbücher
VT	Vetus Testamentum
VT.S	Vetus Testamentum. Supplements
VTSup	→ VT.S
VuF	Verkündigung und Forschung
VWGTh	Veröffentlichungen der Wissenschaftlichen Gesellschaft für Theologie
WBC	Word Biblical Commentary
WMANT	Wissenschaftliche Monographien zum Alten und Neuen Testament
WuD	Wort und Dienst
WUNT	Wissenschaftliche Untersuchungen zum Neuen Testament
ZAR	Zeitschrift für Altorientalische und Biblische Rechtsgeschichte
ZAW	Zeitschrift für die alttestamentliche Wissenschaft
ZBK.AT	Zürcher Bibelkommentare. Altes Testament

Stellenregister

Altes Testament

https://doi.org/10.1515/9783111202228-030

Außerkanonische Schriften / Neues Testament

Alter Orient

Weitere antike Quellen

Nachweis der Erstpublikationen

Secondary Sources Also Deserve to be Historically Evaluated: The Case of the United Monarchy
Davies, P. R./Edelman, D. V. (Hg.), The Historian and the Bible. Essays in Honour of Lester L. Grabbe, LHBOTS 530, New York/London: T&T Clark, 2010, 31–45.

Why a Reform like Josiah's Must Have Happened
Grabbe, L. L. (Hg.), Good Kings and Bad Kings. The Kingdom of Judah in the Seventh Century BCE, European Seminar in Historical Methodology 5, LHBOTS 393, London/New York: T&T Clark, 2005, 27–46.

Ethnische und kultische Konzepte in der Politik Nehemias
Hossfeld, F.-L./Schwienhorst-Schönberger, L. (Hg.), Das Manna fällt auch heute noch. Beiträge zur Geschichte und Theologie des Alten, Ersten Testaments. Festschrift für Erich Zenger, HBS 44, Freiburg u. a.: Herder, 2004, 13–32.

The Controversy about Judean versus Israelite Identity and the Persian Government: A New Interpretation of the Bagoses Story (*Jewish Antiquities* XI.297–301)
Lipschits, O./Knoppers, G./Oeming, M. (Hg.), Judah and the Judeans in the Achaemenid Period. Negotiating Identity in an International Context, Winona Lake: Eisenbrauns, 2011, 483–504.

Die erstmalige Konstituierung des Pentateuch durch die spät-deuteronomistische Redaktionsschicht (K^D bzw. D)
Krause, J. J./Oswald, W./Weingart, K. (Hg.), Eigensinn und Entstehung der Hebräischen Bibel. Erhard Blum zum siebzigsten Geburtstag, FAT 136, Tübingen: Mohr Siebeck, 2020, 129–145.

Der kompositionelle Abschluss des Pentateuchs (Dtn 31–34): Zur Rekonstruktion der nicht-priesterlichen Pentateuchredaktion
Maskow, L./Robker, J. (Hg.), Kritische Schriftgelehrsamkeit in priesterlichen und prophetischen Diskursen. Festschrift für Reinhard Achenbach zum 65. Geburtstag, BZAR 27, Wiesbaden: Harrassowitz, 2022, 273–287.

How Jerusalem's Temple Was Aligned to Moses' Tabernacle: About the Historical Power of an Invented Myth
Niesiołowski-Spanò, Ł./Pfoh, E. (Hg.), Biblical Narratives, Archaeology and Historicity. Essays in Honour of Thomas L. Thompson, LHBOTS 680, London u. a.: T&T Clark, 2020, 198–209.

On the Structure and Formation of the Book of Deutero-Isaiah
Bautch, R. J./Hibbard, J. T. (Hg.), The Book of Isaiah. Enduring Questions Answered Anew. Essays Honoring Joseph Blenkinsopp and His Contribution to the Study of Isaiah, Grand Rapids/Cambridge: Eerdmans, 2014, 21–42.

Ausprägungen der Exodustradition in der Prophetie und in den Psalmen
Ebach, R./Leuenberger, M. (Hg.), Tradition(en) im alten Israel. Konstruktion, Transmission und Transformation, FAT 127, Tübingen: Mohr Siebeck, 2019, 109–142.

https://doi.org/10.1515/9783111202228-031

Israel in der offiziellen Religion der Königszeit
Irsigler, H. (Hg.), Die Identität Israels. Entwicklungen und Kontroversen in alttestamentlicher Zeit, HBS 56, Freiburg u. a.: Herder, 2009, 39–57.

Der Streit der Deuteronomisten um das richtige Verständnis der Geschichte Israels
Mommer, P./Scherer, A. (Hg.), Geschichte Israels und deuteronomistisches Geschichtsdenken. Festschrift zum 70. Geburtstag von Winfried Thiel, AOAT 380, Münster: Ugarit Verlag, 2010, 1–21.

How Radical Must the New Beginning Be? The Discussion between the Deutero-Isaiah and the Ezekiel School
Middlemas, J./Clines, D. J. A./Holt, E. K. (Hg.), The Centre and the Periphery. A European Tribute to Walter Brueggemann, HBM 27, Sheffield: Sheffield Phoenix Press, 2010, 7–21.

Welche Art von Individualität förderte die altisraelitische Familienreligion?
Grund-Wittenberg, A. (Hg.), Religionspraxis und Individualität. Die Bedeutung von Persönlicher Frömmigkeit und Family Religion für das Personkonzept in der Antike, Paderborn: Wilhelm Fink/Brill, 2021, 133–151.

Die soziale und rituelle Bedeutung von Essen und Trinken in der Jakoberzählung
Geiger, M./Maier, Chr./Schmidt, U. (Hg.), Essen und Trinken in der Bibel. Ein literarisches Festmahl für Rainer Kessler zum 65. Geburtstag, Gütersloh: Gütersloher Verlagshaus, 2009, 131–146.

Warum ‚Wozu'? Zur Pragmatik der an Gott gerichteten Fragen in den Klagegebeten der Hebräischen Bibel
Schiffner, K./Leibold, S./Frettlöh, M. L./Döhling, J.-D./Bail, U. (Hg.), Fragen wider die Antworten. Festschrift für Jürgen Ebach zum 65. Geburtstag, Gütersloh: Gütersloher Verlagshaus, 2010, 318–340.

Erotik und Sexualität in den Gesetzen der Torah: Nicht nur ein Störfaktor, sondern auch ein Menschenrecht
Bindrim, D./Grunert, V./Kloß, C. (Hg.), Erotik und Ethik in der Bibel. Festschrift für Manfred Oeming zum 65. Geburtstag, ABIG 68, Leipzig: Evangelische Verlagsanstalt, 2021, 41–57.

Ambivalent Relations between Brothers in the Hebrew Bible
Lemos, T. M./Rosenblum, J. D./Stern, K. B./Ballentine, D. S. (Hg.), With the Loyal You Show Yourself Loyal. Essays on Relationships in the Hebrew Bible in Honor of Saul M. Olyan, AIL 42, Atlanta: SBL Press, 2021, 29–43.

The Legacy of Claus Westermann for Theology and Church
Dell, K. J./Joyce, P. M. (Hg.), Biblical Interpretation and Method. Essays in Honour of John Barton, Oxford: Oxford University Press, 2013, 106–119.

Der Auszug Israels aus Ägypten und das christliche Freiheitsverständnis
Bachmann, V./Schellenberg, A./Ueberschaer, F. (Hg.), Menschsein in Weisheit und Freiheit. Festschrift für Thomas Krüger, OBO 296, Leuven u. a.: Peeters, 2022, 20–34.

Biblische Perspektiven zur Wirtschaftsethik
Casper, M./Gabriel, K./Reuter, H.-R. (Hg.), Kapitalismuskritik im Christentum. Positionen und Diskurse in der Weimarer Republik und der frühen Bundesrepublik, Frankfurt/New York: Campus Verlag, 2016, 387–403.

Muss die exklusive Gottesverehrung gewalttätig sein? Israels steiniger Weg zum Monotheismus
Dobos, K. D./Kőszeghy, M. (Hg.), With Wisdom as a Robe. Qumran and Other Jewish Studies in Honour of Ida Fröhlich, HBM 21, Sheffield: Sheffield Phoenix Press, 2008, 23–40.

Theokratie und Gewaltenteilung: Der sogenannte Verfassungsentwurf des Ezechiel (Ez 40–48)
Trampedach, K./Pečar, A. (Hg.), Theokratie und theokratischer Diskurs. Die Rede von der Gottesherrschaft und ihre politisch-sozialen Auswirkungen im interkulturellen Vergleich, Colloquia historica et theologica 1, Tübingen: Mohr Siebeck, 2013, 55–73.

Eine himmlische UNO: Religiös fundierte Friedensvermittlung nach Jes 2,2–5
Althoff, G. (Hg.), Frieden stiften. Vermittlung und Konfliktlösung vom Mittelalter bis heute, Darmstadt: Wissenschaftliche Buchgesellschaft, 2011, 37–56.